T0214081

Communications
in Computer and Information Science   1140

Commenced Publication in 2007
Founding and Former Series Editors:
Phoebe Chen, Alfredo Cuzzocrea, Xiaoyong Du, Orhun Kara, Ting Liu,
Krishna M. Sivalingam, Dominik Ślęzak, Takashi Washio, Xiaokang Yang,
and Junsong Yuan

More information about this series at http://www.springer.com/series/7899

Vladimir Sukhomlin · Elena Zubareva (Eds.)

Convergent Cognitive Information Technologies

Third International Conference, Convergent 2018
Moscow, Russia, November 29 – December 2, 2018
Revised Selected Papers

 Springer

Editors
Vladimir Sukhomlin ⓘ
Moscow State University
Moscow, Russia

Elena Zubareva ⓘ
Moscow State University
Moscow, Russia

ISSN 1865-0929   ISSN 1865-0937   (electronic)
Communications in Computer and Information Science
ISBN 978-3-030-37435-8   ISBN 978-3-030-37436-5   (eBook)
https://doi.org/10.1007/978-3-030-37436-5

This Springer imprint is published by the registered company Springer Nature Switzerland AG
The registered company address is: Gewerbestrasse 11, 6330 Cham, Switzerland

Preface

This CCIS volume, published by Springer, contains the proceedings of the Third International Scientific Conference on Convergent Cognitive Information Technologies (Convergent 2018), which took place during November 29 – December 2, 2018, at the Lomonosov Moscow State University, Faculty of Computational Mathematics and Cybernetics. The Lomonosov Moscow State University was founded in 1755 and was the first university in Russia. It currently hosts more than 50,000 students. The Lomonosov Moscow State University is one of the major traditional educational institutions in Russia, offering training in almost all branches of modern science and humanities. By providing up-to-date infrastructure, convenient logistics, as well as historical and natural attractions, the venue allowed for the organization of the Convergent 2018 conference to ensure a high standard.

The conference was focused on research and development of scientific and technological foundations of the information society, the key development trends of which are the convergence of various scientific directions: basic and applied technologies; total intellectualization of technologies and services of modern society's ecosystem; and a comprehensive digital transformation of the world economy. The volume contains 35 contributed papers selected from 116 full paper submissions. Each submission was reviewed by at least three Program Committee members, with the help of external reviewers, and the final decisions took into account the feedback from a rebuttal phase. We wish to thank all the authors who submitted to Convergent 2018, the Program Committee members, and the external reviewers.

The series of scientific events relevant to the priority directions for the development of science, technology, and engineering in Russia with in the major modern interdisciplinary field – information and telecommunication systems – brings together representatives from Mathematics, Informatics, Physics and Materials Science, Computer Science, Data Science, and Humanities, from Russia and foreign countries.

The growing integration and interpenetration of technologies such as, computer, communication, instrumentation, software, robotcontroller, nano-, bio-, cognitive, information, printing, etc., leads to accelerated rates of scientific and technological progress and determines the formation of a new complex science-intensive technology areas. These directions should include the Internet of Things, Smart Cities, Big Data, Intelligent Control Systems, Digital Transformation of Transport, and Industrial Clustering Technology of the Digital Economy.

The plenary reports demonstrated the full convergent nature of the scientific and technological development, the most important directions of the digital transformation of various activities, and the formation of new challenges to industry, science, and the economy.

In his speech, Igor Sokolov, Academician of the Russian Academy of Sciences, Director of the Federal Research Center Computer Science and Control of the Russian Academy of Sciences (FRC CSC RAS), analyzed the role of the digital economy of the

Russian program approved by the Government of Russia No. 1632-p dated July 28, 2017, to ensure global competitiveness and national security implementation of the Strategy for the Development of the Information Society in Russia for 2017–2030 (approved by Decree of the President of Russia No. 203 dated May 9, 2017). Further, I. A. Sokolov considered the supreme importance of developing complex information technologies such as, Big Data, the Internet of Things, System Information Security, Artificial Intelligence and Robotics, Blockchains, Cyber-Physical Systems, Automated Production, etc., forming the instrumental basis of the digital economy and having the characteristics of convergence. In conclusion, I. A. Sokolov noted the relevance and timeliness of the conference devoted to basic and applied research in the field of backbone technologies of the digital economy, namely convergent cognitive information technologies.

Vladimir Krupennikov, Deputy of the State Duma of Russia, Deputy Chairman of the Committee of the State Duma of Russia on Information Policy, Information Technologies, and Communications, spoke at the opening of the conference and in his welcoming address stated, inter alia, that lawmakers are currently working intensively on about 50 laws, reflecting the challenges of digital economy. In conclusion, the deputy wished the conference participants a fruitful and successful conference.

Arutyun Avetisyan, Corresponding Member of the Russian Academy of Sciences, Director of the Ivannikov Institute for System Programming of the Russian Academy of Sciences (ISP RAS), made a presentation on the topic: "System Programming as a Key Direction in Countering Cyber Threats." The report aroused great interest from the audience – many conferees called it the best plenary report. The report analyzed the characteristics of modern software, as well as the software crisis associated with information security in the conditions of the digital economy development, which caused an accelerated introduction of information technologies in all spheres of life (robots, intelligent assistants, cyber-physical systems, data energy sources). The causes of defects and critical software vulnerabilities were examined. It was emphasized that defects, in particular, programmer errors and bookmarks in a binary code, are the main source of cyber threats. Classic methods of protection against cyber threats were discussed. The reporter devoted a significant part of the report to reviewing the key areas of countering cyber threats based on the development of new models, methods, and related systems programming technologies that enable in-depth analysis and software transformation in order to detect and eliminate defects, identify the maximum number of errors in executable code, as well as ensuring the sustainability of software systems. The report also evoked interest in the analysis of foreign experience in the development of secure software, including specialized standards (USA), technology for automated search for defects and vulnerabilities in binary code and building patches with software fixes.

Further in the report A. I. Avetisyan identified promising areas of research and development, including: deductive analysis, static analysis, searching for possible defects in the code by patterns, dynamic analysis (fuzzing, symbolic execution, slicing), combined analysis, and static/dynamic analysis using (incomplete) formal models. In conclusion, the areas of research and development in the context of specific work carried out by the Institute of ISP RAS were considered, organizational and methodical theses were formulated to achieve the highest possible level of cybersecurity, prescribing the need for: integrated application of the entire technology stack, continuous search for innovative solutions, and training specialized personnel, on the basis of a distributed center of competence, consolidating the efforts of institutes of the Russian Academy of Sciences, universities, companies, and the state. But in general, institutional mechanisms are needed to ensure the effective participation of Russia in international cooperation, with the aim of long-term transfer of knowledge and technology to Russia, retaining personnel, and creating an enabling environment for exporting innovations, in particular, exporting security.

Andrey Kostogryzov, Honored Scientist of Russia, Doctor of Technical Sciences, Professor, Chief Researcher of the Institute of Informatics Problems, FRC CSC RAS, delivered a fundamental report on the topic "Analytical Forecasting of Risks and Justification of Proactive Provisioning Measures." At the beginning of his report, he made a forecast of the development of the field of information and communication technologies (ICT) for the near future and considered trends in the transformation of production systems and infrastructures with of "smart" systems implementation. It is shown that in view of the constant increasing complexity of systems, in order to ensure competitiveness in the market, constant prediction of risks in the life cycle of systems, their comparison with an acceptable level of risk, justification, and adoption of balanced measures of proactive counteraction to threats are necessary. The report further outlines solutions to these problems based on the principles of systems engineering, modeling the processes of implementing threats and countering threats, constantly predicting risks and justifying proactive measures, applying methods of complexation distribution functions for integrable complex architectures. Further, an overview of optimization problems for risk management in the "process" approach was made using examples of mathematical models and tools created by the author, significantly reducing risks and unnecessary costs, while increasing the degree of scientific validity of technical solutions for creating a number of complex systems from different application areas.

Convergent 2018 was attended by about 300 people. The Program Committee reviewed 147 submissions and accepted 116 as full papers, 10 as short papers, 4 as posters, and 2 as demos; 21 Convergent 2018 submissions were rejected. According to the conference program, these 130 oral presentations (of the full and short papers) were structured into 9 sessions, including Theoretical Questions of Computer Science; Computational Mathematics; Computer Science and Cognitive Information Technologies; Parallel and Distributed Programming; Grid Technologies; Programming on GPUs; Cognitive Information Technologies in Control Systems; Big Data and Applications; the Internet of Things: Standards, Communication, and Information Technologies; Network Applications; Smart Cities: Standards, Cognitive-Information Technologies, and their Applications; Cognitive Information Technologies in Digital Economics; Digital Transformation of Transport; and Applied Optimization Problems.

The conference was attended by leading experts and teams from research centers, universities, the IT industry, institutes of the Russian Academy of Sciences, Russian high-tech companies, and from the near and far abroad countries.

Convergent 2018 was further supported by the following associations and societies: Federal Educational-Methodical Association in higher education for the enlarged group of specialties and areas of training 02.00.00 "Computer and Information Sciences",

Russian Foundation for Basic Research, Fund for Promotion of Internet Media, IT Education, Human Development "League Internet Media", Federal Research Center Computer Science and Control of the Russian Academy of Sciences, Russian Transport Academy, Samsung Research Center, D-Link Corporation, and BaseALT.

March 2019   Vladimir Sukhomlin
                                                              Elena Zubareva

Organization

General Chair

Evgeny Moiseev   RAS, Lomonosov Moscow State University, Russia

Program Committee Co-chairs

Igor Sokolov   Federal Research Center Computer Science
                     and Control of RAS, Russia
Vladimir Sukhomlin   Lomonosov Moscow State University, Russia

Organizing Committee Co-chairs

Evgeny Moiseev   RAS, Lomonosov Moscow State University, Russia
Vladimir Sukhomin   Lomonosov Moscow State University, Russia

Organizing Committee

Leonid Dmitriev   Lomonosov Moscow State University, Russia
Mikhail Fedotov   Lomonosov Moscow State University, Russia
Dmitry Gouriev   Lomonosov Moscow State University, Russia
Evgeniy Ilyushin   Lomonosov Moscow State University, Russia
Sergey Lozhkin   Lomonosov Moscow State University, Russia
Mikhail Lugachyov   Lomonosov Moscow State University, Russia
Vassily Lyubetsky   Kharkevich Institute for Information Transmission
                     Problems, RAS, Lomonosov Moscow State University,
                     Russia
Evgeniy Morkovin   Lomonosov Moscow State University, Russia
Dmitry Namiot   Lomonosov Moscow State University, Russia
Mikhail Posypkin   Computing Center of. A.A. Dorodnicyn, Federal Research
                     Center Computer Science and Control of RAS,
                     Lomonosov Moscow State University, Russia
Alexander Razgulin   Lomonosov Moscow State University, Russia
Vasiliy Tikhomirov   Lomonosov Moscow State University, Russia
Alexander Tomilin   Lomonosov Moscow State University, Russia
Evgeniy Zakharov   Lomonosov Moscow State University, Russia
Elena Zubareva   Lomonosov Moscow State University, Russia

Program Committee

Sergei Andrianov   Saint Petersburg State University, Russia
Sergei Avdonin   University of Alaska Fairbanks, USA

Esen Bidaibekov	Abai Kazakh National Pedagogical University, Kazakhstan
Yousef Daradkeh	Prince Sattam bin Abdulaziz University, Saudi Arabia
Alekzander Emelianov	National Research University - Moscow Power Engineering Institute, Russia
Yuri Evtushenko	Federal Research Center Computer Science and Control of RAS, Russia
Victor Gergel	Lobachevsky State University of Nizhni Novgorod, Russia
Luis Gouveia	University Fernando Pessoa, Portugal
Sava Grozdev	IHEAS, Institute of Mathematics and Informatics, BAS, Bulgaria
Tatyana Gubina	BaseALT, Russia
Dmitry Izmestiev	LANIT Group of Companies, Russia
Evgeniy Khenner	Russian Academy of Education, Perm State National Research University, Russia
Alekzander Kim	The Institute of Electronic Control Computers, Russia
Alexander Klimov	Russian University of Transport (MIIT), Russia
Vladimir Korenkov	Joint Institute for Nuclear Research, Laboratory of Information Technologies, Russia
Sergey Kramarov	Surgut State University, Russia
Tok Ling	National University of Singapore, Singapore
Alexander Misharin	Russian Railways, Russian University of Transport (MIIT), Russia
Valentin Nechaev	MIREA - Russian Technological University, Russia
Diethard Pallaschke	Karlsruhe Institute of Technology, Germany
Oleg Pokusaev	Russian University of Transport (MIIT), Russian Transport Academy, Russia
Gennady Ryabov	RAS, Lomonosov Moscow State University, Russia
Konstantin Samouylov	Peoples Friendship University of Russia, Russia
Manfred Schneps-Schneppe	Ventspils University College, Latvia
Alexey Smirnov	BaseALT, Russia
Leonid Sokolinsky	South Ural State University, Russia
Margarita Sotnikova	Saint Petersburg State University, Russia
Vladimir Sukhomlin	Lomonosov Moscow State University, Russia
Dmitry Tarkhov	Peter the Great St. Petersburg Polytechnic University, Russia
Mourat Tchoshanov	University of Texas at El Paso, USA
Andrey Terekhov	Saint Petersburg State University, Russia
Alexander Vasilyev	Peter the Great St. Petersburg Polytechnic University, Russia
Evgeny Veremey	Saint Petersburg State University, Russia
Vladimir Voevodin	RAS, Lomonosov Moscow State University, Russia
Dmitry Volkov	Institute for Applied Mathematics of the RAS, Open Systems Publishing House, Russia
Alexander Yazenin	Tver State University, Russia

Victor Zakharov	Federal Research Center Computer Science and Control of RAS, Russia
Alexey Zhabko	Saint Petersburg State University, Russia
Yuri Zhuravlev	Federal Research Center Computer Science and Control of RAS, Russia
Elena Zubareva	Lomonosov Moscow State University, Russia

Contents

Big Data and Applications

**The Internet of Things (IoT): Standards, Communication
and Information Technologies, Network Applications**

**Smart Cities: Standards, Cognitive-Information Technologies
and Their Applications**

Cognitive Information Technologies in the Digital Economics

Digital Transformation of Transport

Applied Optimization Problems

Theoretical Questions of Computer Science, Computational Mathematics, Computer Science and Cognitive Information Technologies

Modeling of Financial Asset Prices with Hyperbolic-Sine Stochastic Model

Sergey Shorokhov$^{(\boxtimes)}$ (ID) and Maxim Fomin (ID)

Peoples Friendship University of Russia (RUDN University),
6 Miklukho-Maklaya Street, Moscow 117198, Russian Federation
{shorokhov-sg,fomin-mb}@rudn.ru
http://www.rudn.ru

Abstract. We propose an analytically tractable local volatility model for asset price dynamics leading to volatility smile/skew and fatter-tailed probability distribution. The proposed local volatility model is based on stochastic process of hyperbolic-sine type. We derive the transition probability density function for hyperbolic-sine model and justify that this function has delta function terminal condition at initial time. We compare the probability density functions in Black-Scholes and hyperbolic-sine models to demonstrate that the probability distribution in hyperbolic sine model has some features of fat-tailed distributions. Risk neutral valuation technique is applied to find explicit valuation formula for European call option price in hyperbolic-sine model. In hyperbolic-sine model European call option is more valuable than an identical option in Black-Scholes model for ATM options. We verify that in hyperbolic-sine model Breeden-Litzenberger formula (relation between European call option price and probability density function) holds true. We also examine that Dupire formula correctly recovers volatility function from European call option price in hyperbolic-sine model.

Keywords: Stochastic models · Volatility function · Hyperbolic-sine process · Dupire formula

1 Introduction

Modern mathematical finance is based on the famous constant volatility Black-Scholes (BS) model [1] with risk-neutral asset dynamics given by stochastic differential equation (SDE)

$$dS = r\, S\, dt + \sigma_0\, S\, dW,\ S\left(t_0\right) = S_0,\, r > 0,\, \sigma_0 > 0. \tag{1}$$

But an assumption of constant volatility fails to hold in practice because of the so-called "volatility smiles" [2] and fat tails of financial data distributions [3].

The publication has been prepared with the support of the "RUDN University Program 5–100". The research was funded by RFBR, grant No. 19-08-00261.

V. Sukhomlin and E. Zubareva (Eds.): Convergent 2018, CCIS 1140, pp. 3–10, 2020.
https://doi.org/10.1007/978-3-030-37436-5_1

One of the most natural approaches to these issues is the transition to general model of risk-neutral asset dynamics of the form

$$dS = r\, S\, dt + \sigma\, (S, t)\, S\, dW,\ S\,(t_0) = S_0, \tag{2}$$

with volatility σ being a function of asset price S and time t (local volatility model).

The concept of local volatility model is attributed to Dupire [4]. Local volatility models are commonly used for pricing derivatives, including European call and put options.

The list of analytically tractable local volatility models is rather short. Known examples of analytically tractable local volatility models include shifted lognormal model [5] with volatility function $\sigma_0 \left(1 - \frac{\alpha\, e^{r\, t}}{S}\right)$, $\alpha \in \mathbb{R}$, normal (Bachelier or Cox-Ross) model [6] with volatility function $\frac{\sigma_0}{S}$ and CEV model [6–9] with volatility function $\sigma_0\, S^{\beta}$. Recent developments in local volatility models include application of Weyl-Titchmarsh theory [10,11], quadratic normal volatility models [12,13] and some other methods [14,15]. Another important approach to the problems of volatility smiles and fat-tail distributions are stochastic volatility models [16,17], when volatility itself is a solution of some SDE.

2   Hyperbolic-Sine Local Volatility Model

According to [18], when risk-neutral dynamics of asset price is described by SDE

$$dS = r\, S\, dt + a\,(S,\, t)\, dW, \tag{3}$$

and asset price S can be represented as a function of standard Brownian motion W and time t, i.e. $S = s\,(W,\, t)$, absolute volatility function $a\,(S,\, t)$ in (3) is a solution of second-order nonlinear partial differential equation (PDE)

$$\frac{a^2}{2}\, \frac{\partial^2 a}{\partial S^2} + r\, S\, \frac{\partial a}{\partial S} + \frac{\partial a}{\partial t} - r\, a = 0,\ S > 0,\ t \in [0,\, T]. \tag{4}$$

It can be easily verified that function $a\,(S,\, t) = \sqrt{2\, r\, S^2 + \sigma_0^2}$ is an exact particular solution of (4).

Let the dynamics of asset price S under some risk-neutral measure be given by SDE

$$dS = r\, S\, dt + \sqrt{2\, r\, S^2 + \sigma_0^2}\, dW, \tag{5}$$

where $r > 0$, $\sigma_0 > 0$, W – standard Brownian motion, $S\,(t_0) = S_0 > 0$. Model (5) (HS model) implies underlying stochastic process of hyperbolic-sine type [19]. Volatility function in (5) is equal to

$$\sigma\,(S,\, t) = \sqrt{\frac{\sigma_0^2}{S^2} + 2\, r} \tag{6}$$

and to some extent can model volatility smile/skew (see Fig. 1).

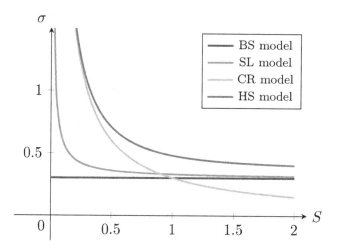

Fig. 1. Volatility functions in local volatility models ($r = 7\%$, $\sigma_0 = 30\%$)

Changing variable S in (5) to $S' = \operatorname{arsinh}\left(\frac{\sqrt{2r}}{\sigma_0}S\right) = \ln\left(\frac{\sqrt{2r}}{\sigma_0}S + \sqrt{1 + \frac{2r}{\sigma_0^2}S^2}\right)$
and applying Ito's Lemma we obtain the following SDE for new variable S'

$$dS' = \sqrt{2r}\, dW \tag{7}$$

with initial condition $S'(t_0) = S_0' = \operatorname{arsinh}\left(\frac{\sqrt{2r}}{\sigma_0}S_0\right)$. From (7) it follows
that the stochastic process $S'(t)$ is distributed normally with expectation
$\operatorname{arsinh}\left(\frac{\sqrt{2r}}{\sigma_0}S_0\right)$ and variance $2r(t - t_0)$, i.e.

$$S'(t) \sim \mathcal{N}\left(\operatorname{arsinh}\left(\frac{\sqrt{2r}}{\sigma_0}S_0\right),\, 2r(t - t_0)\right). \tag{8}$$

3   Transition Probability Density Function in HS Model

The transition probability density function for stochastic process $S'(t)$ is equal
to

$$\rho'(x',\, t,\, S_0',\, t_0) = \frac{1}{2\sqrt{\pi r(t - t_0)}}e^{-\frac{(x' - S_0')^2}{4r(t - t_0)}},\ t \geq t_0. \tag{9}$$

The relation $S(t) = \frac{\sigma_0}{\sqrt{2r}}\sinh S'(t)$ implies that the transition probability
density function (p.d.f.) for $S(t)$ is equal to

$$\rho(x, t, S_0, t_0) = \rho'\left(\operatorname{arsinh}\left(\frac{\sqrt{2r}}{\sigma_0}x\right), t, \operatorname{arsinh}\left(\frac{\sqrt{2r}}{\sigma_0}S_0\right), t_0\right)\frac{d}{dx}\operatorname{arsinh}\left(\frac{\sqrt{2r}}{\sigma_0}x\right)$$

$$= \frac{1}{\sqrt{2\pi}\sqrt{\sigma_0^2 + 2r x^2}\sqrt{t - t_0}}e^{-\frac{1}{4r(t - t_0)}\left(\operatorname{arsinh}\left(\frac{\sqrt{2r}}{\sigma_0}x\right) - \operatorname{arsinh}\left(\frac{\sqrt{2r}}{\sigma_0}S_0\right)\right)^2}. \tag{10}$$

Function ρ, given by (10), is a solution of Fokker-Planck PDE for HS model (5):

$$\frac{\partial \rho}{\partial t} + \frac{\partial}{\partial x}\left(r\,x\,\rho\right) - \frac{1}{2}\frac{\partial^2}{\partial x^2}\left(\left(\sigma_0^2 + 2\,r\,x^2\right)\rho\right) = 0. \tag{11}$$

The expectation of $S\left(t\right)$ is equal to

$$\mathbf{E}\left[S\left(t\right)\right] = \int\limits_{-\infty}^{+\infty} x\,\rho\left(x,\,t,\,S_0,\,t_0\right)dx = S_0 e^{r\,(t-t_0)}. \tag{12}$$

The variance of $S\left(t\right)$ is equal to

$$\mathbf{V}\left[S\left(t\right)\right] = \mathbf{E}\left[S^2\left(t\right)\right] - \left(\mathbf{E}\left[S\left(t\right)\right]\right)^2 = \int\limits_{-\infty}^{+\infty} x^2\,\rho\left(x,\,t,\,S_0,\,t_0\right)dx - S_0^2 e^{2r\,(t-t_0)}$$

$$= S_0^2 e^{4\,r\,(t-t_0)} + \frac{\sigma_0^2}{4\,r}\left(e^{4\,r\,(t-t_0)} - 1\right) - S_0^2 e^{2r\,(t-t_0)}. \tag{13}$$

Obviously, if $t \to t_0$ then $\mathbf{E}\left[S\left(t\right)\right] \to S_0$, $\mathbf{V}\left[S\left(t\right)\right] \to 0$, which means that $S\left(t_0\right)$ has Dirac delta distribution concentrated at point S_0.

As can be seen from Fig. 2, the distribution of $S\left(t\right)$ in HS model (5) exhibit fatter tails, compared to distribution in BS model (1).

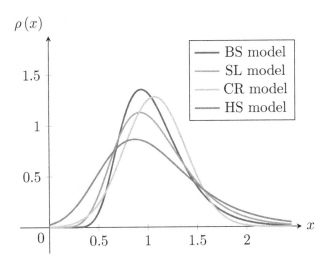

Fig. 2. P.d.f. in local volatility models ($t = 1$, $S_0 = 1$, $t_0 = 0$, $r = 7\%$, $\sigma_0 = 30\%$)

4   Option Pricing in HS Model

In HS model (5) European call option price $c\,(S, t, K, T)$ satisfies Black-Scholes-Merton PDE

$$\frac{\partial c}{\partial t} + r\,S\,\frac{\partial c}{\partial S} + \frac{1}{2}\,\left(\sigma_0^2 + 2\,r\,S^2\right)\,\frac{\partial^2 c}{\partial S^2} - r\,c = 0 \tag{14}$$

with boundary condition $c\,(S, T, K, T) = \max\,(S - K,\, 0)$ and can be determined according to Feynman-Kac formula as

$$c\,(S, t, K, T) = e^{-r(T-t)}\,\mathbf{E}\,[\max\,\{S - K, 0\}] = e^{-r(T-t)} \int_K^{+\infty} (x - K)\,\rho\,(x, T, S, t)\,dx. \tag{15}$$

Changing variable x in (15) to

$$u = \frac{1}{\sqrt{2\,r\,(T - t)}}\,\left(\operatorname{arsinh}\left(\frac{\sqrt{2\,r}}{\sigma_0}\,x\right) - \operatorname{arsinh}\left(\frac{\sqrt{2\,r}}{\sigma_0}\,S\right)\right)$$

we calculate European call option price as follows

$$\begin{aligned}
c\,(S, t, K, T) = {} & \frac{1}{2}\,S\,\left(\Phi\left(\sqrt{2\,r\,(T - t)} - K^*\right) + \Phi\left(-\sqrt{2\,r\,(T - t)} - K^*\right)\right) \\
& + \frac{1}{2}\,\sqrt{\frac{\sigma_0^2}{2\,r} + S^2}\,\left(\Phi\left(\sqrt{2\,r\,(T - t)} - K^*\right) - \Phi\left(-\sqrt{2\,r\,(T - t)} - K^*\right)\right) \\
& - e^{-r\,(T - t)}\,K\,\Phi\left(-K^*\right),
\end{aligned} \tag{16}$$

where

$$K^* = \frac{1}{\sqrt{2\,r\,(T - t)}}\,\left(\operatorname{arsinh}\left(\frac{\sqrt{2\,r}}{\sigma_0}\,K\right) - \operatorname{arsinh}\left(\frac{\sqrt{2\,r}}{\sigma_0}\,S\right)\right).$$

From Fig. 3 it follows that European call options in HS model (5) are more valuable than identical options in BS model (1) when asset price is near strike price (option is "At-The-Money").

5   Breeden-Litzenberger Formula in HS Model

The relationship between European call options prices $c\,(S, T, K, T)$ and risk-neutral transition probability density function $\rho\,(x,\, t,\, S_0,\, t_0)$ is given by Breeden-Litzenberger formula [20]:

$$\frac{\partial^2 c}{\partial K^2} = e^{-r\,(T-t)}\,\rho\,(K, T, S, t). \tag{17}$$

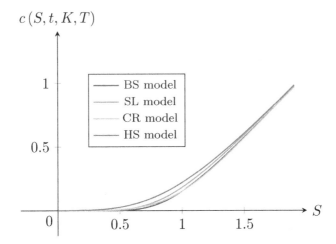

Fig. 3. European call option prices in local volatility models ($t = 0$, $K = 1$, $T = 1$, $r = 7\%$, $\sigma_0 = 30\%$)

Let us check if formula (17) holds true for HS local volatility model. First, we receive

$$\frac{\partial c}{\partial K} = \left(-S \cosh\left(K^* \sqrt{2r\,(T-t)} \right) - \sqrt{\frac{\sigma_0^2}{2r} + S^2}\, \sinh\left(K^* \sqrt{2r\,(T-t)} \right) + K \right)$$
$$\cdot \frac{e^{-\frac{1}{2}\left(K^{*2} + 2r\,(T-t) \right)}}{\sqrt{2\pi}\sqrt{T-t}\sqrt{\sigma_0^2 + 2r\,K^2}} - e^{-r\,(T-t)}\,\Phi\left(-K^* \right).$$

Since K^* can be represented as

$$K^* = \frac{1}{\sqrt{2r\,(T-t)}} \ln \frac{\sqrt{2r}\,K + \sqrt{\sigma_0^2 + 2r\,K^2}}{\sqrt{2r}\,S + \sqrt{\sigma_0^2 + 2r\,S^2}},$$

we receive that

$$K - S \cosh\left(K^* \sqrt{2r\,(T-t)} \right) - \sqrt{\frac{\sigma_0^2}{2r} + S^2}\, \sinh\left(K^* \sqrt{2r\,(T-t)} \right) \equiv 0,$$

hence

$$\frac{\partial c}{\partial K} = -e^{-r\cdot(T-t)}\,\Phi\left(-K^* \right).$$

And further

$$\frac{\partial^2 c}{\partial K^2} = \frac{\partial}{\partial K}\left(-e^{-r\cdot(T-t)}\,\Phi\left(-K^* \right) \right) = -e^{-r\cdot(T-t)}\,\varphi\left(-K^* \right)(-1)\frac{\partial K^*}{\partial K},$$
$$\frac{\partial K^*}{\partial K} = \frac{1}{\sqrt{T-t}}\frac{1}{\sqrt{\sigma_0^2 + 2r\,K^2}}, \quad \varphi\left(x \right) = \frac{1}{\sqrt{2\pi}}\,e^{-\frac{1}{2}x^2},$$

so Breeden-Litzenberger formula (17) holds true for HS local volatility model:

$$\frac{\partial^2 c}{\partial K^2} = e^{-r\,(T-t)}\,\varphi\left(K^*\right)\frac{1}{\sqrt{T-t}}\frac{1}{\sqrt{\sigma_0^2 + 2\,r\,K^2}} = e^{-r\,(T-t)}\rho\left(K,T,S,t\right).$$

6   Dupire Formula in HS Model

The Dupire formula [4, 21] gives us an opportunity to obtain the volatility function $\sigma\left(K,T\right)$ in a local volatility model from European call option price function $c\left(S,t,K,T\right)$

$$\sigma\left(K,T\right) = \sqrt{\frac{\frac{\partial c}{\partial T} + r\,K\,\frac{\partial c}{\partial K}}{\frac{1}{2}\,K^2\,\frac{\partial^2 c}{\partial K^2}}}. \tag{18}$$

Omitting some tedious calculations, we receive the numerator of the fraction in (18) as

$$\frac{\partial c}{\partial T} + r\,K\,\frac{\partial c}{\partial K} = \frac{1}{2}\,\varphi\left(K^*\right)e^{-r\,(T-t)}\frac{\sqrt{\sigma_0^2 + 2\,r\,K^2}}{\sqrt{T-t}},$$

hence the expression under a square root sign in (18) is equal to

$$\frac{\frac{\partial c}{\partial T} + r\,K\,\frac{\partial c}{\partial K}}{\frac{1}{2}\,K^2\,\frac{\partial^2 c}{\partial K^2}} = \frac{\frac{1}{2}\,\varphi\left(K^*\right)e^{-r\,(T-t)}\frac{\sqrt{\sigma_0^2 + 2\,r\,K^2}}{\sqrt{T-t}}}{\frac{1}{2}\,K^2\,e^{-r\cdot(T-t)}\frac{1}{\sqrt{T-t}\sqrt{\sigma_0^2 + 2\,r\,K^2}}\,\varphi\left(K^*\right)} = \frac{\sigma_0^2 + 2\,r\,K^2}{K^2}$$

and Dupire formula recovers the correct expression for volatility function in HS local volatility model:

$$\sigma\left(K,T\right) = \sqrt{\frac{\sigma_0^2}{K^2} + 2\,r}.$$

7   Conclusion

We presented a hyperbolic-sine local volatility model including the transition probability density function as an exact solution of Fokker-Planck PDE and the European call option pricing formula as an exact solution of Black-Scholes-Merton PDE. Hyperbolic-sine local volatility model captures some aspects of the volatility smiles and can be used for pricing different types of options. The model can also be used for credit risk estimation in structural credit risk models.

References

1. Black, F., Scholes, M.: The pricing of options and corporate liabilities. J. Polit. Econ. **81**(3), 637–654. https://doi.org/10.1086/260062
2. Derman, E., Miller, M.B.: The Volatility Smile. Wiley (2016). https://doi.org/10.1002/9781119289258

3. Rachev, S.T., Menn, C., Fabozzi, F.J.: Fat-Tailed & Skewed Asset Return Distributions: Implications for Risk Management, Portfolio Selection, and Option Pricing. Wiley (2005)

4. Dupire, B.: Pricing with a smile. Risk **7**(1), 18–20 (1994)

5. Brigo, D., Mercurio, F.: Fitting volatility skews and smiles with analytical stock-price models. Seminar Paper at Institute of Finance, University of Lugano (2000). http://www.istfin.eco.unisi.ch/seminar-papers-smile.pdf

6. Cox, J.C., Ross, S.A.: The valuation of options for alternative stochastic processes. J. Financ. Econ. **3**(1–2), 145–166. https://doi.org/10.1016/0304-405X(76)90023-4

7. Cox, J.C.: The constant elasticity of variance option pricing model. J. Portfolio Manag. **23**(5), 15–17. https://doi.org/10.3905/jpm.1996.015

8. Emanuel, D.C., MacBeth, J.D.: Further results on the constant elasticity of variance call option pricing model. J. Financ. Quant. Anal. **17**(4), 533–554. https://doi.org/10.2307/2330906

9. Schroder, M.D.: Computing the constant elasticity of variance option pricing formula. J. Finan. **44**(1), 211–219. https://doi.org/10.2307/2328285

10. Li, Y., Zhang, J.E.: Option pricing with Weyl-Titchmarsh theory. Quant. Finan. **4**(4), 457–464. https://doi.org/10.1080/14697680400008643

11. Zhang, J.E., Li, Y.: New analytical option pricing models with Weyl-Titchmarsh theory. Quant. Finan. **12**(7), 1003–1010. https://doi.org/10.1080/14697688.2010.503659

12. Andersen, L.: Option pricing with quadratic volatility: a revisit. Finan. Stochast. **15**(2), 191–219. https://doi.org/10.2139/ssrn.1118399

13. Carr, P., Fisher, T., Ruf, J.: Why are quadratic normal volatility models analytically tractable? SIAM J. Financ. Math. **4**(1), 185–202. https://doi.org/10.1137/120871973

14. Mitra, S.: A review of volatility and option pricing. Int. J. Financ. Markets Deriv. **2**(3), 149–179. https://doi.org/10.1504/ijfmd.2011.042598

15. Deelstra, G., Rayee, G.: Local volatility pricing models for long-dated FX derivatives. Appl. Math. Finan. **20**(4), 380–402. https://doi.org/10.1080/1350486x.2012.723516

16. Gatheral, J.: The Volatility Surface: A Practitioner's Guide. Wiley (2012). https://doi.org/10.1002/9781119202073

17. Javaheri, A.: Inside Volatility Filtering - Secrets of the Skew. Wiley (2015). https://doi.org/10.1002/9781118949092

18. Carr, P., Tari, M., Zariphopoulou, T.: Closed form option valuation with smiles. Preprint, NationsBanc Montgomery Securities (1999)

19. Brigo, D., Mercurio, F., Sartorelli, G.: Alternative asset-price dynamics and volatility smile. Quant. Finan. **3**(3), 173–183. https://doi.org/10.1088/1469-7688/3/3/303

20. Breeden, D.T., Litzenberger, R.H.: Prices of state-contingent claims implicit in option prices. J. Bus. **51**(4), 621–651. https://doi.org/10.1086/296025

21. Derman, E., Kani, I.: Riding on a smile. Risk **7**(2), 139–145 (1994)

On Mathematical Visualization in Education

Alexey Karpov[1], Vladimir Klepov[2], and Alexey Nikitin[3,4]($\boxtimes$)

[1] University of Bonn, Bonn, Germany
`karpovad@yandex.ru`
[2] Yandex, Moscow, Russia
`V.klepov@gmail.com`
[3] Lomonosov Moscow State University, Moscow, Russia
`nikitin@cs.msu.ru`
[4] National Research University Higher School of Economics, Moscow, Russia

Abstract. This article treats the use of modern information technologies in the classroom educational process. It emphasizes the need to combine symbolic and visual mathematics, describes the problems associated with this issue, provides a review of the existing systems and a list of the requirements a modern mathematical visualization system must meet. The article is conceived as a manifesto for the use of mathematical visualization in education. The article then goes on to describe the developments of the authors' research group. The functionality of visualmath.ru website is described. This resource contains an ample collection of visual and text modules for teachers to create presentations based largely on visual materials. The most important part of the article is the description of fast and powerful JavaScript visulatization libraries developed specifically for the project: Skeleton and Grafar. The former is designed to display two-dimensional graphs, while the latter visualizes three-dimensional objects with transparency and illumination effects. Both libraries are capable of processing large element sets in near-real time. In conclusion, selected examples of visualizations created using the libraries use are provided, including the ones used in courses on mathematical analysis and analytical geometry.

Keywords: Information technologies in the education · JavaScript graphics libraries · Mathematical analysis

1 Motivation

1.1 Images in Mathematics

Images in mathematics bridge the gap between symbolism and imagination. David Hilbert [3] notes the conflict between the two trends: mathematicians strive for a logically consistent symbolic abstraction while trying to maintain intuitive understanding of a problem. In ancient India geometric conjectures

© Springer Nature Switzerland AG 2020
V. Sukhomlin and E. Zubareva (Eds.): Convergent 2018, CCIS 1140, pp. 11–27, 2020.
https://doi.org/10.1007/978-3-030-37436-5_2

were proven in a very peculiar manner. Having formulated the premise, the mathematician plotted the shapes necessary for the proof, provided brief comments, and wrote "Watch!" afterwards. It was assumed that the person willing to understand the problem at hand can do so himself by studying the images provided, with no further explanation [7]. As an example, we include a plot (Fig. 1) attributed to Ganesha, 16th century [30].

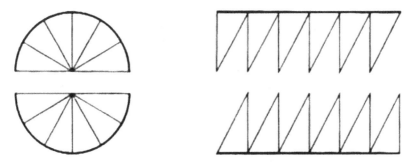

Fig. 1. An illustrated explanation of the area equality between a circle and a rectangle with sides equal to the radius and the half-arc length.

1.2   Symbolic Mathematics

However, after that period the dominant method in mathematics began to change. René Descartes' works on algebraic geometry have turned mathematics into a primarily symbolic science. Images were reduced to guesswork and example aids, losing the role of the primary means of proof. By the end of the 19th century the discovery and further studies of the more abstract objects, such as abstract algebras and higher-dimensional spaces, had made mathematics even less intuitive. Nowadays the less-formal studies would not be considered real mathematics.

Symbolic description of mathematical objects is precise but it takes a lot of training to gain intuition into symbolic manipulations. Scientists can easily lose track of the real-world problem they are solving and come to an absurd conclusion. The key skill of an applied mathematician is correlating the abstraction with the reality. Even in pure mathematics the studies of abstract concepts begin by studying special cases that are easy to understand [2,5]. A famous Russian mathematician and educator Vladimir Arnold referred to mathematics as "experimental science" [11]. Visualization can help resolve these issues. Science is easier and more humane with images. A layman unfamiliar with the notation can readily see similarities between real-world objects and charts, which is a key to introducing younger students to advanced mathematical concepts.

In Sect. 2.1 we highlight the importance of computer technologies in education. In Sects. 2.2, 2.3 and 3.1 we describe the current state of interactive images in classical mathematical education. At the same time, we introduce technical constraints on an interactive system suitable for educational use. A list of popular educational tools that could fit these requirements is provided in Sect. 3.2. After that, we describe our own technical developments in Sects. 3.3 and 3.5. Finally, we show some examples created with these libraries.

2 Visualization in Education

2.1 Computer Technologies in Pedagogy

Computers are responsible for several effects that would transform education in the years to come. Computer Algebra Systems (CAS) and Automated Theorem Proving (APT) software are already capable of solving well formalized problems intractable to humans in an efficient and correct manner. Solutions to numerous problems not solvable symbolically (most prominently, differential equations, including scientific and engineering applications) can be approximated using numerical computing. Future mathematicians need not be trained to carry out computations according to a predefined algorithm with no errors — computers are better suited for such tasks. The key skill of a mathematician working in the industry is to formalize applied problems and to validate the sanity of the computer-produced solution. Mathematical education can no longer ignore these trends, and therefore it needs visualization.

On the other hand, computers can tackle the task of visualizing complex objects with ease. Contemporary scientists process and analyze billions of observations and publish their findings in a comprehensible format. A study scale this wide was unimaginable even a couple of decades ago. No more are mathematicians bound by the rough, static two-dimensional blackboard. In [10] the new wave of interest to mathematical imaging is referred to as the "visualization renaissance". Another advantage of computer graphics is its inherent interactivity. The users can better understand the model at hand while altering the parameters and watching the change induced on the image.

Mathematical visualization still has a lot of ideas to borrow from several connected fields of study. Information graphics is a well-developed and popular topic of study with a high volume of literature summarizing and describing best practices (e.g. the works of Edward Tufte, [6]). Theory of automated visualization is largely confined to proprietary technologies but some academic works are available and we can expect to acquire further material as the patents expire. Finally, software developers and psychologists have advanced the theory of human-computer interaction [1,4] and there is no shortage of the most experimental concepts, such as the use of augmented/virtual reality.

2.2 Problem Statement

In this section we approach to the realm of school and university education. Currently, students and children are dominantly visual learners. However, visual

materials are scarce in classrooms, mostly due to technical and methodological difficulties. In the best case, blackboard sketches or presentations are used.
Movement is usually displayed schematically. We believe that using computer
technologies can greatly boost the students' understanding of the material and
must therefore be pursued by all means.

Several libraries of visual materials exist worldwide such as **MIT Open
Course Ware**, [12], **The d'Arbeloff Interactive Mathematics Project**,
[13] etc. Powerful information systems such as **Wolfram Mathematica**, [14]
allow their users to create new materials themselves. However, the primary focus
of our work is lecture use, and the described solutions are require adaptation for
such cases. Mathematics has a wide array of remarkable pedagogical findings,
scattered throughout the diverse courses, with powerful geometrical ideas beside
them. Unfortunately, the vast majority of these has not been illustrated, while
the rest can be improvement hugely by uncapping the potential of computed-
driven interactive visualization.

2.3   An Interactive System Concept

Our task is to create a framework that allows students understand the educational material deeper. The following diagram shows the current state of the
education process:

$$\text{listen / read} \longrightarrow \text{learn the theorem and its proof} \longrightarrow$$

$$\longrightarrow \text{memorize or remember.}$$

After the *listening/read* step, we suggest that the students should look at
visual explanation of theorems and statements or even to interact with these
images. It helps a person understand the subject better and positively impacts
the effectiveness and the duration of remembering the educational material.

The importance and the quality of illustrations are also emphasized in modern mathematical textbooks distributed by OpenStax, [17].

A large library of so-called visual modules shall be developed soon, covering
at least classical mathematical courses. Each module must include well-arranged
and relevant text.

In addition, there must be a convenient and easy-to-use web platform storing
the visual modules library. The platform is supposed to be used by both students
and lecturers. The lecturers should have access to the library that can be used
to construct a presentation for coming lectures. Later the presentation is to be
demonstrated during a class using the lecturer's computer or mobile device.

At the same time all students with student accounts log in to the platform
using their mobile devices, find the lecturer in the list, and connect to the current
lecture broadcast. The state of the web page on a student's device is synchronized
with the lecturer's page. The lecturer comments the slides content and proves
the theorems/statements, while also showing the visual modules integrated into
the lecture.

The lecturer is able to ask questions or conduct tests during the lecture via the platform. In a short time, they can see the statistics of answers including the number of participants and the number of people who picked a specific option. These interactive tests help lecturers get an instant feedback and thus adjust the course effectively.

3 The Design Requirements and an Overview of the Existing Solutions

3.1 What Should a Visualization System Be Like

A good mathematical visualiazation system bridges the gap between the logic and the intuition. Developing such a system is an inherently interdisciplinary endeavor, taking cues from formal systems, numerical methods, programming, and visual design. It is very rare for a single person to be acquainted with all of these areas, let alone be proficient in these. This calls for a higher-dimensional programming interface that is easily usable by people trained in mathematics with sensible visual defaults, and encouraging simple programming.

The system should make use of its underlying media, the computer. To help the users explore complex mathematical objects, the system should not only be interactive but also function in real time. Another use case computers excel at is creating three-dimensional graphics. As such, computer adds two usable dimensions to a printed graphic: one spatial and one temporal. It will take us, the scientific community, a lot of time to unleash the full potential of this freedom.

The use of the system in education adds further design constraints. As the education should be free and generally available, the system should be cross-platform and accessible, with no major functional deficiencies, on low-end and mobile devices.

To sum up, here is a brief list of design constraints along with the relevant solutions:

- **ease of use**: high-level interface with sensible defaults;
- **availability**: a JavaScript program works across all major devices, aided by the browser runtime;
- **fast 2D graphics**: rely on Scalable Vector Graphics (SVG) [35] for interoperability with standard web technologies and ease of distribution;
- **3D graphics**: WebGL technology. Compatibility with legacy browsers should be provided via canvas or SVG fallbacks [36,37];
- **interactivity**: efficient computational models.

3.2 Overview of the Existing Systems

Major computer mathematical systems support plotting out of the box. Maple [15], MatLab [16], Mathematica [14] are powerful, widely adopted packages. However, their use in educational visualization is limited: even the special educational licenses are expensive, mobile device support is lacking, and the users need to learn a special programing language. Open-source alternatives, such as R [18], Octave [19], Julia [20], only solve the license cost issue.

Mathematical libraries for general-purpose programming languages offer a more pragmatic alternative. SciPy [21] and matplotlib [22] have emerged as the go-to data analysis tools following the increased popularity of python as a scientific computing language. While this is great step forward, python programs are still not easily distributed, especially for mobile devices. Lately there has been a lot of enthusiasm around combining a python back-end with the browser interface using Jupyter and JavaScript extensions such as Bokeh but this solution still offers only limited interactivity.

Distributing visualizations as images and videos is adequate for some cases but offers little to no interactivity to the end user. Computers are capable of much more. Finally, these visualizations still need to be generated somehow — presumably using one of the aforementioned mathematical packages.

The golden standard of web-based visualization is set by d3.js [23], the eighth most starred library on GitHub as of September 2018. The library is built using JavaScript programming language and conventional web technologies. This enables the end users to freely interact with the data looking for interesting patters. While d3 could be our library of choice, it still lacks in certain aspects. The system is built on vector graphics, and displaying three-dimensional objects is not possible without serious rework. Approximating algebraic objects with datasets is a separate complex task not handled by d3.

There are several online systems for mathematical visualization. Desmos offers no 3D capabilites. GraphyCalc [24] only supports explicit functions of two variables. Wolfram Alpha [25] delegates computations and rendering to a server back-end, limiting real-time client interactivity. MathBox is, as of 2018, still an early prototype with unclear development status. Finally, GeoGebra is the system most suitable for our use case but the 3D support appears to be an afterthought.

As shown in this section, the solutions available do not meet our design constraints. In the following sections we go on to describe our own solutions to the problem — JavaScript libraries Skeleton and Grafar Sect. 3.5, suitable for 2D and 3D mathematical visualization, respectively.

3.3   VisualMath.ru Web Application

A discussion of mathematical visualization is inseparable from the educational use cases. As stated in Sect. 2.3, we keep in mind the typical scenario we have all participated in. The students attend the lecture where the lecturer walks them through the necessary theory, supporting his arguments with illustrations.

Our team has already developed a functional prototype of the system described in [46]. It is a conventional client-server application consisting of a REST API and a single page application (SPA). We have chosen the SPA approach because it is well suited for the massively interactive concepts described in Sect. 2.3.

Apart from our custom-made solutions, the application relies heavily on KaTeX for client-side TeX rendering [27]. While omitting some of the more advanced TeX features, it offers an improved performance over MathJax, [28,29]. This library also powers the popular online learning platform, Khan Academy.

Developing a content management interface for lecturers is another high-priority goal of our project. Mathematics professors are often conservative when it comes to technology. Few of us can be truly called open minded. To capture the attention of this audience, we need to put a lot of effort into the ease-of-use. The concept is fairly simple: a lecture is a board, onto which a lecturer places colored cubes, each representing some content module. The content types supported include but are not limited to, illustrations, theoretical blocks, tests. Having assembled the lecture, the content editor proceeds to edit the modules. Importing educational content from the editor's computer is also supported.

The web application prototype implements many of the ideas described. The users can create and edit lectures, show the visual modules to the audience, and run tests to evaluate the students' understanding of the topic (see Fig. 2).

Fig. 2. Creating a lecture on visualmath.ru

For even further immersion of the students, our team has developed an Android application that can be used to view the lectures [38]. The iOS application is currently under development.

3.4 Grafar, a Library for Three-Dimensional Interactive Visualization

Grafar is a JavaScript library for creating interactive three-dimensional visualization developed specifically for VisualMath.ru project. As opposed to Wolfram, the library works in a browser with no proprietary plug-ins. Grafar is also among the fastest visualization libraries: the tests with computing explicitly defined surfaces over 1000×1000 grid have shown usable performance of 30 frames per second.

Grafar is designed from the ground up for mathematical visualization, featuring a high-level interface for working with analytical objects. Instead of generating the dataset to be displayed ad-hoc, the developers define the values of free variables along with their mappings. This model encourages very concise and readable code:

const x = grafar.range(−1, 1, 100).select(); const y = grafar.range(−1, 1, 100).select(); const z = grafar.map([x, y], (x, y) => Math.cos(x) * Math.sin(y)); grafar.pin([x, y, z], surfContainer);

The system relies on a three-step conceptual model of visualization:

- Find an algorithmic form of the objects, compile functions for efficient use on numeric arrays;
- Sample the free variables and find a finite set of points that reasonably approximate the object;
- Render the dataset, respecting inter-point topology.

Theoretically, any visualization library (d3, highcharts, echarts) can be used for the rendering step through custom bindings. However, the problem with plugging generic statistical visualization systems is their focus on aggregated representations over performance. While such preprocessing makes sense when helping users make sens of massive statistical datasets, it is useless for algebraic objects. The primary mathematical use-case is displaying thousands of points moving unpredictably every frame. The existing SVG-based libraries are simply inadequate for this scenario.

Numerical computing, even in the simplest form of applying a complex function over a set of points is not a classical web-development problem either. Grafar uses a concept called Reactive Programming (RP) to efficient implement real-time updates. This paradigm has made its way into mainstream front-end programming lately: the massively popular Vue.js framework [31] uses pull-based RP (the submodel Grafar also uses), while the more experimental cycle.js [33] pushes further the original electrical engineering metaphor. RxJS [32] is the go-to library for state management in Angular applications, with versions for all the major languages developed by Microsoft. While handling complex systems with interconnected dependencies, reactive programming still manages to be easy for the less-technical users: this is the model used by Microsoft Excel to recompute the formulas on source cell updates. Architects employ a visual programming software, Grasshopper, for designing procedural buildings.

Reactive Programming is an umbrella term for programming techniques using explicit Data Flow Graph (DFG). The nodes of such a graph replace the conventional variables, with the edges connecting the variables that depend on one another. This allows for reliable and efficient updates of all the dependent variables when a free variable changes — we locate the node's children and recompute their values, repeating recursively. Not only does this avoid unnecessary recomputation of those variables that do not depend on the changed one but it also allows dead code elimination and automatic parallelization. Finally, as a declarative technique, reactive programming is easy to understand for those already familiar with mathematical notation.

Unfortunately, the existing JavaScript libraries for reactive computations can not be readily used for data volumes of the magnitude encountered routinely in mathematical visualization and numerical computing. Connecting the SciJS ecosystem developed for numerical computing with reactive programming presents an exciting challenge for the open source community, if only too specialized for mainstream adoption.

Finally, Grafar uses WebGL for fast rendering. This technology allows the browser to access the GPU, unleashing the power of massively parallel computations to update the image in real time. Vector graphics used by d3 can not be used to display a large number of objects, while with the native canvas API we are still stuck in the single browser thread for projecting the multidimensional data onto the viewport. There is a multitude of specialized WebGL libraries, most prominent in cartography — MapboxGL.JS and deck.gl are two popular examples.

While the mathematical and scientific imaging possesses a distinctive visual style setting it apart from the commercial information graphics, this more often than not arises unintentionally from the lack of care. Scientists do not assign significant weight to matters of "aesthetics", often falling back to the default values of their chosen plotting library and validating this behavior by their fellow academics. However, the right choices of representations and color maps can make all the difference. Grafar can be used to display higher-dimensional objects in various ways: through small multiples, parallel coordinates or coloring. Optimal color maps can be generated by standalone packages, yielding more attractive and comprehensible results.

Thanks to its massive performance and layered architecture, Grafar can also be used for generic data visualization tasks. Discrete mathematical objects, such as digital signal processing or graph theory, are not out of reach either. Datasets with hundreds of thousands observations can be displayed with a usable frame rate even on lower-end mobile devices.

A stable version of Grafar is distributed through npm, the de-facto package manager of JavaScrtipt development. Source code, written in TypeScript, is available on github, [34].

3.5 Skeleton

Another part of our work is the library for two dimensional visualization called Skeleton. It is a foundation for many of our 2D programs. The library implements our other idea — state synchronization between the lecturer's computer and the student's one. If a lecturer changes coordinates of a graph, moves some elements or interacts with buttons and sliders then exactly the same changes happen on computers (or smartphones) of students simultaneously. The core concept of Skeleton library is being an easy-to-use tool to build mathematical visualizations

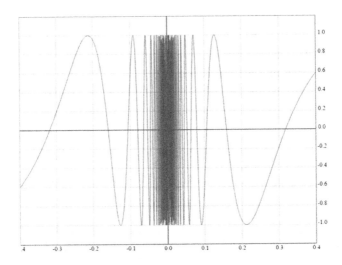

Fig. 3. An example of Skeleton-based program drawing $\sin(1/x)$ function.

(e.g. Fig. 3). Later we realized that the library shows itself best when we create visualization of calculus objects and theorems. Each graph object has its own API making it simple to change the state. As a result, it allows to create animated graphs easily [41]. The synchronization is done by WebSocket browser API [43]. This requires the state of each object, including the graph itself, to be serializable to string. However, the library is not tied to any transport and WebSocket can be replaced with similar tools, both browser-native and libraries, transferring data from server to client in real time. For example, it can be WebRTC which transfers data peer-to-peer [44,45].

4   Results and Conclusion

At the end of the article we provide some example visualizations from the Visual-Math.ru project. Most of them are from the calculus course. Because of our teaching background, this area is better represented in our project than the other university and school courses.

In the first part, there are images of 2D library Skeleton. For some of the images we also comment on rendering time if there is a large number of elements. We used a laptop with Intel Core i5 2.3 GHz, 8 Gb RAM. This setup is typically cost less then 1000$ and usually available for many laptop owners.

In the second part we provide examples of Grafar visualizations. One of the examples contains a comparison with a similar image created in MathWorks' MATLAB.

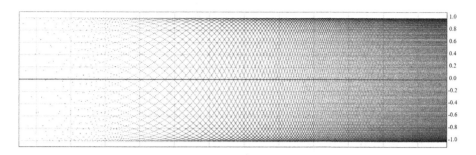

Fig. 4. The sequence $x_n = \sin n$ in logarithmic scale.

4.1 Examples of Skeleton Programs

The first program shows the sequence $x_n = \sin(n)$ in logarithmic scale. The image shows the first 50000 elements of the sequence. The rendering time was 1232 ms.

The image (see Fig. 4) is an example of a sequence having the closed interval $[-1, 1]$ as a set of subsequential limits. In our opinion, the image can help to see this fact clearly.

The next object is a slightly modified Thomae's function in the open interval $(0, 1)$ also known as Riemann function or popcorn function (see Fig. 5).

$$R(x) = \begin{cases} \frac{(-1)^n}{n}, & x = \frac{m}{n} \in \mathbf{Q}, \\ 0, & x \in \mathbf{R} \setminus \mathbf{Q}. \end{cases} \tag{1}$$

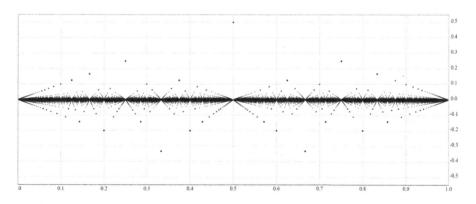

Fig. 5. Thomae's function in the open interval $(0, 1)$.

The Fig. 5 shows that the function is continuous in every irrational point and discontinuous in every rational point. Also it has a supremum and infimum for every interval of the real axis.

A modified Tomae's function is:

$$\widetilde{R}(x) = \begin{cases} n, & x = \frac{m}{n} \in \mathbf{Q}, \\ 0, & x \in \mathbf{R} \setminus \mathbf{Q}. \end{cases} \tag{2}$$

The new function (see Fig. 6) is notable because it is finite but not bounded on any numeric interval. Even a geometrically intuitive person can hardly imagine the appearance of the function. The figure shows all the points in the interval $(0, 1)$ with the denominator not exceeding 1000. The rendering time was 5005 ms.

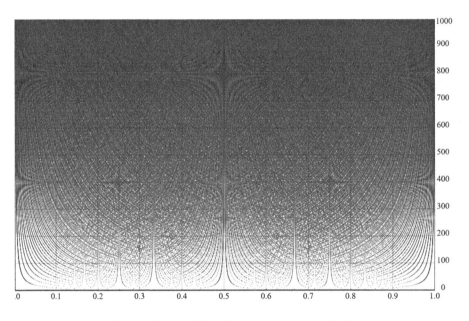

Fig. 6. The modified Tomae's function in $(0, 1)$.

The last figure (see Fig. 7) was captured in the program demonstrating a property of differentiable functions to be linear close to differentiable points. The figure also shows the control elements (dropdowns and buttons) that a lecturer or a student can use to see the property in an animation.

Unfortunately, the animations cannot be shown in this article. You can find some of the animations on a web site «A Programmer Library». For example, our work «9 GIFs on numerical sequences» [40, 41].

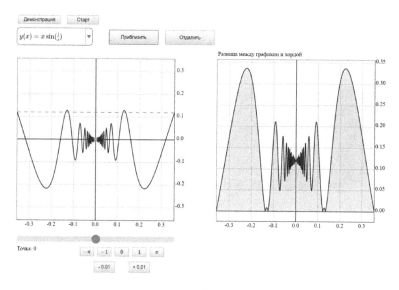

Fig. 7. The function $y = x \cdot \sin \frac{1}{x}$ is not differentiable at $x = 0$.

4.2   Grafar Examples

The figure below shows a volume bounded by the following surfaces:

$$V = \{(x, y, z) \mid x \geq |z| \mid$$

$$x = z^2 + x^2,$$

$$2x = z^2 + x^2,$$

$$0 \leq y \leq 3 - z^2 - x^2\}$$

The left picture of the Fig. 8 shows the domain and the bounding surfaces. The right picture is a projection of the cut orthogonal to the axis Oy to the xOz plane. The program allows to move the cut, the projection. The bounding lines change in real rime.

The next example visualizes the method of Lagrange multipliers. The problem is to find a local maximum of a function $f(x, y) = 2x + 3y$ subject to a condition $x^2 + y^2 = 1$. The function describes a plane and the condition is a cylinder.

The Lagrange functions for this problem are paraboloids of revolution (depending on the multiplier's sign upward- or downward-facing). They have unconditional minimum and maximum at the points of the conditional extremum of the given problem (Fig. 9).

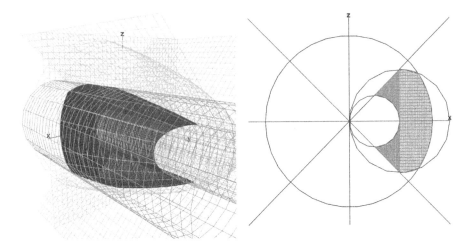

Fig. 8. An illustration on triple integrals

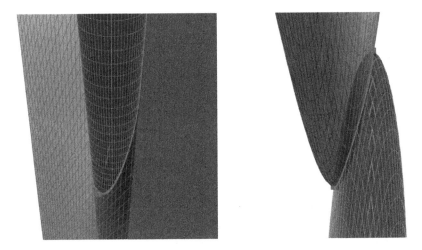

Fig. 9. An illustration on Lagrange multiplier method

The next image illustrates a topic from analytic geometry.
The Fig. 10 shows a one-sheet hyperboloid

$$\frac{x^2}{a^2} + \frac{y^2}{b^2} - \frac{z^2}{c^2} = 1.$$

The program allows to change all the three parameters of the surface in a real time – a, b, c. Students can see how these variables affect the surface.

The last figure compares how the surface looks in

$$x^2 + y^2 + z^2 = a^2, \quad x^2 + y^2 + z^2 = b^2, \quad x^2 + y^2 = z^2,$$
$$x \geq 0, \quad 0 < a < b, \tag{3}$$

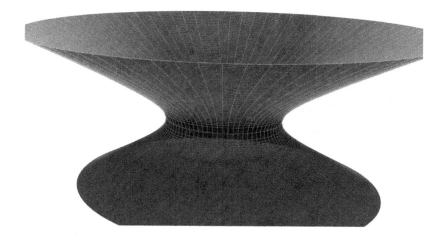

Fig. 10. A one-sheet hyperboloid

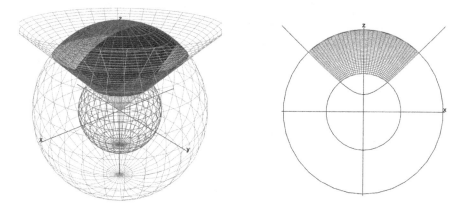

Fig. 11. Scope (3), depicted in the Grafar library.

Grafar (Fig. 11) and in The MathWorks Matlab, [16], (Fig. 12).

As the image beauty is a rather subjective concept, we note that in our project we could not use Matlab system for the reasons described in the part Sect. 3.2. First of all, because Matlab does not work in the browser.

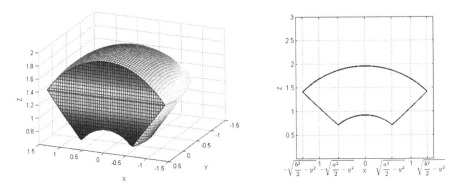

Fig. 12. Scope (3), depicted in the MathWorks Matlab.

Acknowledgements. Authors should note that a very large number of people worked on the project described in this article. Basically these were A. Nikitin's students, who wrote their course works and theses on this topic. We express our deep gratitude to all of them. We would like to single out among them people who participated in the creation of the illustrations involved in this article: N. Kondrashov, A. Korytova, A. Anokhin, M. Gritsaev, I. Kushnir, A. Shemendyuk and M. Lukashova.

References

1. Eick, S.G., Wills, G.J.: High interaction graphics. Eur. J. Oper. Res. **81**(3), 445–459 (1995)
2. de Guzman, M.: The role of visualization in the teaching and learning of mathematical analysis (2002)
3. Hilbert, D., Cohn-Vossen, S.: Geometry and the Imagination, vol. 87. American Mathematical Society (1999)
4. Karadag, Z.: Improving online mathematical thinking. In: 11th International Congress on Mathematical Thinking in Elementary and Advanced Mathematics. Educational Studies in Mathematics, vol. 38, pp. 111–113 (2011)
5. Polya, G.: How to Solve It: A New Aspect of Mathematical Method. Princeton University Press, Princeton (2014)
6. Tufte, E.R., Graves-Morris, P.R.: The Visual Display of Quantitative Information, vol. 2. Graphics Press, Cheshire (1983)
7. Uspenskiy, V.A.: Appologiya matematiki (sbornik statej). ANF, Moscow (2017). (in Russian)
8. Vickers, P., Faith, J., Rossiter, N.: Understanding visualization: a formal approach using category theory and semiotics. IEEE Trans. Vis. Comput. Graph. **19**(6), 1048–1061 (2013)
9. Ziemkiewicz, C., Kosara, R.: Understanding information visualization in the context of visual communication. Technical report, Technical Report CVCUNCC-07-08 (2007)
10. Zimmermann, W., Cunningham, S.: Editors' introduction: what is mathematical visualization. In: Visualization Teaching Learning Mathematics, pp. 1–7 (1991)
11. Arnold, V.I.: Experimentalnaya matematika. FAZIS, Moscow (2005). (in Russian)

12. MIT Open Course Ware. https://ocw.mit.edu/
13. The d'Arbeloff Interactive Mathematics Project. http://web.mit.edu/edtechfair/projects/interactive-math.html
14. Wolfram Mathematica: Modern Technical Computing. https://www.wolfram.com/mathematica/
15. Maple for STEM Education & Research - Maplesoft. https://www.maplesoft.com/MapleEducation/
16. MathWorks - MATLAB & Simulink. https://www.mathworks.com/products/matlab.html
17. OpenStax Access. The future of education. 1999–2018, Rice University. https://openstax.org/subjects/math/
18. R: The R Project for Statistical Computing. https://www.r-project.org/
19. GNU Octave. https://www.gnu.org/software/octave/
20. The Julia Language. https://julialang.org/
21. SciPy.org. https://www.scipy.org/
22. Matplotlib: Python plotting. https://matplotlib.org/index.html
23. D3.js - Data-Driven Documents. https://d3js.org/
24. GraphyCalc - 3D Graphing Calculator. http://www.graphycalc.com/
25. Wolfram|Alpha: Computational Intelligence. http://www.wolframalpha.com/
26. Michael Mikowski, Josh Powell - Single Page Web Applications: JavaScript end-to-end (2013)
27. Khan/KaTeX: Fast math typesetting for the web. https://github.com/Khan/KaTeX
28. KaTeX and MathJax Comparison Demo. https://www.intmath.com/cg5/katex-mathjax-comparison.php
29. KaTeX - a new way to display math on the Web. https://www.intmath.com/blog/mathematics/katex-a-new-way-to-display-math-on-the-web-9445
30. Yushkevich, A.P.: The History of Mathematics in the Middle Ages. Fizmatlit, Moscow (1961). (in Russian)
31. Reactivity in Depth — Vue.js. https://vuejs.org/v2/guide/reactivity.html
32. Angular - The RxJS library. https://angular.io/guide/rx-library
33. Cycle.js. https://cycle.js.org/#-functional-and-reactive
34. Grafar 4 GitHub. https://github.com/thoughtspile/Grafar/
35. Scalable Vector Graphics (SVG) Full 1.2 Specification. https://www.w3.org/TR/SVG12/
36. HTML Canvas 2D Context. https://www.w3.org/TR/2dcontext/
37. WebGL 2.0 Specification. https://www.khronos.org/registry/webgl/specs/latest/2.0/
38. MaximPestryakov/visualmath-android. https://github.com/MaximPestryakov/visualmath-android
39. cherurg/skeleton: The drawing mathematical 2D visualizations. https://github.com/cherurg/skeleton
40. Programmer's library. https://proglib.io/
41. 9 gifs, which illustrate numerical sequences | Programmer's library (in Russian). https://proglib.io/p/sequences/
42. 9 gifs, clearly illustrating the notion of differentiability | Programmer's library (in Russian). https://proglib.io/p/diff/
43. RFC 6455 - The WebSocket Protocol. https://tools.ietf.org/html/rfc6455
44. WebRTC 1.0: Real-time Communication Between Browsers. https://www.w3.org/TR/webrtc/
45. Can I use... WebRTC. https://caniuse.com/#search=webrtc
46. VisualMath.ru: Platform for the blended learning. http://www.visualmath.ru/

Cognitive Computing Cybersecurity: Social Network Analysis

Alimbubi Aktayeva[1,3]([✉]) [iD], Rozamgul Niyazova[2] [iD],
Gulshat Muradilova[1] [iD], Yerkhan Makatov[3] [iD],
and Ulzhan Kusainova[3] [iD]

[1] Sh. Ualikhanov, Kokshetau State University,
Abay Str. 76, 020000 Kokshetau, Kazakhstan
aaktaewa@list.ru, mgs@mail.ru
[2] L. Gumilyov Eurasian National University,
Satpayev Str. 2, 010008 Astana, Kazakhstan
rozamgul@list.ru
[3] Abay Myrzakhmetov Kokshetau University,
Auezov Str. 189, 020000 Kokshetau, Kazakhstan
erhanmk@list.ru, ulzhan97@mail.ru

Abstract. The structure and basic principles of technology for increasing the probability of identifying subjects of information processes of open Internet resources based on ontology methods are considered. Based on this ontology the knowledge base intended for creation of the program systems supporting ensuring information security has been realized. The first step in building the domain theory is a formal description of the domain ontology, i.e. the meaning of all used terms specific to the given subject area. Cognitive ontology's of subject areas are a tool necessary to achieve high pertinence of information retrieval and are needed to describe key concepts of a given subject area. The developed ontological knowledge base has been used when developing the software complex intended for identification of the user of social networks when ensuring information security, monitoring and preventing threats. This article is next in a series of articles by the authors in which they continue to monitor and analyze the current state and new tendencies in the field of information security and safety of information.

Keywords: Ontology · Knowledgebase · Cybersecurity · Social network · Identification · Cognitive computing

1 Introduction

The rapid development of social networks and the ability to collect information from them led to a marked increase in interest in analyzing social networks and the emergence of new methods that are becoming increasingly popular and are used in various fields: to search for experts, to recruit a team of specialists, social recommendations, marketing, communications, advertising and many others.

© Springer Nature Switzerland AG 2020
V. Sukhomlin and E. Zubareva (Eds.): Convergent 2018, CCIS 1140, pp. 28–43, 2020.
https://doi.org/10.1007/978-3-030-37436-5_3

Social networks are more and more widely used in the interests of informational and psychological impact. They provide opportunities in terms of influencing the formation of public opinion, the adoption of political, economic and military decisions, affect the information resources of the enemy and the dissemination of specially prepared information.

Thus, the task of collecting information, monitoring and analyzing social networks for information security is important and relevant. The purpose of this paper is to review and analyze the main tasks and methods of analyzing social networks used to detect, prevent and fight threats in social networks (see Fig. 1).

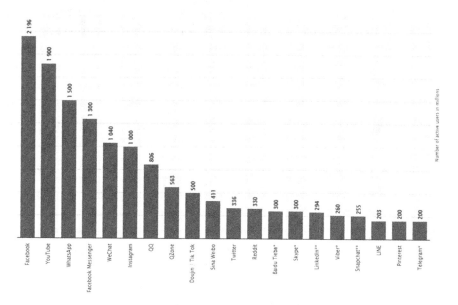

Fig. 1. Most famous social network sites worldwide as of July 2018, ranked by the number of active users (in millions) [22].

A series of massive data breaches last year saw cybersecurity plant its roots firmly in the public eye. The risk to organizations is great and is constantly growing. The simple truth is that threats evolve too rapidly for most cybersecurity systems to keep pace, and the ever-growing amount of data that companies hold (50% annual growth) is only increasing the challenge. The Internet of Things promises to exacerbate this growth even further, bringing with it an explosion in the number of data points. This explosion brings with it many positives, providing a great resource for organizations to learn from.

For example, 42% of cybersecurity professionals working at enterprise organizations claim that they ignore a significant number of security alert, 31% of organizations forced to ignore security alerts claim they ignore 50% or more security alerts because they can't keep up with the overall volume. The 2015 Cost of Data Breach Study by IBM and the Ponemon Institute found that the average total cost of a data breach rose from $3.52 million in 2014 to $3.79 million - and it is affecting everyone (see Fig. 2).

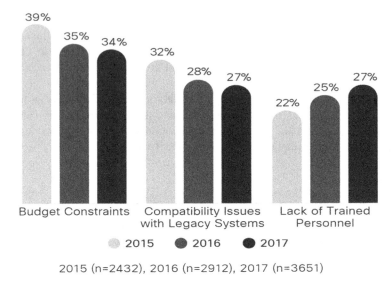

Fig. 2. The greatest obstacle to security: budget constraints [22].

Machine learning is useful for automatically detecting "known-known" threats—
the types of infections that have been seen before (see Fig. 3).

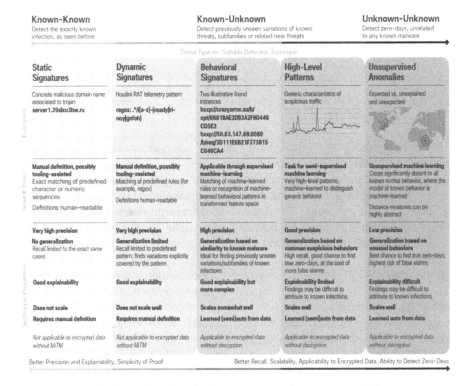

Fig. 3. Machine learning in network security: taxonomy [22].

But its real value, especially in monitoring, encrypted web traffic, stems from its ability to detect "known-unknown threats - previously unseen variant of known threats, malware subfamilies, or related new threats" and "unknown-unknown - net-new malware" threats.

The technology can learn to identify unusual patterns in large volumes of encrypted web traffic and automatically alert security teams to the need for further investigation. Behavior analytics tools are also considered useful when locating malicious actors in networks; 92% of security professionals said these tools work very to extremely well (see Fig. 4).

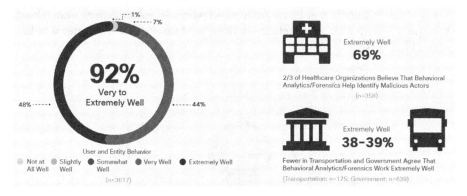

Fig. 4. Most security professionals see value in behavioral analytics tools [22].

Lack of skilled talent tops the list of obstacles in all industries and across all regions. In 2017, the median number of security professionals at organizations was 40, a significant increase from 2016's median number of 33 (see Fig. 5).

Fig. 5. Organizations hire more security professionals [22].

The IoT is still evolving, but adversaries are already exploiting security weaknesses in IoT devices to gain access to systems—including industrial control systems that support critical infrastructure. IoT botnets are thriving because organizations and users are deploying low-cost IoT devices rapidly and with little or no regard for security. IoT devices are Linux- and Unix-based systems, so they are often targets of executable and linkable format (ELF) binaries. They are also less challenging to take control of than a PC, which means it's easy for adversaries to quickly build a large army [17, 18].

IoT devices operate on a 24-hour basis and can be called into action at a moment's notice. And as adversaries increase the size of their IoT botnets, they are investing in more sophisticated code and malware and shifting to more advanced DDoS attacks. Between October 1, 2016, and September 30, 2017, Cisco threat researchers discovered 224 new vulnerabilities in non-Cisco products, of which 40 vulnerabilities were related to third-party software libraries included in these products, and 74 were related to IoT devices [17, 18] (see Fig. 6).

Total Vulnerabilities: 224

Fig. 6. Third-party library and IoT vulnerabilities [22].

The current stage of development of society is characterized by the increasing role of the information sphere, which is a collection of information, information infrastructure, entities engaged in the collection, formation, dissemination, and use of information. Therefore, the tasks of ensuring information security are of particular importance, and in the course of technical progress, this importance will only increase [6, 7, 12, 13, 17, 18].

Among network resources, an increasing role is played by social networks, which, in addition to performing the function of supporting communication, exchanging opinions and receiving information from their members, are increasingly becoming objects and means of information management and an arena of information confrontation (see Fig. 7).

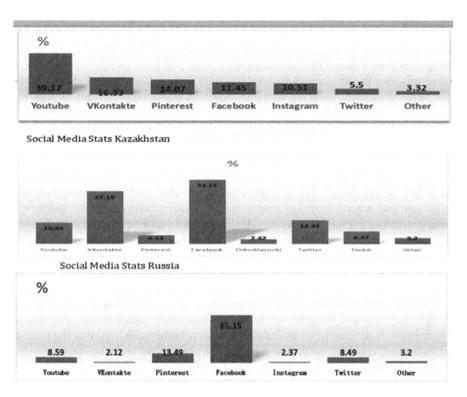

Fig. 7. Social Media Stats Kazakhstan, Russian Federation and Worldwide [17, 18].

Social networks have become an important tool of information influence, including - to manipulate the person, social groups and society as a whole, as well as the field of cyberwar.

A social network is a social structure consisting of a set of subjects and a set of relations defined on it. Formally, a social network is a graph $G(N, E)$, where $N = \{1, 2, \ldots, n\}$ is a finite set of vertices and E is a set of edges reflecting the interaction of agents.

Currently, as rightly noted, there is a lack of a systematic presentation of methods and algorithms for network analysis, suitable for modern social applied research. One of such promising areas of research in this area is the modeling of information security systems using ontologies as specifications of this subject area.

Ontologies allow conceptualizing the subject area, formalizing accumulated knowledge: defining the key concepts of the subject area, defining the semantic relations between the concepts necessary for setting tasks and describing the processes of their solution in a given subject area. In addition, the advantage of using ontologies is the ability to analyze, accumulate and reapply knowledge of the subject area, obtained from different sources.

What is cognitive computing cybersecurity?

As cyber attacks grow in volume and complexity, artificial intelligence is helping under-resourced security operations analysts stay ahead of threats. Curating threat intelligence from millions of research papers, blogs and news stories, artificial intelligence provides instant insights to help you fight through the noise of thousands of daily alerts, drastically reducing response times. A tremendous amount of security knowledge resides sailed in different repositories, such as threat intelligence databases, malware sandbox reports, threat reports released by security vendors, or blogs. Security analysts are required to search these systems manually, keep track of the findings and correlate over them to identify actionable insight.

Cognitive computing is a computerized model that simulates human thought processes. It is a fundamentally Artificial Intelligence that uses data mining, pattern recognition, and natural language processing by utilizing both supervised and unsupervised machine learning techniques. This means that, unlike the static systems currently in place, it evolves as threats evolve, learning from data in real-time to identify previously hidden patterns and anomalous behavior.

By doing this, it can anticipate changes to the cyber landscape, and pinpoint and disrupt unknown threats as they arise. It can also identify the many, many false positives that the data throws up, building a profile of the normal 'pattern of life' for an employee or company, flagging up deviations that could indicate that a system is compromised. It appears to be missing to self-learn in the same way that the human brain works. It can help predict and prevent emerging and undocumented security tatters of time before cognitive computing is a mainstay as a cybersecurity tool. Where human analysts fit into this, time will tell.

The methodologies and technologies on the *Cognitive Cybersecurity* research on to help to detect, understanding and deflecting advanced cybersecurity threats and attacks on their network. It explores challenging research problems posed by building and combining Artificial Intelligence and cognitive methods, scalable big data security analytics as an as graph mining, deep correlation, and provenance analysis, and next-generation defense mechanisms to gain deep intelligence and insights about cyber security threats and attacks as well as threat actors. They are as a contextual and behavioral analysis, machine learning, reasoning, transparent malware analysis, active defense, and cyber deception layers. Current focus areas on the methodologies and technologies at the Cognitive Cybersecurity researches are:

1. Artificial Intelligence-powered and cognitive security offense analytics, cyber threat hunting, and threat intelligence consolidation;
2. Cross-stack cyber deception and active defense techniques;
3. Cybersecurity analytics, event correlation, and provenance tracking on the network and device-level;

4. Next-generation malware analysis;
5. Design of high-speed and scalable data collection platforms for real-time and historical security analytics;
6. Security data visualization and penetration testing (see Fig. 8).

Every day, cybersecurity analysts investigate ongoing incidents that could potentially impact their enterprise. To proactively mitigate their risk, they need to stay current on new types of threats and attack vectors documented in more than 1 million security bulletins, threat reports and news articles published each year.

They sift through mountains of data, false positives, and ever-morphing malware and exploits to identify the few security events that are most likely to be problematic and require fast action.

Advanced analytics and other software tools help security analysts detect anomalies and determine high-risk threats, but the volume of information combined with the rate and sophistication of attacks has made it nearly impossible for any single analyst to keep up. Technology can help, but only to a point.

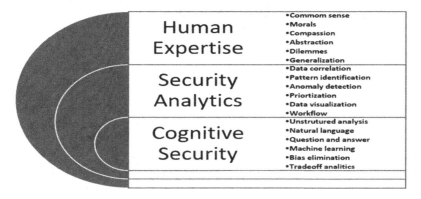

Fig. 8. Cognitive system bridge.

Traditional security relies primarily on structured data that technology can organize and analyze—but that only account for 20% of all the data out there. It's the unstructured knowledge—the other approximately 80% of data delivered in natural language that analysts read and discuss all the time—that often proves most valuable in detecting and stopping threats before they cause harm.

Cognitive computing could tap into and make sense of security data that has previously been dark to an organization's defense, enabling security analysts to gain new insights and respond to threats with greater confidence at scale and speed. Cognitive systems are taught, not programmed, using the same types of unstructured information that security analysts rely on.

Like an analyst cognitive system are taught, the system can learn as it goes, able to recognize terms and make connections between them, so it can understand questions and use reason to provide answers.

The more Cognitive computing works with actual users, such as clients and business partners, the more it will understand the context of the information it's learning. That means it will not only be able to provide more precise answers, but it will also make connections between data points that a security analyst may never have considered.

Cognitive computing can help us keep up with the rate and pace of the threat landscape, especially in the face of a significant cybersecurity skills shortage. Cybersecurity won't replace security analysts, but rather will augment their knowledge so they can more effectively investigate and respond to threats. What would take a security analyst day or weeks to investigate and Cognitive computing will be able to do in minutes or hours.

The security analysts using for Cybersecurity could quickly and accurately analyze graphically representations of emerging threats that might impact their organization. Since Cybersecurity reads the latest reports and applied them to events in the organization's environment, it can respond to natural-language questions. Security professionals will be able to be more proactive, spending less time on the mundane and more on the important work of stopping attacks and protecting their enterprise.

To solve the problem of information retrieval in the social networks of the Internet, three types of ontologies can be used:

1. Hierarchy of domain ontologies;
2. Ontology of Internet resources;
3. Ontology user (see Fig. 10).

The hierarchy of ontologies of subject domains contains ontologies of sections and subsections of a certain domain. To implement the proposed approach, we used the model-theoretic formalization of ontologies [6, 7, 12, 13]. The ontology of the domain is considered as a pair - signature from the set of key concepts of the domain and the set of analytical proposals that are true in this subject domain. This set of analytical proposals determines the meaning of key concepts of the domain (Fig. 9).

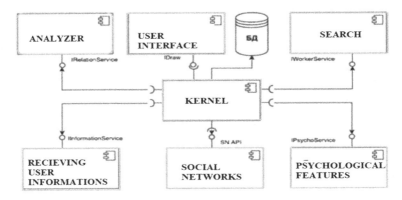

Fig. 9. The system component of the program complex for assessing the security of social networks.

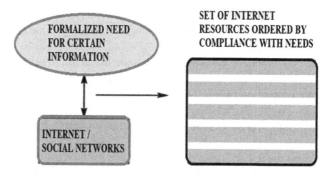

Fig. 10. Formal model Social networks search information.

Pertinence is a measure of search quality; how well the search result satisfies the user's information need, i.e. how much the list of resources given by the search engine corresponds to the information need that the user tried to formulate in this formalized query. Information need of the user can be expressed in a formalized request with varying degrees of completeness and accuracy. Achieving high pertinence is the main task of modern search engines (Fig. 11).

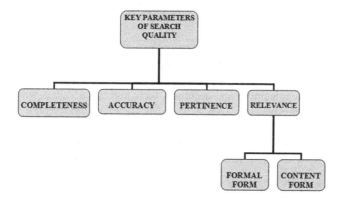

Fig. 11. Common quality parameters of the information - search engines.

Relevance is a measure of how well a list of results responds to a query; determine the order in which search results are presented to the user. Relevance is a narrower concept than pertinence. Distinguish between content and formal relevance - according to the method of its definition.

Formal relevance is a correspondence determined algorithmically by comparing the search prescription and the search image of the document, based on the issuance criterion used in the information retrieval system.

Content relevance - document compliance with the information request, determined in an informal way.

Relevance - a binary relation between a formalized query and the response to this query. The numerical value of relevance depends on three parameters - accuracy, completeness, and ranking.

Ranking - the correctness of the order in which the list of information search results is presented.

Accuracy - the proportion of relevant resources among all resources present in the issue.

Completeness - the proportion of relevant resources present in the issuance among all relevant resources available on the Internet.

The main goal of the research is to develop methods for increasing the pertinence of information retrieval. To obtain high pertinence, we must achieve both high adequacy and high relevance. In order to obtain high adequacy, the user must have:

1. Various and sufficiently rich tools for creating a formalized query;
2. The ability to accurately and fully formulate his information needs.

There are two more characteristics of information retrieval, more deeply revealing relevance and perinterence. Accuracy is a measure of search efficiency, expressed as the ratio of the number of relevant resources found to the total number of resources contained in the search engine output in response to a formalized query.

Completeness is a measure of search efficiency, expressed as the ratio of the number of relevant resources extracted from the search engine from the Internet in response to a formalized query, to the total number of relevant resources contained on the Internet.

Accuracy - the share of pertinent resources among all resources present in the output, and completeness is the share of pertinent resources present in the issue, among all the pertinent resources available on the Internet. Obviously, with such a change in the definitions of completeness and accuracy, their numerical values will also change for specific results of processing specific requests. To make the research more precise, you will need to enter a more formal definition of search performance parameters. This approach is based on the logical analysis of the natural language and the theory of the speech actions [6, 7, 12, 13]. In the information search we consider three entities:

1. Person - a user who wants to get information;
2. Formalized request;
3. And the last, third is the answer to the request, presented in the form of an ordered list of found Internet resources.

Therefore, the first step in searching for information is in formulating a request. The correspondence between the user's information need and the formalized query determines the success of the information search. Let us call the correspondence between the user's information need and a formalized request, the adequacy of the request.

Cognitive ontologies of subject areas are a tool necessary to achieve high pertinence of information retrieval and are needed to describe key concepts of a given subject area.

The purpose of which is to explicitly define the meaning of terms specific to the given subject area; Shows a common vision of such subject areas.

An ontology is an explicit specification of the conceptualization. The need to use ontologies follows from the general formulation of the problem of modeling discrete systems presented in Fig. 12.

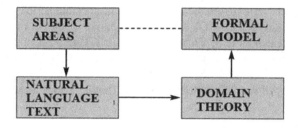

Fig. 12. Statement of the problem of the simulated subject area.

The simulated search domain will be represented as a set of texts in natural language. The task is to build a formal model of this subject area. To do this, you first need to build the domain theory. The first step in building the domain theory is a formal description of the domain ontology, i.e. the meaning of all used terms specific to the given subject area. Let us briefly formulate what the experts mean by the concept of ontology [8]:

1. The ontology - a tool for modeling reality;
2. The ontology describes a specific subject area;
3. The knowledge represented by ontology should be inter-subjective;
4. The ontology should contain a glossary of key concepts and a specification of their meaning.

The formal ontology of the subject domain SD is the pair $O = \langle A, \sigma \rangle$, where σ - a set of key concepts of the domain and A - a set of analytical proposals describing the meaning of these key concepts. In the definition of the domain ontology, the set σ is the signature of the ontology. This means that σ contains only symbols of concepts.

The set A consists of the definitions of the symbols contained in the signature σ. In addition, $\sigma \subseteq \sigma(A)$ holds, but not necessarily true $\sigma = \sigma(A)$. This means that the set of analytical sentences A may contain signature characters that are not symbols of key concepts in the domain. This can happen when, when describing the meaning of signature symbols (that is, symbols of key concepts), we use statements that contain concepts that are not themselves key concepts of a given subject domain.

Definition 1. For the formal ontology $O = \langle A, \sigma \rangle$, the set A does not have to be a theory, i.e. the set A is not necessarily deductively closed.

The simplest type of ontology, defining the meanings of the terms of a certain subject domain, is a glossary (or thesaurus). Of interest is the question of the possibility of representing the meaning of key concepts of an arbitrary domain with the help of a glossary. To answer this question, we consider the formal definition of a glossary of the subject domain. We give a formal definition of a glossary in theoretical-model terms. For this, the following definitions and notation are required:

The signature is a tuple $\sigma = \langle P_1, \ldots, P_n, \ f_1, \ldots, f_k, \ c_1, \ldots, c_m \rangle$, where $P_1, \ldots, P_n$ are predicate symbols; $f_1, \ldots, f_k$ are symbols of functions (operations); $c_1, \ldots, c_m$ are symbols of constants (i.e., selected elements).

Let $S(\sigma)$ denote the set of all sentences, i.e. formulas without free variables, signatures σ.

For a formula ϕ, let $\phi(\sigma)$ be the signature of the formula ϕ, that is, the set of all signature characters in ϕ. Let $\sigma(G)$ denote the signature of the set of formulas G.

For the set of sentences G by $Th(G) = \{\psi \in S(\sigma(G)) | G|\psi\}$ denote a theory that is axiomatically by the set of sentences of T. We denote by $Th(\varphi) = Th(\{\varphi\})$ a theory that is axiomatized by the sentence φ.

The symbol $\subset$ will denote the strict inclusion. That is, $A \subset B$ means that $A \subseteq B$ and $A \neq B$.

Definition 2. Let σ be a signature. The sequence of sentences $\varphi_1, \ldots, \varphi_n \in S(\sigma)$ is called a formal glossary (defining concepts from σ), if:

a) $\sigma(\phi_1) \subset \sigma(\phi_1 \& \phi_2) \subset \ldots \subset \sigma(\phi_1 \& \ldots \& \phi_n) = \sigma$;
b) adding each new sentence ϕ_k conservatively expands the previous set of sentences, i.e.

$$Th(\phi_1 \& \ldots \& \phi_k) = Th(\phi_1 \& \ldots \& \phi_n)S(\sigma(\phi_1 \& \ldots \& \phi_k))$$

Conservative expansion means the following: when defining new concepts, they should not change the meaning of already defined concepts. We have defined the meaning of the term only when later in the glossary its meaning will no longer be redefined, in particular, new information essential to its meaning will not be added. Conservative expansion is a prerequisite in the glossary definition.

Definition 3. We say that a formal glossary $\phi_1, \ldots, \phi_n$ represents a set of sentences G if

$$Th(G) = Th(\phi_1 \& \ldots \& \phi_n)$$

Definition 4. We say that the formal glossary $\phi_1, \ldots, \phi_n$ explicitly defines concepts from σ if there are such formulas $\psi_1, \ldots, \psi_n$ that for any $k > n$, we have

$$\varphi_{k+1} = \forall x \big(P(x) \leftrightarrow \psi_{k+1}(x) \big),$$

$$\text{or } \varphi_{k+1} = \forall x \big((f(x) = y) \leftrightarrow \psi_{k+1}(x, y) \big),$$

$$\text{or } \phi_{k+1} = \forall y \big((c = y) \leftrightarrow \psi_{k+1}(y) \big),$$

where $P, f, c \in \sigma \backslash \sigma(\phi_1 \& \ldots \& \phi_k)$; x - tuple $(n - k)$ variables;

$$\sigma(\psi_{k+1}) \subseteq \sigma(\phi_1 \& \ldots \& \phi_k)$$

The three types of definitions indicated are explicit definitions of the predicate (n-local relation), functions and constants.

2 Summary

To solve the problem of accurate information retrieval, two approaches are connected:

1. Search engine techniques to provide relevant formal query processing;
2. The Interface of Internet directories to provide the user with a clear and convenient interface.

The system of rubrics of social networks is based on a hierarchy of ontologies of subject domains; With the help of this ontology hierarchy, the relevance of the documents found in the selected domain is achieved.

Pertinence of information retrieval is achieved due to the specification of not only the subject area in which information is searched but also the type of Internet resource required, as well as the type of search task that the user wants to solve. For this, the ontology of the Internet and ontology are using user information retrieval systems.

To solve the pressing cybersecurity challenges of today, we need more creative approaches, and the only way to find them is to make new connections, that best describes the value of cognitive computing. The following tools allow us to better explore the combination of structured and unstructured data, be it customer, security, maintenance or financial information:

1. Making Connections with Cognitive Security;
2. Learning from Other Industries;
3. Intelligence Analysis;
4. Predictive Maintenance;
5. Risk Management;
6. Embarking on a Cognitive Journey.

In cybersecurity want to evolve past simply finding problems, no matter how fast, in predicting and preventing them. They want to use intelligence and indicators to take automatic action on potential threats. To solve the pressing security challenges of today and tomorrow, we need more creative approaches. Cognitive cyber intelligence threat, also known as cyber threat intelligence (CTI), is organized, analyzed and refined information about potential or current attacks that threaten.

Then the development of ontologies of subject domains is carried out on the basis of a theoretical model approach to the formalization of ontologies. A domain ontology is represented as a pair - a signature of a domain consisting of key terms and a set of analytical sentences describing the meaning of key terms of the domain.

References

1. III Kelly, J.E.: Computing, cognition and the future of knowing how humans and machines are forging a new age of understanding. In: IBM Research Whitepaper on Cognitive Computing (2015). https://s3.amazonaws.com/academia.edu.documents/44915350/Computing_Cognition_WhitePaper.pdf?AWSAccessKeyId=AKIAIWOWYYGZ2Y53UL3A&Expires=1554458924&Signature=Dt0OTA%2BiCZ0afcE8oUK9sDoYkOc%3D&response-content-disposition=inline%3B%20filename%3DComputing_cognition_and_the_future_of_kn.pdf, https://securityintelligence.com/dyre-wolf/. Accessed 01 Nov 2018
2. III Kelly, J.E., Hamm, S.: Smart Machines: IBM's Watson and the Era of Cognitive Computing. Columbia Business School Publishing, New York (2013)
3. Polanyi, M.: The Tacit Dimension. Routledge & Kegan Paul, London (1966)
4. Kuhn, J., Mueller, L.: The Dyre wolf campaign: stealing millions and hungry for more. IBM Secur. (2015). https://securityintelligence.com/dyre-wolf/. Accessed 01 Nov 2018
5. Wang, L., Raghavan, H., Castelli, V., Florian, R., Cardie, C.: A sentence compression based framework to query-focused multi-document summarization. In: Proceedings of the 51st Annual Meeting of the Association for Computational Linguistics, Sofia, Bulgaria, 4–9 August 2013, vol. 1, pp. 1384–1394 (2013)
6. Aktayeva, Al., Galieva, N., Asanova, K., Naraliev, N., Sundetov, S., Makulbek, N.: Technique of identification of users of social networks over ontologies. Mod. Inf. Technol. IT-Educ. 12(2), 26–34 (2016). (in Russian). http://sitito.cs.msu.ru/index.php/SITITO/article/view/48/35
7. Aktayeva, A., et al.: Cognitive ontology of information security priorities in social networks. In: Proceedings of the International Scientific and Practical Conference Open Semantic Technologies for Intelligent Systems, OSTIS-2017, pp. 365–376 (2017). http://proc.ostis.net/proc/Proceedings%20OSTIS-2017.pdf
8. Schumacher, M.: Toward a security core ontology. Security Engineering with Patterns. LNCS, vol. 2754, pp. 87–96. Springer, Heidelberg (2003). https://doi.org/10.1007/978-3-540-45180-8_6
9. Jutla, D., Bodorik, P., Gao, D.: Management of private data: addressing user privacy and economic, social, and ethical concerns. In: Jonker, W., Petković, M. (eds.) SDM 2004. LNCS, vol. 3178, pp. 100–117. Springer, Heidelberg (2004). https://doi.org/10.1007/978-3-540-30073-1_8
10. Undercoffer, J., Joshi, A., Pinkston, J.: Modeling computer attacks: an ontology for intrusion detection. In: Vigna, G., Kruegel, C., Jonsson, E. (eds.) RAID 2003. LNCS, vol. 2820, pp. 113–135. Springer, Heidelberg (2003). https://doi.org/10.1007/978-3-540-45248-5_7
11. Stepanov, P.A.: Processing automation of natural language texts. Vestnik NSU. Ser.: Inf. Technol. 11(2), 109–115 (2013). (in Russian). http://jit.nsu.ru/article.php?558+en_EN+549
12. Palchunov, D.E., Stepanov, P.A.: The use of model-theoretic methods for extracting ontological knowledge in the domain of information security. Softw. Eng. 11, 8–16 (2013). (in Russian)
13. Golomazov, D.D.: Term extraction from a collection of documents divided into rubrics. Inf. Technol. 2, 8–13 (2010). (in Russian)
14. Kolin, K.K.: Philosophy of information: the structure of reality and the phenomenon of information. Metaphysics 4, 61–84 (2013). (in Russian)
15. Ursul, A.D.: Nature of Information: a Philosophical Essay, 2nd edn. Chelyabinsk (2010). (in Russian)
16. ISO/IEC 27032: Information technology. Security techniques. Guidelines for cybersecurity (2012)

17. Social Media Stats Russian Federation. http://gs.statcounter.com/social-media-stats/all/russian-federation/#monthly-201308-201808-bar. Accessed 01 Nov 2018
18. Cisco Visual Networking Index: Forecast and Trends, 2017–2022 White Paper. https://www.cisco.com/c/en/us/solutions/collateral/service-provider/visual-networking-index-vni/complete-white-paper-c11-481360.html. Accessed 01 Nov 2018
19. Vorozhtsova, T.N.: Ontology as the basis for the development of intelligent cybersecurity systems. Ontol. Des. **4**(14), 69–77 (2014). (in Russian). https://elibrary.ru/item.asp?id=22545616
20. Massel, L.V., Massel, A.G.: Intelligent computing research directions of energy development. Bull. Tomsk. Polytech. Univ. **321**(5), 135–140 (2012). (in Russian). https://elibrary.ru/item.asp?id=18783678
21. Resolution of the Government of the Republic of Kazakhstan of 30.06.2017 no. 407 on Approval of the Cyber Security Concept ("Cybershield Kazakhstan"). (in Russian). https://online.zakon.kz/m/Document/?doc_id=39754354. Accessed 01 Nov 2018
22. Cisco Security Research. https://www.cisco.com/c/en/us/products/security/security-reports.html. Accessed 01 Nov 2018

Application of the Multi-layer Method and Method of Continuing at the Best Parameter to the Solving of a Stiff Equation

Elena Budkina[1] , Evgenii Kuznetsov[1] , Dmitry Tarkhov[2(✉)] ,
Anastasia Gomzina[2] , and Semyon Maltsev[2]

[1] Moscow Aviation Institute (National Research University),
Volokolamskoe shosse 4, 125993 Moscow, Russia
`emb0909@rambler.ru`, `kuznetsov@mai.ru`
[2] Peter the Great St. Petersburg Polytechnic University, Polytechnic Street 29,
195251 St. Petersburg, Russia
`dtarkhov@gmail.com`, `Gomzina.aa@edu.spbstu.ru`,
`semyon.maltsev@gmail.com`

Abstract. By using the example of one rigid boundary value problem for a second order differential equation on a sphere, we compare our two approaches for giving construction of approximate solutions. The first approach consists of using the method of prolongation of the solution by the best parameter. This approach allows us to substantially decrease the number of steps and increase stability of the calculation process with comparison to standard methods. The second approach is linked with the building of an approximated multi-layer solution to the problem and is based on the use of analytical recurrent rations. We build those recurrent ratios based on classic numerical methods, applied to an interval of variable length. In the result, an approximated solution in the form of a table of numbers is substituted with an approximated solution is the form of a function, which is easier to use for adaptation, building graphs and other purposes. Problems related to stiffness of material can be solved by using solution of singularly perturbed differential equations with applying standard methods for the numerical solution of ordinary differential equations, however it can lead to significant difficulties. The first difficulty is the loss of stability of the computational process, when small errors in individual steps lead to an uncontrolled increase in the error of computations as a whole. Another difficulty directly connected with the first one is the need to greatly reduce the integration step, which leads to a strong slowdown of the computational process. In this work, it is shown, that both of our approaches successfully cope with indicated difficulties.

Keywords: Sphere · Stiff equation · Multi-layer method · Best parameter singularly perturbed equation

V. Sukhomlin and E. Zubareva (Eds.): Convergent 2018, CCIS 1140, pp. 44–53, 2020.
https://doi.org/10.1007/978-3-030-37436-5_4

1 Introduction

Studies related to the solution of singularly perturbed equations began to develop at the beginning of the 20th century in the works of Prandtl related to the description of the boundary layer in problems of the motion of a viscous fluid. The formation of the theory of singularly perturbed equations was also presented in the works of Tikhonov [2–4]. He first considered the general form of nonlinear equations and systems with a small parameter with the highest derivative, defined the domain of influence of a solution of a degenerate equation and a degenerate system, and proved first results on the proximity of a solution of a degenerate equation (system of equations) to solving the original problem. He created a well-known scientific school of which Vasilyeva is a prominent representative. Later, she and her students Butuzov, Tupchiev, Nefedov, and others developed the theory of singular perturbations for equations containing small parameters in the higher derivatives. This was done both for ordinary differential equations and for initial-boundary value problems for partial differential equations. In the following, singular equations with a small parameter with the highest derivative will be called singularly perturbed. They obtained fundamental results on the representation of solutions of singularly perturbed problems by asymptotic series of special types. The main results obtained are presented in monographs [5, 6]. In addition to the consideration of problems with boundary layers, in the works of Vasilyeva, Butuzov, and Nefedova, problems with contrasting structures (internal boundary layers) were considered [7]. An overview of the results related to the study of solutions of problems with contrasting structures is given in [8]. In addition to these works, a significant place in the study of the existence of solutions of problems with boundary and internal layers is taken by the monograph of Chang and Howes [9], which outlines the basis of the apparatus of differential inequalities as applied to the proof of the existence of solutions of nonlinear boundary singularly perturbed problems and considers many practical problems applications from mathematical physics. It is also should be noted that today the apparatus of differential inequalities plays a leading role in the study of the existence of a solution of singularly perturbed equations. In the theory of singularly perturbed equations, differential inequalities were first used by Nagumo [10]. In addition, we note the contribution to the theory of singular perturbations of S. A. Lomov and I. S. Lomov, whose monograph [11] contains a mathematical theory of the boundary layer for linear differential equations in one-dimensional and multi-dimensional cases for operators with different properties. Earlier, S. A. Lomov published a monograph [12], in which, in addition to linear differential equations, nonlinear ones were also considered. The continuation of these results over the past 5 years are many works. We note the main. The main results in the field of numerical-analytical methods for solving singularly perturbed equations with boundary and internal layers belong to the school of Tikhonov. In the works of Butuzov and co-authors, the construction of asymptotes for singularly perturbed boundary problems (Dirichlet and Neumann) is considered for elliptic equations with internal and angular boundary layers [13–16], as well as for the first initial-boundary parabolic equation [sixteen]. The method of differential inequalities is used. In addition, boundary-value problems for ordinary differential equations with a multi-band inner layer (contrast structures of the splash and step type) are considered and asymptotic expansions for them are constructed [17].

In this work a singularly perturbed problem is considered [1]

$$\frac{d^2y}{dx^2} = F(x, y, y'), y(0) = 0, y(1) = 0 \tag{1}$$

Where $F(x, y, y') = A(x^2 + y^2 + \left(y'\right)^2 - 4)$, A – large parameter. Let's rearrange (1)

$$\begin{cases} \frac{dy}{dx} = v, \\ \frac{dv}{dx} = F(x, y, v) \end{cases} \tag{2}$$

When $A > 1$ a solution within the integrated function package of Wolfram Mathematica is not found. We will be looking for the solution with the use of two methods: numeric method of prolongation by the best parameter and original approximately-analytical method.

2   Numeric Method of Prolongation by the Best Parameter and Original Approximately Analytical Method

By performing parametrization of the source system (1) we introduce a parameter λ- the best argument [30], such that: $x = x(\lambda)$, $y = y(\lambda)$, $v = v(\lambda)$.

The discrete version of the parameterized task is:

$$\begin{cases} y - y_* - v(x - x_*) = 0, \\ v - v_* - F(x, y, v)(x - x_*) = 0, \\ (x - x_*)^2 + (y - y_*)^2 + (v - v_*)^2 - \Delta\lambda^2 = 0. \end{cases} \tag{3}$$

The symbol "$*$" denotes the solution found in the previous step on λ. The initial boundary problem will be solved by shooting. When solving a problem using the shooting method, the boundary problem is reduced to the initial problem, i.e. boundary conditions are replaced by initial conditions: $y(0) = 0$, $v(0) = p$.

The solution of the initial problem depends on the parameter p, i.e.

$$y = y(\lambda, \ p), \ v = v(\lambda, \ p). \tag{4}$$

In this function (4) must satisfy the boundary conditions $y(0) = 0$, $v(0) = p$, $y(1) = 0$:

$$R(p) = b(y(0, p), v(0, p), y(1, p)) = 0 \tag{5}$$

Parameter p can be found by any iterative method. We used Newton's method:

$$p_{s+1} = p_s - \left[\frac{\partial R}{\partial p}(p_s)\right]^{-1} R(p_s) \tag{6}$$

The convergence of Newton's method depends on the choice of the initial approximation of p_0. In [31] it is proposed in (6) to introduce a new parameter μ:

$$\Phi(p, \mu) = R(p) - (1 - \mu)R(p_0) = 0, \quad \mu \in [0, 1], \tag{7}$$

where p_0 - initial value of the parameter at $\mu = 0$, and for $\mu = 1$ condition (7) is satisfied.

Solving system (6) with

$$0 = \mu_1 < \mu_2 < \ldots < \mu_m = 1, \tag{8}$$

Founding p by using Newton's iterative method.

$$p_{s+1} = p_s - \left[\frac{\partial \Phi}{\partial p}(p_s, \mu)\right]^{-1} \Phi(p_s, \mu). \tag{9}$$

But as parameter μ is not monotonous, it is necessary to perform parameterization (5) according to the best parameter [32]. For this, the solution curve (5) is divided into h elements: $0 = \eta_1 < \eta_2 < \ldots < \eta_h = H$. The solution is in the parameter η. This way in the system (5) $p_r = p(\eta_r)$, $\mu_r = p(\eta_r)$.

Parametrization by the best parameter:

$$R(p) - (1 - \mu)R(p_0) = 0,$$
$$\sum_r (p - p_r^*)^2 + (\mu - \mu_r^*)^2 - \Delta\eta_r^2 = 0 \tag{10}$$

In this case, the Newton method converges regardless of the initial value and the Jacobian of system (9) is not degenerate.

The results of the calculations are shown in Figs. 1 and 2.

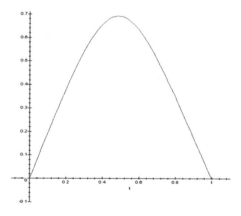

Fig. 1. Graph of approximate solution for the system (4) for $A = 3$.

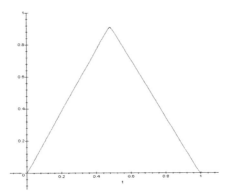

Fig. 2. Graph of approximate solution of the system (4) for $A = 100$.

3 Analytical Solution of the Problem by a Multilayer Method

We will build approximate analytical solutions by using the methods from literature
[18]. The essential part of the approach is to apply the well-known recurrent formulas
for the numerical integration of differential equations to an interval with a variable
upper limit. As a result, an approximate solution can be obtained as a function of this
upper limit. Further, the possibility of constructing a spectrum of mathematical models
that can be chosen with including parameters, which are selected from experimental
data. From the range of models, we can choose the one that is most adequate in
accuracy and complexity.

We explain our method on the example of the classical explicit Euler method.
Consider the Cauchy problem for a system of ordinary differential equations.

$$\begin{cases} \mathbf{y}'(x) = \mathbf{f}(x, \mathbf{y}(x)), \\ \quad \mathbf{y}(x_0) = \mathbf{y}_0 \end{cases} \tag{11}$$

On the interval $D = [x_0; x_0 + a]$. Here $x \in D \subset \mathbb{R}$, $\mathbf{y} \subset \mathbb{R}^p$, $\mathbf{f} : \mathbb{R}^{p+1} \to \mathbb{R}^p$. Classical Euler's method consists of dividing the interval D on n parts:
$x_0 < x_1 < \ldots < x_k < x_{k+1} < \ldots < x_n = x_0 + a$, and of the use of the iteration formula

$$\mathbf{y}_{k+1} = \mathbf{y}_k + h_k \mathbf{f}(x_k, \mathbf{y}_k), \tag{12}$$

where $h_k = x_{k+1} - x_k$; $\mathbf{y}_k$ – approximated to the precise value of the searched solution
$\mathbf{y}(x_k)$.

To attain an approximated solution in the form of a function on the attained dotted
approximations, midpoint method is used (polygonal approximation) or a spline.

We offer a completely different method for building an approximated solution in
the form of a function. With the use of formula (12) we will construct an approximated
solution for problem (11) on the interval $\tilde{D} = [x_0, x]$ with a variable upper limit
$x \in [x_0, x_0 + a]$. Wherein $h_k = h_k(x)$, $\mathbf{y}_k = \mathbf{y}_k(x)$, $\mathbf{y}_0(x) = \mathbf{y}_0$. As the searched

approximated solution, it is offered to use $\mathbf{y}_n(x)$. The simplest option of the algorithm is attained by a uniform division of the interval with step $h_k(x) = (x - x_0)/n$.

For a numerical solution of Cauchy's problem (11) on the interval $[x_0, x_0 + a]$ a wide range of numerical methods is developed [29]. Most of which consists of the division of the given interval by points x_k on intervals of lengths $h_k, k = 1, \ldots, n$ and the use of the recurrent formula:

$$\mathbf{y}_{k+1} = \mathbf{y}_k + F(\mathbf{f}, h_k, x_k, \mathbf{y}_k, \mathbf{y}_{k+1}). \tag{14}$$

Similarly, methods with memory, in which the dependence of the solution is constructed in the next point not only on the solution in the previous point, but also on the solution is a few previous points, is considered.

$$\mathbf{y}_{k+1} = \mathbf{y}_k + F(\mathbf{f}, h_k, x_k, \mathbf{y}_{k-p}, \ldots, \mathbf{y}_k, \mathbf{y}_{k+1})$$

Here operator F defines a specific method. This method is called apparent if $F(\mathbf{f}, h_k, x_k, \mathbf{y}_k, \mathbf{y}_{k+1})$ does depend on $\mathbf{y}_{k+1}$. In this case we apply formula (14) n times to the interval with a variable upper limit $[x_0, x] \subset [x_0, x_0 + a]$. In result, we get a function $\mathbf{y}_n(x)$ that can be considered as an approximated solution to the Eq. (11).

If the function F in (14) depends on $\mathbf{y}_{k+1}$, then the Eq. (14) can be considered an equation relative to $\mathbf{y}_{k+1}$. This equation can allow a precise solution. Therefore, instead of (14) we get a ration of type

$$\mathbf{y}_{k+1} = B(\mathbf{f}, \mathbf{y}_k, h_k, x_k) \tag{15}$$

Formula (15), as before, allows o calculate $\mathbf{y}_n(x)$ and use it as an approximated solution to the problem (11).

If precisely solving of the Eq. (14) relative to $\mathbf{y}_{k+1}$ can not be achieved, then in order to achieve formula (15) we can use an approximation method (Newton's method for example) or a specifically educated neural system, as it is done in [26]. These methods allow us to successfully solve numerous modeling problems [19–24] and problems of model construction with real measurements [25–28]. Let us apply our modification of the trapezoid method [29]

$$y_{k+1}(x) = y_k(x) + 0.5 h_k(x)(v_k(x) + v_{k+1}(x))v_{k+1}(x)$$
$$= v_k(x) + 0.5 h_k(x)(F(x_k(x), y_k(x), v_k(x)) + F(x_{k+1}(x), y_{k+1}(x), v_{k+1}(x))). \tag{16}$$

For our problem $F(x, y, v) = A(x^2 + y^2 + v^2 - 4)$ and (16) leads to a quadratic equation for v_{k+1} which can be easily solved by choosing $h_k = \frac{x - x_0}{n}$, $x_k = x_0 + \frac{k(x - x_0)}{n}$, where parameter n is number of layers in formula.

As am approximate solution we consider $y_n(x)$. Considering that $v(x_0) = 0$, such a point always exists when the boundary conditions of the problem (1) are satisfied by the Rolle theorem. Value of x_0 and $y_0 = y(x_0)$ will be chosen so that the boundary conditions are satisfied $y(0) = 0, y(1) = 0$. As the initial values will be considered

$y_0(x) = y_0$, $v_0(x) = 0$. The solution from [1] is not found, including method of application of the Wolfram Mathematica package. While there is another solution, but it can be obtained with $A > 1$ only by selecting the starting point, i.e. choosing values x_0 and $y_0 = y(x_0)$ so that the boundary conditions are satisfied. Solutions with the first approach and the second with a sufficiently large number of layers $n \geq 4$ differ slightly.

Let us present some results of calculations. By using calculation results and virtue of symmetry of $y_n(x)$, the optimal value of x_0 for the solution, which is constructed by the formula (16), is 0.5 (Fig. 3).

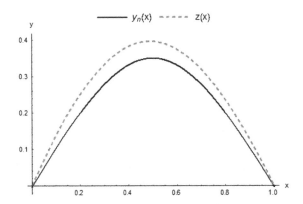

Fig. 3. Graph $y_n(x)$ for $n = 1$ and graph of approximate solution that is built in the Wolfram Mathematica package for $A = 1$

As An increase in the parameters leads to an increase in the error, i.e. to maintain accuracy, it is necessary to increase number, as it was expected (Fig. 4).

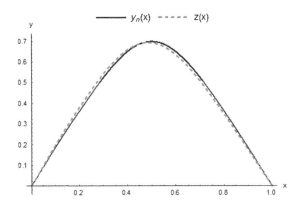

Fig. 4. Graph $y_n(x)$ for $n = 3$ and graph of approximate solution $z(x)$ that is built in the Wolfram Mathematica package for $A = 3$

Increase in the parameter A leads to an increase in the error $y_n(x)$, i.e. for the conservation of accuracy there is a need of increasing the number of layers n (Fig. 5).

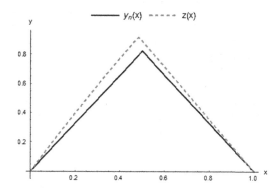

Fig. 5. Graph $y_n(x)$ for $n = 4$ and graph of approximate solution $z(x)$ that is built in the Wolfram Mathematica package for $A = 200$.

Comparing pictures allows us to make two conclusions:

1. The symmetry of the solution relative to $x = 0.5$ with two different methods allows to suggest that the asymmetry of the approximated solutions, constructed in Wolfram Mathematica package, is linked to the package's features, not the problem's.
2. Irrelevant difference in solutions, constructed with completely different approaches, allows us to suppose that the error is therefore irrelevant.

Acknowledgments. This work was funded by RSF (project code 18-19-00474).

References

1. Kachalov, V.I., Besov, M.I.: Method of holomorph regularization in the theory of boundary problems. In: Pontryagin Readings – XXIX, MSU, Moscow (2018) https://elibrary.ru/item.asp?id=34926029. Accessed 21 June 2018. [in Russian]
2. Tikhonov, A.N.: Dependence of solutions of differential equations on a small parameter. Sb. Math. **22**(64)-2, 193–204 (1948). http://www.mathnet.ru/php/archive.phtml?wshow=paper&jrnid=sm&paperid=6075&option_lang=rus. Accessed 21 June 2018. [in Russian]
3. Tikhonov, A.N.: On systems of differential equations containing parameters. Sb. Math. **27**(69)-1, 147–156 (1950). http://www.mathnet.ru/php/archive.phtml?wshow=paper&jrnid=sm&paperid=5907&option_lang=rus. Accessed 21 June 2018. [in Russian]
4. Tikhonov, A.N.: Systems of differential equations containing small parameters for derivatives. Sb. Math. **31**(73)-3, 575–586 (1952). http://www.mathnet.ru/php/archive.phtml?wshow=paper&jrnid=sm&paperid=5548&option_lang=rus. Accessed 21 June 2018. [in Russian]
5. Vasil'eva, A.B., Butuzov, V.F.: Asymptotic methods in the theory of singular perturbations. Higher School, Moscow (1990). [in Russian]

6. Vasilyeva, A.B., Plotnikov, A.A.: Asymptotic theory of singularly perturbed problems. Physics Faculty of Moscow State University, Moscow (2008). [in Russian]
7. Vasil'eva, A.B., Butuzov, V.F., Nefedov, N.N.: Contrast structures in singularly perturbed problems. Fundamentalnaya i prikladnaya matematika = Fund. Appl. Math. **4**(3), 799–851 (1998). http://www.mathnet.ru/php/archive.phtml?wshow=paper&jrnid=fpm&paperid=344 &option_lang=rus. Accessed 21 June 2018. [in Russian]
8. Butuzov, V.F., Vasilyeva, A.B., Nefedov, N.N.: Asymptotic theory of contrast structures (review). Autom. Remote Control **58**(7), 1068–1091 (1997). [in Russian]
9. Chang, K., Howes, F.: Nonlinear singularly perturbed boundary value problems. In: Theory and Applications, Mir, Moscow (1988). [in Russian]
10. Nagumo, M.: Über das Verhalten der Integrals von $\lambda y'' + f(x, y, y', \lambda) = 0$ für $\lambda \to 0$. Proc. Phys. Math. Soc. Jpn. **21**, 529–534 (1939)
11. Lomov, S.A., Lomov, I.S.: Fundamentals of the Mathematical Theory of the Boundary Layer. Publishing House of Moscow University, Moscow (2011). [in Russian]
12. Lomov, S.A.: Introduction to the General Theory of Singular Perturbations. Nauka, Moscow (1981). [in Russian]
13. Butuzov, V.F., Levashova, N.T., Mel'nikova, A.A.: A steplike contrast structure in a singularly perturbed system of elliptic equations. Comput. Math. Math. Phys. **53**(9), 1239–1259 (2013). https://doi.org/10.1134/s0965542513090054
14. Butuzov, V.F., Denisov, I.V.: Corner boundary layer in nonlinear elliptic problems containing derivatives of first order. Model. Anal. Inf. Syst. **21**(1), 7–31 (2014). https://elibrary.ru/item.asp?id=21351116. Accessed 21 June 2018. [in Russian]
15. Butuzov, V.F., Beloshapko, V.A.: Singularly perturbed elliptic Dirichlet problem with multiple root of the degenerate equation. Model. Anal. Inf. Syst. **23**(5), 515–528 (2016). https://doi.org/10.18255/1818-1015-2016-5-515-528. [in Russian]
16. Butuzov, V.F., Bychkov, A.I.: Asymptotics of the solution of an initial-boundary value problem for a singularly perturbed parabolic equation in the case of a triple root of a degenerate equation. Comput. Math. Math. Phys. **56**(4), 593–611 (2016). https://doi.org/10.1134/s0965542516040060. [in Russian]
17. Butuzov, V.F.: On contrast structures with a multi-zone inner layer. Model. Anal. Inf. Syst. **24**(3), 288–308 (2017). https://doi.org/10.18255/1818-1015-2017-3-288-308. [in Russian]
18. Lazovskaya, T., Tarkhov, D.: Multilayer neural network models, based on grid methods. In: IOP Conference Series: Materials Science and Engineering, vol. 158, no. 1, p. 012061 (2016). https://doi.org/10.1088/1757-899x/158/1/012061
19. Tarkhov, D., Shershneva, E.: Approximate analytical solutions of Mathieu's equations based on classical numerical methods. In: Sukhomlin, V., Zubareva, E., Sneps-Sneppe, M. (eds.) Proceedings of the XI International Scientific-Practical Conference "Modern Information Technologies and IT-Education" (SITITO 2016), Moscow, Russia, 25–26 November 2016. CEUR Workshop Proceedings, vol. 1761, pp. 356–362 (2016). http://ceur-ws.org/Vol-1761/paper46.pdf. Accessed 21 June 2018. [in Russian]
20. Vasilyev, A., Tarkhov, D., Shemyakina, T.: Approximate analytical solutions of ordinary differential equations. In: Sukhomlin, V., Zubareva, E., Sneps-Sneppe, M. (eds.) Proceedings of the XI International Scientific-Practical Conference "Modern Information Technologies and IT-Education" (SITITO 2016), Moscow, Russia, 25–26 November 2016. CEUR Workshop Proceedings, vol. 1761, pp. 393–400 (2016). http://ceur-ws.org/Vol-1761/paper50.pdf. Accessed 2018/06/21. [in Russian]
21. Lazovskaya, T., Tarkhov, D., Vasilyev, A.: Multi-layer solution of heat equation. In: Kryzhanovsky, B., Dunin-Barkowski, W., Redko, V. (eds.) NEUROINFORMATICS 2017. SCI, vol. 736, pp. 17–22. Springer, Cham (2018). https://doi.org/10.1007/978-3-319-66604-4_3

22. Borovskaya, O.D., Lazovskaya, T.V., Skolis, X.V., Tarkhov, D.A., Vasilyev, A.N.: Multilayer parametric models of processes in a porous catalyst pellet. Mod. Inf. Technol. IT Educ. **14**(1), 27–37 (2018). https://doi.org/10.25559/sitito.14.201801.027-037

23. Kartavchenko, A.E., Tarhov, D.A.: Comparison of methods for construction of approximate analytical solutions of differential equations on the example of elementary functions. Mod. Inf. Technol. IT Educ. **13**(3), 16–23 (2017). https://doi.org/10.25559/sitito.2017.3.440. [in Russian]

24. Vasilyev, A.N., Svintsov, M.V., Tarkhov, D.A.: Development of analysis of multilayer methods for solving wave equation with special initial conditions. In: Sukhomlin, V., Zubareva, E., Sneps-Sneppe, M. (eds.) Proceedings of the 2nd International Scientific Conference "Convergent Cognitive Information Technologies" (Convergent 2017). Moscow, Russia: 24–26 November 2017. CEUR Workshop Proceedings, vol. 2064, pp. 393–400 (2017). http://ceur-ws.org/Vol-2064/paper16.pdf. Accessed 21 June 2018. [in Russian]

25. Tarkhov, D.A., Kaverzneva, T.T., Tereshin, V.A., Vinokhodov, T.V., Kapitsin, D.R., Zulkarnay, I.U.: New methods of multilayer semiempirical models in nonlinear bending of the cantilever. In: Sukhomlin, V., Zubareva, E., Sneps-Sneppe, M. (eds.) Proceedings of the 2nd International Scientific Conference "Convergent Cognitive Information Technologies" (Convergent 2017), Moscow, Russia, 24–26 November 2017. CEUR Workshop Proceedings, vol. 2064, pp. 143–149 (2017). http://ceur-ws.org/Vol-2064/paper17.pdf. Accessed 21 June 2018. [in Russian]

26. Vasilyev, A.N., Tarkhov, D.A., Tereshin, V.A., Berminova, M.S., Galyautdinova, A.R.: Semi-empirical neural network model of real thread sagging. In: Kryzhanovsky, B., Dunin-Barkowski, W., Redko, V. (eds.) NEUROINFORMATICS 2017. SCI, vol. 736, pp. 138–144. Springer, Cham (2018). https://doi.org/10.1007/978-3-319-66604-4_21

27. Zulkarnay, I.U., Kaverzneva, T.T., Tarkhov, D.A., Tereshin, V.A., Vinokhodov, T.V., Kapitsin, D.R.: A two-layer semi-empirical model of nonlinear bending of the cantilevered beam. In: IOP Conference Series: Journal of Physics: Conference Series, vol. 1044, no. 1, p. 012005 (2018). https://doi.org/10.1088/1742–6596/1044/1/012005

28. Bortkovskaya, M.R., et al.: Modeling of the membrane bending with multilayer semi-empirical models based on experimental data. In: Sukhomlin, V., Zubareva, E., Sneps-Sneppe, M. (eds.) Proceedings of the 2nd International Scientific Conference "Convergent Cognitive Information Technologies" (Convergent 2017), Moscow, Russia: 24–26 November 2017. CEUR Workshop Proceedings, vol. 2064, pp. 150–156 (2017). http://ceur-ws.org/Vol-2064/paper18.pdf. Accessed 21 June 2018. [in Russian]

29. Hairer, E., Norsett, S.P., Wanner, G.: Solving Ordinary Differential Equations I. Nonstiff Problem. Springer, Heidelberg (1987). https://doi.org/10.1007/978-3-662-12607-3

30. Shalashilin, V.I., Kuznetsov, E.: Parametric Continuation and Optimal Parametrization in Applied Mathematics and Mechanics. Springer, Netherlands (2003). https://doi.org/10.1007/978-94-017-2537-8

31. Samoylenko, A.M., Ronto, N.I.: Numerically-Analytical Methods for Investigating Solutions of Boundary-Value Problems. Naukova Dumka, Kiev (1986). [in Russian]

32. Budkina, E.M., Kuznetsov, E.B.: Solution of boundary value problems for differential algebraic equations. In: Proceedings of the 11th International Conference on Computational Mechanics and Contemporary Applied Software Systems, Izd-vo MAI, Moscow, pp. 44–46 (2015). https://elibrary.ru/item.asp?id=24658093. Accessed 21 June 2018. [in Russian]

Forecasting News Events Using the Theory of Self-similarity by Analysing the Spectra of Information Processes Derived from the Vector Representation of Text Documents

Dmitry Zhukov[1]([✉]) [iD], Tatiana Khvatova[2] [iD],
and Konstantin Otradnov[1] [iD]

[1] MIREA - Russian Technological University, Vernadsky Prospekt,
78, 119454 Moscow, Russia
zhukovdm@yandex.ru, const.otradnov@yandex.ru
[2] Peter the Great St. Petersburg Polytechnic University, Polytechnic Street 29,
195251 St. Petersburg, Russia
tatiana-khvatova@mail.ru

Abstract. This paper presents a new methodology developed by the authors to forecast news events based on representing texts as vectors, subtracting information process spectrums from the vectors, and analysing these with the help of self-similarity theory. Spectrum extraction is performed using text processing by applying mathematical linguistics approaches (text markups, normalisation, commenting); the vectors obtained are then clustered according to theme groups and the time of the news appearance. By applying the Hurst self-similarity method to analyse information news process spectrums, their self-similarity features are analysed. The information processes are then classified into two different classes: self-similar and not self-similar. It is proven that if the self-similarity feature is present in the processes investigated, the Hurst self-similarity method (R/S analysis) and almost-periodic functions will enable us to discover the almost periods of repeatability of events, and this will further allow us to forecast their behaviour over time and predict new events.

Keywords: Forecasting news events · Information process spectrum · Self-similarity of an information process · The Hurst method

1 Introduction

The issue of resolving the tasks of forecasting the behavior of systems and of processes belonging to those systems, is undoubtedly important for various spheres of activity – technical, engineering or social. Nowadays, forecasting the behavior of social and economic systems is one of the most under-explored fields of research due to the complexity caused by the presence of human factors, which cause stochasticity (contingency) and ambiguity, i.e. the indeterminacy of potential state outcomes and the ways in which such outcomes could materialize.

© Springer Nature Switzerland AG 2020
V. Sukhomlin and E. Zubareva (Eds.): Convergent 2018, CCIS 1140, pp. 54–69, 2020.
https://doi.org/10.1007/978-3-030-37436-5_5

The evolution of information technologies has led to the emergence of a new class of objects – socio-technical systems, the key representative of which is the internet, and its segments such as news portals and social networks.

The appearance of a news event on these portals can be considered a signal or spectrum of information processes related to this news. While analyzing the spectrums of such signals, two tasks must be resolved. Firstly, the rules of extracting information process spectrums from the textual descriptions appearing in the internet news must be formalized. Secondly, the main characteristics of such processes, i.e. the presence or absence of long-term dependencies and their time intervals, must be defined. The results obtained can be used to forecast emergency situations and natural disasters.

2   Literature Review

Open initial data (for example, social networks and news feeds) can serve as a base for forecasting a wide range of events, for example, outbreaks of diseases [20], election results [2, 3], and protests [4]. There is a real need to develop approaches which shed light on the events preceding the researched events.

Currently, many attempts are made to develop various methods and models of social and economic events forecasting.

In [4] the authors describe a framework (EMBERS) for forecasting civil disorders in various places using a combination of models with heterogeneous input sources, ranging from social networks to satellite images.

In [5] the authors combine multitask learning and dynamic functions from social networks for space-temporal forecasting of events. Generative models are also used in [6] for building a joint model of the temporal evolution of content on a social networks. In [7] the authors develop a generative model for categorical forecasting of events in event flows by using frequent episodes of their occurrence.

Chouhan and Khatri [8] developed a model based on data analysis and machine learning which aims to forecast catastrophes and natural disasters. They suggest analyzing historical data, extracting patterns of events connected with various kinds of disasters, and using these patterns for machine learning (as a teaching sample) and then forecasting future disasters by using current events. The authors collected data from disasters using key search words from the Google search engine. The text documents obtained from the search queries were then processed with mathematic linguistic approaches; finally, using Bayesian classification, false results were eliminated [8]. After the data is collected, it is clustered. From the key words used to generate the search queries, the matrix of transition is built and the matrix of observations is composed from the grouped events. Both matrices are entered to the hidden Markov model to calculate the forecasting model. In the authors' view, this approach enables us to forecast future events and their locations.

Radinsky and Horvitz [9] describe a model of future events forecasting which generalizes the particular patterns of events sequences extracted from the news. The authors have tried to develop a model which considers the connection between past historical events and the prediction of future events. The data they extracted was from 22 years of news, between 1986 and 2008. They suggest [9] that real-world events are generated by the probabilistic models which also generate news messages about these events. The messages from the news events are used to develop a model in the form of the probability $P(ev_j(t + \Delta)|ev_i(t))$ of a future occurrence of an event ev_j at a moment in time $t + \Delta$ and the past event ev_i at a moment of time t. For example, this model shows that there is an 18% probability of draught ev_j after the event of flood ev_i. This probability approximates the connection between the two events occurring in the real world.

Molaei and Keyvanpour [10] propose a systematic classification of event forecasting based on a time series. A time series allows us to identify the connections among data and to forecast various kinds of events. Events from the real world which occur at a certain moment of time are considered. The authors divide all the complexities of event forecasting into two categories: complexities connected with the data and complexities connected with algorithms. The first category is not directly connected with the second. The data for the times series are characterized by a large volume, a large number of dimensions and the permanent need to update them. The second category is connected with difficulties in implementing algorithms for events forecasting in a time series.

Lesko and Zhukov [11] research the structure of a vector information space, obtained from the text description of news and the changes in this structure occurring over time. In this study, the authors propose the possibility of forecasting news events based on the Fourier method of analyzing the complex spectra of vectors, defining the central positions of new clusters evolving with time related to their average direction (the authors call this 'Director').

Lukianov and Grunskaya [12] suggest defining the probabilities of a dangerous geophysical process occurring by using the method of eigenvectors. In their study, the new system for handling a multidimensional time series in order to forecast dangerous geophysical processes is developed. Forecasting events is based on a two-dimensional time series processing, one dimension being a physical value, whilst the other is a digitalized array of previously occurring events.

Preethi, Uma and Kumar [13] have developed a model to identify the cause-consequence connection among events which is further applied to the tone of the event forecast, and forecasting the time between events across social networks. The authors define the cause-consequence connection as the relationship between two events, the cause and the result, wherein the second event results from the first; therefore the cause-consequence connection is useful for forecasting. The model comprises several steps [13]. In the first step, tweets are selected for a given period of time, and key words are extracted from tweets. In the second step, tone – positive, negative or neutral - is defined using the key words extracted. To define the tone of the words, a special classification code is used. This is generated according to the Support Vector Machine (SVM). In the third stage, cause-consequence connections among the key words are defined based on the association rule learning approach which extracts the rules "if-then" from the data. In the fourth step, events forecasting is performed by using a time-series analysis of tweets and cause-consequence connections assessed in the previous step.

In the research [14], a stochastic model of the dynamics of how moods change within social networks is developed. This explores the probability of reaching and exceeding the percolation threshold (PT) of information transmission in a social network with a given network density.

Pang and Zhang [15] describe the model of a leaders' search in social network communities and forecast events where users will repeat the leaders' search. According to the authors, the task of forecasting such events can be resolved by means of binary classification. Logit regression is suggested as the classification algorithm. The classification characteristics are linked to four aspects: a leader, a user, relations between the leader and the user and between the leader and the community itself. A leader's characteristics show how the leader influences people in the community, how many followers he/she has, and what the probability is that users will follow this leader. Leader-user characteristics show the extent to which users trust the leader, whether they are friends, etc. In the authors' view, the proposed model predicts, with an 80% probability, events which will be repeated or followed by users in the wake of the leader. The famousness of the event does not play such a big role; even if the event is not popular, users are likely to be influenced by their leader.

Sidorov [16] suggests using machine learning, particularly regression, for forecasting events within social network communities. The regression learning approach was implemented using a packet gradient descent on the platform .Net and C# language.

Takaffoli, Rabbany and Zaïane [17] develop a library based on machine learning for forecasting events inside communities in a dynamic social network. The library analyses the key characteristics of the community – its structure, history, behavior of its most influential members – and automatically defines the most significant characteristics for each event appearing within a community. The analysis is also based on studying the behavior of community members, because the members play a very important role in the community and shape its structure. The authors also provide several approaches to searching obvious and non-obvious communities inside of the dynamic social networks (a non-obvious community is defined as a more or less stable group of individuals whose reasons to be connected are hard to identify). To forecast events, technologies of machine learning are used such as logit regression and various classification methods. To forecast the size of the community and its degree of solidarity, the Two-Stage Cascade model is applied. In the first stage, the variable of the viability of the community is forecast, and in cases where the variable is positive, during the second stage, the size and solidarity of the community are forecast. The authors present experiments using real life data which show it is possible to precisely forecast events, the vector of their development, and the degree of solidarity within the community. The experiments confirm the relationship between the behaviors of community members - especially among its most influential members - and the future of the community. Takaffoli, Rabbany and Zaïane [17] reveal some evolutionary patterns within and across communities; for example, the degree of integrating new members into a community is a good indicator of its potential for survival; the potential for survival of non-obvious communities depends on certain non-obvious qualities of their members and the internal connections within the community.

Gerber presents research into using tweets with spacio-temporal attributes in order to forecast crime [18]. The author uses Twitter-specific linguistic analysis and statistical modelling to automatically reveal the topics under discussion in big cities. Furthermore, the topics are applied to the crime prediction model. To extract the themes of tweets, Gerber suggests using topic modelling [18]. Prior to topic modelling, tweet texts are tokenized using a special tokenizer and partial linguistic tagger. Ideograms and smileys have a very important role in the analysis, so the specialized tokenizer recognizes smileys as separate tokens. In tweets, smileys possess certain semantic content describing the emotional state of a user, so they are used for tweet theme modelling. To forecast the occurrence of a crime, Gerber defined a one-month training window, then mapped the labelled points (latitude/longitude pairs) across the city borders [18]. The points were derived from two sources: from places of known types of crime within the training window, and from a grid of evenly spaced points at 200-meter intervals, not coinciding with points from the first set. By using these points, a binary classification was obtained.

It is important to note that only a few existing approaches present proof and interpretative analysis to support forecasting. This emphasizes the need to develop new approaches for analyzing initial test data in order to forecast events. It is arguably possible to use a method of pre-processing the initial text data using computer linguistics approaches which represent the data as mathematical vectors and also help to clusterize them. Studying the changes in composition and structure of clusters may allow us to create an efficient forecasting method.

3 The Model for Forecasting News Events Based on Information Process Spectrums Analysis with the Hurst Self Similarity Method

3.1 Extracting Spectrums of Information News Processes from Text Documents

Statistical semantic hypothesis allows us to formalize text document representation as a vector space model. For vector representation of texts, a dictionary of words and terms is required. The essence of the model is as follows: if the total number of different unique words and terms is M, and the number of text documents is N, then X_i, i – varies from 1 to N) can be assigned a vector

$$X_i = \left\{ x_{1,I}, x_{2,I}, \ldots, x_{k,I}, \ldots, x_{M,I} \right\}$$

in which the first element characterizes the frequency of the appearance of the first term in the document, the second element – frequency of the second term, etc. Each element of vector $x_{k,i}$ can take a positive value. All X_i form a matrix 'term – document' (the columns of the matrix are vectors X_i, and the lines define the frequencies of the occurrence of terms in the documents of the collection):

$$
\begin{vmatrix}
x_{1,1} & x_{1,2} & \cdots & x_{1,i} & \cdots & x_{1,N} \\
x_{2,1} & x_{2,2} & \cdots & x_{2,i} & \cdots & x_{2,N} \\
\vdots & \vdots & \cdots & \vdots & \cdots & \vdots \\
x_{j,1} & x_{j,2} & \cdots & x_{k,i} & \cdots & x_{i,N} \\
\vdots & \vdots & \cdots & \vdots & \cdots & \vdots \\
x_{M,1} & x_{M,2} & \cdots & x_{M,i} & \cdots & x_{M,N}
\end{vmatrix}
\tag{1}
$$

In place of $x_{j,i}$ it is possible to use the TFIDF metric which characterizes the weighted normalized appearance of j-word or term (n–gram) from the dictionary into i-document in the collection. Using this metric diminishes the weight of widely used words, which is reasonable, and ultimately increases the accuracy of the information search:

$$
\text{TFIDF} = \text{TF} \times \text{IDF} = \frac{n_j}{\sum_k n_k} \times \log\frac{D}{d},
\tag{2}
$$

where n_j – is the number of times a word appears in the document, $\sum_k n_k$ is the total number of words in the document, D in the total number of documents in the collection, and d is the number of documents containing a certain term.

Before vectorization of the text documents, it is important to conduct a number of preliminary procedures and their linguistic pre-processing:

- Text markup (linearization) is needed in order to recognize and extract words-terms and combined terms (n-grams) from the initial text. While undertaking markups, punctuation and hyphenations are considered; the so-called stop words, i.e. words which do not hold much information but often appear in the text, such as prepositions etc., are ignored.
- Text normalization. While undertaking normalization, grammar information (inclinations, gender, tenses, etc.) is removed from the initial text. Words in different registers, as well as their abbreviations, are aligned to take the same form. In certain cases, normalization can be substituted by stemming or lemmatization which can be considered as a simplified normalization procedure, i.e. analysis without taking the context into account.
- Text commenting. Commenting is particularly important because the same word can be used in the text in its various meanings. Commenting means including metadata with information about various meanings for a word, parts of speech, sentence diagramming, into the document.

After the text markup, normalization and commenting have been performed, each document in the collection is represented by the set of terms belonging to it, and by their frequencies; this allows the creation of a vector space model of the document.

The distance between vectors (cosine similarity) shows the similarity of documents between one another within the collection. The smaller the angle between the vectors, the more similar the documents are:

$$d(x,y) = \frac{x\,y}{\|x\|\|y\|} = \frac{\sum\limits_{i=1}^{n}(x_i y_i)}{\sqrt{\sum\limits_{i=1}^{n} x_i^2}\sqrt{\sum\limits_{i=1}^{n} y_i^2}}, \tag{3}$$

where x is the first vector, y is the second vector, x_i is the coordinate value of the first vector, y_i is the coordinate value of the second vector. The vector space model of the document enables us to resolve the task of classifying documents into meaning groups (clusterizing them), i.e. to resolve the task of uniting similar documents into groups.

To clusterize the documents in this research, the K-means algorithm is used. This widely-used algorithm belongs to the class of hierarchical algorithms and has multiple advantages – it is simple and fast to use, and provides high quality clusterization. One of the weaknesses of this algorithm is the need to input the number of clusters in advance. However, the speed is high - $O(kndi)$, where k is the number of clusters, n is the number of meanings in the vector, d is the number of documents, i is the number of iterations. The aim of the algorithms is to find such cluster centres where the distance between the vector of a cluster document and the vector of the cluster centre would be minimal:

$$\arg\min_{C} \sum_{i=1}^{k} \sum_{x \in C_i} d(x, \mu_i) = \arg\min_{C} \sum_{i=1}^{k} \sum_{x \in C_i} \|x - \mu_i\|, \tag{4}$$

where x is a document, μ_i is i-cluster's centroid, C is the set of documents in the i-cluster.

To compute the distance between a document and the cluster centroid, the squared Euclidean distance $d(x,y)$ is used:

$$d(x,y) = \sqrt{\sum_{i=1}^{n}(x_i - y_i)^2}, \tag{5}$$

where x_i is the coordinate values of the first vector, y_i – the coordinate values of the second vector and n is the dimension of the space.

The centroid, i.e. the arithmetic mean vector of all vectors in the cluster, is computed as follows:

$$C = \frac{C_1 + C_2 + \ldots + C_k}{k} \tag{6}$$

where C_k is the vector of news in a cluster and k is the number of news stored in the cluster.

3.2 Mathematical Model to Analyse the Presence of Long-Term Dependencies in the Spectra of Information Processes

In order to make news events forecasting possible, it is important that there are persistent time dependencies in the behavior of the information processes connected with these news events. To analyze time dependencies, the self-similarity approach theory (R/S analysis) can be applied. To describe the self-similarity of a random process, it is essential to study the aggregated processes constructed by averaging the values of the initial process at various time intervals [21, 22]:

$$X^{(m)} = \left\{ X_k^{(m)} : k = 1, 2, 3, \ldots \right\}; X_k^{(m)} = \frac{\sum_{i=1}^{m} X_{(k-1)\,m+i}}{m} \qquad (7)$$

The number of events occurring at a certain unit of time can be considered as the value of a random process. Therefore, a random process will represent a discrete sequence of values. The argument of this sequence will be represented by the consecutive number of the time unit: $X = \{X_t : t = 0, 1, 2, \ldots\}$.

It is important to note that the aggregated processes will be stationary and have limited covariance:

$$Cov(X_1, X_{i+k}) = (X_1 - \bar{X})(X_{i+k} - \bar{X}) < +\infty$$

with the variance $D(X) = \overline{(X_1 - \bar{X})^2} = \sigma^2$ and autocorrelation function: $r(k) = \frac{Cov(X_t, X_{t+k})}{D(X)}$. The diminishing variance is asymptotically described by the expression $D(X(m)) \approx am - \beta$, $0 < \beta < 1$, $m \to \infty$, i.e. the variation of the aggregated processes – the average samples – decreases more slowly compared to the value inverse to the sample size m. If there is a divergence of the process autocorrelation function: $\sum_k r(k) = \infty$, $r(k) \approx k^{-\beta}$, it is then called a persistent dependency in self-similar processes. This means that the decrease in the autocorrelation function occurs hyperbolically slowly. In this case, an autocorrelation function can be represented as an asymptotic approximation

$$r(k) \sim k - \beta L(k),$$

where $0 < \beta < 1$, $H = 1 - \beta/2$, and L is a slowly changing function, and then $\sum_k k^{-\beta} L(k) = \infty$.

When talking about the fluctuation character of the power spectrum, we mean the analogy of the power spectrum of a flow:

$$f(\omega) \approx c\omega - \gamma, \ \omega \to 0, \ \gamma = 1 - \beta, \qquad (8)$$

when $f(\omega) = \sum_k r(k)e^{-i\omega k}$.

If a random process possesses the features described above, it means that its autocorrelation function coincides with the aggregated processes autocorrelation functions exactly: $r(k) = rm(k)$ or asymptotically $r(k) \rightarrow rm(k)$, when $m \rightarrow \infty$. These relations explain why such a process is called self-similar: correlation characteristics of such processes, averaged across various time intervals, remain the same.

An important parameter characterizing the 'extent' of self-similarity of a random process, is the estimation of the Hurst parameter [22]. The Hurst parameter lies in the interval $0.5 < H < 1$. For processes not possessing the self-similarity feature, the Hurst parameter H equals 0.5, for the fractal processes with persistent dependency, such parameters vary from 0.7 to 0.9.

Let us consider a sample of experimental data with the volume $n: x_1, x_2, \ldots, x_n$ and define the average mean for it $\overline{X_n} = \frac{1}{n} \sum_{k=1}^{n} x_k$; the sample standard deviation $S_n =$

$\sqrt{\frac{1}{n} \sum_{k=1}^{n} x_k^2 - \left(\frac{1}{n} \sum_{k=1}^{n} x_k \right)^2}$ and the deviation:

$$R_n = \max_{\kappa \leq n} \left\{ \sum_{i=1}^{n} X_i - \kappa \overline{\overline{X}} \right\} - \min_{\kappa \leq n} \left\{ \sum_{i=1}^{n} X_i - \kappa \overline{\overline{X}} \right\} \qquad (9)$$

Variability of a self-similar process at an interval n is defined as a non-decreasing function of the interval length R_n. Hurst showed that for self-similar processes with a larger n the following relations are present: $R_n/S_n \approx \{n/2\}H$ or $\ln(R_n/S_n) \approx H \ln(n/2)$, where H is the Hurst parameter. It is derived from the dependency of the logarithm of the average value of the variance and the logarithm of the size of the partition block of the initial data sample. If self-similarity is present, the derived dependency is linear. The extent of self-similarity can be estimated by plotting a graph of $\ln(R_n/S_n)$ related to $\ln(n/2)$ at various n, and computing H as the slope ratio of the line obtained. It is important to note that the set of points obtained will not lie on the same line, this is why they should be approximated by a line, for example, by using the least squares approach. This method of estimating the Hurst parameter is called the R/S-method. It must be noted that this gives only an approximate value for the Hurst parameter, so for a stricter estimation it makes more sense to use several approaches and then to compare the results. One of the possible approaches is the periodogram analysis, the weakness of which is the large volume of computing.

3.3   Research Methodology

To carry out the quantitative research, a collection of 100,000 text documents was extracted from 8 news sites in 2016. The maximum number of words in one document was 10,404, the minimum - 101. The dictionary of terms used included 2,570,724 words and 1,451,828 terms (n–grams). To increase the speed of collecting text and parsing (syntaxes analysis) several parallel 'worker services' for collecting independent news and processing were launched.

To conduct the quantitative experiment and process the data, special software was developed; computing machinery with the following characteristics was used:

- Processor: Core i7-4790 K, 4.0 giga cycle per second, 4 cores.
- Disk size: 80 Hb SSD.
- Operating memory: 16 Hb DDR3.
- Operating system: Ubuntu Linux 16.04.2 LTS.
- The time to perform various operations was:
- Normalization time: 234 s.
- Vectorization time: 18 s.
- Clusterization time: 14756 s.
- Segmentation into days (24 h): 179 s.
- Time for computing the Hurst parameter: 10 s.

News analysis consisted of two stages. In the first stage, pre-processing of news was performed. The news was processed into the feature matrix and clusterized according to themes. From the initial collection of 100,000 news items in 2016, 300 clusters of various themes (topics) were obtained.

The second stage of analysis involved the segmentation of news clusters into subgroups according to days (periods of 24 h) without accumulating news from previous periods. If no accumulation took place, only news from the current day (24 h) was put into the current subgroup. In this way, each cluster was segmented into 365 subgroups.

In the third stage, the spectrum of the information process was constructed. For this, firstly the base vector was formed with every element equal to 1 – this is important to avoid orthogonality with any of the vectors from the text collection. The vectors were then processed by the following algorithm:

- Choose any unprocessed cluster;
- Construct a centroid for each subgroup;
- Calculate the centroid's deviation from the base vector;
- For each cluster, save the list of groups and their deviations; mark the cluster as 'processed';
- If there are still unprocessed clusters, go back to step 1 and continue; otherwise terminate the algorithm.

As a result, for each cluster, the cosines of the angles between the centroid vector of each subgroup and the base vector were calculated.

The parameters of the centroid vectors of cluster subgroups, in addition to the calculated deviations, serve as inputs for the algorithm of self-similarity analysis. The algorithm returns the coefficients of the linear equation $\ln(R_n) \approx \ln(S_n) + H \ln(n/2)$, correlation coefficient for the linear dependency and the Hurst parameter.

The algorithm consists of several steps. In the first step, the input data (the cosines of the angles between the base vector and the vector of cluster centre) are divided into blocks. Each cluster consists of 365 groups. At first, the groups are divided into 183 blocks with the length of two groups per block, then into 122 blocks, with the length of 3 groups per block, etc. until 1 block consists of 365 groups. In the second stage, for each block, a mathematical expectation and variance of the input data (the cosines of the angles between the base vector and the vector of cluster centre) are estimated. For example, the sequence of 365 groups is divided into 52 blocks, each block consisting of 7 subgroups. For each block, the mathematical expectation and variance are calculated, so 52 values of variances are obtained, and their average value is calculated. As a result, for each cluster, we obtain a set of data to construct the linear dependency $\ln(R_n) \approx \ln(S_n) + H \ln(n/2)$ and process the results with the least squares method with the aim of estimating the coefficients of the linear equation.

3.4   Experiential Analysis of the Results Obtained

As an example of a typical spectrum of an information news process, let us consider the data collected for cluster no. 103 which contains 500 items of news about NATO (this is just a spontaneously selected topic which usually provokes a lot of feedback in the mass media).

To better visualize the clusterization quality taken from the 500 news items, the following news titles were selected at random (the Russian news portal vesti.ru was used, so the system of news processing is now developed for Russian texts): NY Times: The unity of NATO began to show signs of strain after political discord with Russia; Grushko: Russia will respond to NATO's measures to expand their presence in the East; NATO admitted their vulnerability to the Russian army; Russia will give a symmetric answer to any strengthening of NATO in the East; WSJ: European countries do not want to help NATO curb Russia; The UK Minister of Defense: the dialogue with Russia is useful, but the policy of delaying is significant, too; Moscow responds to decisions taken at the NATO Summit in Warsaw; NATO promises to increase military presence in the Black Sea region; In the State Parliament of the Russian Federation they announced how Russia may respond to Sweden joining NATO; Mass-media: Obama intends to ask Germany to strengthen the eastern borders of NATO.

Figure 1 presents the spectrum of the discussed information process. If the algorithm of self-similarity described earlier is applied to this data, we will get the data presented in Fig. 2 in logarithmic coordinates.

The dots plotted on the graph in Fig. 2 correspond to the calculations obtained while processing the spectrum of the process presented in Fig. 1 with the Hurst method. The solid lines are the result of statistical data processing.

It is important to note that the process presented in Fig. 2, while being partitioned into blocks of any dimension, is not self-similar. This is proven by the shift of the trend in the area of logarithm from the share of m from all the sequence equal to -4 (see Fig. 2, line No. 1).

To obtain a rough estimate of the time interval after which the self-similarity trend is broken, it is possible to approximate the group of points, situated at the bottom left part of Fig. 2, by a linear dependency, presented by line No. 2 in Fig. 2. The crossover point of lines 1 and 2 gives us the estimate of the time interval wherein the self-similarity trend is broken.

For line No. 1 in Fig. 2, the following equation was obtained: $y = 0.134x - 8.09$ (1) with correlation coefficient 0.957 and Hurst parameter $H = 0.93$. For line No. 2: $y = 0.495x - 6.718$ (2) with correlation coefficient 0.964 and Hurst parameter $H = 0.75$. The crossover point of lines No. 1 and 2, has the coordinate for the

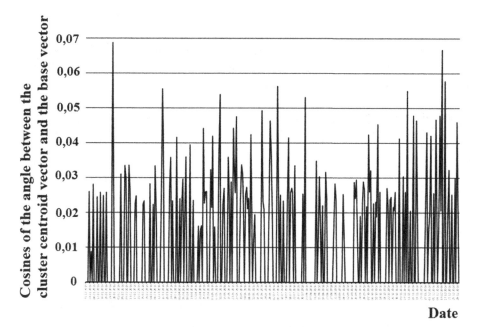

Fig. 1. Spectrum of the information news process describing news events concerning NATO (cluster No. 103).

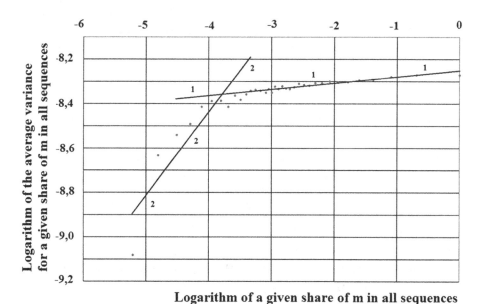

Fig. 2. Graphic dependency between the logarithm of the average variance and the logarithm of the size of the partition block m (calculation of the Hurst parameter for the spectrum of the NATO information news process, cluster No. 103).

logarithm of the size of the partition block $(\ln(m) = -3.80$, therefore $m = 1/\exp(-3.8) \approx 45$ days). This point is calculated if Eqs. (1) and (2) are set equal. At this point, the trend of self-similarity has changed within the spectrum of the investigated information news process. The process itself has a rather obvious 45-day dependency. For news cluster No. 134, describing the news events connected to the Islamic State (a terrorist organization outlawed in Russia), the graphic representation of the information process spectrum will look as presented in Fig. 3, and dependencies of the logarithm of the average variance and the size of the partition block m will look as shown in Fig. 4. News cluster No.134 consists of 491 pieces of news.

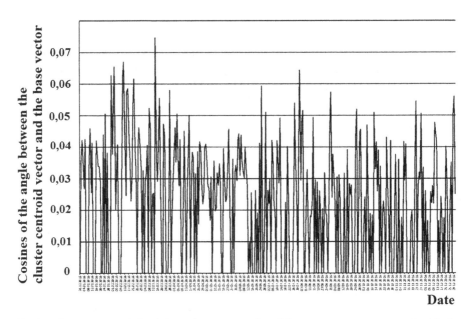

Fig. 3. The spectrum of the information process describing news events connected with the Islamic State (IS, a terrorist organization outlawed in the Russian Federation).

In order to better visualize the quality of the clusterization, the following titles were selected at random from 500 news stories: The Pentagon proclaims that the military operation against IS (IS is a terroristic organization outlawed in the Russian Federation) in Libya is now complete; The first days of the cease-fire in Syria: The Russian Ministry of Defense draws conclusions; The Kremlin called the absence of dialogue with the USA as the reason for IS activation in the Syrian Arab Republic; More than 200 IS militants laid down arms in the Syrian Homs; IS used chemical arms against the opposition in Northern Syria; «Life» published a video of a fight between IS militants and the Syrian army close to Deir ez-Zor; Jehad in the shadow of IS; IS militants in Aleppo fired on philologists. One student died; Zakharova: Militants and arms enter Aleppo via Turkish-Syrian border; Syrian army shelled IS militants from a height near Palmira.

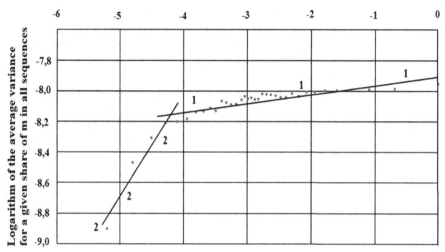

Fig. 4. Graphic representation of the dependency between logarithms of the mean value of the variance and the logarithm of the partition block m (the Hurst coefficient evaluation for the information news process spectrum for cluster No. 134).

The points on the graph presented in Fig. 4 correspond to the estimated values obtained while processing the spectrum presented in Fig. 3 with the Hurst method. Solid lines 1 and 2 are the results of statistical data processing.

For line No. 1 in Fig. 4 the following equation was obtained: $y = 0.049x - 7.919$ with correlation coefficient 0.88 and Hurst coefficient $H = 0.98$. For line No. 2: $y = 0.643x - 5.466$ with correlation coefficient 0.96 and Hurst coefficient $H = 0.68$. The interception point for lines 1 and 2 have a coordinate position for the logarithm of the size of partition block ($\ln(m) = -4.13$, so $m = 1/\exp(-4.13) \approx 62$ days).

At this point the change in the self-similarity trend occurs in the spectrum of the investigated information news process, and the process itself has a distinct 62-day dependency.

The results obtained are valuable in terms of forecasting future news events. In particular, analysis of emergencies, natural disasters and catastrophes over the course of a long period of time (for example, 15–20 years) may enable us to define the time interval of their self-similarity, to forecast the frequency of their occurrence in the future, and accordingly take preventive action.

4   Conclusions

Using the methods of mathematical linguistics - i.e. text markups, normalization, commenting, and applying the procedure of clustering the vectors according to topic groups depending on the time at which the news occurred - enables us to obtain the spectrums of information processes.

By applying the Hurst self-similarity method to analyse information news process spectrums, we can identify their self-similarity and, based on the value of the self-similarity time interval, forecast the behaviour of processes, i.e. the change in trend and disappearance of self-similarity. When conducting the time series analysis (i.e. analysis of the process spectrum) for longer periods of time, other points of the changing trend, as well as other self-similarity intervals of an information process, can be discovered.

Identifying self-similarity features for information processes enables us to classify them into two different classes: self-similar and not self-similar. Further analysis of self-similar processes, using almost-periodic functions, may enable us to find the almost-periods of repeatability of events as described by these. This is very important for forecasting their occurrence in the future. Apart from the method of almost-periodic functions, wavelet analysis can be applied to discover the repeatability of news events. The advantage of wavelet analysis (as well as the method of almost-periodic functions) compared to the Fourier analysis, is that it allows us to follow the change in the spectrum of the non-linear process over time and to define prevailing frequencies (the value inverse to the frequency is the period of a process). Applying the Fourier approach to analyse spectrums of self-similar information processes has limitations because such processes are not a superposition of linear oscillations, but have non-linear character, and this may result in losing information and obtaining incorrect results.

Acknowledgment. This paper was supported by the Russian Foundation for Basic Research (RFBR), grant No. 28.2635.2017/ПЧ.

References

1. Avramov, D., Kaplanski, G., Levy, H.: Talking numbers: technical versus fundamental investment recommendations. J. Bank. Finance **92**(C), 100–114 (2018). https://doi.org/10.2139/ssrn.2648292
2. Premanode, B., Toumazou, C.: Improving prediction of exchange rates using differential EMD. Expert Syst. Appl. **40**(1), 377–384 (2012). https://doi.org/10.1016/j.eswa.2012.07.048
3. Friesen, G.C., Weller, P.A.: Quantifying cognitive biases in analyst earnings forecasts. J. Fin. Markets **9**(1), 333–365 (2006). https://doi.org/10.1016/j.finmar.2006.07.001
4. Mabu, S., Hirasawa, K., Obayashi, M., Kuremoto, T.: Enhanced decision making mechanism of rule-base genetic network programming for creating stock trading signals. Expert Syst. Appl. **40**(16), 6311–6320 (2013). https://doi.org/10.1016/j.eswa.2013.05.037
5. Cambria, E., Schuller, B., Xia, Y., Havasi, C.: New avenues in opinion mining and sentiment analysis. IEEE Intell. Syst. **28**(2), 15–21 (2013). https://doi.org/10.1109/MIS.2013.30
6. Balahur, A., Steinberger, R., van der Goot, E., Pouliquen, B., Kabadjov, M.: Opinion mining on newspaper quotations. In: Proceedings of the International Joint Conference on Web Intelligence and Intelligent Agent Technology (IEEE/WIC/ACM 2009), vol. 3, pp. 523–526. IEEE Computer Society (2009). https://doi.org/10.1109/WI-Iat.2009.340
7. Vanstone, B., Finnie, G.: Enhancing stock market trading performance with ANNs. Expert Syst. Appl. **37**(9), 6602–6610 (2010). https://doi.org/10.1016/j.eswa.2010.02.124

8. Chouhan, S.S., Khatri, R.: Data mining based technique for natural event prediction and disaster management. Int. J. Comput. Appl. **139**(14), 34–39 (2016). https://doi.org/10.5120/ijca2016909102

9. Radinsky, K., Horvitz, E.: Mining the web to predict future events. In: Proceedings of the 6th ACM International Conference on Web Search and Data Mining (WSDM 2013), pp. 255–264. ACM, New York (2013). https://doi.org/10.1145/2433396.2433431

10. Molaei, S.M., Keyvanpour, M.R.: An analytical review for event prediction system on time series. In: Proceedings of IEEE 2nd International Conference on Pattern Recognition and Image Analysis (IPRIA), March 2015, pp. 1–6 (2015)

11. Lesko, S., Zhukov, D.: Trends, self-similarity, and forecasting of news events in the information domain, its structure and director. In: Proceedings of DataCom International Conference on Big Data Intelligence and Computing, 5th International Symposium on Cloud and Service Computing (SC2), pp. 870–873. IEEE, Chengdu (2015). https://doi.org/10.1109/SmartCity.2015.178

12. Lukianov, V., Grunskaya, L.: Forecasting disasters using the 'risk indicator'. In: Proceedings of Physics and Radioelectronics in Medicine and Ecology (FREME 2016), pp. 217–219 (2016). (in Russian)

13. Preethi, P.G., Uma, V., Kumar, A.: Temporal sentiment analysis and causal rules extraction from tweets for event prediction. Procedia Comput. Sci. **48**, 84–89 (2015). https://doi.org/10.1016/j.procs.2015.04.154

14. Zhukov, D., Khvatova, T., Zaltsman, A.: Stochastic dynamics of influence expansion in social networks and managing users' transitions from one state to another. In: Proceedings of the 11th European Conference on Information Systems Management (ECISM 2017), pp. 322–329. ACPI Ltd., Reading (2017)

15. Pang, J., Zhang, Y.: Event prediction with community leaders. In: Proceedings of 10th International Conference on Availability, Reliability and Security, pp. 238–243. IEEE (2015). https://doi.org/10.1109/ARES.2015.24

16. Sidorov, A.K.: Forecasting events' outcomes using intellectual data analysis. In: Proceedings of New Information Technologies Conference, Ryazan State Radiotechnical University, pp. 49–51 (2017). (in Russian)

17. Takaffoli, M., Rabbany, R., Zaïane, O.: Community evolution prediction in dynamic social networks. In: Proceedings of the 2014 IEEE/ACM International Conference on Advances in Social Networks Analysis and Mining (ASONAM 2014), pp. 9–16 (2014)

18. Gerber, M.S.: Predicting crime using Twitter and kernel density estimation. Decis. Support Syst. **61**, 115–125 (2014). https://doi.org/10.1016/j.dss.2014.02.003

19. Feldman, R., Sanger, J.: The Text Mining Handbok. Cambridge University Press, Cambridge (2007)

20. Bezverkhy, O.A., Samohvalova, S.G.: Clustering large amounts of text search queries. Scientists Notes PNU **7**(3), 104–110 (2016). (in Russian). http://pnu.edu.ru/media/ejournal/articles-2016/TGU_7_166.pdf. Accessed 12 Oct 2018

21. Mandelbrot, B.B.: The Fractal Geometry of Nature. W.H. Freeman, San-Francisco (1982)

22. Leland, W.E., Taqqu, M.S., Willinger, W., Wilson, D.V.: On the self-similar nature of ethernet traffic (extended version). IEEE/ACM Trans. Netw. **2**(1), 1–15 (1994). https://doi.org/10.1109/90.282603

Organization of Information System for Semantic Search Based on Associative Vector Space

Valery Sachkov[ID], Dmitry Zhukov[(⊠)][ID], Yury Korablin[ID],
Vyacheslav Raev[ID], and Dmitry Akimov[ID]

MIREA - Russian Technological University,
Vernadsky Prospekt 78, 119454 Moscow, Russia
zhukovdm@yandex.ru, akim-dmitrij@yandex.ru

Abstract. Text arrays, created by the online community, contain specific cognitive capabilities. Analyses cover the following: mass media materials, social networks, forums, blogs, political materials, biographies and diaries, scientific publications, belles-letters and other. As practice shows, standard search systems are not always able to find the required data out of this huge volume of the data file. A difficult task for the automated computer text processing is the semantic analysis, which is interpretation of meaning of the text, its content and semantics. Performance of this task requires knowledge of meaning of words and sentences; the way to describe these values formally, and to carry out operations with them, even their storage in computer memory, cause difficulties. That is why in automated text processing computer is not able to search texts of a certain subject, without explicitly specified keywords or phrases, as well as to find texts with the similar meaning, which is quite difficult for the search procedure. Modern information retrieval systems (IRS) are mainly based on key words. The major features for this approach are frequency of word occurrence in document collection, its uniqueness, morphological and syntactic properties. The problem is that the full-text information retrieval systems initially do not imply any semantic connection between the documents and the information they contain, and do not take into account the context and many other issues of importance for semantic interpretation, which makes full-text information retrieval systems unsuitable solution for contextual search. Semantic information retrieval systems should settle the issue of full-text IRS and assist the computer in formal description of semantic meaning of the documents and the data about it. This paper examines possible organization of semantic information-retrieval system based on associations, and uses associative vector spaces as the basic semantic structures.

Keywords: Semantics · EMD · WMD · Search system · Association · Pre-processor

V. Sukhomlin and E. Zubareva (Eds.): Convergent 2018, CCIS 1140, pp. 70–78, 2020.
https://doi.org/10.1007/978-3-030-37436-5_6

1   Introduction

Processing of huge data files for retrieval of essential knowledge is one of the burning issues of the modern world of the «Big Data» . One of the most valuable types of the generated digital data is the text arrays of documents in natural language.

Text arrays, created by the online community, contain specific cognitive capabilities. Analyses cover the following: mass media materials, social networks, forums, blogs, political materials, biographies and diaries, scientific publications, belles-letters and other. As practice shows, standard search systems are not always able to find the required data out of this huge volume of the data file.

A difficult task for the automated computer text processing is the semantic analysis, which is interpretation of meaning of the text, its content and semantics. Performance of this task requires knowledge of meaning of words and sentences; the way to describe these values formally, and to carry out operations with them, even their storage in computer memory, cause difficulties. That is why in automated text processing the computer is not able to search the texts of a certain subject, without explicitly specified keywords or phrases, and to find texts with similar meaning, which is quite difficult for search procedure.

The most frequent modern programming tools belong to the full-text information-retrieval systems (IRS). Their example is the Internet browser, such as «Google» or «Yandex» . Full-text IRS has developed libraries for basic processing: tokenization, sentence search (Sentence Boundary Disambiguation, SBD), search of named objects (Named entity recognition, NER) and definition of parts of speech (Parts of speech, POS). But the full-text information retrieval systems initially do not imply any semantic connection between documents and information that they contain, and do not take into account the context and many other issues of importance for semantic interpretation, which makes full-text information retrieval systems unsuitable solution for contextual search. Herewith nowadays the most compelling challenge in natural language text processing is the semantic search.

Full-text IRS mainly base on key words. The major features for this approach are frequency of word occurrence in document collection, its uniqueness, morphological and syntactic properties. That is why this paper targets at research in IRS development for semantic text processing in natural language.

2   Objective

Semantic IRS should settle the issue of full-text IRS and assist the computer in formal description of semantic meaning of a document and data about it. Nowadays semantic IRS are not mature, compared to the full-text ones, as the technology of the latter has well-established standards, specifications and tools. One of the attempts to find the solution was creation of Semantic Web concept. But the single standard was not established, all solutions are different, and the developed tools, formats and structures are mainly incompatible. There were some attempts to develop ubiquitous language for sematic structures description, which could solve the problems of incompatibility and diversity of Semantic Web ideas implementation. This initiative had no general support, as the developers are not eager to complicate their life and develop additional infrastructure of their resources for semantic processing.

Full-text and semantic IRS, presently in use, in many cases were not in position to solve the sematic search issue, thereby there is need to search and develop new methods and algorithms of semantic search. Difficulty of such systems is formal presentation of semantic structures and tools for interaction with them. There are a lot of various solutions for such problems; the most common ones are studied below.

One of the implementations is the «Semantic Web» concept [1], which was the base for development of the document model «RDF» [2], storing the semantic structures. The substantial problem of the RDF model is the complex ontology structure, and the SPARQL language, suggested as the standard one for RDF documents processing, has a number of significant faults in grammar and semantics of enquiries.

The example research in this line is described in paper [3], in which the authors develop full-text IRS and equally the semantic IRS based on RDF, for Arabic language, which is the most difficult one for processing at present. One more example of semantic search based on semantic networks ontology is UMLS Semantic Network [4], described in paper [5] where the semantic IRS is developed for search of biomedical data, which do not depend on terms and key words.

Next approach to semantic processing organization can be arranged by means of graphs. In paper [6] authors apply the sematic search approach through development of ontologies based on hierarchical graphs, which is conceptually close to conceptual graphs, suggested by Sowa [7]. This problem is also covered by paper [8], where the authors apply graphs for semantic filtering of requests. In paper [9] authors use «Babelfy» algorithm [10], based on graphs to develop the recommendation system.

Another modern approach to understanding of text semantics and search of words with similar sense and text topic spotting is based on neural network model training. There are 2 competitive approaches, one of which is based on frequency occurrence in the document corpus, another – on forecasting model. The well-known representative of the 1st approach is the Latent Semantic Analysis (LSA) [11], the 2nd one is represented by the algorithm set word2vec [12].

Paper [13] makes introduction to research on forecasting model based on neural networks, where the authors create database of biomedical terms and definitions.

Alternative approaches are studied in paper [14], offering a challenging application of LSTM model [15], using the sematic text processing to create the poem stylistically similar to Byron's one.

The latest methods of semantic text processing are studied in paper [16], with the detailed summary of possible sematic analyses methods for social networks and their development perspectives.

Summing up the above, the development of modern semantic IRS requires the solution, taking account of semantic structure, based on forecastable model of word similarity, fixing the problem of frequency overlaying, as well as possessing the comparison algorithm for 2 documents in natural language.

3 Application of Associative Vector Spaces

Compared to standard search systems, focused on word occurrence frequency, semantic IRS are more disposed to understanding the meanings, hidden in the received documents and user requests by means of adding sematic tags to the texts in order to structure and conceptualize the objects in the documents. People can understand the request based on the context and provide the relevant response.

Associations allow putting aside the direct meaning of the word, making possible its replacement by a set of other words. This effect has reverse-acting; by the bag of words (associations) a person can restore the search word. This feature makes possible for a person to create the search query, having no idea of the key words or terms of the data domain, he is not a specialist in, but obtaining the required result. The word order and their number are not of importance for conceptual search, so the person can communicate with the search engine in natural language, without creation of special search phrase, as the search engine itself processes the query and clears out the extra.

This approach to search management is worlds apart from the management of the current information-retrieval systems and claims attention.

Associative vector space (AVS) is a multi-dimensional vector space, in which every vector contains a set of linguistic units (words or word combinations), corresponding to the associative document context in natural language.

Search of documents in AVS is done not by the key words, but by meaning, and occurs at comparison of associations between the text and the search query, making possible semantic search of texts and documents with similar meaning in natural language.

Associations allow putting aside the direct meaning of the word, making possible its replacement by a set of other words. This effect has reverse-acting; by the bag of words (associations) a person can restore the search word. The applied AVS use the features of paradigmatic and syntagmatic associations.

With AVS, it is possible to create the query with no key word, paying no attention to word order and their number, without any extra processing of the text and the query.

In order to implement the associative-semantic search in AVS, we need the mathematical model, allowing assessment of semantic similarity of two documents by their associations. «Earth movers distance» (EMD) was applied as the distance metrics.

Earth movers distance (EMD) is the diversity assessment method for two multi-dimensional distributions in any attribute space with the distance measure between two single attributes [17]. EMD is calculated based on determination of transportation model [18] of linear programming, with advanced algorithms.

As computations are done for words, the best algorithm for distance calculation with EMD is the modified calculation method Word Mover's Distance (WMD) [19].

Special software, named the "Associative sematic text preprocessor" was developed for implementation of this algorithm and results of its application in development of modern sematic IRS are described in this paper.

Figure 1 presents the conceptual – semantic search algorithm in AVS, implemented in the Associative sematic text preprocessor.

The simplified contextual – semantic search algorithm follows the below steps [20]:

1. Type of vector to store the data is determined.
2. Text is pre-processed: tokenization, stemming, lemmatization, deletion of stop words, etc.
3. Unloading of the required semantic kernel depending on the incoming message subject, selection of semantic kernel by the trained model with the multi-nominal Bayesian classifier algorithm [21].
4. Unloading of the required document package to perform the search.
5. Calculation of the distance matrix for the query in the vector space of the semantic kernel.
6. Creation of association vector for each package document.
7. Calculation of EMD distance.
8. Return of the sorted relevant list of documents, complying with the query.

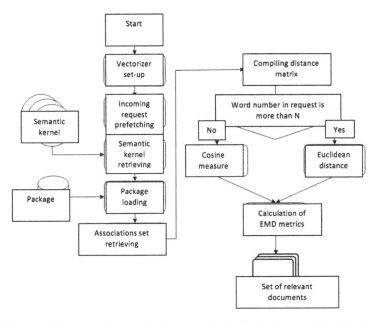

Fig. 1. Conceptual – semantic search algorithm in AVS, implemented in the Associative sematic text preprocessor [20].

Below is description of the key algorithm elements [20]:

- *Semantic kernel* – vector space of the semantic field for search of words and word combinations with similar meaning. It is an ordered set of words or word combinations, giving the most precise description of the object domain, type of activity or the subject. Allows for the most relevant search requests. Sematic kernel contains a central key word, usually the high volume one, and the rest of the key words ranged by decrease of multiple use frequency with the central query in the general collection of documents.

- *Package* – a set of specially arranged documents from the news portal «RIA Novosti», by means of web-craping, with a package of texts, containing 250 thousand of documents in natural language, under 13 main website sections, for 3 years of portal news publications, for which the sematic search is performed.
- *Association assessment module* – the module assessing and filtering the associations found in the sematic kernel
- *EMD metrics* – the dissimilarity assessment method for 2 multidimensional distributions in any attribute space, with the existing distance measure between 2 single attributes. EMD metrics calculates the cost of changes or the required operations for converting of one document into another. EMD calculation is based on transportation model closure.
- *Distance matrix* – matrix of weight of every word in the document for calculation of EMD metrics.

4 Results Obtained

Contextual – semantic search in associative vector space was assessed through search, filtering and ranging of issue-related documents, based on the arranged document packages. User defined the subject in form of a small collection of documents, describing the subject of his concern. Queries were formed automatically based on the submitted collection, and search results are filtered and ranged in compliance with distance metrics in the associative vector space.

For this special purpose there was a wide package of documents compiled from the news portal «RIA Novosti» (https://ria.ru), by means of web-scraping. A package of texts was selected, comprising 250 thousand of documents under the main site sections for 3 years of news publications on the portal.

The subject of the pilot search «Flight accidents», a collection of 10 news documents with various accidents related to aviation, numbers of documents from the «Accidents» package: 119, 121, 332, 342, 347, 355, 504, 559, 661, 948. Algorithm output is presented in Fig. 2.

The results present the smallest EMD distance for the documents selected for search.

The searched documents can miss the key words from the search query, but the content of the document complies with the search domain. This is evidenced by relations of key words, associations and general words from the search data selection and the documents.

Table 1 presents the below relations for query by the 2 documents (119, 121):

- Match of customized words from retrieval – number of matches of the customized words in the document found with the words from the search retrieval, in percentage.
- Use of customized words from the retrieval – number of total customized words matches in the total number of the search retrieval.
- Association matches in the document – index, characterizing commonality of AVS vector of the document found with the AVS search retrieval.

	doc_num	EMD	text
119	119	67.171673	москв 16 — прайм представител межгосударствен авиацион комитет мак принима участ работ комисс миноборон рф расследован катастроф самолет 154 произош соч 25 декабр прошл сообща комитет расследован дан катастроф привлеч специалист лабораторн исследовательск баз науч техническ центр мак отмеча ко...
121	121	78.862919	москв 15 — пассажирск самолет франкфурт — москва немецк авиакомпан Lufthans вечер воскресен соверш аварийн посадк аэропорт домодедово российск столиц перегрев лобов стекл сообщ источник экстрен служб предварительн причин аварийн посадк — перегр лобов стекл — собеседник 22 30 мск московск аэропорт ...
485	485	86.859318	москв 28 — выяснен причин авиакатастроф 154 близ соч продолжа параллельн поисков операц задействова разнородн группиров корабл суд глубоководн аппарат самолет вертолет миноборон мчс фсб росс федеральн регіональн структур поднят внов обнаружен останк погибш направл идентификац москв провед перви...
17173	17173	90.808066	краснодар 14 — татья кузнецов пассажирск самолет Boeing летевш томск суббот вечер пыта ослеп лазер анап сообщ воскресен представител южн транспортн прокуратур инцидент произошел 21 30 мск взлет Boeing рейс анап — томск освещ лазерн луч зелен цвет ослеплен член экипаж полет повлия — рассказа собе...
19281	19281	91.159623	петербург 1 — вертолет ми 8 борт могл наход высокопоставлен чиновник ноч воскресен потерпел крушен мурманск област борт наход 18 дво вых настоя обнаруж тел погибш опозна сообщ источник правоохранительн орган регион тел поднят водолаз поверхн опозна заместител губернатор мурманск област сред — со...
6152	6152	91.611101	москв 20 — специалист межгосударствен авиацион комитет мак воскресен приступ работ бортов самописц разб ростов дон самолет Boeing 737 800 очеред гендиректор авиакомпан Flyduba гейт ал гейт заяв авиакомпан полност доверя российск власт расследован катастроф призва дела поспешн предложен причин ...
6153	6153	93.339509	рост дон 20 — аэропорт ростов дон утр суббот произош крушен пассажирск Boeing официальн закр 08 00 утр понедельник сообщ представител аэропорт ольг ладейщиков аэропорт ростов дон официальн закр 08 00 утр 21 март — пояснл ладейщиков добав связа либ задержк восстановлен взлетн посадочн полос днем ...
6163	6163	95.368322	брянск 19 – гор всеобщ скорб основн дня соцсет росс сообщен крушен ростов дон пассажирск Boeing 737 800 летевш дуб соболезнован родн свидетельств очевидц соседств интернет пространств недоумен повод причин трагед нежелан приня горожан комментар фотограф зимн пейзаж дума город — дом улиц дерев сн...
19238	19238	95.847247	москв 3 — спасател обнаруж черн ящик разб мурманск вертолет ми 8 сообщ источник правоохранительн орган регион извлеч поверхн черн ящик — прибор регистрац параметр полет — собеседник агентств ящик мак расшифровк авиакатастроф произош ноч воскрес...
17375	17375	98.201941	москв краснодар 4 — программ международн гидроавиасалон геленджик скорректирова авар вертолет ми 8 российск авиацион компан панх потерпел источник организатор выставк программ наверн придет измен — призна вертолет ми 8 российск авиацион компан панх потерпел крушен посадк выполнен демонстрацион полет рамк открыт...

Fig. 2. Conceptual – semantic search algorithm output.

2 first lines are worth special attention. Document 119 contains all words from the search retrieval (100%), as well as document 121. But relation of AVS vector in document 121–100%, and in document 119–13%, herewith both have the minimal EMD distance. Further study revealed that match of customized words in the document and the search retrieval varies between 10%–20%, and match of AVS vector between 10%–60%, use of words from the retrieval – from 15% to 55%. Such dispersion showed that matches of words or AVS vectors do not matter, the major feature is the EMD, because the document positioned as the 100th by the EMD, can have matches of words for 60% and AVS for 60%, but fully disagree with the search domain.

Table 1. Rate of the key words, associations and general words from the search retrieval in documents.

Document number	EMD	Match of customized words from retrieval in the document, %	Total words in document	Customized words used from retrieval %	Number of associations in the document	Match of associations in the document and the retrieval, %
119	67.17	100	57	54.3	69	100
121	78.86	100	51	48.6	63	100
485	86.86	11.7	429	47.6	598	68.1
19281	91.16	11.6	328	36.2	480	40.6

5 Conclusion

Experimental results revealed the possibility of using the associative vector spaces in the semantic search information systems. Comparison of frequency of occurrences of words, associations and vectors proved that due to the properties of associations, the word order, as well as their number, does not matter for the associative semantic search (ASP). The results of the TSA algorithm in the associative semantic text preprocessor (ASTP) showed an acceptable result, the ranked documents found correspond to the search domain of the "plane crash". This approach to the organization of the semantic text processing in the natural language deserves attention and further study.

Acknowledgement. The study is performed under financing secured by the Ministry of Education and Science of the Russian Federation for the competitive part of the state assignments to the high schools and scientific organizations for implementation of the pilot scientific projects. Project number 28.2635.2017/ПЧ, title «Development of stochastic self-organization models for the semi structured data and memory implementation in forecasting of news events on the basis of the natural language texts».

References

1. W3C Semantic Web Activity. The World Wide Web Consortium (W3C). https://www.w3.org/2001/sw/. Accessed 25 June 2018
2. Resource Description Framework (RDF): Terms and Abstract Syntax. The World Wide Web Consortium (W3C), 10 February 2004. https://www.w3.org/2007/03/rdf_concepts_ru. Accessed 25 June 2018
3. Sayed, A., Muqrishi, A.A.: IBRI-CASONTO: ontology-based semantic search engine. Egypt. Inform. J. **18**(3), 181–192 (2017). https://doi.org/10.1016/j.eij.2017.01.001
4. The UMLS Semantic Network. https://semanticnetwork.nlm.nih.gov. Accessed 25 June 2018
5. Hanauer, D.A., et al.: Development and empirical user-centered evaluation of semantically-based query recommendation for an electronic health record search engine. J. Biomed. Inform. **67**, 1–10 (2017). https://doi.org/10.1016/j.jbi.2017.01.013
6. Tucar, L., Diaca, P.: Semantic web service composition based on graph search. Procedia Comput. Sci. **126**, 116–125 (2018). https://doi.org/10.1016/j.procs.2018.07.215
7. Sowa, J.F.: Semantics of conceptual graphs. In: Proceedings of the 17th Annual Meeting of the Association for Computational Linguistics, California, pp. 39–44 (1979) https://doi.org/10.3115/982163.982175
8. Wolfengagen, V.E., Kosikov, S.V., Ismailova, L.Y., Aleksandrova, I.A., Zaytsev, A.E.: Semantic filtering of exemplar queries. Procedia Comput. Sci. **123**, 189–194 (2018). https://doi.org/10.1016/j.procs.2018.01.031
9. Dib, B., Kalloubi, F., Nfaoui, E.H., Boulaalam, A.: Semantic-based followee recommendations on Twitter network. Procedia Comput. Sci. **127**, 505–510 (2018). https://doi.org/10.1016/j.procs.2018.01.149
10. Moro, A., Raganato, A., Navigli, R.: Entity linking meets word sense disambiguation: a unified approach. Trans. Assoc. Comput. Linguist. **2**(1), 231–244 (2014)
11. Landauer, T., Foltz, P.W., Laham, D.: Introduction to latent semantic analysis. Discourse Process. **25**(2–3), 259–284 (1998). https://doi.org/10.1080/01638539809545028

12. Mikolov, T., Le, Q.V., Sutskever, I.: Exploiting similarities among languages for machine translation (2013). https://arxiv.org/pdf/1309.4168.pdf. Accessed 25 June 2018

13. Cohen, T., Widdows, D.: Embedding of semantic predications. J. Biomed. Inform. **68**, 150–166 (2017). https://doi.org/10.1016/j.jbi.2017.03.003

14. Shedko, A.Y.: Semantic-map-based assistant for creative text generation. Procedia Comput. Sci. **123**, 446–450 (2018). https://doi.org/10.1016/j.procs.2018.01.068

15. Gers, F.A., Schmidhuber, J., Cummins, F.: Learning to forget: continual prediction with LSTM. Neural Comput. **12**(10), 2451–2471 (1993). https://doi.org/10.1162/089976600300015015

16. Kou, F., Du, J., He, Y., Ye, L.: Social network search based on semantic analysis and learning. CAAI Trans. Intell. Technol. **1**(4), 293–302 (2016). https://doi.org/10.1016/j.trit.2016.12.001

17. Rubner, Y., Tomasi, C., Guibas, L. J.: A metric for distributions with applications to image databases. In: IEEE International Conference on Computer Vision, pp. 59–66 (1998). https://doi.org/10.1109/iccv.1998.710701

18. Hitchcock, F.L.: The distribution of a product from several sources to numerous localities. Stud. Appl. Math. **20**, 224–230 (1941). https://doi.org/10.1002/sapm1941201224

19. Finding similar documents with Word2Vec and WMD. https://markroxor.github.io/gensim/static/notebooks/WMD_tutorial.html. Accessed 25 June 2018

20. Sachkov, V.E.: Application of associative – semantic preprocessor in interactive natural language dialogue systems. In: Proceedings of the Institute of System Programming of the RAS, vol. 30, revision. 4, pp. 195–208 (2018). https://doi.org/10.15514/ispras-2018-30 (4)-13

21. Shimodaira, H.: Text Classification using Naive Bayes. http://www.inf.ed.ac.uk/teaching/courses/inf2b/learnnotes/inf2b-learn-note07-2up.pdf. Accessed 25 June 2018

Algorithm for Solving Ordinary Differential Equations Using Neural Network Technologies

Irina Bolodurina⬤, Denis Parfenov$^{(\boxtimes)}$, and Lubov Zabrodina⬤

Orenburg State University, Pobeda Avenue 13, 460000 Orenburg, Russia
prmat@mail.osu.ru

Abstract. The paper considers the neural network approach for solving the Cauchy problem for ordinary differential equations of the first order based on the representation of the function as a superposition of elementary functions, the algorithm of solving the problem is proposed. The application of the neural network approach allows obtaining the desired solution in the form of a functional dependence that satisfies smoothness conditions. On the basis of a two-layer perceptron, a model of a neural network solution of the problem and a numerical algorithm realizing the search for a solution are built. We developed a program and algorithmic solution of the Cauchy problem. We analyzed the accuracy of the results and its interrelation with the parameters of the neural networks used. The equivalence of the work of the neural network algorithm and the third-order numerical Runge-Kutta algorithm is shown. In addition, the problem of retraining the neural network algorithm for solving the Cauchy problem for first order ordinary differential equations is posed.

Keywords: Ordinary differential equations · Artificial neural network · Optimization methods

1 Introduction

Currently, neural networks are widely used in various fields of science. Such networks are used for solving problems of pattern recognition, time series prediction, network optimization, packet routing, etc. This is due to the fact that neural networks represent a flexible set of tools for solving a variety of data processing and analysis tasks.

Subsequent paragraphs, however, are indented. Artificial neural networks are universal approximants of complex (nonlinear) functional dependencies. Their most important feature is the stability of the neural network model in relation to data errors. Such errors include boundary perturbations, calculation errors, etc. Another important feature of artificial neural networks is the possibility of parallelizing the solution of the problem, as well as the use of a set of networks (including networks of different types). In this matter, the use of neural network technologies in solving various problems is an object of great interest. The effectiveness of using this approach for solving ordinary differential equations (ODE) is expressed in the possibility of representing a solution in the functional dependence form, which satisfies smoothness conditions.

At present, the apparatus for solving ODE by means of numerical methods is widely developed: the finite difference method, the finite element method, the finite

© Springer Nature Switzerland AG 2020
V. Sukhomlin and E. Zubareva (Eds.): Convergent 2018, CCIS 1140, pp. 79–92, 2020.
https://doi.org/10.1007/978-3-030-37436-5_7

volume method, the boundary element method, and so on. Numerical methods make it possible to obtain a discrete representation of the desired solution, which is not sufficient in all applied problems. The main difference between the neural network and numerical approaches is that the neural network technology allows obtaining a functional representation of Cauchy problem solution.

An approach based on using the capabilities of modern neural network technologies used to solve the first-order Cauchy problem is proposed in the framework of the research.

The rest of the paper is organized as follows. Section 2 presents the results of a review of the literature devoted to the consideration of various approaches to solving differential equations based on artificial neural networks. Section 3 describes the basic idea of the neural network approach. Section 4 is devoted to the description of the mathematical formulation of the problem and the functional representation of the desired solution. In Sect. 5, the initial formulation of the problem reduces to the problem of minimizing the error in the approximation of the resulting solution. Section 6 presents a step-by-step algorithm for the neural network approach for solving the first-order Cauchy problem. Section 7 is devoted to describing the practical implementation of the presented algorithm and evaluating the results.

2 Related Work

The neural networks have properties that allow performing optimization procedures. Thus, in the article [1] the authors Bolodurina et al. use the neural network model to optimize the network operation in the infrastructure of the virtual data center. In this regard, we consider the works that allow for neural network optimization of the search for an approximate solution of differential equations.

For example, scientists Mead et al. consider the construction of a direct and non-iterative feedforward neural network with approximate arbitrary coefficients for the solution of ordinary differential equations. The developed method uses a hard limit transfer function, but the construction requires imposing certain constraints on the values of the input, bias, and output weights, and the attribution of certain roles to each of these parameters [2].

Kjaramonte et al. in their research describe the need for more complex activation functions to solve the ODE. The approach used makes it possible to obtain results comparable in error with numerical methods; however, the complete algorithm for solving ODE by means of neural networks is not presented [3].

Other researches use the Kansa method to solve partial differential equations (PDE) by using neural networks, the trust region method of solving problems of minimizing the quadratic error functional is expounded. Zemskova et al. conducted the experiments that combine the above methods for nonlinear parameters. The results of the operation of the algorithms show the effectiveness of the application of neural networks with radial basis functions in the solution of PDE [4].

In the study of Kovalenko et al. are used methods for solving partial differential equations using radial basis function networks (RBF networks), feed-forward neural networks and a modified neural network. The stages of the neural network approach, the adjustment of weights and the problems arising during the research were studied [5].

In the monograph "Principles and Techniques of Neural Network Modeling" by Vasilyev et al. outlined the neural network approach, which makes it possible to solve problems in a uniform manner, without fundamentally reconstructing the algorithms. The problem of choosing a functional basis of a neural network is solved, methods for selecting parameters and structure of a neural network model are described. The authors consider the practical application of the approach to the heat equation [6].

In the study of the Yadav et al. develop an artificial neural network trained by a modified error back propagation algorithm, which is capable of adjusting parameters for modeling the dynamics of the heat equation even with large changes in the boundary conditions without knowledge of system equations [7].

In the study of Vasilyev et al. others considered in detail the problem of finding a function for which the dynamic equation in a certain region and its values in a certain set of points are known. The contribution of the authors of the article was to build a mathematical model of the neural network on heterogeneous data, including differential equations and experimental observations [8].

In the other work, Vasilyev et al. was research the multicomponent systems in the study of regions of a composite type with discontinuous coefficients are presented in the. Authors examined neural network approaches to solving boundary problems of mathematical physics in multidimensional composite domains [9].

In the one more work, Vasilyev et al. considered a method for solving problems in mathematical physics based on the use of normalized radial basis function networks, using the example of elliptic and parabolic problems with known analytical solutions. To solve non-stationary problems, a hybrid algorithm that combines neural network approximation in space with finite-difference time-domain approximation is used [10].

A review of studies has shown that the neural network approach is actively used to solve various kinds of differential equations. Currently, there are methods for solving specific types of problems and a General idea of the solution scheme for problems as a whole, but there is no any step-by-step algorithm based on neural network technology that allows practical implementation of neural network approach in solving ODE. In this regard, this study is aimed at developing an algorithm for solving the Cauchy problem for the first-order ODE.

3 Formulating the Research Problem

The basis for the application of artificial neural networks as universal approximations is Kolmogorov's theorem that any function can be represented as a superposition of continuous functions [11].

According to this theorem, summation operations and composition of functions of one variable are enough to determine the function of several variables.

To apply this property to the solution of the Cauchy problem for ODE of the first order, we consider a two-layer neural network with m inputs and one output.

For definiteness, assume that the transfer functions of the first and output layers are sigmoid.

If any numbers $x_1, \ldots, x_n$ are input, then at the output we get the value of some function $y = F(x_1, \ldots, x_n)$, which is the response of the neural network. It is clear that the result depends on the input signal, and the value of internal parameters of the network, which are the weight coefficients of the neurons.

The exact form of the function:

$$F(x_1, \ldots, x_n) = \sum_{i=1}^{m} w_i^{(1)} \cdot \sigma \left(\sum_{j=1}^{m} x_j \cdot w_{ji}^{(0)} \right), \tag{1}$$

$$\sigma(s) = \frac{1}{1 + e^{\alpha s}}, \tag{2}$$

where $\sigma(s)$ is the sigmoid activation function, $w_{ji}^{(0)}$ are the weight coefficients of the input layer, $w_i^{(1)}$ are the weight coefficients of the hidden layer, x_j are input signals.

Theorem (*on the error of the representation*). Let $y = F(x_1, \ldots, x_n)$ be any continuous function defined on a bounded set, the function σ is defined according to the conditions presented above, then for $\forall \varepsilon > 0$ there exist $n, w_{ji}^{(0)}, w_i^{(1)}$ such that:

$$F(x_1, \ldots, x_n) = \sum_{i=1}^{m} v_i^{(1)} \cdot \sigma \left(\sum_{j=1}^{m} x_j \cdot v_{ji}^{(0)} \right), \tag{3}$$

where $v_{ji}^{(0)}, v_i^{(1)}$ are the sets of numbers that approximate the function to the analytic representation with an error of at most ε in the entire domain of the definition.

In terms of the theory of neural networks, this theorem is formulated as follows: Any continuous function of several variables can be realized with any accuracy by means of a two-layer neural network.

4   Neural Network Approach to Solving the Problem

The proposed approach to the solution will be illustrated in terms of the following definition of the General differential equation:

$$G(\vec{t}, u(\vec{t}), \nabla u(\vec{t})) = 0, \tag{4}$$

taking into account some boundary conditions (for example, Dirichlet or Neumann), where $\vec{t} = (t_1, t_2, \ldots, t_n) \in \mathbb{R}^n, D \subset \mathbb{R}^n$ denotes the domain of definition, and $u(\vec{t})$ is the computable solution.

This approach can also be applied to higher-order differential equations, but we do not consider this kind of problems in this paper.

In order to obtain the solution of the differential equation, we carry out a discretization of the domain D and its boundary S onto the set of points $\widehat{D}$ and $\widehat{S}$, respectively.

Then the problem is transformed into the following system of equations:

$$G(\vec{t_i}, u(\vec{t_i}), \nabla u(\vec{t_i})) = 0, \quad \forall \vec{t_i} \in D, \tag{5}$$

taking into account some boundary conditions.

If $u_t(\vec{t}, \vec{p})$ denotes a solution with an adjustable parameter vector $\vec{p}$, then the problem is transformed into:

$$\min_{\vec{p}} \sum_{\vec{t_i} \in D} G^2(\vec{t_i}, u(\vec{t_i}, \vec{p}), \nabla u(\vec{t_i}, \vec{p})) = 0, \quad \forall \vec{t_i} \in D, \tag{6}$$

in which it is necessary to take into account the limitations imposed by the boundary conditions.

In the proposed approach a recurrent neural network for constructing an approximate solution is used, and a parameter vector $\vec{p}$ corresponds weights and additional parameters of the neural architecture.

We seek the solution $u_t(\vec{t})$ in such a way that it immediately satisfies the boundary conditions from the construction. This condition is achieved by representing the solutions as a sum of two terms:

$$u_t(\vec{t}) = A(\vec{t}) + F(\vec{t}, N(\vec{t}, \vec{p})), \tag{7}$$

where $N(\vec{t}, \vec{p})$ is the output of a single-layer recurrent network with the parameter vector $\vec{p}$ and n input signals determined by the input vector $\vec{t}$.

The function $A(\vec{t})$ does not contain adjustable parameters and satisfies the boundary conditions. The second term in the representation of the solution is that the function F is constructed in such a way that it does not contribute to the boundary conditions (vanishes identically in the domain S), since the function $u_t(\vec{t})$ must satisfy them. This term uses the neural network, weights and rules, which must be corrected when solving the minimization problem.

At this stage, the problem is reduced from the initial problem of bounded optimization to unbounded optimization because of the choice of the form of the desired solution, which satisfies the boundary conditions by construction.

5   The Reduction to the Problem of Minimization

The effective minimization (6) can be considered as a training procedure for a neural network, where the error corresponding to each input vector $\vec{t_i}$, is equal to the value $G\left(\vec{t_i}\right)$, which must be identically equal to zero. The calculation of this error value includes not only the output of the network (as in the case of conventional training), but also the derivative of the output with respect to any of its input signals. Therefore, when calculating the error gradient with respect to the weight coefficients, it is necessary to calculate the gradient of the output function of the neural network in the domain as well as the gradient with respect to its input data (parameters).

Consider in general a multilayer perceptron with n input signals, one hidden layer with m sigmoid activation functions and a linear output block. Of course, one can expand the neural network into more than one hidden layer, to solve ordinary differential equations of a higher order.

For a given vector of input signals $\vec{t} = (t_1, \ldots, t_n)$, the output of the neural network is:

$$N = \sum_{i=1}^{m} w_i^{(1)} \cdot \sigma(z_i), \qquad (8)$$

and z_i is the total input sign of the neural network, having the form:

$$z_i = \sum_{j=1}^{N} w_{ij}^{(0)} \cdot t_j + \tau_i, \qquad (9)$$

where $w_{ij}^{(0)}$ denotes the weight from the neuron of the input layer i to the neuron of the hidden layer j; $w_i^{(1)}$ denotes the weight from the neuron of the hidden layer j directed to the output of the network result; τ_i means the offset of the signal of hidden layer i; $\sigma(z_i)$ is a sigmoid activation function.

Gradient of the network output function in the direction of the input signals of the network will have the form of:

$$\frac{\partial^k N}{\partial t_j^k} = \sum_{j=1}^{m} w_i^{(1)} \cdot w_{ij}^{(0)k} \cdot \sigma_i^k, \qquad (10)$$

where $\sigma_i^k = \sigma(z_i)$ and σ^k denotes the k-th order derivative of the sigmoid.

In addition, the gradient of the network output function with the respect to all input signals has the form:

$$\frac{\partial^{\lambda_1}}{\partial t_1^{\lambda_1}} \frac{\partial^{\lambda_2}}{\partial t_2^{\lambda_2}} \cdots \frac{\partial^{\lambda_n}}{\partial t_n^{\lambda_n}} N = \sum_{j=1}^{m} w_i^{(1)} \cdot P_i \cdot \sigma_i^{(\Lambda)}, \qquad (11)$$

where

$$P_i = \prod_{k=1}^{n} w_{ik}^{(0)\lambda_k} \qquad (12)$$

$$\Lambda = \sum_{i=1}^{n} \lambda_i. \qquad (13)$$

The expression (11) shows that the derivative of the network output function at any of its inputs is equivalent to a recurrent neural network $N_g(\vec{t}_i)$ with one hidden layer which has the same values for the weights $w_{ij}^{(0)}$ and interference τ_i, and with each weight $w_i^{(1)}$ replaced by $w_i^{(1)} \cdot P_i$. In addition, the activation function of each neuron of the hidden layer is replaced by a Λ-th derivative of the sigmoid.

Therefore, the gradient N_g with the respect to the parameters of the original network can be easily obtained in the form of:

$$\frac{\partial N_g}{\partial w_i^{(1)}} = P_i \cdot \sigma_i^{(\Lambda)}, \tag{14}$$

$$\frac{\partial N_g}{\partial w_i^{(1)}} = P_i \cdot \sigma_i^{(\Lambda)}, \tag{15}$$

$$\frac{\partial N_g}{\partial w_{ij}^{(0)}} = t_j \cdot w_i^{(1)} \cdot P_i \cdot \sigma_i^{(\Lambda+1)} + w_i^{(1)} \cdot \lambda_j \cdot w_i^{(1)\lambda_j-1} \left(\prod_{k=1,k\neq j}^{n} w_{ik}^{(0)\lambda_k} \right) \sigma_i^{(\Lambda)}. \tag{16}$$

Once the derivative of the error calculation function with respect to the network parameters is determined, then it is enough to use almost any minimization method. For example, you can use the steepest descent method, the conjugate gradient method, and other methods proposed in the theory of optimization methods. In this paper, we used a gradient projection method that is quadratic convergent and it demonstrates high performance.

The gradient projection method is based on finding the extreme point of the function in the direction of the anti-gradient. The application of this method to the quadratic functions in the field of real numbers defines a finite number of steps.

Algorithm Gradient Projection Method:

1. Set the initial approximation $\vec{x}_0$, the error of calculations ε, specify the descent factor λ and the number of steps of the algorithm $k = 0$.
2. Calculate the initial direction of the anti gradient:

$$j = 0, \vec{S}_k^j = -\nabla f(\vec{x}_k), \vec{x}_k^j = \vec{x}_k, \tag{17}$$

3. Calculate the following approximation:

$$\vec{x}_k^{j+1} = \vec{x}_k^j + \lambda \cdot \vec{S}_k^j, \vec{S}_k^{j+1} = -\nabla f\left(\vec{x}_k^{j+1}\right). \tag{18}$$

If $\left\| \vec{S}_k^{j+1} \right\| < \varepsilon$ or $\left\| \vec{x}_k^{j+1} - \vec{x}_k^j \right\| < \varepsilon$, then $\vec{x} = \vec{x}_k^{j+1}$ is the extreme point (the end of the algorithm).

Otherwise: If $(j+1) < n$, then $j = j+1$ and go to the step 3, otherwise $\vec{x}_{k+1}^j = \vec{x}_k^{j+1}, k = k+1$ and the transition to the step 2.

Note that λ can be chosen as:

− a constant, but in this case method may diverge;

- a fractional step, that is, the length of the step is divided by a certain number during the process of the descent;
- a steepest descent:

$$\lambda^{[j]} = \arg\min_{\lambda} f\left(\vec{x}^{[j]} - \lambda^{[j]}\nabla f\left(\vec{x}^{[j]}\right)\right). \tag{19}$$

It should also be noted that for a given grid of points, the derivatives of the output function of the neural network (or gradient network) with the respect to the parameters can be obtained even in the case of algorithms for parallelizing computations. Also, in the case of an error back propagation algorithm, an online or batch mode for updating the weight can be used.

6 Algorithm of Neural Network Approach for Solving an ODE of the 1st Order

We consider the application of the neural network approach described above to solve the Cauchy problem for the firs-order ODE, which have the form:

$$\begin{cases} \frac{du}{dt} = f(t, u), \\ u(a) = A, \quad t \in [a, b] \end{cases} \tag{20}$$

We will search the solution of the problem (20), in accordance with the theory above, in the form (7):

$$u_t(t) = A + t \cdot N(t, \vec{p}), \tag{21}$$

where $N(t, \vec{p})$ is the output of the recurrent neural network with one input signal t and the parameters of the network $\vec{p}$, which includes the weight coefficients, the learning rate, the number of input signals and the gradient descent multiplier. Note that $u_t(t)$ satisfies the Cauchy problem in construction.

It is natural that the desired solution in the form of (21) will have its accuracy. The error representing the difference between the found solution and the exact one will be determined as follows:

$$E[\vec{p}] = \sum_i \left\{\frac{du_t(t_i)}{dt} - f(t_i, u_t(t_i))\right\}^2, \tag{22}$$

where t_i are the points on the interval [a, b].

Since the following holds:

$$\frac{du_t(t)}{dt} = N(t, \vec{p}) + t \cdot \frac{dN(t, \vec{p})}{dt}, \tag{23}$$

then it is possible to calculate the gradient of the network output function with respect to the vector of its parameters $\vec{p}$ using (10)–(16), depending on the neural network structure used to solve the ODE. The same applies to all subsequent task models.

Algorithm of Neural Network Approach

Step 1:

Select the test set $\{t_j\}$ of the input signals by dividing the definition area into n equidistant points. Generate random weight coefficients of layers $w_{ji}^{(0)}, w_i^{(1)}$.

Step 2:

Calculate the total input feature of the system:

$$\Sigma_i = \sum_j w_{ji}^{(0)} \cdot t_j. \tag{24}$$

Pass the total feature and the set of input signals $\{t_j\}$ to the output layer.

Step 3:

For updating weight coefficients $(w_{ji}^{(0)}, w_i^{(1)})$, use gradient descent for minimization of calculation errors:

$$E[\vec{p}] = \sum_i \left\{ \frac{du_t(t_i)}{dt} - f(t_i, u_t(t_i)) \right\}^2 \to min. \tag{25}$$

Thus, if the error of the neural network increased (the network was overtrained), then finish the series of gradient descent.

Step 4:

We obtain an analytic representation of $u_t(t)$ in the form (21) and the approximation error $E[\vec{p}]$.

End.

Thus, the developed algorithm of the neural network approach (see Fig. 1) will provide a solution to the Cauchy problem for the ODE of the first order in the form of a functional dependence (21).

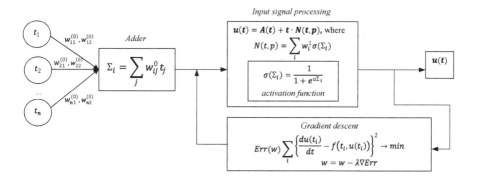

Fig. 1. Schematic representation of the algorithm neural network approach.

7 Experimental Results

Let us investigate the developed neural network algorithm for solving the first-order Cauchy problem for the error of the obtained result, comparing it with the fourth-order Runge-Kutta method, and also find the dependence of the neural network approach on the network parameters used. Consider particular examples of the Cauchy problem for ODE of the 1st order that have an analytic solution.

7.1 Neural Network Approach as an Alternative to Numerical Methods

Let us consider the Cauchy problem:

$$\begin{cases} \frac{du}{dt} - 0,2u = e^{-\frac{t}{5}}\cos t, \\ u(0) = 0, \quad t \in [0, 1]. \end{cases} \tag{26}$$

Analytic solution of the problem (26) has the form:

$$u = e^{-\frac{t}{5}}\sin t. \tag{27}$$

As a result of the work of the considered algorithms, we obtained:

(1) for the Runge-Kutta method of 4th order accuracy:

$$\Delta u_1 = 0.000236713, Count_{N1} = 80.$$

where Δu_1 - error of the numerical solution; $Count_{N1}$ - the number of iterations to achieve the specified accuracy (the number of points in the definition area).

(2) for neural network approach:

$$\Delta u_2 = 0.0004766790, Count_{N2} = 170, Neur = 10.$$

where Δu_2 - neural network error; $Count_{N2}$ - number of iterations; $Neur$ - number of neurons.

The function $u(t)$, which was found as a result of the neural network algorithm, has the form:

$$u_t(t) = t \cdot \left(\sum_{i=1}^{m} w_i^{(1)} \cdot \sigma\left(t \cdot \sum_{j=1}^{m} w_j^{(0)}\right) \right), \tag{28}$$

where $w_j^{(0)}$ - weights of the input layer (Table 1); $w_i^{(1)}$ - output layer weights (Table 2); $m = Neur$ - the number of neurons in the network.

Table 1. Values of the weighting coefficients $w_j^{(0)}$.

j	1	2	3	4	5	6	7	8	9	10
$w_j^{(0)}$	−1.8	1.5	−0.8	−0.8	−0.1	−1.6	0.58	−0.6	1.1	1.5

Table 2. Values of the weighting coefficients $w_i^{(1)}$.

j	1	2	3	4	5	6	7	8	9	10
$w_i^{(1)}$	−0.9	1.2	−1.5	0.9	0.63	3.1	−0.3	−0.7	0.07	−0.4

A graphical representation of the obtained solutions is shown in the Fig. 2.

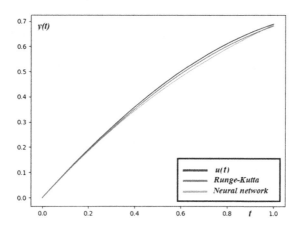

Fig. 2. Graph comparing the solution of the neural network algorithm and the Runge-Kutta method.

Since new random weights are generated each time at the input of the neural network, a series of 10 experiments was carried out, which also had the 4th order of accuracy and retained the $Count_{N2} > Count_{N1}$ property.

Thus, the neural network requires more iterations than the Runge-Kutta method ($Count_{N2} > Count_{N1}$) to achieve the same order of solutions accuracy ($\Delta u_1 \approx \Delta u_2$).

7.2 The Problem of Overtraining the Neural Network on a Particular Example

The condition for the exit from the gradient descent (search for weight coefficients) is of great importance in the development of a neural network algorithm for solving the Cauchy ODE problem of the 1st order. This is due to the fact that the usual convergence condition of the gradient method cannot be applied, since in this case the neural network can recognize examples from the training set, but does not acquire the generalization property. In this case, it is said that the neural network is overtrained. Consider this property on a particular example of the Cauchy ODE problem of the 1st order.

Let us consider the Cauchy problem:

$$\begin{cases} \frac{du}{dt} + 2tu = e^{-t^2} \\ u(0) = 10, \quad t \in [0, 1]. \end{cases} \tag{29}$$

Analytic solution of the problem (27) has the form:

$$u = te^{-t^2} + 10e^{-t^2}. \tag{30}$$

As a result of the neural network algorithm we obtained:

(1) for $Count_{N41} = 150$:

$$\Delta u_{41} = 0.24960104, \ Neur = 4.$$

where Δu_{41} – neural network error; $Count_{N41}$ – number of iterations; $Neur$ – number of neurons (see Fig. 3).

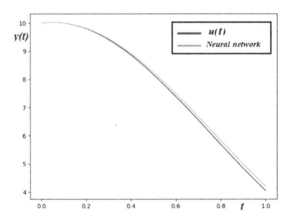

Fig. 3. Graph showing the difference between an exact solution and a neural network solution with a number of iterations of 150.

(2) For $Count_{N42} = 250$:

$$\Delta u_{42} = 25.21320845, \ Neur = 4.$$

where Δu_{24} - neural network error; $Count_{N24}$ - number of iterations; $Neur$ - number of neurons (see Fig. 4).

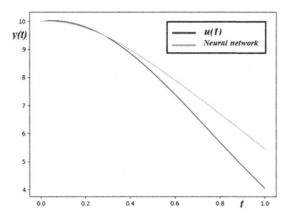

Fig. 4. Graph showing the difference between an exact solution and a neural network solution with a number of iterations of 250.

Thus, it may be concluded that it is necessary to further study the dependence of the parameters of the neural network for each Cauchy problem for ODE. One can set as a parameter the number of neurons, organized within the constraints, as well as other factors, the change of which affects the result.

In view of the possible overtrained the neural network, it is necessary to take into account the error of the deviation of the found solution in parallel to the error of the coefficients in the gradient descent when obtaining the weight coefficients. If the neural network reaches the optimal solution, the gradient descent cycle is completed.

8   Conclusion

A neural network approach to the solution of the Cauchy ODE problem of the 1st order, based on the representation of the function as a superposition of elementary functions, is considered and an algorithm for solving the problem is proposed. The following areas of further research are promising:

- study of the impact of the structure, parameters, and types of activation functions of the neural network on the solution;
- study of the stability of the solution obtained by the neural network method;
- improvement of the presented algorithm at the stage of finding coefficients (the overtrained problem).

Acknowledgments. The research work was funded by the Russian Foundation for Basic Research, according to the research projects No. 16-29-09639, 18-37-00400, 18-07-01446 and the President of the Russian Federation within the grant for state support of young Russian scientists (MK-860.2019.9).

References

1. Bolodurina, I.P., Parfenov, D.I.: Neural network model for optimize network work in the infrastructure of the virtual data center. In: 25th Telecommunications Forum TELFOR: Materials of Forum, Belgrade, Serbia, pp. 1–4 (2017). https://doi.org/10.1109/telfor.2017.8249297
2. Meade, Jr., Fernandez, A.: The numerical solution of linear ordinary differential equations by feedforward neural networks. Math. Comput. Model. **19**(12), 1–25 (1994). https://doi.org/10.1016/0895-7177(94)90095-7
3. Chiaramonte, M., Kiener, M.: Solving differential equations using neural networks. Machine Learning Project, pp. 1–5 (2013). http://cs229.stanford.edu/proj2013/ChiaramonteKiener-SolvingDifferentialEquationsUsingNeuralNetworks.pdf
4. Zemskova, Yu.N., Gorbachenko, V.I., Artyukhina, E.V.: The using of trust neighbourhood method to solution partial differential equation on neural networks with radial basis function. Izv. Penz. gos. pedagog. univ. im.i V. G. Belinskogo, no. 18(22), pp. 151–158 (2010). (in Russian)
5. Kovalenko, A.N., Chernomorets, A.A., Petina, M.A.: On the neural networks application for solving of partial differential equations. Belgorod State University Scientific Bulletin. Series "Economics. Computer Science", no. 9(258), pp. 103–110 (2017). http://dspace.bsu.edu.ru/bitstream/123456789/20389/1/Kovalenko_O_primenenii_17.pdf. (in Russian)
6. Vasilyev, A.N.: Principles and techniques of neural network modeling. In: Vasiliev, A.N., Tarkhov, D.A. (eds.) SPb.: Nestor-History (2014). (in Russian)
7. Yadav, N., Yadav, A., Kumar, M.: An Introduction to Neural Network Methods for Differential Equations. Springer, Heidelberg (2015). https://doi.org/10.1007/978-94-017-9816-7
8. Vasilyev, A.N., Tarkhov, D.A.: Construction of approximate neural network models from heterogeneous data. Matematicheskoe Modelirovaniye [Math. Models Comput. Simul.] **19**(12), 43–51 (2007). (in Russian)
9. Vasilyev, A.N., Tarkhov, D.A.: Neural network approaches to solution of boundary problems in multidimensional composite areas. Izvestiya TSURE, no. 9, pp. 80–89 (2004). (in Russian)
10. Vasilyev, A.N., Tarkhov, D.A.: Neural network as a new universal approach to the numerical solution of problems of mathematical physics. Neurocomputers, no. 7–8, pp. 111–118 (2004). (in Russian)
11. Kolmogorov, A.N.: On the representation of continuous functions of many variables by superposition of continuous functions of one variable and addition. Dokl. Akad. Nauk SSSR **114**(5), 953–956 (1957). (in Russian)

An Equivalence Relation on the Class
of Regular Languages

Boris Melnikov[1]([✉])(ID), Vasily Dolgov[2](ID), and Elena Melnikova[3](ID)

[1] Shenzhen MSU-BIT University, No. 1, International University Park Road, Dayun
New Town, Longgang District, Shenzhen 518172, Guangdong Province, China
bf-melnikov@yandex.ru
[2] Ulyanovsk State Polytechnical University – Terenga Liceum,
No. 32, Severnyy Venec Street, Ulyanovsk 432027, Russia
[3] Russian State Social University, Wilhelm Pieck str., 4, Moscow 129226, Russia

Abstract. This paper introduces a special binary relation on the set
of regular languages, which possesses all three properties of equivalence
relation. That is, this relation separates the whole class of regular languages into non-intersecting classes. In addition, it allows us to consider
only one representative of each class in the description of the regular
languages class, the so-called "simplified" language. Such simplified language corresponds to a "simplified" automaton. This equivalence relation
makes it possible to limit the number of considered regular languages to
a finite number of finite automata with a priori fixed number of states. In
addition, this equivalence relation preserves the relation # considered in
our previous papers, and therefore allows us to use the previous theory.
For example, on the basis of obtained results, we can apply various algorithms of equivalent transformations of nondeterministic finite automata
to simplified them.

Keywords: Regular languages · Nondeterministic finite automata ·
Equivalence relation · Simplification of automata

1 Introduction and Motivation

This paper introduces a special binary relation on the set of regular languages,
which possesses all three properties of the relation of equivalence. That is, this
relation separates the whole class of regular languages into non-intersecting
classes. In addition, it allows us to consider only one representative of each
class in the description of the regular languages class, the so-called *simplified
language*. This notion relies on the joining of *parallel letters*, which, in its turn,
is also an equivalence relation for a given regular language. Apparently, up to
the present time such a concept has not been encountered in the literature. Such
simplified language corresponds to a *simplified automaton*.

This equivalence relation makes it possible to limit the number of considered regular languages to a finite number of finite automata with a priori fixed

© Springer Nature Switzerland AG 2020
V. Sukhomlin and E. Zubareva (Eds.): Convergent 2018, CCIS 1140, pp. 93–107, 2020.
https://doi.org/10.1007/978-3-030-37436-5_8

number of states. In addition, this equivalence relation preserves the relation # considered in our previous papers, and therefore allows us to use the previous theory. For example, on the basis of obtained results, we can apply various algorithms of equivalent transformations of nondeterministic finite automata to simplified automata, such as:

– constructing the equivalent automaton with minimum possible number of states;
– constructing the equivalent automaton with minimum possible number of edges;
– constructing the equivalent universal automaton;
– constructing an automaton according to the basis one . . .

In this way, we obtain objects of the formalism which are more acceptable in terms of some characteristics, for example, with fewer numbers of vertices, edges, etc. In general, simplified automaton is the canonical one for the corresponding language; the simplified language has the same binary relations #, and this fact allows us to use all the previous theory, see [1–5] etc. In fact, we can consider simplified automata instead of usual nondeterministic finite automata.

2   Preliminaries

This section briefly describes the notation and some facts from our previous publications on related topics, see [1] etc. Let

$$K = (Q, \Sigma, \delta, S, F) \tag{1}$$

be some finite automaton (nondeterministic Rabin-Scott's automaton), defining regular language $L = \mathcal{L}(K)$. Q is the set of states, $S \subseteq Q$ and $F \subseteq Q$ are sets of initial and final states respectively. We shall consider transition function δ of automaton (1) as

$$\delta : Q \times \Sigma \to \mathcal{P}(Q),$$

but not as

$$\delta : Q \times (\Sigma \cup \{\varepsilon\}) \to \mathcal{P}(Q),$$

where the notation $\mathcal{P}(Q)$ denotes the superset (the power set) of the set Q; thus, we shall consider automaton without ε-transitions. We will usually write some edge $\delta(q, a) \ni r$ in the form $q \xrightarrow[\delta]{a} r$, or, if it does not cause ambiguity, simply in the form $q \xrightarrow{a} r$.

We also specially note the following important notation. Along with the transition function δ, we shall also use the alternative transition function

$$\gamma : Q \times Q \to \mathcal{P}(\Sigma)$$

corresponding to it.[1] In this case, γ is defined as follows:

$$\gamma(q', q'') \ni a, \quad \text{where } a \in \Sigma, \quad \text{if and only if} \quad \delta(q', a) \ni q''.$$

---

[1] For example, δ corresponds to γ, $\tilde{\delta}$ corresponds to $\tilde{\gamma}$, etc.

In this case, we will sometimes write the automaton (1) in the form

$$K = (Q, \Sigma, \gamma, S, F)$$

(i.e. replacing δ for γ); such a record will not cause confusion.

The mirror automaton for the automaton of (1), i.e.,

$$(Q, \Sigma, \delta^R, F, S),$$

where

$$q' \xrightarrow[\delta^R]{a} q'' \quad \text{if and only if} \quad q'' \xrightarrow[\delta]{a} q',$$

will be denoted by K^R; note that K^R defines the mirror language L^R.

Considering the regular language L to be given and use the notations defined in the cited papers for it. For the considered language L, its automaton of canonical form (CDFA) will be denoted as $\widetilde{L}$. Let automata $\widetilde{L}$ and $\widetilde{L^R}$ for the given language L be as follows:

$$\widetilde{L} = (Q_\pi, \Sigma, \delta_\pi, \{s_\pi\}, F_\pi) \quad \text{and} \quad \widetilde{L^R} = (Q_\rho, \Sigma, \delta_\rho, \{s_\rho\}, F_\rho).$$

Moreover, we do not consider the language $L = \emptyset$, so both these automata *do have* initial states.[2]

Let us recall definitions of binary relation $\#$ and state-marking functions φ^{in} and φ^{out}, see for details [1]. Relation $\# \subseteq Q_\pi \times Q_\rho$ is defined for pairs of states of automata $\widetilde{L}$ and $\widetilde{L^R}$ in the following way: $A \# X$ if and only if

$$\left(\exists uv \in L \right) \left(u \in \mathcal{L}_{\widetilde{L}}^{in}(A), \, v^R \in \mathcal{L}_{\widetilde{L^R}}^{in}(X) \right).$$

Note that such a definition is non-constructive; however, for example, [1] contains also its equivalent constructive variant (i.e., the definition-algorithm).

3   The Concepts of Simplified Automaton and Simplified Regular Language

The main idea of this section can be expressed as follows: for a given regular language, we define some relation ("parallelity") on the set of its letters (Σ), and then we show that "parallel" letters can be united in a way that preserves all important properties of this regular language. Thus, let us firstly define the "simplified" automata and "simplified" languages.

---

[2] Like [1], we name "canonical automaton" a deterministic automaton, containing the minimum possible number of states. Here, also like [1], we do *not* require this automaton to be the everywhere-defined, and, therefore, do not consider the possible "dead state".

Definition 1. Let regular language L be defined over the alphabet Σ, let $a, b \in \Sigma$, and let there exist an automaton $K = (Q, \Sigma, \delta, S, F)$, such that $\mathcal{L}(K) = L$ and $(\forall q \in Q)(\delta(q, a) = \delta(q, b))$. Then we shall call letters a and b *parallel over the regular language* L, and denote this fact as

$$a \overset{L}{\|} b.$$

□

For illustrative purposes, we shall give two more *equivalent* definitions. But we shall not prove this equivalence, since we shall not need the first one, and the second one is obvious.

Definition 2. Letters a and b are *parallel over the regular language* L, if there is a regular expression R_0, which defines L, such that

$$R_0 = R_0((a + b), c_1, \ldots, c_k), \quad \text{where} \quad c_1, c_2, \ldots, c_k \in \Sigma \setminus \{a, b\}.$$

□

Definition 3. Letters a and b are *parallel over the regular language* L, if there is an automaton $K = (Q, \Sigma, \gamma, S, F)$, such that $L_K = L$ and

$$(\forall q_1, q_2 \in Q)(\gamma(q_1, q_2) \ni a \iff \gamma(q_1, q_2) \ni b).$$

□

Let us now define the relation of "parallelity" of letters for an automaton. Let us note that this relation and the relation defined above are in the same correspondence as the notions of regular expression and regular language. Namely, if two letters are parallel over some regular language, nevertheless, this language can be defined by an automaton for which this parallelity does not hold.

Definition 4. Let automaton $K = (Q, \Sigma, \delta, S, F)$, let $a, b \in \Sigma$, and let

$$(\forall q \in Q) \, (\delta(q, a) = \delta(q, b)).$$

Then the letters a and b are *parallel over the automaton* K. We shall denote this fact as

$$a \overset{K}{\|} b.$$

□

We denote hereinafter a deterministic finite automaton (DFA), obtained from K, by $\hat{K}$. Similarly, like for languages, we shall denote the CDFA obtained from K by $\tilde{K}$. Similar upper signs we shall apply to all elements of the 5-tuple forming the automaton.

Proposition 1. If $a \overset{K}{\|} b$, then $a \overset{\hat{K}}{\|} b$ and $a \overset{\tilde{K}}{\|} b$.

Proof.

$$(\forall Q_1 \in \mathcal{P}(Q)) \, (\forall a, b \in \Sigma)$$

$$\left(\hat{\delta}(Q_1, a) = \bigcup_{q \in Q_1} \delta(q, a) \overset{\text{Def.4}}{=} \bigcup_{q \in Q_1} \delta(q, b) = \hat{\delta}(Q_1, b) \right),$$

i.e., when we convert a finite automaton to DFA, then the parallelity preserves, that is

$$a \overset{K}{\|} b \Rightarrow a \overset{\hat{K}}{\|} b.$$

When converting DFA to CDFA, we only join the states of automaton, here

$$\widetilde{\gamma}(r, q_1) = \hat{\gamma}(r, q_1) \cup \hat{\gamma}(r, q_2),$$

where $\hat{\gamma}(r, q_1)$ and $\hat{\gamma}(r, q_2)$ can contain a and b only pairwise. Therefore, the same is true for $\widetilde{\gamma}(r, q_1)$. The same reasoning can be applied for

$$\widetilde{\gamma}(q_1, r) = \hat{\gamma}(q_1, r) \cup \hat{\gamma}(q_2, r).$$

$\square$

Proposition 2. If $a \overset{K}{\|} b$ and $b \overset{K}{\|} c$, then $a \overset{K}{\|} c$.

Proof.

$$(\forall q \in Q) \left(\delta(q, a) \overset{\text{Def.4}}{=} \delta(q, b) \overset{\text{Def.4}}{=} \delta(q, c) \right),$$

i.e., $a \overset{K}{\|} c$.

$\square$

Proposition 3. Let regular language L be given. Let also $a \overset{L}{\|} b$ and $b \overset{L}{\|} c$. Then $a \overset{L}{\|} c$.

Proof. We obtain from Definition 1, that

$$\left(\exists K_1, \ \mathcal{L}(K_1) = L \right) \left(a \overset{K_1}{\|} b \right),$$

and also

$$\left(\exists K_2, \ \mathcal{L}(K_2) = L \right) \left(b \overset{K_2}{\|} c \right).$$

Since $\widetilde{K_1} = \widetilde{K_2} = \widetilde{K}$ (up to redefinition of states – since CDFA is a full invariant of a regular language), then by Proposition 1,

$$a \overset{K_1}{\|} b \Longrightarrow a \overset{\widetilde{K_1}}{\|} b \Longrightarrow a \overset{\widetilde{K}}{\|} b \quad \text{and} \quad b \overset{K_2}{\|} c \Longrightarrow b \overset{\widetilde{K_2}}{\|} c \Longrightarrow b \overset{\widetilde{K}}{\|} c.$$

This implies by Proposition 2, that $a \overset{\widetilde{K}}{\|} c$, and, therefore, by Definition 1, that $a \overset{L}{\|} c$.

$\square$

Thus, the relation $a \overset{L}{\|} b$ is reflexive, symmetric (by definition) and transitive, so it is an *equivalence relation*, and the alphabet Σ can be split into subsets of parallel (over the given language L) letters.

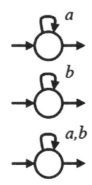

Fig. 1. The given nondeterministic automaton K

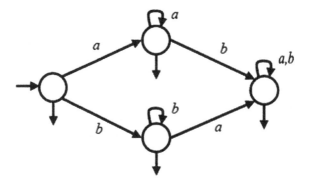

Fig. 2. Deterministic automaton $\hat{K}$

Example 1. Consider regular language over the alphabet $\Sigma = \{a, b\}$, defined by regular expression

$$a^* + b^* + (a + b)^*.$$

It can be defined by automaton K of Fig. 1. From it, we simply obtain the equivalent DFA $\hat{K}$, see Fig. 2:

All states of the last automaton are equivalent (with respect of output language), therefore, after joining them we obtain CDFA $\widetilde{K}$, see Fig. 3:

Thus, the given language L can be defined by an automaton $\widetilde{K}$, where $a \parallel_{L}^{\widetilde{K}} b$. Therefore, by definition, we have $a \parallel_{L} b$ (it was not fully obvious from the initial

Fig. 3. Canonical automaton $\widetilde{K}$

regular expression, but we have obtained this result in a fully automatic way, the way a computer program could have done it). Note that the partition of the alphabet Σ consists of one equivalence set $\{a, b\}$ only, and this partition is due not to the way we define the language (regular expression, NFA, DFA, CDFA), but is an intrinsic property of the language itself.

We shall give two following important propositions. We shall use the first of them in the definition of "simplified" automaton, the second will help us consider the relation $\#$ of the language of this automaton.

Proposition 4. Let $\widetilde{K}$ be the CDFA for the given regular language L. Then for each $a, b \in \Sigma$, the following fact holds:

$$a \overset{L}{\|} b \Longleftrightarrow a \overset{\widetilde{K}}{\|} b,$$

i.e., the parallelity $a \overset{L}{\|} b$ is unambiguously defined by $\widetilde{K}$.

Proof.

$\Rightarrow$ by Definition 1 and Proposition 1;
$\Leftarrow$ by Definition 1. $\qquad\qquad\qquad\qquad\qquad\qquad\qquad\qquad\qquad\qquad\qquad\qquad$ □

Proposition 5. Let L be a regular language over the alphabet Σ, then for each $a, b \in \Sigma$, the following fact holds:

$$a \overset{L}{\|} b \Longleftrightarrow a \overset{L^R}{\|} b,$$

i.e., the parallelity $a \overset{L}{\|} b$ holds also for the mirror language.

Proof.

$\Rightarrow$ Let $a \overset{L}{\|} b$, then for some automaton $K = (Q, \Sigma, \gamma, S, F)$ defining L the following holds: $a \overset{K}{\|} b$. Let us consider automaton

$$K^R = (Q, \Sigma, \gamma^R, S, F),$$

it defines language L^R, then

$$\gamma^R(q_1, q_2) = \gamma(q_2, q_1) \ni a \Longleftrightarrow \gamma^R(q_1, q_2) = \gamma(q_2, q_1) \ni b.$$

$\Leftarrow$ The reverse fact is proved similarly. $\qquad\qquad\qquad\qquad\qquad\qquad\qquad$ □

Example 2. Let us consider automaton K of Fig. 3 and the corresponding language L. As we have already seen, the following holds:

$$a \overset{L}{\|} b \quad \text{and} \quad a \overset{K}{\|} b.$$

The same is true for the language L^R and automaton K^R:

$$a \overset{L^R}{\|} b \quad \text{and} \quad a \overset{K^R}{\|} b$$

(in this case, they are simply equal to L and K respectively).

Thus, we know that every regular language induces some partition of the given alphabet Σ into some subsets of parallel letters, this partition is defined only by the language itself (and the reverse language defines the same partition, see Proposition 5):

$$\Sigma = \bigcup_{i=1}^{n} \sigma_i \,,$$

where

$$\sigma_i \neq \varnothing \,, \quad \sigma_i \cap \sigma_j = \varnothing \quad \text{for} \quad i,j \in \{1,2,\ldots,n\}, \ i \neq j \,;$$

we shall denote this partition as:

$$\bar{\sigma} = \{\,\sigma_1, \sigma_2, \ldots, \sigma_n\,\} \,.$$

Later, we shall consider regular languages and finite automata for the alphabet $\bar{\sigma}$, and we can consider every $\sigma_i \in \bar{\sigma}$ simply as a letter, as well as a subset of Σ.

Below, we suppose that L is a given regular language over the alphabet Σ, $\widetilde{K}$ is the CDFA[3] defining L, and $\bar{\sigma}$ is the partition of Σ corresponding to L. Let us give two other forms of Proposition 4.

Proposition 6. Let $a,b \in \Sigma$. Then $a,b \in \sigma_i$ ($\sigma_i \in \bar{\sigma}$) if and only if $a \overset{\widetilde{K}}{\|} b$.   □

Proposition 7. Let $a,b \in \Sigma$. Then $a,b \in \sigma_i$ ($\sigma_i \in \bar{\sigma}$) if and only if

$$\left(\forall q \in \widetilde{Q}\right) \left(\widetilde{\delta}(q,a) = \widetilde{\delta}(q,b)\right) .$$ □

The proofs of both last propositions are obvious: they are a consequence of Proposition 4 and the definition of parallel letters.

Proposition 7 allows us also to give a definition of the so-called "simplified" automaton over the alphabet $\bar{\sigma}$. Naturally, this automaton defines some regular language, which we shall also call "simplified".

Definition 5. *Simplified automaton* for regular language L, is an automaton

$$\overline{K} = \left(\widetilde{Q}, \bar{\sigma}, \bar{\delta}, \widetilde{S}, \widetilde{F}\right) ,$$

where:

- $\bar{\sigma}$ is the simplified alphabet (for L) defined before;
- $\widetilde{Q}$, $\widetilde{S}$ and $\widetilde{F}$ are elements of 5-tuple of automaton $\widetilde{L}$ also defined before;
- for some $q \in \widetilde{Q}$, $a \in \Sigma$ (where $a \in \sigma_i$) we set

$$\bar{\delta}(q,\sigma_i) = \widetilde{\delta}(q,a).$$

---

[3] Let us note once again, that according to the previous agreement,

$$\widetilde{K} = \left(\widetilde{Q}, \Sigma, \widetilde{\delta}, \widetilde{S}, \widetilde{F}\right) .$$

Note that this definition can be viewed as a process of "combining together" of parallel letters. Doing this, the number of letters of the alphabet can only decrease (since $|\sigma_i| \geq 1$), so the name "simplified" is quite appropriate.

Proof (of the correctness of definition). $\overline{K}$ is defined by regular language L only, since $\widetilde{K}$ is an invariant of L. The equality $\overline{\delta}(q, \sigma_i) = \widetilde{\delta}(q, a)$ is possible, since $\widetilde{\delta}(q, a) = \widetilde{\delta}(q, b)$ when $a, b \in \sigma_i$ (see Proposition 7). □

The definition of automaton $\overline{K}$ and Proposition 7 can be summarized as follows (the proof is evident):

Proposition 8. Consider automata $\widetilde{K}$ and $\overline{K}$ for a given regular language L. Then for each $a \in \Sigma$ and $\sigma_i \in \overline{\sigma}$, the following condition holds:

$$a \in \sigma_i \iff \left(\forall q \in \widetilde{Q}\right) \left(\overline{\delta}(q, \sigma_i) = \widetilde{\delta}(q, a)\right).$$ □

4 Some Complex Properties of the Considered Equivalence Relation

Let us introduce the following notations.

1. Let $a \in \Sigma$, we denote σ_a the subset of Σ ($\sigma_a \in \overline{\sigma}$) containing a.
2. Let $u = a_1 \ldots a_m$, $\overline{u} = \sigma_{a_1} \ldots \sigma_{a_m}$, then we shall write $u \in \overline{u}$. In general, $\overline{u}$ is a word of language $\overline{\sigma}^*$.
3. $\overline{L}$ denotes the language of automaton $\overline{K}$ (the *simplified language*).

We shall prove now, that all the important features of regular language are preserved in the process of combining parallel letters. In particular, automaton $\overline{K}$ is also a CDFA, and language $\overline{L}$ has the same table of relation $\#$ as language L has.

Theorem 1. $\overline{K}$ is deterministic.

Proof. We show that all three properties of deterministic automaton hold:

- $\widetilde{S}$ does not change, i.e. the number of initial states does not exceed 1;
- by the definition of $\overline{K}$, there are no ε-transitions;
- for each $q \in \widetilde{Q}$ and $a \in \sigma_a$, $|\overline{\delta}(q, \sigma_a)| = |\widetilde{\delta}(q, a)| \leq 1$, since $\widetilde{K}$ is deterministic.

□

Theorem 2. Let $u \in \overline{u}$. Then for each $q \in \widetilde{Q}$, the following holds:

$$u \in \mathcal{L}_{\widetilde{K}}^{in}(q) \iff \overline{u} \in \mathcal{L}_{\overline{K}}^{in}(q).$$

Proof.

⇒ Let $u = a_1 \ldots a_m$, $u \in \mathcal{L}_{\widetilde{K}}^{in}(q)$. Then there exists a following path in the automaton $\widetilde{K}$:

$$s \in S \xrightarrow{a_1} q_1 \xrightarrow{a_2} \ldots \xrightarrow{a_m} q \,;$$

and since

$$\overline{u} = \sigma_{a_1} \ldots \sigma_{a_m}, \quad a_i \in \sigma_{a_i}, \quad \overline{\delta}(q, \sigma_a) = \widetilde{\delta}(q, a)$$

(see Proposition 8), the automaton $\overline{K}$ also has a following path:

$$s \in S \xrightarrow{\sigma_{a_1}} q_1 \xrightarrow{\sigma_{a_2}} \ldots \xrightarrow{\sigma_{a_m}} q \,,$$

that is $u \in \mathcal{L}_{\overline{K}}^{in}(q)$.

⇐ The reverse fact is proved similarly.   □

In a perfectly the same manner we can show that the following is true.

Theorem 3. Let $u \in \overline{u}$. Then for each $q \in \widetilde{Q}$, the following holds:

$$u \in \mathcal{L}_{\widetilde{K}}^{out}(q) \Longleftrightarrow \overline{u} \in \mathcal{L}_{\overline{K}}^{out}(q).$$ □

Theorem 4. DFA $\overline{K}$ is a canonical DFA for language $\overline{L}$.

Proof.

– $\overline{K}$ has no unreachable states: let $q \in \widetilde{Q}$, then, since $\widetilde{K}$ is canonical,

$$\mathcal{L}_{\widetilde{K}}^{in}(q) \neq \varnothing;$$

that is, there exists some $u \in \mathcal{L}_{\widetilde{K}}^{in}(q)$. Therefore (by Theorem 2)

$$u \in \mathcal{L}_{\overline{K}}^{in}(q), \quad \text{then} \quad \mathcal{L}_{\overline{K}}^{in}(q) \neq \varnothing,$$

i.e. q is a reachable state of automaton $\overline{K}$.

– $\overline{K}$ has no useless states: this fact is proved similarly to previous one (by Theorem 3).

– $\overline{K}$ has no equivalent (by the output language) states: let us assume the contrary, i.e., let $q_1 \sim q_2$ in automaton $\overline{K}$. That is,

$$\mathcal{L}_{\overline{K}}^{out}(q_1) = \mathcal{L}_{\overline{K}}^{out}(q_2).$$

Then by Theorem 3, we obtain the following:

$$\mathcal{L}_{\widetilde{K}}^{out}(q_1) = \left\{ u \in \Sigma^* \mid u \in \overline{u}, \; \overline{u} \in \mathcal{L}_{\overline{K}}^{out}(q_1) \right\},$$

$$\mathcal{L}_{\widetilde{K}}^{out}(q_2) = \left\{ u \in \Sigma^* \mid u \in \overline{u}, \; \overline{u} \in \mathcal{L}_{\overline{K}}^{out}(q_2) \right\},$$

i.e., $\mathcal{L}_{\widetilde{K}}^{out}(q_1) = \mathcal{L}_{\widetilde{K}}^{out}(q_2)$, then $q_1 \sim q_2$ in automaton $\widetilde{K}$ also, and we come to the contradiction.   □

Thus, the simplified automaton $\overline{K}$ is indeed a canonical one, and it unambiguously defines simplified language $\overline{L}$. Now, we shall prove that the simplified language has the same relation $\#$ as the initial language. At first, we show the connection between L and $\overline{L}$.

Theorem 5. $u \in L \Longleftrightarrow \overline{u} \in \overline{u}$, where $\overline{u} \in \overline{L}$.

Proof. $L = \mathcal{L}_{\overline{K}}^{out}(s)$, where s is the initial state of $\widetilde{K}$. By Theorem 3,

$$u \in \mathcal{L}_{\widetilde{K}}^{out}(s) \Longleftrightarrow \overline{u} \in \mathcal{L}_{\overline{K}}^{out}(s),$$

where $\mathcal{L}_{\overline{K}}^{out}(s) = \overline{L}$. □

Proposition 9. If $v \in \overline{v}$ and $w \in \overline{w}$, then $\overline{v} \cdot \overline{w} = \overline{v \cdot w}$.

Proof. We simply apply the mapping $a \rightarrow \sigma_a$ (where $a \in \Sigma$, $\sigma_a \in \overline{\sigma}$). □

Theorem 6. Languages L and $\overline{L}$ have the same relation $\#$.

Proof. Since L and L^R have the same partition $\overline{\sigma}$ (by Proposition 5), then all the above theorems can be applied to both this languages simultaneously (for L^R, we denote the corresponding automata K^R and $\widetilde{K^R}$).

Let us write the definition of $q_1 \# q_2$ (see [1,4] etc.) and prove that this condition does not change when we convert $\widetilde{K}$ into $\overline{K}$ and back (we use here Theorems 2 and 5).

$\rightarrow$ (i.e., $\widetilde{K} \rightarrow \overline{K}$). For $\widetilde{K}$, we have $q_1 \# q_2$ when

$$(\exists u \in L) \left(u = vw,\ v \in \mathcal{L}_{\widetilde{K}}^{in}(q_1),\ w^R \in \mathcal{L}_{\widetilde{K^R}}^{in}(q_2) \right),$$

then $\overline{u} \in \overline{L}$, and

$$\overline{u} = \overline{v \cdot w} = \overline{v} \cdot \overline{w},$$

where $\overline{w} \in \mathcal{L}_{\overline{K}}^{in}(q_1)$ and $\overline{w}^R \in \mathcal{L}_{\overline{K^R}}^{in}(q_2)$. That is, $q_1 \# q_2$ for language $\overline{L}$ and automaton $\overline{K}$.

$\leftarrow$ (i.e., $\overline{K} \rightarrow \widetilde{K}$). For $\overline{K}$, we have $q_1 \# q_2$ when

$$(\exists \overline{u} \in \overline{L}) \left(u = \overline{v}\overline{w},\ \overline{v} \in \mathcal{L}_{\overline{K}}^{in}(q_1),\ \overline{w}^R \in \mathcal{L}_{\overline{K^R}}^{in}(q_2) \right).$$

Let us take some $v \in \overline{v}$ and $w \in \overline{w}$, then $\overline{u} = \overline{v} \cdot \overline{w} = \overline{v \cdot w}$ and $u = vw \in L$, where $v \in \mathcal{L}_{\widetilde{K}}^{in}(q_1)$, $w^R \in \mathcal{L}_{\widetilde{K^R}}^{in}(q_2)$. That is $q_1 \# q_2$ for the given language L and automaton $\widetilde{K}$. □

5   Equivalent Simplified Languages

Now, we can naturally define the equivalence by simplifying regular languages. These are the languages which have the same simplified language (of course, up to renaming letters of the alphabet $\overline{\sigma}$). More formally:

Definition 6. Languages L_1 and L_2 are equivalent by simplifying, if L_i simplifies to $\overline{L_i}$ over the alphabet $\overline{\sigma_i}$ ($i = 1, 2$), and there exists a bijection

$$\overline{\sigma_1} \longleftrightarrow \overline{\sigma_2},$$

such that this bijection can be extended to $\overline{L_1}$ and $\overline{L_2}$ (i.e., the simplified automata $\overline{K_1}$ and $\overline{K_2}$ are the same up to renaming letters and states).   □

Example 3. Languages

$$L_1 = a^* + b^* + (a + b)^* \quad \text{and} \quad L_2 = c^*$$

are equivalent by simplifying since both languages have the same simplified language $\overline{L_i} = \sigma_i^*$.

The last definition is indeed the definition of equivalence relation, since the simplified language (simplified automaton) is an invariant of regular language, and, therefore, all the regular languages are partitioned into the subsets of languages having the same simplified language.

It is worth noting, that the simplifying of languages can be considered as a first tiny step in the approach to *classification of regular languages*: any regular language can be obtained from some simplified language by the operation, inverse to the operation of simplifying:

$$\sigma_i \to \{ a_{i_1}, a_{i_2}, \ldots, a_{i_n} \}, \quad \text{where} \quad \sigma_i \cap \sigma_j = \varnothing,$$

and so on.

Note also, that it is quite feasible to define a "letter parallel to language", for example for some simple language (e.g., with no Kleene's star) and to extend the above equivalence relation.

Some additional approaches of *classification of regular languages* were given in [4]; in future publications, we are going to combine these classifications.

6   Automata with No Parallel Letters

Since there is no acceptable classification of simplified languages yet, it is important to find some other application of this notion. One of possible applications is the fact that while considering simplified languages we can omit automata with parallel letters. This, in particular, lets us to examine only finite number of automata when we fix their number of states.

The next definition can be considered as an operation of "pre-joining" of parallel (for automaton) letters. The theorem tells us that this pre-joining does not change the simplified automaton.

Definition 7. Let $K = (Q, \Sigma, \delta, S, F)$, $a, b \in \Sigma$, and $a \overset{K}{\|} b$. We also assume, that $\Sigma' = \Sigma' \setminus \{b\}$ and σ' is the corresponding restriction of δ onto the alphabet Σ'. Then we shall say that automaton $K' = (Q, \Sigma', \delta, S, F)$ is obtained from K by joining of parallel letters a and b. □

Theorem 7. Let $K = (Q, \Sigma, \delta, S, F)$, $a, b \in \Sigma$, $a \overset{K}{\|} b$, and automaton K' is obtained from K by joining of parallel letters a and b. Then $\overline{K} = \overline{K'}$.

Proof. We already know, that operations $K \to \hat{K}$ and $\hat{K} \to \widetilde{K}$ preserve the property $a \overset{K}{\|} b$ (see Proposition 1). If we apply the simplifying operation to $\widetilde{K}$ and $\widetilde{K'}$, then automaton $\overline{K'}$ will differ from $\overline{K}$ only by the fact that the set σ_i (where $\sigma_i \ni a, b$) will change for $\sigma_i \setminus \{b\}$, which is insignificant for $\overline{\sigma}$ as an alphabet. □

Thus, each automaton can be reduced, by the series of operations of "pre-joining" letters, to an automaton which has no parallel letters. Doing so, we does not change its simplified automaton (simplified language). This allows us to examine *only finite number of automata* (up to renaming letters and states) with the fixed number of states.

Theorem 8. If n is the number of states of finite automaton, then the number of simplified automata (languages) of all such NFA does not exceed the following value:
$$2^{2^{n^2}-1} \cdot (2^n - 1)^2.$$

Proof. By the previous theorem, the number of simplified automata (languages) does not exceed the number of automata with n states having *no parallel letters*. Now, we shall estimate the last number.

Let the states of automaton
$$Q = \{q_1, q_2, \ldots, q_n\}$$
be ordered in some way (we shall not consider permutations of this set), and
$$K = (Q, \Sigma, \gamma, S, F).$$

Then we shall map every letter $a \in \Sigma$ (the number $|\Sigma|$ will be defined later) to a binary matrix of the size $n \times n$ (see Fig. 4), where each element b_{ij} is equal 0 or 1; we set $b_{ij} = 1$, if the following condition is satisfied:
$$a \in \gamma(q_i, q_j).$$

This matrix fully defines the occurrence of a given letter in an automaton. Evidently, that the letters with equal matrices are parallel (over K), and, vice versa, if matrices are not equal, then the corresponding letters are not parallel (over K). Hence, the number of non-parallel letters is no greater than 2^{n^2}.

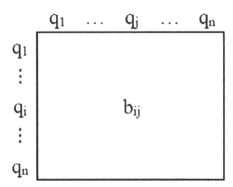

Fig. 4. Binary matrix defines the occurrence of letter in an automaton

The null matrix can be excluded (because the letter is *not* in the automaton), that is

$$|\Sigma| \leq 2^{n^2} - 1.$$

We should also take into account that every letter is either *present* in automaton, or *not* (we do not consider the renaming of letters). Therefore, the number of ways to define γ is

$$2^{2^{n^2}-1}.$$

Both S and F have $2^n - 1$ ways (we also exclude the null set). Multiplying this numbers, we obtain

$$2^{2^{n^2}-1} \cdot (2^n - 1)^2. \qquad \square$$

7 Conclusion

Thus, we defined in this paper a simplified automaton. We proved, that this automaton is a canonical one for the corresponding language. Hence, it unambiguously defines simplified language, and we can consider equivalent simplified languages. Moreover, the initial regular language and corresponding simplified one have equal relations #, which allows us to use all the previous theory by just considering simplified automata instead of finite automata. We studied automata with no parallel letters and obtained an upper bound on the number of simplified languages with a priori fixed number of states of the given nondeterministic finite automaton.

In the future publications, we are planning to shall give some *computational* results on the number of simplified languages when the automaton for the considered language has exactly two states. This results surprisingly confirm the aforementioned upper bound. It is worth noting, that we can apply "simplifying" to almost any notion in the theory of regular languages. For example we can study "simplified universal automaton", see [3], etc. As we said before, we also are going to combine two classifications of regular languages, i.e., the classification considered in this paper and also one which can be obtained on the basis of [4].

References

1. Melnikov, B.: Once more on the edge-minimization of nondeterministic finite automata and the connected problems. Fundam. Informaticae **104**(3), 267–283 (2010)
2. Melnikov, B., Tsyganov, A.: The state minimization problem for nondeterministic finite automata: the parallel implementation of the truncated branch and bound method. In: Proceedings of the International Symposium on Parallel Architectures, Algorithms and Programming, PAAP-2012, Taipei, Taiwan, pp. 194–201 (2012)
3. Melnikov, B., Dolgov, V.: Some more algorithms for Conway's universal automaton. Acta Univ. Sapientiae, Informatica. **6**(1), 5–20 (2014)
4. Melnikov, B.: The complete finite automaton. Int. J. Open Inf. Technol. **5**(10), 9–17 (2017)
5. Melnikov, B.: The star-height of a finite automaton and some related questions. Int. J. Open Inf. Technol. **6**(7), 1–5 (2018)

A Semiotic Model Mapping and Reduction Properties

Igor Fiodorov[1(✉)] 🆔 and Aleksandr Sotnikov[2] 🆔

[1] Plekhanov Russian University of Economics, Stremyannyi per. 36,
117997 Moscow, Russia
Igor.Fiodorov@mail.ru
[2] Joint Supercomputer Center of the Russian Academy of Sciences,
Leninsky Prospect 32a, 119334 Moscow, Russia
ASotnikov@jscc.ru

Abstract. In this paper, we investigate semiotic models used in the computer industry, by means of linguistic approach, considering a computer modeling notation as an artificial modeling language, which, compared to a natural language of human communication, sacrifices its beauty and imagery for the sake of accuracy and unambiguity. The research is carried out in the context of Frege's triangle, its vertexes represent three sets of different nature: material objects, ideal concepts, and signs. We suggest separating relations inter elements of one set, and a mapping describing the correspondence between the elements of different sets. Three sides of Frege's triangle can be interpreted as mappings: conceptualization - assigns an object to a concept, semantic - link a concept to a sign, representation - connects a sign of a model to an object of a subject area. An analysis of mappings inter three sets of different nature allows making a judgment on model quality. In the case of computer modeling notations all mappings should be morphisms that carry the relations between the elements of one set to the relations between the elements of the other. Finally, we make a proposition that syntax and semantics of a computer modeling notation can be formalized by use of Bunge-Wand-Weber upper-level ontology.

Keywords: Semiotic model · Syntax · Semantic · Ontology

1 Introduction

H. Stachowiak differentiates natural model, having the same physical nature as an original, and semiotic one made of signs [1]. He suggests three fundamental properties that make a model: mapping, reduction and pragmatism. Attempts to understand these properties by direct matching a model with an original fail [2, 3]. In this paper, we investigate semiotic models used in technical science, i.e. in computer industry, by means of linguistic methods. Compared to a natural language of human communication an artificial modeling notation sacrifices its beauty and imagery for the sake of accuracy

A. Sotnikov—The work was done within the framework of the state assignment (research topic: 065-2019-0014 (reg. no. AAAA-A19-119011590097-1).

V. Sukhomlin and E. Zubareva (Eds.): Convergent 2018, CCIS 1140, pp. 108–115, 2020.
https://doi.org/10.1007/978-3-030-37436-5_9

and unambiguity. We limit observation to the modeling of material objects, leaving ideal world out of concern. Due to the limits of this paper, we introduce only general ideas. We make a proposition that syntax and semantics of an artificial modeling notation can be formalized by means of linguistic methods and with a use of Bunge-Wand-Weber upper-level ontology.

2   Related Research

Shreider reveals a similarity between semiotic and algebraic models [4]. He affirms that a model can be characterized by a list of those relations between objects of subject area which that model can represent. Classification of relations is subject to a research of: philosophers, terminologist, developers of IT and DBMS [5, 6]. R. Chaffin and D. Herrmann provide a list of 31 semantic relations [7]. We single out main problems of that classification, authors: (1) mix entities of a different nature (material objects, ideal concepts and signs); (2) base the classification on expert opinion; (3) made grouping bottom-up; (4) consider taxonomy of models outside the semiotic theory.

According to Gastev consistency between a model and an original can be characterized using the algebraic notion of morphism [2]. Gurr declares that a syntax of a notation can be explained if we manage to restore relations between objects of a subject area [3].

Aiming to evaluate whether a model provides a clear representation of a real-world, Wand and Weber «rely on basic notions from the mathematics of mappings» [8]. For this, they analyze a mapping from a set of signs forming modeling alphabet to a set of concepts founding ontology. However, they regard ontology just as a thesaurus, do not consider relations between concepts.

Guizzardi believes that semantics, syntax and pragmatics of a modeling notation should be consistent with ontology, but he denies an unambiguous connection between concrete syntax and ontological model [9].

All referenced studies regard diverse mappings and understand morphism differently. We carry out this research in the context of Frege's triangle (see Fig. 1), that illustrates a principle how an analyst percept a subject area. Let distinguish three sets of different nature: material objects, ideal concepts and signs. Three sides of the triangle can be interpreted as mappings: conceptualization - assigns an object to a concept, semantic - link a concept to a sign, representation - connects a sign of a model to an object of a subject area. We can assert that C. Gurr studies the representation mapping,

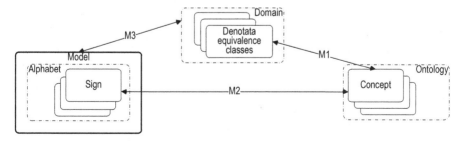

Fig. 1. Frege's triangle

particularly its algebraic morphism, while Y. Wand and R. Weber analyze the semantic mapping, understand morphism in the context of the set theory.

Here and after we imply a morphism as a relation preserving linear transformation from one mathematical structure to another one so that relations in the source domain are mapped to equivalent relations in the destination or codomain [10].

3   Relations

Let evaluate relations between elements of three genera: material objects, concepts and signs. Our classification is not exhaustive; it aims to demonstrate an approach. We limit ourselves to n-ary relations, where n $\leq$ 2.

3.1   Relations Inter Objects of a Subject Area

A classification of relations proposed here differs from the known in that it is based on a matching of object's properties and exclude connections that should be attributed to mappings. Let consider Bunge-Wand-Weber upper-level ontology [8]. According to M. Bunge, the world around us is made of things. Things are considered to be a separate, independent, sustainable object. Therefore we will use a term an object as a synonym of a thing. An object can be either simple or complex; the latter can be divided into a set of subobjects. A property is an attribute of an object. Property can't have properties. We assume that a unary relation represents a property of an object.

A property can be inherent to an individual object, for example, a dimension or a color characterize each separate object, or mutual, characterizing a set of objects, for example, a distance or a weight are defined for pairs of objects. A distinction between inherent and mutual properties is important for a further observation.

First, we consider inherent properties. Two or more objects can share certain intrinsic property, we call it an association. For example, to be a driver means that a person and his license have similar owner's name. Several objects sharing a specific intrinsic property form a group, while all and necessarily all objects possessing a characteristic property form a class [11]. We say that in regard to characteristic property all objects of a class are equivalent to each other. If we are able to define a system of characteristic properties we can partition the subject area into non-intersecting classes. These are internal relations, their holding is in some sense in the nature of their relata [12].

Second, we consider the mutual properties – they link objects, not belonging to one class, for example, all objects moving at a particular speed.

Third, we consider both: inherent and mutual properties. On one hand, this combination can define objects from different classes belonging to a larger whole. That is a part-whole relation. On the other, it can define the order of the objects within a set.

Bunge strongly recommends separate an aggregate formed by independent elements, its state at any time is equal to the sum of the states of all components and a system whose state is not additive [13]. Bunge calls a relation between interacting objects a bonding, we call it a functional relation. If we agree to neglect any kind of spontaneous change (due to aging or degradation) we can say that an object can change only due to the functional relation. Functional relations can affect either inherent of mutual properties. A change of an inherent property results in a state transition, while a change of a mutual property results in a shift of spatial or temporal characterization. For example, an operation changes a state of an object, while logical operator changes its spatiotemporal position.

3.2   Relations of Ontology Concepts

According to Guarino, «ontologies are a means to formally model the structure of a system, i.e., the relevant entities and relations that emerge from its observation» [14]. Ontology is not limited to a thesaurus; it also reproduces the relations between objects of a subject area [15]. Thus a mapping that connects an object of a subject area with the corresponding concept must be a structure-preserving morphism.

3.3   Relations Between Signs of a Model

Consider the fragment of the Frege's triangle shown in Fig. 2. The links between signs of the alphabet can be interpreted as a concrete syntax of a notation, and the links inter the concepts can be treated as an abstract syntax. We require the semantic mapping to be a morphism, it transfers relations between concepts onto relations of signs. Thus, the concrete syntax can be formalized by examining the relation between ontology concepts. The semantics of the sign is determined by a content of a corresponding concept.

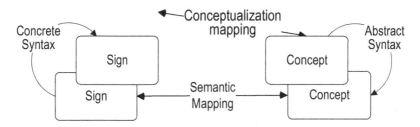

Fig. 2. Abstract and concrete syntax.

4   Model Mapping Property

The idea of the proposed approach is in replacing a representation mapping with two adjacent: conceptualization and semantic mappings.

We assume that a set of objects forming a subject area can be divided into disjoint subsets, called equivalence classes so that an object belongs to an equivalence class if and only if it possesses a characteristic property. Let state, if M_i and M_j are equivalence classes and M is the entire domain, then:

$$M = \bigcup_i M_i \quad \text{and} \quad M_i \cap M_j = \varnothing, \ i \neq j \tag{1}$$

4.1   Conceptualization Mapping

A conceptualization mapping aligns each class with an appropriate concept. All objects belonging to one class must reference single concept. First, we evaluate possible mappings:

- *Equipotency* (bijection) – each equivalence class is mapped onto the individual concept.
- *Indiscernibility* (surjection) – one concept map different equivalence classes, which is unacceptable.
- *Uncertainty* (injection) – different concepts map to a single equivalence class, which can cause errors.
- *Meaningless reality* – some real-world objects have no related concepts, cannot be mapped into a model.
- *Empty notion* – a concept cannot be associated with a relevant object.

Not all of the above combinations are permissible in modeling notation. Ontology by convention is a complete and unambiguous definition of a subject domain, therefore uncertainty and indiscernibility cases should be instantly discarded [15]. Ontology always includes a finite number of notions, so we can speak about the scope or size of ontology as compared to a subject domain. If ontology includes an empty notion, this means that the ontology's scope exceeds the size of a domain. We consider a model erroneous if it contains something that the original does not have. For example, a centaur or mermaid are acceptable concepts in a natural language but are disallowed in notation. If the ontology scope is smaller than the domain size, then meaningless reality appears, some denotatum cannot be mapped into a model. It's quite a common case when a model discards those real objects, which are not important for modeling objectives. We believe that ontology is not limited to a thesaurus, which means that the conceptualization mapping should preserve relations between the real world objects and transfer them onto the relations between concepts. In case of equipotency, a conceptualization mapping is an isomorphism – all concepts are mapped to appropriate classes and all conceptual relations between classes are mapped into appropriate relations between concepts. In case of meaningless reality, a conceptualization mapping is a homomorphism – some equivalence classes do not have a necessary concept and particular conceptual relations remain undefined.

4.2   Semantic Mapping

Now let us have a look at the semantic mapping connecting signs of a modeling notation and concepts of the ontology. First, we consider a mapping of two sets. The following alternatives can be discerned:

- *Unambiguity* (monosemy) – a sign has only one meaning.
- *Ambiguity* (polysemy) – a sign has several meanings, we assume this improper.
- *Equivalence* (synonymy) – different signs have similar or equivalent meanings.
- *Meaninglessness* (anasemy) – some signs have no meaning; we assume this unacceptable.
- *Deficiency of representational ability of a language* – some ontology notions have no appropriate sign.

In artificial modeling notation an ambiguity and equivalence must be excluded. Any sign must have only one meaning, two objects of different classes cannot be represented by a similar sign. The meaninglessness of a sign is also unacceptable as it demonstrates the bad design of a modeling notation. Synonymy, when different signs have the same meaning, is not prohibited, but makes a model difficult to understand.

Now we consider a semiotic mapping as a morphism that transfers relations between individual concepts on the relations between corresponding signs of the alphabet. We notice that relations between signs of the alphabet can be interpreted as a concrete syntax of a notation while links between concepts can be interpreted as an abstract syntax. Thus, relations between ontology concepts define a syntax of notation.

4.3   Representation Mapping

The peculiarity of a model is that it can include several similar signs of the alphabet all of them referencing different objects of reality that belong to one equivalence class. We will assume:

- *Significance* – each sign represents one denotate.
- *Synonymy* (ambivalence) – several signs corresponds a single denotate.
- *Ambivalence* – one sign represents several denotates.
- *Empty sign* – the sign doesn't represent any denotate.
- *Vacancy* – the denotate have no sign

A model is created using an alphabet of a modeling notation. Each sign of a model should display exactly one denotate of a prototype. A model can include several identical alphabet characters. All denotate, symbolized by one sign of an alphabet, belong to the equivalence class, which map a certain concept.

5   Model Reduction Property

Let assume an analyst has chosen an appropriate modeling notation and correctly applies it – follows semantic and syntactic rules of a notation. Suppose a conceptualization mapping is a morphism that renders subject area onto ontology concepts:

$$M1 : Object \rightarrow Concept \tag{2}$$

Assume a semantic mapping is a morphism that relates a set of alphabet signs with a set of ontology concepts:

$$M2 : Concept \rightarrow Sign \tag{3}$$

According to morphisms multiplication theorem, their composition is also a morphism [2]:

$$M1 * M2 = M3 : Model \rightarrow Subject\,Area \tag{4}$$

Thus, if conceptualization and semantic mapping are both are an isomorphism, their consistent application is also isomorphism and a model equals original. If one is isomorphism while second is a homomorphism (or both homomorphism), their product is a homomorphism, in this case, a model is similar to the original, but not equal. If at least one of the mappings is not morphism, then a model differs from an original [2]. The correspondence between an original and a model may be characterized as follows:

- The truth in a model is that common, which coincide in a model and a reality
- The missing in a model is something that exists in reality but is absent in a model.
- The false is something that exists in a model but is absent from an original.

How can we discard some details so that the model is true? We distinguish two options: reduction of concepts and reduction of relations.

Let consider reduction of concepts. As we have seen a model can represent a reality if conceptualization mapping and/or semantic mapping are a morphism. In case of meaningless reality – some real-world objects have no related concepts, cannot be mapped into a model. For example, original BWW ontology doesn't have a concept «actor», thus notations based on this ontology are not capable to present a participant of interaction. We call it a deficiency of representational ability of a notation – there is no appropriate language sign for some ontology notions.

A reduction of relations means that a model represents only part of relations that exist in an original. For example, what differentiates ontology, partonomy, thesaurus, lists. etc.? Each of them is capable to represent only particular relations. Following Shreider [4] we use a signature of a model – it lists types of those relations that are preserved in a model. Thus a signature allows differentiating between partonomy, thesaurus, etc.

6 Conclusion

This paper presents a new approach to the analyses of semiotic models. Its novelty is in the fact that we apply linguistic methods to study an artificial modeling notation. Within frames of this discussion, we have analysed a semiotic model mapping and reduction properties. We suggest:

- Separate relations and mappings. As result, we can see that so-called semantic relations, for example, a synonymy, are in fact, a type of semantic mapping.
- Analyse mappings inter three sets of different nature: material objects, ideal concepts and signs.
- Consider a mapping as a morphism that carries the relations between the elements of one set onto the relations between the elements of the other.
- Analyse relations between objects of a subject area top down, taking a top-level Bunge-Wand-Weber ontology as a foundation.
- Base a classification of relations on a matching of objects properties. This way a total number of relations types can be decreased.
- Use a signature to differentiate various models types.
- Model reduction property is subdivided into a reduction of relations and a reduction of concepts.

We prove the hypothesis that semantics and syntax of the modeling language can be justified using an ontology and three mappings connecting real-world objects, concepts of ontology and signs of a modeling notation. Thus, the semantics of the sign is determined through the content of the notion, associated with the corresponding concept of the ontological model, while the syntax of this notation is defined by the relations existing between concepts. The pragmatics of the model is a subject of a further research.

References

1. Thalheim, B.: General and specific model notions. European Conference on Advances in Databases and Information Systems. ADBIS 2017. Advances in Databases and Information Systems. LNCS, vol. 10509, pp. 13–27. Springer, Cham (2017). https://doi.org/10.1007/978-3-319-66917-5_2

2. Gastev, Y.: Homomorphisms and Models: Logical and Algebraic Aspects of Modeling. Nauka, Moscow (1975). (in Russian)

3. Gurr, C.A.: On the isomorphism, or lack of it, of representations. In: Marriott, K., Meyer, B. (eds.) Visual Language Theory, pp. 293–305. Springer, New York (1998). https://doi.org/10.1007/978-1-4612-1676-6_10

4. Shreider, Y.A., Sharov, A.A.: Systems and Models. Radio i Svyaz', Moscow (1982).(in Russian)

5. Storey, V.C., Thalheim, B.: Conceptual modeling: enhancement through semiotics. In: Mayr, H., Guizzardi, G., Ma, H., Pastor, O. (eds.) Conceptual Modeling. ER 2017. Lecture Notes in Computer Science, vol. 10650, pp. 182–190. Springer, Cham (2017). https://doi.org/10.1007/978-3-319-69904-2_15

6. Nuopponen, A.: Tangled web of concept relations. Concept relations for ISO 1087-1 and ISO 704. In: 2014 Terminology and Knowledge Engineering, Berlin, pp. 10–p (2014)

7. Stock, W.G.: Concepts and semantic relations in information science. J. Am. Soc. Inform. Sci. Technol. **61**(10), 1951–1969 (2010). https://doi.org/10.1002/asi.21382

8. Wand, Y., Weber, R.: Thirty years later: some reflections on ontological analysis in conceptual modeling. J. Database Manag. **28**(1), 1–17 (2017). https://doi.org/10.4018/JDM.2017010101

9. Guizzardi, G.: Ontological foundations for structural conceptual models. Ph.D. thesis, University of Twente, Enschede, The Netherlands (2005)

10. Jacobson, N.: Basic Algebra I. Dover Books on Mathematics. Dover, New York (2009)

11. Palomäki, J., Kangassalo, H.: That IS-IN isn't IS-A: a further analysis of taxo-nomic links in conceptual modelling. In: Ramirez, C. (ed.) Advances in Knowledge Representation. Chap. 1, pp. 3–18. InTech (2012). https://doi.org/10.5772/36484

12. Marmodoro, A., Yates, D. (eds.): The Metaphysics of Relations. Oxford University Press, Oxford (2016)

13. Bunge, M.: Treatise on basic philosophy. In: Ontology II. A World of Systems, vol. 4. D. Reidel Publishing, New York (1979)

14. Guarino, N., Oberle, D., Staab, S.: What is an ontology? In: Staab, S., Studer, R. (eds.) Handbook on Ontologies. IHIS, pp. 1–17. Springer, Heidelberg (2009). https://doi.org/10.1007/978-3-540-92673-3_0

15. Nayhanova, L.V.: Main aspects of construction of high level ontologies and subject area, pp. 452–479. Informika, Prosveshchenie, Moscow (2005). (in Russian)

Cognitive Information Technologies
in Control Systems

Spectral MIMO H∞-Optimization Problem

Evgeny Veremey⬤ and Yaroslav Knyazkin⁽⊠⁾⬤

Saint-Petersburg State University, University Avenue 35, Peterhof,
198504 Saint Petersburg, Russia
yaroslavknyazkin@gmail.com

Abstract. This paper is devoted to the problem of spectral H∞-optimal control synthesis for LTI plants. This problem is significant in situations when spectral features of the external disturbance are not completely given. H∞-optimization problem has been paid very serious attention for the past decades and it can be solved with the help of well-known numerical methods, based on Riccati equations or linear matrix equations (LMI), but these approaches are not absolutely universal, because there are irregular situations, such as problems with no noisy measurement signal. Implementation of the spectral methods, based on parameterization of the set of transfer functions of the closed-loop system and polynomial factorization makes possible to avoid mentioned difficulties, but most of the research in this area are devoted to the plants with scalar control signal that significantly restricts its area of implementation. The approach, proposed in this paper, makes possible to overcome these difficulties. Some theoretical aspects, including matrix Nevanlinna-Pick rational function interpolation, are discussed and computational scheme for the optimal control design is formulated. Applicability and effectiveness are illustrated by the numerical example with implementation of MATLAB package.

Keywords: Optimization · Linear-quadratic problem · H infinity control · Interpolation

1 Introduction

Problem of the optimal rejection of external disturbances has been a hot research area since pioneer works of N. Wiener and A. Kolmogorov. Effectiveness of the designed control laws is often expressed by linear quadratic functionals, characterizing tradeoff between reduction of the external disturbance influence and control intensity. It is notable, that minimization of such functional can be considered as both H_2 optimization problems and H∞ ones. These methods have been paid serious attention in such monographs as [1, 2]. Most of them are devoted to techniques, based on solving of algebraic matrix Riccati equation (2-Riccati approach) or linear matrix inequalities (LMI-technique).

It is notable that there are situations, where implementation of these well-known methods is non-effective or even impossible. Various H-optimization problems with no noisy measurement signal are typical examples of such issues. These difficulties can be successfully overcome by using of special spectral approaches in frequency domain, based on parameterization of the closed-loop system transfer functions set and

© Springer Nature Switzerland AG 2020
V. Sukhomlin and E. Zubareva (Eds.): Convergent 2018, CCIS 1140, pp. 119–131, 2020.
https://doi.org/10.1007/978-3-030-37436-5_10

polynomial factorization. Nowadays, there exist such methods of H_2 and H_∞ optimization problems (including their special cases) solution, but all developed H_∞ control synthesis algorithms [3–9] have restricted area of implementation, because they can be used only for plants with scalar control signal. The main object of this research is to overcome mentioned difficulty and propose more generally applicable solution.

In our opinion, this method has three main features. Firstly, it is parameterization technique, used in the first time in [10], which allows to apply spectral H-optimization methods for MIMO (Multiple Input – Multiple Output) plants. Sincerely, it includes solving of algebraic matrix Riccati equation that increases computational effort. Secondly, matrix Nevanlinna-Pick interpolation is implemented to calculate transfer function of the optimal closed-loop system. Finally, similarly to the approaches, expanded in [4, 5], the proposed method guarantees non-uniqueness of the optimal controller that expands its area of application and can be useful for solution of cognitive problems in control systems.

The paper is organized as follows. In the next section, equations of a controlled plant are presented and problem of the H_∞-optimal control design is formulated. Section 3 is devoted to the description of the implemented parameterization technique and an alternative statement of the problem, which is considered as interpolation one. In Sect. 4 we adduce condition of the matrix Nevanlinna-Pick problem solvability and formulae for its commutating. Section 5 is devoted to computation of the optimal closed-loop system transfer function and calculation of the controller, providing it. In Sect. 6, the numerical example of optimal controller design is presented. Finally, Sect. 7 concludes this paper by discussing the overall results of the investigation and possible directions of the future research.

2 Problem Statement

Let us introduce a linear time invariant plant

$$\begin{aligned}\dot{\mathbf{x}} &= \mathbf{A}\mathbf{x} + \mathbf{B}\mathbf{u} + \mathbf{H}\mathbf{d}(t)\,, \\ \mathbf{y} &= \mathbf{C}\mathbf{x}\,,\end{aligned} \tag{1}$$

where $\mathbf{x} \in R^n$ is the state space vector, $\mathbf{u} \in R^r$ is the control, $\mathbf{d} \in R^{n_d}$ is the external disturbance and $\mathbf{y} \in R^m$ is output measured signal. All components of the matrices $\mathbf{A}, \mathbf{B}, \mathbf{C}, \mathbf{H}$ are known constants, the pairs $\{\mathbf{A}, \mathbf{B}\}$ and $\{\mathbf{A}, \mathbf{C}\}$ are controllable and observable respectively.

External disturbance $\mathbf{d}(t)$ for the system (1) is treated as output of the filter with transfer function

$$\mathbf{S}_1(s) = \mathbf{N_d}(s)/T_\mathbf{d}(s)\mathbf{i}_1\,, \tag{2}$$

where $\mathbf{N_d}(s)$ is $(n_\mathbf{d} \times n_\mathbf{d})$ transfer function, $T_\mathbf{d}(s)$ is Hurwitz polynomial and $\mathbf{i}_1$ is signal with unknown frequency spectrum. The parameters $\mathbf{N_d}(s)$, $T_\mathbf{d}(s)$ present known spectral features of $\mathbf{d}(t)$ and if they are fully unknown then $\mathbf{S}_1(s) \equiv \mathbf{I}$. Note that $\mathbf{S}_1^{-1}(s)$ is stable transfer function, i.e. $\det(\mathbf{N_d}(s))$ is Hurwitz polynomial.

The controller is to be designed in the form

$$\mathbf{u} = \mathbf{W}(s)\mathbf{x} = \mathbf{W}_2^{-1}(s)\mathbf{W}_1(s)\mathbf{x}, \text{ or } \mathbf{u} = \tilde{\mathbf{W}}(s)\mathbf{y} = \mathbf{W}_2^{-1}(s)\tilde{\mathbf{W}}_1(s)\mathbf{y} \qquad (3)$$

where $\mathbf{W}_1(s)$, $\mathbf{W}_2(s)$ are $(r \times n)$ и $(r \times r)$ polynomial matrices and choice of $\mathbf{W}(s)$ should minimize the following mean-square functional

$$I(\mathbf{W}) = \lim_{T \to \infty} \frac{1}{T} \int_0^T (\mathbf{x}^T\mathbf{R}\mathbf{x} + k^2\mathbf{u}^T\mathbf{Q}\mathbf{u})\, dt, \qquad (4)$$

where $\mathbf{R}, \mathbf{Q}$ are symmetric positive definite matrices and k is a given positive value. We cannot calculate the accurate value of the functional I, because the external disturbance $\mathbf{d}(t)$ has unknown frequency spectrum, but we can minimize its upper bound. Let us rewrite the expression (4) in frequency domain

$$I = \frac{1}{j\pi} \int_0^{j\infty} tr[\mathbf{S}_2^*(s)\mathbf{S}_1^*(s)\mathbf{F}_0^*(s)\mathbf{F}_0(s)\mathbf{S}_1(s)\mathbf{S}_2(s)]\, ds = \|\mathbf{F}_0(s)\mathbf{S}_1(s)\mathbf{S}_2(s)\|_2^2, \qquad (5)$$

where $\mathbf{F}_0(s)$ is a such transfer function that

$$\mathbf{F}_0^*(s)\mathbf{F}_0(s) = \mathbf{F}_{\mathbf{x}}^T(-s)\mathbf{R}\mathbf{F}_{\mathbf{x}}(s) + k^2\mathbf{F}_{\mathbf{u}}^T(-s)\mathbf{Q}\mathbf{F}_{\mathbf{u}}(s), \text{ where} \qquad (6)$$

$$\begin{aligned} \mathbf{F}_{\mathbf{x}}(s) &= (s\mathbf{I} - \mathbf{A} - \mathbf{B}\mathbf{W})^{-1}\mathbf{H}, \\ \mathbf{F}_{\mathbf{u}}(s) &= \mathbf{W}(s\mathbf{I} - \mathbf{A} - \mathbf{B}\mathbf{W})^{-1}\mathbf{H}, \end{aligned} \qquad (7)$$

and unknown transfer function $\mathbf{S}_2(s)$ is shaping filter of the signal $\mathbf{i}_1$. Consider upper limit of I

$$J(\mathbf{W}) = \|\mathbf{F}_0(s)\mathbf{S}_1(s)\|_\infty^2 = \max_{\omega \in [0,\infty)} \|\mathbf{F}_0(j\omega)\mathbf{S}_1(j\omega)\|^2. \qquad (8)$$

As a result, the problem reduces to the following one:

$$J(\mathbf{W}) \to \min_{\mathbf{W} \in \Omega_W}, \qquad (9)$$

where $\Omega_{\mathbf{W}}$ is set of the stabilizing controllers (3). This set is such that all the roots of characteristic polynomial $\Delta(s)$ of the closed-loop system

$$\Delta(s) = (A_s(s))^{1-r} \det(\mathbf{W}_1\mathbf{B}_s - \mathbf{W}_2(s)A_s(s)), \text{ where} \qquad (10)$$

$$\mathbf{B}_s(s) \equiv A_s(s)(s\mathbf{I} - \mathbf{A})^{-1}\mathbf{B}, \ A_s = \det(\mathbf{A}), \qquad (11)$$

are located in the open left-half complex plane.

3 Spectral Approach to H∞ Optimization

These transfer functions $\mathbf{F_x}(s)$, $\mathbf{F_u}(s)$ can be parameterized with implementation of the approach, first presented in the monograph [10]. Despite the technique, used in [3–9], this method includes solution of the algebraic matrix Riccati equations that results in increasing of computational complexity but it can be used in case of multidimensional control signal. Let us introduce the adjustable function-parameter

$$\Phi(s) = \alpha(s)\mathbf{F_x}(s) + \beta(s)\mathbf{F_u}(s), \tag{12}$$

where $\alpha(s)$, $\beta(s)$ are $(r \times n)$ and $(r \times r)$ polynomial matrixes. These parameters can be calculated in the same way as proposed in [9, 10]. Firstly, let us solve the following matrix Riccati equation

$$\mathbf{S}\mathbf{A} + \mathbf{A}^T\mathbf{S} - \frac{1}{k^2}\mathbf{S}\mathbf{B}\mathbf{Q}^{-1}\mathbf{B}^T\mathbf{S} + \mathbf{R} = 0, \tag{13}$$

and calculate them as follows

$$\alpha(s) = \alpha_0 = \frac{1}{k^2}\mathbf{Q}^{-1}\mathbf{B}^T\mathbf{S}, \ \beta(s) = \beta_0 = \mathbf{I}. \tag{14}$$

Then we introduce the notations

$$\begin{aligned}
\Theta(s) &= A_s(s)\beta(s) + \alpha(s)\mathbf{B}_s(s), \\
\mathbf{H}_s(s) &\equiv A_s(s)(s\mathbf{I} - \mathbf{A})^{-1}\mathbf{H}, \ \mathbf{P}(s) \equiv (s\mathbf{I} - \mathbf{A}),
\end{aligned} \tag{15}$$

present the plant (1) in frequency domain

$$(s\mathbf{I} - \mathbf{A})\mathbf{F_x} - \mathbf{B}\mathbf{F_u} = \mathbf{H}, \tag{16}$$

and express transfer functions $\mathbf{F_x}$, $\mathbf{F_u}$, using formulae (7), (16)

$$\begin{pmatrix} \mathbf{F_x} \\ \mathbf{F_u} \end{pmatrix} = \mathbf{M}_\Phi^{-1}\begin{pmatrix} \mathbf{H} \\ \Phi \end{pmatrix}, \text{ where } \mathbf{M}_\Phi = \begin{pmatrix} s\mathbf{I} - \mathbf{A} & -\mathbf{B} \\ \alpha_0 & \beta_0 \end{pmatrix}. \tag{17}$$

Inverse matrix $\mathbf{M}_\Phi^{-1}$ can be calculated by Frobenius formula of block matrix inversion

$$\mathbf{M}_\Phi^{-1} = \begin{pmatrix} \mathbf{P}^{-1} - \mathbf{P}^{-1}\mathbf{B}(\beta + \alpha\mathbf{P}^{-1}\mathbf{B})^{-1}\alpha\mathbf{P}^{-1} & \mathbf{P}^{-1}(\beta + \alpha\mathbf{P}^{-1}\mathbf{B})^{-1} \\ -(\beta + \alpha\mathbf{P}^{-1}\mathbf{B})^{-1}(s)\alpha\mathbf{P}^{-1} & (\beta + \alpha\mathbf{P}^{-1}\mathbf{B})^{-1} \end{pmatrix}, \tag{18}$$

where $\mathbf{P} = s\mathbf{I} - \mathbf{A}$. Taking into account the equality

$$(\beta(s) + \alpha(s)\mathbf{P}^{-1}\mathbf{B})^{-1} = A_s(s)(A_s(s)\beta(s) + \alpha(s)\mathbf{B}(s))^{-1} = A_s\Theta^{-1}(s), \tag{19}$$

we can transform the expression (18) to the form

$$\mathbf{M}_\Phi^{-1} = \begin{pmatrix} \mathbf{P}^{-1} - \mathbf{B}_s(s)\Theta^{-1}(s)\alpha(s)\mathbf{P}^{-1} & \mathbf{B}_s(s)\Theta^{-1}(s) \\ -A_s(s)\Theta^{-1}(s)\alpha(s)\mathbf{P}^{-1} & A_s(s)\Theta^{-1}(s) \end{pmatrix}. \tag{20}$$

Then substitute the calculated matrix $\mathbf{M}_\Phi^{-1}$ to (17) and express of $\mathbf{F_x}(s)$, $\mathbf{F_u}(s)$ as functions of $\Phi(s)$:

$$\begin{aligned} \mathbf{F_x} &= \mathbf{F_x}(\widetilde{\Phi}) = \mathbf{H}_s(s)/A_s(s) + \mathbf{B}_s(s)\Theta^{-1}(s)\widetilde{\Phi}(s), \\ \mathbf{F_u} &= \mathbf{F_u}(\widetilde{\Phi}) = A_s(s)\Theta^{-1}(s)\widetilde{\Phi}(s), \end{aligned} \tag{21}$$

where $\widetilde{\Phi} = (\Phi - \alpha_0 \mathbf{P}^{-1}\mathbf{H})$. Also we introduce auxiliary notations

$$\begin{aligned} \mathbf{B}_\delta &= D_{1s}(s\mathbf{I} - \mathbf{A} + \mathbf{B}\alpha_0)^{-1}\mathbf{B}, \\ D_s &= \det(s\mathbf{I} - \mathbf{A} + \mathbf{B}\alpha_0), \end{aligned} \tag{22}$$

to transform the transfer function $\Theta^{-1}(s)$ in simpler form

$$\begin{aligned} \Theta^{-1}(s) &= (\alpha_0 \mathbf{B}_s + IA_s)^{-1} = A_s^{-1}\mathbf{I} - A_s^{-1}\alpha_0(\mathbf{B}_s\alpha_0 + IA_s)^{-1}\mathbf{B}_s \\ &= A_s^{-1}\mathbf{I} - A_s^{-1}\alpha_0(\mathbf{I} + \mathbf{P}^{-1}\mathbf{B}\alpha_0)^{-1}\mathbf{P}^{-1}\mathbf{B} = A_s^{-1}\mathbf{I} - A_s^{-1}\alpha_0(\mathbf{P} + \mathbf{B}\alpha_0)^{-1}\mathbf{B} \\ &= A_s^{-1}\mathbf{I} - A_s^{-1}\alpha_0 D_s^{-1}\mathbf{B}_\delta = \tfrac{1}{A_s D_s}(D_s\mathbf{I} - \alpha_0 \mathbf{B}_\delta). \end{aligned} \tag{23}$$

Note that choice of the parameters $\alpha(s)$, $\beta(s)$ by the formulae (14) results in the equality, proven in [9]

$$\Theta_*^{-1}(\mathbf{B}_s^*\mathbf{R}\mathbf{B}_s + k^2\mathbf{Q}A_s^*A_s)\Theta^{-1} = k^2\mathbf{Q}, \tag{24}$$

that significantly simplifies the following calculations. Now let us consider the expression from integrand in (5)

$$\mathbf{F}_0^*\mathbf{F}_0 = \mathbf{F_x}^*\mathbf{R}\mathbf{F_x} + k^2\mathbf{F_u}^*\mathbf{Q}\mathbf{F_u}, \tag{25}$$

and convert it to the form, used in the papers [3–10]

$$\mathbf{F}_0^*\mathbf{F}_0 \equiv (\mathbf{T}_1^* + \widetilde{\Phi}^*\mathbf{T}_2^*)(\mathbf{T}_1 + \mathbf{T}_2\widetilde{\Phi}) + \mathbf{T}_3, \text{ where} \tag{26}$$

$$\begin{aligned} \mathbf{T}_1(s) &= (k\sqrt{\mathbf{Q}})^{-1}\Theta_*^{-1}\mathbf{B}_s^*\mathbf{R}\mathbf{H}_s/A_s(s) \\ &= (k\sqrt{\mathbf{Q}})^{-1}\tfrac{(D_s^*\mathbf{I} - \mathbf{B}_\delta^*\alpha_0^T)}{A_s A_s^* D_s^*}\mathbf{B}_s^*\mathbf{R}\mathbf{H}_s, \quad \mathbf{T}_2(s) = k\sqrt{\mathbf{Q}}, \\ \mathbf{T}_3(s) &= (\mathbf{H}_s^*\mathbf{R}\mathbf{H}_s)/A_s A_s^* - \mathbf{T}_1^*(s)\mathbf{T}_1(s). \end{aligned} \tag{27}$$

Remark. It is notable that the summand $\mathbf{T}_3(s)$ is divided to the polynomials A_s (and A_s^*) totally. Transfer functions $\mathbf{F_x}$, $\mathbf{F_u}$ are received as a result of linear fractional transformation (17) of the parameter $\Phi(s)$, so characteristic polynomial of the closed-loop system is product of the denominators of $\Phi(s)$ and the matrix $\mathbf{M}_\Phi$. It does not depend on the polynomial $A_s(s)$. Consider the summand $(\mathbf{T}_1 + \mathbf{T}_2\widetilde{\Phi})$, taking into account the equality (24):

$$
\begin{aligned}
(\mathbf{T}_1 + \mathbf{T}_2\widetilde{\Phi}) &= (k\sqrt{\mathbf{Q}})^{-1}[\Theta_*^{-1}\mathbf{B}_s^*\mathbf{R}\mathbf{P}^{-1}\mathbf{H} - k^2\mathbf{Q}\,\alpha_0\mathbf{P}^{-1}\mathbf{H} + k^2\mathbf{Q}\Phi] \\
&= (k\sqrt{\mathbf{Q}})^{-1}\Theta_*^{-1}[\mathbf{B}_s^*\mathbf{R}\mathbf{P}^{-1}\mathbf{H} - (\mathbf{B}_s^*\mathbf{R}\mathbf{B}_s + k^2\mathbf{Q}A_s^*A_s)\Theta^{-1}\alpha_0\mathbf{P}^{-1}\mathbf{H} + k^2\mathbf{Q}\Phi],
\end{aligned}
$$

and rewrite two first summands in square brackets similarly to [10]

$$
\begin{aligned}
&(k\sqrt{\mathbf{Q}})^{-1}\Theta_*^{-1}[\mathbf{B}_s^*\mathbf{R} - (\mathbf{B}_s^*\mathbf{R}\mathbf{B}_s + k^2\mathbf{Q}A_s^*A_s)\Theta^{-1}\alpha_0]\mathbf{P}^{-1}\mathbf{H} \\
&= (k\sqrt{\mathbf{Q}})^{-1}\Theta_*^{-1}\{\mathbf{B}_s^*\mathbf{R}[\mathbf{I} - \mathbf{B}_s\Theta^{-1}\alpha_0] - k^2\mathbf{Q}\alpha_0 A_s^*A_s\}\mathbf{P}^{-1}\mathbf{H} \\
&= (k\sqrt{\mathbf{Q}})^{-1}(\mathbf{I} + \alpha_0\mathbf{P}^{-1}\mathbf{B})_*^{-1}\mathbf{B}^*\mathbf{P}_*^{-1}\mathbf{SCS}_1 \\
&= (k\sqrt{\mathbf{Q}})^{-1}\mathbf{B}^*(\mathbf{P} + \mathbf{B}\alpha_0)_*^{-1}\mathbf{SCS}_1.
\end{aligned}
$$

Denominators of the functions $(\mathbf{T}_1 + \mathbf{T}_2\widetilde{\Phi})$, $\mathbf{F_x}$, $\mathbf{F_u}$ (and, so, $\mathbf{F}_0^*\mathbf{F}_0$) do not depend on the $A_s(s)$ and so, characteristic polynomial of

$$
\mathbf{T}_3(s) \equiv \mathbf{F}_0^*\mathbf{F}_0 - (\mathbf{T}_1^* + \widetilde{\Phi}^*\mathbf{T}_2^*)(\mathbf{T}_1 + \mathbf{T}_2\widetilde{\Phi}),
$$

does not divide on A_s.

The problem (9) can be transformed to the equivalent form

$$
J = J(\Phi(s)) \rightarrow \min_{\Phi \in \Omega_\Phi}, \tag{28}
$$

where Ω_Φ is set of parameters $\Phi(s)$ with Hurwitz characteristic polynomials. One can see that the summand $\mathbf{T}_3(s)$ in the formula (27) does not depend on the parameter $\widetilde{\Phi}(s)$ and the value

$$
J_{\min} = \max_{\omega \in [0,\infty)} (\text{tr}\{S_1^*(j\omega)\mathbf{T}_3(j\omega)S_1(j\omega)\}) = \text{tr}\{S_1^*(j\omega_0)\mathbf{T}_3(j\omega_0)S_1(j\omega_0), \tag{29}
$$

is lower bound of the functional J. Let us consider the choice of the function-parameter $\widetilde{\Phi}(s)$ such that

$$
J(\widetilde{\Phi}(s)) < \rho^2, \quad \rho^2 = J_{\min} + \varepsilon, \varepsilon \geq 0,
$$

instead the problem (28), using a technique, implemented in [6].

Problem (28) obviously reduces to search of the minimum value $\rho^2 = \rho_0^2$ (and, respectively, $\varepsilon \geq 0$), guarantying solvability of the following problem:

$$
\begin{aligned}
&J_0(\widetilde{\Phi}(s)) = J(\widetilde{\Phi}(s)) = \min_{\Phi \in \Omega_\Phi} \{ \rho^2 : \exists\Phi \in \Omega_\Phi : \forall\omega \in [0,\infty) \\
&\left\| (\mathbf{T}_1(j\omega) + \mathbf{T}_2(j\omega)\widetilde{\Phi}(j\omega))S_1(j\omega) \right\|^2 + \text{tr}\,(S_1^*(j\omega)\mathbf{T}_3(j\omega)S_1(j\omega)) \leq \rho^2 \}.
\end{aligned} \tag{30}
$$

4 Polynomial Matrix Interpolation Technique

Let us rewrite the expression (30) as

$$\left\|(\mathbf{T}_1(j\omega) + \mathbf{T}_2(j\omega)\widetilde{\Phi}(j\omega))S_1(j\omega)\right\|^2 \le \rho^2 - \mathrm{tr}\,(S_1^*(j\omega)\mathbf{T}_3(j\omega)S_1(j\omega)), \qquad (31)$$

then introduce the polynomial $R_\rho(s)$ and transfer function $\widetilde{L}(s)$, such as

$$\frac{R_\rho(s)R_\rho(-s)}{D_s D_s^* T_d T_d^*} = \rho^2 - \mathrm{tr}\,(S_1^*(s)\mathbf{T}_3(s)S_1(s)), \ \widetilde{L}(s) = \frac{D_s T_d}{R_\rho} \cdot \frac{D_s^*}{D_s}, \qquad (32)$$

(the second factor of $\widetilde{L}(s)$ allows to avoid divisibility of the $\mathbf{T}_1(s)$ denominator to the polynomial D_s^* that is necessary below). As a result, the expression (31) can be transformed to the form

$$\left\|(\mathbf{T}_1(s) + \mathbf{T}_2(s)\widetilde{\Phi}(s))S_1(s)\widetilde{L}(s)\right\|_\infty^2 \le 1. \qquad (33)$$

One can see that factor outside the parameter $\widetilde{\Phi}$ reduces to zero in the complex points $s = g_i$ $(i = \overline{1,n})$, such as $D_s(-g_i) = 0$, i.e. roots of the polynomial $D_s(-s)$, and values of the expression $\mathbf{Z}(s)$

$$\begin{aligned}
\mathbf{Z}(s) &= (\mathbf{T}_1(s) + \mathbf{T}_2(s)\widetilde{\Phi}(s))S_1(s)\frac{D_s^* T_d}{R_\rho(s)} \\
&= ((k\sqrt{\mathbf{Q}})^{-1}\frac{(D_s^*\mathbf{I} - \mathbf{B}_\delta^*\alpha_0^T)}{A_s A_s^*}\mathbf{B}_s^*\mathbf{RH}_s + k\sqrt{\mathbf{Q}}D_s^*\widetilde{\Phi})\frac{\mathbf{N_d}}{R_\rho(s)},
\end{aligned} \qquad (34)$$

in the points g_i can be calculated as follows

$$\mathbf{Z}_i = (k\sqrt{\mathbf{Q}})^{-1}\frac{(D_s^*\mathbf{I} - \mathbf{B}_\delta^*\alpha_0^T)}{A_s A_s^*}\mathbf{B}_s^*\mathbf{RH}_s\frac{\mathbf{N_d}}{R_\rho(s)}\bigg|_{s=g_i}, \ (i = \overline{1,n}). \qquad (35)$$

As a result, problem (30) can be considered as the search of the stable matrix transfer function $\mathbf{Z}(s)$, satisfying the conditions

$$\|\mathbf{Z}(s)\|_\infty^2 \le 1, \ \mathbf{Z}(g_i) = \mathbf{Z}_i. \qquad (36)$$

It is well-known statement of fractionally rational matrix interpolation problem, described in details in [12, 13]. Let us note that the similar method (classical Nevanlinna-Pick interpolation) has been successfully implemented in the previous research, devoted to H_∞ optimization [6, 7], but most of the proposed algorithms can be applied only to the plants with scalar control signal, than significantly restricts area of their field of application. The interpolation technique, used in this paper, is a special case of the two-sided Nudelman Problem. Let us introduce the notations

$$\mathbf{C}_- = [\mathbf{I}_{n_d} \ \mathbf{I}_{n_d} \ldots \mathbf{I}_{n_d}], \tag{37}$$

is $n_d \times n \cdot n_d$ matrix,

$$\mathbf{C}_+ = [\mathbf{Z}_1 \ \mathbf{Z}_2 \ldots \mathbf{Z}_n], \tag{38}$$

is $r \times n \cdot n_d$ matrix, and

$$\mathbf{A}_\pi = \begin{bmatrix} g_1 \mathbf{I}_{n_d} & & \\ & \ddots & \\ & & g_n \mathbf{I}_{n_d} \end{bmatrix}, \tag{39}$$

is $n \cdot n_d \times n \cdot n_d$ block diagonal matrix and implement the following theorem, presenting the necessary and sufficient conditions of the matrix Nevanlinna-Pick problem (36) solvability [12]. There exists a rational function $\mathbf{Z}(s)$ that interpolates the set $\langle g_i, \mathbf{Z}_i \rangle$, analytic in closed right half-plane and satisfies the condition (36), if and only if the Pick Matrix

$$\Lambda_{i,j} = \left[\frac{\mathbf{I} - \mathbf{Z}_i^H \mathbf{Z}_j}{\bar{g}_i + g_j} \right]_{1 \le i,j \le n}, \tag{40}$$

is positive definite. In this case, there is a 2×2 block matric transfer function

$$\Xi(s) = \mathbf{I}_{r+n_d} + \begin{bmatrix} \mathbf{C}_+ \\ \mathbf{C}_- \end{bmatrix} (s\mathbf{I}_{n \cdot n_d} - \mathbf{A}_\pi)^{-1} \Lambda^{-1} [-\mathbf{C}_+^H \ \mathbf{C}_-^H], \tag{41}$$

and solutions of the Nevanlinna-Pick interpolation problem become

$$\mathbf{Z}(s) = [\Xi_{1,1}(s)\Psi(s) + \Xi_{1,2}(s)][\Xi_{2,1}(s)\Psi(s) + \Xi_{2,2}(s)]^{-1}, \tag{42}$$

where $\Psi(s)$ is an arbitrary $r \times n_d$ asymptotically stable transfer function, satisfying

$$\|\Psi(s)\|_\infty \le 1.$$

5   Transfer Matrices of the Optimal Closed-Loop Systems

Note, that the theorem, cited above, specifies direct way to calculation of transfer functions of the optimal closed-loop system. Let us consider that there exist solution $\mathbf{Z}(s) = \mathbf{Z}_1(s)/Z_2(s)$ of the Nevanlinna-Pick problem (26) for the parameter ρ. Consider the following equality

$$(\mathbf{T}_1(s) + \mathbf{T}_2(s)\widetilde{\Phi}_0(s))\mathbf{S}_1(s)\frac{D_s^* T_d}{R_\rho(s)} = \frac{\mathbf{Z}_1(s)}{\mathbf{Z}_2(s)}, \text{ or} \tag{43}$$

$$\left((k\sqrt{\mathbf{Q}})^{-1}\Theta_*^{-1}\mathbf{B}_s^*\mathbf{R}\mathbf{H}_s\frac{1}{A_s} + k\sqrt{\mathbf{Q}}\widetilde{\Phi}_0(s)\right)\mathbf{N_d}(s)\frac{D_s^*}{R_\rho(s)} = \frac{\mathbf{Z}_1(s)}{\mathbf{Z}_2(s)},$$

and receive the function-parameters $\widetilde{\Phi}_0(s)$ and $\Phi_0(s)$

$$\widetilde{\Phi}_0(s) = (k\sqrt{\mathbf{Q}})^{-1}\frac{\mathbf{Z}_1(s)}{\mathbf{Z}_2(s)}\left(\frac{\mathbf{N_d}(s)D_s^*}{R_\rho(s)}\right)^{-1} - (k^2\mathbf{Q})^{-1}\Theta_*^{-1}\mathbf{B}_s^*\mathbf{R}\mathbf{H}_s\frac{1}{A_s}, \tag{44}$$

$$\Phi_0(s) = (k\sqrt{\mathbf{Q}})^{-1}\frac{\mathbf{Z}_1(s)}{\mathbf{Z}_2(s)}\left(\frac{\mathbf{N_d}(s)D_s^*}{R_\rho(s)}\right)^{-1} - (k^2\mathbf{Q})^{-1}\mathbf{B}^*(\mathbf{P} + \mathbf{B}\alpha_0)_*^{-1}\mathbf{SH}. \tag{45}$$

Let us demonstrate that denominator of $\Phi_0(s)$ is Hurwitz polynomial. Divisibility of $\widetilde{\Phi}_0(s)$ numerator to the polynomial D_s^* directly follows from (35), (36). Denominator of $\Phi_0(s)$ does not contain neither multiplier D_s^* nor A_s, and we can see that characteristic polynomial of the closed-loop system is

$$\Delta(s) = Z_2(s)\det(\mathbf{N_d}(s))D_s.$$

Finally, substitute calculated $\widetilde{\Phi}_0(s)$ to the Eq. (21) and receive dynamics of the optimal closed-loop system

$$\begin{aligned}\mathbf{F_x} &= \mathbf{F_x}(\widetilde{\Phi}) = \mathbf{H}_s(s)/A_s(s) + \mathbf{B}_s(s)\Theta^{-1}(s)\widetilde{\Phi}_0(s),\\\mathbf{F_u} &= \mathbf{F_u}(\widetilde{\Phi}) = A_s(s)\Theta^{-1}(s)\widetilde{\Phi}_0(s).\end{aligned} \tag{46}$$

Similarly to the research [4], computation of the transfer functions (46) of the optimal closed-loop system does not provide the complete solution of the problem and it is necessary to provide it with the help of the controller (3). Let us implement the known optimum condition [4]: the controller (3) provides the optimal transfer functions (46) for the closed loop system (1), (3) if and only if its transfer matrix $\mathbf{W}(s)\mathbf{x} = \mathbf{W}_2^{-1}(s)\mathbf{W}_1(s)$ satisfies the following main polynomial equation (MPE):

$$\mathbf{W}_1(s)\widetilde{\mathbf{F}}_\mathbf{x}(s) - \mathbf{W}_2(s)\widetilde{\mathbf{F}}_\mathbf{u}(s) = \mathbf{0}, \tag{47}$$

where polynomial matrices $\widetilde{\mathbf{F}}_\mathbf{x}(s)$, $\widetilde{\mathbf{F}}_\mathbf{u}(s)$ represent numerators of the optimal transfer functions $\mathbf{F_x}(s)$, $\mathbf{F_u}(s)$ (46).

Remark. It was noted in [4] that numerators and denominator of the functions $\mathbf{F_x}(s)$, $\mathbf{F_u}(s)$ can have common multiplier $C_0(s)$, which can be no Hurwitz. Solving of this problem needs background study, and only the easiest way to avoid this difficulty is presented in this paper. If we choose such order $n_\mathbf{W}$ of the controller $\mathbf{W}(s)$, that deg $\Delta(s) = n + n_\mathbf{W}$, then $C_0(s) \equiv const$.

Let us remark, that the transfer functions $\mathbf{F_x}(s)$, $\mathbf{F_u}(s)$ can be such that design of controller $\mathbf{W}(s)$ in the desired structure (e.g.) is impossible. One of ways to overcome this difficulty is to deform the spectral power density (2) by multiplying on the polynomial matrix $\widehat{\mathbf{N}}_\mathbf{d}(s)$ and using the filter

$$\widetilde{\mathbf{S}}_1(s) = \widetilde{\mathbf{N}}_\mathbf{d}/T_\mathbf{d} = \mathbf{N_d}\widehat{\mathbf{N}}_\mathbf{d}(s)/T_\mathbf{d}, \tag{48}$$

instead $\mathbf{S}_1(s)$ in the calculations above. Note that the transfer function $\widetilde{\mathbf{S}}_1^{-1}(s)$ must be stable one.

6 Example of Synthesis

Let us demonstrate implementation of the proposed approach for the solution of the H_∞-optimization problem with the model (1) and the functional (4), having the following parameters:

$$A = \begin{pmatrix} -0.0936 & 0.63 & 0 \\ 0.048 & -0.072 & 0 \\ 0 & 1 & 0 \end{pmatrix}, B = \begin{pmatrix} 0.0196 & 0.0133 \\ 0.0160 & 0.0192 \\ 0 & 0 \end{pmatrix}, H = \begin{pmatrix} 0.4100 \\ 0.0076 \\ 0 \end{pmatrix},$$

$$C = I, R = \begin{pmatrix} 0 & 0 & 0 \\ 0 & 0 & 0 \\ 0 & 0 & 1 \end{pmatrix}, Q = I, k = 0.1.$$

External disturbance have not any spectral features, i.e. $\mathbf{N_d}(s) \equiv 1$, $T_\mathbf{d}(s) = 1$. Let us establish the condition that transfer function of the optimal controller $\mathbf{W}(s)$ should have proper elements and deform $\mathbf{N_d}(s)$, using $\widetilde{\mathbf{N}}_\mathbf{d} = s + 1$ instead of it. Then we compute transfer functions from the formulae (11):

$$A_s(s) = s^3 + 0.8106s^2 + 0.0367s,$$

$$B_s(s) = \begin{pmatrix} 0.019s^2 + 0.0237s & 0.0133s^2 + 0.0217s \\ 0.016s^2 + 0.0024s & 0.0192s^2 + 0.0024s \\ 0.016s + 0.0024 & 0.0192s + 0.0024 \end{pmatrix}, H_s = \begin{pmatrix} 0.41s^2 + 0.3s \\ 0.0076s^2 + 0.02s \\ 0.0076s + 0.02 \end{pmatrix},$$

solution of the matrix Riccati Eq. (13)

$$S = \begin{pmatrix} 0.1290 & 0.4938 & 0.2902 \\ 0.4938 & 4.5622 & 3.7407 \\ 0.2902 & 3.7407 & 3.7492 \end{pmatrix},$$

and parameters α_0, β_0 from (14)

$$\alpha_0 = \begin{pmatrix} 1.035 & 8.237 & 6.536 \\ 1.012 & 9.416 & 7.568 \end{pmatrix}, \ \beta_0 = \begin{pmatrix} 1 & 0 \\ 0 & 1 \end{pmatrix}.$$

Then we receive values $J_{min} = 0.3542$, $\omega_0 = 0$. Calculate transfer functions of the optimal closed loop system

$$\mathbf{F_u} = \frac{1}{\Delta(s)} \begin{pmatrix} -0.179s^6 - 1.23s^5 - 2.122s^4 - 1.551s^3 - 0.539s^2 - 0.087s - 0.0051 \\ -0.119s^6 - 1.137s^5 - 2.09s^4 - 1.564s^3 - 0.5477s^2 - 0.088s - 0.0052 \end{pmatrix},$$

$$\mathbf{F_x} = \frac{1}{\Delta(s)} \begin{pmatrix} 0.41s^6 + 1.343s^5 + 1.733s^4 - 1.112s^3 + 0.369s^2 + 0.060s + 0.0036 \\ 0.0076s^6 + 0.0347s^5 + 0.0329s^4 + 0.0101s^3 + 0.0009s^2 \\ 0.0076s^4 + 0.0347s^3 + 0.0329s^2 + 0.0101s^1 + 0.0009 \end{pmatrix},$$

$$\Delta(s) = s^7 + 3.37s^6 + 4.575s^5 + 3.223s^4 + 1.261s^3 + 0.2714s^2 + 0.0294s + 0.00124,$$

set order of the controller $n_W = 4$ and compute its parameters:

$$\mathbf{W_2} = (s^4 + 2.185s^3 + 1.567s^2 + 0.4225s + 0.0351) \cdot \mathbf{I},$$
$$\widetilde{\mathbf{W}}_1 = \begin{pmatrix} -0.0436s^4 - 2.522s^3 - 2.308s^2 - 0.627s - 0.050 \\ -0.2903s^4 - 2.451s^3 - 2.339s^2 - 0.6304s - 0.051 \end{pmatrix} \cdots$$
$$\cdots \begin{pmatrix} -0.11s^4 + 0.645s^3 + 0.782s^2 + 0.243s + 0.0244 \\ -0.238s^4 + 0.412s^3 + 0.536s^2 + 0.102s - 0.0006 \end{pmatrix}.$$

Let us demonstrate the frequency response: $A_\omega = \|\mathbf{F}_0(j\omega)\mathbf{S}_1(j\omega)\|_2^2$ on the Fig. 1. It can be seen that $A_\omega \leq J_a$ and it possesses the maximal value on the zero frequency.

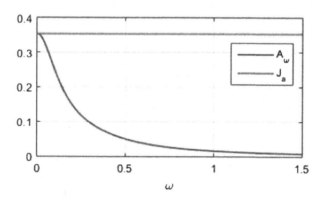

Fig. 1. Frequency response A_ω and J_a.

7 Conclusion

A novel spectral approach in frequency domain to H_∞-optimal control synthesis is proposed and described in details in this paper. The demonstrated method can be applied to a wide spectrum of practical control issues concerned with disturbance without certain general frequency.

Polynomial model presentation and the special parameterization technique for the transfer matrices of the closed-loop system are used in the proposed method. The dynamics of the optimal closed-loop system can be obtained by the method, based on matrix Nevanlinna-Pick interpolation technique. Non-uniqueness of the optimal controller makes possible to construct it in the desired structure that can offer significant advantage. Also the developed method does not include repeated solution of the algebraic matrix Riccati equations that can improve its computational effectiveness. Working capacity and effectiveness of the proposed approach are demonstrated by the numerical example with implementation of MATLAB package.

Finally, let us mention some possible directions of future research. First of all, singular case [7] requires special attention. . Robust features, transport delays and more complicated representation of the external disturbance also can be taken into account.

References

1. Doyle, J.C., Francis, B.A., Tanenbaum, A.R.: Feedback Control Theory. Mac Millan, New York (1992)
2. Bhattacharyya, S., Datta, A., Keel, L.: Linear Control Theory: Structure, Robustness and Optimization. CRC Press, Taylor & Francis Group, Boca Raton (2009)
3. Veremey, E.I.: Efficient spectral approach to SISO problems of H_2-optimal synthesis. Appl. Math. Sci. **79**(9), 3897–3909 (2015). https://doi.org/10.12988/ams.2015.54335
4. Veremey, E.I.: H_2-optimal synthesis problem with nonunique solution. Appl. Math. Sci. **10**(38), 1891–1905 (2016). https://doi.org/10.12988/ams.2016.63120
5. Veremey, E.I.: RMS Multipurpose Optimization. St. Petersburg, SPbU (2017). (in Russian)
6. Veremey, E., Sotnikova, M.: Spectral approach to H_∞-optimal SISO synthesis problem. WSEAS Trans. Syst. Control **9**(43), 415–424 (2014). https://doi.org/10.12988/ams.2015. 54335
7. Veremey, E.: Irregular H_∞-optimization of control laws for marine autopilots. In: Constructive Nonsmooth Analysis and Related Topics (Dedicated to the Memory of VF Demyanov) (CNSA), pp. 1–4. IEEE, Saint-Petersburg (2017). https://doi.org/10.1109/cnsa. 2017.7974028
8. Veremey, E.I., Smirnov, M.N., Smirnova, M.A.: Synthesis of stabilizing control laws with uncertain disturbances for marine vessels. In: 2015 International Conference "Stability and Control Processes" in Memory of VI Zubov (SCP), pp. 606–608 (2015). https://doi.org/10. 1109/scp.2015.7342219
9. Veremey, E.I., Knyazkin, Y.V.: H_∞-optimal synthesis problem with nonunique solution. In: Sukhomlin, V., Zubareva, E., Sneps-Sneppe, M. (eds.) Proceedings of the 2nd International scientific conference "Convergent Cognitive Information Technologies" (Convergent 2017), Moscow, Russia, 24–26 November 2017, CEUR Workshop Proceedings, vol. 2064, pp. 270–276 (2017). http://ceur-ws.org/Vol-2064/paper32.pdf. Accessed 21 Oct 2018

10. Aliev, F.A., Larin, V.B., Naumenko, K.I., Suncev, V.I.: Optimization of Linear Time-Invariant Control Systems. Naukova Dumka, Kyiv (1978). (in Russian)
11. Aliev, F.A., Larin, V.B.: Parametrization of sets of stabilizing controllers in mechanical systems. Int. Appl. Mech. **44**(6), 599 (2008). https://doi.org/10.1007/s10778-008-0085-3
12. Coelho, C.P., Phillips, J.R., Silveira, L.M.: Passive constrained rational approximation algorithm using Nevanlinna-Pick interpolation. In: Proceedings 2002 Design, Automation and Test in Europe Conference and Exhibition, Paris, France, pp. 923–930 (2002). https://doi.org/10.1109/date.2002.998410
13. Ball, J., Gohbergl, I.: Interpolation of Rational Matrix Functions. Birkhäuser, Basel (2013). https://doi.org/10.1007/978-3-0348-7709-1

Path Planning of Mobile Robot Based on an Improved Ant Colony Algorithm

Chong Pan[1] , Hongbo Wang[1(✉)] , Jinxin Li[1] ,
and Maxim Korovkin[2]

[1] Jilin University, Qianjin Str. 2699, Changchun 130012, Jilin, China
panchong9617@163.com, wang_hongbo@jlu.edu.cn
[2] Saint-Petersburg State University, Universitetskaya nab. 7-9,
198504 Saint Petersburg, Russia
maxik@vrm.apmath.spbu.ru

Abstract. The ant colony algorithm (ACO) is an intelligent optimization algorithm inspired by the behavior of ants searching for food in the nature. As a general stochastic optimization algorithm, the ant colony algorithm has been successfully applied to TSP, mobile robot path planning and other combinatorial optimization problems, and achieved good results. But because the probability of the algorithm is a typical algorithm, the parameters set in the algorithm is usually determined by experimental method, leading to the optimization of the performance closely related to people's experience, it is difficult to optimize the algorithm performance. Moreover, the traditional ant colony algorithm has many shortcomings, such as long convergence time and easiness to fall into the local optimal solution. In order to overcome these shortcomings, in this paper, a large number of experimental data are analyzed to obtain the main appropriate parameters of the ant colony algorithm, such as the number M of ants, the number K of iterations, the influence factor α and β, and a new pheromone updating method that is related to the sine function is proposed in this paper, the simulation results show that the improved algorithm can accelerate the speed by 60%, and the global optimal solution can be found more easily than the original ant colony algorithm.

Keywords: Ant colony algorithm · Path planning · Update pheromone

1 Introduction

The path planning technology of mobile robot [1] is that the robot independently plans a safe running route according to the perception of the environment by its own sensors, and efficiently completes the operation tasks. The path planning of mobile robot mainly solves three problems: first, enable the robot to move from the initial point to the target point; second, using certain algorithm makes the robot to avoid obstacles, and have to go through some necessary points to finish the corresponding task, at present, the commonly used mobile robot global path planning method are many, such as *grid method* [2], the *artificial potential field method* [3], *neural network algorithm* [4], A^* *algorithm* [5], the *genetic algorithm* [6] and *ant colony algorithm* [7] and the *particle*

© Springer Nature Switzerland AG 2020
V. Sukhomlin and E. Zubareva (Eds.): Convergent 2018, CCIS 1140, pp. 132–141, 2020.
https://doi.org/10.1007/978-3-030-37436-5_11

swarm algorithm [8], etc.; third, on the premise of completing the above tasks, optimize the running trajectory of the robot as much as possible. Robot path planning technology is one of the core technologies in the research of intelligent mobile robot.

Ant colony algorithm is a probabilistic algorithm used to find the optimal path. This algorithm has the characteristics of distributed computing, information positive feedback and heuristic search, and is essentially a heuristic global optimization algorithm in evolutionary algorithm. *Ant colony system* is an improved ant colony algorithm proposed by Dorigo and Gambardella et al. [9], which mainly modifies the rules of state transformation and pheromone update. *Sorting based ant system* was proposed by Bulinheimer et al. [10], which refers to the concept of sequencing in genetic algorithm. German scholar Thomas Stutzle and others put forward *Max-Min Ant System* [11] which can avoid the premature convergence of the search process effectively by increasing the pheromone on the optimal path and limiting the range of pheromone. Wang et al. put forward a real-coded genetic algorithm and an improved isochron method on ship the optimal path [12, 13].

A new pheromone updating method is proposed in this paper, which makes the volatility of pheromones change with ant algebra by introducing sinusoidal function.

2 Traditional Ant Colony Algorithm

At the initial moment, m ants were randomly placed in the city, and the initial value of pheromones on each route was the same. Each ant randomly chose the next road, and its probability formula was formula (1).

$$p_{ij}^k(t) = \begin{cases} \frac{[\tau_{ij}(t)]^\alpha [\eta_{ij}(t)]^\beta}{\sum_{s \in a_k} [\tau_{is}(t)]^\alpha [\eta_{is}(t)]^\beta}, & \text{if } j \in a_k \\ 0, & \text{otherwise} \end{cases} \tag{1}$$

where τ_{ij} is the pheromone on edge (i,j), $\eta_{ij} = 1/d_{ij}$ is the heuristic function for transferring from city i to city j, α is the information heuristic factor, while β is the expected heuristic factor, a_k is the city set that ant k is allowed to visit in the next step, and the tabu t_{ak} records the cities that ant k is currently passing through.

Once an ant passes through a path, the pheromones evaporate, ρ is volatility coefficient, and running at a rate of zero less than or less than one. Formula (2) is the information element updating formula.

$$\tau_{ij}(t+1) = (1-\rho)\,\tau_{ij}(t) + \sum_{k=1}^{m} \Delta\,\tau_{ij}^k(t) \tag{2}$$

where $\Delta\tau_{ij}^k$ is the pheromone of the k-th ant to it passes through the edge (i,j), defined as formula (3).

$$\Delta\tau_{ij}^k = \begin{cases} 1/d_{ij} & \text{if edge } (i,j) \text{ is on the path } T^k \\ 0, & \text{otherwise} \end{cases} \tag{3}$$

3 Selection of the Main Parameters in Algorithm

The main parameters of ant colony algorithm are the number M of ants, the pheromone volatilization factor ρ, information heuristic factor α, expectation heuristic factor β and pheromone intensity factor Q. In order to determine the optimal combination of the main parameters in the algorithm, a simple 20×20 two-dimensional grid was used to experiment. Finally, a set of optimal parameter values are found by adjusting the values of the main parameters to the shortest path in various cases.

3.1 Selection of the Number M of Ants

By changing the number M of the ants in each experiment and ensure that all the other parameters are the same, mobile robot finds the shortest path through the ant colony algorithm that is shown in Fig. 1 below:

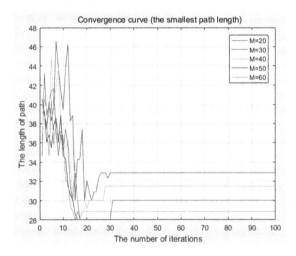

Fig. 1. The shortest path found under the different ant numbers.

It can be seen from the Fig. 1, when the number of ants M is different, several experiments get the different shortest path. When the ant number M value is 50, the shortest path length is 28.04, so selecting the number of ants $M = 50$ in the next experiment.

3.2 Selection of the Pheromone Volatilization Factor ρ

For the selection of pheromone volatility coefficient, nine groups of experimental data, 0.1–0.9, were selected and ten experiments were carried out for each group of data. The shortest path and the convergence curve of each test were recorded respectively.

Table 1. The shortest path and the convergence iterations of each ρ.

ρ	0.1	0.2	0.3	0.4	0.5	0.6	0.7	0.8	0.9
The smallest path length	>29.21	28.21	28.15	28.10	28.10	28.15	28.45	28.51	Non
The number of iterations	>100	82	54	40	38	24	33	42	>100

From the Table 1, it can be concluded that when the pheromone volatilization factor ρ is 0.5, the shortest path can be 28.10, and the convergent iterations can be at least 38, so $\rho = 0.5$.

3.3 Selection of the Heuristic Factors

The information heuristic factor α is selected as 1, 2 and 3 to the experiment, as shown in the Fig. 2, it can be seen that the smallest path length is the minimum when α is equal to 1, and the minimum cannot be obtained when the other values are taken.

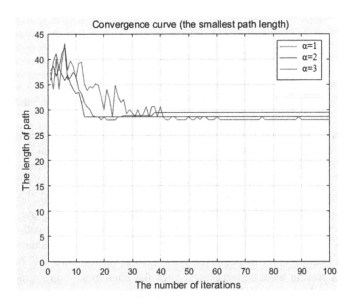

Fig. 2. The shortest path found under the different information heuristic factor α.

The expectation heuristic factor β is selected as 3, 5, 7 and 9 to the experiment, as shown in the Fig. 3, it can be seen that the smallest path length is the minimum when β is equal to 7, and the minimum cannot be obtained when the other values are taken.

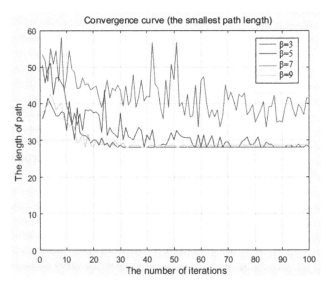

Fig. 3. The shortest path found under the different expectation heuristic factor β.

4   Improved Ant Colony Algorithm

Due to the shortcomings of traditional ant colony algorithm such as too long convergence time and easy to fall into the local optimal solution, the following improvement strategies are proposed:

In this paper, introducing a sine function that can make pheromone volatilization coefficient of rho and ants associated algebra k, the initial time, k value is small, the value of the sine function approximation is equal to zero, the pheromone almost nonvolatile, ants according to the pheromone concentration on the initial moment every path to find the shortest path, and leave pheromone on the path to walk, because of the shortest path pheromone concentration is greater than the other path, and the positive feedback mechanism of ant colony algorithm, making the shortest path pheromone concentration increasing, with the increase of ants algebra k value, pheromone volatilization coefficients rho began to play a role, pheromones are beginning to evaporate, To prevent local convergence, when the pheromone concentration in each path is evaporated, the rest of the pheromone and left in the wake of the ant walk this path pheromone, the experimental simulation results are shown below.

4.1   Only to Improve the Pheromone Volatilization Factor ρ

In order to study the influence of the introduced sine function on the important parameters in the ant colony algorithm, We applied the improved method to the pheromone volatilization factor ρ and the pheromone intensity factor Q. This section focuses on the effects of improving the pheromone volatilization factor ρ. We can multiply the sine function $\sin((k/K)(pi/2))$ by the original pheromone volatilization factor ρ, where k is the current ant generation, and K is the total generation of the ant set. It can make the pheromone volatilization factor ρ change with the ant generation K. It is brought into the formula of the pheromone concentration as shown in formula (4) and the improved pheromone concentration formula (5) is finally obtained.

$$\tau = (1 - \rho)\tau + \Delta\tau \tag{4}$$

$$\tau = (1 - \sin((k/K)(pi/2))\rho)\tau + \Delta\tau \tag{5}$$

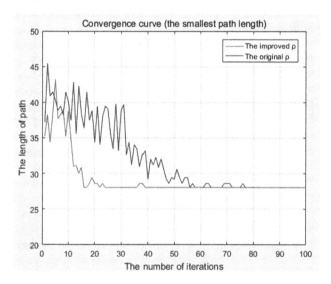

Fig. 4. Trend of convergence curve by improving the pheromone volatilization factor ρ.

Only to improve the pheromone volatilization factor ρ, it can be seen in Fig. 4 that the rate of convergence of the improved algorithm is faster than the original algorithm, the original ant colony algorithm converges to 28.63 in 78th generation, and the improved ant colony algorithm converges to 28.63 in 40th generation. It can be concluded from this, only to improve the way of updating the pheromone volatilization factor ρ can obviously accelerate the convergence speed of the ant colony algorithm.

4.2   Only to Improve the Pheromone Intensity Factor Q

This section focuses on the effects of improving the pheromone intensity factor Q. The pheromone intensity factor Q is a factor that is applied to the increases $\Delta\tau$ of the pheromone concentration as shown in formula (6). Using the same method as in Sect. 4.1, and the improved increases of the pheromone concentration is finally obtained as formula (7).

$$\Delta\tau = \Delta\tau + \frac{Q}{L}, \tag{6}$$

$$\Delta\tau = \Delta\tau + \frac{\sin((k/K)(pi/2))Q}{L}. \tag{7}$$

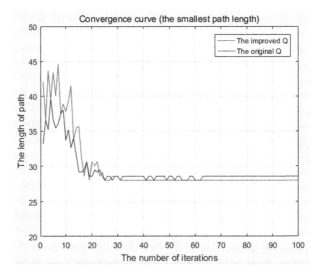

Fig. 5. Trend of convergence curve by improving the pheromone intensity factor Q.

Only to improve the pheromone intensity factor Q, it can be seen in Fig. 5 that the original ant colony algorithm converges to 28.63 in 63th generation, and the improved ant colony algorithm converges to 28.04 in 32th generation. It can be concluded from this, only to improve the pheromone intensity factor Q can obviously accelerate the convergence speed of the ant colony algorithm and find the smaller path.

4.3   Improve the Pheromone Volatilization Factor ρ and the Pheromone Intensity Factor Q at the Same Time

In this section, we will apply the improved method to both the pheromone volatilization factor ρ and the pheromone intensity factor Q. By comparing the original algorithm with the improved algorithm, the following experimental results can be obtained.

The pheromone volatilization factor ρ and the pheromone intensity factor Q were improved in the algorithm at the same time. It can be seen from Fig. 6, the yellow line is the trajectory of the robot that the original ant colony algorithm found, the red line is the trajectory of the robot that the improved ant colony algorithm found. By comparing the length of the two trajectories, the improved ant colony algorithm can find a shorter trajectory.

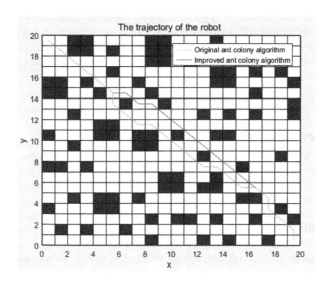

Fig. 6. The trajectory of the robot. (Color figure online)

While the pheromone volatilization factor ρ and the pheromone intensity factor Q were improved of the algorithm at the same time, it can be seen from Fig. 7, the original ant colony algorithm converges to 28.63 in 70th generation, and the improved ant colony algorithm converges to 28.04 in 28th generation. It can be concluded from this, improve the pheromone volatilization factor ρ and the pheromone intensity factor Q at the same time can greatly accelerate the convergence speed of the ant colony algorithm and find a shorter path.

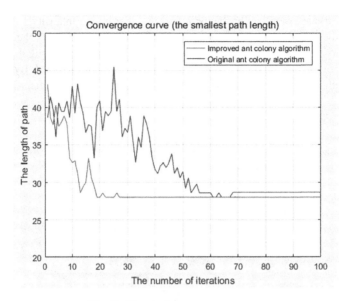

Fig. 7. Trend of convergence curve.

5 Conclusion

In this paper, an improved ant colony algorithm for mobile robot path planning is proposed. Improved ant colony algorithm is mainly from two aspects: the pheromone volatilization factor ρ and the pheromone intensity factor Q, and simulation results show that the improved ant colony algorithm convergence speed is faster, and can find the shortest path. The current research is mainly about two-dimensional planar environment. In the future, ant colony algorithm can be applied to three-dimensional space for path planning.

References

1. Hong, S., Lianjun, H., Xiaohui, Z.: Research on path planning for the mobile intelligent robot. In: Proceedings of the 2009 WRI World Congress on Computer Science and Information Engineering, Los Angeles, CA, pp. 121–124 (2009). https://doi.org/10.1109/csie.2009.221
2. Zhu, L., Fan, J.-Z., Zhao, J., Wu, X.-G., Liu, G.: Global path planning and local obstacle avoidance of searching robot in mine disasters based on grid method. J. Cent. South Univ. (Sci. Technol.) **42**(11), 3421–3428 (2011)
3. Adeli, H., Tabrizi, M.H.N., Mazloomian, A., Hajipour, E., Jahed, M.: Path planning for mobile robots using iterative artificial potential field method. Int. J. Comput. Sci. **8**(4), 28–32 (2011)
4. Althoefer, K.: Neuro-fuzzy motion planning for robotic manipulators. Ph.D. thesis, King's College, London (1997)

5. Nosrati, M., Karimi, R., Hasanvand, H.A.: Investigation of the (Star) search algorithms: characteristics, methods and approaches. World Appl. Program. **2**(4), 251–256 (2012)
6. Goldberg, D.E.: Genetic Algorithm in Search Optimization and Machine Learning, vol. **xiii**, no. (7), pp. 2104–2116. Addison Wesley, Boston (1989)
7. Dorigo, M., Maniezzo, V., Colorni, A.: Ant system: optimization by a colony of cooperating agents. IEEE Trans. Syst. Man Cybern. Part B (Cybern.) **26**(1), 29–41 (1996). https://doi.org/10.1109/3477.484436
8. Kennedy, J., Eberhart, R.: Particle swarm optimization. In: Proceedings of ICNN 1995 - International Conference on Neural Networks, Perth, WA, Australia, vol. 4, pp. 1942–1948 (1995). https://doi.org/10.1109/icnn.1995.488968
9. Dorigo, M., Gambardella, L.M.: Ant colony system: a cooperative learning approach to the traveling salesman problem. IEEE Trans. Evol. Comput. **1**(1), 53–66 (1997). https://doi.org/10.1109/4235.585892
10. Bulinheimer, B., Hartl, R.F., Strauß, C.: A new rank based version of the ant system: a computational study. Cent. Eur. J. Oper. Res. Econ. **7**(1), 25–38 (1997)
11. Stutzle, T., Hoos, H.H.: Max-min ant system. Future Gener. Comput. Syst. **16**(9), 889–914 (2000)
12. Wang, H., Li, X., Li, P., Veremey, E., Sotnikova, M.: Application of real-coded genetic algorithm in ship weather routing. J. Navigation **71**(4), 989–1010 (2018). https://doi.org/10.1017/S0373463318000048
13. Wang, H., Li, P., Xue, Y., Korovkin, M.V.: Application of improved isochron method in ship's minimum voyage time weather routing. Vestnik Sankt-Peterburgskogo Universiteta. Seriya 10. Prikladnaya Matematika. Informatika. Protsessy Upravleniya **13**(3), 286–299 (2017). https://doi.org/10.21638/11701/spbu10.2017.306. (in Russian)

Algorithm for Customers Loss Minimization with Possible Supply Chain Disruption

Elena Lezhnina⬥, Yulia Balykina⬥, and Timur Lepikhin$^{(\boxtimes)}$⬥

Saint-Petersburg State University, University Avenue 35, Peterhof,
198504 Saint Petersburg, Russia
t.lepihin@spbu.ru

Abstract. Continuous development of companies in various sectors of the economy has led to an expansion of the processes they implement. With the increase in the number of logistic processes of the company, there is a need for their optimization, with a subsequent reduction in the costs of their provision. Logistic costs can reach up to forty-five percent of the company's general administrative expenses. As of today, there are many approaches to setting and solving the problem for optimization of logistics systems. In this paper, the authors suggest a set of different strategies for selecting suppliers in the market, taking into account a number of constraints, in particular, the supplier's required reliability, as well as the goods pricing strategy, provided that such goods are competitive. The main objective of the research is to solve the problem of the optimal choice of the quantity of goods in the order with supplier losses minimization. The goal is achieved by choosing the optimal or the so-called economical order size, at which the supplier's losses will be minimal. To determine the optimal order size, a modified Harris-Wilson formula for the economic order quantity is used. Two types of the problem are considered: a model in the absence of supply disruption and a model with probable supply disruptions. Scenarios of a customer's behavior are suggested for possible supply disruptions, such as the supplier equipment failure or transportation problems. Using the proposed algorithm, the customer can develop a relevant stock forming strategy.

Keywords: Loss minimization · Supply chain disruption · Game theory approach

1 Introduction

Continuous development of companies in various sectors of the economy has led to an expansion of the processes they implement. In particular, the logistics process of the company is a whole set of nested processes. As a consequence, with the increase in the number of such processes, there is a need for their optimization, with a subsequent reduction in the costs of their provision and, accordingly, an increase or stabilization of revenues.

As is well known, logistic costs can reach up to forty-five percent of the company's general administrative expenses. Therefore, setting the task of minimizing costs in the optimization of logistic systems is particularly relevant. Currently, there are many

V. Sukhomlin and E. Zubareva (Eds.): Convergent 2018, CCIS 1140, pp. 142–149, 2020.
https://doi.org/10.1007/978-3-030-37436-5_12

approaches to setting and solving the problem for optimization of logistics systems. The first work on mathematical modeling of inventory control was written by Harris. The Harris-Wilson formula is a traditional method of finding the optimal balance between the cost of shipping and storing goods in order to minimize total costs and determine the optimal lot size for the goods. This formula is known as the Economic Order Quantity Formula (EOQ) [1].

One of the main directions in developing approaches to solving the problems of inventory management and optimizing costs is game theory and its applications. Nevertheless, to solve composite problems, it is possible to combine the methods of game theory with the methods of optimal control theory, which successfully cope with various types of problem statements in which it is necessary to determine the parameters that contribute to the achievement of a given extremum of the function being studied.

The first task of analyzing the inventory control model, solved with the help of game theory, was described by the Parlar [2]. Models with one player who takes decisions that describe many important aspects but do not take into account the behavior of other players in the market are described in 1963 by Hadley and Whitin [3], Hax and Candea in [4] and in 1994 in the work of Tersine [5].

At present, an approach based on the use of noncooperative game theory for the analysis of supply chain models is quite common. In this approach, the idea of strategic equilibrium is used as a rational game solution. Many concepts of equilibrium are considered in the works of van Damme [6].

The static models of Cournot (1838) and Bertrand (1883) were described long before the emergence of game theory methods. Since price control is a simpler process than control of the quantity of the goods produced, in this study the Bertrand oligopoly is adopted. For the quality of the optimality principle, the Nash equilibrium was chosen [7].

It is worth paying special attention to the problem of delivery disruption. Since the functioning of a company is connected with a lot of factors independent of direct business participants, which may include diverse events such as natural disasters, strikes, technical problems at work, and others, mathematical models of these processes require to be presented as a random processes [8]. These negative random processes can lead to serious financial losses, as noted by Hendrik and Singal [9], and can be described using probabilistic models. In particular, in [8] it was suggested to define a delivery disruption as a random event, which interrupts the functioning of the supply chain for a time period of random length. There are various strategies for mitigating the consequences of such supply disruptions that companies can choose [10]. One of them is to create a certain stock of goods, serving as a buffer when supplies stop.

In this work, the authors suggest a set of different strategies for selecting suppliers on the market, taking into account a number of constraints, in particular, the supplier's required reliability, as well as a pricing strategy that must be established for goods, provided that such goods are competitive.

The aim of the research is to solve the problem of the optimal choice of the quantity of goods with due consideration of the supplier loss minimization.

2 Mathematical Formalization

The main optimization task in hand is to minimize supplier losses. The goal is achieved by choosing the optimal or the so-called economical order size, at which the supplier's losses are minimal.

Let us consider two options of setting the problem: a model in the absence of supply disruption and a model with probable supply disruptions.

2.1 Model with no Supply Disruption

The classical formula for an optimal size of the order is expressed by formula (1):

$$Q^* = \sqrt{\frac{2CR}{H}}, \tag{1}$$

where Q^* - economic order quantity, C - costs of placing an order, R - annual demand for a product, H - the cost of storing a unit of goods per year.

As one of the parameters, expression (1) contains the demand for a product, which, inversely proportional to the classical case depends on its value.

When constructing the order size formation algorithm, a two-step model is considered, first described in [11] for single-product consignments and further expanded for multi-product lots in [12].

The general scheme of the algorithm consists of the following steps:

1. the economical size of the order is determined in general form (1);
2. a non-cooperative game is built and competitive prices for the product are determined, taking into account the prices of this product (good) from other games, which ensures strategic equilibrium in the market;
3. final determination of the economic size of the order by substituting the obtained price values in the demand function.

Let us consider this algorithm in more detail. The model of the market in which n retailers sell m products is explored: $i = \overline{1, n}, j = \overline{1, m}$. A retailer i decides how many products he will order for the period T: $q_i = (q_{i1}, \ldots, q_{im})$, $i = \overline{1, n}$ – the vector of product quantity.

Having received the ordered goods, the player i assigns a price for each product, according to which he will sell it in the following form: $p_i = (p_{i1}, \ldots, p_{im})$, $i = \overline{1, n}$ - the vector of prices for the goods.

$D_{ij}(p_{i1}, \ldots, p_{im})$ is the demand function for the goods j at the price offered by the player i.

When analyzing price competition (not only in the Bertrand model), the demand for the company's products also depends on the prices assigned by other players. The cost function of the player i is expressed by the following formula:

$$TC_i(p_{i1},\ldots,p_{im},q_1) = \sum_{j=1}^{m}\left(c_j D_{ij}(p_{i1},\ldots,p_{im}) + c_{ij}^0 \frac{D_{ij}(p_{i1},\ldots,p_{im})}{q_{ij}} + c_{ij}^H \frac{q_{ij}}{2}\right), \quad (2)$$

where c_{ij}^0 - cost of order placement by the seller i for a unit of goods j, c_{ij}^H - cost of storing a unit of goods j for the seller i.

Since at prices below marginal costs the seller bears losses for any positive sales volume, the prices selected by him satisfy the following restriction:

$$p_{ij} > c_j + c_{ij}^0 + c_{ij}^H, \ i = \overline{1,n}, \ j = \overline{1,m}$$

Then the payoff function in the game of the i-th player is calculated by the formula (3):

$$\Pi_i(p_{i1},\ldots,p_{im}) = \sum_{j=1}^{m} p_{ij} D_{ij}(p_{i1},\ldots,p_{1m}) - TC_i(p_{i1},\ldots,p_{im},q_{i1},\ldots,q_{im}) \quad (3)$$

2.2 Model with Probable Supply Disruptions

In real conditions, market participants may face such a phenomenon as supply disruption. Supply disruptions can be a result of both external causes (for example, natural disasters) and internal problems of the supplier company (failure of equipment, etc.). Traditionally, in the literature the period when a supplier is available for an order is called wet-, on-, up-interval. The period when deliveries are impossible are called dry-, off, down-interval. Atan and Snyder [13] offered to simulate the alternation of on- and off-periods in the form of a Markov chain. The duration of the periods is subject to an exponential distribution law with parameters μ (recovery rate) and λ (disruption rate). By β we define a probability that the supplier is in the "off" period. Then, by the property of Markov chains, we have an expression for the probability of the "off" period in the following form:

$$\beta = \frac{\lambda}{\lambda+\mu}\left(1 - e^{-(\lambda+\mu)\frac{Q}{D}}\right) \quad (4)$$

It follows from formula (4) that the planned interval between deliveries $\frac{Q}{D}$ can increase by an amount $\frac{\beta}{\mu}$. In accordance, the expected cost of the cycle is:

$$TC_i(p_{i1},\ldots,p_{im},q_i) =$$
$$= \sum_{j=1}^{m}\left(c_j D_{ij}(p_{i1},\ldots,p_{im}) + c_{ij}^0 \frac{D_{ij}(p_{i1},\ldots,p_{im})}{q_{ij}} + c_{ij}^H \frac{q_{ij}}{2} + p_j \frac{D_{ij}(p_{i1},\ldots,p_{im})\beta}{\mu}\right).$$
$$(5)$$

Thus, the cost of the cycle is increased by the amount $p_j \frac{D_{ij}(p_{i1},\ldots,p_{im})\beta}{\mu}$.

Since function (5) is quasi-convex, it has a local extremum (minimum).

During the game, each participant solves two problems: to choose the optimal size of the order and to assign the optimal (competitive) price for the goods being sold. We call $q_i = (q_{i1}, \ldots, q_{im})$ a vector of internal player strategy and $p_i = (p_{i1}, \ldots, p_{im})$ – vector of external player strategy.

In the first step of the game, each participant i solves the internal task of determining the economic order quantity:

$$\min_{(q_{i1}, \ldots, q_{im})} TC_i(p_{i1}, \ldots, p_{im})$$

$$= \min_{(q_{i1}, \ldots, q_{im})} \sum_{j=1}^{m} \left(c_j D_{ij}(p_{i1}, \ldots, p_{im}) + c_{ij}^0 \frac{D_{ij}(p_{i1}, \ldots, p_{im})}{q_{ij}} + c_{ij}^H \frac{q_{ij}}{2} + p_j \frac{D_{ij}(p_{i1}, \ldots, p_{im})\beta}{\mu} \right)$$

Taking into account the complexity of the function (5), the solution can be obtained using numerical methods. Nevertheless, we can greatly simplify this task, using the approximation proposed by Snyder [13]. The author approximates the probability β by a value $\beta' = \frac{\lambda}{\lambda + \mu}$.

Then the optimal order size (economic order quantity) according to Harris formula is equal to:

$$q_{ij}^* = \sqrt{\frac{2c_{ij}^0 D_{ij}(p_{i1}, \ldots, p_{im})}{c_{ij}^H} + A^2 + B} - A \tag{6}$$

where $A = \frac{\beta' D_{ij}(p_{i1}, \ldots, p_{im})}{\mu}$, and $B = \sqrt{\frac{2D_{ij}^2(p_{i1}, \ldots, p_{im})p_{ij}}{c_{ij}^H \mu}}$.

Substituting the value q_{ij}^* obtained in (6) into the cost formula (5), we obtain a new function in the form (7):

$$TC_i^*(p_{i1}, \ldots, p_{im})$$

$$= \sum_{j=1}^{m} \left(c_j D_{ij}(p_{i1}, \ldots, p_{im}) + c_{ij}^0 \frac{D_{ij}(p_{i1}, \ldots, p_{im})}{q_{ij}} + c_{ij}^H \frac{q_{uo}^*}{2} + p_j \frac{D_{ij}(p_{i1}, \ldots, p_{im})\beta}{\mu} \right) \tag{7}$$

And, consequently, a new profit function in the form (8):

$$\tilde{\Pi}_i(p_{i1}, \ldots, p_{im}) = \sum_{j=1}^{m} p_{ij} D_{ij}(p_{i1}, \ldots, p_{1m}) - TC_i^*(p_{i1}, \ldots, p_{im}) \tag{8}$$

As a result, we get a non-cooperative game of n players (price competition) in the following form:

$$\Gamma = \left\langle N, \{\tilde{\Pi}_i\}_{i=1}^{N}, \{\Omega_i\}_{i=1}^{N} \right\rangle$$

where $N = \overline{1, n}$ – a set of players, $\Omega_i = \{p_i | p_i \subset [0, \infty)\}$ – sets of strategies for the i-th player, $\tilde{\Pi}_i(p_{i1}, \ldots, p_{im})$ - a payoff function of player i, that depends on only external strategies $(p_{i1}, \ldots, p_{im}) \in \Omega_1 \cdot \Omega_2 \cdot \ldots \cdot \Omega_n$.

For each player i we need to find a strategy $p_i \in \Omega_i$, that provides a solution of our optimal problem in the following way:

$$\tilde{\Pi}_i(p_{i1}, \ldots, p_{im}) \to \max_{(p_{i1}, \ldots, p_{im})} \tag{9}$$

The Nash equilibrium situation $(p_1^*, \ldots, p_n^*)$ will be a solution of a system of n equations of the form:

$$\frac{\partial \tilde{\Pi}_i(p_{i1}, \ldots, p_{im})}{\partial p_{ij}} = 0, \ i = \overline{1, n} \tag{10}$$

Taking into account the complexity of Eq. (10) in general form, it is necessary to apply numerical integration (for example, using MATLAB).

After finding the equilibrium situation $(p_1^*, \ldots, p_n^*)$ in the game Γ, it becomes possible to determine the numerical values q_{ij}^* by the formula (6).

3 Forming a Strategy of Behavior

In view of the above, we have two situations: a model with a probable supply disruption and a model with no such supply. In the case of a model with supply disruptions, as discussed above, there is an increase in costs. In this way, the customer decision to choose this or that model is characterized by its attitude towards risk. Thus, the customer can either risk and not increase the costs of settling possible disruptions, or consider this problem, thereby reducing his profit.

As a rule, in real life several suppliers are represented on the market. Suppose a customer can choose from t suppliers, the cost k of the product is known for each supplier, and the parameters β_k, μ_k, λ_k, $k = \overline{1, t}$ are also known.

3.1 First Strategy

First, we consider the case of choosing a supplier. The player must evaluate the parameters β_k. If β_k are small enough, then the customer can neglect the risk and solve the optimization problem in the absence of the disruption risk, while choosing the supplier with the minimum prices c_j^k. In a different situation, if the parameters β_k are not sufficiently small, it is necessary to take into account all parameters simultaneously. Therefore, it is necessary to solve k problems of minimizing costs and maximizing profits in the form of:

$$TC_i^k(p_{i1}, \ldots, p_{im})$$

$$= \sum_{j=1}^{m} \left(c_j D_{ij}(p_{i1}, \ldots, p_{im}) + c_{ij}^0 \frac{D_{ij}(p_{i1}, \ldots, p_{im})}{q_{ij}} + c_{ij}^H \frac{q_{ij}^*}{2} + p_j \frac{D_{ij}(p_{i1}, \ldots, p_{im})\beta_k}{\mu_k} \right)$$

$$\arg \max_{(p_{i1}, \ldots, p_{im})} \tilde{\Pi}_i(p_{i1}, \ldots, p_{im}) = \sum_{j=1}^{m} p_{ij} D_{ij}(p_{i1}, \ldots, p_{im}) - TC_i^k(p_{i1}, \ldots, p_{im})$$

Then the player should chose a supplier that gives the best profit.

3.2   Second Strategy

For the second strategy, the customer can change the supplier at any time of the order. In this case, the customer's behavior strategy is changing somewhat. The customer ignores the risk and chooses the supplier with the lowest prices c_j^k. When the "dry" period occurs, the player must decide how to proceed further. Either the player can wait for the delivery to be restored during the likely period $\frac{\beta_k}{\mu_k}$, sustaining losses, or switch to another supplier. Therefore, the following values should be compared:

1. Possible losses $\frac{\beta_k}{\mu_k}$ are defined in the form:

$$L_i^k = \frac{\Pi_i^k(p_{i1}, \ldots, p_{im})}{T} \cdot \frac{\beta_k}{\mu_k} ,$$

where $\Pi_{i^*}^{k^*}(p_{i1}, \ldots, p_{im})$ is the solution of problem (9), i^* - customer under consideration, k^* - current supplier.

2. Then the losses are considered when ordering from another seller (more risky or with higher prices):

$$\Pi_{i^*}^l(p_{i1}, \ldots, p_{im}) - \Pi_{i^*}^{k^*}(p_{i1}, \ldots, p_{im}),$$

where $l = \overline{1, t}$, $l \neq k^*$.
We choose a case with least losses.

4   Conclusion

In this article, a scenario of the customer's behavior is suggested for possible supply disruptions, such as the supplier equipment failure or transportation problems. Using the proposed algorithm, the customer can manage the process of stocks forming: either secure himself against such disruptions, creating a buffer stock, or switch his supply chain to another supplier.

References

1. Harris, F.W.: What quantity to make at once. In: The Library of Factory Management, vol. V. Operation and Costs, pp. 47–52. A. W. Shaw Company, Chicago (1915)

2. Parlar, M.: Game theoretic analysis of the substitutable product inventory problem with random demands. Nav. Res. Logistics 35(3), 397–409 (1988). https://doi.org/10.1002/1520-6750(198806)35:3%3c397:AID-NAV3220350308%3e3.0.CO;2-Z

3. Haldey, G.F., Whitin, T.M.: Analysis of Inventory Systems. Prentice-Hall, Englewood Cliffs (1963)

4. Hax, A.C., Candea, D.: Production and Inventory Management. Prentice-Hall, Englewood Cliffs (1984)

5. Tersine, R.J.: Principles of Inventory and Materials Management. Elsevier North Holland, Amsterdam (1994)

6. van Damm, E.: Stability and Perfection of Nash Equilibria. Springer, Heidelberg (1991). https://doi.org/10.1007/978-3-642-58242-4

7. Nash, J.F.: Non-cooperative games. Ann. Math. 54, 286–295 (1951). https://doi.org/10.2307/1969529

8. Bertrand, J.: Theorie mathematique de la richesse sociale. J. des Savants 67, 499–508 (1883)

9. Snyder, L.V., Atan, Z., Peng, P., Rong, Y., Schmitt, A.J., Sinsoysal, B.: OR/MS models for supply chain disruptions: a review. IIE Trans. (Institute of Industrial Engineers) 48(2), 89–109 (2016). https://doi.org/10.1080/0740817x.2015.1067735

10. Hendricks, K.B., Singhal, V.R.: The effect of supply chain glitches on shareholder wealth. J. Oper. Manag. 21(5), 501–522 (2003). https://doi.org/10.1016/j.jom.2003.02.003

11. Wang, Y., Gilland, W., Tomlin, B.: Mitigating supply risk: dual sourcing or process improvement? Manuf. Serv. Oper. Manag. 12(3), 489–510 (2010). https://doi.org/10.1287/msom.1090.0279

12. Gasratov, M., Zakharov, V.: Games and inventory management. In: Dynamic and Sustainability in International Logistics and Supply Chain Management. Cuvillier Verlag, Gottingen (2011)

13. Lezhnina, E.A., Zakharov, V.V.: The Nash equilibrium in multy-product inventory model. Contrib. Game Theory Manag. 7, 191–200 (2014)

Regulation of the Crowd Dynamic Objects Flight Through the Narrow Tunnel

Alexey Zhabko$^{(\boxtimes)}$ [iD], Olga Chizhova [iD], and Oleg Tikhomirov [iD]

Saint-Petersburg State University, University Avenue 35,
Peterhof 198504, Saint Petersburg, Russia
{a.zhabko,o.chizhova,o.tikhomirov}@spbu.ru

Abstract. Mathematical models of dynamic processes described by systems of differential-difference equations of delay type with a linearly increasing aftereffect are considered. Such a class of systems has been investigated significantly worse than the class of systems with limited aftereffect. However, in recent times many new applications have appeared in the controlled dynamic processes described by such systems. This paper is devoted to the study of the asymptotic stability of the zero solution of homogeneous differential-difference systems with several concentrated linearly increasing delays. The theoretical basis of the study is the approach of B.S. Razumikhin, which made it possible to obtain coefficient sufficient conditions for asymptotic stability. Further analysis of the asymptotic stability of nonlinear systems with unlimitedly increasing delay can be based on an adaptation of the Lyapunov-Krasovsky approach. As an application, we consider a dynamic model of the span of a large family of UAVs over a limited tunnel, which is described by a system of differential-difference equations with concentrated constant and linearly increasing delays. The approach used in the work can be applied to the analysis of stability, including systems with distributed delay.

Keywords: Mathematical modeling · Differential-difference system · Linearly increasing time-delay · Stability · Dynamics

1 Introduction

The class of differential equations with a time proportional delay is studied much worse than the class of equations with a constant delay. Equations with a linearly increasing delay are distinguished from a class of equations with a bounded time-variable delay in that the solution history, which influences the dynamics of this solution at the current time, increases indefinitely with time. Hence, it turns out to be impossible to apply certain research methods to equations with increasing, including linearly increasing delay.

The most studied among the equations with linearly increasing delay are linear equations. But in some cases it is necessary to consider systems in which the right-hand parts does not have linear terms, or the matrix with linear terms does not allow using stability and instability theorems in a linear approximation [1]. In these cases, the first, in a broad sense, approximation is a system of equations with homogeneous right-hand sides. Note that the Laplace transform method used to study linear equations with constant delay is not applicable to such equations with homogeneous right-hand sides.

© Springer Nature Switzerland AG 2020
V. Sukhomlin and E. Zubareva (Eds.): Convergent 2018, CCIS 1140, pp. 150–155, 2020.
https://doi.org/10.1007/978-3-030-37436-5_13

Theorems on the stability of homogeneous systems without delay were proved in the works of Zubov, Malkin, Krasovskii [2–4]. A refinement of the known stability criteria for the first, in a broad sense, approximation of systems without delay is given in the paper of Aleksandrov [5]. However, nonlinear equations and systems of such equations containing linear time delays, until recently, remain virtually unexplored. In [6], some sufficient conditions are given for the stability and instability of a scalar equation with a homogeneous right-hand side and one linear delay.

In this paper, we consider new mathematical model described by a system of differential-difference equations with a constant and linearly increasing delay. Such models appear in the analysis of the situation of traffic jams in dynamic processes. For example, if you increase the density of traffic on a circular road, or when a large crowd leaves public institutions, and so on. Here, the dynamics of the span of a large family of UAVs through a long tunnel are analyzed. For such dynamical systems with mixed delay, sufficient conditions for asymptotic stability are formulated and the corresponding theorems are proved.

2 Mathematical Model

Consider the groups of UAVs moving along a path divided into homogeneous sections. Let us enumerate these sections from 1 to N. Let $r_i(t)$ and $V_i(t)$ denote the average density and average velocity of the flow group in section i at the moment t. Let $c_i(t)$ denote the average flux density at the beginning of the i-th section, and $d_i(t)$ denote the average density at the end of the $(i-1)$-th segment.

Assumption 1. The maximum possible speed on this path is V_0.

Assumption 2. By $\tilde{V}(r)$ we denote the dependence of the average velocity of a group of drones on the flux density.

Suppose the function $\tilde{V}(r)$ with $r > \tilde{r}_0$ is determined by the equality

$$\tilde{V}(r) = \frac{V_0 \cdot \tilde{r}_0}{\tilde{r}_0 + a(r - \tilde{r}_0)}$$

If $\dot{\tilde{r}}_{is}$ is the average rate of increase in the flux density between the site with the number s and the site with the number i at time $\bar{t}$, then writing the balance equations between the average densities $y_s(t)$ $(s = 1, \ldots, N)$ of the flow of drones at time t in the s-th area, we obtain the equations

$$\dot{y}_s(t) = f_s(y_s(t), u_s(t)), \quad u_s = u_s(t, y_1(t - h_{s1}), \ldots, y_N(t - h_{sN}))$$

in which $h_{si} = h_{si}^0 + \gamma_{si}(t - \bar{t})$, and $h_{ss} = 0$.

Next, we analyze the conditions for the asymptotic stability of the first in the broad sense approximation in the neighborhood of the equilibrium position. Namely, stability of homogeneous differential-difference systems with several linearly increasing concentrated delays is investigated.

3 Homogeneous System Stability

Consider a scalar equation with linearly increasing delays of the following form:

$$\dot{x} = a_0 x^\mu(t) + a_1 x^\mu(\alpha_1 t) + a_2 x^\mu(\alpha_2 t) \tag{1}$$

We assume that $\mu = p/q$ is a rational number with an odd numerator and an odd denominator, in addition $\mu > 1$. The coefficients a_0, a_1, a_2 will be considered real numbers, and the parameters α_1, α_2 – also real and satisfying the conditions $0 < \alpha_j < 1$; $j = 1, 2$.

Define the initial function $\varphi : [\alpha t_0; t_0] \to R; \varphi(t_0) = x_0; t_0 > 0$ and apply the Razumikhin approach [7] to clarify the question of the asymptotic stability of the zero solution of Eq. (1). A similar approach to the study of the asymptotic stability of the zero solution of an equation with a homogeneous right-hand side and one linear delay was used in [8, 9].

Along with Eq. (1), we consider the equation

$$\dot{x} = a_0 x^\mu(t) \tag{2}$$

with the same restrictions on the values of a_0 and μ. If we choose a definite positive Lyapunov function in the form $v(x) = x^{\mu+1}$, then it is obvious that the zero solution of Eq. (2) will be asymptotically stable under condition $a_0 < 0$, and

$$\left. \frac{dv(x)}{dt} \right|_{(2)} = a_0(\mu + 1)x^{2\mu}(t)$$

Theorem 1. A zero solution of Eq. (1) is asymptotically stable if the inequality

$$a_0 + (|a_1| + |a_2|)B_1^\mu < 0$$

is true for some $B_1 > 1$.

Proof. Using the Razumikhin condition

$$x^{\mu+1}(\alpha_j t) \leq Bx^{\mu+1}(t), \quad B > 1 \tag{3}$$

and considering the condition $a_0 < 0$ to be satisfied, we find the derivative of the function $v(x)$ on the solutions of the Eq. (1). Then we get

$$\left. \frac{dv(x)}{dt} \right|_{(1)} \leq (\mu + 1)\left(a_0 x^{2\mu}(t) + |a_1||x^\mu(t)x^\mu(\alpha_1 t)| + |a_2||x^\mu(t)x^\mu(\alpha_2 t)|\right) \tag{4}$$

We introduce the value of $B_1 > 1$, such that $B_1^{\mu+1} = B$. Then from inequality (3) it immediately follows that $|x^\mu(\alpha_j t)| \leq |B_1 x(t)|^\mu$, $j = 1, 2$. Now from inequality (4) will follow

$$\left.\frac{dv(x)}{dt}\right|_{(1)} \le (\mu+1)\left(a_0 + (|a_1|+|a_2|)B_1^\mu\right)x^{2\mu}(t).$$

Hence the statement of the theorem obviously follows.
Consider now equation

$$\dot{x} = \sum_{k=0}^{N} a_k x^\mu(\alpha_k t) \tag{5}$$

where $a_0 < 0$ and the remaining parameters satisfy the analogous conditions of Eq. (1).

Theorem 2. A zero solution of Eq. (5) is asymptotically stable if the inequality

$$a_0 + B_1^\mu \sum_{k=1}^{N} |a_k| < 0$$

is true for some $B_1 > 1$.

Proof is a natural generalization of the proof of Theorem 1.

Next, we investigate for asymptotic stability the zero solution of the following system of equations

$$\dot{x} = A_0 x^\mu(t) + \sum_{k=1}^{N} A_k x^\mu(\alpha_k t) \tag{6}$$

Here $x(t)$ is a vector of dimension n, $(x^\mu(t))^T = (x_1^\mu(t), x_2^\mu(t), \ldots, x_n^\mu(t))^T$, A_k are real matrices of a corresponding dimension, the parameters α_k and μ satisfy the same conditions as before. Along with system (6), we will consider an appropriate system that does not contain delays

$$\dot{x} = A_0 x^\mu(t) \tag{7}$$

It is known that if the matrix $A_0 + A_0^T$ is Hurwitz, then the zero solution of system (7) is asymptotically stable. Moreover, there are two homogeneous, definitely positive functions $v(x)$ and $w(x)$, for which the relation $\left.\frac{dv}{dt}\right|_{(7)} = -w(x)$ is satisfied, and also the following estimates are true

$$\begin{aligned} c_1\|x\|^{\mu+1} &\le \|v(x)\| \le c_2\|x\|^{\mu+1}, \\ c_3\|x\|^\mu &\le \left\|\frac{\partial v}{\partial x}\right\| \le c_4\|x\|^\mu, \\ p_1\|x\|^{2\mu} &\le \|w(x)\| \le p_2\|x\|^{2\mu}. \end{aligned} \tag{8}$$

Enter the value $\bar{A} = \max_{k=1,\ldots,N} \|A_k\|$.

Theorem 3. Let the zero solution of system (7) be asymptotically stable. Then the zero solution of system (6) is asymptotically stable if the inequality

$$-p_1 + \bar{A} N c_4 \left(\frac{Bc_2}{c_1} \right)^{\frac{\mu}{\mu+1}} < 0$$

is true.

Proof. It is obvious that

$$\frac{dv(x)}{dt}\bigg|_{(6)} = -w(x) + \sum_{k=1}^{N} \frac{\partial v}{\partial x} A_k x^{\mu}(\alpha_k t) \leq -w(x) + \bar{A} \sum_{k=1}^{N} \frac{\partial v}{\partial x} x^{\mu}(\alpha_k t) \qquad (9)$$

From the condition of Razumikhin and the first of inequalities (8) it follows that $c_1 \|x(\alpha_k t)\|^{\mu+1} \leq Bc_2 \|x(t)\|^{\mu+1}$, whence we will have the estimate $\|x(\alpha_k t)\|^{\mu} \leq \left(\frac{Bc_2}{c_1} \right)^{\frac{\mu}{\mu+1}} \|x(t)\|^{\mu}$.

Substituting this estimate into inequality (9) and taking into account the second and third inequalities (8), we finally get

$$\frac{dv}{dt}\bigg|_{(6)} \leq \left[-p_1 + \bar{A} N c_4 \left(\frac{Bc_2}{c_1} \right)^{\frac{\mu}{\mu+1}} \right] \|x(t)\|^{2\mu}$$

which completes the proof.

4 Conclusion

In this paper, we obtain sufficient conditions for the asymptotic stability of the homogeneous differential-difference systems with linearly increasing delay, based on the approach of B.S. Razumikhin. In the future, it is supposed to extend the method of Lyapunov-Krasovsky functionals, justified for systems with limited delay, to the systems considered in the article, and to obtain necessary and sufficient conditions for the stability of such systems.

References

1. Bellman, R., Cooke, K.L.: Differential-Difference Equations. Academic, New York (1963)
2. Zubov, V.I.: The Methods of A.M. Lyapunov and Their Applications. Noordhoff, Groningen (1964)
3. Malkin, I.G.: Theory of the Motion Stability. Gostekhizdat, Moscow-Leningrad (1952). (in Russian)
4. Krasovskii, N.N.: On Stability in First Approximation. Prikladnaya Matematika i Mekhanika **XIX**(5) (1955). (in Russian)

5. Aleksandrov, A.: Stability of the motions of non-autonomous dynamical systems. St. Petersburg State University Publishing House, St. Petersburg (2004). (in Russian)
6. Zhabko, A.P., Chizhova, O.N.: Stability analysis of a homogeneous differential-difference equation with a linear delay. In: Bulletin of St. Petersburg University. Series 10: Applied Mathematics, Computer Science, Control Processes, no. 3, pp. 105–115 (2015). (in Russian)
7. Razumikhin, B.S.: Stability of time delay systems. Prikladnaya Matematika i Mekhanika **20**(4), 500–512 (1956). (in Russian)
8. Zhabko, A.P., Chizhova, O.N.: Razumikhin approach to analyses of the differential-difference systems with linearly increasing time-delay. In: Proceedings of the 20th International Workshop on Beam Dynamics and Optimization (BDO), Saint-Petersburg, pp. 1–2 (2014) https://doi.org/10.1109/bdo.2014.6890103
9. Zhabko, A.P., Chizhova, O.N., Zaranik, U.P.: Stability analysis of the linear time delay systems with linearly increasing delay. Cybern. Phys. **5**(2), 67–72 (2016). (in Russian)

Financial Risk Assessment in the SiU8 Futures Trading Using Neural Network Based on the SAR-Method

Nikolay Lomakin$^{(\boxtimes)}$ (iD)

Volgograd State Technical University, Lenin Avenue 28,
400005 Volgograd, Russia
tel9033176642@yahoo.com

Abstract. The theoretical basis for the SAR-model applied for calculating the financial risk of time series of exchange instruments has been considered. The article describes the AI neural network for assessing financial risk in the course of exchange trading in a SiU8 US dollar futures contract on the Moscow Exchange by the MoExSAR method in order to minimize the risk.

There has been suggested and proven a hypothesis that the Kohonen map neural network enables forecasting the extent of loss in the course of exchange trading in a SiU8 US dollar futures contract on the Moscow Exchange by the MoExSAR method, as well as predicting the financial instrument price, which is of practical importance for successful trading.

The relevance is due to the fact that in the conditions of increasing volatility in the USD futures contract price, the risk of financial losses and its value increase, with the artificial intelligence systems applied being of great importance to forecast financial risk using the SAR model.

Assessing the extent of loss on financial risk using the neural network forecast of the financial instrument price has practical significance in the conditions of market uncertainty. The neural network that allows predicting both the SiU8 futures contract price and financial risk losses in the trading process has been successfully developed.

Keywords: Neural network · Time series · Financial risk · SAR method · Exchange · SiU8 futures contract · Artificial intelligence

1 Introduction

The relevance is due to the fact that in the conditions of high volatility in the stock exchange instruments and strengthening of all types of risk, it is important to apply artificial intelligence systems to predict the SiU8 futures contract price and financial losses on risk using the SAR-method.

The SAR-method has been taken as the basis for a quantitative assessment of financial risks in practice. Quite often, in terms of assessing the risks, an investor is interested in the anticipated values of the loss rather than probability of the loss itself.

© Springer Nature Switzerland AG 2020
V. Sukhomlin and E. Zubareva (Eds.): Convergent 2018, CCIS 1140, pp. 156–162, 2020.
https://doi.org/10.1007/978-3-030-37436-5_14

This is explained by the fact that in some cases the probability of loss may be slight, but the extent of loss is so severe that the consequences of an adverse result can be considered catastrophic.

Sometimes in such situations, the investor neglects the risk due to its being low and thus makes a mistake, since because of the disastrous effects; the risk itself constitutes a real danger to the financial standing of the company.

2   Results and Discussion

To develop the program proposed, the theoretical foundations of the SAR-model applied for calculating the financial risk of time series stock exchange instruments were considered.

Results:

1. The article presents the AI neural network developed for assessing financial risk in the course of exchange trading in the SiU8 US dollar futures contract on the Moscow Exchange MoEx using the SAR-method to minimize it.
2. There has been suggested and proven a hypothesis that the Kohonen map neural network enables forecasting the extent of financial loss when trading in the SiU8 futures contract, as well as getting forecast of the financial instrument price, which is of practical importance for successful trading.
3. The relevance of the study is due to the fact that in the conditions of increasing volatility in the USD futures contract price, the risk of financial loss and its value increase, and the artificial intelligence systems applied to forecast financial risk using the SAR model is of great importance.

3   Discussion

Financial risk is known to be associated with the probability of loss of financial resources (cash). Practice shows that in terms of assessing the risks, an investor is interested in the anticipated values of the loss rather than probability of the loss itself. Since in some cases, the probability of loss may be slight, but the extent of loss is so severe that the consequences of an adverse result can be catastrophic. In such cases, the investor may neglect the risk itself, due to its being low and thus makes a mistake. Because of disastrous effects, the risk of that kind is a severe danger to the investor's financial standing. Therefore, necessary is a risk assessment that takes into account the extent of possible loss. Such a method for assessing financial risk is the so-called SaR method (Shortfall-at-Risk) [1].

That is, the SaR method is used in addition to the ValueatRisk (VaR) that is based on the definition of the functional relationship of the risk probability. This method is widely used by commercial banks [2]. It seemed appropriate to put forward and prove the hypothesis that the "Kohonen map" neural network can predict financial losses on the risk of a change in the price of a time series SiU8 futures contract using the SAR method.

Studies show that works of many Western and Russian authors are devoted to this issue. For example, Lomakin and Grishankin et al. considered stock exchange transactions with securities of a company as a tool to reduce financial risks [3]; Pavlov successfully conducted a research study of financial risks of an organization using an artificial intelligence system [4]. Amirli and Lomakin conducted an assessment of losses on the financial risk in stock trading by the neural network based on the SAR method [5]. The risk assessment is important in determining the probability of bankruptcy in solving other problems [6].

As practice shows, a research study of financial risks in stock trading is of great interest. To develop a program for assessing financial risks based on a neural network using the SAR method, initial data were taken on the MOEX exchange using the QUIK terminal for the SiU8 financial instrument (Fig. 1).

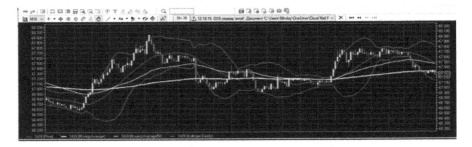

Fig. 1. The SiU8 graph.

In XL, calculations were made of the parameters necessary, i.e., expected value, standard deviation, quantile and SaR (Table 1).

Table 1. The values for financial risk, i.e., expected value, standard deviation, quantile and SaR.

	A	B	C	D	E	F	G	H	I	J	K	L
1	ClosePrice	RSI	BBh	BBm	BBl	Date	r,%		Мат ожид.	Станд.откл.	Квантиль(99)	
2	67259	32,64808	67484,3	67827,48	67141,12	20180817	0,24%		0,17%	0,00962559	-0,020642925	
3	67100	46,39638	67127,55	67245,97	67009,13	20180816	-0,64%					
4	67534	47,00109	67641,25	67892,56	67389,94	20180815	1,26%		Pt+1	65870,5775		
5	66686	42,32425	66753,1	66923,56	66582,64	20180814	-2,15%		Pt+5	64154,393		
6	68134	44,18321	68280,2	68477,65	68082,75	20180813	0,17%					
7	68021	61,74449	68011,85	68130,32	67893,38	20180810	1,50%				Относит,%	SaR(абсолютн, руб.)
8	67011	71,73214	66828,45	67054,76	66602,14	20180809	1,74%		VaR(t+1)	-0,020859	-1388,42	-1444,812002
9	65854	73,22151	65508,65	65936,12	65081,18	20180808	3,17%		VaR(t+5)	-0,0472583	-3104,61	-3230,697851
10	63802	50,65646	63801,7	63837,78	63765,62	20180807	-0,42%					
11	64069	60,41439	64006,75	64122,44	63891,06	20180806	0,63%		Макс	Мин	Интервал	Кол-во интерв
12	63664	60,94406	63587,15	63656,6	63517,7	20180803	-0,08%		3,17%	-2,15%	0,53%	10
13	63716	47,05092	63777,65	63846,72	63708,58	20180802	0,53%					
14	63378	64,75071	63344,55	63418,08	63271,02	20180801	0,79%		Макс	№ группы	Границы доходностей	
15	62881	65,48632	62762,25	62891,95	62632,55	20180731	0,42%		3,17%	1	-2,15%	
16	62615	40,34726	62613,25	62673,71	62552,79	20180730	-0,85%			2	-1,62%	
17	63149	48,16269	63140,7	63208,92	63072,48	20180727	-0,26%		Мин	3	-1,09%	
18	63314	57,01263	63246,95	63316,5	63177,4	20180726	0,19%		-2,15%	4	-0,55%	
19	63196	34,92123	63333,4	63446,63	63220,17	20180725	-0,79%			5	-0,02%	
20	63696	68,07191	63604,7	63923,34	63286,06	20180724	0,38%		Интервал	6	0,51%	
21	63452	51,80298	63430,6	63486,27	63374,93	20180723	-0,67%		0,53%	7	1,04%	
22	63877	46,17623	63920,2	64007,61	63832,79	20180720	-0,33%			8	1,57%	
23	64090	57,01509	64043,9	64231,47	63856,33	20180719	1,10%			9	2,10%	
24	63389	43,46104	63419,45	63495,38	63343,52	20180718	0,59%			10	2,10%	

Based on the data calculated, an input file was generated for the neural risk model of the SiU8 financial instrument (Table 2).

Table 2. Input file for the neural SaR model of the SiU8 financial instrument.

	A	B	C	D	E	F	G	H	I	J	K
1	ClosePrice	RSI	BBh	BBm	BBl	Интервал	Мат ожид.	Станд.откл	Квантиль(99)	VaR(t+1)	SaR(t+1)
2	67259	32,64808	67484,3	67827,48	67141,12	-0,02148	0,00175	0,009626	-0,02064292	-0,02086	-1388,42
3	67259	32,64808	67484,3	67827,48	67141,12	-0,02148	0,001899	0,014494	-0,02148132	-0,02172	-1444,81

The data obtained were presented in the form of a Kohonen map (Fig. 2).

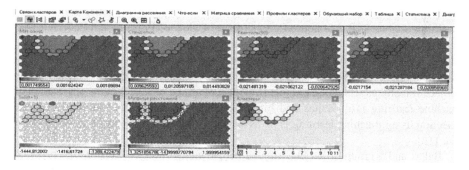

Fig. 2. The Kohonen map.

The "what-if" function allowed getting the forecast values of the absolute values of possible financial losses (Fig. 3).

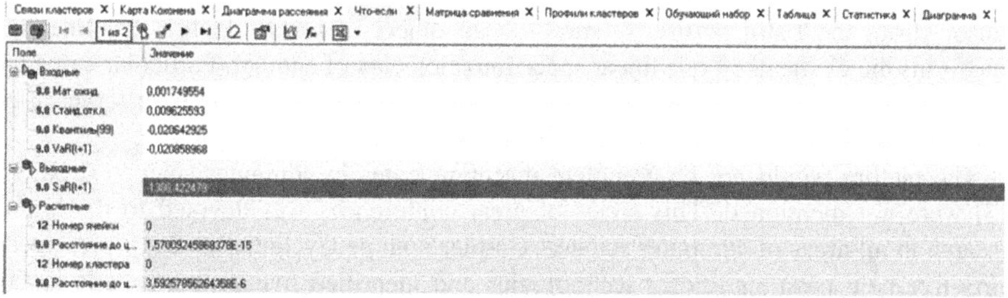

Fig. 3. Forecast for financial loss values using the "what-if" function.

With an open long position of the SiU8 futures contract, with the price of 67,259 RUB, the forecast for the financial losses value was 1388.42 RUB or 2.0642% for the next 15-min timeframe. The predicted loss value was calculated by the neural network based on the input parameters, i.e., expected value of 0.001749554, standard deviation of −0.009625593, quantile [99] 0.020642925 and VaR [i + 1] −0.085858968.

The studies showed that many authors devoted their works to the problem concerned. There is some development of approaches observed in studying the problems of financial risk. So, the portfolio theory by Markowitz [7] and a simplified model of portfolio analysis by Sharpe [8] laid the foundations for assessing financial risk. In the works of modern authors we can see a solution to more specific issues of financial risk management. For example, Stix proposed his own approach in calculating risk [9]; Knight offered his own approaches in the study of risk, uncertainty and profit [10].

Of scientific interest are the results of the study conducted by Ruppert regarding statistics and data analysis for financial engineering [11], as well as the work by Jensen with colleagues who proposed a pricing model for capital assets [12].

In their scientific work, Fama and Mac Bes came to the conclusion that it is necessary to consider risk as a category that is experiencing return and balance [13], whereas Zhang offered to focus on the study of the cost premium, which is also of no small importance [14]. We appreciate the point of view of Frazinni and Pedersen who believe the role of the beta portfolio of financial instruments to be important [15].

As the studies show, the most important direction in the development of the artificial learning systems in managing financial risk is machine learning, which is the subject of many papers. For example, Breyman identified obstacles in the application of machine learning [16]. Baltas and his colleagues investigated the problem of stock selection using machine learning [17], as well as investment issues with a low level of risk [18].

Baltas and a group of his like-minded people came to the conclusion that it would be expedient to combine smart beta factors, which made it possible to take a different look at many problems, including the problem of managing the financial risk of a portfolio [19]. The studies show that there is a new trend in the development of machine learning, which was noted by Jones in his guide for beginners in the field of artificial intelligence, machine learning and cognitive computing [20]. The placement of IBM open source projects can play an important role in the AI development [21], so intensive research in the field of tensor calculations can be a vivid example of it [22]. Tensor (from the Latin *tensus*, " tense") is an object of linear algebra that linearly transforms the elements of one linear space into elements of another. Particular cases of tensors are scalars, vectors, bilinear forms, etc. The term "tensor" also often serves as a short variant for the term "tensor field" that the tensor analysis deals with.

The picture would not be complete if lecture notes in computer science (LNCS) [23] were not mentioned. This series of great conferences was devoted to the latest research in all areas of computer science. Gartner's Hype Cycle Curve 2018 presented thirty-five new most significant technologies and identified five distinct trends in IT development that will erase the boundaries between man and machine. The latest technologies, such as artificial intelligence (AI), will be the driver that will allow companies to achieve ubiquitous presence. Artificial intelligence systems enable an investor to continuously interact with the ecosystems of his business in order to function successfully in the foreseeable future [24]. These trends include AI democratization, digital ecosystems, self-employed biohacking, immersive technologies and ubiquitous infrastructure. The Internet of Things is one of the IT-phenomena that develop with the growth of the information consumed, rather than with the advent of new technology gadgets [25].

4 Conclusion

Based on the study conducted, we can draw the following conclusions.

First, there is a further development of the neural networks in financial risk management; the prediction of losses on the financial instrument volatility risk is important.

Secondly, there was proved a hypothesis that the "Kohonen map" neural network enables a forecast for the extent of loss on the SiU8 futures contract price volatility. So, with the open long position of the SiU8 futures contract, the price of which being 67,259 RUB, the forecast of the financial losses value was -1388.42 RUB, or 2.0642%.

Acknowledgments. The work was supported by the Russian Foundation for Basic Research, project no. 18-010-01210-A ("A cognitive approach to the theoretical and methodological foundations of the strategic development of small business in the digital economy system with account of the drift risks").

References

1. Vasiliev, V.A., Letchikov, A.V., Lyalin, V.E.: Mathematical models for assessing and managing risks of commercial entities. Audit Financ. Anal. **4**, 200–237 (2006). (in Russian)
2. Zhdanov, V.: Value at risk (VAR) method. http://www.beintrend.ru/value-at-risk-varvar. Accessed 21 Sept 2018. (in Russian)
3. Lomakin, N.I., Grishankin, A.I., Maksimova, O.N.: Exchange operations with the company's securities as a tool to reduce financial risks. In: Proceedings of the IX Interregional Scientific-Practical Conference. The Interaction Between Enterprises and Universities: Science, Personnel and Innovation, Volzhsky, 18–19 April 2013, pp. 174–177. VPI (branch) VSTU, Volgograd (2013). (in Russian)
4. Pavlov, V.O., Lomakin, N.I.: Investigation of the financial risks of an organization using an artificial intelligence system. In: Terelyansky, P.V. (ed.) Proceedings of the 1st International Scientific-Practical Conference. Step into the Future: Artificial Intelligence and the Digital Economy. State University of Management, Moscow, no. 3, pp. 321–326 (2017)
5. Amirli, S., Lomakin, N.I.: The loss assessment in stock trading from the financial risk with the neural network based on the SAR method. In: Gorokhov, A.A. (ed.) Proceedings of the 8th International Scientific-Practical Conference. Trends in the Development of Modern Society: Managerial, Legal, Economic and Social Aspects, 20–21 September 2018. Southwest State University, Kursk, pp. 146–150 (2018)
6. Lomakin, N.I., et al.: Neural network for assessing the bankruptcy risk of an enterprise. Certificate of registration. Computer software, no. 2018611016, 22 January 2018. Russian Federation, VSTU (2018)
7. Markowitz, H.M.: Portfolio selection. J. Finan. **7**(1), 77–91 (1952)
8. Sharpe, W.F.: A simplified model for portfolio analysis. Manage. Sci. **9**(2), 171–349 (1963). https://doi.org/10.1287/mnsc.9.2.277
9. Six, G.: A calculus of risk. Sci. Am. **278**(5), 92–97 (1998)

10. Knight, F.H.: Risk, Uncertainly and Profit. Houghton Mifflin Company, Boston (1921)
11. Ruppert, D.: Statistics and Data Analysis for Financial Engineering. Springer, New York (2011). https://doi.org/10.1007/978-1-4419-7787-8
12. Jensen, M.C., Black, F., Scholes, M.S.: The capital asset pricing model: some empirical tests. In: Jensen, M.C. (ed.) Studies in the Theory of Capital Markets. Praeger, New York (1972)
13. Fama, E.F., MacBeth, J.D.: Risk, return and equilibrium: empirical tests. J. Polit. Econ. **81**(3), 607–636 (1973)
14. Zhang, L.: The value premium. J. Finance **60**(1), 67–103 (2005). https://doi.org/10.1111/j.1540-6261.2005.00725.x
15. Frazzini, A., Pedersen, L.H.: Betting against beta. J. Finan. Econ. **111**(1), 1–25 (2014). https://doi.org/10.1016/j.jfineco.2013.10.005
16. Breiman, L.: Bagging predictors. Mach. Learn. **24**(2), 123–140 (1996). https://doi.org/10.1023/A:1018054314350
17. Baltas, N., et al.: Quantitative Monographs. Stock Selection Using Machine Learning. UBS Global Research (2015)
18. Baltas, N., Jessop, D., Jones, C., Lancetti, S., Winter, P., Holcroft, J.: Quantitative Monographs. Low-Risk Investing: Perhaps not Everywhere. UBS Global Research (2015)
19. Baltas, N., et al.: Academic Research Monitor. Combining Smart Beta Factors. UBS Global Research (2016)
20. Jones, M.T.: A guide for beginners in the field of artificial intelligence, machine learning and cognitive computing (2017). https://developer.ibm.com/articles/cc-beginner-guide-machine-learning-ai-cognitive/. Accessed 21 Sept 2018
21. Open source projects from IBM. https://developer.ibm.com/open/code/. Accessed 21 Sept 2018
22. Awesome TensorFlow. https://github.com/jtoy/awesome-tensorflow. Accessed 21 Sept 2018
23. LNCS. http://www.springer.com/lncs. Accessed Sept 2018
24. Gartner named five trends in the development of new technologies that will erase the boundaries between man and machine. https://www.crn.ru/news/detail.php?ID=128821. Accessed 21 Sept 2018
25. The main IT trends in 2017. https://geekbrains.ru/posts/2017_whats_new. Accessed 21 Sept 2018

Some Questions of Trajectory Control of Quadrotor Motion

Natalia Zhabko⬤, Timur Lepikhin$^{(\boxtimes)}$⬤, and Maxim Korovkin⬤

Saint-Petersburg State University, University Avenue 35, Peterhof,
198504 Saint Petersburg, Russia
{n.zhabko, t.lepihin, m.korovkin}@spbu.ru

Abstract. The paper presents an approach to provide the motion of a quadrotor along a given trajectory under the influence of step perturbations. The proposed approach is based on the use of a speed regulator, introduced in the works of Veremey E.I. as one of the elements of a special multi-purpose structure controller. Due to its structure, the speed controller gives for the closed-loop system the property of astatism for regulated variables, which means that the error between the actual motion and the desired trajectory converges to zero in the presence of step disturbances. In this work the controller that provides a quadrotor motion along a given trajectory, is based on four linear simplified mathematical models. Each of such simplified models describes the motion for one of the regulated variables and is used to design control law for each specific scalar regulated variable, that gives the astatism property for this variable. As a result the controller is formed to regulate the position in space and the yaw angle of quadrotor. In the end the paper presents graphs of transients of changes in position and orientation in the space under the action of the proposed control to illustrate its effectiveness; simulation is carried out in MATLAB-Simulink environment for a particular quadrotor model.

Keywords: Quadrotor · Optimal control · Control system design · Astatism · Dynamics · Stabilization · Speed control

1 Introduction

It is well known that unmanned aerial vehicles, including multirotor aerial vehicles, are now widely used in various fields of human activity. The intensive use of such devices generates a large number of mathematical and engineering problems in the field of modeling, control theory, signal and image processing, and related directions. In the control theory arising tasks can be associated with the automation of various stages of controlling the apparatus and implementing specified movements, using specific information while ensuring a given movement, increasing the efficiency of solving specific tasks and saving resources. At the same time, the development of own unmanned aerial vehicles or the use of ready-made vehicles, among which there are inexpensive options, are quite affordable. Such popularity of the considered devices leads to the fact that it does not cease to be relevant to the topic related to the study of various issues of the development of algorithms and the search for new solutions,

V. Sukhomlin and E. Zubareva (Eds.): Convergent 2018, CCIS 1140, pp. 163–174, 2020.
https://doi.org/10.1007/978-3-030-37436-5_15

which is reflected in a fairly large number of publications. Among the existing works, in particular, there are publications on the use of various control techniques, including LQR optimization, H_∞-optimization, methods of nonlinear control theory, neural networks, and others for solving various problems of controlling the dynamics of devices. Some solutions are described in [1–5], including trajectory-control. This work is inspired by the works of Veremey E.I. and provides separate control laws for any regulated variable on the base of the so-named speed control law, that is presented and discussed in works of Veremey E.I., where such structure serves as an element of multi-purpose control law. In this paper the problem of trajectory tracking control for quadrotor is discussed and the main purpose of using of speed laws is to provide of step disturbances attenuation. A description of the general principles of construction of such regulators and features of their application in the tasks of controlling the dynamics of ships, for example, can be found in [6–8], the issue of the synthesis of an astatic controller for multi-rotor aircraft based on the use of elements of such a multi-purpose structure is described in [5]. The paper is organized in the following way. Firstly, the mathematical model of quadrotor is described, than the proposed control strategy is discussed, and finally the illustrations of controller design and conclusions are presented.

2 Mathematical Model

As a basic mathematical model of a quadrotor we consider the system of ordinary nonlinear differential equations of the 18th total order that describes the motion of an object as a controllable rigid body that performs longitudinal displacements along the coordinate axes and rotational motions along the Euler angles:

$$
\begin{aligned}
\ddot{x} &= \tfrac{1}{M}\sum_{1}^{4} F_i(\cos\varphi\cos\psi\sin\theta + \sin\varphi\sin\psi) + d_1, \\
\ddot{y} &= \tfrac{1}{M}\sum_{1}^{4} F_i(\cos\varphi\sin\psi\sin\theta - \sin\varphi\cos\psi) + d_2 \\
\ddot{z} &= \tfrac{1}{M}\sum_{1}^{4} F_i(\cos\varphi\cos\theta) - Mg + d_3, \\
\ddot{\varphi} &= \tfrac{1}{J_\varphi}(F_3 - F_4)L + d_4, \\
\ddot{\theta} &= \tfrac{1}{J_\theta}(F_1 - F_2)L + d_5, \\
\ddot{\psi} &= \tfrac{1}{J_\psi}(F_1 + F_2 - F_3 - F_4)\rho + d_6,
\end{aligned}
\tag{1}
$$

Here (x, y, z) – the quadrotor coordinate vector, (φ, θ, ψ) – the angles of roll, pitch and yaw respectively, M is the mass of the plant, g is the acceleration due to gravity, $(J_\varphi, J_\theta, J_\psi)$ – the moments of inertia on the roll, pitch and yaw, L – the distance from the center of mass to the engine. The structural diagram of a quadrotor as a control object is shown on the Fig. 1. Here F_i – thrust force of i-th engine, i – index from 1 to 4 for Quadrotor. The functions d_i, $i = \overline{1,6}$ specify the disturbances that can be caused, for example, by gusts of wind, and can be represented in the form of step functions $d_i = A_i \cdot 1(t)$, $A_i = const$, $i = \overline{1,6}$.

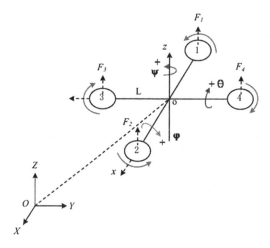

Fig. 1. Quadrotor scheme.

The thrust produced by each propeller is described by the equation in the following form:

$$F_i = K \frac{\omega}{s + \omega} u_i ,$$ (2)

where ω – drive frequency, K – some positive factor, $i = \overline{1, 4}$.

The actuator dynamics can be described by the equation $\delta_i = \frac{\omega}{s+\omega} u_i$, $i = z, \varphi, \theta, \psi$, that in the state space can be represented in the form:

$$\dot{\delta}_i = -\omega \delta_i + \omega u_i$$ (3)

Then we can introduce new control signals:

$$\begin{bmatrix} F_1 + F_2 + F_3 + F_4 \\ F_3 - F_4 \\ F_1 - F_2 \\ F_1 + F_2 - F_3 - F_4 \end{bmatrix} = K \frac{\omega}{s + \omega} \begin{bmatrix} 4u_z \\ 2u_\varphi \\ 2u_\theta \\ 4u_\psi \end{bmatrix}$$ (4)

Now, from the Eq. (4) and taking into account (3), it is possible to express the thrust of each engine as a function of the dynamics of the drives.

Thus the thrust forces of the engines can be expressed by the equations:

$$\begin{aligned} F_1 &= K(\delta_z + \delta_\psi + \delta_\theta), \\ F_2 &= K(\delta_z + \delta_\psi - \delta_\theta), \\ F_3 &= K(\delta_z - \delta_\psi + \delta_\varphi), \\ F_4 &= K(\delta_z - \delta_\psi - \delta_\varphi). \end{aligned}$$

Numerical experiments in this work are carried out on the basis of data on a specific quadrotor described in [2].

The values of the parameters for quadrotor are as follows $M = 1.4$ kg, $J_\varphi = 0.03$ kg $\cdot$ m^2, $J_\theta = 0.03$ kg $\cdot$ m^2, $J_\theta = 0.03$ kg $\cdot$ m^2, $J_\psi = 0.04$ kg $\cdot$ m^2, $\rho = 4$ N $\cdot$ m, $K = 120$ N, $\omega = 15$ rad/s.

The following restrictions on the variables are taken into account: $F_i \leq Mg$, $|u_i| \leq 15$, $i = \overline{1,4}$.

The designed controller is based on the simplified model of the plant, that we can get in the assumption of the motion in horizontal plane when $F_1 + F_2 + F_3 + F_4 \approx mg$, and the small angles of pitch, roll and yaw $\theta \approx 0$, $\varphi \approx 0$ and $\psi \approx 0$.

In such case we can find from the system (1) the separate linear systems to approximate the motion in X and Y directions

$$\ddot{x} = g\theta, \tag{5}$$

$$\ddot{y} = -g\varphi, \tag{6}$$

height dynamics

$$\begin{aligned} \dot{z}_1 &= z_2, \\ \dot{z}_2 &= \tfrac{4K}{M}\delta_z - g, \\ \dot{\delta}_z &= -\omega\delta_z + \omega u_z, \end{aligned} \tag{7}$$

roll dynamics

$$\begin{aligned} \dot{\varphi}_1 &= \varphi_2, \\ \dot{\varphi}_2 &= \tfrac{2LK}{J_\varphi}\delta_\varphi, \\ \dot{\delta}_\varphi &= -\omega\delta_\varphi + \omega u_\varphi \end{aligned} \tag{8}$$

pitch dynamics

$$\begin{aligned} \dot{\theta}_1 &= \theta_2, \\ \dot{\theta}_2 &= \tfrac{2LK}{J_\theta}\delta_\theta, \\ \dot{\delta}_\theta &= -\omega\delta_\theta + \omega u_\theta \end{aligned} \tag{9}$$

yaw dynamics

$$\begin{aligned} \dot{\psi}_1 &= \psi_2, \\ \dot{\psi}_2 &= \tfrac{4K\rho}{J_\psi}\delta_\psi, \\ \dot{\delta}_\psi &= -\omega\delta_\psi + \omega u_\psi \end{aligned} \tag{10}$$

here the new variables $z_1 = z$, $z_2 = \dot{z}$, $\varphi_1 = \varphi$, $\varphi_2 = \dot{\varphi}$, $\theta_1 = \theta$, $\theta_2 = \dot{\theta}$, $\psi_1 = \psi$, $\psi_2 = \dot{\psi}$ are used and the equations are supplemented by the actuator dynamics (3), each scalar signal u_z, u_φ, u_θ, $u_\psi \in E^1$ is used to control respectively the height, roll, pitch and yaw.

3 Control System Design

First we give a description of the structure and properties of the speed regulator [5, 8] for the SISO-system, on which the proposed control scheme is based. In [5], the speed controller was used to ensure stabilization of the orientation and a given height of the quadrotor.

We assume that the mathematical model of the control object is represented by LTI-system:

$$\dot{\mathbf{x}} = \mathbf{A}\mathbf{x} + \mathbf{B}\delta + \mathbf{H}_w\mathbf{f}_w(t),$$
$$\dot{\delta} = u, \tag{11}$$
$$y = \mathbf{C}x,$$

where matrices $\mathbf{A}, \mathbf{B}, \mathbf{H}_w, \mathbf{C}$ have constant components. Here $\mathbf{x} \in \mathbf{E}^n$ – is a state space vector, $u \in \mathbf{E}^1$ – is a deviation of control signal, $\delta \in \mathbf{E}^1$ – actuator state, $y \in \mathbf{E}^1$ – measured variable is used for control design, it is accepted as a controlled, $\mathbf{f}_w \in \mathbf{E}^l$ – is a vector of external disturbances, in this case it is a wind. Here, together with the equations of the object, the differential equation of the actuator dynamics is given.

The mathematical model of the control law for the presented linear model of the object is given by the following equations:

- equation of observer device:

$$\dot{\mathbf{z}} = \mathbf{A}\mathbf{z} + \mathbf{B}\delta + \mathbf{H}(y - \mathbf{C}z), \tag{12}$$

- equation of speed control:

$$u = \mu\dot{\mathbf{z}} + \nu y \tag{13}$$

Here matrices $\mathbf{H}, \mu, \nu$ are unknown and must be found in the process of control design, based on the requirements imposed on the dynamics of the object in the absence and presence of external disturbances.

These matrices are searched sequentially according to the following scheme.

First, the control law is constructed in the form of feedback on the state at a zero command signal and in the absence of external disturbance in the following form:

$$u = \mathbf{K}_x\mathbf{x} + \mathbf{K}_\delta\delta, \tag{14}$$

where $\mathbf{K}_x$ и $\mathbf{K}_\delta$ – constant matrices with elements, the choice of which is to perform based on the requirement of providing the necessary speed in a closed non-linear system while ensuring the asymptotic stability of the closed linear system (11), (14). Further, on the basis of the found matrices $\mathbf{K}_x$ and $\mathbf{K}_\delta$, the matrices μ, ν in the speed law (13) are uniquely determined by fixing a part of the controlled variables in Eq. (11) and representing the others in accordance with object Eq. (11) depending on the derived state variables:

$$u = \mu \dot{\mathbf{x}} + v y \tag{15}$$

This form of representation of the control signal gives a closed-loop system the property of astatism on a regulated variable, that is, a zero equilibrium position on a regulated variable in the presence of constant disturbances at the input.

This is due to the fact that in system (11), considered together with Eq. (14), along the constant solution, we have $vy = 0$ no matter what kind of step perturbation in the form $\mathbf{f}_w = \mathbf{f}_0 \cdot 1(t)$ for a constant vector $\mathbf{f}_0 \in \mathbf{E}^l$ is at the input. As a rule, the property of astatism is provided in linear control by introducing integral components of the regulated variables into the control law, which leads to an increase in the order of the system. At the same time, the most commonly used PID controller, as is well known, has a number of drawbacks, including it does not provide sufficient flexibility and robustness of a closed system.

Now you can take into account that the state variables are measured using noise and additionally inject an asymptotic observer into the control loop. The matrix $\mathbf{H}$ in the observer must be chosen so as to ensure that the characteristic polynomial of the matrix $\mathbf{A} - \mathbf{HC}$ is Hurwitz, after which the transition to the equation of the speed control law of the form (13) is performed.

Equations (12)–(13) can be converted to an equivalent form to be implemented:

$$\dot{\mathbf{z}} = \mathbf{A}\mathbf{z} + \mathbf{B}\delta + \mathbf{H}(y - \mathbf{C}\mathbf{z}),$$
$$\dot{\delta} = \mathbf{K}\mathbf{z} + \mathbf{K}_0\delta + v_0 y,$$

where $\mathbf{K} = \mu(\mathbf{A} - \mathbf{HC})$, $\mathbf{K}_0 = \mu \mathbf{B}$, $v_0 = \mu \mathbf{H} + v$.

Let us turn to the regulator design to control the motion of a quadrotor on a given trajectory in space. For this aim firstly the state feedback control laws are designed for height and yaw angle separately for systems (7) and (10)

$$u_z = K_{1z} z + K_{2z} \dot{z} + K_{0z} \delta_z , \tag{16}$$

$$u_\psi = K_{1\psi} \psi + K_{2\psi} \dot{\psi} + K_{0\psi} \delta_\psi. \tag{17}$$

If the task is to provide the motion defined by the functions of time determining the orientation in space and a given height, it is similarly possible to perform the design of control laws for state variables of systems (8) and (9). However, in this case, we will assume that it is required to provide motion along a given trajectory in space at a given constant yaw angle (can also be given as a function of time with some modification of the control law), and we will perform control laws design of coordinates in the horizontal plane in the following forms:

$$u_{\theta x} = K_{\theta x1} \theta + K_{\theta x2} \dot{\theta} + K_{\theta x3} x + K_{\theta x4} \dot{x} + K_{\theta x5} \delta_{\theta x}, \tag{18}$$

$$u_{\varphi y} = K_{\varphi y1} \varphi + K_{\varphi y2} \dot{\varphi} + K_{\varphi y3} y + K_{\varphi y4} \dot{y} + K_{\varphi y5} \delta_\varphi. \tag{19}$$

the control laws (18), (19) are formed on the basis of linear systems obtained by combining Eqs. (5) and (9) and (6) and (8), respectively.

For systems (7)–(10), taking as inputs the variable states of the drives in the variables height, roll, pitch and yaw angles, the following asymptotic observers are formed:

$$
\begin{aligned}
\dot{p}_{1s} &= p_{2s} + h_{1s}(s - p_{1s}), \\
\dot{p}_{2s} &= b_s \delta_s + h_{2s}(s - p_{1s}),
\end{aligned}
\tag{20}
$$

$s = z, \psi$, variables p_{1s} – are the estimations of variables $s = z, \psi$, and p_{2s} – are estimations of their derivatives. For the coordinates in the horizontal plane for Eq. (5) and for pitch:

$$
\begin{aligned}
\dot{\hat{x}}_1 &= \hat{x}_2 + h_{1x}(x_1 - \hat{x}_1), & \dot{p}_{1s} &= p_{2s} + h_{1s}(x_1 - \hat{x}_1), \\
\dot{\hat{x}}_2 &= g p_{2s} + h_{2x}(x_1 - \hat{x}_1), & \dot{p}_{2s} &= b_s \delta_s + h_{2s}(x_1 - \hat{x}_1).
\end{aligned}
\tag{21}
$$

$s = \theta$, variables p_{1s} – are the estimations of variables $s = \theta$, and p_{2s} – are estimations of their derivatives. Similarly, the coordinates in the horizontal plane for Eq. (6) and for roll:

$$
\begin{aligned}
\dot{\hat{y}}_1 &= \hat{y}_2 + h_{1y}(y_1 - \hat{y}_1), & \dot{p}_{1s} &= p_{2s} + h_{1s}(y_1 - \hat{y}_1), \\
\dot{\hat{y}}_2 &= -g p_{2s} + h_{2y}(y_1 - \hat{y}_1), & \dot{p}_{2s} &= b_s \delta_s + h_{2s}(y_1 - \hat{y}_1),
\end{aligned}
\tag{22}
$$

$s = \varphi$, variables p_{1s} – are the estimations of variables $s = \phi$, and p_{2s} – are estimations of their derivatives.

Here $p_s = (p_{1s}\, p_{2s})^T$, $s = z, \varphi, \theta, \psi$, $\hat{x} = (\hat{x}_1\, \hat{x}_2)^T$ и $\hat{y} = (\hat{y}_1\, \hat{y}_2)^T$, and $\hat{x}_1$ – is the estimation of variable x, $\hat{x}_2$ – is the estimation of its derivative, $\hat{y}_1$ – is the estimation of variable y, $\hat{y}_2$ – is the estimation of its derivative, $b_\theta = \frac{2LK}{J_\theta}$ $b_z = \frac{4K}{M}$ $b_\varphi = \frac{2LK}{J_\varphi}$ $b_\psi = \frac{4K\rho}{J_\psi}$. The final choice of coefficients in the observers $h_{1j}, h_{2j}, j = z, \varphi, \theta, \psi, x, y$, as well as other non-fixed coefficients in Eqs. (16)–(22), can be carried out in the process of numerical experiments with a nonlinear closed system with all the limitations and must provide asymptotic stability for the closed-loop system (5)–(10), (16)–(22).

Each of the control laws (16)–(19) is firstly represented in the form (15), for each system we proceed to the form (13). For example, for a regulated longitudinal coordinate, we first obtain the control law in the form:

$$
u_{\theta x} = \frac{1}{g} K_{\theta x1} \ddot{x} + K_{\theta x2} \dot{\theta} + K_{\theta x3} x + K_{\theta x4} \dot{x} + \frac{1}{a_\theta} K_{\theta x5} \ddot{\theta},
$$

and then, substituting in above relation instead of the derivatives themselves, their estimations coming from observers, we turn to the control in the following form:

$$
u_{\theta x} = \frac{1}{g} K_{\theta x1} \dot{\hat{x}}_2 + K_{\theta x2} \dot{p}_{10} + K_{\theta x3} x + K_{\theta x4} \dot{\hat{x}}_1 + \frac{1}{a_\theta} K_{\theta x5} \dot{p}_{20}.
\tag{23}
$$

Considering the control law (23) together with the observer (21) to estimate the longitudinal coordinate x, roll angle θ and their derivatives $\dot{x}$ and $\dot{\theta}$, we obtain an LTI system with input x and output $u_{\theta x}$, that can be set using its transfer function $K(p)$:

$$u_{\theta x} = K(p)x , \quad p = \frac{d}{dt}. \tag{24}$$

Closed-loop system (5), (9), (24) is asymptotically stable and, moreover, by construction, astatism is achieved in it for regulated variable x. The equation for the error in x for closed-loop system takes the form:

$$(E - W_{u_{\theta x}\theta x}(p)K(p))x = 0,$$

where $W_{u_{\theta x}\theta x}(p)$ – is the transfer function of system from input $u_{\theta x}$ to regulated output x:

$$x = W_{u_{\theta x}\theta x}(p)u_{\theta x}, \quad W_{u_{\theta x}\theta x}(p) = \mathbf{C}_{\theta x}(pE - \mathbf{A}_{\theta x})^{-1}\mathbf{B}_{\theta x}, \quad p = \frac{d}{dt}.$$

where $\mathbf{A}_{\theta x} = \begin{pmatrix} \mathbf{A}_\theta & \mathbf{0}_{2x2} & \mathbf{B}_\theta \\ \mathbf{B}_{x0} & \mathbf{A}_x & \mathbf{0}_{2x1} \\ \mathbf{0}_{1x2} & \mathbf{0}_{1x2} & \omega \end{pmatrix}$, $\mathbf{B}_{\theta x} = \begin{pmatrix} \mathbf{0}_{4x1} \\ \omega \end{pmatrix}$, $\mathbf{C}_{\theta x} = (0 \ \ 0 \ \ 1 \ \ 0 \ \ 0)$,

$\mathbf{A}_\theta = \mathbf{A}_x = \begin{pmatrix} 0 & 1 \\ 0 & 0 \end{pmatrix}$, $\mathbf{B}_\theta = \begin{pmatrix} 0 \\ b_\theta \end{pmatrix}$, $\mathbf{B}_x = \begin{pmatrix} 0 \\ g \end{pmatrix}$, $\mathbf{B}_{x0} = (\mathbf{B}_x \ \ \mathbf{0}_{2x1})$.

Now we suppose that it is required to ensure the motion of the quadrotor along the trajectory defined by the functions of time with respect to regulated variables. This requirement can be expressed by the following expressions:

$$\begin{aligned} e_x &= x - x_z(t) \underset{t\to\infty}{\to} 0, \\ e_y &= y - y_z(t) \underset{t\to\infty}{\to} 0, \\ e_z &= z - z_z(t) \underset{t\to\infty}{\to} 0, \\ e_\psi &= \psi - \psi_z(t) \underset{t\to\infty}{\to} 0, \end{aligned} \tag{25}$$

where $x_z(t)$, $y_z(t)$, $z_z(t)$ and $\psi_z(t)$ – are a sufficient number of times continuously differentiable functions defining the desired trajectory with respect to the corresponding variables, $e_x(t)$, $e_y(t)$, $e_z(t)$ и $e_\psi(t)$ – errors, characterizing the deviation of monitored variables from a given trajectory at the current time t. In fact, in addition to relations (25), it is required that the error functions fall into a given neighborhood of zero in a certain finite time, while the transients in the given motion modes satisfy the necessary requirements. Let us construct a new regulator with regulated variable x in the following form:

$$u_{\theta x} = K(p)(x - x_z(t)) + W^{-1}_{u_{\theta x}\theta x}(p)x_z(t), \tag{26}$$

where $W^{-1}_{u_{\theta x}\theta x}(p)x_z(t)$ – is an additional program component control. The equation in a closed-loop system with respect to the error e_x with such control will take the form:

$$(E - W_{u_{\theta x}\theta x}(p)K(p))e_x = 0,$$

that is, for the error e_x the corresponding condition in (25) is fulfilled, moreover, for this variable e_x the astatism is provided.

By performing similar constructions for all noted variables, it is possible to obtain four separate laws of motion control on the trajectory for each regulated variable, thereby ensuring the fulfillment of conditions (25). In this case, the control laws the change in the height and angle of the course will have a slightly simpler form, since for their construction models of lower order (7) and (10) will be used.

4 Numerical Results

To implement the proposed trajectory-control scheme, we will form the basic control laws (15)–(18) based on the solution of the linear quadratic controller (LQR) synthesis problem of the following form:

$$J = J(\mathbf{K}_j) = \int\limits_0^\infty \left(\mathbf{x}^T\mathbf{Q}_j\mathbf{x} + u^T R_j u\right) dt \to \min_{\mathbf{K}_j \in \Omega}.$$

where Ω – is an area of asymptotic stability of the corresponding closed system in the parameter space, $j = z, \varphi y, \theta x, \psi$. Matrix $\mathbf{Q}_j$ is a diagonal, it is each time is chosen with non-negative weights on the diagonal, and, together with the corresponding scalar positive value R_j, defines a compromise between stabilization accuracy and intensity of control law for each variable, making it possible to achieve acceptable performance under the given constraints on the control variables.

The numerical values of the parameters of the basic regulators for all the studied variables, obtained by numerical simulation, are presented below:

$$\mathbf{Q}_z = \begin{bmatrix} 14\cdot10^6 & 0 & 0 \\ 0 & 10.5\cdot10^6 & 0 \\ 0 & 0 & 0 \end{bmatrix}, \; R_z = 8\cdot10^7$$

$$\mathbf{Q}_\psi = \begin{bmatrix} 1.0009 & 0 & 0 \\ 0 & 20 & 0 \\ 0 & 0 & 10000 \end{bmatrix}, \; R_\psi = 10^5$$

$$\mathbf{Q}_{\theta x} = \mathbf{Q}_{\varphi y} = \begin{bmatrix} 1.5 & 0 & 0 & 0 & 0 \\ 0 & 10 & 0 & 0 & 0 \\ 0 & 0 & 1 & 0 & 0 \\ 0 & 0 & 0 & 10 & 0 \\ 0 & 0 & 0 & 0 & 1 \end{bmatrix}, \; R_{\varphi y} = R_{\theta x} = 10^7$$

In Figs. 2 and 3 it is shown the dynamic processes in variables z and y, x. The illustrations are made for a movement characterized by the presence of constant perturbations at the entrance for the desired trajectory $x_z(t) = \sin\left(\frac{\pi}{15}\right)$, $y_z(t) = \sin\left(\frac{\pi}{15}\right)$, $z_z(t) = \sin\left(\frac{\pi}{10}\right)$ at the desired angle $\psi_z(t) = 13°$. Transient processes in deviations of the yaw, roll and pitch are shown in Fig. 4.

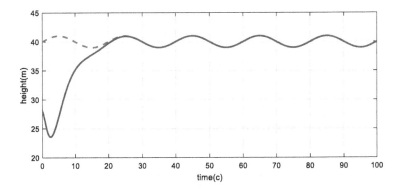

Fig. 2. Transient process of height changing.

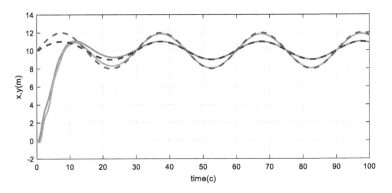

Fig. 3. Transients change the coordinates in the horizontal plane.

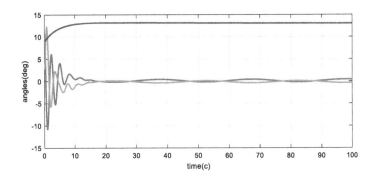

Fig. 4. Transient changes of roll, yaw and pitch.

Analysis of the graphs shows that the developed control laws ensure the movement of the regulated variables along the desired trajectory given by the time functions, while demonstrating a fairly good speed. At the same time, in regulated variables, the processes are endowed with the property of astatism, that is, in the presence of constant perturbations, the actual motion approaches the given one with a very small error.

For comparison in Fig. 5 it is shown the dynamic processes for variables y, x with the control laws for these variables, but in form that not provides the astatism for regulated variables. As it can be seen, in this case, the actual motion deviates strongly enough from the given one.

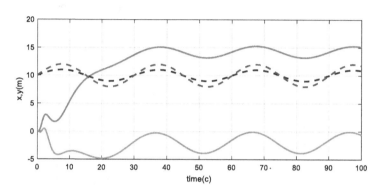

Fig. 5. Transients change the coordinates in the horizontal plane without astatism.

Acknowledgments. This work is supported by the Russian Foundation for Basic Research under grant 17-07-00361 A.

References

1. Besnard, L., Shtessel, Y.B., Landrum, B.: Control of a quadrotor vehicle using sliding mode disturbance observer. In: Proceedings of the 2007 American Control Conference, New York, USA, 11–13 July 2007, pp. 5230–5235 (2007). https://doi.org/10.1109/acc.2007.4282421
2. Liu, C., Pan, J., Chang, Y.: PID and LQR trajectory tracking control for an unmanned quadrotor helicopter: experimental studies. In: Proceedings of the 35th Chinese Control Conference (CCC), Chengdu, China, 27–29 July 2016, pp. 10845–10850 (2016). https://doi.org/10.1109/chicc.2016.7555074
3. Hernandez-Martinez, E.G., Fernandez-Anaya, G., Ferreira, E.D., Flores-Godoy, J.J., Lopez-Gonzalez, A.: Trajectory tracking of a quadrocopter UAV with optimal translation control. IFAC-ParersOnline **48**(19), 226–231 (2015). https://doi.org/10.1016/j.ifacol.2015.12.038
4. Lepikhin, T.A.: The analysis of Quadrocopter and Hexacopter dynamics. In: AIP Conference Proceedings, vol. 1738, p. 160005 (2016). https://doi.org/10.1063/1.4951938

5. Zhabko, N.A., Lepikhin, T.A.: Astatic controller synthesis for quadrocopter motion control. In: Sukhomlin, V., Zubareva, E., Sneps-Sneppe, M. (eds.) Proceedings of the 2nd International Scientific Conference "Convergent Cognitive Information Technologies" (Convergent'2017), Moscow, Russia, 24–26 November 2017. CEUR Workshop Proceedings, vol. 2064, pp. 255–263 (2017). http://ceur-ws.org/Vol-2064/paper30.pdf. Accessed 21 June 2018. (in Russian)

6. Veremey, E.I., Sotnikova, M.V., Eremeev, V.V., Korovkin, M.V.: Modal parametric optimization of control laws with special structure. In: Proceedings of the 14 International Conference on Control, Automation and Systems (ICCAS 2014), Korea, 22–25 October 2014, pp. 1278–1283 (2014). https://doi.org/10.1109/iccas.2014.6987753

7. Veremey, E.I., Korovkin, M.V., Sotnikova, M.V.: Ships' steering in accurate regime using autopilots with special structure of control law. IFAC-PapersOnline **48**(16), 7–12 (2015). https://doi.org/10.1016/j.ifacol.2015.10.250

8. Veremey, E.I.: Dynamical correction of control laws for marine ship's accurate steering. J. Mar. Sci. Appl. **13**(2), 127–133 (2014). https://doi.org/10.1007/s11804-014-1250-1

Dynamics Characteristics Optimization for the UAV Ensemble of Motions

Sergey Zavadskiy$^{(\boxtimes)}$ and Timur Lepikhin

Saint-Petersburg State University, University Av. 35, Peterhof,
198504 Saint Petersburg, Russia
{s.zavadsky, t.lepihin}@spbu.ru

Abstract. The tasks of multicopters control are considered as an area for application of modern theoretical approaches to the control system design. The paper considers the multicopter control system, which includes a subsystem of equilibrium stabilization and an executive subsystem. The executive system is responsible for changing the position of the apparatus in space according to the commands of the operator. The program list of control commands and a wide range of perturbations affecting the multicopter are forming a whole ensemble of movements of the UAV. The equations of the control system expand the vector of states of the multicopter. The coefficients in the control regulator are adjusted to provide the desired dynamics characteristics of the ensemble of movements. The novelty of this approach is that the problem of simultaneous optimization of the executive and stabilizing subsystems has been presented. Ensemble of program and perturbed motions of the multicopter is described by guarantee upper estimations. The results of practical calculations for a particular UAV are presented. The simulation demonstrates the ensemble dynamics before and after optimization. Transient diagrams show an optimized response to the operator's control commands. The analytical part of the work was carried out for a multicopter with an arbitrary even number of screws more than three.

Keywords: UAV · Optimal control · Control system design · Multicopter · Dynamics · Stabilization

1 Introduction

Recently, unmanned aerial vehicles of multicopter type have become widespread. The most common multicopters are those with four screws. But also multicopters with a different number of screws arranged in pairs symmetrically are quite popular [1]. Multicopter necessarily equipped with modern electronics responsible for management processes [2]. To create a complete hardware or software implementation, it is necessary to equip the controller with a control program [3]. The control laws for such programs must be well calculated and meet the high requirements for the stability of the device, the accuracy of command execution and the saving of energy costs [4, 5]. The stabilization subsystem should work out a wide range of random perturbations [6]. At the same time, for the executive subsystem there is a voluminous list of program instructions [7, 8]. Therefore, the development of optimization approaches to the

© Springer Nature Switzerland AG 2020
V. Sukhomlin and E. Zubareva (Eds.): Convergent 2018, CCIS 1140, pp. 175–186, 2020.
https://doi.org/10.1007/978-3-030-37436-5_16

optimization of the ensemble of transients of the control object is actual. Modern optimal control system synthesis is based on wide range of methods: PID control [9, 10], MPC predictive methods [11, 12], LQG synthesis [4, 13], nonlinear control [14], H2-optimal synthesis [15, 16] and control of guaranteed estimation [17, 18]. But concurrent optimization of program and perturbed ensemble of motions is not enough considered.

The aim of the work is simultaneous optimization of the program and disturbed motions of the multicopter.

2 Mathematical Model of UAV

Consider the principles and equations of motion of the multicopter [19]. The propeller motors rotate at a variable speed and create the necessary traction and torque. Motors are located in pairs in opposition to each other and symmetrically with respect to the center of mass. In each pair, one motor has an even number $i = 2, 4, .., m$, and the opposite one has an odd number $j = 1, 3, .., m - 1$, where m – an even number of multicopter screws. Let us list the phase variables describing the position and state of the aircraft in space. Coordinates in space are x, y, z m, from the origin frame of reference; speed of the device along the axes of the reference frame, respectively u, v, w m/sec; angles of Euler tilt of the apparatus relative to the reference frame axes: ψ – a yaw angle, rad., θ – a pitch angle, rad., φ – a roll angle, rad; angular velocity of rotation p, q, r rad/sec. These values correspond to the rate of change of the Euler angles. The device moves along any of these phase coordinates as a result of changes in the angular rotational speeds of the screws Ω_i, $i = 1, .., m$.

The thrust produced by the motor is presented in form:

$$F_i = b_i \Omega_i^2,$$

where b_i – a given constant coefficient of traction. The total thrust module is calculated as:

$$T = \sum_{i=1..m} b_i \Omega_i^2. \tag{1}$$

For each UAV, the diagonal components I_x, I_y, I_z, kg • m^2, the inertia tensor $J = \begin{pmatrix} I_x & 0 & 0 \\ 0 & I_y & 0 \\ 0 & 0 & I_z \end{pmatrix}$ are identified. They are treated as given constants. The problems of multicopter model identification are considered in [19–21]. The rotational speed of the screws is identified as the LTI of the subsystem in the form:

$$\dot{\Omega}_i = -\mu_i \Omega_i + \eta_i U_i, \quad i = \overline{1, m}, \tag{2}$$

where U_i is the control voltage, supplied to the i -th motor; μ_i, η_i – constants identified for a specific motor. Additional specified constant parameters for a multicopter are l –

the beam frame size; this is the distance between the motors and the center of mass; d – the aerodynamic drag coefficient; and M is the mass of the apparatus. Multicopter hardware sensors allow you to measure and report the position of the object and altitude to the control system, accelerometers measure accelerations along the axes, a 6-axis gyro produces Euler angles and angular rotation speeds. Thus, the composition of observations contains 12 values.

Let us consider the equations of motion for the UAV:

$$\begin{cases} \dot{x} = u, \\ \dot{y} = v, \\ \dot{z} = w, \end{cases} \tag{3}$$

$$\begin{cases} \dot{\phi} = p, \\ \dot{\theta} = q, \\ \dot{\psi} = r, \end{cases} \tag{4}$$

$$\begin{cases} \dot{p} = \frac{lb}{I_x} \left(\sum_{i=2,4,..,m} \Omega_i^2 - \sum_{j=1,3,..,m-1} \Omega_j^2 \right) - qr \frac{(I_x - I_y)}{I_x}, \\ \dot{q} = \frac{lb}{I_y} \left(\sum_{i=2,4,..,m} \Omega_i^2 - \sum_{j=1,3,..,m-1} \Omega_j^2 \right) - pr \frac{(I_x - I_z)}{I_y}, \\ \dot{r} = \frac{d}{I_z} \left(\sum_{i=1,..,m} \Omega_i^2 \right), \end{cases} \tag{5}$$

$$\begin{cases} \dot{u} = rv - qw - g\sin(\theta), \\ \dot{v} = pw - ru + g\cos(\theta)\sin(\varphi), \\ \dot{w} = qu - pv + g\cos(\theta)\cos(\phi) - \frac{b}{M} \left(\sum_{i=1..m} \Omega_i^2 \right), \end{cases} \tag{6}$$

where g is gravitational constant.

We introduce the vector $f(t)$ of external perturbations affecting the object. Then we get the dynamic system of equations in the following form:

$$\begin{aligned} \dot{X} &= F(X, U_1, .., U_m) + f(t), \\ Y &= C_{obj}X, \end{aligned} \tag{7}$$

where $X = [xyz\phi\psi\theta wrqpuv \, \Omega_1..\Omega_m]^T \in R^n$ – state space vector for considering control object, $n = 12 + m$ – system dimension, $f(t) \in R^n$ – vector of external disturbances, $Y = [xyz\phi\psi\theta wrqpuv]^T \in R^{12}$ - observe vector, that is provided by structure and sensors of UAV, matrix of observations are shown below:

$$C_{obj} = \begin{pmatrix} 1 & \cdots & 0 \\ 0 & \ddots & 0 & O_{[12 \times m]} \\ 0 & \cdots & 1 \end{pmatrix},$$

where $O_{[12 \times m]}$ – zero block with 12 rows and m columns.

2.1   The Problem of Stabilization the External Disturbances

The equations of motion can be linearized in relative to the equilibrium position, in which the apparatus is immobile in the air. This position corresponds to the phase state space point

$$X_{eq} = [x = 0, y = 0, z = 0, \phi = 0, \psi = 0, \theta = 0, w = 0, r = 0, q = 0, p = 0, u = 0,$$
$$v = 0, \ \Omega_{01}, .., \Omega_{0m}]^*,$$

$$(8)$$

where $\Omega_{01}, \ldots, \Omega_{0m}$ – initial velocities for the motors providing immobility in the air. LTI system in the deviation form is presented by formula:

$$\dot{X} = A_{obj}X + B_{obj}U + f(t),$$
$$X(0) = X_0,$$
$$Y = C_{obj}X,$$

$$(9)$$

where X_0 – deviation from equilibrium position X_{eq} at initial time moment, A_{obj} – the Jacobian of the system (9) calculated at the point X_{eq}:

$$A_{obj} = \begin{pmatrix} \frac{\partial F_1(X_{eq})}{\partial X_1} & \cdots & \frac{\partial F_1(X_{eq})}{\partial X_n} \\ \vdots & & \vdots \\ \frac{\partial F_n(X_{eq})}{\partial X_1} & \cdots & \frac{\partial F_n(X_{eq})}{\partial X_n} \end{pmatrix}, \ B_{obj} = \begin{pmatrix} O_{[12 \times m]} \\ \eta_1 & \cdots & 0 \\ 0 & \ddots & 0 \\ 0 & \cdots & \eta_m \end{pmatrix}.$$

$$(10)$$

Because in practice, multicopters are unstable objects, the matrix A_{obj} has positive eigenvalues, and the system needs to be stabilized. For considering multicopters with number of motors $m \geq 4$, the system (10) is controllable, and pair (A_{obj}, C_{obj}) is observable. The system's disturbances can be stabilized with control law in the form joining observer and regulator [4, 22]:

$$\dot{Z} = A_{cntr}Z + B_{cntr}Y,$$
$$U = C_{cntr}Z,$$

$$(11)$$

where $Z \in X^r$ the state vector of regulator, r – the dimension of regulator, U – the vector of control voltage, $A_{cntr}, B_{cntr}, C_{cntr}$ – constant regulator matrices that need to be defined. The formulation of the control law coefficients optimization problem does not depend on the dimension r. Such approach makes possible to connect object of high dimension with the regulator of decreased dimension, what is necessary for extremely complex real-time electro-physical devices of a high dimension, for example [23, 24]. A good approximation for a multicopter dynamics can also have high dimension.

2.2   Programmable Motion

The program control commands from the operator panel can be entered in the controller equations as an additional constant error signal $Y_{prog} \in R^{12}$ in the following form:

$$\dot{Z} = A_{cntr}Z + B_{cntr}(Y - Y_{prog}),$$
$$U = C_{cntr}Z. \tag{12}$$

The vector Y_{prog} components determine which desired values are required for the observed values of the multicopter. An example, a given constant positive pitch angle will cause continuous movement of the device forward with a certain speed, similarly for a roll angle – movement to the side. To set the roll angle as 1 rad., we should specify $Y_{prog} = [0\,0\,0\,1\,0\,0\,0\,0\,0\,0\,0\,0]^T$. Other parameters and their values are set similarly.

2.3   Optimization of Movement Ensemble and Control System Design

The Linear system with feedback has the following view:

$$\begin{pmatrix} \dot{X} \\ \dot{Z} \end{pmatrix} = \begin{pmatrix} A_{obj}X + B_{obj}C_{cntr}Z \\ B_{cntr}C_{obj}X + A_{cntr}Z \end{pmatrix} + \begin{pmatrix} f(t) \\ -B_{cntr}Y_{prog} \end{pmatrix}, \tag{13}$$

$$X(0) = X_0,$$
$$Z(0) = O_{[r \times 1]}, \tag{14}$$

$$Y = C_{obj}X,$$
$$U = C_{cntr}Z. \tag{15}$$

At practice we have a set of initial values of X_0, set of program signals Y_{prog} and arbitrary external disturbances $f(t)$. The set of disturbances is $\Phi = \{X_0, Y_{prog}, f(t)\}$.

This set corresponds to an ensemble of motions for the system in deviations (13) in form: $\{X(t) = X(t, X_0, Y_{prog}, f(t))\}$ [25].

It is possible to formulate upper estimation for observable parameters Y and minimize them. We use a function $num(x)$ that returns a number of phase component x in the state space vector X.

Statement: For each $\{X_0, Y_{prog}, f(t)\}$ that is provided by constraint

$$X_0^* G_1 X_0 + \begin{bmatrix} f(t) \\ Y_{prog} \end{bmatrix}^* G_2 \begin{bmatrix} f(t)^* & Y_{prog}^* \end{bmatrix}^* \leq 1, \tag{16}$$

where G_1, G_2 are symmetric constant weight matrices with non-negative definite values, then for all trajectories of phase variable $x(t)$ from vector $X(t, X_0, Y_{prog}, f(t))$ the following expression is satisfied:

$$\left| x(t, X_0, Y_{prog}, f(t)) \right| < = S_x(t), \tag{17}$$

where $S_x(t) = \sqrt{D(t)[num(x), num(x)]}$, where $D(t)$ – is a non-negative solution of equation:

$$\dot{D} = PD + DP^* + \begin{bmatrix} E_{[n \times n]} \\ -B^*_{cntr} \end{bmatrix}^* G_2 \left[E_{[n \times n]} - B^*_{cntr} \right]^*, \quad D(0) = G_1, \qquad (18)$$

In the book [25] the various statements are considered and proofs are given. In the presented statement, the vector of external influences is extended by the vector of program signals Y_{prog}. Constant matrices G_1, G_2, in the statement, are set by the researcher in such a way as to determine the desired set of signals:

$$\Phi = \Phi(G_1, G_2) \supset \{X_0, Y_{prog}, f(t)\}.$$

It follows from the statement that the trajectories of the remaining components of the observations and control voltages can be limited in the same way:

For each $X_0, Y_{prog}, f(t) \in \Phi(G_1, G_2)$, with the following conditions $|x(t)| < = S_x(t)$, $|y(t)| < = S_y(t)$, $|z(t)| < = S_z(t)$, ..., $|U_1(t)| < = S_{U_1}(t)$, ..., $|U_m(t)| < = S_{U_m}(t)$, we have an expression: $S_{U_i}(t) = \sqrt{(C_{cntr}D(t)C^*_{cntr})}\,[i, i]$.

We introduce a functional that estimates the quality of the dynamics of an ensemble of motions, and set the task of minimizing this:

$$I = \int_0^T k_1 S_x(t) + k_2 S_y(t) + \ldots + k_{12+m} S_{U_m}(t)\, dt \;\rightarrow\; \min, \qquad (19)$$

where $k_1, k_2, .., k_{12+m}$ − non-negative weighting coefficients estimating the contribution of observed values to control accuracy and the contribution of control voltages to energy costs, $[0, T]$ − a modeling period. Such a functional assesses the quality of transients and energy costs.

Optimization of the functional is possible in various ways: searching for a global minimum, gradient methods, stochastic search, machine learning methods, etc.

3   Example of Modeling in MATLAB

Practical optimization was carried out for quadrocopter. The results of the comparison are given for the original controller [4] and optimized. The device has the following parameter values:

$m = 4$, $\Omega_{01} \cong \ldots \cong \Omega_{0m} = 463.7$ rad/sec, $l = 27.5$ cm,
$b = 1.5099 \cdot 10^{-5}$ kg $\cdot$ m, $M = 1.3333$ kg, $d = 4,399 \cdot 10^{-7}$ kg $\cdot$ m^2 sec^{-1},
$I_x = 0.0091$ kg $\cdot$ m^2, $I_x = 0.0091$ kg $\cdot$ m^2, $I_x = 0.0149$ kg $\cdot$ m^2.

The set of perturbations $\Phi(G_1, G_2)$ is the same for the initial and optimized control and its matrix are given by diagonal elements. For G_1 the diagonal elements are (0 0 0.049 0.029 0.015 0.015 0 0 0 0 0 0 0 0 0 0 0 0 0). For G_2 the diagonal elements are equal to (0.01 0.01 0.01 0.01 0.01 0.01 0.01 0.01 0.01 0.01 0.01 0.01 0.01 0.01 0.01 0.01 0.01 0.01 0.01 10 10 10 10 10 10 10 10 10 10 10 10). In this practical experiment, emphasis is placed on achieving the desired Euler angles, angular velocities, and the altitude of the quadrocopter, while moving the copter over the site is permissible arbitrarily far. Therefore the optimizing estimations are chosen as $S_z(t)$, $S_\varphi(t)$, $S_\theta(t)$, $S_\psi(t)$, $S_p(t)$, $S_q(t)$, $S_r(t)$, $S_w(t)$, and also to reduce the energy costs in the functional (19), estimates for the control voltages $S_{U_i}(t)$ with $i = \overline{1,4}$ are taken into account. The graphs show the dynamics of ensembles of Quadrocopter movements with a constant set of perturbations $\Phi(G_1, G_2)$ with initial control and optimized (Figs. 1 and 2).

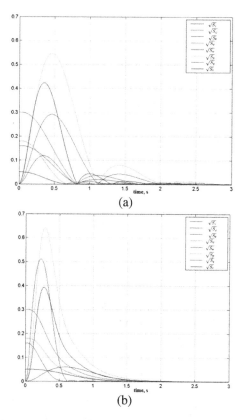

(a)

(b)

Fig. 1. Estimates of the observed values of the ensemble of motions of the multicopter with (a) the initial regulator, (b) the optimized regulator.

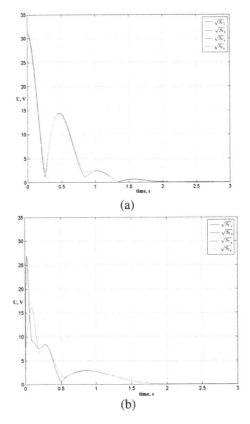

Fig. 2. Estimates of the control voltages of the four motors for the whole ensemble of the multicopter with (a) the initial regulator, (b) the optimized regulator.

Table 1. The values of the integral quality criterion with the initial and optimized control law.

Regulator	Value	Accuracy	Energy spent
Initial	679.3334	0.0493	679.2847
Optimized	204.8343	0.0334	204.8009

Table 1 contains the numerical value of the functional, as well as the values of control accuracy and energy costs. For an optimized regulator, there is an improvement in the dynamics of transient processes, as well as an increase in the accuracy of control while reducing energy costs. Practical tests have shown that this was made possible by reducing overshoot and vibrational effects in transient processes. Since the optimization of both program and disturbed motions was simultaneously carried out, it is also interesting to simulate the response of a quadrocopter to control commands. As an example, the commands to achieve a specified speed in the vertical direction w_{prog}, to achieve a specified value at the Euler angles ψ_{prog}, θ_{prog}, φ_{prog}.

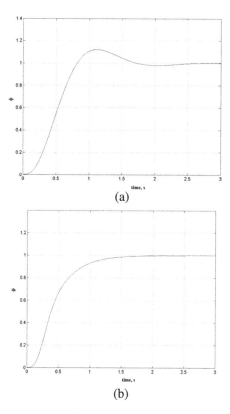

Fig. 3. Response to the programmed step input of the roll angle $\varphi_{prog} = 1$, with (a) initial control law, (b) optimized control law.

These commands are interesting in that they set the desired speed of the object along three directions of space. Most often, in practice, the operator from the remote panel sets the desired speed by the deviation of the joystick in each direction. Commands can be modeled as system responses to step signal Y_{prog}. To simulate the angle of roll, stepwise action $Y_{prog} = [0\,0\,0\,1\,0\,0\,0\,0\,0\,0\,0\,0]^T$ is used (Fig. 3).

To model the rate of altitude change, the stepwise action has the form $y_{prog} = [0\,0\,0\,0\,0\,0\,1\,0\,0\,0\,0\,0]^T$ (Fig. 4).

The response graphs show a more efficient achievement of the program mode while maintaining the speed of execution while reducing overshoot. This is a positive result of simultaneous optimization of program and perturbed movements.

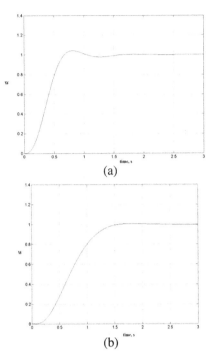

Fig. 4. The response to the programmed step input of the magnitude of the vertical velocity w, with $w_{prog} = 1$m/sec, (a) the initial control, (b) the optimized control.

4   Conclusion

An approach is proposed for modeling, comparing and optimizing the ensemble of program and disturbed motions of the multicopter. The equations of dynamics (3)–(6) are considered in general for a multicopter with four or more even number of screws, which are arranged in pairs symmetrically. Equation of the control and the stabilization law (11)–(12) expands the state space vector of the object (9). The dimension of the regulator is not constrained, which allows you to select the regulator, depending on the hardware controller's processor power. The ensemble of movements (17)–(18) of the apparatus is modeled as a response of the system to a set (16) containing perturbations and program signals. The estimates (17) characterize the dynamics of the whole ensemble, and the functional (19) estimates the accuracy of control and the energy costs for the whole ensemble. Practical calculations for a quadrocopter with the specified parameters show a qualitative and quantitative improvement in the dynamics of transient processes with a simultaneous decrease in energy costs.

References

1. Holda, C., Ghalamchi, B., Mueller, M.W.: Tilting multicopter rotors for increased power efficiency and yaw authority. In: 2018 International Conference on Unmanned Aircraft Systems, ICUAS 2018, vol. 8453359, pp. 143–148 (2018) https://doi.org/10.1109/icuas.2018.8453359

2. Silano, G., Aucone, E., Iannelli, L.: CrazyS: a software-in-the-loop platform for the Crazyflie 2.0 nano-quadcopter. In: MED 2018 - 26th Mediterranean Conference on Control and Automation, vol. 8442759, pp. 352-357 (2018) https://doi.org/10.1109/med.2018.8442759

3. Mhdawi, A.K.A., Al-Raweshidy, H.: SDQ-6WI: software defined quadcopter-six wheeled IoT sensor architecture for future wind turbine placement. IEEE Access **6**, 53426–53437 (2018). https://doi.org/10.1109/ACCESS.2018.2871271

4. Zavadskiy, S., Sharovatova, D.: Improvement of quadrocopter command performance system. In: Stability and Control Processes in Memory of V.I. Zubov (SCP), pp. 609–610 (2015) https://doi.org/10.1109/scp.2015.7342220

5. Lepikhin, T.A.: The analysis of Quadrocopter and Hexacopter dynamics. In: AIP Conference Proceedings, vol. 1738, p. 160005 (2016). https://doi.org/10.1063/1.4951938

6. Betancourt-Vera, J., Castillo, P., Lozano, R., Vidolov, B.: Robust control scheme for trajectory generation and tracking for quadcopters vehicles: Experimental results. In: 2018 International Conference on Unmanned Aircraft Systems, ICUAS 2018, vol. 8453482, pp. 1118–1124 (2018). https://doi.org/10.1109/icuas.2018.8453482

7. Cantieri, A.R., et al.: A quadcopter and mobile robot cooperative task using visual tags based on augmented reality ROS package. Stud. Comput. Intell. **778**, 185–208 (2018). https://doi.org/10.1007/978-3-319-91590-6_6

8. Hatem, I., Jamal, M., Murhij, Y., Ali, Z.: Low-cost quadcopter indoor positioning system based on image processing and neural networks. Mech. Mach. Sci. **58**, 243–257 (2018). https://doi.org/10.1007/978-3-319-89911-4_18

9. Sanders, B., Vincenzi, D., Holley, S., Shen, Y.: Traditional vs gesture based UAV control. In: Advances in Human Factors in Robots and Unmanned Systems. AHFE 2018. Advances in Intelligent Systems and Computing, vol. 784, pp. 15–23 (2018) https://doi.org/10.1007/978-3-319-94346-6_2

10. Thien, R.T.Y., Kim, Y.: Decentralized formation flight via PID and integral sliding mode control. Aerosp. Sci. Technol. **81**, 322–332 (2018). https://doi.org/10.1016/j.ast.2018.08.011

11. Mendoza-Soto, J.L., Alvarez-Icaza, L., Rodríguez-Cortés, H.: Constrained generalized predictive control for obstacle avoidance in a quadcopter. Robotica **36**(9), 1363–1385 (2018). https://doi.org/10.1017/S026357471800036X

12. Dubay, S., Pan, Y.-J.: Distributed MPC based collision avoidance approach for consensus of multiple quadcopters. In: IEEE International Conference on Control and Automation, ICCA, vol. 8444273, pp. 155–160 (2018). https://doi.org/10.1109/ICCA.2018.8444273

13. Masse, C., Gougeon, O., Nguyen, D.-T., Saussie, D.: Modeling and control of a quadcopter flying in a wind field: a comparison between LQR and structured ∞ control techniques. In: 2018 International Conference on Unmanned Aircraft Systems, ICUAS 2018, vol. 8453402, pp. 1408–1417 (2018) https://doi.org/10.1109/icuas.2018.8453402

14. Joukhadar, A., AlChehabi, M., Stöger, C., Müller, A.: Trajectory tracking control of a quadcopter UAV using nonlinear control. In: Rizk, R., Awad, M. (eds.) Mechanism, Machine, Robotics and Mechatronics Sciences. MMS, vol. 58, pp. 271–285. Springer, Cham (2019). https://doi.org/10.1007/978-3-319-89911-4_20

15. Veremey, E., Knyazkin, Y.: Siso problems of h2-optimal synthesis with allocation of control actions. WSEAS Trans. Syst. Control **12**, 193–200 (2017)

16. Zhabko, N.A., Lepikhin, T.A.: Astatic controller synthesis for quadcopter motion control [in Russian]. In: Sukhomlin, V., Zubareva, E., Sneps-Sneppe, M. (eds.) Proceedings of the 2nd International Scientific Conference "Convergent Cognitive Information Technologies" (Convergent 2017), Moscow, Russia, 24–26 November 2017. CEUR Workshop Proceedings, vol. 2064, pp. 255-263 (2017). http://ceur-ws.org/Vol-2064/paper30.pdf. Accessed 21 Jun 2018

17. Ananyev, B.: About control of guaranteed estimation. Cybern. Phys. 7(1), 18–25 (2018)

18. Talagaev, Y.: State estimation, robust properties and stabilization of positive linear systems with superstability constraints. Cybern. Phys. 6(1), 32–39 (2017)

19. Pairan, M.F., Shamsudin, S.S.: System identification of an unmanned quadcopter system using MRAN neural. In: IOP Conference Series: Materials Science and Engineering, vol. 270, no. 1, p. 012019 (2017). https://doi.org/10.1088/1757-899X/270/1/012019

20. Rastgoftar, H., Atkins, E.M.: Continuum deformation of a multiple quadcopter payload delivery team without inter-agent communication. In: 2018 International Conference on Unmanned Aircraft Systems, ICUAS 2018, vol. 8453433, pp. 539–548 (2018). https://doi.org/10.1109/icuas.2018.8453433

21. Tikhonov, N.O., Lepikhin, T.A., Zhabko, N.A.: Mathematical modelling of tricopter [in Russian]. In: Sukhomlin, V., Zubareva, E., Sneps-Sneppe, M. (eds.) Proceedings of the 2nd International Scientific Conference "Convergent Cognitive Information Technologies" (Convergent 2017), Moscow, Russia, 24–26 November 2017. CEUR Workshop Proceedings, vol. 2064, pp. 335-340 (2017) http://ceur-ws.org/Vol-2064/paper39.pdf. Accessed 21 Jun 2018

22. Boiko, I., Chehadeh, M.: Sliding mode differentiator/observer for quadcopter velocity estimation through sensor fusion. Int. J. Control 91(9), 2113–2120 (2018). https://doi.org/10.1080/00207179.2017.1421775

23. Zavadskiy, S.V.: Concurrent optimization of plasma shape and vertical position controllers for ITER tokamak. In: 20th International Workshop on Beam Dynamics and Optimization (BDO), pp. 196–197 (2014). https://doi.org/10.1109/bdo.2014.6890102

24. Ovsyannikov, D.A., Zavadskiy, S.V.: Optimization approach to the synthesis of plasma stabilization system in tokamak iter. Probl. At. Sci. Technol. 116(4), 102–105 (2018)

25. Kirichenko, N.: Introduction to the Motion Stabilization Theory, Kiev (1978). [in Russian]

Application the Evolutional Modeling to the Problem of Searching the Optimal Sensors Location of Fire-Fighting System

Galina Malykhina$^{(\boxtimes)}$ ⓘ and Alena Guseva ⓘ

Peter the Great St. Petersburg Polytechnic University, Polytechnic Street 29,
195251 Saint Petersburg, Russia
fmalykhina@gmail.com, Alyona-kitty@rambler.ru

Abstract. The aim of the study is to develop an evolutionary algorithm for the optimal sensors' location in multi-sensory systems for early detection of fires in rooms. The legislative acts regulating the sphere of fire safety in Russia are given. It is indicated that there is no justification for choosing the location of fire detectors. An evolutionary algorithm for the optimal placement of sensors controlling such fire factors as temperature, concentration of carbon dioxide and visibility, depending on the density of the smoke. The article describes the process of developing an evolutionary algorithm and its application to the problem of finding the optimal location. Methods of evolutionary modeling, such as genetic methods, genetic programming, methods of particle swarm optimization and methods of "colony of ants", and their basic applications are described. The main operators of the genetic algorithm, such as reproduction, crossing and mutation, and their modifications are considered. We propose our own modification method for applying it for the current task. In the super-computer center of the Peter the Great Polytechnic University, we model fires of several types of materials: rags, gasoline, oil, diesel fuel, electric cables. The simulation results were used as data to verify the algorithm. The results of testing the algorithm on model data are presented. It shows the gain in response time of the fire extinguishing system to the occurrence of fire when the sensors are located, calculated by the genetic algorithm, in comparison with the usual uniform arrangement.

Keywords: Fire simulation · Evolutionary modeling · Genetic algorithm · Multicriteria sensors · Optimal positioning

1 Introduction

In accordance with Art. 5 [1] each protection object must have a fire safety system, which includes a fire prevention system, a fire protection system and a set of organizational and technical measures to ensure fire safety. The main purpose of the fire protection system according to Art. 52 [1] is the protection of people and property from the effects of dangerous fire factors.

To increase the speed of reaction of the fire detection system, it is necessary to arrange the available sensors to minimize the reaction time. The fire detector is an

© Springer Nature Switzerland AG 2020
V. Sukhomlin and E. Zubareva (Eds.): Convergent 2018, CCIS 1140, pp. 187–199, 2020.
https://doi.org/10.1007/978-3-030-37436-5_17

integral part of an automatic fire-extinguishing installation or warning system. In most cases, they are installed on the ceiling, with rare exceptions; they are also installed on the walls, and must cover the entire area of the room with its action. If, when a fire starts, the smoke from it will spread in the dead zone of the sensors and the temperature will rise there too, the fire will spread until the temperature from it or the smoke is reached by the sensors, but the damage will already be much greater. The smoke can also be dissipated by a draft, and its concentration under the ceiling will not be sufficient to trigger the sensor. The same can be with temperature. It goes without saying that at some point in time the fire will reach the scale that all sensors will send the necessary signals. But, again, the delay even for a second can be fatal.

Today, the rules specified in the code of rules 5.13.130.2009 [2] are in force. Here the requirements for different rooms are detailed: among other things, with inclined, latticed ceilings, with a non-standard shape, etc. It will take a change to this set of rules # 1, which has been in force since 20.06.2011 - many adjustments necessary for design have been made here. The minus of these documents is that they, strictly speaking, are limited only by requirements. And often it is necessary to simulate the possible processes that occur during a fire to adequately draw up a project. Unfortunately, the set of rules does not contain their description. Detectors of what type should be installed on this or that object are described in sufficient detail in Table M1 "Selection of the types of fire detectors depending on the purpose of the protected room and the type of fire load". And with this, as a rule, problems do not arise. But to correctly install point detectors, observing all the requirements, having sustained the necessary distances - often raises a number of questions. In document SR 5.13.130.2009 there is no clear indication of the location of the detectors, only about their number. This is bad, since the features of the protected room are not taken into account, which entails an increase in the system response time, and as a result, the efficiency of its operation. The purpose of this study is to develop an evolutionary algorithm for the optimal arrangement of sensors to reduce the reaction rate of the fire fighting system to the occurrence of a fire.

The optimal arrangement of sensors is affected by several factors:

- probability of occurrence of a fire in a certain place of a room with coordinates (x_1, x_2);
- type of source of ignition and quantity of combustible materials;
- the size of the room and the location of ventilation.

The task of finding the optimal location belongs to the class of so-called NP-complete problems, the solution of which can not be found without a full search of options. Among these tasks, in particular, multicriteria optimization when placing sensors.

It is known that with a large dimension, the implementation of the search of variants is practically impossible because of the extremely high time costs. In this situation, an alternative approach to solving the above problems is the application of methods of evolutionary computation [3, 4]. The genetic algorithm allows solving a lot of optimization problems that can not be solved by standard optimization methods [5]. The application of the genetic algorithm will significantly reduce the amount of computation, which is very important for the creation of robotic fire systems. Existing variants of genetic algorithms cannot be directly applied when searching the optimal sensors location. Therefore, the problem of developing an algorithm for the optimal arrangement of sensors in a multicriteria early warning system for ignition is urgent [6, 7]. The solution of this problem involves the creation of a computer model of the process of starting a fire because of ignition different types of materials and obtaining performance indicators of the proposed solution.

2   Method of Decision-Making About Occurrence of Fire

A Priori Knowledge. Fire can appear anywhere in the room with coordinates $\mathbf{x} = [x_1, x_2]^T$ and its neighborhood. The probability of a fire is different and is related to the purpose of the room and the presence of possible sources of ignition in it. For example, if the room is operated with fuel or lubricating oil, the most likely occurrence of a fire in the vicinity of the potential spill if you store rags that are wiping spilled combustible materials - in the storage area, if there is power equipment - at the junction of power cables or shields. The probability of ignition at an arbitrary point in the room with coordinates $\mathbf{x}$ is a mixture of Gaussians:

$$p(\mathbf{x}) = \frac{1}{C}\sum_{i=1}^{C} P(i) \frac{1}{2\pi|\mathbf{\Sigma}_{ci}|^2} \exp\left(-\frac{1}{2}(\mathbf{x} - \mathbf{x}_{ci})^T \mathbf{\Sigma}_{ci}^{-1}(\mathbf{x} - \mathbf{x}_{ci})\right), \qquad (1)$$

where $\mathbf{x}_{ci}$ - coordinates of a centre of $i - s$ type of ignition, $\mathbf{\Sigma}_{ci}$ - covariance matrix $i - s$ ignition, C – number of centers of ignition, which should be considered for the study room.

Probability of ignition in the neighborhood $\delta_{\mathbf{x}}$ points with coordinates $\mathbf{x}$:

$$P(\mathbf{X}_i) = \int_{\delta_{\mathbf{x}}} p(\mathbf{x})d\mathbf{x} \qquad (2)$$

The algorithm for detecting a fire consists in the continuous and simultaneous monitoring of several potential fire factors (smoke, heat, carbon monoxide) and the formation of a reliable fire alarm signal with a minimum delay after the occurrence of a fire. For each factor, the standardized, program-defined value, upon which a fire alarm is declared, is the "delta factor" - the magnitude of the change in the fire factor relative to the current value. This approach is based on monitoring the finite difference in the values of all the facts of the fire.

When we determining the optimal arrangement of the sensors, it is necessary to take into account the type of ignition. For example, in the case of combustible-lubricating materials, there is a rapid increase in temperature in the neighborhood of the fire; when the rags burn, the temperature is lower, but the smoke is higher; when the cables are ignited, the smoke most rapidly grows.

Minimizing the time of detection of ignition is associated with a large computational cost, so to find the optimal solution it is advisable to apply the evolutionary algorithm.

3 Justification of the Choice of Evolutionary Optimization Algorithm

All evolutionary algorithms use the principles of biological evolution - a combination of mutation, natural selection and reproduction. The main problem solved by using such algorithms is optimization, that is, a gradual improvement of something based on the given criteria. The basic optimization problem is posed as a mathematical programming problem:

$$\underset{X \in D_x}{extr} \ F(X), \tag{3}$$

where $D_x = \{X | \varphi(X) \rangle 0, \ \psi(X) = 0\}$, $F(X)$ - fitness function, X – vector of params, $\varphi(X)$ and $\psi(X)$ – constraint functions, D_x – an admissible region in the parameter space. Formula (1) can also be interpreted as the task of finding the extremum of the fitness function by varying the parameters within the permissible range.

Evolutionary algorithms are used in a situation where it is possible to formulate criteria for a good solution, but it is difficult to come up with it. Our main criterion is the minimum response time of the sensor system to the occurrence of a fire in different parts of the room.

Currently, four main groups of evolutionary methods are being studied and developing - genetic methods (Genetic Algorithms—GA), genetic programming, methods for optimizing the swarm of particles (Particles Swarm Optimization—PSO) and methods of "colony of ants" (Ant Colony Optimization—ACO).

The author of GP G. J. Koza defined genetic programming as an application program that uses the principles of evolutionary adaptation to the construction of a procedural code [8, 9]. Genetic programming is used when it comes to computer programs. At present, using genetic programming, a number of results have been obtained that surpass those obtained by humans. For example, sorting networks have been created, a quantum algorithm for Grover's problem, etc.

The PSO algorithm was originally described as applied to the problems of mathematical biology in 1987 [10]. Information on algorithms and solution results using PSO methods of a number of optimization problems is given, for example, in [11, 12]. The PSO (Particles Swarm Optimization) method simulates the behavior of multiple agents seeking to reconcile their state with the state of the best agent.

For the first time the idea of using an analogy with the behavior of an ants colony for solving optimization problems was expressed in 1992 [13]. The application of the ACO methods is illustrated by the examples of the traveling salesman problem [14], cutting and packing [15], etc. An overview of the ACO methods is given in [16].

At present, in computer-aided design and control systems, most attention is paid to genetic methods, often referred to by genetic algorithms. The use of genetic algorithms for the solution of optimization problems was initiated by Holland in 1975 [17]. A fundamental contribution to the development of GA was made by Goldberg [18].

To apply any of the evolutionary algorithms, you need:

1. Form the set of parameters;
2. Develop an algorithm for computing the fitness function;
3. Form an algorithmic implementation of the evolutionary method.

The general scheme of the evolutionary algorithm is shown in Fig. 1.

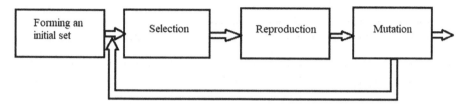

Fig. 1. General scheme of the evolutionary algorithm

Evolutionary calculations are one of the possible heuristic approaches to the solution of multimodal (having several local extremes) optimization problems of large dimension due to a combination of randomness and determinism elements exactly as it does in living nature [19]. Like any method that uses an element of randomness, evolutionary calculations do not guarantee the detection of a global extreme of the objective function (optimal solution) for a certain time. Their main advantage is that they allow finding "good" solutions to very difficult problems in less time than other methods. The methods of evolutionary computation proved to be quite effective for solving a number of real problems of engineering design, planning, routing and placement, managing securities portfolios, forecasting, and in many other areas. Since we have access to such a resource as a supercomputer center, we can allow parallel calculations and use a larger amount of the initial population. Parallelization methods are given in [20–23].

4   Application of the Genetic Algorithm to the Problem of the Optimal Sensors Location

4.1   Forming an Initial Set of Sensor Group Locations

The sensors in the simulated room are located on a grid whose cell size is 10×10 cm. Accordingly, the coordinates of the sensors in the initial population must satisfy the following parameters:

$$x_1 = k * 10,$$
$$x_2 = n * 10,$$

where $k \in \left[0; \frac{X_{max}}{10}\right]$, $n \in \left[0; \frac{Y_{max}}{10}\right]$.

The initial population will be represented by a four-dimensional array of the following type:

$$S = \left(\left((X_1), \ldots, (X_M)\right)_1, \left((X_1), \ldots, (X_M)\right)_2, \ldots, \left((X_1), \ldots, (X_M)\right)_N\right). \quad (4)$$

where M – the desired number of sensors in the room, N initial population size, $X_i = (x_1, x_2)^T$ – coordinates of sensors.

4.2   Fitness Function for Estimating the Average Reaction Time of a Set of Sensors for Fire Start for Various Sources of Ignition

The purpose of optimizing the location of the sensors is the fastest detection of a different kind of ignition. Therefore, the fitness function is the average fire detection time, depending on the geometry of the room, the location of combustible materials, the type of ignition, the coordinates of the sensors. Obtaining the objective function is associated with a large amount of computation. At the first stage, it is necessary to simulate the ignition process in a room with a given geometry, based on the solution of the Navier-Stokes equations.

The result of the solution is a four-dimensional tensor with the following dimensions: coordinate along the length and along the width of the room; temperature, concentration of CO and smoke; time (Fig. 2).

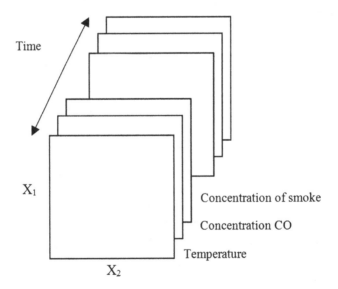

Fig. 2. Four-dimensional tensor of fire factors

The decision function may contain several criteria that take into account the type of ignition. In a simplified form, the criteria for making a decision on ignition can use different thresholds for different types of ignition:

$$
\begin{aligned}
Fire_{cable}(n) &= (\Delta T(n) > \Delta T_{\theta 1}) \wedge (\Delta CO(n) > \Delta CO_{\theta 1}) \wedge (\Delta Sm(n) > \Delta Sm_{\theta 1}), \\
Fire_{CO}(n) &= (\Delta T(n) > \Delta T_{\theta 2}) \wedge (\Delta CO(n) > \Delta CO_{\theta 2}) \wedge (\Delta Sm(n) > \Delta Sm_{\theta 2}), \\
Fire_{Rag}(n) &= (\Delta T(n) > \Delta T_{\theta 3}) \wedge (\Delta CO(n) > \Delta CO_{\theta 3}) \wedge (\Delta Sm(n) > \Delta Sm_{\theta 3}), \\
Fire &= Fire(cable) \vee Fire(CL) \vee Fire(Rag),
\end{aligned}
\tag{5}
$$

where $\Delta T(n)$, $\Delta CO(n)$, $\Delta Sm(n)$ - he results of changes in temperature, concentration of carbon monoxide and smoke concentration, at a discrete point in time n, obtained during modeling, ΔT_{θ_j}, ΔCO_{θ_j}, ΔSm_{θ_j} thresholds for making a decision on ignition $j - s$ type. For example, when $j = 1$ our decision is $Fire(cable)$ cable fires, when $j = 2 -$ decision is $Fire(CL)$ the ignition of combustive-lubricating substances, when $j = 3 -$ decision is $Fire(Rag)$ ignition of burning rags.

The criteria (5) correspond to the decision to ignite after exceeding the thresholds by measuring results from three sensors. For faster detection, a criterion for exceeding the threshold with measurements from one or two sensors can be used, for example:

$$
Fire(.) = (\Delta t > \Delta t_{\theta 1}) \vee (\Delta CO > \Delta CO_{\theta 1}) \wedge (\Delta Sm > \Delta Sm_{\theta 1});
\tag{6}
$$

Taking into account the accepted decision criterion and the distribution of the ignition probabilities at different points of the room, defined by the formula (1), the average decision making on ignition depends on the distance to the sensor and on the time quantum n from the moment of ignition:

$$
\begin{aligned}
\Delta T_{avg}(\mathbf{x}, n) &= E_i\{\Delta T(\|\mathbf{x}_i - \mathbf{x}\|, n)\}, \\
\Delta CO_{avg}(\mathbf{x}, n) &= E_i\{\Delta CO(\|\mathbf{x}_i - \mathbf{x}\|, n)\}, \\
\Delta Sm_{avg}(\mathbf{x}, n) &= E_i\{\Delta Sm(\|\mathbf{x}_i - \mathbf{x}\|, n)\},
\end{aligned}
\tag{7}
$$

where $E_i\{\Delta Q(\|\mathbf{x}_i - \mathbf{x}\|, n)\}$ - mean fire factor increment $Q \in \{T, CO, Sm\}$ for a given probability distribution of the origin at time n at a distance $\|\mathbf{x}_i - \mathbf{x}\|$ from the source of ignition.

The purpose of optimizing the location of the sensors is to find the minimum time for detecting a fire when using a certain criterion from a set of decision criteria:

$$
F(\mathbf{x}) = \min_n \left[Fire(\Delta T_{avg}(\mathbf{x}, n), \Delta T_{avg}(\mathbf{x}, n), \Delta T_{avg}(\mathbf{x}, n)) \right].
\tag{8}
$$

The decision if fire start is not necessarily based on predicates (3,4); in our study, a neural network approach is also used.

4.3   Selection

Selection is the choice of sets of locations that will participate in the creation of the next generation. There are different methods of selection. Some of the most common methods are tournament selection ("Tournamentselection") [24] and roulette wheels ("Roulettewheel") [25]. For our problem, we chose two other methods. We estimate the effectiveness of each.

Ranging. Based on the value of the fitness function, we order the sets of sensors. The probability of choosing a particular set depends only on the position in the set of sets, and not on the value of its objective function.

The Boltzmann Method. We use the same approach as in the optimization of "annealing modeling". This method for controlling the process introduces the concept of "artificial temperature" T. From a certain moment, we reduce (according to the chosen law) and change the probability of selection of individuals. Thus, the probability of selecting an individual with the value of fitness-function is $f(u_i)$:

$P_s(a_i) = \frac{1}{N} \left(\exp(f(u_i)/T) \times \left(\overline{\exp(f(u_i)/T)} \right)^{-1} \right)$, where $\overline{\exp(f(u_i)/T)}$- average value

$\exp(f(u_i)/T)$ for the current population. This makes it possible at the final stage to narrow down the search in the most promising area of search, while maintaining a sufficient degree of diversity in the population.

When using the Boltzmann method, the algorithm converges to a minimum faster than using the method of ranking. The following graph shows the dependence of the speed of execution of the algorithm on the number of initial samples using Boltzmann methods and ranking (Fig. 3).

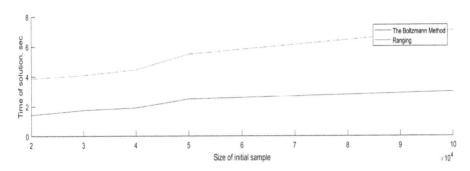

Fig. 3. Dependence of the speed of the algorithm on the choice of reproduction method.

4.4   Crossing

Before crossing, you need to decide on the method of choice. There are two possible options:

- *Panmixia* (random choice). We choose randomly from the population obtained at the previous step. Efficacy decreases with an increase in the number of the initial population N.
- *Selective selection.* Parents become individuals whose target function values are not more than the average for the population. Thus one individual can enter into several pairs.

Since to search for one minimum and use of a large initial capacity of the population does not fit panmixia, we will use the selective choice.

In the theory of genetic algorithms, the following methods of crossing are considered.

- *Binary recombination.* Conditionally, it is possible to divide the binary combination methods into 2 types. For recombinations of the first type, we use a part of the genes of one parent and part of the genes of the other, and as a result we obtain two individuals, some of whose genes coincide with the parents.
- *Homogeneous crossing-over* is characterized by the fact that as a result of crossing only 1 specimen is obtained. For each gene of this individual, by selecting a random mask it is determined which parent gene of which individual will be taken.
- *Recombination of actual values.* There is a discrete, intermediate, and linear recombination. With discrete recombination, the gene value of the offspring is randomly selected from the parents' genes.

In connection with the specific nature of the input vectors, none of the methods can be directly applied. Therefore, the crossing is carried out as follows. Since the genome we have is a sensor, we will evaluate its response rate to the occurrence of a fire. That is, we alternately compare the two parent genes as in a homogeneous crossing-over, and choose the best reaction time. Further, as in the case of intermediate recombination, we choose the coefficient for the coordinates in the space of this sensor. As a result, the gene of the offspring will differ from the parent gene by a certain number of sensor locations.

4.5 Mutation

There are several ways to mutate. The choice of a suitable mutation operator is solved within the framework of the task [26, 27]. With probability of P_m, we will choose the m child to mutation. The classical types of mutation due to the specifics of the data cannot be given, therefore as a mutation we use the coordinate shift to a certain random factor α.

5 Using the Developed Genetic Algorithm to Find the Optimal Sensors Locations in the Simulated Room

We simulated nine fires in different location. In each location we ignited various combustible materials. Only the initial intensity and area of ignition remained the same for each experiment. Figure 4 shows a 3D model of a room with selected sources of ignition.

The data of these fires were used to calculate the fitness function of the genetic algorithm.

According to the norms of SP 5.13130.2009, in one small room it is necessary to install either three analog non-addressable fire sensors, included in the "AND" scheme, or two addressable fire sensors, included in the "AND"("OR") scheme, depending on the program of operation duplication registered in the installation of the address PPC [1]. Modeling of a room of 5 × 7 m with three sensors was done. In the case of a

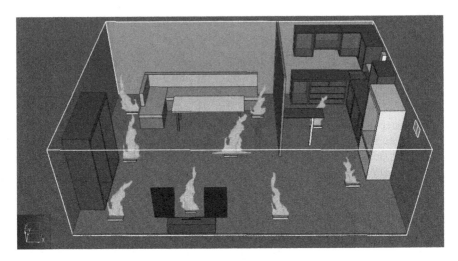

Fig. 4. Location of ignition sources.

uniform arrangement of three sensors at points with coordinates (2.5, 1.5), (2.5, 3.5) and (2.5; 5.0), the average reaction time for ignition is 43.78 s.

The average response time using the developed genetic algorithm, depending on the size of the initial population, is shown in Fig. 5.

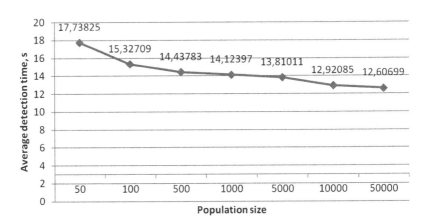

Fig. 5. Average response time, depending on the size of the initial population.

On the Fig. 5 we can see that if we increase the size of the initial population the time of fire detection become shorter. The difference in the response time between the uniform arrangement and the arrangement calculated by the genetic algorithm is on average more than two times.

With the optimal arrangement of the three sensors shown in Fig. 6, the average reaction time decreased to 12.6 s.

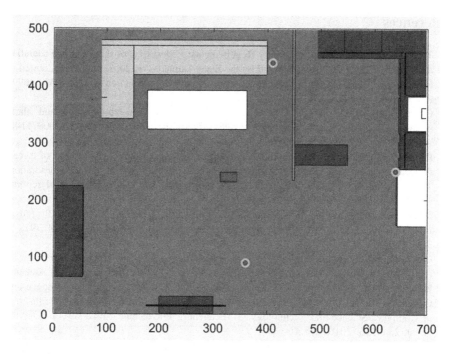

Fig. 6. The location of the three sensors, calculated by the genetic algorithm.

6 Conclusion

Using the genetic algorithm with the proposed objective function allowed us to optimize the location of the fire system sensors in the room and to reduce the mean time of detection of fire by an average of 50%.

It took several minutes to simulate the combustion of substances of different types to calculate the fitness function of the genetic algorithm. For modeling, we use the FDS (Fire Dynamics Simulator) program running on the supercomputer center SPbPU on the several nodes of the computational cluster with using the OpenMP technology.

Using the network of fire alarm sensors, connected by ZigBee wireless interface, allows us to move the sensors along the ceiling on the rails laid on it and monitoring changes occurring in the room during the entire operation time. Robotic mobile fire systems can include an algorithm for optimizing the position of sensors, which reduces the number of sensors, shorten the polling time, and reduce the time of detection of the fire.

A modification of the genetic algorithm suitable for solving the problem of the optimal arrangement of sensors in the fire-fighting system has been developed. The calculation of the fitness function for a genetic algorithm takes into account not only the features of the room itself, but also the likelihood of a fire and the characteristics of the combustible material. The choice of the method of reproduction for this type of problem is justified. The method of crossing was modified, to work with a set of sensors, rather than a gene.

References

1. Technical Regulations on Fire Safety Requirements: Feder. Law of the Russian Federation no. 123-FZ of July 22, 2008; adopted by the State. Duma 07/04/2008; approved Council of Federation 11.07.2008. http://www.consultant.ru/document/cons_doc_LAW_78699/. Accessed 15 Aug 2018. [in Russian]
2. СП 5.13130.2009 Systems of fire protection. Automatic fire-extinguishing and alarm systems. Designing and regulations rules. http://docs.cntd.ru/document/1200071148. Accessed 15 Aug 2018. [in Russian]
3. Pernin, C.G., Comanor, K., Menthe, L., Moore, L.R., Anderson, T.: Allocation of forces, fires, and effects using genetic algorithms (Technical report (RAND)). RAND Corporation, TR-423-A, Santa Monica, California (2008). https://www.rand.org/pubs/technical_reports/TR423.html. Accessed 15 Aug 2018
4. McDermott, J., Castelli, M., Sekanina, L., Haasdijk, E., García-Sánchez, P. (eds.): EuroGP 2017. LNCS, vol. 10196. Springer, Cham (2017). https://doi.org/10.1007/978-3-319-55696-3
5. Goldberg, D.E.: Genetic Algorithms in Search, Optimization, and Machine Learning, 1st edn. Addison-Wesley Publishing Company Inc., Boston (1989). The University of Alabama
6. Nevelsky, A.S., Malykhina, G.F.: Ship's wireless fire system. In: Computer Science and Cybernetics (ComCon-2016). Proceedings of the student scientific conference of the Institute of Computer Science and Technology. St. Petersburg Polytechnic University of Peter the Great, 234–236 (2016). [in Russian]
7. Guseva, A.I., Malykhina, G.F., Militsyn, A.V.: Algorithms of the early warning on fire in the premises of the vessel. In: Malykhin, G.F. (ed.) Complex Protection of Objects of Information - 2016. Proceedings of the All-Russian Scientific and Practical Conference with International Participation, pp. 39–43 (2016). [in Russian]
8. Koza, R.: Genetic Programming II: Automatic Discovery of Reusable Programs. The MIT Press, London (1994)
9. Loseva, E.D., Lipinsky, L.V.: Ensemble of networks with application of multi-objective self-configurable genetic programming. Vestnik SibGAU **17**(1), 67–72 (2016)
10. Deneubourg, J.-L., Goss, S., Pasteels, J.M., Fresneau, D., Lachaud, J.-P.: Self-organization mechanisms in ant societies (II): learning in foraging and division of labor. In: From Individual to Collective Behavior in Social Insects. Birkhauser, Basel (1987)
11. Eberhart, R.C., Kennedy, J.: A new optimizer using particles swarm theory. In: Proceedings of the Sixth International Symposium on Micro Machine and Human Science, Nagoya, Japan, pp. 39–43 (1995). https://doi.org/10.1109/mhs.1995.494215
12. Eberhart, R.C., Dobbins, R.W., Simpson, P.: Computational Intelligence PC Tools. Academic Press, Boston (1996)
13. Dorigo, M.: Optimization, learning and natural algorithms. Ph.D. thesis, Dipartimento di Electronica, Politecnico di Milano (1992)
14. Dorigo, M., Gambardella, L.: Ant colonies for the traveling salesman problem. Technical report, TR/IRIDIA/1996-3 Université Libre de Bruxelles (1996)
15. Valeyeva, A.F.: Ant colony algorithm for the 2-D bin-packing problems. Inf. Technol. **10**, 36–43 (2005)
16. Dorigo, M., Caro, G., Gambardella, L.: Ant algorithms for discrete optimization. Artif. Life **5**(2), 137–172 (1999). https://doi.org/10.1162/106454699568728
17. Korneev, V.V., Gareev, A.F., Vasyutin, S.V., Raikh, V.V.: Database: Intellectual Information Processing. Publishing House Knowledge, Moscow (2001). [in Russian]

18. Holland, J.: Adaptation in Natural and Artificial Systems. University of Michigan Press, Ann Arbor (1975)
19. Goldberg, D.E.: Genetic Algorithms in Search, Optimization, and Machine Learning. Addison-Welsey, Boston (1989)
20. Rodriguez, M.A., Escalante, D.M., Peregrin, A.: Efficient distributed genetic algorithm for rule extraction. Appl. Soft Comput. **11**(1), 733–743 (2011). https://doi.org/10.1016/j.asoc. 2009.12.035
21. Alba, E., Tomassini, M.: Parallelism and evolutionary algorithms. IEEE Trans. Evol. Comput. **6**(5), 443–462 (2002). https://doi.org/10.1109/TEVC.2002.800880
22. Zhongyang, X., Zhang, Y., Zhang, L., Niu, S.: A parallel classification algorithm based on hybrid genetic algorithm. In: Proceedings of the 6th World Congress on Intelligent Control and Automation, Dalian, China, pp. 3237–3240 (2006)
23. Knysh, D.S., Kureichik, V.M.: Parallel genetic algorithms: a survey and problem state of the art. J. Comput. Syst. Sci. Int. **49**(4), 579–589 (2010). https://doi.org/10.1134/S1064 230710040088
24. Eremeev, A.V.: A genetic algorithm with tournament selection as a local search method. J. Appl. Industr. Math. **6**(3), 286–294 (2012). https://doi.org/10.1134/S1990478912030039
25. Abd Rahman, R., Ramli, R., Jamari, Z., Ku-Mahamud, K.R.: Evolutionary Algorithm with Roulette-tournament selection for solving aquaculture diet formulation. Math. Prob. Eng. **2016**, 3672758 (2016). https://doi.org/10.1155/2016/3672758
26. Rutkovskaya, D., Pilinsky, M., Rutkovsky, L.: Neural networks, genetic algorithms and fuzzy systems. Hotline-Telecom, Moscow (2004). [in Russian]
27. Gen, M., Cheng, R.: Genetic Algorithms and Engineering Design. Wiley, New York (1997)

Adaptive System Monitoring of the Technical Condition Technological Objects Based on Wireless Sensor Networks

Aleksey Vinogradenko[1]([✉]) [ID], Pavel Budko[1] [ID],
and Vladimir Fedorenko[2] [ID]

[1] Military Telecommunication Academy Named After the Soviet Union Marshal
Budienny S.M, Tikhoretsky Av. 3, 194064 St. Petersburg, Russia
Vinogradenko.a@inbox.ru, budko62@mail.ru
[2] North Caucasus Federal University, Pushkina Str. 1, 355009 Stavropol, Russia
fovin_25@mail.ru

Abstract. An analysis was made of existing control systems and telemetry. There are requirements for modern geographically distributed telemetry systems. Simulation of an adaptive system for monitoring the technical condition of technological objects based on wireless sensor networks is considered as a decomposition of particular problems of forming, processing and transmitting measurement information using the methods of the theory of random processes, queuing theory and methods of the theory of signal transmission. We described a method for reducing the redundancy of measurement information in the monitoring systems of the technical condition of technological objects due to its operation in emergency and pre-emergency alarm modes, as well as taking into account external factors. It has been determined that the priority of service requests coming from sensors is characterized by the growth dynamics of the monitored parameter to the established tolerance, which is confirmed by the application service model. It is shown that the system for monitoring the technical condition of technological objects can be made in the form of application service systems, which are a queuing system that registers the flow of accident signals - applications and determine their priorities. Based on the analysis of the use of wireless sensor networks, the possibility of their integration into a simulated system for monitoring the technical condition of geographically distributed control objects is shown. It is shown that for an ordered polling of the elements of the sensor network, a polling system with dynamically changing parameters can be used. A group polling method is described in various polling modes with a fixed number of sensors registering an alarm signal, which makes it possible to significantly increase the efficiency of testing, taking into account possible errors in the transmission of measurement information.

Keywords: Technical condition · Adaptive monitoring system · Sensors · Measurement information · Sensor networks · Polling

© Springer Nature Switzerland AG 2020
V. Sukhomlin and E. Zubareva (Eds.): Convergent 2018, CCIS 1140, pp. 200–210, 2020.
https://doi.org/10.1007/978-3-030-37436-5_18

1 Introduction

In the operation of various types of complex technological objects and systems, an important place is given to their technical condition (TC) monitoring, the equipment installed on them, as well as to operational control of production processes, automation of the experiment, detection of deviations of monitored values, measurements of deviated parameters and their registration. A particular importance is assumed by operational control systems, telemetry, used to prevent emergencies at geographically distributed technological facilities, equipped with a large number of sensors that are remote from data processing centers (DPCs) [1–3]. At the same time, strict requirements are imposed on the efficiency and reliability of information delivery via wireless data transmission network (WDTN) channels for well-timed stopping the threat of accidents.

Analysis of the existing telemetric systems (TMS) used in various industries and for military purposes to measure technical parameters, process and exchange measurement information (MI) with the data center, showed a lack of consideration of pre-emergency conditions, as well as low testing efficiency [4–7]. In addition, the presence of a large number of sources of MI, sent to a single data center, necessitates the dispatching of information flows from sensors registering the technical parameters of objects of control in telemetry systems (TMS) [8–11].

For the timely detection and transmission of the alarm signal from the OK signal, it is necessary to have a system for sensors' scanning for the presence of an MI that is relevant for transmission.

In monitoring systems, sensors use different polling rules for ordered polling, which are similar to polling systems for computer network elements and are called polling [12]. In addition to the similarity in mathematical models with priority queuing systems (QS), priorities in the polling systems are assigned according to a certain rule, and their parameters can change dynamically.

The study is aimed at the development of an adaptive system for monitoring the TC of technological objects, exchanging MI, taking into account its priority, the dynamics of changes in polling parameters, and errors in the process of transferring MI to the data center.

In order to comply with modern standards and requirements, the developed system for monitoring the TC of technical objects must meet the following conditions:

1. transmit the current MI in on-line mode;
2. to carry out simultaneous interrogation of several sensors in order to save time for guaranteed detection of alarms;
3. maintaining a balance in reducing the redundancy of MI and preserving the completeness of monitoring the TC of technological objects.

The feasibility of the proposed monitoring system is based on the use of methods of the theory of random processes, queuing theory and methods of the theory of signal transmission.

2 Determining the Priority of MI in Identifying Alarm Signals

Control devices in a simulated vehicle monitoring system of TC of technological objects are a series of sensors and controllers that record their signal parameters and compare them with acceptable limits [13]. In case of exceeding this level, the sensor makes a negative decision on the received MI flow, that is, a failure occurs.

The output of any parameter of the received measuring signal $X_i(t)$ beyond the appropriate limits $\underline{X_i}(t)$, $\overline{X_i}(t)$ should be considered as an alarm signal coming from the sensor. Exceeding the permissible values is determined by comparing these parameters with the established tolerances. In this case, overshoots occur, that is, the intersection of the measured processes in a controlled object given limits. The frequency of overshoots is a random phenomenon, therefore, the failure of the equipment is a random event [14].

Thus, overshoots are a random flow of requests (requirements) for making decisions on servicing an element of a controlled technological object that enters the QS. The intensity of such requests is determined by the number of sensors, the temporal characteristics of controlled random processes and the number of established tolerance levels for each process. Given the random nature of the receipt of applications for services coming from the object of control, a situation arises in which several applications for service are simultaneously received. This results in a queue of requests.

The waiting time for requests in the queue may exceed a certain amount, which may entail a loss of the value of this application, as in this case there is a delay in starting the service (decision-making) of the controlled object.

The flow of applications received by the QS has intensity λ, and the flow of services has intensity μ. Then, $\mu = 1/t_{srv}$, where t_{srv} is the service time of one application. Taking into account the fact that the application contains N symbols, $t_{srv} = N \cdot T_c$ where T_c is the duration of one character of the request. In the presence of erroneously recorded emissions (symbols) $T_c = h_{add}^2 E_n/P_c$, where $h_{add}^2 = P_c \cdot T_c/E_n = -2\ln(2P_{err\_add})$, the intensity of request operation: $\mu = P_c/h_{add}^2 E_n N$. Knowing the duration of one character of the request, you can determine the allowable waiting time (the minimum remaining) for servicing the next request:

$$T_{c\_allow} = -(4E_n/P_c) \cdot \ln(P_{err\_add}). \tag{1}$$

Thus, it is possible to predict the withdrawal of applications from the queue, taking into account external factors (errors), and, therefore, to maintain the relevance (value) of MI, which contributes to a more efficient operation of technological systems and facilities.

In existing telemetry systems, each parameter of an object is controlled with a period T_0, regardless of its rate of change. However, with an increase in the rate of change of individual parameters, they can reach acceptable values in a time shorter than a fixed period T_0. In this case, the control system will not be able to promptly respond to unacceptable changes in the parameter, which will lead to the failure of the controlled object.

For the operative control of the object's state, the measurement and the subsequent evaluation of the parameter are carried out with a frequency proportional to the rate of change of the parameter. Depending on the output speed (time Δt_1, Δt_2 reaching the allowable value) of the monitored parameter U beyond the allowable limits, the signal priority is determined, which is set due to the multilevel tolerance system (Fig. 1) [15]. This makes it possible to predict: the less time before reaching the controlled parameter, the higher the priority of the application. Such an approach makes it possible to identify pre-emergency conditions of objects of control.

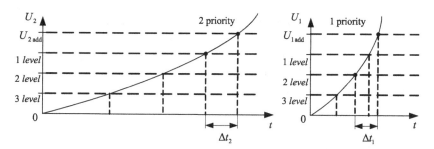

Fig. 1. Comparison of the priority of requests depending on the dynamics of the controlled parameter out of acceptance band.

To reduce the redundancy of MI while maintaining the completeness of control of objects via a communication network, it is advisable to transfer not all the results of parameter measurements, but only messages about the output of parameters of the object being monitored beyond the established tolerances [16]. Such an approach would reduce the message volume transmitted via wireless data networks [17].

In the course of analyzing the process of removing MI sensors about controlled objects, an approach to solving this problem is presented by representing the entire sensor link of a simulated vehicle monitoring system as a fault management system, where the controllers are service channels (Fig. 2). At the same time, applications of lower priorities that have left the queue reappear with the new iteration of emissions [18, 19]. This QS is a state graph of the subsystem when servicing applications received from objects of control, including the state without messages, pre-emergency, emergency and emergency-pre-emergency states, characterizing any state of the telemetry systems touch level.

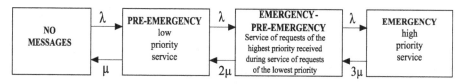

Fig. 2. State graph of the monitoring subsystem when servicing requests received from objects of control.

The priority of service requests coming from the sensors is determined by the growth dynamics of the monitored parameter to the established tolerance. This makes it possible to predict: the less time before reaching the controlled parameter, the higher the priority of the request.

Such a forecast is provided by the request serving model [20], which allows controlling two flows of requests with different priorities, operating in three modes (Fig. 3). Operating requests of high and low priorities received from sensors in this model is carried out in requests operating units. The principle of operation of such a model is as follows: in the case of receipt of high-priority request (after the arrival of low-priority requests), operation of low-priority requests will be terminated, incoming high-priority requests will be served, impulses from the outputs of the released request service units will be sent through the first OR element to the first output of the model. At the same time, as soon as the service of the high priority request is completed in the request service unit, where the operation of the low priority request was terminated, the operation of the low priority request is resumed and the third output of this unit closes.

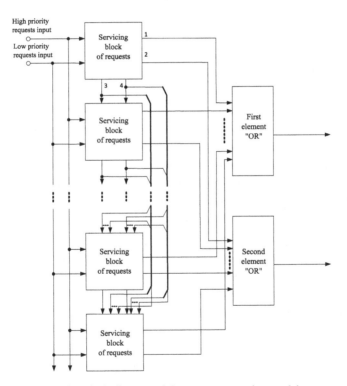

Fig. 3. Block diagram of the request operation model.

Newly received low priority requests will go through all the operation units of requests that are engaged in operating both low- and high-priority requests, and will be accepted for operation if there are free units that are determined when polling previous request operation units. If, during the operation period of high and low priority requests, high priority requests arrive, then in those blocks that receive high priority requests, the operation of low priority requests will stop again, and high priority requests will be operated.

3   Sensor Network Monitoring System

As noted above, for the transmission of MI received from sensors, wireless data transmission channels (satellite communication networks, specialized packet radio networks, broadband wireless networks, sensor networks) can be used. The territorial diversity of technological objects, the harsh conditions of its operation and the need to ensure safe operation have led to the widespread use of wireless sensor networks (WSN).

Therefore, the WSN, as a distributed network of sensor nodes that collect data on the parameters of control objects and transfer them to the data center by relaying from node to node, fully meets the requirements for automating monitoring processes. Sensor nodes can be installed stationary or be able to arbitrarily move in a certain space without disturbing the logical connectivity of the network, in this case the sensor network does not have a fixed topology and has a self-organizing structure [21].

The network node contains: a number of sensors (sensors) that receive data from the external environment; microcontroller; memory device; transceiver; self-contained power supply; executive mechanisms for the transfer of control actions from network nodes to the external environment. Of great importance are the methods of integrating sensors that measure the values of primary electrical quantities that are functionally dependent on the monitored parameters.

The wireless sensor is a board on which digital and analog-to-digital converters, a microprocessor, operational and flash memory, an interface unit, a transceiver, a power source, and sensors are located.

The interface block contains other input/output ports, for example, programming or connecting an external sensor.

The radio modem includes a low-power transceiver and a microcontroller, which, in turn, incorporates a processor, random-access and permanent storage devices, an analog-to-digital converter, an interrupt-handling unit, a certain range of interfaces, and other peripheral nodes.

As options, the sensor may include a visualization unit for displaying the current state of the device and an input unit for changing operating modes, rebooting, etc. [22].

The main processing of data received by the sensor and including sensor information, as well as information about the state of the sensors and the results of the data transfer process, is performed by the network node.

The monitoring system under development assumes the presence of several thousand sensors transmitting information over wireless networks about the occurrence of emergency situations at a technological facility. The approach to solving the problem of the most rapid detection of sensors that fix alarm signals is the development of a dynamically changeable polling system.

4   Implementation of the Collection and Processing of MI at the Network Level

As already noted, emissions are a random flow of requests (requirements) for making decisions on the maintenance of a controlled object. Such a system consisting of several sensors that "generate" request flows, and a sensor node that performs their polling, can be thought of as a polling system with a specific service discipline.

In the majority of works devoted to the development and study of various models of WDT systems [23, 24], methods of ordered polling have been developed, in which the number of sensors detecting the emission of a controlled parameter is comparable to their total number. However, for a simulated monitoring system that includes thousands of sensors within the WSN, this approach will be ineffective, since the time taken to survey sensors will be proportional to their total number, and, therefore, critically long. Thus, it is necessary to develop such a polling method based on group polling, when several sensors simultaneously transmit MI, which will significantly reduce the time required to identify sensors that fix alarm signals.

Consider the WSN, operating B objects, on the j-th object the are n_j sensors installed $j = 1, \ldots, B$; $n^* = \max\limits_j n_j$ - the maximum possible number of sensors on one technological object is assumed to be relatively small. Thus, there are $t = \sum\limits_{j=1}^{A} n_j$ sensors and it is required to develop a rule of their scanning for the most rapid identification S_j of sensors transmitting the accident signal.

Suppose that B is large, and the maximum number of simultaneously triggered sensors in the event of an emergency is relatively small. In this case, we include in the group of sensors being surveyed only those that will fix the alarm signal simultaneously.

It should be noted that the probability of an emergency in the network p_d is not known, but it is known that it is rather small: $p_d \leq p_d^0$, where p_d^0 is some given probability. However, the use of the upper limit of this probability in the polling control algorithm for calculating the permissible number of sensors fixing the accident signals is not effective, since the group polling method used is sensitive to the expected number of sensors. This is due to the fact that if the estimated number of sensors fixing the alarm signals is incorrect, the information content of the survey data drops significantly. This situation is most typical for distributed TMS, and the probability of an accident in its local area is small [25].

In the event of an emergency at the j-th object, the z_j sensors are simultaneously triggered, where z_j is a discrete random variable with distribution on the $\{1, \ldots, n_j\}$ set. The distribution of the value depends on the relevant object, the cause of the emergency, the location of the sensors, etc. All these circumstances are usually unknown or it is difficult to consider them.

Therefore, an assumption is considered that the probability of actuation of all sensors on a single object is high enough. The condition of the sensors is described by $x_1, \ldots, x_i$ variables that take the value "0" or "1". The value "0" indicates the passive state of the sensor, and "1" indicates the operating state of the sensor, which records the alarm signals. The ordered set of working sensors is denoted by S.

Group polling is set using the vector $a = (a_1, \ldots, a_t)$, where a_t takes the values "0" or "1". The value $a_t = 1$ means that the t-th sensor does not participate in the polling. If N is the number of polls, then all polls are given by the Boolean matrix of polls $A = (a^j, \ldots, a^N)^T$, where a^j is the vector of j-th polling. If there is at least one alarm signal in the group of polled sensors, then we note the presence of an alarm signal, that is, as "1". If there is no such sensor in the group, then it does not receive a single signal, which is interpreted as "0". Thus, as a response from the sensors of the j-th group, the result will be formed as

$$f_j = (a_1^j \wedge x_1) \vee (a_t^j \wedge x_1), \tag{2}$$

where $\wedge$ – Boolean product, $\vee$ – Boolean sum.

It is also assumed that errors in the transmission of MI are possible in the network. This means that the value of the function f_j is known with some error: each poll results in a distortion of the result regardless of the polls in accordance with the stochastic transition matrix.

$$W = \begin{pmatrix} 1 - \beta_0 & \beta_0 \\ \beta_1 & 1 - \beta_1 \end{pmatrix}, \tag{3}$$

where β_0 – probability of reception mispresentation "0", and β_1 – probability of reception mispresentation "1".

Therefore, the result of the j-th polling will be g_j that takes the values "0" or "1" in accordance with the matrix W regardless of the values in other observations, assuming that f_j are fixed.

In the case when the number of sensors on all technological objects is the same, we will select control objects for which the sensors will be polled, and further, on each of these objects we will choose one polled sensor. Therefore, no more than one sensor can participate in each polling at a single site. To create such a matrix, it is necessary to select the scanned sensor at each site. That is, if an object participates in a polling - $a_j^k = 1$, where k is the number of the polling, and j is the number of the object, then among the sensors of the j - object, the scanned sensor is randomly selected.

To simplify the identification procedure, the decision on the activity of a specific sensor is made on the basis of "factor analysis" [26] using the maximum likelihood method, but it does not search for a sensor fixing the accident, but search is made for an object with similar operating sensors. In this case, when identifying the active sensor of the object, information will be requested from all the other sensors of the object, but through another channel. Obviously, there is some redundancy here, but it only leads to the establishment of a small number of additional polls, which will be disabled if the object is identified incorrectly.

To decide whether an object is active or not, the following data is used: $x_{00}(i)$ - the number of observations on the j-object when no sensor was polled and the result of the polling turned out to be $g = 0$; $x_{10}(i)$ - the number of observations when at least one sensor was not polled on the i-object, and the result of the polling $g = 0$; $x_{01}(i)$ - the number of observations when no sensor was surveyed on the i-object, and the result of the polling $g = 1$ and $x_{11}(i)$ - the number of observations when at least one sensor was surveyed on the i-object and the result of the polling is $g = 1$. Since the results of observations are assumed to be independent, then $x_{00}(i)$, $x_{10}(i)$, $x_{01}(i)$ and $x_{11}(i)$ - form sufficient statistics.

Thus, after conducting N pollings fir each of t sensors there are calculated values of $x_{00}(i)$, $x_{10}(i)$, $x_{01}(i)$ and $x_{11}(i)$ and on their base the likelihood ratios are determined

$$L(i) = a_{00}x_{00}(i) + a_{10}x_{10}(i) + a_{01}x_{01}(i) + a_{11}x_{11}(i), \tag{4}$$

Then

$$a_{00}^0 = \log\frac{1 - \beta_0 - p^0(1 - \beta_0 - \beta_1)}{1 - \beta_0 - p^0(1 - \beta_0 - \beta_1)}, \tag{5}$$

$$a_{01}^0 = \log\frac{p^0(1 - \beta_0 - \beta_1) + \beta_0}{p^0(1 - \beta_0 - \beta_1) + \beta_0}, \tag{6}$$

$$a_{10}^0 = \log\frac{\beta_1}{1 - \beta_0 - p^0(1 - \beta_0 - \beta_1)}, \tag{7}$$

$$a_{11}^0 = \log\frac{1 - \beta_0}{\beta_0 - p^0(1 - \beta_0 - \beta_1)}, \tag{8}$$

where $p^0 = 1 - (1 - p_0)^{s_0-1}$.

Based on the error value of the first kind, the threshold values L_0 are calculated, beyond which the logarithm of the likelihood ratio $L(i)$ makes a decision that the sensor detects the alarm signal. Further, the decision on the presence of an emergency at the facility is made in the case when at least one sensor is recognized as active.

Thus, in geographically-distributed systems of monitoring the TC of technological objects, the use of the group polling method is fully justified. For splitting a multitude of sensors into objects of control, it is advisable to use a factorial method of processing the results of observations or other methods that take into account the correlation of the response of all sensors located on the corresponding technological object in emergency situations.

5 Conclusion

A simulated monitoring system of TC of technological facilities, built on the basis of the WNS, will allow timely detection of an emergency situation, as well as the efficient use the allocated network resource by reducing the redundancy of MI, not only at the sensor level, but also at the network level. To reduce the redundancy of MI on the WNS, it is advisable to transmit only messages about the output of monitored parameters beyond the established tolerances, and the dynamics of their deviations indicate a pre-emergency condition of the technological object. The specificity of the construction and operation of the WNS allows you to consider them as QS, where the role of serving elements is played by controllers that provide service for the application for some time. The use of group polling systems in the WNS in various polling modes with a fixed number of sensors registering an alarm can significantly increase the efficiency of testing, taking into account possible errors in the transmission of MI.

References

1. Budko, P.A.: Model of the automated control system of technical condition of land robotic complexes. In: Proceedings of the 2nd Interuniversity Scientific and Practical Conference Problems of Technical Providing Troops in Modern Conditions, St. Petersburg, pp. 145–149 (2017). in Russian
2. Vinogradenko, A.M., Veselovsky, A.P., Buryanov, O.N.: Operating control of technical condition of mobile electrotechnical objects. In: Proceedings of the III All-Russian Scientific and Practical Conference Modern Problems of Creation and Operation of Arms, Military and Special Equipment, St. Petersburg, pp. 178–184 (2016). in Russian
3. Budko, N.P., et al.: Way of the distributed control and adaptive management of multilevel system and the device for his implementation [Sposob raspredelennogo kontrolya i adaptivnogo upravleniya mnogourovnevoy sistemoy dlya ego osushestvleniya]. Patent RF, no. 2450447 (2012). in Russian
4. Budko, P.A., Vinogradenko, A.M., Litvinov, A.I., Yurov, A.S.: Way of monitoring of precritical condition of controlled objects. Sens. Syst. **184**(9), 8–14 (2014). in Russian
5. Budko, P.A., et al.: Detection of an accident conditions of the marine robotic complex (system) according to the multi-stage control procedure on the basis of wavelet transform application. Mar. Radio Electron. **4**(58), 20–23 (2016). in Russian
6. Vinogradenko, A.M., Buryanov, O.N., Veselovsky, A.P.: Way of operating control of technical condition of mobile specifics. In: Proceedings of the VIII All-Russian Scientific and Practical Conference Machines and Mechanisms Reliability and Durability, Ivanovo, pp. 34–36 (2017). in Russian
7. Vinogradenko, A.M., Ladonkin, O.V., Yurov, A.S.: The system of monitoring of technical condition of military mobile objects with use of wireless technologies. T-Comm. Telecommun. Transp. **1**, 51–55 (2015). in Russian
8. Vinogradenko, A.M., Fedorenko, I.V., Galvas, A.V.: Multiphase organization of service in information and telemetry systems. Inform. Syst. Technol. **59**(3), 121–125 (2010). in Russian
9. Vinogradenko, A.M.: The model of the system of monitoring of controlled objects of the control point management. Neurocomputers. Dev. appl. **1**, 44–51 (2016). in Russian
10. Budko, P.A.: Complex use of diverse communication channels for management of robotic complexes on the basis of uniform system of radio monitoring. H&ES Res. **9**(1), 18–41 (2017). in Russian
11. Vinogradenko, A.M.: Formation of a multichannel telemetry system as a multi-criteria problem of resource allocation in a single information and control space. H&ES Res. **5**(2), 10–15 (2013). in Russian
12. Vishnevsky, V.M., Semenova, O.V.: Polling systems: theory and application in broadband and wireless networks. Tehnosfera, Moscow (2007). in Russian

13. Budko, N.P., Budko, P.A., Vinogradenko, A.M., Litvinov, A.I.: Sposob i ustroystvo avtomatizirovannogo kontrolya tehnicheskogo sostoyaniya elektrooborudovaniya [Way and the device of the automated control of technical condition of electric equipment]. Patent RF, no. 2548602 (2015). in Russian

14. Volkov, L.I.: Management of operation of aircraft complexes. Visshaya shkola, Moscow (1987). in Russian

15. Vinogradenko, A.M., Fidorenko, I.V.: Sistema dlya kontrolya parametrov tehnologicheskih ob'ektov [System for control of parameters of technological objects]. Patent RF, no. 96676 (2010). in Russian

16. Fedorenko, V.V.: The time-probability characteristics of a telemetric signal with the variable number of bits. In: Proceedings of the Vserossiykoy Scientific and Practical Conference Control Problems in Technical Systems, St. Petersburg, pp. 151–155 (2017)

17. Yashin, A.I.: Simulation modeling of automated control system of technical condition of elements of distributed radio centers. Mar. Radio Electron. **63**(1), 32–37 (2018)

18. Budko, P.A., Vinogradenko, A.M., Kuznetsov, S.V., Goydenko, V.K.: Realization of a method of multilevel complex control of technical condition of a sea robot. Syst. Control Commun. Secur. **4**, 71–101 (2017). in Russian

19. Budko, P.A., et al.: Method of multivariate statistical control of technical condition of radio-electronic equipment on the basis of integration of indications of several types of sensors. Sens. Syst. **223**(3), 3–11 (2018). in Russian

20. Fedorenko, V.V., Vinogradenko, A.M., Budko, N.P., Listova, N.V.: Model' obsluzhivaniya zayavok [Request service model]. Patent RF, no. 87277 (2009). in Russian

21. Kucheryaviy, A.E., Prokopyev, A.V., Kucheryaviy, E.A.: Self-organizing networks. St. Petersburg, Lubacich (2011). in Russian

22. Design of wireless sensor networks (2012). http://isca.su/index.php. Accessed 05 Nov 2018

23. Vishnevsky, V.M., Portnoy, S.L., Shahnovich, I.V.: Encyclopedia WiMAX. Tehnosfera, Moscow (2009). in Russian

24. Slelarchik, K.: Model of maintenance and repair system, taking into account the features of operation of communication systems based on hardware and software and components of collecting information about the state of the network. In: Technologies and means of communication, no. 4, pp. 57–63 (2017). in Russian

25. Malikova, E.E., Tsitovich, I.I.: Strategy group polling in a broadband wireless network monitoring. Rev. Appl. Ind. Math. **17**(2), 284–285 (2010). in Russian

26. Malikova, E.E.: Method of increasing the capacity of telemetry and monitoring systems based on wireless networks. T-Comm Telecommun. Transp. **7**, 37–39 (2010)

Disaster Tolerance of On-Board Control Systems for Ground Robots

Nikita Bocharov[1]([⊠]) [iD], Vasiliy Vorobushkov[2] [iD],
Nikolay Paramonov[1] [iD], and Oleg Slavin[3] [iD]

[1] PJSC «Brook INEUM», Vavilova Str. 24, 119334 Moscow, Russia
bocharov.na@phystech.edu
[2] JSC «MCST», Nagatinskaya Str. 1, Build. 23, 117105 Moscow, Russia
[3] Federal Research Center «Computer Science and Control»
of Russian Academy of Sciences, Vavilova Str. 40, 119333 Moscow, Russia

Abstract. Modern ground robotic systems can be operated in harsh conditions, as well as in combat conditions, which can provoke numerous equipment failures, both natural and intentional, as a result of which the question of ensuring the disaster tolerance of the control system of the robotic complex is raised. An essential, but not resolved issue of creating control systems of robotic systems is equipping with computer equipment that is developed on the basis of domestic microprocessors and domestic software. This article proposes methods and algorithms that are the basis for the creation of disaster-tolerant control systems for ground robots based on domestic computers and software. The authors have developed algorithms for increasing the reliability of onboard control systems to catastrophic faults and numerical results of increased reliability of these systems using the developed methods were obtained. The use of domestic computers and certified software "Elbrus" allows us to talk about the prospects of solving problems of import substitution in the field of robotics. The authors believe that the following provisions and results are new in this work: the definition of the onboard computer system disaster tolerance is introduced, algorithms are developed to ensure the disaster-tolerance of the onboard computer system using the computers and software series "Elbrus".

Keywords: Onboard control systems · Disaster tolerance · Reconfiguration · Robotics

1 Introduction

Modern ground robotic system (GRS) can be operated in harsh conditions, as well as in combat conditions, which can provoke numerous failures, both natural and intentional, as a result of which the question of ensuring the disaster tolerance of the control system of the robotic complex is raised. We will assume that disaster tolerance is the ability to continue the work of the robot in the event of sudden catastrophic failures in the shortest period of time. An essential, but not resolved issue of creating control systems of robotic systems is equipping with computers and software developed on the basis of domestic microprocessors and domestic software [1].

V. Sukhomlin and E. Zubareva (Eds.): Convergent 2018, CCIS 1140, pp. 211–222, 2020.
https://doi.org/10.1007/978-3-030-37436-5_19

Since robotics is one of the promising areas of application of computer systems (CS) and general software (GS) of the Elbrus [2–4], one of the purposes of this work was to study the applicability of CS and GS "Elbrus" [5] to ensure the disaster tolerance of onboard computer systems.

The remainder of the paper is organized as follows. In Sect. 2, we introduce the definition of disaster tolerance of an onboard computer system. Section 3 describes reliability indicators. Section 4 describes robot modes. Section 5 describes the main part of proposed method. Sections 6–8 describe additional algorithms to ensure successful work of the proposed method.

2 The Concept of Disaster Tolerance

The difference between the concepts of "fault tolerance" and "disaster tolerance" is that in the concept of "fault tolerance" the emphasis is on restoring performance after single, random, unrelated component failures. The technology of processing such failures assumes, as a rule, that the backup components of each subsystem are introduced into the work, or the remaining components of the repeatedly duplicated subsystem redistribute work among themselves regardless of what is happening at this time in other subsystems.

In the concept of "disaster tolerance" applied to the onboard computer systems of GRS, the main thing is the preservation of data and the continuation of work in conditions of mass and, possibly, intentional failures of systems and related subsystems. Intentional failures can be caused by deliberate damage, such as a projectile hitting a communications subsystem, or by the failure of any components as a result of a collision. As the main indicator in this case, the indicator of availability of the computer system is used, which characterizes the degree of possibility of performing the task in a reasonable time and with the required level of performance. In the context of this article, the components of the availability of a computing system are dependability measure of hardware and software of the computer system, as well as the performance of the system, which varies depending on the backup scheme and the number of failures.

3 Reliability Indicators

The onboard computer system is essentially a system with non-recoverable elements, since the replacement of failed elements in an autonomously functioning robot is impossible. The reliability of such systems is determined by the following indicators:

- reliability function $P(t)$;
- failure probability $Q(t)$;
- failure density $f(t)$;
- failure rate $\lambda(t)$;
- mean operating time to failure t_m.

These indicators are defined as follows:

$$P(t) = 1 - \frac{n(t)}{N} = 1 - Q(t);$$

$$f(t) = -\frac{dP(t)}{dt};$$

$$\lambda(t) = \frac{f(t)}{P(t)};$$

$$t_m = \int_0^\infty tf(t)dt.$$

When solving the problem of disaster resistance, it is necessary to take into account that in addition to the main (natural) flow of failures, which are the consequence of errors, failures, etc., there is a flow of failures caused by targeted attempts to damage the robot. Such failures can be, for example, the result of a shot at a robot or crash. We will call this flow a flow of catastrophic failures. Will denote the flow rate of natural failures as λ_1, and the flow rate of catastrophic failures as λ_2. Thus, the total flow of failures for the onboard computer system will be determined by the expression:

$$\lambda = \lambda_1 + \lambda_2$$

There are many related works devoted to ensuring the fault tolerance of onboard computer systems, so the method proposed in this article focuses on the tolerance to flow of catastrophic failures. Also note that when operating the robot in a combat situation or otherwise threatening the robot, the failure rate of the catastrophic failure flow will be significantly higher than failure rate of the natural failure flow, i.e. $\lambda_2 \gg \lambda_1$. We can assume, that the components of the onboard computer system have sufficiently high reliability to ensure the operation of the robot under normal conditions in which there are only natural failures. Thus, the considered problem of ensuring disaster tolerance is reduced to increasing the reliability function in case of a high intensity and brief failure flow.

4   GRS Modes

Applicable to the military GRS (MGRS) after early failure period, we will assume that MGRS can operate in one of three modes, characterized according to the prevailing situation and the corresponding catastrophic failure flow:

- *Preparation mode.* The robot is moving to its goal, actively using its systems of technical vision, making detailed maps of the terrain and so on. In this mode the flow of catastrophic failures is at almost zero level, i.e. $\lambda_2 \to 0$, and the flow of natural failures is at the usual level. The risk of physical damage or unauthorized access to the control system is minimal. We will consider this case obvious, because ensuring disaster tolerance is equivalent to ensuring fault tolerance.

- *Combat readiness mode.* The robot is located near the combat zone and should be ready to switch to combat mode. In this mode the level of catastrophic failures increases, therefore, appropriate methods should be used to ensure timely switching to combat mode with the increased threat of catastrophic failures. The risk of physical damage or unauthorized access to the control system increases, compared to preparation mode ($\lambda_2 > \lambda_1$).
- *Combat mode.* The robot is directly threatened by hostile elements, there is a high risk of serious physical damage or unauthorized access to the control system. In this mode, the flow rate of catastrophic failures λ_2 increases to its maximum value and becomes much larger than the flow of natural failures ($\lambda_2 \gg \lambda_1$).

5 Disaster Tolerance of the Onboard Computer System

The use of a single computing module (CM) as an onboard computing system has an obvious disadvantage. When the robot is operating in preparation mode, the level of the failure flow is low, and reliable operation of the onboard control system MGRS will be provided for a period approximately equal to the mean time between failures. However, with a sudden increase of the flow of failures in case of a transition to combat readiness mode and especially to the combat mode, ensuring the disaster tolerance of the onboard computer system of the MGRS is just impossible. Any external influence can lead to a complete fault of the onboard computer system and, consequently to the termination of robot operation. This circumstances is the main reason for the need to use various kinds of redundancy in the design of MGRS.

Redundancy is common method for ensuring additional reliability of an object. The method is implemented through the use of additional tools and capabilities that are redundant to the minimum required to perform the required functions. The most common implementation of the redundancy method is to include additional objects in parallel with the object of reservation that fully or partially duplicate its functions, and are able to take over its tasks in case of failure.

The following types of redundancy are used for GRS:

- hardware (schematic, structural);
- time;
- information;
- functional;
- load.

The simultaneous use of two or more types of redundancy is preferable, as it provides a greater effect in improving reliability. But the main contribution retains the hardware redundancy, and it should be implemented first.

Hardware redundancy is used to back up all critical components of onboard computer systems, starting with the CM and ending with the communication lines.

Information, functional and load redundancy are implemented using appropriate algorithms that ensure the operation of the onboard computer system of the GRS in case of failure of a part of the equipment. These algorithms are discussed below.

With the implemented redundancy, the failure of the control system of the GRS as a whole occurs only after the failure of the main CM and all backups. The main CM is considered to be the module that is necessary to perform the required functions without using the reserve.

In practice, there are the following methods of reservation:

- by object type

  - full redundancy;
  - partial redundancy;

- by redundancy rate (k – is the ratio of the number of backup elements to the number of main elements)

  - redundancy with integral rate;
  - redundancy with fractional rate;

- by the method of backups inclusion
- continuous redundancy

  - hot redundancy;
  - warm redundancy;
  - cold redundancy;

- substitution redundancy

For a preliminary assessment of the benefits of redundancy, it is assumed that when operating in combat mode, the probability of failure of the CM is 30%. Then the probability of failure of the system without redundancy will be 70%, and the system with one backup CM – 91%. If you add a second backup computing module, then the probability of failure of such a system is already 97.3%. From this we can see that the presence of even one backup device decreases the probability of failure of the system by more than 20%.

Figure 1 shows the graphs of the reliability function of the system with the substitution redundancy and with the continuous redundancy at different redundancy rates n. The dependency graphs show that substitution redundancy is a more efficient way to improve the reliability of the system, as compared to redundancy with a constantly included reserve. Its effectiveness grows with $\lambda_0 t$. However, the constantly included reserve has big advantage if the entire computing module is reserved. While the main element is not out of order, you can use more computing power to solve onboard problems and improve the efficiency of the robot. As computational resource is one of the main necessities of GRS the continuous redundancy remains the best way to improve reliability.

Different backup methods must be used to back up different components of the onboard computer network. For example, it does not make sense to use a partial redundancy for a CM, as this will greatly complicate its design and construction, and thus increase the probability of its failure, which will compensate for all the advantage obtained during the redundancy.

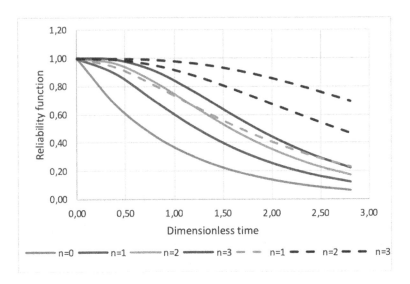

Fig. 1. Dependence of the reliability function on dimensionless time with substitution redundancy (dash) and with continuous redundancy (solid) for different redundancy rate.

6 The Algorithm of Reconfiguration of the Onboard Computer Network After Failure

In case of failure in a redundant computing system, it is necessary to perform the appropriate reconfiguration, which will take into account the reduced performance of the onboard network or the failure of communication channels. Developed appropriate algorithm is explained below.

By onboard computer network, we mean a multi-machine computer complex (MMC), which includes many machines of the same type (class), combined in network to establish the configuration, exchange service messages of the real-time operating system (RTOS) and messages of functional programs by standard LAN channels, as well as optical channels. Multi-machine complexes, on the basis of which real-time systems are implemented, are essentially specialized local networks, with a number of stringent requirements for the composition of physical communication channels, the speed of information transmission, reliability and speed of message delivery.

The concept of architecture implemented on the basis of homogeneous CM is illustrated in Fig. 2, which shows an example of onboard computing network (OCN) and the major connections that implement one of the redundancy schemes.

Each CM is connected to all the others via LAN. The channels of the local network are primarily intended for the transmission of multi-machine complex control information, diagnostic and debugging information about the operation of the real-time system.

If failure in one of the primary CS occurs, the corresponding functional program code restarts from the last agreed checkpoint on the backup one. At the same time, the

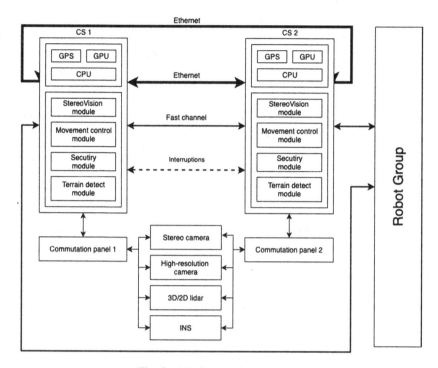

Fig. 2. MMC. Functional scheme.

RTOS takes the failed CM out of work, and the backup one, which assumes the main functions, assigns the status of the main one.

For fast restart in case of failure it is supposed to use hardware and software which control actions by the OS kernel on installation of the system watchdog timer. A watchdog timer is a set of hardware and software that allows you to restart the OS due to a software or hardware error.

In case of using as RTOS "Elbrus", the process of working with the watchdog timer is as follows. The user process-daemon notifies the watchdog driver at regular intervals via a special device */dev/watchdog* that it is still working. When such notification is received, the driver programs the watchdog timer in a such way as to delay the restart of the OS for a while. If for some reason the notification has not occurred, the watchdog timer will restart the OS after the specified interval has elapsed.

The transfer of calculations from the primary CM to the backup one can be performed both automatically (in case of failure of the main machine) and by the operator, but the restoration of the same configuration after repair is carried out only by the operator's commands.

The possibility of forming the required topology of links is determined by the capabilities of cascading modules of S-bus expansion.

The other types of machines can be connected to CM-based networks using standard Ethernet networking tools, as well as through fast channels, the use of which will allow to implement branched connections with various devices in specific OCN.

The way to ensure the configuration of the OCN is the use of software to solve the problems of commutation of the components described above. Configuration is performed by exchanging service messages over a standard LAN network. The initial information required for configuration in the process of initialization of functional programs is formed in the configuration file describing the MMC and the commutation paths between them.

Initialization of MMC is generally performed according to the following scheme. First, the standard system software runs a real-time program on the main CM, then from this program the initialization and launch of real-time programs on other CMs happens, by referring to the appropriate RTOS interface procedure. The initial data for initialization must be contained in the configuration file.

In the initialization process, a structure is created on the host machine that describes the network configuration, as well as the RTOS daemon process. The same structures and processes are created on all MMC nodes connected via a standard network.

In addition to daemons the RTOS on each machine runs "real time program" to work in real-time. Real time program on other machines also refers to this RTOS interface procedure, which provides her access to already established structures for cooperation in the OCN.

After the OCN is successfully initialized and programs are run in real time, the CMs interact at the functional program level. Thus, there is a synchronization of the computational process at the level of functional programs.

Organization of point-to-point interaction between CMs during real-time operation is performed by using RTOS interface procedures for synchronous and asynchronous I/O (writing, reading, I/O control and waiting) in accordance with the logic of interaction of various functional programs.

7 Distributed Data Storage

The use of a redundant computing system poses the problem of distributed data storage. According to [6–8] at the moment there are no reliable, formally and mathematically proven distributed databases with equivalent rights/functions. Only the "dedicated" master database (master) and slave database are available. The exchange of information in this architecture between the databases is called master-slave replication [6].

The main problem of using distributed databases is ensuring consistency of data [9]. It requires a large number of service messages to achieve data consistency (for example, to make sure that the data available to the robot is still relevant), that in the case of a group of robots and, accordingly, slow and not always stable communication channels, does not allow to achieve a high level of performance. Among the models considered in [9], the output consistency model is ideally suited for the task of ensuring the disaster tolerance of onboard computer systems. This model does not require as many data transfers as the model of strict, sequential or weak consistency, but at the same time minimizes the time during which a node possesses unique information (which is important to ensure the stability of the system to the failures of individual nodes), because at the time of exiting the critical section, changes made to the shared memory must be propagated to the rest of the network.

The most obvious solution to the problem of managing distributed data is to choose one of the CSs as Server and perform all data operations through it (Fig. 3). For example, when a consistency model requires a certain node (e.g. node 2) to update some shared data, the node will obtain this data from a server node (node 1). And vice versa, if the model requires the node (e.g. node 2) to propagate its updated data to all other nodes, the node must delegate this task to the server node (node 1), sending it both the task and the data. The server node will contact the other nodes and send them the necessary data. An isolated server node in a distributed system is potentially dangerous, as a dedicated node becomes a weak point of the system – failure of it can lead to failure of the entire system. This can be prevented by reserving a server node (Fig. 4).

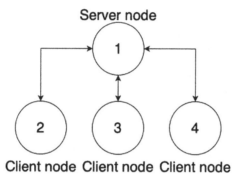

Fig. 3. Model with central server node.

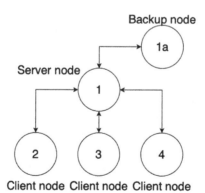

Fig. 4. Fault tolerant model with central server node.

One of the CMs is marked as "mirror" of the server node. And now, when the server node (node 1) performing any data write operation, server node first informs its mirror (node 1a), and only after receiving accept response from the mirror node continues its work. If the mirror node fails, the server node will notice it by the operation timeout trigger and mark another node as mirror.

Using full replication will allow multiple nodes to not only read but also write the same data at the same time. To maintain consistency in this case, all write operations must be ordered in some way. To do this, the server adds a number to each notification that increases with each sending. Using this number, nodes can be sure that they receive notifications in the correct order (and if they miss any of them, they can request it again by specifying the appropriate number in the request).

As the data is distributed across all nodes, the failure of any of them is reversible without additional algorithm improvements. The server can be restored just like any other node, since all it needs to "know" other than the shared memory state is the last number used by its predecessor.

Thus, the implementation of the above algorithms ensures the safety of data in case of failure of any CMs in the GRS. If necessary, the algorithm can be scaled by increasing the number of backup nodes.

8 Load Distribution in Case of Failure

In the event of the failure of a part of the robot's redundant control system, the computing resources may no longer suffice to ensure the fulfillment of its tasks. In this case, you can either limit the robot's tasks to the required minimum (for example, pave the way to the repair station or remain in place as a data translator between robots in the group), or use the free computing resources of other CMs and distribute the tasks to them.

The generalized algorithm of decision-making on reconfiguration consists of the following steps:

1. A boolean vector R is formed, reflecting changes in the state of the OCN. S is the set of operable CMs. Index i-1 denotes the previous iteration of the algorithm, and i – the current one. "1" means that there have been changes in the state of the OCN compared to the previous iteration.

$$R = \left\{ \begin{array}{l} 1, S_i \neq S_{i-1} \\ 0, S_i = S_{i-1} \end{array} \right\}$$

2. Depending on the state of the vector R, the decision is made on whether to change the state of the OCN and to reconfigure according to the reconfiguration table or some optimality criterion.
3. The algorithm of reconfiguration selected in step 2 is implemented. Vector R is reset. In case of successful completion of the reconfiguration, go to step 1. In case of failure go to step 4.
4. Reconfiguration is not possible due to insufficient hardware resources or failure of a highly critical function. Issue of a fault signal of the robot. The end of the operation of the robot.

Steps 1–3 are performed cyclically throughout the life of the system. The decision to issue a fault signal can be made already at step 1 when analyzing the input data on failures. For example, when all CMs fail on one robot, it makes no sense to attempt reconfiguration. To implement this, in addition to analyzing the vector R, it is necessary to check the specified limits on the number of failures. In addition, you can add additional options to the list of possible states of the OCN, in which the possibility of performing functions with a high priority will be checked without their optimal distribution. This can be useful in complex systems with a large number of CMs, in which there is a possibility of such distribution in order to maintain its performance in multiple failures.

9 Conclusion

In this article the method of disaster tolerance of the OCN of GRS is considered. The authors introduced the definition of the term of disaster tolerance of the OCN, considered the ways to ensure it using redundancy of different types. Appropriate algorithms were proposed, taking into account the special features of "Elbrus" hardware and software.

The use of domestic hardware and certified "Elbrus" software shows the potential of solving the robotic tasks according to import substitution policy.

Acknowledgments. This work was supported by Russian Foundation for Basic Research (project №17-29-03297).

References

1. Glukhov, V., Bychkov, I., Trushkin, K.: Trusted hardware and software platform "Elbrus". Domestic solution for ASU TP KVO. Informatizatsiya i Sistemy Upravleniya v Promyshlennosti **1**(49), 66–71 (2014). (in Russian)
2. Paramonov, N., Rjevsky, D., Perekatov, V.: Trusted software and hardware environment "Elbrus" on-board computing means robotic complexes. Questions Radio Electron. = Voprosy radioelektroniki **3**, 159–169 (2015). (in Russian)
3. Bocharov, N., Paramonov, N., Timofeev, G., Panova, O.: Performance of the computer systems with Elbrus-8S processor on the robotic systems tasks. Nanoindustry **S**(82), 79–84 (2018). (in Russian)
4. Bocharov, N., Paramonov, N., Aleksandrov, A., Slavin, O.: Solving of tasks of cognitive control a robots group in multi-core microprocessors «Elbrus». In: Sukhomlin, V., Zubareva, E., Sneps-Sneppe, M. (eds.) Proceedings of the 2nd International Scientific Conference on Convergent Cognitive Information Technologies (Convergent 2017), Moscow, Russia, 24–26 November 2017. CEUR Workshop Proceedings, vol. 2064, pp. 234–244 (2017). http://ceur-ws.org/Vol-2064/paper28.pdf. Accessed 15 Aug 2018. (in Russian)
5. Alfonso, D., et al.: Eight-core «Elbrus-8C» processor microarchitecture. Questions Radio Electron. = Voprosy radioelektroniki, **3**, 6–13 (2016). (in Russian)
6. Shilkin, E., Klopov, I., Ostroukhov, A., Klevetov, D.: Architecture of distributed databases and roles in the implementation of group management of robots. Mod. Sci. Pract. **6–7**(23), 12–17 (2017). (in Russian)

7. Beloglazov, D.A., et al.: Group Control on Moving Objects in Uncertain Environments. Fizmatlit Publishers, Moscow (2015). (in Russian)
8. Kalyaev, I.A., Gayduk, A.R., Kapustin, S.G.: Models and Algorithms of Group Control in Robot Groups. Fizmatlit Publishers, Moscow (2009). (in Russian)
9. Boiko, P.: Maks DSM: distributed shared memory system for multi-agent systems in IoT, Ph. D. thesis. St. Petersburg University, St. Petersburg (2018). (in Russian)

Application of the Asymptotic Observers for the Stabilization of the Time-Delay Linear Equations

Ruslan Sevostyanov$^{(\boxtimes)}$ (ID) and Liliya Shayakhmetova (ID)

Saint-Petersburg State University, Unversitetskaya Str. 7-9,
199034 Saint-Petersburg, Russia
sevostyanov.ruslan@gmail.com

Abstract. Stabilization of the time-delay linear systems by using the static feedback is possible only for the limited value of the time delay in the control channel. In case of the exceeding such limit the further stabilization is impossible. However, the delay limit could be increased by using the number of asymptotic observers of the special kind. The basic idea lies in the equivalence of any realization of the system with certain transfer function which leads to the possibility of distribution of the delay by the several observers. Each observer has lesser delay value so overall limit is decreased. Theoretically, if there are enough observers it is possible to stabilize the system with arbitrary big delay. Moreover, such approach can improve dynamical characteristics in cases where delay value is small enough for the system to be stabilizable. The paper describes the structure and the synthesis method for such observers. The results of the experiments with the computer model are given for the demonstration of the derived regulator's efficiency.

Keywords: Control theory · Feedback · Linear systems · Stabilization · Delay · Asymptotic observer

1 Introduction

The presence of the delays is inevitable in almost every system of the real world. Besides natural reasons there is one more source of the delays caused by the development of the electronics and ubiquitous usage of the microcontrollers and computers. It is so called computational delay and it arises from the fact that control algorithms and also processing and transmission of the digital signals takes nonzero time.

In some cases delay can make improvements in dynamics of the automatic control system, but more often the effect of the delay presence is negative, leading to decrease in the control quality and to loosing stability. Therefore we need to consider delay in design and realization of the automatic control systems.

There exist different methods to consider delays in feedback. One of the most widely known approaches is delay compensation [1] based on usage of the future plant's state computed with the help of the mathematical model of the plant. This method assuming usage of the regulator with own dynamics. Such method allow to

© Springer Nature Switzerland AG 2020
V. Sukhomlin and E. Zubareva (Eds.): Convergent 2018, CCIS 1140, pp. 223–230, 2020.
https://doi.org/10.1007/978-3-030-37436-5_20

keep the transfer matrix of the initial system without the delay and it can be base on the usage of the dynamic regulator as initial feedback [2]. However compensation in this case can be sensitive to inaccuracy in the mathematical model, i.e. there might be possible problems with robust stability.

It might be simpler and more reliable to use classic static feedback based on current plant state. Despite the simplicity in realization of the regulator the feedback synthesis process can be quite complicated because the delay system, in fact, has infinite number of eigenvalues. Besides that there is known problem that using the static feedback it is impossible to stabilize the system with arbitrary delay value. However the problem must be solved if we use the output of the asymptotic observer of the special kind [3] as the feedback input. Basically, if we use enough number of observer, we can stabilize the system with any arbitrary delay value, or we can improve the stability degree of the system with the given delay. This paper describes the structure of such asymptotic observers and also explores the effect of their usage for stabilization of the linear delay equation.

2 Task Description

Let us consider linear equation

$$\dot{x}(t) = ax(t) + u(t - \tau), a > 0, \tau > 0. \tag{1}$$

We need to achieve stability of the system (1) with the given delay value τ, wherein it is desired to provide given stability degree $\sigma_r = \mathrm{Re}(\lambda)$ where λ is the Eq. (1) rightmost eigenvalue;

Let us make the closed-loop system from (1) by applying the feedback

$$u(t) = kx(t), \tag{2}$$

Where k is the arbitrary rational number.

Stabilization of the system (1), (2) by choosing k is possible only if the following condition [3] is true:

$$a\tau < 1. \tag{3}$$

In this case the maximal degree of stability, which we can achieve, is described by the expression

$$\sigma_r^* = a - \frac{1}{\tau}. \tag{4}$$

Condition (3) can be improved by the following idea. Let us assume that we are measuring not the actual state $x(t)$, but some output

$$y(t) = cx(t). \tag{5}$$

System (1), (5) may be described by the transfer function

$$\frac{Y(s)}{U(s)} = \frac{ce^{-s\tau}}{s-a}. \tag{6}$$

Let $c = 1$. Let us notice that any system

$$\begin{aligned}
\dot{x}(t) &= ax(t) + u(t - \tau_1), \\
y(t) &= x(t - \tau_2), \\
\tau_1 + \tau_2 &= \tau,
\end{aligned} \tag{7}$$

is a realization of (6). Consider the asymptotic observer

$$\dot{z}(t) = az(t) + u(t - \tau_1) + h(z(t - \tau_2) - y(t)). \tag{8}$$

Let us make closed-loop system from (7) by the feedback

$$u(t) = kz(t). \tag{9}$$

In this case maximal degree of stability would be

$$\sigma_r^* = \max(a - \frac{1}{\tau_1}, a - \frac{1}{\tau_2}). \tag{10}$$

It is obvious that the optimal value $\sigma_r^* = a - \frac{2}{\tau}$ is achieved if $\tau_1 = \tau_2 = \frac{\tau}{2}$ and condition (3) is of the form

$$a\tau < 2. \tag{11}$$

Described approach can be generalized. If we take enough number of observers like (8) and each one with its own delay distribution, then we can achieve arbitrary degree of stability and arbitrary value in the right side of the inequality (11). For example let us consider the system with two observers

$$\begin{aligned}
\dot{x}(t) &= ax(t) + kz_1(t - \frac{1}{3}\tau), \\
y(t) &= x(t - \frac{2}{3}\tau), \\
\dot{z}_1(t) &= az_1(t) + kz_1(t - \frac{1}{3}\tau) + h(z_1(t - \frac{1}{3}\tau) - z_2(t)), \\
\dot{z}_2(t) &= az_2(t) + kz_1(t - \frac{2}{3}\tau) + h(z_2(t - \frac{1}{3}\tau) - y(t)).
\end{aligned} \tag{12}$$

For system (12) we get $\sigma_r^* = a - \frac{3}{\tau}$ and condition (3) of the form $a\tau < 3$.

If we continue derivations analogous to (12), then we can apply feedback using the system of three asymptotic observer of the form

$$\dot{x}(t) = ax(t) + kz_1(t - \tfrac{1}{4}\tau),$$
$$y(t) = x(t - \tfrac{3}{4}\tau),$$
$$\dot{z}_1(t) = az_1(t) + kz_1(t - \tfrac{1}{4}\tau) + h(z_1(t - \tfrac{1}{4}\tau) - z_2(t)),$$ (12a)
$$\dot{z}_2(t) = az_2(t) + kz_1(t - \tfrac{2}{4}\tau) + h(z_2(t - \tfrac{1}{4}\tau) - z_3(t)),$$
$$\dot{z}_3(t) = az_3(t) + kz_1(t - \tfrac{3}{4}\tau) + h(z_3(t - \tfrac{1}{4}\tau) - y(t)).$$

For system (12a) we get $\sigma_r^* = a - \tfrac{4}{\tau}$ and condition (3) of the form $a\tau < 4$.

Finally let us generalize the structure of the observer to provide $\sigma_r^* = a - \tfrac{N+1}{\tau}$ and condition (3) in form $a\tau < N + 1$, where N is the number of asymptotic observer. Let us introduce the notation

$$\mathbf{z}(t) = \begin{pmatrix} z_1(t) \\ z_2(t) \\ \cdots \\ z_N(t) \end{pmatrix}, \mathbf{z}_\tau(t) = \begin{pmatrix} z_1(t - \frac{1}{N+1}\tau) \\ z_1(t - \frac{2}{N+1}\tau) \\ \cdots \\ z_1(t - \frac{N}{N+1}\tau) \end{pmatrix}, \mathbf{\gamma}(t) = \begin{pmatrix} z_2(t) \\ z_3(t) \\ \cdots \\ z_N(t) \\ y(t) \end{pmatrix},$$

$$A_{NxN} = \begin{pmatrix} a & 0 & \cdots & 0 \\ 0 & a & \cdots & 0 \\ \vdots & \vdots & \ddots & \vdots \\ 0 & 0 & \cdots & a \end{pmatrix}, K_{NxN} = \begin{pmatrix} k & 0 & \cdots & 0 \\ 0 & k & \cdots & 0 \\ \vdots & \vdots & \ddots & \vdots \\ 0 & 0 & \cdots & k \end{pmatrix},$$

$$H_{NxN} = \begin{pmatrix} h & 0 & \cdots & 0 \\ 0 & h & \cdots & 0 \\ \vdots & \vdots & \ddots & \vdots \\ 0 & 0 & \cdots & h \end{pmatrix}.$$

With this we can write the general form of the closed-loop system of the linear equation with the feedback based on the system of asymptotic observer as the following:

$$\dot{x}(t) = ax(t) + kz_1(t - \tfrac{1}{N}\tau),$$
$$y(t) = x(t - \tfrac{N-1}{N}\tau),$$
$$\dot{\mathbf{z}}(t) = \mathbf{A}\mathbf{z}(t) + \mathbf{K}\mathbf{z}_\tau(t) + \mathbf{H}(\mathbf{z}(t - \tfrac{1}{N}\tau) - \boldsymbol{\gamma}(t)). \tag{13}$$

We should notice that analogous derivations can be used for generalization of the regulator (13) to the case of linear delay systems.

3 Computer Modelling

Consider the equation

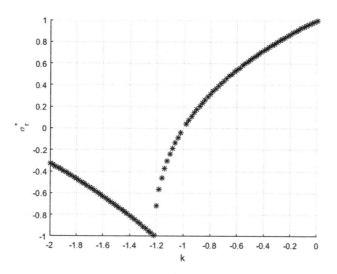

Fig. 1. Function $\sigma_r^*(k)$ with $N = 1$ and $\tau = 1$.

$$\dot{x}(t) = x(t) + u(t - \tau). \tag{14}$$

Assume $\tau = 1$ and the initial state $x_0(t) = 1, t \in [-\tau, 0]$. Let us make closed-loop system from (14) by the feedback (2). In this case we can achieve only $\sigma_r^* = 0$ by $k = -1$, i.e. there just stability, but not the asymptotic stability.

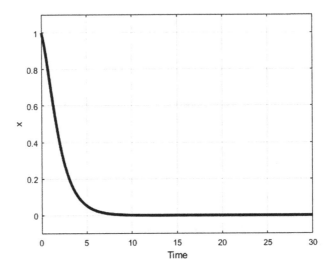

Fig. 2. Output dynamics with $N = 1$ and $\tau = 1$.

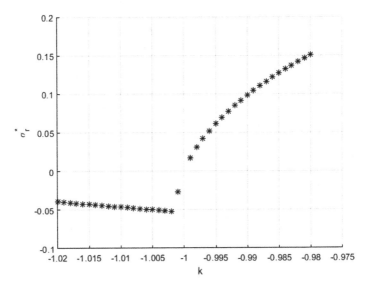

Fig. 3. Function $\sigma_r^*(k)$ with $N = 1$ and $\tau = 1.9$.

Let us apply feedback (13) with $N = 1$ and $h = k$. The function $\sigma_r^*(k)$ is demonstrated on the Fig. 1. As we can actually see, minimal value $\sigma_r^* = -1$ is achieved with $k = -1.22$. Dynamics of the closed-loop system in show on Fig. 2. It can be seen that there is actual asymptotic stability, the value of x converges to zero.

On the other hand, as we stated below, usage of one observer can increase the limit of the delay value at which there is still possibility to provide asymptotic stability up to the value $\tau = 2$. Let $\tau = 1.9$. Function $\sigma_r^*(k)$ for this case is shown on Fig. 3. The best

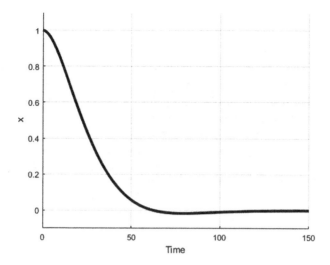

Fig. 4. Output dynamics with $N = 1$ and $\tau = 1.9$.

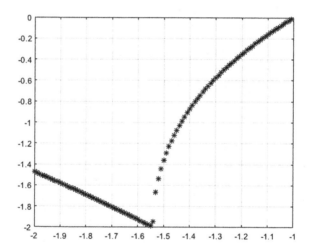

Fig. 5. Function $\sigma_r^*(k)$ with $N = 2$ and $\tau = 1$.

value $\sigma_r^*(k) = -0.05$ is achieved with $k = -1.002$. Transition process in this case is demonstrated on Fig. 4 and it takes quite a long time. Nevertheless, without application of the asymptotic observer in this the stabilization would be impossible at all.

Further increasing the number of observers, as we stated below, leads to improvement of the degree of stability and also to increase of available delay value limit. For demonstration let us compute function $\sigma_r^*(k)$ for values $N = 2$ and $\tau = 1$ (Fig. 5). Here we get the best value $\sigma_r^* = -2$ with $k = -1.55$.

230 R. Sevostyanov and L. Shayakhmetova

4 Conclusion

In this work we presented the extension of the visual line following algorithm using visual feedback and multipurpose regulator to the case of the underactuated system. Multipurpose regulator is supplemented by integral part to provide constant linear velocity of robot's motion along the line. Influence of the tunable parameters on the control motion dynamics is described. The efficiency of the proposed method is shown by the experiments with the computer model. For the further directions of the research we can mark out the problems of the automatic tuning of the tunable matrices depending on the certain requirements to the controlled motion quality. The interesting problems are also arising from the task of the periodic external disturbances compensation and the influence of the feedback delay to the system's dynamics.

References

1. Krstic, M.: Delay Compensation for Nonlinear, Adaptive, and PDE Systems. Birkhäuser, Basel (2009). https://doi.org/10.1007/978-0-8176-4877-0
2. Michiels, W., Engelborghs, K., Vansevenant, P., Roose, D.: Continuous pole placement for delay equations. Automatica **38**(5), 747–761 (2002). https://doi.org/10.1016/S0005-1098(01)00257-6
3. Veremey, E.I.: Compensative output regulators for LTI-systems with late control systems. In: Proceedings of the X International scientific conference PMTUKT-2017. Nauchnaya kniga, Voronezh, pp. 106–110 (2017). [in Russian]

Multi-purpose Control of a Moving Object Using Computer Vision Algorithms

Margarita V. Sotnikova$^{(\boxtimes)}$

Saint-Petersburg State University, Saint-Petersburg, Russia
m.sotnikova@spbu.ru

Abstract. The article is devoted to the design of control systems for moving objects using computer vision algorithms. The relevance of this research area is associated with the increasing use of autonomous vehicles for solving practically important tasks without human intervention. However, many of these tasks are impossible or inefficient to solve without using of visual information.

The problem of visual positioning of a moving object equipped with an onboard video camera is considered. The purpose of the control is to provide the desired position of some observed object in the image plane of the camera. A mathematical model of the joint dynamics of a moving object and a set of observed points in the image plane is derived. Such joint dynamics are taken into account in control design because the camera, mounted on board, has restrictions on freedom of movement in space and on the speed of these movements.

A multi-purpose approach to the synthesis of the control law is proposed, allowing to ensure the fulfillment of a set of requirements for the quality of processes in a closed-loop system in various regimes. The choice of adjustable elements of a multi-purpose structure is discussed. The application of the approach is illustrated by an example of control of a wheeled robot. The results of simulation performed in MATLAB/Simulink environment are presented.

Keywords: Multi-purpose control · Computer vision · Visual positioning · External disturbances · Moving object · Wheeled robot

1 Introduction

Nowadays the autonomous moving objects are extensively used in practice, in particular in the areas where human operation is impossible or undesirable. The autonomy of these objects is implemented by means of special sensors installed on board and getting the information about the surrounding world. In many applications the visual information obtained from cameras plays a crucial role and can be effectively used in feedback control.

Supported by RFBR, research project № 18-37-00463.

The three basic approaches to visual feedback control or visual servo control are presented in papers [1–3]. The first method named IBVS (Image based visual servo control) is based on the minimization of the difference between actual and desirable position of the observed object on the image plane of the camera. The second approach named PBVS (Position based visual servo control) utilizes visual information for the three-dimensional reconstruction of the observed scene and then the obtained geometrical information is used in control algorithms. In the framework of the third approach the elements of the first two approaches are combined, so it represents the combination of the image-based and position-based approaches. It can be noted that in the second approach the poblems of computer vision and control are separated, while in the first and third approaches, visual information is used directly in the feedback loop to form a control signal.

In this paper the issues related to the first approach are investigated. The problem of visual positioning of a moving object is considered. The control objective consists of providing the desired position of the observed object in the image plane of the onboard camera. Unlike previously obtained results [4], here the mathematical model of the joint dynamics of a moving object and the observed points in the image plane is taken as a basis for control system design. The use of such joint model is necessary, since the moving object imposes a constraints on the freedom and on the velocity of camera motion in space.

It is proposed to use a multi-purpose structure for control system design, which makes it possible to reduce the overall extremely complex problem of analytical synthesis to a sequence of local optimization problems [5]. The most important feature of the multi-purpose approach is that it allows us to provide the fullfilment of a set of requirements imposed on the performance of a closed-loop system in a various regimes, including the motion under the influence of external disturbances. The choice of adjustable elements of a multi-purpose structure is discussed and the corresponding computational algorithm for their search is formed.

The practical application of the proposed approach is illustrated by the example of control of a wheeled robot. The results of the simulation performed in the MATLAB/Simulink environment are presented.

2   Statement of Visual Positioning Problem

Let consider a mathematical model of the moving object dynamics

$$\mathbf{M}\dot{\nu} = -\mathbf{D}\nu + \tau + \tau_e(t), \tag{1}$$

where $\mathbf{M} = \mathbf{M}^T$ is a positive definite inertia matrix, $\mathbf{D}$ is a positive definite damping matrix, $\nu \in E^n$ is a vector of linear and angular velocities, $\tau \in E^n$ and $\tau_e(t) \in E^n$ are control input and external disturbances respectively.

Let assume that the moving object is equipped with an onboard camera. This camera is fixed and can move and rotate only together with the object, that is, it does not have additional degrees of freedom. The object of observation is in the field of view of the camera at each time instant. This observed object has certain geometric characteristics and position in space.

Let $\mathbf{s}$ be a vector representing the projection of the observed object on the image plane. The components of such a vector, in particular, can be projections (x_i, y_i), $i = \overline{1, N}$ of interest points of the object on the image plane [6]. The change in vector $\mathbf{s}$ is related with the motion of a camera in space that is described by the following system of differential equations:

$$\dot{\mathbf{s}} = \mathbf{L}_s\left(\mathbf{s}, \mathbf{Z}_c\right)\nu + \mathbf{d}_c(t). \tag{2}$$

Here $\mathbf{Z}_c$ is a vector containing the applicate Z_i, $i = \overline{1, N}$ of each of the observed points in the camera coordinate system, $\mathbf{d}_c(t)$ is an external disturbance, $\mathbf{L}_s\left(\mathbf{s}, \mathbf{Z}_c\right)$ is an interconnection matrix whose components are given in [1]. The expressions for the elements of this matrix are derived on the basis of the laws of theoretical mechanics and the perspective projection model [7]. In addition to system (2), let also consider the equations for vector $\mathbf{Z}_c$:

$$\dot{\mathbf{Z}}_c = \mathbf{L}_Z\left(\mathbf{s}, \mathbf{Z}_c\right)\nu + \mathbf{d}_Z(t), \tag{3}$$

where $\mathbf{L}_Z\left(\mathbf{s}, \mathbf{Z}_c\right)$ is a matrix whose components is described in [1], $\mathbf{d}_Z(t)$ is an external disturbance. As a result, Eqs. (1)–(3) constitute the full mathematical model of the control object. It is important to note that these equations should be considered together, since Eq. (1) actually makes an additional differential connections with respect to model (2). In the following it is supposed that the vectors ν, $\mathbf{s}$ and $\mathbf{Z}_c$ can be mearused.

The purpose of the control is to achieve the desired vector $\mathbf{s}_d$, that is, the desired projection of the observed object in the image plane. Formally, it can be represented as follows:

$$\lim_{t \to +\infty} \mathbf{s}(t) = \mathbf{s}_d. \tag{4}$$

The essence of the problem of visual positioning is the synthesis of nonlinear feedback of the form

$$\begin{aligned} \dot{\rho} &= \mathbf{f}\left(\rho, \tau, \mathbf{s}, \mathbf{Z}_c, \mathbf{s}_d\right), \\ \tau &= \mathbf{g}\left(\rho, \tau, \mathbf{s}, \mathbf{Z}_c, \mathbf{s}_d\right), \end{aligned} \tag{5}$$

where $\rho \in E^k$ is a state vector of the regulator. The regulator (5) must provide that the following requirements hold:

(1) control objective (4) is achieved;
(2) the asymptotic stability for the closed-loop system (1–3), (5);
(3) astatism with respect to controlled output vector $\mathbf{s}$ in the presence of constant or slowly varying external disturbances;
(4) filtering the external disturbances in the control signal channel in the presence of oscillatory disturbances.

The classical solution of the considered problem is the synthesis of control based on the IBVS method (image-based visual servo control) [1]. In the framework of this approach the control signal is formed in such a way as to provide an exponential decrease in the error that determines the difference between the desired and the actual position of the observed object in the image plane. It is important to note that this method implies that the camera has six degrees of freedom and can move freely in the configuration space, that is, there are no additional differential constraints in the form of dynamics Eq. (2).

In paper [4] was proposed the approach to control system design, which is based on the separation of two loops – the first loop to control the velocity of the moving object, and the second loop to control the motion of an observed points in the image plane. This approach is effective if the control object has low inertia and powerful actuators.

Unlike to the mentioned approaches, this paper proposes a multi-purpose approach to the synthesis of the control law on the basis of a complete joint nonlinear mathematical model (1)–(3). The issues of the choice of adjustable elements of multi-purpose structure are discussed. The purpose of this adjustment is to provide a set of the requirements imposed on the performance of the closed loop system.

3   Control System Design Using Multi-purpose Approach

Consider the mathematical model of the dynamics of the moving object and the image points represented by the formulas (1)–(3). It can be noted that this model is essentially nonlinear. Let constant vectors s_d and $\mathbf{Z}_c^d$ determines the final desired poition of the observed object with respect to the camera frame.

Now let us introduce a simplified linear model on the basis of Eqs. (1) and (3) in the following form:

$$\begin{aligned} \mathbf{M}\dot{\nu} &= -\mathbf{D}\nu + \tau + \tau_e(t), \\ \dot{\mathbf{e}} &= \mathbf{L}_{s0}\nu + \mathbf{d}_c(t), \end{aligned} \tag{6}$$

where $\mathbf{L}_{s0} = \mathbf{L}_s\left(\mathbf{s}_d, \mathbf{Z}_c^d\right)$ is a constant matrix computed for the final position of the camera, $\mathbf{e} = \mathbf{s} - \mathbf{s}_d$ is an error vector. Model (6) approximately represents the dynamics of the control object, and it is the most accurate in the vicinity of the equilibrium position $\nu_0 = \mathbf{0}$, $\mathbf{s}_0 = \mathbf{s}_d$. Let us assume this model as a basis for control system design.

Consider the multi-purpose structure of the control law [8,9]. Within the framework of stated problem and taking into account the Eq. (6), it is represented by the following system of differential equations:

$$\begin{aligned} \mathbf{M}\dot{\mathbf{z}}_\nu &= -\mathbf{D}\mathbf{z}_\nu + \tau + \mathbf{H}_\nu\left(\nu - \mathbf{z}_\nu\right), \\ \dot{\mathbf{z}}_e &= \mathbf{L}_{s0}\mathbf{z}_\nu + \mathbf{H}_e\left(\mathbf{e} - \mathbf{z}_e\right), \\ \dot{\mathbf{p}} &= \alpha\mathbf{p} + \beta_\nu\left(\nu - \mathbf{z}_\nu\right) + \beta_e\left(\mathbf{e} - \mathbf{z}_e\right), \\ \xi &= \gamma\mathbf{p} + \mu_\nu\left(\nu - \mathbf{z}_\nu\right) + \mu_e\left(\mathbf{e} - \mathbf{z}_e\right), \\ \tau &= -\mathbf{K}_\nu\mathbf{z}_\nu - \mathbf{K}_e\mathbf{z}_e + \xi. \end{aligned} \tag{7}$$

Here $\mathbf{z}_\nu \in E^n$ and $\mathbf{z}_e$ are the state vectors of asymptotic observer, $\mathbf{p} \in E^{n_p}$ is a state vector of the dynamical corrector. The first two equations in the multi-purpose structure (7) are the equations of the asymptotic observer, the next two equations represents the dynamical corrector, and the last equation forms control signal. Adjustable elements of the multi-purpose structure (7) consists of the following elements:

(1) matrices $\mathbf{K}_\nu$ and $\mathbf{K}_e$ of the basic control law;
(2) matrices $\mathbf{H}_\nu$ and $\mathbf{H}_e$ of the asymptotic observer;
(3) matrices $\alpha, \beta_\nu, \beta_e, \gamma, \mu_\nu, \mu_e$ of the dynamical corrector.

The search for these adjustable elements, based on the requirements for the closed-loop system performance in the different regimes of motion, constitute the essence of the problem of multi-purpose synthesis.

In futher discussion, the dynamical corrrector equations are also represented in the following equivalent tf-form:

$$\xi = \mathbf{K}_1(s)\,(\nu - \mathbf{z}_\nu) + \mathbf{K}_2(s)\,(\mathbf{e} - \mathbf{z}_e),\tag{8}$$

where $\mathbf{K}_1(s) = \gamma \left(\mathbf{E}_{n_p} s - \alpha\right)^{-1} \beta_\nu + \mu_\nu$, $\mathbf{K}_2(s) = \gamma \left(\mathbf{E}_{n_p} s - \alpha\right)^{-1} \beta_e + \mu_e$ are the transfer matrices, s is a Laplace variable.

Let us consider sequentially the issues of choosing adjustable elements of a multi-purpose structure (7). The most important feature of the multi-purpose structure is that the search for its adjustable elements can be performed sequentially, as shown in [10].

3.1   Synthesis of the Basic Control Law and the Asymptotic Observer

Let us consider the basic regime of motion of a closed-loop system. This regime is described by Eq. (6) in the absence of external disturbances, under non-zero initial conditions $\nu_0 \neq \mathbf{0}$, $\mathbf{e} \neq \mathbf{0}$ and with the basic regulator of the form

$$\tau = -\mathbf{K}_\nu \nu - \mathbf{K}_e \mathbf{e}.\tag{9}$$

Let introduce a positive definite quadratic form

$$V = \frac{1}{2}\mathbf{e}^T\mathbf{e} + \frac{1}{2}\nu^T\mathbf{M}\nu.$$

Calculating its derivative on the motion of a closed-loop system, we obtain

$$\dot{V}|_{(6)} = -\nu^T\mathbf{D}\nu + \nu^T\left(\mathbf{L}_{s0}^T\mathbf{e} + \tau\right).$$

From here it follows that we can choose the matrices of a basic regulator (9) in the following way:

$$\mathbf{K}_e = \mathbf{L}_{s0}^T,\ \mathbf{K}_\nu \succ 0,$$

where $\mathbf{K}_\nu$ is the any positive definite matrix. In this case we have $\dot{V}|_{(6)} \leq 0$, hence the equilibrium position of a closed-loop system (6), (9) is stable. It can be noted that the closed-loop system (6) and (9) in the absence of external disturbances has a zero equilibrium position $\nu_0 = \mathbf{0}$, $\mathbf{e} = \mathbf{0}$, and therefore $\mathbf{s}_0 = \mathbf{s}_d$, so the control objective (4) is achieved. Since the model (6) is linear and stationary, the asymptotic stability of the equilibrium position is guaranteed if the eigenvalues of the matrix of the closed-loop system (6), (9) are located in the open left half-plane of the complex plane.

Let now consider the issue of the choice of the matrices $\mathbf{H}_\nu$ and $\mathbf{H}_e$ of asymptotic observer. In accordance to (7) the equations of asymptotic observer are as follows:

$$
\begin{aligned}
\mathbf{M}\dot{\mathbf{z}}_\nu &= -\mathbf{D}\mathbf{z}_\nu + \tau + \mathbf{H}_\nu \left(\nu - \mathbf{z}_\nu\right), \\
\dot{\mathbf{z}}_e &= \mathbf{L}_{s0}\mathbf{z}_\nu + \mathbf{H}_e \left(\mathbf{e} - \mathbf{z}_e\right).
\end{aligned}
\tag{10}
$$

Let introduce the vectors of observation errors: $\mathbf{e}_\nu = \nu - \mathbf{z}_\nu$, $\mathbf{e}_s = \mathbf{e} - \mathbf{z}_e$. Then, taking into account (6) and (10), we can form equations with respect to observation errors:

$$
\begin{aligned}
\mathbf{M}\dot{\mathbf{e}}_\nu &= \left(-\mathbf{D} - \mathbf{H}_\nu\right)\mathbf{e}_\nu, \\
\dot{\mathbf{e}}_s &= \mathbf{L}_{s0}\mathbf{e}_\nu - \mathbf{H}_e\mathbf{e}_s.
\end{aligned}
\tag{11}
$$

From (11) we can see that the convergence of observation errors $\mathbf{e}_\nu$ and $\mathbf{e}_s$ to zero is guaranteed for any choice of the positive definite matrices $\mathbf{H}_\nu$ and $\mathbf{H}_e$.

3.2 Synthesis of the Dynamical Corrector

The main purpose of the dynamical corrector is to provide the desired dynamics of a closed-loop system in the presence of external disturbances. In the framework of this paper, the synthesis of a dynamical corrector is aimed at providing two properties of a closed-loop system: astatism on the controlled vector $\mathbf{s}$ in the presence of constant or slowly varying external disturbances, and filtration of external disturbances in the control channel in the presence of oscillating disturbances.

Consider firstly the case of constant external disturbances. Let assume that $\tau_e = \tau_{e0}$ and $\mathbf{d}_c = \mathbf{d}_{c0}$ are constant vectors. Taking into account (7) and (8), the expression for the control signal can be represented in the form

$$
\tau = -\mathbf{K}_\nu\mathbf{z}_\nu - \mathbf{K}_e\mathbf{z}_e + \mathbf{K}_1(s)\left(\nu - \mathbf{z}_\nu\right) + \mathbf{K}_2(s)\left(\mathbf{e} - \mathbf{z}_e\right).
\tag{12}
$$

Next, let us form the equations of the system closed by regulator (12). As a result, using (6) and (10), and also the entered designations for vectors $\mathbf{e}_\nu$ and $\mathbf{e}_s$, we obtain

$$
\begin{aligned}
\mathbf{M}\dot{\mathbf{e}}_\nu &= \left(-\mathbf{D} - \mathbf{H}_\nu\right)\mathbf{e}_\nu + \tau_{e0}, \\
\dot{\mathbf{e}}_s &= \mathbf{L}_{s0}\mathbf{e}_\nu - \mathbf{H}_e\mathbf{e}_s + \mathbf{d}_{c0}, \\
\mathbf{M}\dot{\mathbf{z}}_\nu &= -\mathbf{D}\mathbf{z}_\nu + \mathbf{H}_\nu\mathbf{e}_\nu - \mathbf{K}_\nu\mathbf{z}_\nu - \mathbf{K}_e\mathbf{z}_e + \mathbf{K}_1(s)\mathbf{e}_\nu + \mathbf{K}_2(s)\mathbf{e}_s, \\
\dot{\mathbf{z}}_e &= \mathbf{L}_{s0}\mathbf{z}_\nu + \mathbf{H}_e\mathbf{e}_s.
\end{aligned}
\tag{13}
$$

The equilibrium position of the closed-loop system (13) can be found by equating its right-hand parts to zero. Doing so, from the first two equations we obtain

$$
\begin{aligned}
\left(-\mathbf{D} - \mathbf{H}_\nu\right)\mathbf{e}_{\nu 0} + \tau_{e0} &= \mathbf{0}, \\
\mathbf{L}_{s0}\mathbf{e}_{\nu 0} - \mathbf{H}_e\mathbf{e}_{s0} + \mathbf{d}_{c0} &= \mathbf{0},
\end{aligned}
\tag{14}
$$

where $\mathbf{e}_{\nu 0}$ and $\mathbf{e}_{s0}$ are equilibrium positions for vectors of errors. From (14) we get that there is a bijection between the non-zero disturbance vectors τ_{e0}, $\mathbf{d}_{c0}$ and non-zero error vectors $\mathbf{e}_{\nu 0}$, $\mathbf{e}_{s0}$. In this connection, the vectors $\mathbf{e}_{\nu 0}$, $\mathbf{e}_{s0}$ can be interpreted as a disturbances in the third and fourth equations of system (13). Keeping this in mind, from forth equation we have

$$\mathbf{z}_{\nu 0} = -\left(\mathbf{L}_{s0}^T \mathbf{L}_{s0}\right)^{-1} \mathbf{L}_{s0}^T \mathbf{H}_e \mathbf{e}_{s0} = \mathbf{T} \mathbf{e}_{s0}, \tag{15}$$

where $\mathbf{T} = -\left(\mathbf{L}_{s0}^T \mathbf{L}_{s0}\right)^{-1} \mathbf{L}_{s0}^T \mathbf{H}_e$ is an auxiliary designation. Substituting (15) in the third equation of the system (13) and taking into account the equality $\mathbf{z}_{e0} = \mathbf{e}_0 - \mathbf{e}_{s0}$, we find

$$\mathbf{K}_e \mathbf{e}_0 = (\mathbf{K}_e - \mathbf{D}\mathbf{T} - \mathbf{K}_\nu \mathbf{T} + \mathbf{K}_2(0)) \, \mathbf{e}_{s0} + (\mathbf{H}_\nu + \mathbf{K}_1(0)) \, \mathbf{e}_{\nu 0}.$$

Therefore, the astatic property is satisfied for any disturbances τ_{e0}, $\mathbf{d}_{c0}$, if the following conditions are hold

$$\mathbf{K}_2(0) = -\mathbf{K}_e + \mathbf{D}\mathbf{T} + \mathbf{K}_\nu \mathbf{T}, \quad \mathbf{K}_1(0) = -\mathbf{H}_\nu. \tag{16}$$

Thus, the matrices $\alpha, \beta_\nu, \beta_e, \gamma, \mu_\nu, \mu_e$ of the dynamical corrector must satisfy the conditions (16), which provides the astatism of the controlled output $\mathbf{s}$ with respect to the constant disturbances τ_{e0}, $\mathbf{d}_{c0}$.

Let now consider a case of oscillating disturbances. For simplicity, we assume that the disturbances $\tau_e(t)$ and $\mathbf{d}_c(t)$ are harmonic oscillations with frequency ω_0. In the subsequent discussion the additional conditions on the transfer matrices $\mathbf{K}_1(s)$ and $\mathbf{K}_2(s)$ are derived. These conditions provides filtering of an external disturbances with frequency ω_0 in the control signal channel.

To this end, let us consider the equations of the asymptotic observer in the system (7) and express the values of the vectors $\mathbf{z}_\nu$ and $\mathbf{z}_e$. As a result, we obtain

$$\begin{aligned} \mathbf{z}_\nu &= \mathbf{T}_{11}(s)\mathbf{e}_\nu + \mathbf{T}_{12}(s)\mathbf{e}_s, \\ \mathbf{z}_e &= \mathbf{T}_{21}(s)\mathbf{e}_\nu + \mathbf{T}_{22}(s)\mathbf{e}_s, \end{aligned} \tag{17}$$

where $\mathbf{T}_{11}(s)$, $\mathbf{T}_{12}(s)$, $\mathbf{T}_{21}(s)$, $\mathbf{T}_{22}(s)$ are the auxiliary transfer functions, expressions for which are determined by (15). Substituting (17) to the equation for the control signal (12), we have

$$\begin{aligned} \tau = &(-\mathbf{K}_\nu \mathbf{T}_{11}(s) - \mathbf{K}_e \mathbf{T}_{21}(s) + \mathbf{K}_1(s)) \, \mathbf{e}_\nu + \\ &+ (-\mathbf{K}_\nu \mathbf{T}_{12}(s) - \mathbf{K}_e \mathbf{T}_{22}(s) + \mathbf{K}_2(s)) \, \mathbf{e}_s. \end{aligned}$$

Then the condition of filtering the external disturbances $\tau_e(t)$ and $\mathbf{d}_c(t)$ at a given frequency ω_0 takes the form

$$\begin{aligned} \mathbf{K}_1(j\omega_0) &= \mathbf{K}_\nu \mathbf{T}_{11}(j\omega_0) + \mathbf{K}_e \mathbf{T}_{21}(j\omega_0) = \mathbf{R}_1 + j\mathbf{I}_1, \\ \mathbf{K}_2(j\omega_0) &= \mathbf{K}_\nu \mathbf{T}_{21}(j\omega_0) + \mathbf{K}_e \mathbf{T}_{22}(j\omega_0) = \mathbf{R}_2 + j\mathbf{I}_2. \end{aligned} \tag{18}$$

Here $\mathbf{R}_1$, $\mathbf{R}_2$ and $\mathbf{I}_1$, $\mathbf{I}_2$ are the matrices with real components representing real and imaginary parts of complex numbers.

As a result, the properties of astatism and filtering are provided by the multi-purpose control law (7) if the transfer matrices $\mathbf{K}_1(s)$ and $\mathbf{K}_2(s)$ of the dynamical corrector are satisfied to the conditions (16) and (18).

Let consider the issue of synthesis of the dynamical corrector in state-space form that satisfies conditions (16) and (18). The essence of this problem is to choose such matrices $\alpha, \beta_\nu, \beta_e, \gamma, \mu_\nu, \mu_e$ of the corrector that ensure fulfillment of the mentioned conditions.

First of all, we can note that the stability of the equilibrium position of a closed-loop system (6), (7) is guaranteed if matrix α is Hurwitz. Let us select the dimension of the state vector of the corrector $n_p = 3$ and set an arbitrary Hurwitz matrix α of size 3×3. Let also take the following matrices values: γ is a matrix, which rows are equal to the vectors $\gamma_i = (0, 0, 1)$, $i = \overline{1, n}$, and $\mu_\nu = \mathbf{0}$, $\mu_e = \mathbf{0}$. Thus, only vectors β_ν, β_e remain unknown.

Taking into account (16) and (8), we obtain

$$\gamma \alpha^{-1} \beta_\nu = \mathbf{H}_\nu, \quad \gamma \alpha^{-1} \beta_e = -\mathbf{K}_e + \mathbf{D}T + \mathbf{K}_\nu \mathbf{T}. \tag{19}$$

Similarly, on the basis of equality (18), we derive the conditions

$$\begin{aligned}
\gamma \left(\mathbf{E}_{n_p} j\omega_0 - \alpha\right)^{-1} \beta_\nu &= \mathbf{R}_1 + j\mathbf{I}_1, \\
\gamma \left(\mathbf{E}_{n_p} j\omega_0 - \alpha\right)^{-1} \beta_e &= \mathbf{R}_2 + j\mathbf{I}_2.
\end{aligned} \tag{20}$$

Let introduce the following notations:

$$\alpha^R = Re\left(\mathbf{E}_{n_p} j\omega_0 - \alpha\right)^{-1}, \quad \alpha^I = Im\left(\mathbf{E}_{n_p} j\omega_0 - \alpha\right)^{-1}.$$

Then the Eq. (20) can be represented as follows:

$$\begin{aligned}
\gamma \alpha^R \beta_\nu &= \mathbf{R}_1, \quad \gamma \alpha^I \beta_\nu = \mathbf{I}_1, \\
\gamma \alpha^R \beta_e &= \mathbf{R}_2, \quad \gamma \alpha^I \beta_e = \mathbf{I}_2.
\end{aligned} \tag{21}$$

Considering together (19) and (21), we obtain two systems of linear equations with the same square matrix of size 3×3 to search for unknown vectors β_ν and β_e. The matrix of these systems is equal to

$$\mathbf{A} = \begin{pmatrix} \gamma \alpha^{-1} \\ \gamma \alpha^R \\ \gamma \alpha^I \end{pmatrix}. \tag{22}$$

If the matrix (22) is non-singular, then both linear systems have a unique solution defining the unknown vectors β_ν and β_e.

As a result, the considered procedure allows to design a mathematical model of dynamical corrector in the state space form in accordance with Eq. (7). The matrices $\alpha, \beta_\nu, \beta_e, \gamma, \mu_\nu, \mu_e$ of this representation is chosen in accordance with the conditions of astatism (16) and disturbance filtering (18). It can be mentioned that the proposed procedure can be easily extended to the case of polyharmonic external disturbances.

4   Practical Example

Let us illustrate the proposed approach for control system design by an example of wheel robot control. The mathematical model of its dynamics is represented by equation [11]:

$$\dot{\nu} = \tau + \tau_e(t). \tag{23}$$

where $\nu = (u, v, r)^T$ is a robot velocity, $\tau_e(t)$ is an external disturbance. The dynamics of an observed points in the image plane of onboard video camera is described by Eq. (2). The joint system of equations (23) and (2) represents a full mathematical model, which is used as the basis for the construction of a multi-purpose control law (7).

Let us assume that the camera observe four points in three-dimensional space that are the vertices of a square. The initial and the final positions of this square in the image plane are shown in Fig. 1. In accordance with the proposed approach, we can design multi-purpose control law (7). The result of its application is represented in Figs. 1 and 2. The trajectories of a points on the image plane are shown in Fig. 1 and the corresponding robot motion can be seen in Fig. 2. From the figures it can be noted that the desired position of the observed object in the image plane is achieved. The developed multi-purpose control algorithm possess also the properties of stability, astatism and filtering.

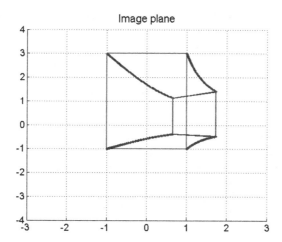

Fig. 1. Trajectories of a points in the image plane.

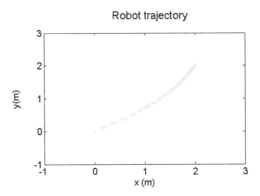

Fig. 2. Robot trajectory.

5   Conclusion

In this paper the approach for control system design in visual positioning problem is proposed. The method is based on a joint mathematical model of the dynamics of a moving object and the dynamics of points in the image plane of the onboard camera, as well as a multi-purpose structure of the control law. The design procedure takes into account the requirements of the closed-loop system astatism for controlled output and filtering of external disturbances in the control channel. The computational algorithm for searching the matrices of a dynamical corrector is developed. This algorithm allows to ensure the fulfillment of the imposed requirements. The application of the approach is demonstrated by the example of wheeled robot control.

References

1. Chaumette, F., Hutchinson, S.: Visual servo control: basic approaches. IEEE Robot. Autom. Mag. **13**(4), 82–90 (2006)
2. Chaumette, F., Hutchinson, S.: Visual servo control: advanced approaches. IEEE Robot. Autom. Mag. **14**(1), 109–118 (2007)
3. Malis, E., Chaumette, F., Boudet, S.: 2 1/2 D visual servoing. IEEE Trans. Robot. Autom. **15**(2), 238–250 (1999)
4. Veremey, E.I., Sotnikova, M.V.: Visual image based dynamical positioning using control laws with multipurpose structure. IFAC Proc. Vol. **48**(16), 184–189 (2015)
5. Veremey, E.I.: Lineynye sistemy s obratnoi svyaz'yu. Izdatel'stvo Lan', Saint-Petersburg (2013)
6. Lowe, D.G.: Distinctive image features from scale-invariant keypoints. Int. J. Comput. Vis. **2**(60), 91–110 (2004)
7. Szeliski, R.: Computer Vision: Algorithms and Applications. Springer-Verlag, London (2011). https://doi.org/10.1007/978-1-84882-935-0
8. Veremey, E.I.: Dynamical correction of positioning control laws. IFAC Proc. Vol. **46**(33), 31–36 (2013)

9. Veremey, E.I.: Separate filtering correction of observer-based marine positioning control laws. Int. J. Control **90**(8), 1561–1575 (2017)
10. Veremey, E.I.: Dynamical correction of control laws for marine ships' accurate steering. J. Mar. Sci. Appl. **13**(2), 127–133 (2014)
11. Siciliano, B., Khatib, O. (eds.): Handbook of Robotics. Springer, Heidelberg (2008). https://doi.org/10.1007/978-3-540-30301-5

Stabilization of the Underactuated Robot on the Visual Trajectory

Ruslan Sevostyanov$^{(\boxtimes)}$ (iD)

Saint-Petersburg State University, Unversitetskaya Str. 7–9,
199034 Saint-Petersburg, Russia
sevostyanov.ruslan@gmail.com

Abstract. The article considers the problem of moving and stabilizing under-actuated wheeled robot on the visual curve in the motion plane. The curve is detected by the video camera mounted on the robot. The task is solved with the help of the approach named visual servoing which uses the visual information in the feedback. The aim of the visual serving is to minimize the difference between desired and the actual position of the set of the points on the image. The main feature of the proposed solution is considering a number of requirements to the robot's dynamic including the reaction on the presence of the external disturbances. Thereby the regulators of special kind called multipurpose structure are used which makes possible to decompose the basic set of requirements into smaller independent tasks. Additional complication is the underactuated nature of the considered robot. Efficiency of the derived regulator is shown through the experiments with computer model.

Keywords: Control theory · Feedback · Stabilization · Computer vision

1 Introduction

Development of the electronics and applied math methods leads to the growth of using information from the video cameras in the tasks of the automatic motion control of the different objects. As an example we can give autonomous cars, manipulators on the automated factories and the competitions of the autonomous robots soccer. Besides those situations in which the images are used only to get the information about the current state of the plant one can highlight the separate class of the methods which use the visual information directly for the feedback loop. Such methods are called Visual Servoing in literature [1]. Shortly they can be described as the minimization of the difference between desired and actual position of the set of the point on the image. There are a lot of publications about the control of the fully actuated plants so far, however the situations in which the amount of the control inputs less than the number of the states of freedom of the controlled system are still being developed and need further research.

On the other hand the requirements for the motion control quality and for the reactions on different disturbances such as wind, nonsmooth surface or hull vibrations are constantly growing, becoming stricter. Thereby we need to apply approaches that can take into account the whole set of requirements and restrictions for the controlled

© Springer Nature Switzerland AG 2020
V. Sukhomlin and E. Zubareva (Eds.): Convergent 2018, CCIS 1140, pp. 242–250, 2020.
https://doi.org/10.1007/978-3-030-37436-5_22

motion dynamics. In this case we can use the feedback of the special type which is called multipurpose regulators [2]. Besides the orientation to the multimode such regulators are noticeable because they allow to split the initial complex task to the simpler subtasks which can be solved in a certain sense independently.

This paper extends the method described in the work [3] to the case of the underactuated robot moving along the visual curve line which lies in the robot's motion plane using the visual servoing approach paired with the multipurpose regulator.

2 Task Description

Let us the mobile robot controlled by setting the left and right wheels velocities (so called unicycle model). It could be either the tracked robot or the three-wheeled robot in which the third wheel (usually mounted in front or rear) spins independently.

Mathematical model of the robot is described by the equations [4]:

$$\dot{\upsilon} = A\upsilon + B\tau + d(t),$$
$$\dot{\eta} = R(\eta)\upsilon, \tag{1}$$

where $\upsilon = (v, \omega)^T$ – velocity vector, v – linear velocity, ω – angular velocity; $\tau = (\tau_v, \tau_\omega)^T$ – control vector: τ_v – the sum of the motors voltages, τ_ω – the difference of the voltages; $\eta = (x, y, \varphi)^T$ – position of the mass center and the robots heading angle; $d(t)$ – external disturbance vector; A – diagonal matrix of the friction coefficients; B – diagonal matrix of the control coefficients. There is nonlinearity in the system (1) is described by the matrix

$$R(\eta) = R(\phi) = \begin{pmatrix} \sin(\phi) & 0 \\ \cos(\phi) & 0 \\ 0 & 1 \end{pmatrix}. \tag{2}$$

On the robots hull there is a video camera rigidly fixed downward on the height . We will assume that in the field of the camera's view there always is some continuous visual curve line. Let us set a task of moving the robot along the given curve. Along with this the robot must move at the constant velocity. Line following must be provided considering possible presence of the constant external disturbances. Motion and reaction on disturbance must meet some specified requirements.

3 Visual Servoing

To provide line following it is necessary for the line projection on the camera image to go through point $P^* = (0, y_{\max})$ where $y_{\max}$ – maximal y-axis value on the image plane. It is also necessary for the robot's direction to coincide with the direction of the tangent line of the trajectory at the specified point which is described by the angle θ. Let

$\bar{P} = (\bar{x}, \bar{y})$ be the actual position of the lowest point of the visual line in the image plane. Then we can find the difference between desired and actual parameters

$$
\begin{aligned}
e_x &= \bar{x}, \\
e_y &= \bar{y} - y_{\text{max}}, \\
e_\theta &= \theta.
\end{aligned}
\tag{3}
$$

Next, in accordance with the perspective transformation formulas and also considering the camera position we can set up correspondence between the points in the robot's motion plane and their projections on the image plane:

$$
\begin{aligned}
x &= \frac{X}{h}, \\
y &= -\frac{Y}{h},
\end{aligned}
\tag{4}
$$

where (x, y) – coordinates of the point in the image plane, (X, Y) – coordinates of the point in the motion plane.

Taking into account formulas (1) and (4) we can describe the motion dynamics of the arbitrary point on the image and the rotation dynamics of the arbitrary vector with the formulas

$$
\begin{aligned}
\dot{x} &= \frac{v \sin \varphi}{h} + \omega y, \\
\dot{y} &= -\frac{v \cos \varphi}{h} - \omega x, \\
\dot{\varphi} &= -\omega.
\end{aligned}
\tag{5}
$$

From (3) and (5) it follows, that the dynamics of differences may be described by the equations

$$
\begin{aligned}
\dot{e}_x &= \frac{v \sin \varphi}{h} + \omega(e_y + y_{\text{max}}), \\
\dot{e}_y &= -\frac{v \cos \varphi}{h} - \omega e_x, \\
\dot{e}_\theta &= -\omega.
\end{aligned}
\tag{6}
$$

Introducing the notation

$$
\mathbf{e} = \begin{pmatrix} e_x & e_y & e_\theta \end{pmatrix}^T, \quad
\mathbf{L}(\mathbf{e}) = \begin{pmatrix} \dfrac{\sin \phi}{h} & -\dfrac{\cos \phi}{h} & 0 \\ e_y + y_{\text{max}} & -e_x & -1 \end{pmatrix}^T
\tag{7}
$$

We can rewrite Eqs. (6) in the matrix form

$$e_x = \bar{x},$$
$$e_y = \bar{y} - y_{\max}, \tag{8}$$
$$e_\theta = \theta.$$

The idea of the Visual Servoing approach is in the constructing velocity vector v in the form

$$v^* = -\mu L^+ e, \tag{9}$$

where $\mu > 0$ – arbitrary parameter, purpose of which will be described later, $()^+$ – Moore-Penrose pseudo inversion operator.

Substituting (9) into (8), we get simple linear equation

$$\dot{e} = -\mu e. \tag{10}$$

It is obvious that for any value $\mu > 0$ the system (10) is asymptotically stable. Thus assigning velocity vector in form (9) provides asymptotic convergence of the differences to zero. However, besides that there is a task of providing robot's motion at the constant velocity v_d, therefore, in fact, we need to provide velocity vector as

$$v^* = -\mu L^+ e + v_d. \tag{11}$$

4   Multipurpose Regulator

Now let us consider the task of providing the desired velocity vector (11). Since line following and the reaction on the constant external disturbances must follow the set of requirements, let us introduce regulator of multipurpose structure in the form

$$\dot{z}_v = Az_v + B\tau + R^T(\eta)K_1(\eta - z_\eta),$$
$$\dot{z}_\eta = R(\eta)z_v + K_2(\eta - z_\eta),$$
$$\dot{\gamma} = K_v(z_v - v^*), \tag{12}$$
$$\tau = -K_d(z_v - v^*) - K_i\gamma + F(\tfrac{d}{dt})(\eta - z_\eta).$$

First two equations of the system (12) represent asymptotic observer. Positive definite diagonal matrix K_1 and K_2 are parameters which, on the one hand, determine the rate of convergence of the system state estimation, but in fact these matrices are responsible for reaction on the external step disturbances. The third equation is the integral part which is necessary for providing the motion with the constant speed along the line, positive definite matrix K_v is of diagonal structure. Finally, the fourth equation if the control signal. Last element in this equation is the dynamic corrector which, on the one hand, provides astatism, but on the other hand it can provide certain reaction on the periodic disturbances. In this work we use the corrector only to provide astatism. We can represent the corrector in the state space, so the whole regulator takes form

$$
\begin{aligned}
\dot{z}_v &= Az_v + B\tau + R^T(\eta)K_1(\eta - z_\eta), \\
\dot{z}_\eta &= R(\eta)z_v + K_2(\eta - z_\eta), \\
\dot{\gamma} &= K_v(z_v - v^*), \\
\dot{p} &= A_p p + B_p(\eta - z_\eta), \\
\xi &= C_p p + D_p(\eta - z_\eta), \\
\tau &= -K_d(z_v - v^*) - \gamma + \xi,
\end{aligned}
\tag{13}
$$

where matrices A_p, B_p, C_p и D_p satisfy the condition

$$
F(s) = C_p(Es - A_p)^{-1}B_p + D_p,
\tag{14}
$$

and the matrix A_p must be Hurwitz.

To provide astatism the dynamic corrector must satisfy certain conditions itself. Following derivations analogous to work [2] we get

$$
F(0) = B^{-1}(A - BK_d)R^T(\varphi_0)K_2 - B^{-1}R^T(\varphi_0)K_1.
\tag{15}
$$

5   Computer Modeling

We will assume that the visual line is just straight line. Matrices A and B of the system (1) are unit matrices. The height of the camera is $h = 0.1$ m. First let us consider the situation in which the robot starts moving 0.5 m to the left of the line and directed parallel to it. The desired speed is $v = 10$ m/s. There are not external disturbances. Tunable parameters of the regulator have the following values:

$$
K_1 = K_2 = E, \quad K_v = 0.5, \quad K_i = \begin{pmatrix} 2 & 0 \\ 0 & 0 \end{pmatrix}, \quad K_d = \begin{pmatrix} 1 & 0 \\ 0 & 0.1 \end{pmatrix}, \quad \mu = 6,
$$

$$
A_p = -B_p = -E_{3\times3}, \quad C_p = \begin{pmatrix} 0 & 1 & 0 \\ 0 & 0 & 1 \end{pmatrix}, \quad D_p = \begin{pmatrix} 0 & -4 & 0 \\ 0 & 0 & -3.1 \end{pmatrix}.
$$

Figures 1 and 2 represent the dynamics of the robot in the corresponding situation. It can be seen that the robot actually achieves the line and moves along it. The desired linear velocity is also achieved.

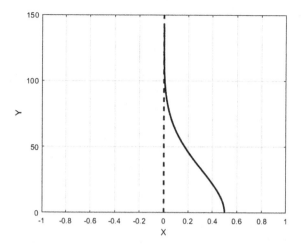

Fig. 1. Robot's trajectory without disturbances.

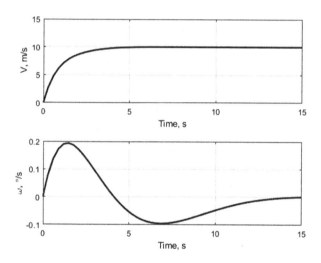

Fig. 2. Robot's dynamics without disturbances.

Now let us consider the situation in which robot starts already on the line and there are external disturbances $d(t) = (\,0.1 \quad 0.05\,)^T$ influences on robot. Figures 3 and 4 demonstrate dynamics of the system without changes in parameters from the previous situation. We can notice appearance of the significant overshoot while achieving the trajectory, however with the help of the dynamic corrector providing astatism the robot manages to achieve the line and desired velocity.

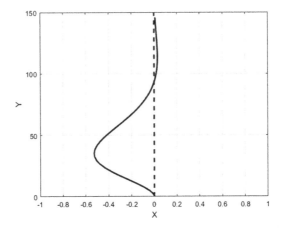

Fig. 3. Robot's trajectory in the presence of constant external disturbances.

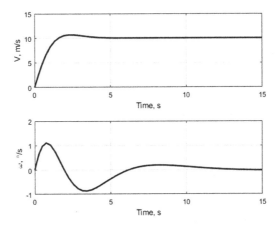

Fig. 4. Robot's dynamics in the presence of constant external disturbances.

We should notice that changing the μ parameter or the coefficients from the control signal equation doesn't provide significant improvement on line following dynamics and the velocities dynamics getting worse. We can achieve improvement by changing asymptotic observer matrices. Let $K_1 = 8E$. As we can see from Figs. 5 and 6 there is significant improvement in line following overshoot. Moreover, linear velocity dynamics is almost unaffected and intensity in angular velocity decreases. Therefore we can actually achieve the desired dynamics in reaction to the constant external disturbances through changing tunable parameters of the asymptotic observer.

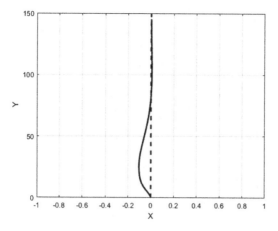

Fig. 5. Robot's trajectory in the presence of constant external disturbances with the matrix K_1 of the asymptotic observer changed.

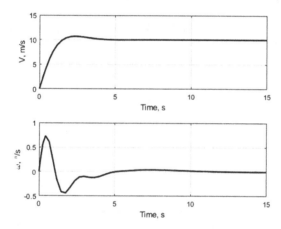

Fig. 6. Robot's dynamics in the presence of constant external disturbances with the matrix K_1 of the asymptotic observer changed.

6   Conclusion

In this work we presented the extension of the visual line following algorithm using visual feedback and multipurpose regulator to the case of underactuated system. Multipurpose regulator is supplemented by integral part to provide constant linear velocity of robot's motion along the line. Influence of the tunable parameters on the control motion dynamics is described. The efficiency of the proposed method is shown by the experiments with the computer model. For the further directions of the research we can mark out the problems of the automatic tuning of the tunable matrices depending on the certain requirements to the controlled motion quality. The interesting problems are also the question of the periodic external disturbances compensation and the influence of the feedback delay to the system's dynamics.

Acknowledgments. The research work was funded by the Russian Foundation for Basic Research, according to the research project No. 18-37-00463.

References

1. Chaumette, F., Hutchinson, S.: Visual servo control. i. basic approaches. IEEE Robot. Autom. Mag. **13**(4), 82–90 (2006). https://doi.org/10.1109/mra.2006.250573
2. Veremey, E.I.: Dynamical correction of positioning control laws. IFAC Proc. Volumes **46**(33), 31–36 (2013). https://doi.org/10.3182/20130918-4-JP-3022.00019
3. Sotnikova, M.V.: Algorithm for visual path following by wheeled fully actuated robot [in Russian]. In: Vestnik Sankt-Peterburgskogo Universiteta. Seriya 10. Prikladnaya Matematika. Informatika. Protsessy Upravleniya, no. 1, pp. 99–108 (2016)
4. Carona, R., Aguiar, A.P., Gaspar, J.: Control of unicycle type robots: tracking, path following and point stabilization. In: Proceedings of IV Jornadas de Engenharia de Electronica e Telecomunicacoes e de Computadores, pp. 180–185. ISEL, Lisbon (2008)

Simplified Rotor Angular Velocity Estimation for a Permanent Magnets Synchronous Motor by Current and Voltage Measurements

Anastasiia O. Vediakova[1] and Alexey A. Vedyakov[2]([⊠])

[1] Department of Computer Applications and Systems, St. Petersburg
State University, 7/9 Universitetskaya nab., St. Petersburg 199034, Russia
vediakova@gmail.com
[2] Faculty of Control Systems and Robotics, ITMO University,
Kronverkskiy Pr., 49, St. Petersburg 197101, Russia
vedyakov@corp.ifmo.ru

Abstract. This paper is devoted to the rotor angular velocity estimation of the permanent-magnet synchronous motor (PMSM). It is an actual problem, for example, in sensorless control. We consider a classical, two-phase model in the stator frame of the unsaturated, non-salient PMSM in the state-space representation. All parameters of the model except the stator windings resistance and rotor inertia are assumed to be known. On the first step, we find the relation between measured signals and angular velocity and excluding the unknown parameters of the motor. This relation is simplified using properties of the measured signals and represented as the first-order regression model, where the unknown parameter is the angular velocity. On the next step, we propose the estimation scheme, which is based on the gradient descent method. The efficiency is illustrated through a set of numerical simulations.

Keywords: Sensorless control · Permanent magnet synchronous motor · Parameter identification · Real-time

1 Introduction

The rotor angular velocity estimate can be used in the control loop instead of the measured value, for sensor fault detection or as a reserve system. It is actively studied as part of sensorless (self-sensing) algorithms, where mechanical variables, such position and speed, estimate by currents and voltages measurements [8].

Sensorless control has several benefits. Transducers mounting requires additional space for sensing element and wiring. High-resolution sensors are

This article is supported by the Ministry of Science and Higher Education of the Russian Federation, ПНИЭР unique identifier RFMEFI57818X0271.

V. Sukhomlin and E. Zubareva (Eds.): Convergent 2018, CCIS 1140, pp. 251–260, 2020.
https://doi.org/10.1007/978-3-030-37436-5_23

usually expensive. Estimators and observers can be used to decrease the cost of the drive system and increase the failure tolerance.

In this paper, the speed estimation for a permanent-magnet synchronous motor (PMSM) is considered. The overview of the main approaches is presented in [2]. We mention the following results. The observer-based position estimator is described in [4,5]. The main problem of such methods is performance degradation at low- and zero-speed. Methods presented in [9,10] use high-frequency signal injection, which improves performance for the low speeds. However, it requires additional hardware effort and cannot be used on the speeds near the maximum.

This work uses the relation between the rotor angular velocity and currents and voltages, which is described in [1]. In the mentioned paper the third order regression model was obtained, where parameters depend on the rotor angular velocity. In this paper, the order is decreased to one. All parameters of the mathematical model are assumed to be known except the stator windings resistance and rotor inertia. Although resistance can be measured, it depends on the temperature and changes over operating time.

2   Problem Statement

Consider a classical, two-phase $\alpha\beta$ model of the unsaturated, non-salient, PMSM given by [6] and [8]

$$\dot{\lambda}(t) = v(t) - Ri(t), \tag{1}$$
$$j\dot{\omega}(t) = -f\omega(t) + \tau_e(t) - \tau_l(t), \tag{2}$$
$$\dot{\theta}(t) = \omega(t), \tag{3}$$

where $\lambda(t) = [\lambda_1(t)\,\lambda_2(t)]^T \in \mathbb{R}^2$ is the stator flux, $i(t) = [i_1(t)\,i_2(t)]^T \in \mathbb{R}^2$ are the currents, $v(t) = [v_1(t)\,v_2(t)]^T \in \mathbb{R}^2$ are the voltages, R is the stator winding resistance, $j > 0$ is the rotor inertia, $\theta(t) \in \mathbb{S} = [0, 2\pi)$ is the rotor phase, $\omega(t) \in \mathbb{R}$ is the mechanical angular velocity, $f \geq 0$ is the viscous friction coefficient, $\tau_l(t) \in \mathbb{R}$ is the load torque, $\tau_e(t) \in \mathbb{R}$ is the torque of electrical origin.

The state-space representation of (1)–(3) has the following form [1]

$$L\frac{di(t)}{dt} = -Ri(t) - \lambda_m\omega(t)C'(\theta) + v(t), \tag{4}$$
$$j\dot{\omega}(t) = -f\omega(t) + \lambda_m i^T(t)C'(\theta) - \tau_l(t), \tag{5}$$
$$\dot{\theta}(t) = \omega(t), \tag{6}$$

where $L \in \mathbb{R}_+$ is the stator inductance, λ_m is the constant flux generated by permanent magnets,

$$C'(\theta) = \begin{bmatrix} -n_p\sin(n_p\theta) \\ n_p\cos(n_p\theta) \end{bmatrix} = n_p JC(\theta) = dC/d\theta, \tag{7}$$

$J \in \mathbb{R}^{2 \times 2}$ is the rotation matrix

$$J = \begin{bmatrix} 0 & -1 \\ 1 & 0 \end{bmatrix}, \quad C(\theta) = \begin{bmatrix} \cos(n_p\theta) \\ \sin(n_p\theta) \end{bmatrix}, \tag{8}$$

$n_p \in \mathbb{N}$ is the number of pole pairs.

The objective is to find the estimate $\hat{\omega}(t)$ of the constant angular velocity ω that provides exponential convergence of the error $\tilde{\omega}(t) = \omega - \hat{\omega}(t)$ to zero, *i.e.* there exist positive constants C and a such that

$$\|\tilde{\omega}(t)\| \leq Ce^{-at}, \tag{9}$$

$\|\cdot\|$ is some norm of the vector, under the following assumptions.

Assumption 1. *All model* (1)–(2) *parameters except the stator winding resistance R and the rotor inertia j are known.*

Assumption 2. *The currents $i(t)$ and voltages $v(t)$ are measured.*

Assumption 3. *The rotor angular velocity $\omega(t)$ is constant.*

The Assumption 2 is satisfied in the usual operation mode. In some cases $v(t)$ are not measured directly, but estimated with sufficiently high accuracy.

3 Main Result

Following [1] consider the equation based on (4)

$$Ri(t) + L\frac{di(t)}{dt} - v(t) = -\lambda_m \omega C'(\theta). \tag{10}$$

Applying the filter as proposed in [7]

$$(\cdot)_f = \frac{1}{Tp+1}(\cdot), \tag{11}$$

where $p = d/dt$ and $T \in \mathbb{R}_+$ is a design parameter, to (10) gives

$$R\frac{1}{Tp+1}i(t) + L\frac{p}{Tp+1}i(t) - \frac{1}{Tp+1}v(t) = -\lambda_m \omega \frac{1}{Tp+1}C'(\theta). \tag{12}$$

Substituting vectors components yields

$$R\zeta_1(t) + \xi_1(t) = \mu \sin(n_p\omega t + \alpha) + \varepsilon_1(t), \tag{13}$$
$$R\zeta_2(t) + \xi_2(t) = -\mu \cos(n_p\omega t + \alpha) + \varepsilon_2(t), \tag{14}$$

where $\varepsilon_1(t)$ and $\varepsilon_2(t)$ are exponentially decaying terms, because filter (11) is stable,

$$\zeta_1(t) = \frac{1}{Tp+1}i_1(t), \tag{15}$$

$$\xi_1(t) = L\frac{p}{Tp+1}i_1(t) - \frac{1}{Tp+1}v_1(t), \tag{16}$$

$$\zeta_2(t) = \frac{1}{Tp+1}i_2(t), \tag{17}$$

$$\xi_2(t) = L\frac{p}{Tp+1}i_2(t) - \frac{1}{Tp+1}v_2(t), \tag{18}$$

$$\mu = \lambda_m n_p \omega / \sqrt{1 + n_p^2 \omega^2 T^2}, \tag{19}$$

$$\alpha = \theta(0) - \arctan(n_p \omega T), \tag{20}$$

where $\mu \in \mathbb{R}$, $\alpha \in \mathbb{R}$ are transfer coefficient and phase shift respectively for (11) and sinusoidal signal with frequency $n_p \omega$.

Let us rewrite $\zeta_1(t)$, $\zeta_2(t)$ и $\xi_1(t)$, $\xi_2(t)$ explicitly

$$\zeta_1(t) = \frac{a_i}{\sqrt{T^2\omega^2 n_p^2 + 1}}\cos\left(n_p\omega t + \varphi_i - \tilde{\alpha}\right)$$

$$= \frac{a_i}{\sqrt{T^2\omega^2 n_p^2 + 1}}\left(\cos\left(n_p\omega t + \varphi_i\right)\tilde{b} + \sin\left(n_p\omega t + \varphi_i\right)\tilde{a}\right)$$

$$= \frac{1}{\sqrt{T^2\omega^2 n_p^2 + 1}}\left(i_1(t)\tilde{b} + i_2(t)\tilde{a}\right), \tag{21}$$

$$\zeta_2(t) = \frac{1}{\sqrt{T^2\omega^2 n_p^2 + 1}}\left(i_2(t)\tilde{b} - i_1(t)\tilde{a}\right), \tag{22}$$

$$\xi_1(t) = \frac{La_i\omega n_p}{\sqrt{T^2\omega^2 n_p^2 + 1}}\cos\left(n_p\omega t + \varphi_i + \frac{\pi}{2} - \tilde{\alpha}\right)$$

$$- \frac{a_v}{\sqrt{T^2\omega^2 n_p^2 + 1}}\cos\left(n_p\omega t - \tilde{\alpha}\right)$$

$$= \frac{L\omega n_p}{\sqrt{T^2\omega^2 n_p^2 + 1}}\left(i_1\tilde{a} - i_2\tilde{b}\right) - \frac{1}{\sqrt{T^2\omega^2 n_p^2 + 1}}\left(v_1\tilde{b} + v_2\tilde{a}\right), \tag{23}$$

$$\xi_2(t) = \frac{L\omega n_p}{\sqrt{T^2\omega^2 n_p^2 + 1}}\left(i_2\tilde{a} + i_1\tilde{b}\right) - \frac{1}{\sqrt{T^2\omega^2 n_p^2 + 1}}\left(v_2\tilde{b} - v_1\tilde{a}\right), \tag{24}$$

where $\tilde{a} = \sin\left(\arctan(n_p\omega T)\right)$, $\tilde{b} = \cos\left(\arctan(n_p\omega T)\right)$, $\tilde{\alpha} = \arctan(n_p\omega T)$.

Excluding R from (13)–(14) and neglecting the exponentially decaying terms we obtain

$$\xi_1(t)\zeta_2(t) - \xi_2(t)\zeta_1(t) = \mu\zeta_2(t)\sin(n_p\omega t + \alpha) + \mu\zeta_1(t)\cos(n_p\omega t + \alpha), \tag{25}$$

where $\xi_1(t)\zeta_2(t) - \xi_2(t)\zeta_1(t)$, $\zeta_1(t)$, and $\zeta_2(t)$ are measured signals, μ and $n_p\omega$ are unknown parameters.

Remark 1. The stator windings inductance can be excluded form (13)–(14) instead of R.

3.1 Angular Velocity Estimation

This section aims to find a linear regression model with constant parameters depending on the unknown angular velocity ω.

Substituting (21)–(24) into the left part of (25) yields

$$
\begin{aligned}
\xi_1(t)\zeta_2(t) - \xi_2(t)\zeta_1(t) &= \frac{L\omega n_p}{T^2\omega^2 n_p^2 + 1}\left(-i_1^2 - i_2^2\right) \\
&\quad + \frac{1}{T^2\omega^2 n_p^2 + 1}\left(v_2 i_1 - v_1 i_2\right) \\
&= -\left(\frac{a_i^2 L\omega n_p + a_i a_v \sin\phi_i}{n_p^2\omega^2 T^2 + 1}\right),
\end{aligned} \tag{26}
$$

where ϕ_i is the phase current shift, a_i and a_v are currents and voltages amplitudes respectively

$$
a_i = \sqrt{i_1^2 + i_2^2}, \tag{27}
$$

$$
a_v = \sqrt{v_1^2 + v_2^2}, \tag{28}
$$

$$
\sin\phi_i = \frac{i_2 v_1 - i_1 v_2}{a_i a_v}. \tag{29}
$$

Substituting (21)–(24) into the right part of (25) gives

$$
\begin{aligned}
\mu\zeta_2(t)&\sin(n_p\omega t + \alpha) + \mu\zeta_1(t)\cos(n_p\omega t + \alpha) \\
&= \frac{\mu}{\sqrt{T^2\omega^2 n_p^2 + 1}}\left[\left(i_2\tilde{b} - i_1\tilde{a}\right)\sin\left(n_p\omega t - \tilde{\alpha}\right)\right. \\
&\quad \left. + \left(i_1\tilde{b} + i_2\tilde{a}\right)\cos\left(n_p\omega t - \tilde{\alpha}\right)\right] \\
&= \frac{\mu}{\sqrt{T^2\omega^2 n_p^2 + 1}}\left[i_1\cos\left(n_p\omega t\right) + i_2\sin\left(n_p\omega t\right)\right] \\
&= -\frac{\lambda_m n_p\omega a_i}{T^2\omega^2 n_p^2 + 1}\sin\phi_i.
\end{aligned} \tag{30}
$$

Combining (26) and (30) we obtain

$$
-\frac{a_i^2 L\omega n_p + a_i a_v \sin\phi_i}{n_p^2\omega^2 T^2 + 1} = -\frac{\lambda_m n_p\omega a_i}{T^2\omega^2 n_p^2 + 1}\sin\phi_i, \tag{31}
$$

$$
a_v \sin\phi_i = \omega n_p\left(\lambda_m \sin\phi_i - a_i L\right). \tag{32}
$$

The Eq. (31) can be represented in the linear regression form

$$\psi(t) = \theta\varphi(t),\qquad(33)$$

where $\psi(t) = a_v \sin\phi_i$ is the regressand, $\theta = \omega$ is the unknown parameter, $\varphi(t) = n_p(\lambda_m \sin\phi_i - a_i L)$ is the regressor.

Various approaches can be used to estimate the unknown parameter θ. We propose the estimation algorithm, which is based on the standard gradient method [3]:

$$\dot{\hat{\theta}}(t) = k\varphi(t)\left(\psi(t) - \hat{\theta}(t)\varphi(t)\right),\qquad(34)$$

where $\hat{\theta}(t)$ is the estimate of the parameter θ, $k \in \mathbb{R}_+$ is a constant gain.

The estimation converges to zero exponentially fast

$$\left\|\theta - \hat{\theta}(t)\right\| \le C_1 e^{-\rho_1 t},\qquad(35)$$

where C_1 and ρ_1 are some positive constants, if the following conditions are satisfied [3]:

1. The regressor $\varphi(t)$ is bounded.
2. There exist the positive constant D, such that

$$\int_0^t \varphi^2(\tau)d\tau \ge Dt.\qquad(36)$$

The regressor in (33) is constant and bounded. Inequality (36) holds for $\varphi(t) \not\equiv 0$. The objective (9) is achieved.

4   Numerical Examples

In this section, we present simulation results that illustrate the efficiency of the proposed estimation algorithm. All simulations have been performed in Mathworks MATLAB Simulink.

The model (4)–(6) parameters, which was used in the simulation, are shown in the Table 1.

Open-loop controller was used in the all experiments

$$v_1(t) = A(t)\cos(\xi(t)t),\qquad(37)$$
$$v_2(t) = A(t)\sin(\xi(t)t),\qquad(38)$$

where

$$A(t) = \frac{\lambda_1\lambda_2}{(p+\lambda_1)(p+\lambda_2)}A_0(t),\qquad(39)$$

$$\xi(t) = \frac{\lambda_1\lambda_2}{(p+\lambda_1)(p+\lambda_2)}\xi_0(t),\qquad(40)$$

Table 1. Parameters of the motor FAST1M6030 and external load.

Parameter (units)	Value
Inductance L (mH)	3.4
Resistance R (Ω)	0.47
Rotor inertia j (kg m^2)	$1.6 * 10^{-3}$
Pairs of poles n_p (–)	3
Magnetic flux λ_m (Wb)	0.4
Viscous friction coefficient f (N·m s/rad)	0.001
External load τ_l (N·m)	0.01

$A(t) = 60$, λ_1 and λ_2 are the tunable parameters; $A_0(t)$ and $\xi_0(t)$ are the desired amplitude and frequency of the voltage signals in steady state.

The experimental results for piecewise constant angular velocity (in the steady state), which have step change at time 200 s, are shown in Fig. 1. The following form of $\xi_0(t)$ was used

$$\xi_0(t) = \begin{cases} 60, 0 \leq t < 200s, \\ 66, 200s \leq t. \end{cases} \tag{41}$$

The estimation gain k was equal to 20. In this case, the estimation error $\tilde{\omega}(t)$ converges to zero in steady state.

In the second case, estimation of the time-varying rotor speed is investigated. The control signals were produced using

$$\xi_0(t) = 60 + \zeta_0(t), \tag{42}$$

$$\zeta_0(t) = \begin{cases} 0, 0 \leq t < 50s, \\ 0.06 \sin(0.2t), 50s \leq t. \end{cases} \tag{43}$$

To increase performance of the estimator, the value of k was increased up to 50. The behaviours of the angular velocity signal $\omega(t)$, estimate $\hat{\omega}(t)$, and estimation error $\omega(t) - \hat{\omega}(t)$ are depicted in Fig. 2. There is a small estimation error, which depends on properties of the rotor speed and the estimator performance.

In Fig. 3 the behaviour of the estimate based on the corrupted by exponentially correlated noise $\delta(t)$ current signal $i(t)$ is illustrated. The noise signal $\delta(t)$ was modelled by a shaping filter $W(s) = 0.005/(0.00004s^2 + 0.0006s + 1)$ with frequency-bounded input white noise of power $N = 0.1$. Simulation parameters were the following

$$\xi_0(t) = 20, \quad k = 5. \tag{44}$$

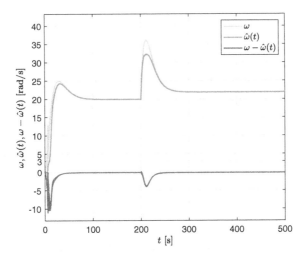

Fig. 1. The angular velocity, estimation, and estimation error

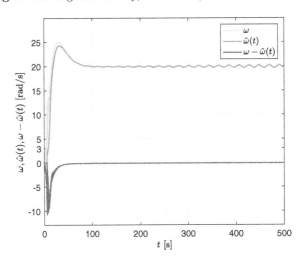

Fig. 2. The angular velocity, estimation, and estimation error for the time-varying rotor speed

In the case of noised measurements, the estimate $\hat{\omega}(t)$ does not converge to $\omega(t)$ and is also corrupted by noise. However, it is bounded.

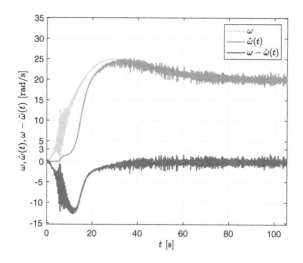

Fig. 3. The angular velocity, estimation, and estimation error for the case with additive noise in the measured signal $i(t)$

5   Conclusion

The simplified estimator for the PMSM rotor angular velocity based on currents and voltages measurements is described. All parameters of the drive are assumed to be known except the stator windings resistance and the rotor inertia.

For the rotation with constant angular velocity is proved that the velocity estimation error converges to zero exponentially fast. The estimator can handle cases with time-varying rotation frequency and noises in the measured signals. The estimation error in such cases is bounded, but don't converge to zero.

For the known stator windings resistance and unknown inductance the estimator can be accordingly modified. From Eqs. (13)–(14) one or another parameter can be excluded.

Future investigations will be devoted to the angular velocity estimation for the case with unknown permanent magnets flux constant λ_m and the stator windings inductance L. Also, time-varying rotation frequency will be considered.

References

1. Alexey, V., Anastasiia, V., Alexey, B., Anton, P., Mikhail, K.: Frequency estimation of a sinusoidal signal with time-varying amplitude and phase. In: 17th IFAC Workshop on Control Applications of Optimization (CAO 2018), pp. 304–309 (2018)
2. Bazylev, D., Vukosavic, S., Bobtsov, A., Pyrkin, A., Stankovic, A., Ortega, R.: Sensorless control of pm synchronous motors with a robust nonlinear observer. In: 2018 IEEE Industrial Cyber-Physical Systems (ICPS), pp. 304–309 (2018). https://doi.org/10.1109/ICPHYS.2018.8387676
3. Ioannou, P.A., Sun, J.: Robust Adaptive Control, vol. 1. PTR Prentice-Hall, Upper Saddle River (1996)

4. Kim, H., Son, J., Lee, J.: A high-speed sliding-mode observer for the sensorless speed control of a pmsm. IEEE Trans. Industr. Electron. **58**(9), 4069–4077 (2011). https://doi.org/10.1109/TIE.2010.2098357

5. Kommuri, S.K., Veluvolu, K.C., Defoort, M.: Robust observer with higher-order sliding mode for sensorless speed estimation of a PMSM. In: 2013 European Control Conference (ECC), pp. 4598–4603. IEEE (2013). https://doi.org/10.23919/ECC.2013.6669214

6. Krause, P.C.: Analysis of Electric Machinery. McGraw-Hill, New York (1986)

7. Middletone, R., Goodwin, G.: Adaptive computed torque control for rigid link manipulators. In: 1986 25th IEEE Conference on Decision and Control, vol. 25, pp. 68–73. IEEE (1986). https://doi.org/10.1109/CDC.1986.267156

8. Nam, K.: AC Motor Control and Electrical Vehicle Applications. CRC Press, Boca Raton (2010)

9. Raca, D., Garcia, P., Reigosa, D.D., Briz, F., Lorenz, R.D.: Carrier-signal selection for sensorless control of pm synchronous machines at zero and very low speeds. IEEE Trans. Ind. Appl. **46**(1), 167–178 (2010). https://doi.org/10.1109/TIA.2009.2036551

10. Wallmark, O., Harnefors, L.: Sensorless control of salient pmsm drives in the transition region. IEEE Trans. Industr. Electron. **53**(4), 1179–1187 (2006). https://doi.org/10.1109/TIE.2006.878315

Big Data and Applications

On Data Analysis of Software Repositories

Dmitry Namiot$^{(\boxtimes)}$ ⓘ and Vladimir Romanov ⓘ

Lomonosov Moscow State University, Leninskie Gory, 1,
GSP-1, 119991 Moscow, Russia
dnamiot@gmail.com, vladimir.romanov@gmail.com

Abstract. This article discusses the analysis of software repositories using data analysis methods. A review is made of methods for analyzing programs based on information retrieved from the program code stored in code repositories. A review is made of methods for analyzing programs based on information retrieved from the program code stored in repositories. The article reviews the works that apply methods of classification, clustering and depth learning in software development. For example, for classifying and predicting errors, changing the properties of code in the process of its evolution, detecting design flaws and debts, assist for code refactoring. The main ultimate goal for all models is, of course, an automation of programming. In practice, we are talking about more simple tasks. This includes, for example, information retrieval (program code), error prediction, clone detection, link analysis, evolution analysis, etc. Firstly, we discuss recurrent neural networks and their deployment for the analysis of software repositories. In the simplest case, recurrent networks model a programming language as a sequence of characters. Also, the paper covers clustering and topic modeling.

Keywords: Data science · Recurrent neural networks · Classification · Clustering · Software metrics · Architectural technical debt · Software repositories · Software engineering

1 Introduction

This article discusses software engineering tasks related to the analysis of data that can be extracted from software repositories. The collections of program texts are the source of data for various tasks related to the development of software. The idea is that metrics that can be obtained from program texts or, for example, Java bytecode, can serve as a source of useful conclusions about the programs themselves (collections of programs).

As metrics, there can be, for example, what is directly measured (calculated) from the source code. For example, the metrics are the number of rows, the number of modules, the number of objects with different access modifiers, etc. Another possibility is in some way artificially defined measurements (so-called feature selection) [1]. For example, some introduced metrics could be just aggregates for other metrics.

The models that are built here can be very diverse. The goal of this article is to create a survey of models used in this field.

The main ultimate goal for all models (as, indeed, for most other tasks of software engineering) is, of course, an automation of programming. At present, this is still far

V. Sukhomlin and E. Zubareva (Eds.): Convergent 2018, CCIS 1140, pp. 263–272, 2020.
https://doi.org/10.1007/978-3-030-37436-5_24

away. In practice, we are talking about more mundane tasks. This includes, for example, information retrieval (program code), error prediction, clone detection, link analysis, evolution analysis, and the like.

One of the advanced examples is presented, for example, in [2]. The developer of video games Ubisoft introduced the program Commit Assistant, which actively blocks encoding errors. This tool is designed to detect errors before developers even commit them in the game code. The system was trained on the data accumulated over 10 years about where previous errors were made in the code, and what modifications were applied to correct these errors. This allows the Commit Assistant to predict when a programmer may face the risk of introducing a similar error. The authors note the possibility of the system to find 60% of errors and, accordingly, save up to 20% of the time of developers.

Interest in the use of formal models in software engineering existed, naturally, for a long time. Another example is the book [3] of 1986, which covers quite a few aspects, such as, for example, verification and transformation of programs.

In other words, this article is our first attempt to review a new direction, which can be characterized as the use of data analysis methods for software engineering tasks.

2   Recurrent Neural Networks

Recurrent Neural Network (RNN) is a class of neural networks where the links between elements form a certain directed sequence. This makes it possible to process successive chains of events.

Below is an example of RNN, which models the language as a sequence of characters. The network is taught in large text and gets the probability distribution of the next character in a sequence specified by the sequence of previous symbols. This will allow us to generate new text one character per step.

The following illustration is taken from [4]. As a working example it is assumed that we have only a lexicon of four possible letters "h e l o", and we wanted to train RNN on the training sequence "hello". This training sequence is actually a source of 4 separate learning examples:

1. The probability of occurrence of "e" should be determined taking into account the context "h"
2. "l" should be probable in the context of "he"
3. "l" should also be likely given the context of "hel", and, finally,
4. "o" should probably be defined in the context of "hell".

Next, we use a vector of four elements, where 1 in the corresponding position corresponds to one of the symbols of our alphabet. The input (Fig. 1) is fed with vectors, where only one symbol is represented. At the output, we see vectors with calculated preferences for subsequent symbols.

In this example, it is very easy to understand how such a network is arranged. Further, as indicated in [4], the network can be trained on program texts (since this is also a language). In the original for training, C code was used from the Linux source repository. For 477 Mb of source code, an RNN model with 10 million parameters was

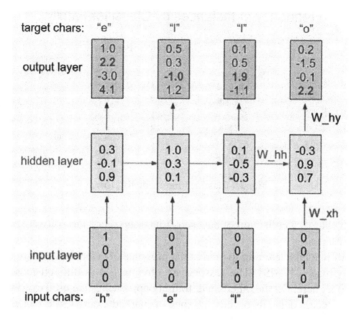

Fig. 1. The size of the input and output is 4, one hidden level of 3 neurons [4]. W_xh and W_hy are weights.

built. As a result, the model can generate "plausible" texts in C programs. But it is more interesting, for example, to show possible errors, based on the fact that the actual following of symbols in the program being tested does not match the calculated preferences.

The paper [5] provides an overview of the use of deep training models for the analysis of software repositories. The authors give an overview of N-gram models of formal languages (programming languages) [6–14]. In this case, their significant shortcomings are noted (for example, the need to take into account the context and semantics). Accordingly, they are opposed to just a recurrent neural network. Concretely, in [5] the Java programming language is considered. Areas of application that are considered by the authors: code review and code suggestion.

3 Other Machine Learning Models

A large review of the various models of machine learning that are used in predicting the presence of defects (errors) in the modules of software systems is given in [15]. It presents the collection of works, which differ both in the metrics that are used to describe the program modules, and on the classifiers used. Figure 2 is a summary table on the use of classification methods:

Frequency of Instances by Classifier Family

	Instances	Percent
DecTree	172	28.7
Regression	136	22.7
Bayes	124	20.7
CBR	77	12.8
Search	41	6.8
ANN	28	4.7
SVM	17	2.8
Benchmark	5	0.8

Fig. 2. Classification methods [15].

As a data source, a collection of data sets, (datasets) related to software engineering [16] can be used.

The use of machine learning to predict the presence of errors in software modules is a popular approach [17–19]. The reasons are obvious - it is difficult to suggest any analytical model here. On the other hand, training approaches are used everywhere and, accordingly, success depends on the presence of marked examples. It can also be said that it is difficult to identify common approaches to the choice of characteristics of the code under investigation. Precisely, we can say that this approach deals, first of all, with the static characteristics of the code. But, and this is noted in the works, the reliability of the code can depend, for example, on the frequency and nature of the updates. We can say that this direction - prediction of the presence of errors and evaluation of the reliability of software modules requires a separate review. An interesting question, in particular, whether such models can exist without binding to the programming language?

Part of the analysis of possible metrics is interesting in [20], where a rather detailed analysis of the influence of architecture on the evolution and quality of the software system is given. The authors of the work proceed from the assumption that joint changes affecting several modules that determine the architecture of the system are more likely to introduce errors than changes occurring within such a module. The paper reviews the metrics used to measure the connectivity of modules, as well as an overview of the architectural types used to visualize the properties of the architecture of the system. The proposed metrics were used to predict architectural defects based on the results of the correlation analysis of the history of module changes. As examples for such analysis, a number of widely used open source software systems were used.

In [21], the problem of architectural technical debt is considered, when it is not an optimal solution for the architecture of the system for a temporary, often justified, acceleration of development. Subsequently, such a decision begins to increasingly complicate the development and require corrections in the architecture of the system.

To assess the growth of this debt, the metric is used - the average number of modified components with each fixation of the code in the repository (ANMCC - average number of modified components per commit). However, the history of code changes is often not available for all code. Based on the analysis of 13 projects with open source code, modularity measurement metrics have been found whose values correlate with the values of the ANMCC metric. Thus, only one version of the software system is needed to assess the technical debt.

In [22], signs of bad code (the so-called bad smell) are discussed. Many of them are calculated on the basis of metrics and can be used in machine learning. Then in the work, the comparative analysis of the tools allowing to carry out detection of a bad code in program repositories is made.

Of course, as the characteristics of machine learning can be considered the relationship between the projects of ecosystems. An ecosystem here is a group of projects that are jointly developed and developed in the same environment. The relationship between projects developed in GitHub is discussed in detail in [23]. The capabilities of this repository allow you to analyze not only technical dependencies (between project components) but also social (between owners and project developers.) The work analyzes the correlation between technical and social dependencies, as well as ways to visualize such dependencies. project and their followers (Fig. 3).

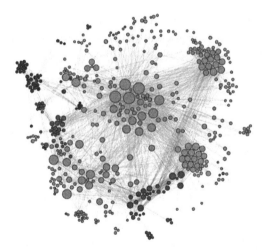

Fig. 3. Map of communication between project developers and their followers.

Figure 4 shows a map of the dependencies of the ecosystem projects.

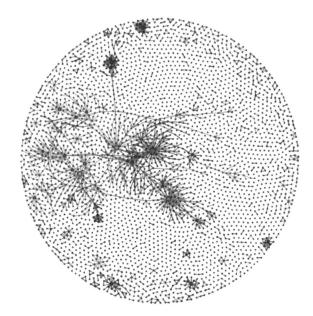

Fig. 4. Map of ecosystem projects.

In the work [24] surveyed 167 articles from the software engineering literature that make use of topic models. A topic model is a method designed to automatically extract topics from a corpus of text documents. Here, a topic is a collection of words that co-occurred frequently in the documents of the corpus. Due to the nature of language usage, the words that constitute a topic are often semantically related.

Topic models were originally developed as a means of automatically indexing, searching, clustering, and structuring large corpora of unstructured and unlabeled documents. Within the topic modeling framework, documents can be represented by the topics within them, and thus the entire corpus can be indexed and organized in terms of this discovered semantic structure.

In the article were identified and described the research trends in the area of mining unstructured repositories using topic models. Set of attributes was defined that allow characterizing each of the surveyed articles. Additionally six facets of related attributes where defined. The facets described and evaluated related work that uses topic models to mine software repositories and perform some software engineering tasks.

4   Clustering

We called this section one of the most frequently used approaches. Technically, this may involve more methods. Here we should start with [25] and an accessible dissertation from one of its authors [26]. This is an IR-model (Information Retrieval) for a large program code from the software repository. In particular, in these papers a technique is proposed for eliminating duplication of data based on the analysis of the history of changing large code.

The next model work in this series is an article [27]. Here the authors propose probabilistic models for extracting information about topics and authors from program texts. Areas of application: automatic annotation of program modules, developer activity statistics, analysis of program similarities, comparison of programmers' work, etc. To conduct research, an infrastructure was developed that allows you to store in the relational database the source code downloaded from the Internet repositories of more than 10,000 projects in the Java language, containing millions of lines of code written by 9,000 authors. In Fig. 5, for example, the clustering is shown authors for implementing Eclipse 3.0.

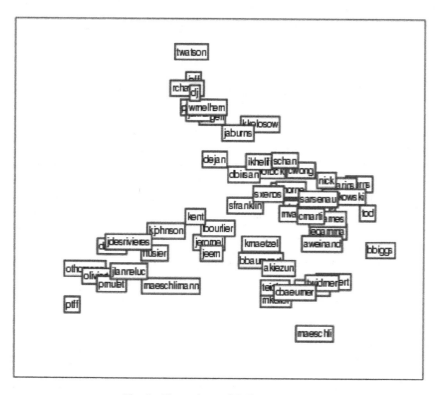

Fig. 5. The authors of Eclipse 3.0 [27].

Classical algorithms of clustering applied to problems of software quality analysis are considered in [28]. The paper describes object-oriented static metrics used to evaluate the quality of software. First, we identify the emissions of metric values and then classify the classes using the K-means method. Classification trees are then constructed to identify those metrics that determine the class's membership of the cluster.

And, finally, the most fundamental and complete overview of the application of clustering in software engineering is presented in [29]. Also here is extensive information on the algorithms of clustering.

The paper examines three main areas for using cluster analysis in software engineering: reflection analysis, software evolution analysis, and information recovery. The goal of the reflexive analysis is the restoration of the architecture of the software module. Components must be associated with elements of a hypothetical architecture.

In the evolution of software components, clustering is used, for example, to reduce the complexity of the code (regrouping modules), to determine the duplicate code, and so on.

Information recovery (reverse engineering) is the restoration of components or the extraction of systemic abstractions. For example, modules are defined in the system based on the clustering of the dependencies found, and so on.

Areas of application of the methods are as follows:

- classification and prediction of errors
- determination of the characteristic of code change in time
- evaluation of code uniformity (definition of "different" fragments)
- automatic detection of design errors
- automatic issuance of recommendations for code refactoring

The work [30] presents a framework that assists software engineers in recovering a software project's architecture from its source code. The architectural recovery process is an iterative one that combines clustering based on contextual and structural information in the code base with incremental developer feedback.

In the article described a framework based on our novel *CCHD algorithm*, short for Coordinated Clustering of Heterogeneous Datasets, which clusters a software project's source code in order to discover its inherent architecture. In addition to automatically producing a coherent software architecture, the framework provides a mechanism to maintain the quality of the extracted architecture by placing newly developed code into appropriate architectural components.

References

1. Guyon, I., Elisseeff, A.: An introduction to variable and feature selection. J. Mach. Learn. Res. **3**(7–8), 1157–1182 (2003). https://doi.org/10.1162/153244303322753616
2. AI Predicts Coding Mistakes Before Developers Make Them. https://futurism.com/ai-predicts-coding-mistakes-before-developers-make-them. Accessed 09 Nov 2018
3. Rich, C., Waters, R.C. (eds.): Readings in Artificial Intelligence and Software Engineering. Morgan Kaufmann Publishers Inc., San Francisco (1986)
4. The Unreasonable Effectiveness of Recurrent Neural Networks. http://karpathy.github.io/2015/05/21/rnn-effectiveness/. Accessed 09 Nov 2018
5. White, M., Vendome, C., Linares-Vásquez, M., Poshyvanyk, D.: Toward deep learning software repositories. In: Proceedings of the 2015 IEEE/ACM 12th Working Conference on Mining Software Repositories, Florence, pp. 334–345 (2015). https://doi.org/10.1109/msr.2015.38

6. Hindle, A., Barr, E.T., Su, Z., Gabel, M., Devanbu, P.: On the naturalness of software. In: Proceedings of the 34th International Conference on Software Engineering (ICSE), Zurich, pp. 837–847 (2012). https://doi.org/10.1109/icse.2012.6227135

7. Nguyen, T.T., Nguyen, A.T., Nguyen, H.A., Nguyen, T.N.: A statistical semantic language model for source code. In: Proceedings of the 9th Joint Meeting on Foundations of Software Engineering (ESEC/FSE 2013), pp. 532–542. ACM, New York (2013). https://doi.org/10.1145/2491411.2491458

8. Afshan, S., McMinn, P., Stevenson, M.: Evolving readable string test inputs using a natural language model to reduce human oracle cost. In: Proceedings of the 2013 IEEE Sixth International Conference on Software Testing, Verification and Validation, Luxembourg, pp. 352–361 (2013). https://doi.org/10.1109/icst.2013.11

9. Movshovitz-Attias, D., Cohen, W.W.: Natural language models for predicting programming comments. In: Proceedings of the 51st Annual Meeting of the Association for Computational Linguistics, Sofia, Bulgaria, pp. 35–40. Association for Computational Linguistics (2013)

10. Allamanis, M., Sutton, C.A.: Mining source code repositories at massive scale using language modeling. In: Proceedings of the 10th Working Conference on Mining Software Repositories (MSR 2013), San Francisco, CA, USA, May 2013, pp. 207–216 (2013)

11. Campbell, J.C., Hindle, A., Amaral, J.N.: Syntax errors just aren't natural: Improving error reporting with language models. In: Proceedings of the 11th Working Conference on Mining Software Repositories (MSR 2014), pp. 252–261. ACM, New York (2014). https://doi.org/10.1145/2597073.2597102

12. Tonella, P., Tiella, R., Nguyen, D.C.: Interpolated n-grams for model based testing. In: Proceedings of the 36th International Conference on Software Engineering (ICSE 2014), pp. 562–572. ACM, New York (2014). https://doi.org/10.1145/2568225.2568242

13. Tu, Z., Su, Z., Devanbu, P.: On the localness of software. In: Proceedings of the 22nd ACM SIGSOFT International Symposium on Foundations of Software Engineering (FSE 2014), pp. 269–280. ACM, New York (2014). https://doi.org/10.1145/2635868.2635875

14. Allamanis, M., Barr, E.T., Bird, C., Sutton, C.: Learning natural coding conventions. In: Proceedings of the 22nd ACM SIGSOFT International Symposium on Foundations of Software Engineering (FSE 2014), pp. 281–293. ACM, New York (2014). https://doi.org/10.1145/2635868.2635883

15. Shepperd, M., Bowes, D., Hall, T.: Researcher bias: the use of machine learning in software defect prediction. IEEE Trans. Softw. Eng. **40**(6), 603–616 (2014). https://doi.org/10.1109/TSE.2014.2322358

16. The tera-PROMISE Repository. http://openscience.us/repo. Accessed 09 Nov 2018

17. Malhotra, R.: A systematic review of machine learning techniques for software fault prediction. Appl. Soft Comput. **27**, 504–518 (2015). https://doi.org/10.1016/j.asoc.2014.11.023

18. Di Martino, S., Ferrucci, F., Gravino, C., Sarro, F.: A genetic algorithm to configure support vector machines for predicting fault-prone components. In: Caivano, D., Oivo, M., Baldassarre, M.T., Visaggio, G. (eds.) PROFES 2011. LNCS, vol. 6759, pp. 247–261. Springer, Heidelberg (2011). https://doi.org/10.1007/978-3-642-21843-9_20

19. Laradji, I.H., Alshayeb, M., Ghouti, L.: Software defect prediction using ensemble learning on selected features. Inf. Softw. Technol. **58**, 388–402 (2015). https://doi.org/10.1016/j.infsof.2014.07.005

20. Kouroshfar, E., Mirakhorli, M., Bagheri, H., Xiao, L., Malek, S., Cai, Y.: A study on the role of software architecture in the evolution and quality of software. In: Proceedings of the 2015 IEEE/ACM 12th Working Conference on Mining Software Repositories, Florence, pp. 246–257 (2015). https://doi.org/10.1109/msr.2015.30

21. Li, Z., Liang, P., Avgeriou, P., Guelfi, N., Ampatzoglou, A.: An empirical investigation of modularity metrics for indicating architectural technical debt. In: Proceedings of the 10th International ACM SIGSOFT Conference on Quality of Software Architectures (QoSA 2014), pp. 119–128. ACM, New York (2014). https://doi.org/10.1145/2602576.2602581
22. Fernandes, E., Oliveira, J., Vale, G., Paiva, T., Figueiredo, E.: A review-based comparative study of bad smell detection tools. In: Proceedings of the 20th International Conference on Evaluation and Assessment in Software Engineering (EASE 2016), Article 18, p. 18. ACM, New York (2016). https://doi.org/10.1145/2915970.2915984
23. Blincoe, K., Harrison, F., Damian, D.K.: Ecosystems in GitHub and a method for ecosystem identification using reference coupling. In: Proceedings of the 2015 IEEE/ACM 12th Working Conference on Mining Software Repositories, Florence, pp. 202–211 (2015). https://doi.org/10.1109/msr.2015.26
24. Chen, T.H., Thomas, S.W., Hassan, A.E.: A survey on the use of topic models when mining software repositories. Empirical Softw. Eng. 21(5), 1843–1919 (2016). https://doi.org/10.1007/s10664-015-9402-8
25. Thomas, S.W., Hassan, A.E., Blostein, D.: Mining unstructured software repositories. In: Mens, T., Serebrenik, A., Cleve, A. (eds.) Evolving Software Systems, pp. 139–162. Springer, Heidelberg (2014). https://doi.org/10.1007/978-3-642-45398-4_5
26. Thomas, S.W.: Mining unstructured software repositories using IR models. Ph.D. thesis, Queen's University, Canada (2012)
27. Linstead, E., Rigor, P., Bajracharya, S., Lopes, C., Baldi, P.F.: Mining internet-scale software repositories. In: Platt, J., Koller, D., Singer, Y., Roweis, S. (eds.) Advances in Neural Information Processing Systems 20, pp. 929–936. Curran Associates, Red Hook (2008). http://papers.nips.cc/paper/3171-mining-internet-scale-software-repositories.pdf
28. Papas, D., Tjortjis, C.: Combining clustering and classification for software quality evaluation. In: Likas, A., Blekas, K., Kalles, D. (eds.) SETN 2014. LNCS (LNAI), vol. 8445, pp. 273–286. Springer, Cham (2014). https://doi.org/10.1007/978-3-319-07064-3_22
29. Shtern, M., Tzerpos, V.: Clustering methodologies for software engineering. Adv. Softw. Eng. 2012, 1 (2012). Article ID 792024. https://doi.org/10.1155/2012/792024
30. Naim, S.M., Damevski, K., Hossain, M.S.: Reconstructing and evolving software architectures using a coordinated clustering framework. Autom. Softw. Eng. 24(3), 543–572 (2017). https://doi.org/10.1007/s10515-017-0211-8

Development of BI-Platforms
for Cybersecurity Predictive Analytics

Sergey Petrenko[1] and Krystina Makoveichuk[2(✉)]

[1] Innopolis University, Universitetskaya Str. 1, 420500 Innopolis, Russia
s.petrenko@innopolis.ru
[2] V.I. Vernadsky Crimean Federal University,
Sevastopolskaya Str. 2-A, 298635 Yalta, Russia
christin2003@yandex.ru

Abstract. The distribution of analytical information systems, the so-called BI platforms (BI – business intelligence) in leading state and commercial companies, allows the top-managers and analysts to work in real time with large information volumes (Big Data). However, the issue of choosing tools for secure access to these new sources of corporate data becomes relevant. The trend of recent years is the integration of business security software products, and the transition from specialized analytical solutions to multipurpose BI platforms. The article considers approaches to providing security in information systems of banks and electronic commerce using multipurpose BI-platforms. The analysis of key problems in arrangement of the Big Data was performed and the problems of implementation, operation and maintenance of BI systems were identified. The analysis of the advantages of the systems of the class Advanced Analytics (Big Data, NoSQL-storages, processing of streaming data on-line) over traditional BI-systems (ETL + SQL + reports) is made. The system features of the BI-platform of security are considered: typical agents and formats of data loading agents, possible types and model of data, the structure of the computing cluster and the gateway. An algorithm for detecting security incidents is given. It has been proven that in order to reduce the dependence level on foreign technologies, the public sector should completely switch to work with Russian software and hardware platform developers. In turn, the commercial segment should also facilitate the transition to Russian developments and more actively use them in their activities.

Keywords: Business intelligence · Security · BI-platform · Analytical information systems · Dashboard · Big Data · Algorithm

1 Introduction

1.1 Possible State of Art

At present, security services of leading state companies and enterprises are increasingly paying their attention to the new analytical information systems, the so-called business intelligence platforms (BI- platforms). BI-systems allow to the top-managers and analysts to work in real time with large information volumes (Big Data). At the same

© Springer Nature Switzerland AG 2020
V. Sukhomlin and E. Zubareva (Eds.): Convergent 2018, CCIS 1140, pp. 273–288, 2020.
https://doi.org/10.1007/978-3-030-37436-5_25

time, tools for secure access to business data sources that have advanced possibilities for consolidating, analyzing and presenting information are especially relevant. The security trend of recent years is the software integration and the transition from specialized analytical solutions to multi-purpose BI platforms. Consider what BI platforms may be in-demand for the Russian security services.

1.2 BI-Security Platform Requirements

Currently, leading Russian state and military companies are mainstreaming the various business intelligence systems from traditional ones of the Business Intelligence class (ETL + SQL + reports) to more advanced systems of Advanced Analytics class (Big Data, NoSQL-storage, thread-specific data processing online).

According to TATA Consultancy Services [1, 7], which summarized data for 1217 companies from 4 world regions (USA, Europe, Asia and Latin America), about half of the companies experienced difficulties in obtaining and analyzing "big data". The investment volume in business analytics varies considerably among different companies: for half of them, it amounts to more than $ 10 million. In addition, companies that receive revenue through the Internet, invest in the development of business intelligence systems even more financial resources.

The research revealed the following key problems in arrangement the Big Data (in descending order of priority):

- Low computing speed for Big Data and its high variability;
- Time consuming data sources identifying for analysis;
- Complexity of recruiting employees, able to analyze Big Data;
- High laboriousness of creating visual representations for the results of data processing.

In the Information Week study conducted in 2013, 248 companies from various fields, including the state financial sector, took part. The study results revealed the following key problems:

- Low quality of source data (59%);
- Software complexity for data analysis by employees who do not have special training (46%);
- Difficulties in deploying the solution to the entire organization (42%).

At the same time, BI-systems users expect the development of the system functional in the following aspects:

- Visualizations (sparklines, heatmaps, treemaps);
- Analysis (forecasting, statistical analysis, etc.);
- Applying interactive dashboards.

According to the well-known analytical company Gartner [1], the basis for successful BI-projects is a qualitative and understandable presentation of the results and conclusions from BI-studies: 70–80% of projects that do not pay due attention, end in failure.

TDWI (The Data Warehousing Institute) estimated that poor quality and non-transparency of the presented results and conclusions, based on the gathered information, do not allow responsible executives to make high-quality decisions timely. According to Gartner, the best tool that allows quickly and clearly conveying useful information and conclusions from the BI-system to the making decisions person in the company is dashboard: 94% of respondents said that dashboard has become an integral part of their BI project success.

Finally, the study [1, 2, 5–7], which involved 752 companies from around the world, shows that even large companies face difficulties in analyzing large data amounts. More than 41% of companies said they do not derive maximum benefit from continually collected data. At the same time, 67% of respondents noted that it is important for them to process data in real time. However, attempts to increase the processing data speed lead to a number of problems. Among the main difficulties the respondents said the following:

- 41% - insufficient skills;
- 39% - delays related to cleaning up and data validation;
- 32% - lack of necessary technologies.

Thus, if we summarize the results of the above-mentioned and other relevant studies, the main problems of implementing, operating and maintaining BI-systems are as follows.

Existing BI-systems are not able to perform calculations on large data amounts quickly enough. According to experts [1, 2, 5–7], the amount of data generated around the world in 2013 was more than 7,000 petabytes, and the annual growth rate of this parameter exceeded 40%. More than 80% of BI-experts believe that existing systems do not have enough computing speed. According to the Gartner forecast [1], while maintaining the growth rates of data generation, 33% of companies by 2017 will not be able to analyze data because of the inability of existing BI-systems to quickly process such volumes.

Calculations in BI-systems often produce incorrect results due to poor data quality. The analysis is complicated by the fact that 60% of calculations must be made according to poor quality, unreliable data [1, 2, 5–7], so IT-specialists put the data quality problem in the second place among all the complexities when using analytics. Almost 30% of respondents found the data of their companies unsuitable for analysis with the help of existing BI-systems.

Developing procedures for converting and cleaning up the source data is time-consuming and costly. In large companies, up to 70% of the study time is spent preparing data for analysis. More than 90% of companies use ETL-solutions for transforming data. ETL costs take more than 65% of the data management budget and are up to $ 67,000 per TB per year.

Companies don't have specialists skilled to develop mathematically correct algorithms and data analysis methods. About 41% of large companies named the lack of such specialists a key problem in the implementation of existing BI-systems, and by 2018 only in the US, a shortage of almost 200,000 specialists in this field is expected [1, 2, 5–7].

Analysis takes a long time, and its results are received by business users too late.

More than 40% of the surveyed companies do not have BI-systems capable of making calculations quickly enough. Among executives, more than 70% believe that faster data analysis would help them to improve the company's efficiency, while 26% of companies believe that speeding up payments is the key driver success of working with Big Data [1, 2, 5–7].

The analysis results are often incomprehensible and impractical. Almost 42% of users are dissatisfied with the conclusions they can see on their dashboards, while 28% of respondents admitted that the analysis results do not allow them to obtain maximum information from the collected data.

Existing BI systems do not provide users with the necessary visualization tools. Currently, almost 50% of existing BI-systems display information in the form of reports, rather than dashboards, while 43% of users are dissatisfied with the visualization tools used. Another 44% users lack the predictive dashboard function, and 61% are sure that dashboards do not provide enough information to make decisions [1, 2].

The analysis results and conclusions are presented in an uncomfortable form and therefore often remain unrequited. About 46% of the interviewed companies stated that the interface complexity is the main problem in using BI-systems. Studies note three key disadvantages of existing interfaces:

- no complex visualization views;
- interactive functions are not developed;
- access from mobile devices is restricted.

To solve the identified problems of implementation, operation and maintenance of modern BI-systems, the following technical solutions and corresponding technological trends for the development of advanced AA class BI-systems are offered [1, 2, 5–7].

First, most CIOs of large companies began to abandon ETL-technology, arguing that 70–80% of the costs associated with BI are spent on permanent rewriting and adaptation of ETL-systems. The possible way to reduce costs is associated with the following new approach: data is directly uploaded to a distributed cluster of analytics and storage, where aggregation, sorting, transformation and primary data analysis are implemented. Time delays can thus be reduced by a factor of 5–10, since the data at the conversion and download stage do not leave the analytic cluster; also, no additional costs are required for ETL-systems software and hardware.

Secondly, the single storage database was replaced with a distributed NoSQL storage. Today, the typical infrastructure of a large company contains between 300 and 500 internal systems, therefore it is rather difficult to store data in a single database. As a solution, 53% of companies made attempts to implement NoSQL-storage and 43% of them expect to receive ROI more than 25%.

Third, analytics should be performed in a distributed cluster. Due to the high cost of processing in BI-systems, companies use on average not more than 12% of their data for analytics. Nevertheless, 12% of companies are already applying a new approach, when harmonization and data enrichment, as well as most of the analytics is performed not in a separate BI-system, but in a distributed analytical cluster that stores, processes and provides data to users.

Fourthly, a massive escape from static graphs to interactive online dashboards on a variety of output devices began. Static reports and graphs do not allow us to use up-to-date information, so 75% of companies preferred to use dashboards continually. But dashboards by themselves are not a panacea, interactive solutions are needed to investigate the causes that led to result-based parameters. In addition, 70% of users prefer to see analytics on mobile devices.

2 BI-Security Platform Startup

Using the example of the Liberty Grant BI-platform, we summarize the requirements and specification of a possible multi-purpose BI-security platform. Doing so, we will take into account that this platform should allow performing high-speed calculations for solving the problems of Russian security services based on a functional library of algorithms and analytical applications (such library has a wide range of the expressive capabilities), for example:

- Analysis of the information technology protection effectiveness;
- Analysis of the computer systems' performance;
- Monitoring of IS threats;
- Analysis of information security tools and CIPF;
- IS analysis, etc.

Typically, BI-platforms are based on the following technologies [5–8, 12, 13]:

- Mixed processing of streaming and packet data;
- Creation of complex analytical procedures from the completed algorithmic blocks;
- Multi-level parallelization of calculations with the provision of high data locality;
- Distributed data storage, parameters and calculation results, parameters and metadata;
- Disclosure of deviations and non-standard behavior of the analyzed parameters;
- Disclosure of formats, structure and correlations in the source data, etc.

The typical BI-platform content can consist of data loading and visualization agents (Fig. 1), which go to the high-speed distributed storage directly from external systems; in this storage, processing is carried out using computing cluster procedures. In this case, during the periods of the peak load absence in the repository, there is a data harmonization process, as well as other procedures of the computing BAM (Bidirectional associative memory) core. Analytical shell tools request data prepared for more advanced analytics, the results of which are passed to the display agents. Dashboard, as one of the most convenient types of up-to-date information visualization, allows the user to interactively monitor parameter changes and to investigate the causes of them.

BAM can integrate applications that are designed to perform applied information security tasks for both state companies and enterprises in various fields of activity.

As components (load agents) (Fig. 2 and Table 1), you can use software adapters to connect to different data sources, for example:

- Connectors for various databases, such as MySql, MsSql, Oracle, MongoDB, MsAccess, PostgreSQL;
- Some CRMs (such as SAP, Oracle, etc.) and SIEM (such as HP, IBM, EMC, etc.);

- Files and data streams (such as UDP, TCP, xls, txt, csv, dif);
- Popular web-interfaces (such as SOAP, XML-RPC, REST, WSDL, UDDI, etc.).

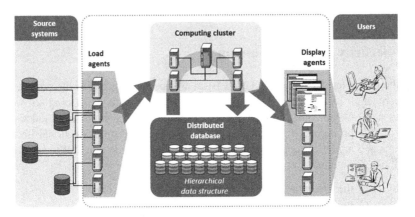

Fig. 1. A sample common context-dependent on domain area of knowledge representation in a single ontology.

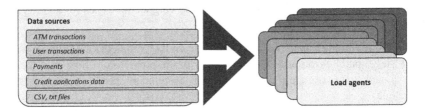

Fig. 2. Typical data loading agents.

Table 1. Open data sets of the FSTEC of Russia.

Databases	CRM and SIEM	Files	Data streams and data buses	Web-services protocols
MySql	SAP	csv	TCP	SOAP
MsSql	Oracle	xls	UDP	XML-RPC
Oracle	HP	txt	Oracle	REST
PostgreSQL	IBM	XML	Tibco	WSDL
MsAccess	EMC	dif		UDDI
MongoDB	etc.			

Depending on the source, the connector device (Fig. 3) can be very different and include:

- Connection driver;
- Source structure description;
- Data format description;
- Query pool;
- Multiplexer (makes it possible to group some requests into one, and then to parse the overall response into several).

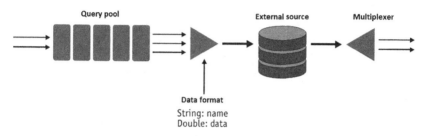

Fig. 3. Functional connector diagram.

A specialized database developed for high-speed computations over multidimensional data can be used in BI-platform. For example, as a data model and storage format, HDF5 can be used (Fig. 4), which:

- Allows processing a wide range of multidimensional data, storing a rich metadata history;
- Has a wide selection of predefined data formats, as well as the feasibility to create custom formats;
- Supports parallelization at all work stages without exception: from uploading to data transfer.

In this case, the system allows storing various information types (Fig. 5):

- Raw harmonized data;
- Aggregates;
- Time-series;
- User data;
- Metadata;
- Safety information.

Various structures are used for storage:

- B-trees;
- hash-tables;

- heaps;
- arrays;
- graphs.

The computing cluster's structure of a typical BI-platform is shown in Fig. 6.

In this case, the coordinating function in the system is performed by a gateway (Fig. 7):

- Evenly distributes user computing tasks to the nodes of the computing cluster;
- Performs the functions of routing data between the local storage databases of processing nodes.

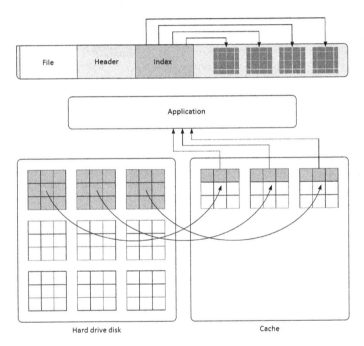

Fig. 4. A feasible data model of the BI security platform.

Data models		
Distributed filesystem		
Security data		
Metadata	Internal data	User data
Dictionaries	Aggregators	Logical object
Source data		Temporary data

Fig. 5. Feasible data types of the BI security platform.

In this case, the computing cluster itself can consist of a number of nodes. Here, each computing node is controlled by a micro-hub component, which is responsible for starting the server and managing its operation. Each micro-hub can launch several analytical procedures - the pipelines, consisting of several separate computing tasks. In addition, each noted task is a standard analytical block (clustering, classification, identifying of main components and outliers, data normalization, etc.), and the output of one block is input for the next.

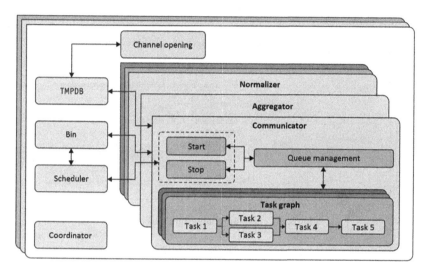

Fig. 6. The computing cluster's structure of the BI-security platform.

The system can perform automatic asynchronous parallelization of the pipelines to servers (Figs. 7, 8 and 9), as well as the same parallelization of separate blocks of a single pipeline between processors and cores within the server. Micro-hubs create buffer stores for greater parallelization efficiency between blocks of pipelines.

In addition to parallelizing the pipelines, the system can achieve acceleration in data processing due to the special organization of the on-line server space. So, each of the computing nodes has a local database (cache) containing data with whom the pipeline blocks will operate. The distribution gateway uses the semantic analysis to determine in advance and transmit to the cache the data required for calculations.

Note that the main visualization tool is a dashboard - a flexibly customizable operational panel for monitoring the situation in real-time mode. Access to the dashboard is via the web-interface or with native applications. For different types of users, the system allows creating several dashboard configurations, consisting of a filtering panel and a set of widgets, whose layout is described in the layout JSON file, which determines the location of graphic elements on the dashboard.

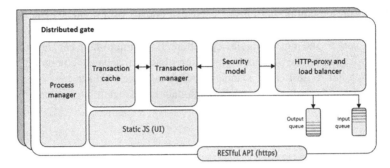

Fig. 7. The structure of the BI-security platform gateway.

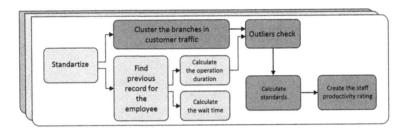

Fig. 8. A computing algorithm's example.

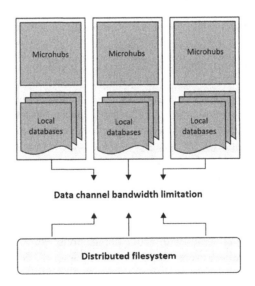

Fig. 9. Data processing.

3 Expected Results

The filtering panel allows narrowing the data set on which the parameters are calculated to specific attribute values.

Here, the widget is a GUI element that allows displaying information useful to the user and system-defined information in a given format. The widget contains a set of parameter values, a chart, and allows changing the section for values' output.

A large set of standard and specialized diagrams can be integrated into the system, such as:

- Histogram;
- Bar chart;
- Bar chart with quartiles;
- Bullet chart;
- Compound duration of the process stages;
- Diagram of the process routes;
- Gantt chart;
- Process graph, etc.

The dashboard view is fully described using the layout. Layout is a universal tool for customizing the dashboard view and allows users to flexibly personalize the informative space for their needs.

Dashboards can have their own hierarchy. For example, from a top-level dashboard with a set of aggregated parameters, you can go to the lowest level and see what the parameter values are.

To connect to an external system, you need to install a module of the corresponding connector on the system side, configure the data transmission channel and set the update rate (or configure triggers).

When the system receives an incoming request to receive data, Gateway checks the addressant data correctness and opens the data download session to the distributed storage. Distributed storage provides scalability, reliability and fault tolerance of the system.

Different data from the storage can be processed by different system blocks with different intensity, therefore the system contains mechanisms that allow reducing the time of request and data transfer:

- Requests to the repository are saved in order to avoid repeated unloading of the same data;
- User request parameters and the results of their processing are saved;
- Multi-level caching is used, which allows you to make a compromise between the speed and the data volume.

The system can contain a wide variety of customizable triggers for various events to launch processing. So, after the data was saved in the repository, the insertion trigger can launch a number of procedures from the computing core, for example, advanced algorithms of the analytic shell.

Here the computing core (built-in handlers) can consist of procedures (Figs. 10, 11 and 12), which help to put the data in a more convenient form for further study (Fig. 13).

1. Quality estimation of data incoming from heterogeneous sources through multiple connectors, puts in correspondence to the data received a set of permissible analytical operations on them, depending on the availability of the necessary fields and attributes.
2. Compiling metadata, that is, information about the data itself. Here is an automatic recognition of types and data formats (structural metadata). Metadata is also collected about individual records for subsequent cataloging and quick access.
3. Harmonization is the data transformation to a unified view while storing the semantic significance by reducing the dimension and put to the final set of types and formats detected automatically. The harmonization procedure can reduce the number of problems associated with heterogeneity of sources, but unlike ETL, it does not set the goal of put all the data to previously known formats.
4. Forming the time-series - sequences of data values at equal discrete time intervals. A such time-series creation allows further application of a set of analytical procedures, including regression analysis, prediction of future values on a retrospective basis, disclosure of seasonality, autocorrelation analysis, autoregressive prediction (f. e., ARIMA algorithm).
5. Searching and cleaning up from the outlayers, which can significantly distort the real parameter value (for example, the average). On the other hand, the search for outliers often reveals best practices or potential problem areas and failures [3, 4, 9–14].

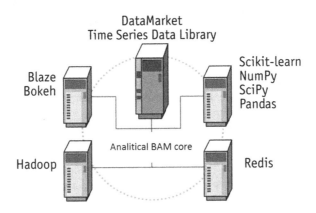

Fig. 10. Analytical core's composition of the BI security platform.

The system uses data that have passed by the harmonization in an easily scalable analytical shell. Thus, the system allows going beyond the standard "what happened?" and get answers to the questions "why did it happen?", "what happens if the trend continues?", "what will happen in the future?" and "what is the best output?". For this purpose, the following software packages are integrated into the system:

- Mathematical modeling;
- Analysis and optimization;
- Calculating the number and developing strategies;
- Predicting development trends;
- Searching for "hidden" patterns, data mining;
- Machine learning;
- Detecting non-standard behavior;
- Detecting security incidents, etc.

Fig. 11. Adapting data models.

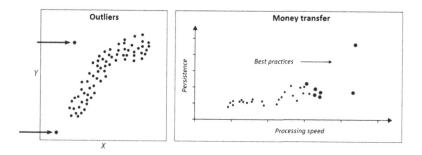

Fig. 12. Representation of calculation results.

Here the main system interface is a dashboard with diagrams for the most important business parameters. Dashboard is an interactive tool that allows the user to choose a data section, filter, and decompose the parameter. The user can also look at problematic areas using regulations, benchmarking or incident reporting.

Choosing a section (Fig. 13) allows user to see the same parameter from the different point of view: the he selects "by RDD" in the combo box of the dashboard section selection for monitoring threats, the widget displays all the important information for each of the RDDs.

For a more detailed exposure in a particular parameter, in order to study it from different points of view and in dynamics, the dashboard performs decomposition, allowing to "fall" in the parameter to an each employee, process, a specific document

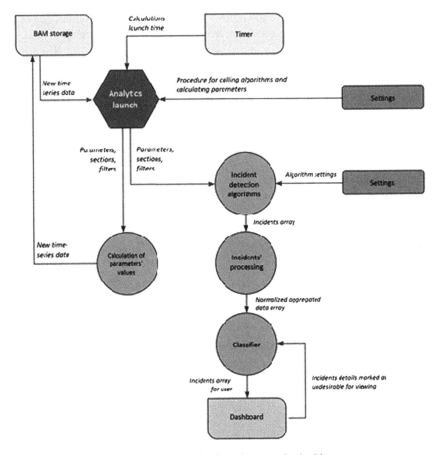

Fig. 13. Algorithm for detecting security incidents.

and each operation. With this detail, you can see all the problems on the dashboard, identify the reasons for their occurrence, and understand how to fix them.

It is possible to create specialized applications (based on the system) to solve specific security services tasks, first of all, to assess the effectiveness of monitoring IS threats [3, 4, 9–14].

Details of the composition, structure, and functionality of the discussed BI security platform can be found in the works.

4   Conclusion

The largest implementations of BI-systems fall on state companies and enterprises. As a rule, customers use several analytical systems simultaneously. For example, in Wells Fargo introduced the system Tableau, SAS BI, Teradata, in Royal Bank of Canada - SAS, Teradata, Esperant. Barclays introduced the systems Tableau, SAS BI and Microsoft Technologies.

The Russian market volume in 2012 amounted to about $ 1.3 billion dollars and continues to grow at 15% per year. In 2012, more than 250 projects were implemented, the total number of projects was more than 1400. In 2013, only in the field of public administration, more than 450 projects were implemented, which is 35% of all projects implemented in Russia. The growth rate of investments in BI is more than 100% per year.

Sberbank is actively implementing business intelligence systems (67 projects), VTB24 (39), Uralsib (24), and public control authorities: the Russian Ministry of Finance (13 projects), the Russian Ministry of Health (4), the Federal Property Management Agency (4). More than 20 companies-users of BI-systems own 100 or more licenses.

In general, the dynamics of the BI-systems market is positive: from $ 14 billion in 2013 to $ 20 billion in 2018. At the same time, the growth BI market rate of Advanced Analytics (AA) class significantly exceeds the growth market rates for traditional BI systems and IT in general and account for more than 33% annually. In particular, significant growth is observed in the segments Big Data, NoSQL, Real-time analysis. It is projected that by 2020 the volume of the BigData-systems market will amount to $ 20 billion against 4 billion in 2013. The growth rate (27%) is 4 times higher than the growth BI market rate. In 2013, the share of companies that planned investments in BigData increased from 58% to 64%. Also, the NoSQL storage market is growing: by 2017, it will amount to $ 1.2 billion, compared with $ 0.3 billion in 2013, which corresponds to an increase of 40% per year.

Today, customers increasingly prefer cloud solutions: 63% of companies see significant advantages in cloud analysis computing technologies. As a result, by 2017, the volume of the cloud analytics market is expected to amount 3.65 billion dollars against 1.2 billion in 2013, which corresponds to a 30% growth annually. Moreover, by 2017, 50% of analytics will account for streaming data. 67% of the companies surveyed consider it important to process and analyze data in real time. As a result, many companies that work in Advanced Analytics show very high business growth rates, for example, QlikTech (23%), Pitney Bowes (38%), Tibco (50%), Tableau (76%).

With regard to Russian security services that provide adequate security for banking transactions and electronic commerce, it is also necessary to consider the following. According to the approved "Fundamentals of the Russian Federation state policy in the field of international information security for the period until 2020", much attention is now given to the information technology security and import substitution in technological platforms.

It implicitly, that critical and sensitive information should be processed by software and hardware complexes exclusively from Russian manufacturers and suppliers.

To reduce the dependence level on foreign technologies, the public sector should completely switch to work with Russian software and hardware platform developers. In turn, the commercial segment should also facilitate the transition to Russian developments and more actively use them in their activities. Thus, the most popular in the short term will be Russian BI-systems for Big Data work, independent of foreign hardware and software [3, 4, 9–12, 14].

For the first time such systems began to appear on the BI-systems market. For example, the hardware and software complex "INNA" for Big Data work under the control of the "Elbrus" OS based on the Linux 2.6.33 kernel and the Russian processor "Elbrus 2C+" by MCST. The mentioned BI-system undergoes certification tests on safety requirements of Russian FSTEC on the 2nd level of undocumented features control and the 2nd class of unauthorized access security.

References

1. Forecast: enterprise software markets, worldwide, 2011–2016, 4Q12 update (2012). https://www.gartner.com/doc/2272115/fore-cast-enterprise-software-markets-worldwide/. Accessed 13 Sept 2018
2. Are business intelligence dashboards on the brink of extinction? (2012). https://www.smartdatacollective.com/are-business-intelligence-dashboards-brink-extinction/. Accessed 13 Sept 2018
3. Biryukov, D.N., Lomako, A.G.: Approach to building a cyber threat prevention system. Problems of Information Security. Computer Systems, no. 2, pp. 13–19 (2013). (in Russian)
4. Biryukov, D.N., Rostovtsev, Y.G.: An approach to construction of consistent theory of anticipatory behavior scenarios in conflict situations. SPIIRAS Proc. 1(38), 94–111 (2015). https://doi.org/10.15622/sp.38.6. (in Russian)
5. Plattner, H.: A Course in In-Memory Data Management: The Inner Mechanics of In-Memory Databases, 2nd edn. Springer, Heidelberg (2014). https://doi.org/10.1007/978-3-642-55270-0
6. Plattner, H., Zeier, A.: In-Memory Data Management: An Inflection Point for Enterprise Applications. Springer, Heidelberg (2011). https://doi.org/10.1007/978-3-642-19363-7
7. Darmont, J., Loudcher, S.: Utilizing Big Data Paradigms for Business Intelligence. IGI Global (2018). https://doi.org/10.4018/978-1-5225-4963-5
8. Lee, J., et al.: SAP HANA distributed in-memory database system: transaction, session, and metadata management. In: Proceedings of the 2013 IEEE 29th International Conference on Data Engineering (ICDE), pp. 1165–1173 (2013). https://doi.org/10.1109/icde.2013.6544906
9. Makoveychuk, K.A., Petrenko, S.A., Petrenko, A.S.: Modeling of self-recovery of computations under perturbation conditions, information systems and technologies in modeling and control. In: Proceedings of the All-Russian Scientific-Practical Conference, pp. 162–166 (2017). (in Russian)
10. Makoveychuk, K.A., Petrenko, S.A., Petrenko, A.S.: Modeling the recognition of destructive effects on computer calculations. In: Proceedings of the All-Russian Scientific-Practical Conference "Information Systems and Technologies in Modeling and Control", pp. 155–161 (2017). (in Russian)
11. Makoveychuk, K.A., Petrenko, S.A., Petrenko, A.S.: Organization of calculations with memory. In: Proceedings of the All-Russian Scientific-Practical Conference "Information Systems and Technologies in Modeling and Control", pp. 260–266 (2017). (in Russian)
12. Li, K., et al.: Tool support for secure programming by security testing. In: Proceedings of the 2015 IEEE Eighth International Conference on Software Testing, Verification and Validation Workshops (ICSTW), pp. 1–4 (2015) https://doi.org/10.1109/icstw.2015.7107462
13. Herschel R.T.: Organizational Applications of Business Intelligence Management: Emerging Trends. IGI Global (2012). https://doi.org/10.4018/978-1-4666-0279-3
14. Petrenko, S.A., Stupin, D.D.: National early warning system on cyber - attack: a scientific monograph. In: Boev, S.F. (ed.). Publishing House "Athena", University of Innopolis, Innopolis (2017). (in Russian)

Improving the Target Quality Chat-Bots on the Basis of Linguistic Metametric Text

Dmitry Zhukov⬤, Yury Korablin⬤, Vyacheslav Raev⬤, and Dmitry Akimov$^{(\boxtimes)}$⬤

MIREA – Russian Technological University, Vernadskogo Av. 78,
119454 Moscow, Russia
`akim-dmitrij@yandex.ru`

Abstract. The paper discusses the methods and technologies used for chat bots, taking into account the specifics of Internet communications, for conscious dialogue with a given goal. The methods of formalizing the creation of pages of virtual personalities are discussed in detail. Information presentations of speech behavior meta-metrics for the implementation of a chat bot efficiency model based on the analysis of short messages are considered.

As sources of attributive sense formation, not values in the generally accepted understanding, but individually-specific categorical scales, serve as an instrument for identifying, classifying and evaluating the subject's significant characteristics of objects and phenomena of virtual reality. The goal of creation of models by the subject (agent) is formalized, which consists in obtaining a forecast, that is, a new information object (message or algorithm of actions).

The phenomenological correspondence with the results of the research of SP was established by S.P. Rastorguev in the part of the model for transforming the virtual world. A technological solution is proposed on the basis of the search model of the associative context in the semantic kernel.

Keywords: Chat bot · Active search · Virtual personalities · Contextual analysis · Text messages · Dialogue · Chat systems · Chat · Metadata

1 Introduction

The main volume of Internet communications currently accounts for social networks. The core of a social network is a graph consisting of virtual personalities: users and agents of influence.

A virtual person is a chat bot knowledge base and at the same time a page on social networks that contains personal information.

The task of enumerating the detection of virtual entities of a social network is extremely time-consuming and often limited by the computing capabilities of the hardware platform [1].

It is impossible to create an account in a social network without specifying a first and last name, respectively, these attributes will always be in the "user page" entity. According to them, virtual entities are distinguished from other types of entities when listing all identifiers in a social network.

© Springer Nature Switzerland AG 2020
V. Sukhomlin and E. Zubareva (Eds.): Convergent 2018, CCIS 1140, pp. 289–295, 2020.
https://doi.org/10.1007/978-3-030-37436-5_26

When using virtual personalities interacting through messages or comments, there is a need for analyzing texts for subsequent reviewing, as well as forming content on a social network page.

For the user of a social network, it is necessary that the virtual personality has some confidence. As a rule, it is possible to build a trust model based on the static and dynamic characteristics of the user's page [2].

2 Stages of the Formation of a Virtual Personality Through the Analysis of Speech Behavior

Often, the same software agent can communicate on behalf of several virtual personalities on the network [3]. As a rule, he pursues the goal to ask a few questions based on the level of user confidence in the dialogue. There are virtual personalities that allow you to conduct a dialogue with a living person without an operator [4].

The main stages are:

1. Automated text analysis of chat messages.
2. Conducting a dialogue in natural language on behalf of a person on a given problem with special programs.
3. Automatic calculation of the text metrics of the interlocutor (user).
4. Automatic generation of messages.

Such virtual personalities are simple chat bots, for technical and information support of IRC chats, chat bots of social networks (for example, bots of Vkontakte "vbots", performing certain commands, mainly for entertainment or receiving news), as well as more complex conversational programs that can really simulate dialogue and answer arbitrary questions [5]. The most famous conversational bot is the CleverBot application, developed as a web application by the British scientist Rollo Carpenter (date, link). Since its inception, the bot has "conducted" more than 65 million conversations. Working with the knowledge base, he constantly updates it through communication with users.

The bot learns to communicate with people, but its capabilities are still limited: it is a stationary application installed on its web platform and not able to act independently. Therefore, the so-called "avatar" appears in the concept of a virtual entity, which compensates for the above deficiency [6].

3 Development of Speech Behavior Analysis MetaMetrics

Let us give a list of the main text metrics for the formation of a virtual personality based on information from the text of the interlocutor [7].

The developed metametrics will allow to build on their values logical laws dividing the space of virtual personalities into fuzzy classes: "defiantly trusting" and "not causing trustworthy" (Table 1).

Table 1. The main text metrics.

Marker	MetaMetrics	Algorithm for calculating the coefficient
M1	Estimation of income based on social network profile information	Correlation integral characteristic of the descriptive part of photographs
M2	Completeness of the page	The sum of the points of completeness of filling in all the analyzed fields of the social network page
M3	Completeness of personal information for the page	The total points of completeness of filling in all the analyzed fields of personal information of a social network page
M4	Characteristic sociability of the user	The average number of messages published by a social network user on his page for specified periods
M5	Quantitative evaluation of individuals with similar interests	The number of social network users who added the analyzed user page "as a friend"
M6	User social significance	The number of social network users who marked the analyzed page as interesting
M7	Average user sociability	The frequency of publications on the user page
M8	Used platforms	Code of the platform, most often used to view and edit your social network page
M9	Evaluation of the user's communication style	Average values of the number of tonal words and punctuation marks in published user messages.
M10	Evaluation of personal qualities of the user	Codes published by the user of information about themselves, like: political views, worldview, attitudes towards smoking and alcohol

The automated system for generating responses of Virtual Personalities (VPs) consists of the following main components [8]:

- connector to chat subsystem;
- text analysis subsystem;
- chat bot subsystem.

When an application for creating a Virtual Personality (VP) arrives in the system, the system connects to the chat API, searches for the user template pages using key information, retrieves the user's dialogue text, retrieves the vector of meta metrics and makes a decision on the formation of the Virtual Personality (VP) or rejecting the application [9].

The result of the work of the VP formation subsystem is the recommendations for forming responses in the chat. The general format of interaction with API - social network interfaces [10]:

- type of request - POST/GET;
- protocol - HTTPS;
- request format - XML.

Before you start working in social networks, you must log in. Authorization in a social network occurs through interaction with the API [11]. To work with it, many social networks require preliminary registration of the application, and provide it with a unique identifier [12].

General algorithm:

1. Accessing the API with the provision of the application identifier;
2. Getting a session ID from the API;
3. Sending an authorization request for overhead lines. Opening of the authorization web page;
4. In case of successful authorization - getting the identifier of the user session;
5. In case of unsuccessful authorization - go to step 3.

4 Using Third-Party Page Metadata to Increase Trust in Dialogue

When conducting a dialogue, it is useful to use the metadata of the user's page for understanding the interests, activity, sociability, mode, and other supporting characteristics that will increase the credibility of the dialogue.

The chat bot administrator sets the location (city), age, gender, user's list of interests (science, robots, electronics, etc.), the system searches for chats, and after that it provides the result of their work - evaluating the interlocutor's text for appropriateness conducting a dialogue on a given topic [13, 14]. Having the additional information obtained in this way, the Administrator makes a decision on the expediency of conducting a dialogue with the found chat user.

To determine the level of interest, it is necessary to analyze the messages published by the users of the social network VKontakte on the pages of the social network user profiles belonging to the training sample (Figs. 1 and 2).

The end result of the algorithm development is a dialogue between the VP and the user, during which phrases on the subject concerned with the target characteristics were selected and defined [15].

Target characteristics can be a set of words in a user's message from the target dictionary or new knowledge about the user's opinion.

In a multidimensional space, Lambda Wilks statistics [16] is used as a criterion for checking the differences between real and virtual personality messages. The Lambda Wilks criterion can be used in the chat bot quality assessment model. We use it in conjunction with the correlation analysis of parts of speech chat bot and the real user dialogue (Fig. 3).

The obtained correlation diagram allows you to clearly demonstrate the proximity of the chatbot dialogue and the real user. The higher the correlation coefficient, the more likely part of the speech is used in the dialogue.

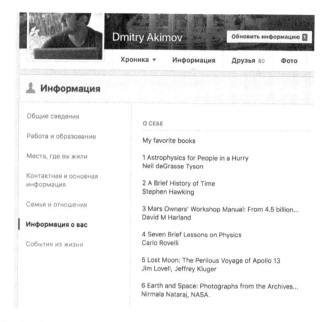

Fig. 1. An example of information about interests in social networks.

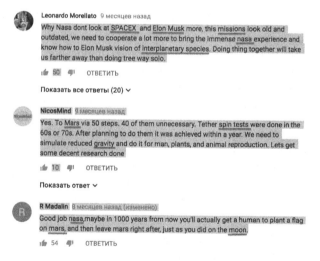

Fig. 2. The result of the formation of messages with the translation of theses and phrases, taking into account the theme of space in the conversational sequence.

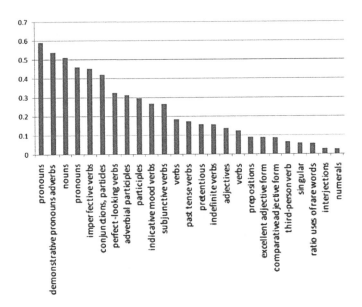

Fig. 3. Combined intra-group syntactic correlations between chatbot messages and real users.

5   Conclusion

The metrics of constructing pages of virtual personalities on the Internet are given. Metrics allow you to create a virtual identity page, thereby increasing the chat bot's ability to achieve the goal to find out the necessary information from the user. The paper does not consider the model of the formation of the dialogue and features of building answers, such studies will be presented in the following works. Additionally, the possibility of using metadata analysis from a user's page in a social network to form topics of dialogue interesting to the user was investigated. Practical issues can be used in dialogue systems with dynamically formed criteria for goal setting. In contrast to "vbots" and CleverBot, a chat bot with analysis of metadata in social networks will allow users to be identified who will be interested in conducting a dialogue on a given topic, and accordingly the probability of obtaining the necessary information will increase.

Acknowledgement. The study is performed under financing secured by the Ministry of Education and Science of the Russian Federation for the state assignments to the high schools and scientific organizations. Project number 2.5676.2017/БЧ.

References

1. Kusner, M.J., Sun, Y., Kolkin, N.I., Weinberger, K.Q.: From word embeddings to document distances. In: Proceedings of the 32nd International Conference on Machine Learning, Lille, France, 2015. JMLR: W&CP, vol. 37, pp. 957–966 (2015)

2. Van Dijk, T.A.: Critical Discourse Analysis. In: Tannen, D., Schiffrin, D., Hamilton, H. (eds.) The Handbook of Discourse Analysis, pp. 352–371. Blackwell, Oxford (2001)

3. Potapov, D.A., Akimov, D.A.: Identification speech design improves the accuracy of the information search system. In: Modern Science: Actual Problems of Theory and Practice. Series: Natural and Technical Sciences, no. 1, pp. 41–43 (2017). [in Russian]

4. Landauer, T.K., Foltz, P.W., Laham, D.: Introduction to latent semantic analysis. Discourse Processes **25**(2–3), 259–284 (1998). https://doi.org/10.1080/01638539809545028

5. Levy, O., Golberg, Y., Dagan, I.: Improving distributional similarity with lessons learned from word embeddings. Trans. Assoc. Comput. Linguist. **3**, 211–225 (2015)

6. Morozova, Y.I.: Construction of semantic vector spaces different subject areas. In: The Scientists of the IPI RAS. Collection of Reports, Moscow, pp. 4–11 (2012). (in Russian)

7. Resource Description Environment (RDF): Concepts and Abstract Syntax, The World Wide Web Consortium (W3C) (2004). https://www.w3.org/TR/rdf11-concepts/. Accessed 12 Sept 2018

8. Sachkov, V.E., Gilmutdinova, E.F., Matyash, E.D., Akimov, D.A.: Processing and computer analysis of natural language texts. In: Modern Science: Actual Problems of Theory and Practice. Series: Natural and Technical Sciences, no. 12, pp. 57–64 (2016). (in Russian)

9. Semantic Channel. https://en.wikipedia.org/wiki/Semantic_Channel. Accessed 12 Sept 2018

10. Serban, I.V., Lowe, R., Henderson, P., Charlin, L., Pineau, J.: A survey of available corpora for building data-driven dialogue systems. CoRR, vol. abs/1512.05742 (2015). https://arxiv.org/abs/1512.05742. Accessed 12 Sept 2018

11. Serban, I.V., Sordoni, A., Bengio, Y., Courville, A., Pineau, J.: Building End-to-end dialogue systems using the generative hierarchical neural network models. CoRR, vol. abs/1507.04808 (2015). https://arxiv.org/abs/1507.04808. Accessed 12 Sept 2018

12. Mikolov, T., Le, Q.L., Sutskever, I.: Exploiting similarities among languages for machine translation. CoRR, vol. abs/1309.4168 (2013). https://arxiv.org/pdf/1309.4168.pdf. Accessed 12 Sept 2018

13. W3C Semantic web activity. The World Wide Web Consortium (W3C). https://www.w3.org/2001/sw/. Accessed 12 Sept 2018

14. Wallace, R.S.: The Anatomy of A.L.I.C.E. In: Epstein, R., Roberts, G., Beber, G. (eds.) Parsing the Turing Test, pp. 181–210. Springer, Dordrecht (2009). https://doi.org/10.1007/978-1-4020-6710-5_13

15. Weizenbaum, J.: Computer Power and Human Reason: From Judgment to Calculation. W. H. Freeman and Company, New York (1976)

16. Basics of discriminant analysis. http://masters.donntu.org/2005/kita/kapustina/library/discr_an.htm. Accessed 12 Sept 2018

New Methods of the Cybersecurity Knowledge Management Analytics

Sergey Petrenko[1][(✉)] ⓘ, Krystina Makoveichuk[2] ⓘ,
and Alexander Olifirov[2] ⓘ

[1] Innopolis University, Universitetskaya Str. 1, 420500 Innopolis, Russia
s.petrenko@innopolis.ru
[2] V.I. Vernadsky Crimean Federal University,
Sevastopolskaya Str. 2-A, 298635 Yalta, Russia
christin2003@yandex.ru, alex.olifirov@gmail.com

Abstract. The article discusses the possibilities of using Master Data Management (MDM) technology to solve the problem of developing a corporate (institutional) state system segment to detect, prevent and eliminate the cyber - attack consequences (hereinafter - SOPKA). Typical objectives of semantic cyber security MDM is identified in article. The semantic cyber security MDM means a data management system that operates rules of the object behavior and interaction in cyberspace to solve the SOPKA problems in order to prevent the protected critical infrastructure transition to catastrophic states. Cyber security ontology (meta-ontology) as the knowledge presentation way about qualitative characteristics and quantitative patterns of information confrontation is proposed. Shown, that by combining cyber security data from various external and internal information sources and corresponding rules to detect, prevent, and eliminate the cyber-attacks consequences into a single semantic domain model, it is possible to build the required intellectual (and, in the future, cognitive) information space, then to develop the appropriate artificial cognitive agents and the corresponding intelligent "semantic cyber security MDM" software and hardware complex to support SOPKA operations as a whole. The basic development principles of the "semantic cyber security MDM" software and hardware complex are formulated. The possible architecture of the "Warning-2016" software and hardware complex that is intended for early cyber-attack warning on corporate and institutional information resources of the Russian Federation is shown. It is based on SAP HANA, and the required semantic MDM is implemented on the basis of SAP NetWeaver Master Data Management (SAP NW MDM).

Keywords: Cybersecurity master data · Cybersecurity ontology · Semantic analysis of big cybersecurity data · Cybersecurity knowledge management · Convergent NBIC technologies · Big data technologies · Master data management system

© Springer Nature Switzerland AG 2020
V. Sukhomlin and E. Zubareva (Eds.): Convergent 2018, CCIS 1140, pp. 296–310, 2020.
https://doi.org/10.1007/978-3-030-37436-5_27

1 Introduction

1.1 Possible State of Art

In this section, Master Data Management (MDM) SOPKA is an information system that accumulates input data from various external and internal data sources (Internet/Intranet and IoT/IoT), ensures centralized data storage and provision in standardized form to make reliable decisions and support the operational SOPKA activities.

The MDM in IT is traditionally used for a data management about products (PIM) and clients (Customer Data Management, CDI). At the same time, MDM is a part of the process-oriented information technology group, and it plays an important role in solving analysis and data processing problems. In practice, the MDM implementation risks are estimated as small, and implementation time as acceptable (Fig. 1). It is believed that MDM technology is relevant, primarily for large organizations with a number of large-scale distributed applications more than three. According to Gartner (Fig. 2), a modern MDM solution should:

- Provide opportunities to manage the information quality;
- Provide loading, integration and synchronization of large arrays and data streams;
- Support workflow management processes and related services;
- Have high performance, availability and security;
- Support automated modes of data collection, processing, storage and analysis;
- Meet technological standards and best practices.

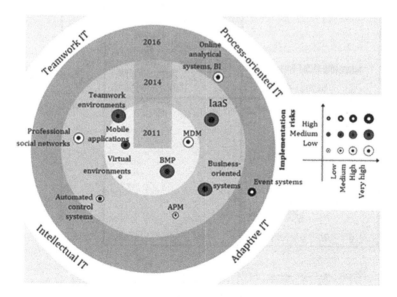

Fig. 1. The MDM place and role in IT.

The main MDM development trends and prospects are:

- MDM applications shift from the business intelligence and decision support to operational activities that directly affect business results;
- Transition from narrow subject-matter solutions (mainly clients or products) to multi-domain solutions (several data types at once: products, customers, finance, security, etc.);
- "Social" MDM uses a modern opportunity of teamwork, social networks and instant messengers to automate master data processing;
- Data governance (unified corporate data management) is an extension of the master data management principles for a wide range of corporate data;
- MDM integration into the corporate business process management system and corporate cybersecurity systems;
- Including constant information (Reference data) along with conditionally-constant information (customers, products, etc.) in the MDM sphere;
- MDM adaptation to work with big data and streaming data processing;
- MDM implementation in the form of appropriate cloud services: SaaS, PaaS or IaaS;
- Evolution from syntactic to semantic technologies analysis and data processing.

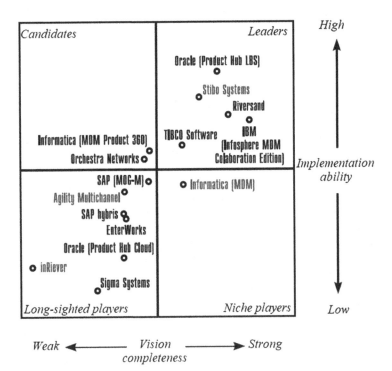

Fig. 2. The "magic" MDM Gartner quadrant.

At the same time, the semantic MDM prospects can be estimated from the Gartner "interest curve" (Fig. 3).

Let us consider that MDM technology shifted from a "lively interest" area to the "mature" technologies field, and the "semantic analysis and data processing" technology is only gaining popularity or is at the meridian of the increased specialists attention in the IT and cybersecurity domains. The semantic cybersecurity MDM means a data management system that operates rules of the object behavior and interaction in cyberspace to solve the SOPKA problems in order to prevent the protected critical infrastructure transition to catastrophic states [19].

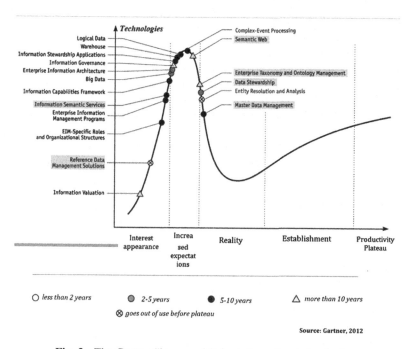

Fig. 3. The Gartner "hype cycle" for information technologies.

Typical objectives of semantic cybersecurity MDM include:

- Construction and support of the cybersecurity ontologies that are information confrontation object models, required to solve SOPKA problems;
- Storage model unification of the cybersecurity data coming from external and internal providing systems, for example SIEM, IDS/IPS, information security tools from unauthorized access, cryptographic information security systems, etc.;
- Standardization of internal cybersecurity data exchange protocols;
- Regulating the processes of maintaining cybersecurity databases and knowledge bases;
- Decision-making support in SOPKA based on the information confrontation semantics, presented in the corresponding cyber security ontology, etc.

1.2 Cybersecurity Ontology

As a rule, the knowledge presentation way about qualitative characteristics and quantitative patterns of information confrontation is not clearly indicated in SOPKA. In our opinion, it is reasonable to use cyber security ontology (meta-ontology) for this. According to Thomas Grubber, the cyber ontology is a certain conceptualization specification of the information confrontation domain. This specification can be given analytically, for example, based on the algorithms theory and mathematical logic, as well as graphically, using some schemes that reflect traditional linguistic methods and textual information process methods [2, 6, 10–12, 14, 16–18]. The key here is an ontology specification language selection, which allows processing the domain machine-interpreted semantics.

Currently, there are three main ontology description language classes:

- Traditional languages based on the specification (*Ontolingua, CycL*), descriptive logic (*LOOM*), frames (*OKBC, OCML, Flogic*);
- More Web-based languages (*XOL, SHOE, UPML*);
- Special languages (*RDF, RDF SPARQL, SWRL, DAML, OIL, OWL*). For example SPARQL can be used to execute logical queries, Semantics-SDK and Owlim can be used to implement rule-based logic output, and Pellet, FaCT++ and Hermi to implement semantic tableau based logic output. At the same time, the OWL API framework integration is possible to introduce the ontology in memory, to modify the ontology at the object level, etc.

Two approaches to ontology are also distinguished in accordance with the IDEF5 standard of ontological analysis (IICE, 1994) and on the recommendations basis of The World Wide Web Consortium (2009).

In the literature, the following ontology construction methods are presented (Table 1):

- *Uscold and King method* (Uschold et al. 1998) [21];
- *Grüninger and Fox approach* (Gruninger et al. 1995) [22];
- *CycL method* (Lenat et al. 1989) [23];
- *Kactus method* (Schreibe et al. 1995) [24];
- *Sensus method* (Swartout et al. 1997) [25];
- *On-To-Knowledge approach* (Staab et al. 2001) [26];
- *Methontology method* (Ferndndez et al. 2006), etc. [27]

In the works of Russian authors, ontologies are presented on the basis of:

- *Finite automata* (Kryvyi 2008, Beniaminov 2003) [28];
- *Lexical syntactic patterns* (Anisimov 2002, Rabchevsky 2009) [29];
- *Product systems* (Nayhanova 2008) [30];
- *Linguistic methods* (Mozzherina 2011) [31];
- *Information granularity* (Tarasov 2012), etc. [32]

Table 1. Known ontology construction ways.

Method name	Completion degree	Implementation complexity	Method flexibility	Software dependence	Life cycle support	Scientific support	Detailed elaboration	Method compatibility
TOVE	Demonstration prototype	Average	Yes	**Does not depend**	No	Yes	Yes	No
Enterprise model approach		Average	Yes	Depends	No		Yes	No
METHONTOLOGY		Average	Yes	Depends	**Yes**		**No**	No
KBSI IDEF5		Average	Yes	Depends	No		Yes	No
Ontolingua		**High**	Yes	Depends	No		Yes	**Yes**
Common KADS and KAKTUS		Average	Yes	Depends	No		**No**	No
PLINIUS		Average	**No**	Depends	No		Yes	No
ONIONS		Average	**No**	Depends	No		**No**	**Yes**
Mikrokosmos		Average	**No**	Depends	No		Yes	No
MENELAS		Average	**No**	Depends	No		**No**	No
SENSUS		**High**	Yes	**Does not depend**	No		Yes	**Yes**
Cye methodology		Average	Yes	Depends	No		Yes	No
UPON		Average	Yes	Depends	**Yes**		Yes	No
101 method		Average	Yes	Depends	No		Yes	No
On-To-Knowledge		Average	**No**	Depends	**Yes**		Yes	No

For example, in the work of Tarasov, [20] the research results in the field of the cognitive agents and mobile robots theory are presented, which, in contrast to reactive agents functioning according to the "stimulus-reaction" scheme, are given a well-developed, dynamic external environment model. Here the cognitive function provides a robot with the learning processes of the outside world, other agents, as well as its self-knowledge. Cognitive processes cover an agent environment perception, generalized internal representation formation, interaction and behavior principles understanding, and training. In fact, the "data-information-knowledge" transitions (Gergey 2004), which are necessary for the efficient agent operation, are implemented in these processes. V.B. Tarasov cognitive robots are able to receive and process heterogeneous information from a human operator in a limited natural language in the form of target designations and instructions, from sensor system actuators and from their own knowledge base.

For the interactive cognitive robot management, it is proposed to develop common ontologies that ensure effective communication between a person and a robot when the latter performs complex tasks in an inaccurate and incompletely defined environment. The main attention is paid to the meta-ontologies formation by granular information representations (in the form of intervals, fuzzy sets, linguistic variables, fuzzy algebraic systems, as well as the space ontology development in the robotics field based on the G. Leibniz and S. Lesnevsky ideas.

Let us note that the granulation meta-ontology and space ontology developed by V. B. Tarasov and his students can be applied to cognitive hardware-software SOPKA agents. The possible architecture of such an artificial cognitive agent is shown in Figs. 4 and 5. In addition to such known artificial agent features as intentionality, activity, reactivity, autonomy and communication skills, an important ability to granulate incoming information will be added.

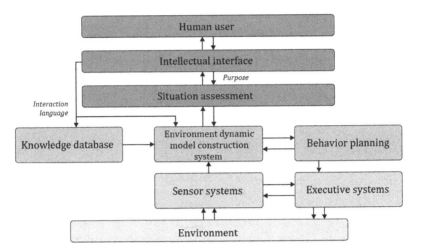

Fig. 4. The information interaction scheme of the cognitive agent with the environment.

The analysis shows that by combining cybersecurity data from various external and internal information sources and corresponding rules to detect, prevent and eliminate the cyber - attacks consequences into a single semantic domain model, it is possible to build the required intellectual (and, in the future, cognitive) information space, then to develop the appropriate artificial cognitive agents and the corresponding intelligent "Semantic cybersecurity MDM" software and hardware complex to support SOPKA operations as a whole.

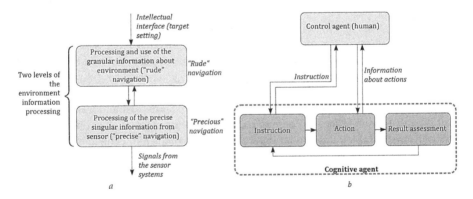

Fig. 5. Artificial cognitive a, b agents architecture.

2 Cybersecurity MDM Principles

We formulate the basic development principles of the "Semantic cybersecurity MDM" software and hardware complex [1, 3–5, 7–9, 13, 15], designed to manage the main (master) SOPKA data:

1. Cybersecurity data consolidation from external information sources in the connected Internet and IIoT networks and internal providing information security tools from unauthorized access, cryptographic information security, SIEM class systems and the SOPKA itself into a single information environment;
2. Presentation of the consolidated cybersecurity data from the mentioned external and internal systems and means in the form of a single object-oriented cybersecurity data model;
3. Ontological representation of information confrontation objects, that is a semantic models and submodels of various domains use to store the mentioned information objects;
4. Vision contextuality of the information confrontation objects, that is the objects representation solely in connection with the goals and objectives of the state and corporate SOPKA;
5. Knowledge orientation, that is a knowledge transfer (object behavior and interconnection rules) from the logic of providing application-based cyber-security applications to a single object database.

We will comment on a number of the above-mentioned principles to establish the "Semantic Cybersecurity MDM" software and hardware complex. A consolidated cyber security data repository for each SOPKA segment or center should be the only place where data will be added, modified or deleted. In other words, the "Semantic Cybersecurity MDM" software and hardware complex should be an independent class of technical systems that is not subordinate to any cybersecurity application system, for example, IDS/IPS or SIEM. The decision rule transfer to the cybersecurity data models level will make them available for all SOPKA systems and tools. Orientation towards the semantic model construction of information confrontation will allow providing the maximum automation level, as the particular solutions, once included in the semantic cybersecurity database, will be properly formalized and reused in various SOPKA applications.

Thus, the "Semantic Cybersecurity MDM" software and hardware complex allows forming and maintaining a consolidated space of aggregated cybersecurity data to support the operational activities of each corporate or institutional segment or SOPKA center. Cybersecurity data for each of the above segments are collected from various external and internal provision systems and accumulated in a single permanent storage location. It is inadvisable to transfer a part of the data beyond the mentioned consolidated space, as this will lead to a connection disruption between the cyberspace objects and automatically to the integrity violation of the information confrontation knowledge system that will limit the developing software and hardware complex capabilities.

The domain model presented in the "Semantic Cybersecurity MDM" software and hardware complex should be capable of adaptation and self-organization, timely display the appearance of new objects and relationships, changes in the object behavior rules in cyberspace and their relationships among themselves. In other words, the semantic MDM should be an intellectual decision-making support environment in SOPKA, regardless of the information confrontation nature and specific content in cyberspace. Contextual representation of the internal the information domain objects structure of the information confrontation must dynamically change depending on the decision to detect, prevent and eliminate the cyber-attacks consequences.

A key characteristic of the "Semantic Cybersecurity MDM" software and hardware complex is the ontological information confrontation objects representation in cyberspace. Without the mentioned ontological model construction, it is impossible to formalize the objects interrelationships with other entities since the compatibility rules for the two objects are determined by the combined compatibility of their constituent parts. At the same time each object meaning is shown in its semantic links with other information confrontation objects. Obviously, when constructing a semantic information confrontation model within the local MDM system of a single segment or the SOPKA center, it will be necessary to operate with terms and definitions from various knowledge fields, and then to combine the mentioned local MDM systems together, for example, using Semantic Web technology.

In a long term, the semantic cybersecurity MDM should be considered as:

- Common language for communication between various applied systems to ensure cybersecurity;
- Method set to maintain specialized databases and cybersecurity directories;
- Technological solution set that provides the creation of a single information space to support the SOPKA operations.

2.1 MDM Cybersecurity System Example

Let us consider the prospective system draft of the "Warning-2016" software and hardware complex that is intended for early cyber - attack warning on corporate and institutional information resources of the Russian Federation.

The possible architecture of the "Warning-2016" software and hardware complex is shown in Fig. 6.

It is based on SAP HANA, and the required semantic MDM is implemented on the basis of SAP NetWeaver Master Data Management (SAP NW MDM). The typical components of the software and hardware complex system architecture are briefly described.

The "Big Data Collection" component is developed based on SAP HANA EIM and NetWeaver Process Orchestration.

Here, SAP HANA EIM "Data Services" (solution of the class Extract/Transform/Leverage, ETL) collects data from various sources. In this case, both standard adapters like Oracle, MS SQL, DB2, Hive, as well as specialized adapters can be used. If necessary, the new adapter development is possible. SAP HANA EIM can perform batch downloading of large data amounts on a schedule up to the online mode (for different data types, different loading time intervals can be configured). When implementing new systems, it will be preferable to organize direct access to databases via the ODBC interface.

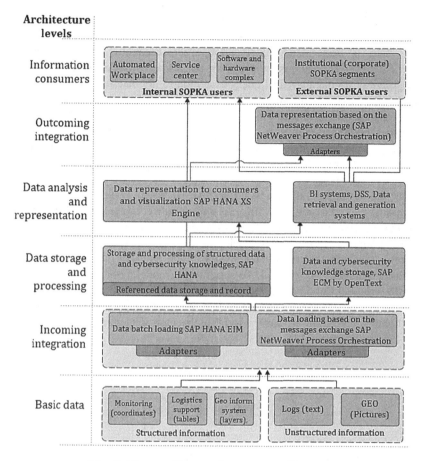

Fig. 6. The cognitive warning system architecture.

SAP NetWeaver Process Orchestration is used to integrate with systems that support queuing and messaging engines. Exchange can occur either in synchronous or asynchronous modes. Process Orchestration (PO) provides mechanisms for guaranteed message delivery, including from/to systems in networks with irregular communications. The messages that cannot be immediately processed are saved in the queue for further sending when the connection is resumed. In this case, ordered message delivery is supported (EO - Exactly_Once, EOIO - Exactly_Once_In_Order). The PO ready-made adapters: File/FTP (S), JDBC, JMS, SOAP, WS (WS Reliable Messaging), HTTP (S), Mail (Mail Servers via SMTP, IMAP4, POP3), SFTP, OData, REST and etc. are used for this integration. If necessary, it is possible to modify their functionality or create a new adapter. The structured data is then loaded into the SAP HANA data storage, and the unstructured data is loaded into SAP Extended ECM by OpenText. When connecting new systems to upload data via messaging, the use of web services technology (for example, SOAP, WS) and XML format will be a more preferable option.

The Data Storage component is developed on the SAP HANA basis, which can function in RAM. Due to this, SAP HANA overcomes the main drawback of traditional DBMSs that is performance degradation when accessing the disk subsystem. Another SAP HANA feature is the use of the so-called "columned: data storage, which allows speeding up the analytical query execution to the database many times.

Within the project framework, a single data model is used in SAP HANA to store consolidated data from various information sources. To do this, we analyze the input data, design the logical repository structure, and create the physical structure of tables and DBMS views. Here the data is stored in specialized formats (on columns, with compression, etc.), but is represented in the form of a classical relational structure from the user/developer point of view.

Thus, the developing storage based on SAP HANA provides the maximum speed of processing and accessing data arrays, as well as data compression. At the same time, due to the relational presentation form, data access will be carried out in the logical structure optimal for the analytics development.

For this, appropriate analytical tools like the SQL query language, which is de facto the industry standard, can be used. To simplify the modeling process, a so-called data "generalized model can be used (Fig. 7), whereas SAP HANA Studio is quite suitable to develop a physical data model. Note that with the Graph Engine help, there is a possibility to store data in a graphical form. In this case, data graph access is performed by XS Engine interfaces.

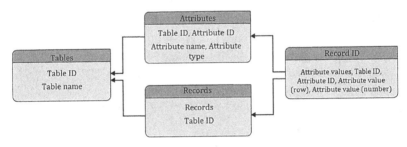

Fig. 7. The "generalized data model" scheme.

It will be necessary to implement a maintenance system of common directories and classifiers (NSI system) to load consistent data from various sources in SAP HANA. For this purpose, the following data entities are provided in the data model: a directory list, a characteristic list of the objects contained in directories, acceptable characteristic value lists, etc. It is also necessary to have recoding tables between similar directories from different systems. Here the "Semantic Cybersecurity MDM" software and hardware complex is exactly designed to manage the basic (master) cybersecurity data to support the SOPKA operation as a whole.

Note that SAP HANA supports the developed fault tolerance mechanisms. When one of the working servers is failed, the backup server connects to the malfunctioning server data and begins to perform its functions. Thus, the system is fault-tolerant (Fig. 8).

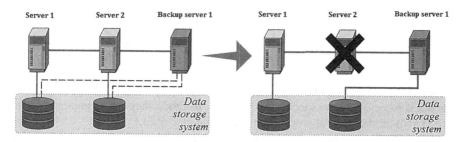

Fig. 8. Fault tolerance scheme.

In addition, it is possible to implement a disaster tolerant solution by deploying identical SAP HANA installations in two remote data centers with the organization of continuous data replication from the first data center to the second one. When one of the data centers fails, the system continues to function.

Note that, depending on the bandwidth of the existing communication channels, synchronous or asynchronous replication mode can be used.

Switching from one data center to another is also possible by using a so-called virtual IP address or IP spoofing through DNS (Fig. 9).

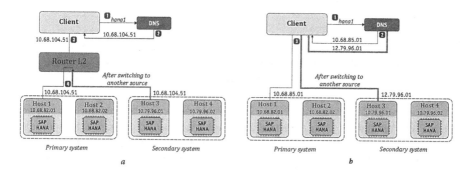

Fig. 9. Possible switching schemes.

To store and manage unstructured information (text documents, audio and video files), it is reasonable to use SAP Extended ECM by Open Text. To scale Open Text, its components (both back-end and front-end) are installed on different servers in such a way that separate servers are responsible for processing user requests and forming interfaces for the latter, while others are in charge of managing the documents storage, building indexes, searching documents, etc. To provide fault tolerance in the 24/7 mode, the Open Text back-end components can be deployed in the HA cluster architecture in Active-Passive mode. For front-end components, constant maintenance is achieved by using backup installations that can be put into balancing at any time when one of the major installations components fails. Switching clients between Open Text installations (if you disconnect one of the installations) are implemented similarly to the case with SAP HANA systems (using a virtual IP address, an IP spoofing).

The "Forecast Analytics" component is developed on the SAP Business Objects BI Platform basis. The named platform supports such functions as generating reports of random complexity, uploading reports in various formats, automatic reports distribution to information consumers, and etc. BI Platform complements the SAP HANA XS Engine functionality in terms of data analysis and reporting.

SAP HANA has an accessible library of predictive algorithms (PAL) available for use. If it is necessary to use specific mathematical methods, they can be implemented in SAP HANA in the form of so-called function libraries (AFL).

Users will be able to access the stored information through software or interactive user interfaces implemented using SAP HANA XS Engine, integrated in the SAP HANA application server. To implement interactive user interfaces, it is suggested to use SAP UI 5 interface element libraries. Using UI5, interfaces can be developed with the automatic adaptation function to the size of the device used to output information (wall panel, desktop monitor, tablet screen, etc.). At the same time, information access will be regulated in accordance with user access rights. When accessing data through software interfaces to ensure guaranteed content delivery to consumers, access can be provided using the SAP NetWeaver Process Orchestration component.

Outbound integration is also implemented by SAP NetWeaver Process Orchestration means.

3   Conclusion

The scientific and technical novelty of the "Semantic Cybersecurity MDM" software and hardware complex is to apply the process approach in constructing ontological information confrontation models. The proposed solution essence can be briefly expressed as "semantic cybersecurity management" or, more fully, "the repeated application methodology of knowledge about information confrontation quantitative patterns and qualitative characteristics". The transition to the semantic technologies application in the SOPKA design is a critically important innovation that determines the main development vector in this sphere in the midterm and is a technological advantages source of the systems to detect, prevent and eliminate the cyber - attack consequences on corporate and institutional information resources of the Russian Federation. At the same time, the appropriate scientific support is, primarily, methods for representing information confrontation knowledge using ontologies, relevant ontological engineering and semantic search methods.

References

1. Petrenko, A.S., Bugaev, I.A., Petrenko, S.A.: Master data management system SOPKA. Zaŝita informacii. Inside **5**(71), 37–43 (2016). (in Russian)
2. Massel, A.G., Tyuryumin, V.O.: Events ontologies and their application for description of energy security threats. In: Proceedings of the Microwave & Telecommunication Technology (CriMiCo), 24th International Crimean Conference, pp. 443–444 (2014). https://doi.org/10.1109/crmico.2014.6959470

3. Barabanov, A.V., Markov, A.S., Tsirlov, V.L.: Statistics of software vulnerability detection in certification testing. J. Phys: Conf. Ser. **1015**(4), 042033 (2018). https://doi.org/10.1088/1742-6596/1015/4/042033

4. Biryukov, D.N., Lomako, A.G., Rostovtsev, Yu.G.: The appearance of anticipating cyber threats risk prevention systems. SPIIRAS Proc. **2**(39), 5–25 (2015). https://doi.org/10.15622/sp.39.1. (in Russian)

5. Vorobiev, E.G., Petrenko, S.A., Kovaleva, I.V., Abrosimov, I.K.: Organization of the entrusted calculations in crucial objects of informatization under uncertainty. In: Proceedings of the 20th IEEE International Conference on Soft Computing and Measurements, SCM, St. Petersburg, Russia, 24–26 May 2017, pp. 299–300 (2017). https://doi.org/10.1109/scm.2017.7970566

6. Kotenko, I., Polubelova, O., Saenko, I., Doynikova, E.: The ontology of metrics for security evaluation and decision support in SIEM systems. In: Proceedings of the 2013 International Conference on Availability, Reliability and Security, Regensburg, Germany, pp. 638–645 (2013). https://doi.org/10.1109/ares.2013.84

7. Kotenko, I.V.: Intelligent mechanisms of cybersecurity management, in risk and security management. Proc. Inst. Syst. Anal. Russ. Acad. Sci. **41**, 74–103 (2009). (in Russian)

8. Massel, L.V., Voropay, N.I., Senderov, S.M., Massel, A.G.: Cyber danger as one of the strategic threats to Russia's energy security. Voprosy kiberbezopasnosti = Cybersecurity **4** (17), 2–10 (2016). https://doi.org/10.21681/2311-3456-2016-4-2-10. (in Russian)

9. Massel, L.V.: Problems of smart grid creation in Russia from the perspective of information technologies and cyber security. In: Proceedings of the All-Russian Seminar with International Participation, Methodological Issues of Research into the Reliability of Large Energy Systems, Reliability of Energy Systems: Achievements, Problems, Prospects, vol. 64, pp. 171–181. ISEM SB RAS, Irkutsk (2014). (in Russian)

10. Massel, L.V., Vorozhtsova, T.N., Pjatkova, N.I.: Ontology engineering to support strategic decision-making in the energy sector. Ontol. Des. **7**(1), 66–76 (2017). https://doi.org/10.18287/2223-9537-2017-7-1-66-76. (in Russian)

11. Massel, L.V.: Fractal approach to structuring knowledge and examples of its applications. Ontol. Des. **6**(2), 149–161 (2016). https://doi.org/10.18287/2223-9537-2016-6-2-149-161. (in Russian)

12. Guarino, N., Musen, M.: Applied ontology: the next decade begins. Appl. Ontol. **10**(1), 1–4 (2015). https://doi.org/10.3233/AO150143

13. Guarino, N.: Services as activities: towards a unified definition for (public) services. In: 2017 IEEE 21st International Proceedings of the Enterprise Distributed Object Computing Workshop (EDOCW), Quebec City, QC, Canada, 10–13 October 2017, pp. 102–105 (2017). https://doi.org/10.1109/edocw.2017.25

14. Petrenko, S.A., Makoveichuk, K.A.: Ontology of cyber security of self-recovering smart GRID. In: Proceedings of the VIII All-Russian Scientific and Technical Conference on Secure Information Technologies (BIT 2017), Bauman Moscow State Technical University, Moscow, Russia, 6–7 December 2017, vol. 2081, pp. 98–106. CEUR Workshop Proceedings (2017). http://ceur-ws.org/Vol-2081/paper21.pdf. Accessed 21 Sept 2018

15. Petrenko, S.: Big Data Technologies for Monitoring of Computer Security: A Case Study of the Russian Federation. Springer, Cham (2018). https://doi.org/10.1007/978-3-319-79036-7

16. Gruber, T.: A translation approach to portable ontology specifications. Knowl. Acquis. **5**(2), 199–220 (1993). https://doi.org/10.1006/knac.1993.1008

17. Gruber, T.: Toward principles for the design of ontologies used for knowledge sharing? Int. J. Hum.-Comput. Stud. **43**(5–6), 907–928 (1995). https://doi.org/10.1006/ijhc.1995.1081

18. Vorozhtsova, T.N.: Ontology as the basis for the development of intelligent cybersecurity systems. Ontol. Des. **4**(14), 69–77 (2014). (in Russian)

19. The concept of the state system for detecting, preventing and eliminating the effects of computer attacks on information resources of the Russian Federation, no. K 1274, 12 December 2014. (in Russian). http://www.scrf.gov.ru/security/information/document131/. Accessed 21 Sept 2018

20. Tarasov, V.B.: From multiagent systems to intellectual organizations. Editorial URSS, Moscow, Russia (2002). (in Russian)

21. Uschold, M., King, M.: Towards a methodology for building ontologies. In: Workshop on Basic Ontological Issues in Knowledge Sharing (1995)

22. Gruninger, M., Fox, M.S.: Methodology for the design and evaluation of ontologies. In: Workshop on Basic Ontological Issues in Knowledge Sharing, IJCAI-95 (1995). http://www.eil.utoronto.ca/wp-content/uploads/enterprise-modelling/papers/gruninger-ijcai95.pdf

23. Lenat, D.B., Guha, R.V.: The evolution of CycL, the Cyc representation language (1991). https://dl.acm.org/citation.cfm?id=122308

24. Schreiber, G., Wielinga, B., Jansweijer, W.: The KACTUS View on the 'O' Word. University of Amsterdam, Social Science Informatics, Roetersstraat 15, NL-1018 WB Amsterdam, The Netherlands (1995). https://pdfs.semanticscholar.org/d835/8a9eeb2c763c06aaa51ec3877501abde380a.pdf

25. Swartout, B., et al.: Toward Distributed Use of Large-Scale Ontologies (1996). http://ksi.cpsc.ucalgary.ca/KAW/KAW96/swartout/Banff_96_final_2.html

26. Sure, Y., Staab, S., Studer, R.: On-to-knowledge methodology (OTKM). In: Staab, S., Studer, R. (eds.) Handbook on Ontologies. INFOSYS, pp. 117–132. Springer, Heidelberg (2004). https://doi.org/10.1007/978-3-540-24750-0_6. https://www.semanticscholar.org/paper/On-To-Knowledge-Methodology-(OTKM)-Sure-Vetter-Staab/5882b6408fa3d5a0df2d625f29681f470311b91e

27. Fernandez, M., Gomez-Perez, A., Juristo, N.: METHONTOLOGY: from ontological art towards ontological engineering, AAAI Technical report SS-97-06 (1997). Compilation copyright © 1997, AAAI (http://www.aaai.org). All rights reserved. http://oa.upm.es/5484/1/METHONTOLOGY_pdf

28. Krivoi, S.L.: Finite-state automata in information technologies. Cybern. Syst. Anal. (5), 3–20 (2011). https://link.springer.com/article/10.1007/s10559-011-9347-x

29. Anisimov, A.V., Marchenko, A.A.: System for processing texts in a natural language. In: Artificial Intelligence. National Academy of Sciences of Ukraine. Institute for Artificial Intelligence, pp. 157–163 (2002). http://lingvoworks.org.ua/index.php?option=com_content&view=article&id=54:2009-06-12-08-35-12&catid=2:misc&Itemid=3

30. Nayhanova, L.V.: Osnovnye aspekty postroeniya ontologiy verkhnego urovnya i predmetnoy oblasti [Main aspects of construction of high level ontologies and subject area]. In: Internet Portals: Content and Technologies, pp. 452–479. Informika, Prosveshchenie (2005). (in Russian)

31. Mozzherina, E.: An approach to improving the classification of the New York Times annotated corpus. In: International Conference on Knowledge Engineering and the Semantic Web KESW 2013: Knowledge Engineering and the Semantic Web, pp. 83–91 (2013). https://link.springer.com/chapter/10.1007/978-3-642-41360-5_7

32. Fedotova, V., Tarasov, V.B.: Development and interpretation of spiral lifecycle's model: a granular computing approach. Part 1. Lifecycle granulation and spiral representation. In: Proceedings of the Seventh International Conference on Soft Computing, Computing with words and Perceptions in System Analysis, Decision and Control (ICSCCW 13), pp. 431–440, September 2013

The Internet of Things (IoT): Standards, Communication and Information Technologies, Network Applications

On a New Approach to Neighbor Discovery as Data Sharing Tool

Dmitry Namiot[1] [iD] and Manfred Sneps-Sneppe[2(✉)] [iD]

[1] Lomonosov Moscow State University,
Leninskie Gory, 1, GSP-1, 119991 Moscow, Russia
dnamiot@gmail.com
[2] Ventspils University of Applied Sciences,
Inženieru Str. 101a, 3601 Ventspils, Latvia
manfredss@venta.lv

Abstract. In this paper, we propose and discuss a new approach to data sharing among mobile subscribers. Our idea is to use the neighbor discovery phase in wireless networks. It simulates a peer-to-peer network that will work without any telecommunication infrastructure. A single mobile phone (smartphone) will be sufficient both for creating a node of such telecommunication network and for publishing (distributing) information. What is important here, the usage of the standard neighbor discovery mechanism does not assume the preloading some mobile applications. Our idea is to share user-defined information during the basic neighbor discovery phase. In this case, the parties involved in the process should be able to read the shared data directly from the process of discovering for neighboring nodes. Our proposal is the further development of ideas related to context-aware systems based on network proximity principles.

Keywords: WiFi · Bluetooth · Network proximity · BLE · Services

1 Introduction

Neighbor discovery is the determination of all nodes in the network a given node may directly communicate with [1]. Usually, the knowledge of neighbors in the networks is important for routing and medium-access control protocols. Obviously, the nodes should discover their neighbors as fast as possible in order to save energy. The fast discovery lets other protocols (e.g., routing protocols) quickly start their execution.

For that, nodes should use (transmit) some identification during the discovery process. Our idea is to use this identity information (or some add-ons for this information) for transferring user-defined data.

To explain the essence of our approach, let us start with some review of neighbor discovery algorithms. This topic is a subject of several papers [2–4]. Neighbor discovery works at a protocol level. The typical example shows Fig. 1. Some node A name is inserted in the neighbor list of some node B based solely upon successful reception of a packet sent by node A. For example, the Internet Engineering Task Force (IETF) proposes to perform Neighbor Discovery at IP Layer [5]. It means that the corresponding protocol assumes a broadcast capability and Media Access Control,

© Springer Nature Switzerland AG 2020
V. Sukhomlin and E. Zubareva (Eds.): Convergent 2018, CCIS 1140, pp. 313–325, 2020.
https://doi.org/10.1007/978-3-030-37436-5_28

which handles contention. For wireless networks (it is our primary goal) neighbor discovery may not be contention based due to energy constraints. In case of broadcasts, the largest energy cost is for collisions support (to support retransmission in the case of a collision). Therefore, wireless networks may use a transmission scheme, which avoids collisions at modulation level. It could be based on a simultaneous transmission of signatures, for example.

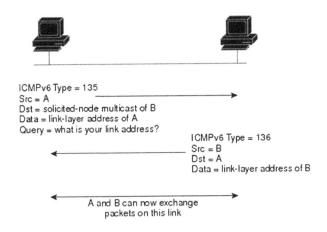

ICMPv6 Type = 135
Src = A
Dst = solicited-node multicast of B
Data = link-layer address of A
Query = what is your link address?

ICMPv6 Type = 136
Src = B
Dst = A
Data = link-layer address of B

A and B can now exchange
packets on this link

Fig. 1. Neighbor discovery in IPv6 [6].

Neighbor discovery can be supervised or unsupervised. In supervised mode, there is a central node (e.g., an access point) which processes the signals received from all other nodes. Actually, this central node determines the network configuration and maintains neighbor lists. In an unsupervised mode, there is no central controller and each node discovers its own neighbors. The more, a neighbor discovery could be synchronous or asynchronous, could be one-directional as well, because each node discovers those nodes it can receive from.

The rest of the article is structured as follows. In Sect. 2, we describe similar works. Section 3 is devoted to neighbor discovery and data sharing for Bluetooth and Bluetooth Low Energy. In Sect. 4, we discuss the neighbor discovery (and its usage for data sharing) in Wi-Fi.

2 On Related Works

2.1 On Facebook Patents

In this connection, we could mention several interesting approaches, papers, and projects. Firstly, it is Mobile Networking in Proximity (MNP), which denotes the exchange of data between devices without available Internet connections. There is a large group of papers [7–10], including a line of patents from Facebook, described systems that allow individuals and advertisers to connect directly to physically close users (devices) that have, for example, similar interests or are open to receiving certain advertisements (Fig. 2). Wireless devices 310, 315, and 320 are located within a single network hop of the wireless device 305, as also indicated by the circle 360. Similarly, wireless devices 325, 330, 335, and 340 are located within a two-hop radius of device 305, since they are separated from the wireless device 305 by two hops, as also indicated by the circle 370. Other devices, such as 345, 350, 355 and 357, are outside the two-hop radius.

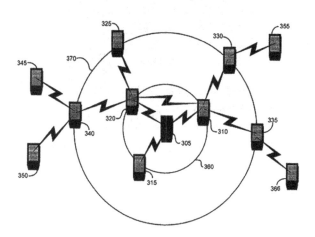

Fig. 2. Wireless social networking [12].

Within the proposed system, the wireless device will establish a connection with other wireless devices nearby, and it will be a direct connection between the devices. Each device can be connected to one or more other devices, depending on the density of users in a certain area, and each of the devices will be open for sending, receiving and transmitting messages as part of the network.

2.2 Wi-Fi and Bluetooth Proximity Mean

In general, mesh networks such as Mobile Ad hoc NETwork (MANET), Vehicular Ad hoc NETwork (VANET) as the above-mentioned Social Mesh Networks (SMN) including neighbor discovery elements being based on peer-to-peer data transfers.

A big group of services belongs to network proximity associated with Wi-Fi, Bluetooth, and Bluetooth Low Energy. For example, in the case of Core Bluetooth, we can switch a Bluetooth device in so-called discoverable mode (Fig. 3).

In this mode, other devices can see device name and address (it is neighbor discovery), as well as obtain RSSI (the signal strength). Note that network proximity in general (and Bluetooth proximity too) has nothing to do with the connectivity [12]. It is just about getting information (obtaining identity) about nearby devices.

For Wi-Fi proximity, we can also detect addresses (MAC-address) and signal strength (RSSI) for access points (wireless nodes). Note, that it could be an existing wireless node and/or access point especially created for proximity measurements.

Fig. 3. Bluetooth discoverable mode [13].

Comparing with Bluetooth proximity, Wi-Fi based network proximity could be used on the bigger distance (Wi-Fi distance versus Bluetooth distance).

The biggest disadvantage for Wi-Fi proximity is the lack of possibility to create Wi-Fi access point programmatically. In other words, the special node for proximity measurement could not be created dynamically in case of Wi-Fi. There is no API for creating Wi-Fi access point (mobile hotspot) on Android OS automatically. Alternatively, Bluetooth proximity works on the smaller distance (Bluetooth distance) but it is possible to create Bluetooth objects (tags) programmatically [14].

2.3 Apple iBeacons

From the point of view of applied services, this topic refers to the context-aware (context-dependent) programming [15] and ambient mobile intelligence systems [16]. These articles are typical works in which the idea of network proximity is promoted. Based on network proximity, the location information (geo-location) is replaced by the availability ("visibility") of a wireless network.

Of course, iBeacon from Apple could be mentioned among these technologies. The basic element here is a tag based on Bluetooth Low Energy (BLE) technology [17]. Each such tag distributes some unique identifier (UUID) and two integer values. It is not directly about neighbor discovery, but this process lets for neighbors to discovery a tag. Thus, translated data become available to mobile devices in the vicinity of the tag and can be used as keys to search for information. Translated integer values (so-called minor and major) are the perfect example of customized identity information circulated during neighbor's data exchange.

2.4   Google's BLE Tag

Google's BLE tag (named *EddyStone*) directly distributes some URL [18] as a customized identity. In general, Google proposes an own protocol for BLE and defines a
message format for proximity beacon messages. In general, the pattern is similar to the
classical iBeacons. Eddystone broadcast some ID, and an application uses obtained ID
for getting data from the cloud or performing some actions. The URL here is just a
special case of ID. Also, Google provides Proximity Beacon API for setting attachment
(data associated with) for BLE tags. This API lets developers register tags, associate
data with tags (add attachments in Google's terms), retrieve data from tags (retrieve
attachments), and monitor beacons. The attachment (data) is a string up to 1024 bytes
long. It could be a plain string, JSON data or even encoded binary data. All attachments
are stored in Google's scalable cloud (in other words, outside of the tag). Google
Physical Web project is an example of the integration of Web technologies and the
physical world. As per Google's vision, the Physical Web is an example of discovery
service. In the Physical Web model, a smart Physical Object broadcasts relevant URLs
that any nearby device can receive. It is very important also that user's phone can
obtain advertised URL without connecting to the tag [18]. It is illustrated in Fig. 4.

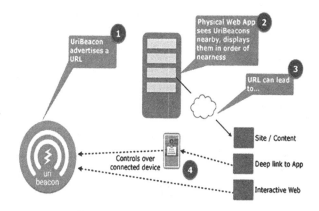

Fig. 4. The physical web: how it works in four steps.

2.5   Beacon Stuffing

Next idea in this context is so-called beacon stuffing approach [19]. This is a low-
bandwidth communication protocol for IEEE 802.11 networks that allows mobile
customers to communicate with Wi-Fi access points without establishing Wi-Fi connections. Beacon stuffing allows customers to receive information from the nearest
access points, to receive even if they are disconnected or when they connect to another
access points. The authors proposed a scheme that supplements the 802.11 standard
and works by overloading the control frames of the 802.11 protocol without violating
the standard. The idea is that according to the Wi-Fi specifications, the mobile device
and the access point exchange service packets (the so-called Probe Request).

Technically, it could be also described as customized identity in neighbor's data exchange. This approach is used in a fairly large number of projects. For example, in [20], the authors offer an Open Source solution for beacon stuffing.

2.6 SSID Use

In the paper [21], the authors use data coding in the access point identifier (SSID) to transmit information about moving objects. In the paper [27], the authors encode location information within SSID (Fig. 5).

Override SSID (most often - in manual mode) is a widely used approach for sharing any information to mobile device owners in the immediate environment of the access point. In the paper [22], numerous examples of the use of political slogans (expressions of support for a certain candidate) in US political companies are given. In the note [23], this approach is illustrated by advertising and marketing. Other examples are provided in web resources [24, 25]. In the paper [26], the authors propose to use SSID as a key for forming an URL with contact information. SSID acts as the digital business card of the owner of the access point.

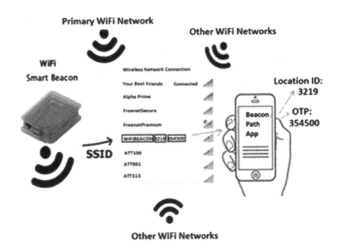

Fig. 5. Encoding location info [27].

3 On a New Approach to Neighbor Discovery in Bluetooth

Before explaining our approach, we have to give some details on Bluetooth technology. Depending on a required functionality, any BLE device may operate in one of three different modes for the neighbor discovery: advertising, scanning, and initiating:

- BLE device in advertising mode (advertiser) periodically transmits advertising information in three advertising channels and listens afterward expecting for responses from other devices.

- A device in scanning mode (so-called scanner) periodically scans the advertising channels and listens to advertising information from others devices.
- As per initiators, they are quite similar, but they can respond to specific types of advertising packets only [28] (Fig. 6).

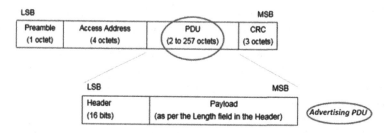

Fig. 6. Bluetooth advertising package [29].

Note the already existing Payload field. As per specification, the advertising header defines several segments. One of the segments is Length field (6 bits). It defines the size of the payload for the different PDU types. In Bluetooth low energy there are two reasons to advertise/broadcast:

- to establish a bi-direction connection between devices
- to broadcast information without ever connecting to another device

Our approach is based on the second use case. It corresponds to PDU types *ADV_NONCONN_IND* and *ADV_SCAN_IND*.

For BLE advertising, we can use 31 byte. For the practical programming on Android platform, we have used the following packages:

- *android.bluetooth.le.AdvertiseCallback,*
- *android.bluetooth.le.AdvertiseData,*
- *android.bluetooth.le.AdvertiseSettings,*
- *android.bluetooth.le.BluetoothLeAdvertiser.*

Pre-requisites include Android SDK 27 [30].

The mobile user is authorizing in the application using the Facebook authorization service. In other words, the user is authorized in the application by entering own identification on the Facebook website.

If this was successful, then Facebook returns the so-called Facebook ID - user UID in the system. There are no rights to the application for accessing the user's data on Facebook. Facebook is used just for identity confirmation. Of course, technically any other social network (e.g., Linkedin) could be used here. This UID is 8 bytes.

The application creates a package for advertising as a string with the standard prefix and UID obtained on the previous step. This is the subject of advertising.

Another application, having received such an advertising package (filtered by the standard prefix), will be able to extract a UID from it and use it to form a link (URL) to a profile in the social network of the user who sent this advertisement. For example, in the case of Facebook this URL for any given UID looks as follows:

https://facebook.com/profile.php?id=UID

It is possible to get also some public information about this user (profile). E.g., the following URL could be used for getting a public photo from any given profile:

http://graph.facebook.com/UID/picture?type=square

It means that application will be able to create a list of links to social network profiles of mobile users who decided to provide themselves to other mobile users in the field. This is a kind of a mark of presence. At the same time, there is no connection between mobile devices and there is no transfer of data from social networks to the 3-rd party applications. For direct interaction, users use links to the profiles of other users and communicate further already entirely according to the rules (and limitations) of social networks.

Essentially, the main idea is to translate such user identification, which is sufficient to use it later for peer-to-peer interaction within any existing applications. In other words, the service itself does not provide interaction. It only allows potential participants of interaction to exchange addresses. The absence of direct interaction makes it possible to exclude the connection of devices via Bluetooth, which ensures safety.

For the transmission of long texts, we can divide them into smaller-length packages (strings), the final symbol of which indicates the need for concatenation of the next packet upon receipt. In this way, the recipient can assemble individual parts into the full text.

Applied model is obvious here. It's just about a broadcast publication of some kind of text information. We should note several important points:

- In such services, there is no need to organize the coordinated work of the transmitter and receivers of information. It's enough just to repeat the whole text several times. Then any receiver involved in the process in the middle of the transmission (which appeared near the receiver after the broadcast starts) will receive and display only a portion of the information for the first time, and then receive and display the entire text. This will be a complete imitation of the information tape on the scoreboard.
- Next, there may be several transmitters. Receivers will distinguish them by the addresses that are present in the advertising packages.
- It is obvious as well that we can support the presentation in the text of some structured information. For example, when displaying the received text, it automatically selects phone numbers, email addresses, and so on. This will allow us to display the data most convenient for later use (make it possible to directly call the number, etc.)

Other service possibilities are related to relaying messages. It is just a retranslation. The advertising message received from the broadcaster can be distributed by the recipient already on its own behalf. Accordingly, the broadcaster will have the opportunity to reach other mobile devices that were not originally in the zone of its availability. Technically, everything also consists in marking the received packet as intended for retransmission. Accordingly, such packages can be filtered also by the recipient and used to form their own advertising package.

3.1 On Implementation

Time delays for advertising in three channels (37, 38, 39) are illustrated in Fig. 7.

According to the Bluetooth standard, the *advInterval* should be an integer multiple of 0.625 ms in the range of 20 ms to 10.24 s, the *advDelay* should be within the range of 0 ms to 10 ms, and the *scanInterval* and *scanWindow* shall be less than or equal to 10.24 s [31].

Initially (according to the standard), these figures determined the performance of the process of finding neighbors (potential delay in disclosing information). In the case of our artificial network, the figures determine the speed of information transfer.

Bluetooth, version 5, introduces two sets of advertising channels - primary and secondary. Bluetooth 5.0 adds new extended Advertising PDUs, e.g., *AUX_SYNC_IND* used for periodic Advertising where unidirectional data is sent at fixed intervals.

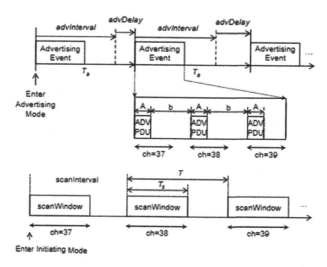

Fig. 7. Advertising process (the upper part) and scanning/initiating process (below) [31].

The link layer packet format is almost identical to packet from Bluetooth 4.0, except the size of the preamble. Thus, the above described our models for applied services are completely valid, and advertised data could be bigger.

4 On a New Approach to Neighbor Discovery in Wi-Fi

We offer some new fitches for neighbor discovery in WI-FI. Classically, Wi-Fi networks operate in a centralized mode. Therefore, we have a special node (access point) that is responsible for media access coordination. Messages are transmitted from devices to access point or vice versa. So neighbor discovery here is a process where some node discovers an access point and starts the connectivity process.

The customization process here is just a customization of access point announcement. This is described in sufficient details above, including in our own works.

4.1 Probe Request

Next moment should be discussed here is so-called probe request. Wi-Fi probe request is a special packet (frame) sent by a client station and requesting information from an access point. It could be either a specific access point (with the given SSID), or all reachable access points, specified with the broadcast SSID. The requested information includes the supported data rates. So, in Wi-Fi networks we could have passive (waiting for the beacon frame from access points) or active (request information from access points) clients.

Note that such packets can be listened to by other computers on the network (not just by the access point). And SSID presence in probe request opens the way for sending some custom information. It is similar to the above-mentioned examples of SSID customization.

4.2 Beacon Stuffing

A much deeper level of Wi-Fi probe requests customization provided by so-called beacon stuffing [19, 20]. It is about embedding additional information inside 802.11 beacons and probe responses. Beacon stuffing raises two important questions. Firstly, it is the compatibility of this approach with various network devices. The second is the struggle of manufacturers of mobile operating systems with tracking mobile users. Accordingly, mobile operating systems can have their own policy with respect to such requests (often - just do not send them), or randomly change the address of the sender. The latter makes it impossible to track all packets from one sender.

4.3 Wi-Fi Direct

It is a direct device-to-device communication in Wi-Fi. It is a Wi-Fi standard enabling devices to connect easily with each other without requiring a wireless access point. Wi-Fi direct supports service discovery. Service description here is just a map (a set of <key, value> pairs). In practice, this allows for arbitrary user information. As above, only the process of obtaining information about the service is interesting here, without establishing a connection between devices (for which, in fact, this service is intended). It is, probably, the best suited for custom neighbor advertising solution. Any mobile application can dynamically create service advertising with various keys and pass this information to the listening devices. As we mentioned above with Bluetooth, these capabilities are useful for communication between applications, even when no local network or hotspot is available.

4.4 Wi-Fi Aware

The last technology in this line is Wi-Fi Aware (Wi-Fi Neighbor Awareness Networking or NAN). According to the Wi-Fi Alliance, Wi-Fi Aware and Wi-Fi Direct are complementary technologies. Wi-Fi Direct is a way for devices to connect with peripherals like printers or cameras, while Wi-Fi Aware is primarily about device-to-device communications. As per the global model, once a Wi-Fi Aware connection has been established, a user could use Wi-Fi Direct to print or share large amounts of information. Thus, neighbor's discovery principles here are similar to Wi-Fi direct.

4.5 On Implementation

For example, Android API has a mechanism for finding other nearby devices. The process starts when one device publishes one or more discoverable services. In the full model, when a device subscribes to one or more services and enters the publisher's Wi-Fi range, the subscriber receives a notification that a matching publisher has been discovered. After the subscriber discovers a publisher, the subscriber can either send a short message or establish a network connection with the discovered device [32]. In our model, everything stops at the discovering stage. A service "discovery" is equals for getting a message from the publisher. For example, in Android API any published service has been defined by own *PublishConfig* object [32]. Our application can redefine *toString()* method with own data. This will be exactly the information that we want to transfer to the "subscriber". The subscription process itself will be stopped. Upon the fact of finding the service, the "subscriber" will receive all the necessary information.

From what we know at the time of this writing, this is the first such use of Wi-Fi services, confirmed by practical experiments. Because there is no connectivity, it is much more secure than the standard full cycle defined for Wi-Fi Aware. Because there is actually no service (just a service description) this can be designed easier and faster. The important point is also that programmatically (dynamically) we cannot create a Wi-Fi node (access point), and software creation of a service is quite possible. Accordingly, we can also dynamically change the service description and using Wi-Fi NAN, devices can be both publishers and subscribers.

5 Conclusion

In this article, we described a new class of mobile services (a new model for creating mobile services), based on using the process of searching for neighboring nodes (services) to transfer custom user information. In the work, our diverse efforts on models of services based on network proximity are generalized, expanded and presented on a unified basis. The result is a new model of systems for distributing local (in terms of location) information. The proposed systems can operate without a telecommunications infrastructure. In general, this approach can be described as the software creation of network nodes or services (Bluetooth, Wi-Fi) identification and descriptions of which are available while searching for neighbor nodes (services) in wireless networks. This identification (description) is used to transmit custom user information. The possible use cases include personal communications, business to consumers (B2C), and business to business (B2B) applications.

References

1. Angelosante, D., Biglieri, E., Lops, M.: Full length article: neighbor discovery in wireless networks: a multiuser-detection approach. Phys. Commun. **3**(1), 28–36 (2010). https://doi.org/10.1016/j.phycom.2009.08.005
2. Cornejo, A., Viqar, S., Welch, J.L.: Reliable neighbor discovery for mobile ad hoc networks. Ad Hoc Netw. **12**, 259–277 (2014). https://doi.org/10.1016/j.adhoc.2012.08.009
3. Gu, Z., Wang, Y., Hua, Q.-S., Lau, Francis C.M.: Neighbor discovery in wireless sensor networks. Rendezvous in Distributed Systems, pp. 243–251. Springer, Singapore (2017). https://doi.org/10.1007/978-981-10-3680-4_19
4. Lavanya, C.B., Asha, K.N., Asha, R.K.P.: A study on energy efficient routing techniques for wireless adhoc network. Int. J. Sci. Eng. Res. **6**(3), 648–651 (2015)
5. ICMPv6 Router Advertisement and Router Solicitation Messages. http://www.tcpipguide.com/free/t_ICMPv6RouterAdvertisementandRouterSolicitationMess.htm. Accessed 16 Oct 2018
6. IPv6 Configuration Guide, Cisco IOS Release 15.2 M&T. https://www.cisco.com/c/en/us/td/docs/ios-xml/ios/ipv6/configuration/15-2mt/ip6-15-2mt-book/ip6-neighb-disc.html. Accessed 16 Oct 2018
7. Bland, A.: FireChat – the messaging app that's powering the Hong Kong protests. The Guardian, 29 (2014)
8. Namiot, D.: On mobile mesh networks. Int. J. Open Inf. Technol. **3**(4), 38–41 (2015)
9. Mobile & Ad Hoc Network. https://www.slideshare.net/cprakash2011/lecture-1-mobile-and-adhoc-network-introduction. Accessed 16 Oct 2018
10. Kopekar, S., Kumar, A.: A study of ad-hoc wireless networks: various issues in architectures and protocols. Int. J. Comput. Appl. **122**(6), 36–40 (2015). https://doi.org/10.5120/21708-4824
11. Bill, D.S.: Wireless social networking. U.S. Patent no. 7,720,037, 18 May 2010
12. Namiot, D., Sneps-Sneppe, M.: On Bluetooth proximity models. In: Advances in Wireless and Optical Communications (RTUWO), Riga, pp. 80–84 (2016). https://doi.org/10.1109/rtuwo.2016.7821860
13. Android 101. https://www.androidcentral.com/android-101-how-pair-bluetooth-headset-0. Accessed 16 Oct 2018
14. Sneps-Sneppe, M., Namiot, D.: On physical web models. In: Proceedings of the 2016 International Siberian Conference on Control and Communications (SIBCON), Moscow, pp. 1–6 (2016). https://doi.org/10.1109/sibcon.2016.7491675
15. Namiot, D., Sneps-Sneppe, M.: Context-aware data discovery. In: Proceedings of the 2012 16th International Conference on Intelligence in Next Generation Networks, Berlin, pp. 134–141 (2012). https://doi.org/10.1109/icin.2012.6376016
16. Namiot, D., Sneps-Sneppe, M.: On mobile wireless tags. Autom. Control. Comput. Sci. **49**(3), 159–166 (2015). https://doi.org/10.3103/S0146411615030062
17. Köhne, M., Sieck, J.: Location-based services with iBeacon technology. In: Proceedings of the 2014 2nd International Conference on Artificial Intelligence, Modelling and Simulation, Madrid, pp. 315–321 (2014). https://doi.org/10.1109/aims.2014.58

18. Namiot, D., Zubareva, E.: On one approach to delivering information to mobile users. Int. J. Open Inf. Technol. **5**(8), 12–17 (2017). (in Russian). http://injoit.ru/index.php/j1/article/view/472/448

19. Chandra, R., Padhye, J., Ravindranath, L., Wolman, A.: Beacon-stuffing: Wi-Fi without associations. In: Eighth IEEE Workshop on Mobile Computing Systems and Applications, Tucson, AZ, pp. 53–57 (2007). https://doi.org/10.1109/hotmobile.2007.16

20. Zehl, S., Karowski, N., Zubow, A., and Wolisz, A.: LoWS: a complete open source solution for Wi-Fi beacon stuffing based Location-based Services. In: Proceedings of the 2016 9th IFIP Wireless and Mobile Networking Conference (WMNC), Colmar, pp. 25–32 (2016). https://doi.org/10.1109/wmnc.2016.7543926

21. Liu, Z., Wu, M., Zhu, K., Zhang, L.: SenSafe: a smartphone-based traffic safety framework by sensing vehicle and pedestrian behaviors. Mob. Inf. Syst. **2016**, 7967249, 13 p. (2016). https://doi.org/10.1155/2016/7967249

22. Maffei, L.: Using a Wi-Fi Network's Name To Broadcast A Political Message (2017). http://www.npr.org/sections/alltechconsidered/2017/02/07/513240428/using-a-wi-fi-networks-name-to-broadcast-a-political-message. Accessed 16 Oct 2018

23. Scott, D.M.: Cyber graffiti with WiFi network names as advertising (2011). http://www.webinknow.com/2011/02/cyber-graffiti-with-wifi-network-names-as-advertising.html. Accessed 16 Oct 2018

24. Chen, J.: Clever SSIDs That Scare Off Leeches Or Send A Message (2011). https://www.lifehacker.com.au/2011/10/clever-ssids-that-scare-off-leeches-or-send-a-message/. Accessed 16 Oct 2018

25. Aylward, L., Gallagher, S.: Scare your neighbors with a spooky Halloween network name (2014). https://arstechnica.com/information-technology/2014/10/scare-your-neighbors-with-a-spooky-halloween-network-name/. Accessed 16 Oct 2018

26. Agarwal, A.: Let Others Contact You Through Your Own Wi-Fi Network (2012). https://www.labnol.org/internet/share-wifi-with-neighbors/21024/. Accessed 16 Oct 2018

27. Huseynov, E., Seigneur, J.: Beacon authpath: augmented human path authentication. In: Proceedings of the 2016 IEEE 10th International Conference on Application of Information and Communication Technologies (AICT), Baku, pp. 1–5 (2016). https://doi.org/10.1109/icaict.2016.7991702

28. Liu, J., Chen, C., Ma, Y.: Modeling neighbor discovery in bluetooth low energy networks. IEEE Commun. Lett. **16**(9), 1439–1441 (2012). https://doi.org/10.1109/LCOMM.2012.073112.120877

29. Warne, W.: Bluetooth low energy - It starts with advertising (2017). http://blog.bluetooth.com/bluetooth-low-energy-it-starts-with-advertising. Accessed 16 Oct 2018

30. Android Bluetooth Advertisements. https://github.com/googlesamples/android-Bluetooth Advertisements. Accessed 16 Oct 2018

31. Liu, J., Chen, C., Ma, Y.: Modeling and performance analysis of device discovery in bluetooth low energy networks. In: Proceedings of the 2012 IEEE Global Communications Conference (GLOBECOM), Anaheim, CA, pp. 1538–1543 (2012). https://doi.org/10.1109/glocom.2012.6503332

32. Wi-Fi Aware Overview. https://developer.android.com/guide/topics/connectivity/wifi-aware. Accessed 16 Oct 2018

Smart Cities: Standards, Cognitive-Information Technologies and Their Applications

Research of Urban Residents Involvement in Environmental Processes Using a Mobile Environmental Application

Alexander Varnavsky[(⊠)] [ID]

National Research University Higher School of Economics,
Myasnitskaya Str. 20, 101000 Moscow, Russia
avarnavsky@hse.ru

Abstract. Recently there are works devoted to the possibility of using mobile applications for monitoring the environment and helping citizens in certain situations related to the environmental condition. The use of these applications by urban residents will allow them to be involved in environmental processes and, consequently, increase the environmental and social responsibility of citizens. The aim of the work is to study the increase of citizens' involvement in environmental processes using a mobile environmental application that displays information on air pollution in the city districts. To assess the current behavior of respondents in environmental situations, as well as behavioral changes when using mobile applications, a questionnaire consisting of 5 sections has been developed. An experiment was conducted with the participation of a group of respondents. The results of the analysis have showed the influence of factors and indicators on the results of answering questions. 5 clusters are distinguished in which the behavior of respondents differ. Accordingly, for each cluster a level of social responsibility of respondents can be assessed. It is shown that all respondents can be divided into 3 groups: the group of respondents No. 1 for whom using of the mobile application is not able to involve them in environmental processes, the group of respondents No. 2 for whom using of the mobile application can strongly involve them in environmental processes, the group of respondents No. 3, for which the use of mobile applications can involve them in environmental processes, but not to a great extent.

Keywords: Mobile environmental application · Environmental responsibility · Behavior in environmental situations

1 Introduction

At present, the actual task is to control the quality of urban air in industrial cities or cities with a population of more than 1 million people. At the same time, such control is carried out by municipal services. The results of monitoring can be published on the municipal of city services for example, [1], and be used by various Internet-technologies for conservation applications [2], including developing and perspective technologies [3].

© Springer Nature Switzerland AG 2020
V. Sukhomlin and E. Zubareva (Eds.): Convergent 2018, CCIS 1140, pp. 329–338, 2020.
https://doi.org/10.1007/978-3-030-37436-5_29

Recently there are works devoted to the possibility of using mobile applications for monitoring the environment and helping citizens in certain situations related to the environmental condition. So the work [4] describes the experience in the development of information systems for the processing and analysis of spatial data using a mobile application for environmental monitoring. The work [5] is devoted to the development a Mobile GIS-based tool containing maps of monitoring asthma attacks based on environmental and local factors that will be generated using predictive algorithms. Changing the behavior and decision-making by the participants of the experiment using the mobile application in evacuating due to the tsunami has been evaluated in the work [6].

There are works aimed at assessing the use of mobile technologies for environmental education [7].

It can be noted that a questionnaire is often a tool for studying the environmental behavior of citizens, their attitude towards environmental problems and other aspects. To implement the questioning, survey are created that can be of various types. For example, in [8], online- survey were created to identify citizens' preferences and study environmental decision-making. This service is designed to provide the necessary information to understand the context of the decision so that participants can learn about the tasks set, improve reflexive thinking, so that participants can create their preferences and motivating the experience to overcome the difficulty and repeatability of the task [8].

In [9], Jones et al. discusses a tool for interactive web-visualization of social survey data related to environmental problems. The possibility of taking into account human motives and actions in environmental situations is described. The tool was used for a survey of water-related questions administered to 6000 adults [9].

In [10], Marcon et al. carried out developing questions for the questionnaire to assess the perception of environmental health hazards in environmental research. This score can be used to rate risk perception and assess its effects empirically [10].

In [11], Jennings et al. conducted a research that used a survey of environmental service workers' knowledge and opinions regarding environmental cleaning. The findings from this survey suggest the need for further education of environmental service workers regarding the different types of pathogens that are spread by contaminated environmental surfaces and which of these are killed with bleach [11].

In [12], Orenstein et al. derived and tested a new construct that measures the way individuals perceive the environment, which authors call "environmental tastes". An attempt has been made to apply this construct for evaluation the factors that influence environmentally significant behavior and opinions [12].

Presently in the literature, increasingly questions are raised regarding an enhancement of the social responsibility of elements of society: citizens and organizations without which it is impossible to develop Russia generally, the processes in the country and the potential of each person [13]. The social responsibility of organizations and companies is impossible without taking care of the environment, solving environmental problems and reducing a harmful effect on the environment. Those, one of the areas of social responsibility is environmental social responsibility [14].

Often in Russia, public authorities do not listen to the opinion of public organizations and solve environmental issues without public participation. It is considered that to increase social and environmental responsibility, it is necessary to raise public awareness of citizens, actively involving the population in environmental processes; to promote the ideas of environmental social responsibility in the business community.

Thus, the task of increasing the social responsibility of citizens due to their inclusion in environmental processes is relevant.

Article [15] describes the mobile environmental application that takes environmental information about air pollution in the vicinity of a user and other areas of the city from a server and displays it on a smartphone screen. The use of this application by urban residents will allow them to be involved in environmental processes and, consequently, increase the environmental and social responsibility of citizens. However, studies of the effectiveness of this process are not described in the literature.

The aim of the work is to study the increase of citizens' involvement in environmental processes using a mobile environmental application that displays information on air pollution in the city districts.

2 Research Tool

The study was carried out by questioning a group of respondents with the presentation of a mobile environmental application.

2.1 Mobile Environmental Application

The developed mobile environmental application [10] is shown in Fig. 1. The application is based on connecting to a server that contains environmental information about air pollution in the city districts, reading the necessary information and displaying point scale and graphical estimates of the air pollution level on the smartphone screen in the area of the user's location and in other areas of the city. Accordingly, the user can obtain information about the level of air pollution in districts of the city on the scale: "Clean" - "Slightly polluted" - "Medium polluted" - "Heavily soiled" - "Very heavily polluted".

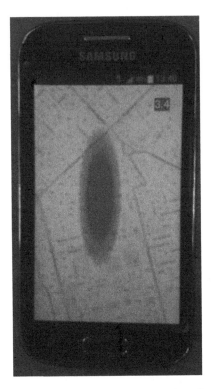

Fig. 1. Developed mobile environmental application.

2.2 Questionnaire

To assess the current behavior of respondents in environmental situations, as well as behavioral changes when using mobile applications, a questionnaire consisting of 5 sections has been developed.

1. Information about the respondent, in which the respondent indicates gender, age, a place of residence, a form of activity.
2. Respondent's attitude to the environment and environmental information, the assessment of his health, in which the respondent indicates interest in environmental information, the impact of factors on human health, visits to Internet resources which provide information on air pollution, as well as self-assessment of one's health.
3. Current behavior of the respondent in environmental situations, in which the respondent indicates the existence of ecological situations and behavior in life, the consumption of organic products and water, the value of the budget for organic products, the attitude to the potential acquisition of an apartment in one or another district of the city, the choice of a city for residence and work.
4. Attitude to the mobile environmental application and its functions, in which the respondent indicated interest in such an application, the willingness to install free of

charge or to buy, the potential goals of installing the application, the desired functions.

5. Behavior of the respondent in environmental situations when using the mobile application and providing him with environmental information, in which the respondent indicated his behaviors when signaling the application about the deterioration of air quality in his area of residence.

The total number of questions in the questionnaire was 30.

3   Research Procedure

To research the increase of citizens' involvement in environmental processes using the mobile environmental application, an experiment has been conducted with the participation of a group of respondents.

1. *Method of conducting*

- *Participants.* The participants of the experiment were 70 students of 2–4 undergraduate courses of the National Research University "Higher School of Economics", living in Moscow and the Moscow Region. The number of males – 46, female – 24. The average age of participants was 20.3 ± 0.7 year.
- *Materials.* To conduct the experiment, we have used the developed questionnaire and the mobile environmental application.
- *Exploratory procedure.* Test subjects have filled out the first 3 sections of the questionnaire, answering questions about themselves, their attitude to ecology and environmental information, self-assessment of health, current behavior in environmental situations. Then the mobile application and its description have been presented to them. After that, respondents have filled out the remaining 2 points of the questionnaire, answering questions about the attitude to the submitted mobile environmental application and its functions, behavior in environmental situations when using the mobile application and providing it with environmental information.

2. *Results*

55.7% of respondents do not read environmental literature, articles on environmental issues, the environmental impact on health. At the same time, 64.3% of all respondents are interested in the environmental impact on human health. 15.7% of them know about the existence of websites and sources of information, from which daily it is possible to learn the average amount of air pollution in the city districts, while those who at least periodically visit such sources are significantly less.

According to subjective feelings, 17.1% of respondents rate the air in their area of residence as "Clean", 41.4% - "Slightly polluted", 32.9% - "Medium polluted", 8.6% - "Heavily polluted". 11.4% of respondents believe that the influence of air quality on human health is weak, 35.7% - that the influence is average, 41.4% - that the influence is strong, 11.5% - that the influence is very strong. 4.3% of respondents believe that the influence of urban air quality is not on their health, 37.1% - that the influence is weak,

38.6% - that the influence is average, 10.0% - that the influence is strong, 10.0% - that the influence is very strong. At the same time, 5.7% of respondents rate their health as poor, 41.4% average, 48.6% good, 4.3% very good.

Only 22.9% of the respondents have indicated that they had situations in which they had changed their behavior concerning the planned behavior, due to urban air pollution.

77.1% of respondents would have established themselves the described mobile environmental application, if it had been free. The rest of them have considered this application not necessary or not ready to pay for it. 47.1% of respondents would pay for the application.

An analysis of answers to questions about how soon the actions would be taken, if the application constantly shows the level of air pollution in the area of residence as "Heavily polluted ", showed that 25% of respondents would do nothing within 2 weeks, and 44% will take any action within 1 week. If the application constantly shows the level of air pollution in the area of residence as "very heavily polluted," only 9% of respondents will not do anything within 2 weeks, and 75% will take any action within 1 week.

One of the questions of the questionnaire is as follows. "Suppose, the application began to show that the air in your region is "very heavily polluted". And it have been lasting for several days. A neighbor came to you, who also had a mobile application installed, and he suggested to collect a group of neighbors and go to the environmental service together. Do you think this idea is reasonable? And will you agree to help him?" This question is intended to assess the potential involvement of a respondent in environmental and social processes. 12.9% of respondents answered that they would not waste time and help their neighbor, since this is unlikely to help, 18.6% is that although it is correct, they will not help their neighbors, because he will manage without themselves, 68.5% is what will help the neighbor.

44.3% of respondents are not afraid of running in a park in which air is medium polluted, 21.4% - in which air is heavily polluted, 4.3% - in which air is very heavily polluted.

4   Processing of Results

At the first stage of data processing, the presence of an interrelation and the dependence/independence of selected indicators were determined. In this case, for different groups of variables, the correlation, variance analysis and Fisher's exact test were used. We noted the basic facts of the existence of interrelations and the dependence of the variables.

There is an interrelation between reading environmental literature by respondents and changing their behavior in environmental situations ($p < 0.05$). Such respondents are also more likely to help a neighbor to apply to the environmental service for air pollution ($p < 0.05$). The quality of air in a park for running ($p < 0.01$), in a place of residence ($p < 0.05$) is important for respondents who would help their neighbor address the environmental service in case of air pollution, they can take this fact into account when buying or renting housing ($p < 0.05$).

Respondents who are not interested in the environmental impact of human health assessed the air in the area of residence mainly as slightly polluted or medium polluted. Respondents who are interested in this issue rated the air in the area of residence as clean, slightly polluted or medium polluted. The significance level of differences in this case between groups of respondents $p < 0.05$.

It can also be noted that the respondents' interest in environmental issues determines their choice of a place of residence ($p < 0.05$), a park for running ($p < 0.05$), installation of this mobile environmental application ($p < 0.01$). Such an influence was also revealed for such an indicator as the prejudice about the influence of air quality on human health.

In addition, respondents' answers showed that there is a connection between the choice of park for running by the criterion of air purity with the budget, which they are willing to spend on organic products and clean water ($p < 0.05$).

We perform a cluster analysis for the respondents' answers. The analysis result in the form of dendrogram is shown in Fig. 2. As a result of the analysis, all respondents are divided into 5 clusters, which combine close answers of respondents.

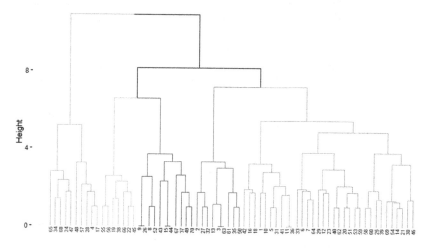

Fig. 2. Cluster dendrogram of respondents.

We describe each cluster.

47.1% of respondents got to the first cluster. These respondents are not characterized by a tendency to the prevalence of reading environmental literature, but a large majority of them are interested in the influence of environmental factors on human health. Most of these respondents evaluate the air in their area of residence as clean and a small proportion of respondents evaluate it as slightly polluted. They consider that the effect of air quality on human health is moderate or strong. They evaluate their health as average or good. They consider that the urban air has little or moderate influence on their state of health. If the mobile application shows deterioration in the quality of urban air in the area of residence, then the vast majority of them will either wait several days for the situation to change, or will call or write a letter to the environmental service. Moreover, if a neighbor comes to them with a request to go to the environmental service together, most of them will agree to help him.

12.9% of respondents got to the second cluster. Most of the respondents do not read the ecological literature, among them there is no prevalence in the interest in the influence of environmental factors on human health. Most of these respondents evaluate the air in the area of residence as moderately polluted, and some respondents evaluate as highly polluted. They consider that the effect of air quality on human health is moderate or strong. They evaluate their health as average or good. A large majority consider that the impact of urban air on their health state is average. If the mobile application shows deterioration in the quality of urban air in the area of residence, all respondents of this cluster will take action, including going to the environmental service. If a neighbor comes to them with a request to go to the environmental service together, they will all agree to help him.

14.3% of respondents got to the third cluster. Most of these respondents are interested in the problems of the influence of environmental factors on human health, but among them there is no prevalence in reading environmental literature. They evaluate the air in the area of residence from clean to heavily polluted without any predominance of any assessment. They consider that the effect of air quality on human health is strong or very strong. Most of them evaluate their state of health as good. A large majority consider that impact of urban air on their state of health is strong or very strong. If the mobile application shows a deterioration in the quality of urban air in the area of residence, the majority of respondents in this cluster will take action, including going to the environmental service. If a neighbor comes to them with a request to go to the environmental service together, they will all agree to help him.

In the fourth cluster got 15.7% of respondents. Most of the respondents do not read environmental literature, although about half of them are interested in the problems of the influence of environmental factors on human health. A large majority of them evaluate the air in their area of residence as slightly polluted. A large majority consider that the effect of air quality on human health is weak. Most of them evaluate their health as average. They consider that impact of urban air on their health state is missing or weak. If the mobile application shows a deterioration in the quality of urban air in the area of residence, the majority of respondents in this cluster will limited to a letter or a call to the environmental service. If a neighbor comes to them with a request to go to the environmental service together, most of them will not agree to help him.

The fifth cluster got 10.0% of respondents. The respondents not read the environmental literature and is not interested in the problems of the influence of environmental factors on human health. Such respondents evaluate the air in the area of residence as slightly polluted or moderately polluted. A large majority consider that the impact of air quality on human health is average. They evaluate their health as average or good. They consider that the impact of urban air on their health state is average. If the mobile application shows a deterioration in the quality of urban air in the area of residence, then such respondents will prefer to wait a few days and not take any action. If a neighbor comes to them with a request to go to the environmental service together, they will not agree to help him.

Thus, 5 clusters are distinguished in which the behavior of respondents differ. Accordingly, for each cluster a level of social responsibility of respondents can be assessed. The respondents of the first cluster, which is the most numerous, are not ready to go to the environmental service if the situation worsens, but if such a proposal comes from a neighbor, then together they don't mind to do it together. The respondents of the second and third clusters are ready to go to the environmental service themselves, and go there with a neighbor, if such a proposal follows. The respondents of these clusters have the highest level of social responsibility. At the same time, respondents of these clusters differ in that they differently assess the degree of influence of urban air on human health in general and on their health in particular. So respondents of the third cluster more strongly assess the degree of such influence. The respondents of the fourth cluster, in the event of deterioration of the ecological situation, will limited to a letter or a call to the environmental service; they will not go to the environmental service with a neighbor, if such an offer follows from them. The respondents of the fifth cluster, which is the smallest, will not take any actions themselves and will not help their neighbor. The respondents of this cluster have the lowest level of social responsibility.

Based on the selected clusters, all respondents can be divided into 3 groups depending on how much the use of the mobile application will affect the change in their behavior. The first group (No. 1) will be the fifth cluster respondents whose behavior will not change. The second group (No. 1) will include respondents whose behavior may change a lot. This group consists of the second and third cluster respondents. The third group (No. 1) will be the respondents of the first and fourth cluster, whose behavior change will be either slight or will depend on others.

Such a division into clusters and groups allows not only to describe the respondents, but also to create strategies for working with each cluster. This will allow to understand the reasons for the behavior of city citizens and develop an optimal strategy to increase the motivation and level of social responsibility of the population.

5 Conclusion

The work evaluates the use of the mobile environmental application to involve urban residents in environmental processes. The results of the analysis have showed the influence of factors and indicators on the results of answering questions. It is shown that all respondents can be divided into 3 groups: the group of respondents No. 1 for whom using of the mobile application is not able to involve them in environmental processes, the group of respondents No. 2 for whom using of the mobile application can strongly involve them in environmental processes, the group of respondents No. 3, for which the use of mobile applications can involve them in environmental processes, but not to a great extent. Using the logistic model, we can assess the influence of reading the environmental literature of the respondent, the respondent's interest in the environmental health problems, the air purity in the area of residence, the agreement with the theory of the effect of air quality on human health on the degree of citizen involvement in environmental processes.

Thus, using the mobile environmental application, it is possible to involve citizens in environmental processes and thereby we can increase their social responsibility.

References

1. Castell, N., Kobernus, M., Liu, H.-Y., Schneider, P., et al.: Mobile technologies and services for environmental monitoring: the Citi-Sense-MOB approach. Urban Clim. **14**(3), 370–382 (2015). https://doi.org/10.1016/j.uclim.2014.08.002
2. Hipólito, J.F.: Multimedia mobile services with applications in environment. Technol. Forecast. Soc. Chang. **74**(6), 854–865 (2007). https://doi.org/10.1016/j.techfore.2006.10.004
3. Granell, C., Havlik, C., Schade, S., Sabeur, Z., et al.: Future internet technologies for environmental applications. Environ. Model Softw. **78**, 1–15 (2016). https://doi.org/10.1016/j.envsoft.2015.12.015
4. Akhmetov, B., Aitimov, M.: Data collection and analysis using the mobile application for environmental monitoring. Proc. Comput. Sci. **56**, 532–537 (2015). https://doi.org/10.1016/j.procs.2015.07.247
5. Khasha, R., Sepehri, M.M., Mahdaviani, S.A., Khatibi, T.: Mobile GIS-based monitoring asthma attacks based on environmental factors. J. Clean. Prod. **179**, 417–428 (2018). https://doi.org/10.1016/j.jclepro.2018.01.046
6. Leelawat, N., Suppasri, A., Latcharote, P., Abe, Y., Sugiyasu, K., Imamura, F.: Tsunami evacuation experiment using a mobile application: a design science approach. Int. J. Disaster Risk Reduct. **29**, 63–72 (2018). https://doi.org/10.1016/j.ijdrr.2017.06.014
7. Uzunboylu, H., Cavus, N., Ercag, E.: Using mobile learning to increase environmental awareness. Comput. Educ. **52**(2), 381–389 (2009). https://doi.org/10.1016/j.compedu.2008.09.008
8. Aubert, A.H., Lienert, J.: Gamified online survey to elicit citizens' preferences and enhance learning for environmental decisions. Environ. Model Softw. **111**, 1–12 (2019). https://doi.org/10.1016/j.envsoft.2018.09.013
9. Jones, A.S., Horsburgh, J.S., Jackson-Smith, D., Ramírez, M., et al.: A web-based, interactive visualization tool for social environmental survey data. Environ. Model Softw. **84**, 412–426 (2016). https://doi.org/10.1016/j.envsoft.2016.07.013
10. Marcon, A., Nguyen, G., Rava, M., Braggion, M., Grassi, M., et al.: A score for measuring health risk perception in environmental surveys. Sci. Total Environ. **527–528**, 270–278 (2015). https://doi.org/10.1016/j.scitotenv.2015.04.110
11. Jennings, A., Sitzlar, B., Jury, L.: A survey of environmental service workers' knowledge and opinions regarding environmental cleaning. Am. J. Infect. Control **41**(2), 177–179 (2013). https://doi.org/10.1016/j.ajic.2012.03.012
12. Orenstein, D.E., Katz-Gerro, T., Dick, J.: Environmental tastes as predictors of environmental opinions and behaviors. Landsc. Urban Plan. **161**, 59–71 (2017). https://doi.org/10.1016/j.landurbplan.2017.01.005
13. Kolk, A.: The social responsibility of international business: from ethics and the environment to CSR and sustainable development. J. World Bus. **51**(1), 23–34 (2016). https://doi.org/10.1016/j.jwb.2015.08.010
14. Dey, P.K., Petridis, N.E., Petridis, K., Malesios, C., et al.: Environmental management and corporate social responsibility practices of small and medium-sized enterprises. J. Clean. Prod. **195**, 687–702 (2018). https://doi.org/10.1016/j.jclepro.2018.05.201
15. Varnavsky, A.: Wearable electronics for efficiency increase of prevention and diagnosis of ecologically caused diseases. In: Proceedings of the I International Forum Instrumentation Engineering, Electronics and Telecommunications – 2015 (IEET-2015), Izhevsk, Russia, 25–27 November 2015, pp. 194–200 (2016)

Using Augmented Reality Technology to Improve the Quality of Transport Services

Dmitriy Skorokhodov[1,2], Yaroslav Seliverstov[1,3(✉)],
Svyatoslav Seliverstov[1,3], Ilya Burov[4], Eugenia Vydrina[5],
Nikolay Podoprigora[6], Natalia Shatalova[1], Victoria Chigur[7],
and Anastasia Cheremisina[5]

[1] Solomenko Institute of Transport Problems of the Russian
Academy of Sciences, 12-th Line VO 13, 199178 Saint-Petersburg, Russia
skorohodda@mail.ru, silver8yr@gmail.com,
Seliverstov_s_a@mail.ru, shatillen@mail.ru
[2] Saint Petersburg Electrotechnical University "LETI",
Professora Popova Str. 5, 197376 Saint-Petersburg, Russia
[3] Peter the Great Saint-PetersburgPolytechnical University,
Polytechnicheskaya Str. 29, 195251 Saint Petersburg, Russia
[4] The Bonch-Bruevich Saint-Petersburg State University
of Telecommunications, Prospect Bolshevikov 22/1,
193232 Saint-Petersburg, Russia
Burov@mail.ru
[5] Russian State Hydrometeorological University, Malookhtinsky Av. 98,
195196 Saint-Petersburg, Russia
Jenek_55@mail.ru, piterugby@gmail.com
[6] Saint Petersburg State University of Architecture and Civil Engineering,
2-nd Krasnoarmeiskaya Str. 4, 190005 Saint-Petersburg, Russia
dekanat_mf@rshu.ru
[7] Saint-Petersburg State University,
Universitetskaya Emb. 7-9, 199034 Saint-Petersburg, Russia
ars8ars@mail.ru

Abstract. The problem of marking the area of the preferred route by means of mobile technology of augmented reality for public transport routes is considered. The analysis of modern theoretical and applied solutions of using the technology of augmented reality in mobile applications is carried out. The task is to reduce the time interval for the search for the route of public transport and the decision to choose a vehicle for an ignorant urban resident, in the conditions of a limited time resource. A theoretical method for marking the routes of public transport on the basis of the transport utility function is proposed. An algorithm is developed for marking the routes of public transport. The software implementation of the algorithm in mobile execution is performed in the Unity and Vuforia environment, using the Yandex API. The problem of finding information on the routes of passenger transport and the problem of improving the perception of transport information through its visual display on a mobile device are solved. A comparison is made between the speed of the developed technology and the existing solutions by the time criterion. Recommendations on the further use of the developed approaches are discussed.

© Springer Nature Switzerland AG 2020
V. Sukhomlin and E. Zubareva (Eds.): Convergent 2018, CCIS 1140, pp. 339–348, 2020.
https://doi.org/10.1007/978-3-030-37436-5_30

Keywords: Augmented reality · Public transport · Mobile applications

1 Introduction

The development of information technologies and the digitalization of the urban transport environment opens new opportunities for improving the quality of transport services for the urban population [1, 2]. And, if the problems of finding preferred routes were solvable within the boundaries of the existing information tools that were in the arsenal of transport science [3, 4], then the tasks of marking the preferred travel area and chains of transport activity [5] remained up to the present time not solvable.

With the advent of new information solutions, the scientific direction "Travel behavior" becomes the leader in the number of scientific and technological implementations that can change the urban environment.

One such technology is the "Augmented Reality". Augmented and virtual reality have become global trends that have an impact comparable to the influence of the Internet and smartphones. The technology of augmented reality enriches the natural environment of a person, makes it more valuable.

At the moment, there are already many applications that simplify the transport behavior of the urban population.

For example, in work [6], scientists proposed pedestrian navigation system Navar, which uses the technology of augmented reality markers to mark the path. In addition to marker markup, Navar displays text explanations consisting of a list of stops. In work [7] the automobile system AR-HUD is presented. This system imposes virtual objects on the windshield of the driver, complements information on vehicles, road signs, road markings and various situations, and, thereby, improves driving safety. In work [8], New York scientists developed a prototype of a mobile application with Augmented Reality technology that presents information about the campus, marking objects inside it. In [9], a navigation tourist mobile application based on augmented reality is presented. This application contains video, including 3D animation, with routes throughout the city containing all the historic buildings. Each image has a QR code, which gives access to text and multimedia information through the website created for this project. In work [10], Japanese scientists developed an application that allows you to hide a person from the screen of your mobile phone, at the time you point the camera at him, by superimposing a special background on it to the color of the environment. In [11] a mobile guide-guide on the island of Corfu with augmented reality is presented.

The analysis shows that the technology of augmented reality is intensively developing in all areas of social activity.

However, to the present day, highly specialized technological solutions of the "Augmented Reality" have not been demonstrated in the tasks of marking the preferred area for users moving using public transport. Such decisions would improve the quality of transport services for the population. The present article is devoted to solving this class of problems.

2 Problems and Methods

Within the framework of the theory of *"Travel behavior"* [12, 13] the task is to reduce the time spent on finding a route for public transport and making a decision on choosing a vehicle for an ignorant urban resident, in the conditions of a limited time resource.

Let us describe the following situation. Every tourist who has arrived in an unfamiliar city is familiar with the situation when it is required to choose a suitable route and the type of public transport to get to the destination. Approaching the bus stop, and seeing how an unfamiliar bus approaches, the tourist has to choose to enter it and already inside the bus to ask the passengers whether he is going to the desired destination or to skip this bus, finding out from nearby passengers or in the Internet environment about the route of this transport facilities.

In the basis of the technological solution, we put the method of marking the preferred travel area, previously considered in [3].

The preferred travel area (Fig. 1) is a spatially limited area of the object's movement, in which the characteristics of its objects satisfy the personal preferences of the user.

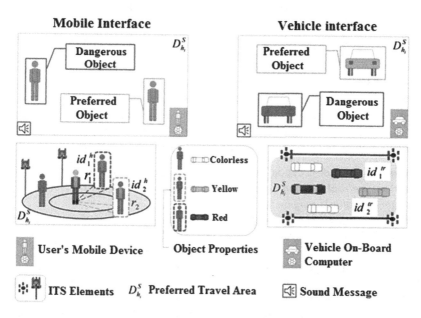

Fig. 1. A preferred travel area (Identifying object properties).

Marking the preferred travel area maximizes the user's transport utility function.

The transport utility function of the user $\Phi_{h_{id}}$ takes the preferred value of $B_t^{\mathrm{Pr}\,ef}$ when the characteristics of the path Ch $(\rho^s\,;\,\rho^d)$ and the properties of the objects E $(\rho^s\,;\,\rho^d)$ entering it satisfy the personal preferences of the user on the way from the departure point ρ^s to the arrival point ρ^d, according to (1):

$$F_{h_{id}} = \lim B_t^{h_{id}}\left(\rho_{h_{id}}^s;\rho_{h_{id}}^d\right) = B_t^{\mathrm{Pr}\,ef}\left(\rho_{h_{id}}^s;\rho_{h_{id}}^d\right)$$

$$\left(\begin{array}{ccc} & F\left[\rho_{h_{id}}^s;\rho_{h_{id}}^d\right] & \\ Ch_{h_{id}}^{\mathrm{Pr}\,ef} & \cap & CH \end{array}\right) = E_{h_{id}}^{\mathrm{Pr}\,ef}\left(\rho_{h_{id}}^s;\rho_{h_{id}}^d\right) \quad (1)$$

where h_{id} - is the user with the id number $\left(\rho_{h_{id}}^s;\rho_{h_{id}}^d\right)$ - the initial and final part of the path, respectively $Ch_{h_{id}}^{\mathrm{Pr}\,ef}$ - preferred characteristics of the user's path $F_{h_{id}}$ - the functional of the markup system and the user's area of travel.

The task of marking the preferred travel area is resolved programmatically in *Unity* and *Vuforia*, using the *Yandex* API. With reference to the problem under consideration, under the marking of the preferred travel area, we will understand the addition of the public mode image, the digital annotation of its route when the cell phone camera is pointed at its number. Consider a general algorithm for solving this problem.

3   Algorithm

The algorithm for marking the route of urban public transport using the technology of augmented reality is shown in Fig. 2.

The algorithm is executed in the following sequence.

1. Determine the geo-location of the user's mobile device. Implemented using libraries: *android.location.Location; android.location.LocationListener; android. location.LocationManager.*
2. Turn on the camera of the mobile device (*Android/iOS*). It is implemented using the following methods: *System.Collections.Generic; System. Runtime. InteropServices; System.Text.RegularExpressions; UnityEngine.*
3. Introduction of the camera to the number of public transport.
4. Display the number on the screen number of the vehicle. It is implemented using the following methods: *UnityEngine; Trackable-Behavior.*
5. The user checks the correctness of the recognized vehicle number. It is implemented using the following method: *UnityEngine.*
6. Display the mobile device route of the vehicle, if the number is correct. It is implemented using the *UnityEngine* method.
7. If the vehicle number is not recognized correctly, return to step 5.
8. Display of the mobile device route of the vehicle. Implemented using the *com.google.android method. maps.MapActivity.*

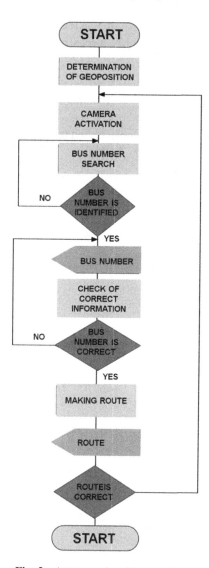

Fig. 2. Augmented reality algorithm.

Defining the geography with the help of Yandex maps, we choose only the public transport numbers passing nearby, which speeds up the work and accuracy of the definition of public transport.

4   Software Example

The parts of the program code, for example, to find the desired number and transfer the number by pressing are shown in Figs. 3 and 4.

```
69      private void OnTrackingFound()
70      {
71          Renderer[] rendererComponents = GetComponentsInChildren<Renderer>(true);
72          Collider[] colliderComponents = GetComponentsInChildren<Collider>(true);
73
74          // Enable rendering:
75          foreach (Renderer component in rendererComponents)
76          {
77              component.enabled = true;
78          }
79
80          // Enable colliders:
81          foreach (Collider component in colliderComponents)
82          {
83              component.enabled = true;
84          }
85
86          Debug.Log("Trackable " + mTrackableBehaviour.TrackableName + " found");
87      }
88
89
90      private void OnTrackingLost()
91      {
92          Renderer[] rendererComponents = GetComponentsInChildren<Renderer>(true);
93          Collider[] colliderComponents = GetComponentsInChildren<Collider>(true);
94
95          // Disable rendering:
96          foreach (Renderer component in rendererComponents)
97          {
98              component.enabled = false;
99          }
100
101         // Disable colliders:
102         foreach (Collider component in colliderComponents)
103         {
104             component.enabled = false;
105         }
106
107         Debug.Log("Trackable " + mTrackableBehaviour.TrackableName + " lost");
108     }
109
110     #endregion // PRIVATE_METHODS
111     }
112 }
113
```

Fig. 3. The script responsible for finding the desired number.

```
5    public class Move : MonoBehaviour
6    {
7        int k = 0;
8        void Update()
9        {
10           if (Input.touchCount == 1) SetTarget();
11           if (Input.GetMouseButton(0)) SetTarget();
12
13       }
14
15       void SetTarget()
16       {
17           RaycastHit hit;
18
19           if (Physics.Raycast(Camera.main.ScreenPointToRay(Input.mousePosition), out hit))
20           {
21               if (hit.collider.tag == "123")
22               {
23                   var bus = Instantiate(Resources.Load("bus123"));
24                   k++;
25                   if (k > 1)
26                   {
27                       if (bus) Destroy(bus);
28                   }
29               }
30               if (hit.collider.tag == "322")
31               {
32                   var bus = Instantiate(Resources.Load("bus333"));
33                   k++;
34                   if (k > 1)
35                   {
36                       if (bus) Destroy(bus);
37                   }
38               }
39
40           }
41       }
42   }
```

Fig. 4. The script for transferring the number by pressing.

When the smartphone camera is pointing to a number or QR-code belonging to a bus, trolleybus or tram, it is highlighted, and if this number is recognized correctly, the user accepts the received API and gets the ready route of the bus (trolleybus or tram) (Figs. 5 and 6).

Fig. 5. Pointing the camera at the bus number.

Fig. 6. Display of the bus route.

5   Results and Comparisons

Comparison of the developed technology with existing solutions. Analysis of the effectiveness and efficiency of the application was made in St. Petersburg (Kolpino settlement) at the Vokzalnaya Ploshchad stop on October 18, 2017 under conditions of average visibility (cloudy sky) at 10:00 am.

Considered 4 options for determining the route:

1. Determination of the route by QR-code;
2. Scan the number and launch the application;
3. Search for a number on the Internet using the *Yandex* search engine;
4. An interview standing next to passengers.

The first two options are implemented in the application described above, the third and fourth corresponds to how the problem of route determination is being solved now. The analysis of the results is presented in Table 1.

Table 1. Estimating the effectiveness of the application by the criterion of time.

Name of actions	App in process		Possible decisions	
	QR-code	Scan of number	Internet search	Ask passenger
Opening app	5–8 s	5–8 s	3–5 s	20–40 s (depends on if passenger is on bus-stop and if he knows he route)
Giving information	0	0	5 s	
The speed of making route	1 s	1 s	2–3 s	
Giving information in bad weather circumstances	0	Depends on the condition of TC and precipitation	5–8 s	
In sum min, sec	6	6	15	20
In sum max, sec	9	9	21	40

Thus, the developed application allows you to quickly and visually build a public transport route: 9 s against 15 and 20 s. Using QR code is preferable in conditions of poor visibility, since the QR code can be located behind the glass, next to the vehicle number. This arrangement protects it from dirt and dying, and thereby minimizes the probability of a number identification error.

6   Conclusion

We demonstrated the effectiveness of the application of the technology of augmented reality in improving the quality of servicing public urban transport passengers.

Using the augmented reality for routing, using the *Yandex maps* API, *Unity* and *Vuforia*, the determination of the geo position and the output of the routes of the required public transport takes place in seconds. This technology can be used to solve a wide class of urban transport problems.

References

1. Seliverstov, Y.A., Malygin, I.G., Komashinskiy, V.I., Tarantsev, A.A., Shatalova, N.V., Petrova, V.A.: The St. Petersburg transport system simulation before opening new subway stations. In: Proceedings of 2017 XX IEEE International Conference on Soft Computing and Measurements (SCM), St. Petersburg, pp. 284–287 (2017). https://doi.org/10.1109/scm.2017.7970562

2. Seliverstov, S.A., Seliverstov, Y.A., Tarantsev, A.A., Grigoriev, V.A., Elyashevich, A.M., Muksimova, R.R.: Elaboration of intelligent development system of megalopolis transportation. In: Proceedings of 2017 IEEE II International Conference on Control in Technical Systems (CTS), St. Petersburg, pp. 211–215 (2017). https://doi.org/10.1109/ctsys.2017.8109528

3. Seliverstov, Y.A., Seliverstov, S.A., Lukomskaya, O.Y., Nikitin, K.V., Grigoriev, V.A., Vydrina, E.O.: The method of selecting a preferred route based on subjective criteria. In: Proceedings of 2017 IEEE II International Conference on Control in Technical Systems (CTS), St. Petersburg, pp. 126–130 (2017). https://doi.org/10.1109/ctsys.2017.8109506

4. Seliverstov, Y.A., et al.: Development of management principles of urban traffic under conditions of information uncertainty. In: Kravets, A., Shcherbakov, M., Kultsova, M., Groumpos, P. (eds.) Creativity in Intelligent Technologies and Data Science. CIT&DS 2017. Communications in Computer and Information Science, vol. 754, pp. 399–418. Springer, Cham (2017). https://doi.org/10.1007/978-3-319-65551-2_29

5. Seliverstov, Y.A., Seliverstov, S.A., Komashinskiy, V.I., Tarantsev, A.A., Shatalova, N.V., Grigoriev, V.A.: Intelligent systems preventing road traffic accidents in megalopolises in order to evaluate. In: Proceedings of 2017 XX IEEE International Conference on Soft Computing and Measurements (SCM), St. Petersburg, pp. 489–492 (2017). https://doi.org/10.1109/scm.2017.7970626

6. Królewski, J., Gawrysiak, P.: Public transport navigation system with augmented reality interface. In: Proceedings of the 5th International Conference on Convergence and Hybrid Information Technology. ICHIT 2011, Daejeon, Korea, 22–24 September 2011, pp. 545–551 (2011). https://doi.org/10.1007/978-3-642-24106-2_69

7. Abdi, L., Ben Abdallah, F., Meddeb, A.: In-vehicle augmented reality traffic information system: a new type of communication between driver and vehicle. Procedia Comput. Sci. **73**, 242–249 (2015). https://doi.org/10.1016/j.procs.2015.12.024

8. Feiner, S., MacIntyre, B., Höllerer, T., Webster, A.: A touring machine: prototyping 3D mobile augmented reality systems for exploring the urban environment. Pers. Technol. **1**(4), 208–217 (1997). https://doi.org/10.1007/BF01682023

9. Fino, E.R., Martín-Gutiérrez, J., Fernández, M.D.M., Davara, E.A.: Interactive tourist guide: connecting web 2.0, augmented reality and QR codes. Procedia Comput. Sci. **25**, 338–344 (2013) https://doi.org/10.1016/j.procs.2013.11.040

10. Hasegawa, K., Saito, H.: Diminished reality for hiding a pedestrian using hand-held camera. In: Proceedings of 2015 IEEE International Symposium on Mixed and Augmented Reality Workshops, Fukuoka, pp. 47–52 (2015). https://doi.org/10.1109/ismarw.2015.18

11. Kourouthanassis, P., Boletsis, C., Bardaki, C., Chasanidou, D.: Tourists responses to mobile augmented reality travel guides: the role of emotions on adoption behaviour. Pervasive Mobile Comput. **18**, 71–87 (2015). https://doi.org/10.1016/j.pmcj.2014.08.009

12. Sierpiński, G., (ed.): Intelligent transport systems and travel behaviour. In: Proceedings of the 13th Scientific and Technical Conference Transport Systems. Theory and Practice 2016, Katowice, Poland, 19–21 September 2016. AISC, vol. 505. Springer, Cham (2016). https://doi.org/10.1007/978-3-319-43991-4

13. Huelsen, M.: Knowledge-Based Driver Assistance Systems. Traffic Situation Description and Situation Feature Relevance. Springer, Karlsruhe (2014). https://doi.org/10.1007/978-3-658-05750-3

Cognitive Information Technologies in the Digital Economics

About the Digital Economy Software

Manfred Sneps-Sneppe[1] ⓘ, Dmitry Namiot[2] ⓘ,
Vladimir Sukhomlin[2,3] ⓘ, and Elena Zubareva[2,3(✉)] ⓘ

[1] Ventspils University of Applied Sciences, Inženieru Street 101a,
Ventspils 3601, Latvia
manfredss@venta.lv
[2] Lomonosov Moscow State University, Leninskie Gory, 1, GSP-1,
119991 Moscow, Russia
dnamiot@gmail.com, sukhomlin@mail.ru,
e.zubareva@cs.msu.ru
[3] Federal Research Center «Computer Science and Control»
of Russian Academy of Sciences, Vavilova Street 40, 119333 Moscow, Russia

Abstract. The article discusses software tasks that should be resolved to implement the Digital Economy of the Russian Federation Program. The DE program identifies nine major digital technologies crucially depending on highly developed software. The article notes that information infrastructure is a crucial element of the Digital Economy. But is such an infrastructure created in Russia? The important point here is the advanced development of telecommunication networks of the new generation, providing any user anywhere universal broadband access to an unlimited range of services. Without the advanced development of these networks, the ubiquity of IT and the global Internet is impossible, since the Internet is the sum of technologies working on top of a telecommunication network.

The article proceeds to the question of choosing the architecture of information systems. This term refers to the architecture of an enterprise, a sector of a national economy, a ministry, or even an entire country. Software in all cases can be the same (similar), and in order to save we should choose a single architecture. The article discusses the Zachman model, DoDAF architecture, Lifecycle Modeling Language and criticizing of these models. The main problem is the complexity of the proposed solutions. Further in work questions of programming of systems of the Internet of Things are considered. Here we are talking about the development and adoption of a standard architecture that will allow us to re-use the developed software.

Keywords: Digital Economy · Software

1 Introduction

The article discusses software tasks that should be resolved to implement the Digital Economy of the Russian Federation Program (hereinafter the DE Program) [1]. The DE program identifies nine major digital technologies that are crucially dependent on highly developed software (SW):

© Springer Nature Switzerland AG 2020
V. Sukhomlin and E. Zubareva (Eds.): Convergent 2018, CCIS 1140, pp. 351–364, 2020.
https://doi.org/10.1007/978-3-030-37436-5_31

- big data;
- neurotechnology and artificial intelligence;
- distributed registry systems;
- quantum technologies;
- new production technologies;
- industrial internet;
- components of robotics and sensorics;
- wireless technology;
- virtual and augmented reality technology.

We are interested above all in the success of domestic production of software and hardware. Here is an example of a table with planned results for the main goal of the DE Program - to develop our own production called "Ensured unity, sustainability and security of the information and telecommunications infrastructure of the Russian Federation at all information space levels. It should be noted that, in accordance with the DE Program, the main task of the information and telecommunication infrastructure is access to the Internet.

Table 1 allows you to make preliminary judgments about the essence of the CE Program, and they look discouraging: in our opinion, the Program has not paid due attention to the development of the domestic communications industry, and without proper procedures it is impossible to create an information infrastructure that is a crucial element of the digital economy. Consequently, the indicators on the share of domestic products planned for 2024 are unlikely to be met.

Table 1. Planned results of the DE Program (fragment).

	2018	2020	2022	2024
The share of the internal network traffic of the Russian segment of the Internet network routed through foreign servers,%	50	35	25	10
Cost share purchased by federal executive authorities, executive authorities of subjects, state corporations, companies with state participation of computer, server and telecommunication equipment of foreign production,%	94	90	75	50
Cost share of purchased and (or) leased by federal executive authorities, executive authorities of subjects, state corporations, companies with state participation of foreign software,%	50	30	20	10

Further, in Sect. 2, critical comments were made to the DE Program in the "infrastructure of the digital economy" direction. Sections 3, 4, 5 and 6 discuss the architecture of information systems. Section 7 focuses on programming the Internet of Things (IoT). Section 8 deals with open interfaces, and Sect. 9 deals with training issues for the digital economy.

2 Criticism of the DE Program in the "Digital Economy Infrastructure" Direction

Let us focus on one of the five directions of the DE Program - information infrastructure. According to the International Academy of Telecommunications expert Boris Lastovich [2], the new social formation, which, in fact, is the information society, as well as its component - the digital economy - can be developed only on the basis of modern information and communication infrastructure. Has such an infrastructure been created in Russia?

Our regulator, the Ministry of Digital Development, Communications and Mass Communications of the Russian Federation (MinComSvyaz) has avoided the term "ICT" in recent years, without taking into account that the basis of the information and communication infrastructure, information space of any country is high-speed telecommunication networks of the new generation NGN, providing the user anywhere universal broadband access to an unlimited range of services and other benefits of telecommunications and ICT. Without the advanced development of these networks, the ubiquity of IT and the global Internet is impossible, since the Internet is the sum of technologies working on top of a telecommunication network.

Unlike traditional networks, NGN networks, as well as services provided on their basis, are convergent and can form a single digital space of a country regardless of the type of network, operator, user connection method (fixed, Wi-Fi or mobile) and the services provided. They also serve as a transport environment for long-distance/international telephone connections and any other types of communications.

In our country, the construction of new generation networks is initially conducted by private capital in order to gain profit from the provision of access to the Internet and related services. It is conducted without taking into account the tasks of creating the basis of the country's digital infrastructure - the single telecommunication network of the Russian Federation, as required by the current law "On Communications" and the interests of the state and society.

Vivid evidence of the spontaneity development is provided by fiber-optic tampering posts on the roofs of buildings in Russian cities, the fuzzy architecture, location and connectivity of traffic exchange nodes of the composite network, and the impossibility of managing it even in emergency situations.

Certainly modern communication networks in Russia owe their unprecedented rapid spread to the competitive market and the lack of administrative barriers. In just 15 years, more than 50% of households received fixed access to the digital environment — many times more than telephones were installed in 120 years. Together with mobile access, the development of cellular networks of 3G and 4G generations and the mass distribution of smartphones, the total broadband access has exceeded 80%, and the number of users - individuals reached 100 million.

But this impressive statistics is provided by a set of commercial networks. This conglomerate of private fragments of the global Internet cannot be used as an infrastructure for special networks, systems and processes that require high reliability and security of information exchange, which fully applies to the tasks of the digital economy development program.

Let's go pick out two specific tasks that are set by the Program, but they are meaningless without a single telecommunication network of the Russian Federation.

1. "To provide satellite coverage of the entire territory of Russia" - it is a necessary thing, but not the main thing, since this link cannot work without terrestrial broadband networks.
2. "To introduce the 5G mobile radio technology". 5G is a technology of mass broadband mobile access and it works on gigabit fiber-optic networks. It is not clear who and how will "introduce" it in market conditions.

In addition, the analysis of the current state of regulatory documents of the Ministry of Communications follows the insistent demand for the development of a new version of the Law "On Communications", taking into account new realities, including the regulation of packet switching technologies, which underlies the DE Program.

3   Information Systems Architecture: Zachman Model

Creating the information infrastructure of the digital economy, which we have discussed, is the first task of the DE Program. Next - to choose the architecture of information systems. This term refers to the architecture of an enterprise, a sector of a national economy, a ministry, or even an entire country. Software in all cases can be very similar, and in order to save we should choose a single architecture.

In 1987, an article by Zakhman "The structure of the architecture of information systems" appeared and foe the firdt time the concept of "enterprise architecture" was introduced [3]. Zachman has been involved in the implementation of IBM information systems for many years and rethought their architecture. He proposed an idea that for the IT industry is comparable to the Periodic Table of Mendeleev. He invented a new description of such complex systems as a transnational corporation. Thus, he became the "father" of enterprise architecture (Enterprise Architecture, EA). Since the publication of the "Zachman model" has undergone significant changes, various modifications have appeared (in the works of 1992–96). For example, formalized graphics tools have been added.

The Zachman model was used by major corporations such as General Motors, Bank of America, and others. The Zachman model served as the basis for NIST to create the Federal Enterprise Architecture Framework (FEAF), the Open Group Architecture Framework (TOGAF) and, most importantly, the methodology for describing the architecture of the US Department of Defense (DoDAF - Department of Defense Architecture Framework).

J. Zachman defined the enterprise architecture as "a set of descriptive representations (models) that are applicable to describe the Enterprise in accordance with the requirements of management personnel (quality) and can develop over a certain period (dynamism)." The term "architecture" is not accidental, it emphasizes the existing analogy between the internal structure of an abstract object — an enterprise and a complex artificial object, such as a building or an orbital international space station (ISS).

The main idea of the model is to ensure the possibility of a consistent description of each individual aspect of the system in coordination with all others [4]. For any fairly complex system, the total number of links, conditions, and rules usually exceeds the possibilities for simultaneous consideration. At the same time, a separate from others consideration of each aspect of the system most often leads to non-optimal solutions, both in terms of performance and cost of implementation.

4 About the Development of DoDAF

The development of the DODAF architecture has been going on for over 25 years, with thousands of developers participating in it. In the course of development, the Ministry of Defense was repeatedly criticized for "wasting" money. The newest review of the state (as of July 2017) of works in the field of enterprise architecture [5] has the curious name "Enterprise Architecture Structures: A New Age Fad". The review presents a paradoxical judgment: a historical analysis shows that using the DoDAF in the US Department of Defense provides "the most exciting example of continuously increasing time and money investment in [enterprise architecture], but still obtaining the same unsatisfactory results."

Difficulty with programming DoDAF is not at all difficult to explain. Description DoDAF contains 57 volumes. It is only natural that it won't be easy to make programmers to strictly take into account such cumbersome instructions. They also do not tend to follow the complex programming language SysML for the same reasons.

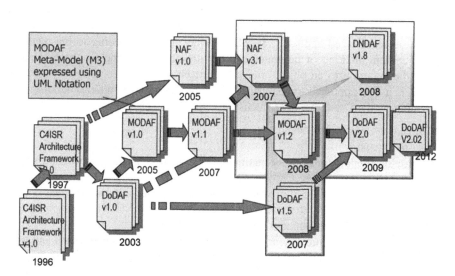

Fig. 1. The evolution of the architectural structures of defense departments. Here: DODAF - US Department of Defense Architecture Framework, MODAF - British Ministry of Defence Architecture Framework, NAF - NATO architecture (deployed in Afghanistan), DNDAF - Canada architecture.

One of the most ardent critics is Stephen Dem. He himself is a multi-year developer of C4ISR and DoDAF architectures. He has been developing information systems for the defense industry for over 40 years. We give a picture (Fig. 1) from his presentation entitled "Does the DODAF architecture need more?" [6]. Unlike many critics of the information systems of complex enterprises, including the defense ministries, the criticism of Stephen Dema is positive: it offers a new language for describing complex systems LML (Lifecycle Modeling Language).

5 LML

Availability of a single language for describing information systems is extremely important for the success of the DE Program, therefore we will give a detailed description of it. And software developers will have to evaluate its feasibility for the needs of the DE Program.

Lifecycle Modeling Language (LML) is an open standard modeling language designed for system engineers. It supports the full life cycle of the system: from concept development to its replacement with a new product. The specification was published on October 17, 2013 [7]. User Guide published in 2014 [8].

The goal of the language is to replace the predecessor languages, such as UML and SysML, which, according to the LML developers, unnecessarily complicate the system development process. LML integrates logical constructs with an ontology to collect information.

SysML is mostly constructs and it has a limited ontology, while DoDAF Meta-Model 2.0 (DM2) has nothing but an ontology. Instead, LML simplifies both constructs and ontologies to make them more complete, but also more convenient to use. There are only 12 primary entity classes. One of the shortcomings of SysML is eliminated - using an object-oriented approach. SysML was developed according to the methodology of system thinking of programmers, but no other discipline for the entire life cycle of the system uses an object-oriented approach.

LML is a new approach to analyzing, planning, defining, designing, building and maintaining modern systems. LML focuses on six goals (Fig. 2):

1. To make it easy to understand
2. Easy to expand
3. To provide support for both a functional and object-oriented approach in a single project.
4. Be a language that can be understood by most system stakeholders, not just system engineers.
5. Maintain the system throughout the life cycle
6. To support both evolutionary and revolutionary changes in system plans and projects throughout the entire service life of the system.

Ontology. Ontologies provide a set of defined terms and relationships between terms for collecting information describing the physical, functional, operational, and software aspects of a system. The usual ways of describing such ontologies are three concepts:

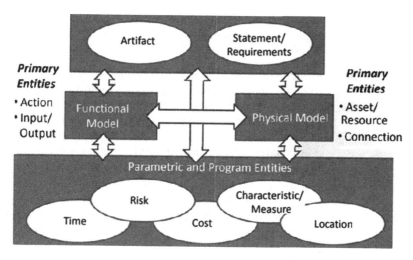

Fig. 2. LML model.

"Entity", "Relationship" and "Attribute" (ERA). The ERA complex is often used to define database schemas. LML extends the ERA scheme by adding the notion of "Attributes on Relationship", thereby reducing the number of required "entities" in ERA. In accordance with the basic idea of LML, these four concepts: "*Entity*", "*Relationship*", "*Attribute*" and "*Attribute on Relationship*" are equivalent elements of the English language: noun, verb, adjective and adverb (noun, verb, adjective and adverb).

Entity (Noun). An entity is defined as something uniquely identifiable and it can exist by itself. There are a total of 12 parent entities in LML:

Action,	Connection,	Location,
Artifact,	Cost,	Risk,
Asset,	Decision,	Statement and
Characteristic,	Input/Output,	Time.

Several child entities are defined to provide accounting of the information needed by users. Child entities, in turn, have their own attributes and attitudes toward parents, plus additional attributes and relationships that make them unique.

Attribute (Adjective). Attributes are used like adjectives in ordinary language. Entities (nouns) may have names, numbers, and description attributes. The intrinsic characteristic or quality of an entity is an attribute. Each attribute has a name that uniquely identifies it within the entity. Attribute names are unique within an entity, but can be used in other entities. The name gives an overview of the attribute information. The attribute data type indicates the data associated with this attribute.

Relationship (Verb): Relationship works the same way as a verb – it connects nouns or, in other words, entities. Relationships provide an easy way to see how entities connect. Relationship names are unique across the LML schema.

Attributes on Relationships (Adverb). The classic ERA model does not have the concept of "relationship attributes". This is a significant addition to language tools. In the same way that attributes relate to entities, the "attribute of a relationship" has a name unique to its relationship, but should not be unique to other relationships.

The LML language can be found in the document [9]. The developers assure that LML can be translated into UML, SysML, DoDAF (DM2) and other languages. The first development tools in LML - Innoslate [10] are already openly available. Innoslate is the first tool to implement the new Lifecycle Modeling Language (LML). Innoslate integrates systems engineering software with requirements management requirements, requirements analysis and collaboration tools. All this is contained in a single solution. Innoslate provides a future standard for modeling complex systems on the Model-Based Systems Engineering (MBSE) approach. Innoslate is a cloud-based web application developed by the new company SPEC Innovations.

6   Criticism of the Zachman Model

One of the critics of the Zahman model is Svyatoslav Kotushev (a graduate of MTUCI, now working in Australia). We give his analysis of the state of affairs in the field of information systems architecture [11].

The discipline of enterprise architecture (EA, enterprise architecture) is closely associated with numerous tools that help architects plan the work of an organization and create their information systems. However, for a very long time, according to Kotushev, we see a rather curious situation, which can be described as absurd, paradoxical or even schizophrenic. Namely, one set of tools is declared as fundamental to the discipline of EA, consistently promoted as a global standard of EA and widely taught in different EA courses, but in fact this set of tools is largely, if not completely, useless for practical purposes.

At the same time, another set of tools is an actual combination of existing best EA practices that work successfully in many organizations, but these tools are barely discussed and do not have reasonable descriptions for novice architects and students that they could learn from. In addition, these two EA toolkits do not overlap with each other. We are talking about the Zakhman model as a prominent representative of fake tools, on the one hand, and the Business Model Capability Model (VSM) as a real, in practice approved tool, on the other.

Currently, the Zachman model has about 4,000 links to Google Scholar and is outlined in many books of up to 750 pages. At the same time, even its origins are not known about the BCM model. For example, BCM is not mentioned in any existing EA structures. Only in the articles of 2009 was it possible to find his description as an already well-known industry phenomenon and not as something new.

Like the Zachman model, other well-known and aggressively promoted EA tools, including, among others, TOGAF, FEAF and ArchiMate, are, according to Kotushev, counterfeit tools (albeit with some reservations). They are also characterized by a set of attributes as the Zachman model, marketing hype, deliberate uncertainty, empty promises and the lack of real practical examples. These tools are mostly useless and practically have no practical value, but only create information noise and distort discourse in the discipline of EA.

Another thing is the BCM model. This is a real tool. Unlike the completely "metaphysical" Zachman model with inexplicable practical significance, the use of the advantages of the BCM model can be explained in clear, simple words - even for "mere mortals". On one page, you can show the hierarchy of all business opportunities of an organization along the BCM model, which provides a simple, comprehensive view of business processes and contributes to the strategic dialogue between business and IT (Fig. 3).

Fake Tools	Real Tools
Origin: Created artificially "top-down" by consultancies and gurus without any empirical justifications	**Origin:** Emerged naturally in industry "bottom-up" out of the real-life experience of multiple practicing architects
Motivation: Purely commercial, used to sell trainings, certifications, software tools and consulting services	**Motivation:** Purely practical, used to solve organizational problems and not distributed on a commercial basis
Promotion: Very actively promoted and discussed, positioned as industry standards and proven instruments	**Promotion:** Never promoted, disseminated quietly from architects to architects mostly through collaboration
Description: Described in detail, many comprehensive sources, courses and trainings available	**Description:** Barely described and codified, no comprehensive information sources available
Notable Example: The Zachman Framework	**Notable Example:** The Business Capability Model
Fundamental "ontology" having no practical implications and no specific use cases in organizations	Practical, highly intuitive and widely used instrument for improving strategic business and IT alignment
Other Examples: TOGAF, FEAF, ArchiMate, etc.	**Other Examples:** Solution overviews and business cases, color-coded TRMs, architecture debt, etc.
Metaphor: "Pampered, lazy and unemployed noblemen of aristocratic origin"	**Metaphor:** "Talented, hard-working and self-made orphans"
Role: Purely symbolic, hardly influence actual EA best practices, let alone define these practices	**Role:** Represent true best practices constituting the genuine body of knowledge on.EA
Attitude: Ignore these tools or learn them carefully, do not try to implement their advice in organizations	**Attitude:** Learn, describe and share these tools with other members of the broader EA community
Future: Sooner or later will fade away and be forgotten as all the previous once-famous management fads	**Future:** Sooner or later will be studied in detail, codified and included in "EA 101" courses and textbooks

Fig. 3. Comparison of the fake and real architecture of the DE Program [11].

Given the importance of choosing information systems architecture for the DE Program, we'll give S. Kotushev the main advice that domestic experts should critically discuss: instead of trying to harmonize their practice with unrealistic suggestions (such as the Zachman model), EA architects should trust their own opinion, focus on the developments that have been tested in their organizations, and then share these best practices with the broader community of experts to share experiences and avoid duplication of development.

7 About Internet of Things Programming

The most important section of the DE Program is the Internet of Things (IoT). It should be noted the following. This is a section in which international standardization efforts have advanced far enough. And this is the section that is perhaps the most suitable for implementing what is called a digital platform. The Internet of Things acts, for example, as a basic platform (one can say - measuring level, data level) for the Smart City [12]. Accordingly, without the adoption of a single architecture at the national level, no reuse of software is possible [13].

It should also be noted that this is a moment that is well understood in the world and there are already quite a lot of solutions in this direction [14]. As a matter of fact, standardization in IoT is precisely the development of a reference architecture [15]. Unfortunately, this is precisely the moment that is completely absent from domestic programs on the digital economy (at least in their current state). For unknown reasons, it all comes down to the development of examples (usually referred to as cases), compatibility issues are not addressed in any way, architectural issues are not considered on principle [16].

To the extent of what is included in educational programs on IoT, it is possible to mention the work [17, 18]. The sections of the educational program correspond to the IoT functional analysis map (Fig. 4).

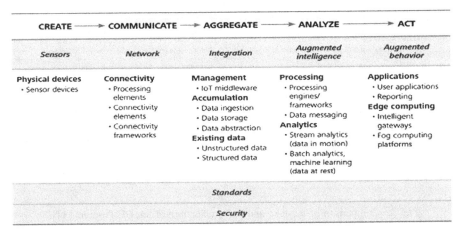

Fig. 4. Functional analysis of IoT [19].

Technically, for the selected reference model (architecture) IoT programming is the programming of mash-ups [20]. As an example of programming for IoT, the work of the W3C consortium [21] can be noted. A more blanket term is Web of Things, a term used to describe approaches, architectural styles of software, and programming patterns that allow real-world objects to be part of the WWW world. Web of Things provides an application layer, i.e. the goal is to simplify the creation of IoT applications.

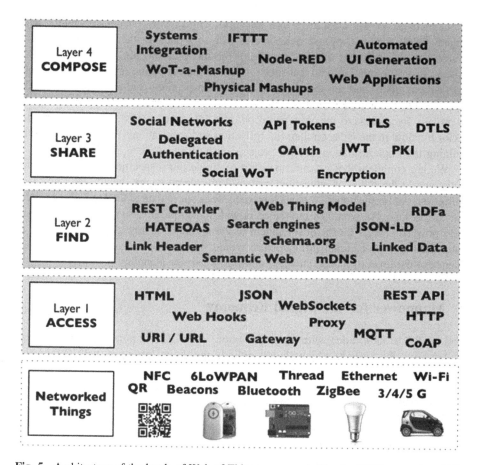

Fig. 5. Architecture of the levels of Web of Things as presented by the W3C consortium [22].

Instead of reinventing completely new standards, Web of Things aims to reuse existing tools and well-known Web standards (eg, REST, HTTP, JSON), semantic Web (eg, JSON-LD, Microdata), real-time Web (eg, Websockets) and social Web tools (Fig. 5).

8 About Open Interfaces

The success of the DE Program depends on the activity of programmers, on their involvement in the development of new applications, and this requires open interfaces to information systems. The issue of open interfaces is critically discussed in the article "Digital economy: goals and means" [23].

Big Data (Big Data) is the first of the list of innovative priorities included in the concept of the digital economy according to the Government. What can the state do? - asks E. Loginov.

Objectives for Big Data are social networks, large banks, telecom operators, and federal retail chains. They use quite successfully big data for their commercial purposes. The state also has a huge resource of the most various big data, ranging from state archives, continuing with statistics on transactions in public registries and ending with data on goods and services at the level of tax inspection. And why not plan on six years (and this is a huge period of time in the innovation sphere) 5–6 specific projects to provide free access to this data based on open interfaces (APIs), giving the private sector freedom in the ideas on their interpretation and application? What prevents from painting the implementation of such projects in the form of plans in the Program?

We are confident that it would be right to single out a specific series of big data initiatives in the fields of education, meteorology, demography, health care, and tax collection. And if the potential of such projects does not remain at the level of domestic use by the state, but would be embodied in widespread public tools, this would be the most powerful driver for the development of the digital economy. At the same time, a natural buildup of national infrastructure would be an unobtrusive statistical consequence at the level of a state strategy, and not a task for planning.

9   Manpower for the Digital Economy

And finally, let us will deal with the central issue of the DE Program - the improvement of the education system, which should provide the digital economy with competent personnel.

Here are the main events from the Federal project "Personnel for the Digital Economy" for the period 10/01/2018–12/31/2024 [24]:

- To provide assistance to citizens, including older ones, in mastering the core competencies of the digital economy;
- To formulate and introduce into the education system the requirements for key competencies of the digital economy for each level of education, ensuring their continuation;
- The system of higher and secondary vocational education works in the interests of preparing and adapting citizens to the conditions of the digital economy and training competent specialists for the digital economy.

We have previously reviewed training programs for the training of staff for the digital economy in articles [25].

10   Conclusions

- The major work in the field of the digital economy, which, in our opinion, applies to all its areas, is the development of unified software: a unified information model, a unified architecture, a unified description language. The presence of a single model will allow coordinating the efforts of developers in different areas and will ensure the development of uniform software tools.

- The DE program name nine major end-to-end digital technologies (big data; neurotechnology and artificial intelligence; distributed registry systems and others). It should be noted that in the Program itself it is difficult to notice the manifestation of these end-to-end technologies, and in the light of the critical comments made on the Program, they are a random set of modern world technologies and, perhaps, not the most important from the point of view of the national economy.

- Preliminary thoughts on the essence of the DE Program look discouraging: the Program does not provide the revival of the communications industry at all. Consequently, the indicators on the share of domestic products planned for 2024 are unlikely to be met.

- On the grounds of the analysis of the current state of regulatory documents of the Ministry of Communications, we can conclude that there is an insistent demand for the development of a new version of the Zocon "On Communications" taking into account the new realities, including the regulation of packet switching technologies, which is the basis for the DE Program.

References

1. Program "Digital Economy of the Russian Federation". Order of the Government of the Russian Federation of 28.07.2017 no. 1632-p. http://static.government.ru/media/files/9gFM4FHj4PsB79I5v7yLVuPgu4bvR7M0.pdf. Accessed 12 Oct 2018. (in Russian)
2. Lastovich, B.: ICT infrastructure of the digital economy, Prostye istiny. IKS no. 7–8 (2017) http://www.iksmedia.ru/articles/5434122-IKTinfrastruktura-cifrovoj-ekonomik.html. Accessed 12 Oct 2018. (in Russian)
3. Zachman, J.A.: A framework for information systems architecture. IBM Syst. J. 26(3), 276–292 (1987). https://doi.org/10.1147/sj.263.0276
4. Karpenko, S.: Using the Zachman model for designing an enterprise IT architecture (2011) http://www.management.com.ua/ims/ims177.html/. Accessed 12 Oct 2018. (in Russian)
5. Kotusev, S.: Enterprise architecture frameworks: the fad of the century. Br. Comput. Soc. (BCS) (2016) http://www.bcs.org/content/conWebDoc/56347/. Accessed 12 Oct 2018
6. Dam, S.H.: Do we still need a DoD architecture framework? In: Dam, S.H. (ed.) DoD Architecture Framework 2.0 – A Guide to Applying System Engineering to Develop Integrated, Executable Architectures, p. xi. SPEC Innovations, Manassas (2015)
7. Lifecycle Modeling Language (LML) Specification 1.0. (2013) http://www.lifecyclemodeling.org/spec/LML_Specification_1_0.pdf. Accessed 12 Oct 2018
8. Dam, S.H.: DoD Architecture Framework 2.0 – A Guide to Applying System Engineering to Develop Integrated, Executable Architectures. SPEC Innovations, Manassas (2015)
9. Dam, S.H., Vaneman, W.K.: A new open standard: lifecycle modeling language (LML) a language for simple, rapid development, operations and support, 25 January 2014. http://cdn2.hubspot.net/hub/316256/file-493267217-pdf/LML_Overview_for_Lifecycle_Management_WG-Dam_and_Vaneman.pdf?t=1391103350000/. Accessed 12 Oct 2018
10. Innoslate. http://www.systemsengineeringtool.com/innoslate/. Accessed 12 Oct 2018
11. Kotusev, S.: Fake and real tools for enterprise architecture. Br. Comput. Soc. (BCS) (2018) http://www.bcs.org/content/conWebDoc/59399. Accessed 12 Oct 2018

12. Kuprijanovskij, V.P., et al.: Smart cities as the "capitals" of the digital economy. Int. J. Open Inf. Technol. **4**(2), 41–52 (2016). http://injoit.ru/index.php/j1/article/view/269/214. (in Russian)
13. Namiot, D.E., Kuprijanovskij, V.P., Sinjagov, S.A.: Info-communication services in the smart city. Int. J. Open Inf. Technol. **4**(4), 1–9 (2016). http://injoit.ru/index.php/j1/article/view/281/236. (in Russian)
14. Sneps-Sneppe, M.A.: How to build a Smart City Part 2. Organization «oneM2M» as a prototype in the field of smart city standards. Int. J. Open Inf. Technol. **4**(2), 11–17 (2016). http://injoit.ru/index.php/j1/article/view/265/210. (in Russian)
15. Namiot, D.E., Sneps-Sneppe, M.A.: On international standards for M2M. T-Comm: Telecommun. Transp. **8**(12), 62–67 (2014). https://elibrary.ru/item.asp?id=22821399&. (in Russian)
16. Namiot, D.E., Sneps-Sneppe, M.A.: On the domestic standards for Smart Cities. Int. J. Open Inf. Technol. **4**(7), 32–37 (2016). http://injoit.ru/index.php/j1/article/view/312/255. (in Russian)
17. Namiot, D., Sneps-Sneppe, M., Daradkeh, Y.I.: On Internet of Things education. In: Proceedings of the 2017 IEEE 20th Conference of Open Innovations Association (FRUCT), St. Petersburg, 2017, pp. 309–315 (2017). https://doi.org/10.23919/fruct.2017.8071327
18. Sneps-Sneppe, M., Namiot, D., Sukhomlin, V.: On telecommunication software engineering education. In: Proceedings of the 2017 IEEE 20th Conference of Open Innovations Association (FRUCT), St. Petersburg, 2017, pp. 705–713 (2017). https://fruct.org/publications/abstract20/files/Sne.pdf
19. Holdowsky, J., Mahto, M., Raynor, M.E., Cotteleer, M.: Inside the Internet of Things (IoT). In: Deloitte Insights, 21 August (2015). http://dupress.com/articles/iot-primer-iot-technologies-applications. Accessed 12 Oct 2018
20. Namiot, D., Sneps-Sneppe, M.: On Internet of Things programming models. In: Vishnevskiy, V.M., Samouylov, K.E., Kozyrev, D.V. (eds.) DCCN 2016. CCIS, vol. 678, pp. 13–24. Springer, Cham (2016). https://doi.org/10.1007/978-3-319-51917-3_2
21. Voskov, L.S., Pilipenko, N.A.: Web of things - a new stage of the Internet of Things. Qual. Innov. Educ. **2**, 44–49 (2013). (in Russian)
22. Guinard, D., Trifa, V.: Building the Web of Things: With Examples in Node.js and Raspberry Pi. Manning Publications, New York (2016)
23. Loginov, E.: Digital economy: goals and means. In: Loyp Agency, 16 November (2017). https://loyp.ru/vision/it-and-automation/digital-economy-goals-and-tools.html. Accessed 12 Oct 2018. (in Russian)
24. Event plan in the direction of "Personnel and Education" programs "Digital Economy of the Russian Federation" http://static.government.ru/media/files/k87YsCABuiyuLAjcWDFILE h6itAirUX0.pdf. Accessed 12 Oct 2018. (in Russian)
25. Sneps-Sneppe, M.A., Sukhomlin, V.A., Namiot, D.E.: On the program "Digital Economy of the Russian Federation": how to create an information infrastructure. Int. J. Open Inf. Technol. **6**(3), 37–48 (2018) http://injoit.ru/index.php/j1/article/view/544/526. (in Russian)

Digital Transformation of Transport

Big Data Processing of Commodity Flows in the Transport and Economic Balance of the Russian Federation

Oleg Evseev[1]([⊠]) , Vasily Murashov[1] , Alexander Zaboev[1] ,
Anton Zemtsov[1] , Victor Buslov[1] , Alexander Shubin[1] ,
Alexander Schirov[2] , Anton Shubin[3] , Anton Urazov[3] ,
and Elena Anikina[3]

[1] Scientific Center for Complex Transport Problems of the Ministry of Transport
of the Russian Federation, 3, Pushkarev lane, 107045 Moscow, Russia
{evseev,aza}@mintrans.org
[2] Institute for Economic Forecasting, Russian Academy of Science,
Nakhimovsky Avenue 47, 117418 Moscow, Russia
schir@ecfor.ru
[3] LLC "Geogracom", Office 4297, Warsawskoye Freeway 42,
115580 Moscow, Russia

Abstract. Planning and forecasting transportation using econometric and mathematical tools based on the spatial input-output tables and knowledge of transportation effects is an important task for improving transport and regional economics. The spatial input-output tables of Russia further called the transport and economic balance of the Russian Federation aggregate the actual and forecast volumes of freight traffic between the regions of the country by rail, road, inland water and maritime transport by types of commodities. The actual information on freight traffic covering the period from 2007 to 2017 bases on statistics for industrial production, domestic and external trade, construction, agriculture, energy, as well as transport statistics and takes into account the relationship between production and consumption, import and export of goods. The features of the Russian statistical accounting specify the order of Big-data processing while calculating the balance.

The transport and economic balance of the Russian Federation provides the forecast of interregional trade flows, transportation infrastructure loading, changes in transport network capacity, transportation costs and time. The forecast of cargo load and interregional freight flows covers the period up to 2030. The forecast model uses Russian economy growth scenarios of the Ministry of Economic Development of Russia, as well as regional economic development scenarios including changes in the technological and transport connectivity of main cargo generating industries.

Keywords: Big data · Traffic flows · Forecasting · Transport · Transport policy · Transport statistics · Transport connectivity and economic relations · Spatial Input-output tables · Transport and economic balance · Transport planning · Transport models

© Springer Nature Switzerland AG 2020
V. Sukhomlin and E. Zubareva (Eds.): Convergent 2018, CCIS 1140, pp. 367–383, 2020.
https://doi.org/10.1007/978-3-030-37436-5_32

1 Introduction

Sustainable and efficient functioning of the transport system is an important focus of the economic policy of any country. It is the target of national strategies, plans and transport development programs, as other documents setting the main priorities of the state transport policy. These plans are based on forecasts of demand for transport services, production, consumption and shipping of main goods, prospects for development of international trade, investment, etc.

In the Russian Federation, and earlier in the Soviet Union, issues of transport development based on economic and mathematical models of planning and forecasting, as well as transport intersectoral balance accounting, were developed by the Institute of Complex Transport Problems of the USSR State Planning Committee (IKTP) [2], and Central Economics and Mathematics Institute of the Academy of Sciences of the USSR (CEMI) [6, 7].

The balance approach was implemented for transport and economic links planning not only in the USSR, but also in the member states of former Council for Mutual Economic Assistance (CMEA).

During the 20 years after USSR dismissed on the way to the transition to market economy, methods based on spatial input-output tables were no longer used in the transport work forecasting. The economic growth of the 21th century and the even more rapid growth of oil and gas, coal, steel, mineral fertilizers exports volume, caused the greater transport network loading and occurring of "bottlenecks". All of these required a revision of the approaches to transport policy and transport planning methods.

The transport strategy of the Russian Federation for the period up to 2030, approved by the decree of the Government of the Russian Federation of November 22, 2008 No. 1734-p, as amended by the Government of the Russian Federation of June 11, 2014 No. 1032-p, designated a balanced, advanced infrastructure development as the most important strategic target for the transport system development. Realization of this goal means coordinated integrated development of all elements of the transport infrastructure based on spatial (interregional) input-output tables.

That means to develop a statistical accounting system, mathematical methods of forecasting and modeling describing needs of economic and population sectors for transport services and the dynamics of the freight base [8].

Transport and economic balance (TEB) is a form of spatial input-output tables for planning and forecasting of transport connectivity and economic relations, expressing the ratio between the size of production and consumption of goods and the need for the volume of transport work for their import or export.

2 Research Objectives

The research target is the creation of methodological approach, mathematical tools and TEB's design procedures based on the data of the official statistical observation of economics and transport sector in the Russian Federation. The incompleteness and inaccuracies of the source statistical data for building a model of demand for freight transport, as well as mismatch between groups of production output and cargos items on modes of transport were the challenges on the beginning phase of the research.

The practical objective was to build a balance, describing the transportation of goods between all Russian regions over the past 10 years, as well as to forecast transport flows for the medium and long term.

The TEB should provide:

- a strong correlation between the forecasts of the transportation volume and expected indicators of socio-economic development and trade;
- correlation with international strategies and forecasts for the development of regional and world trade, energy and commodity markets;
- the usability of econometrics tools for forecasting the volumes of transportation and their directions in relation to indicators of socio-economic development;
- the applicability of integrated approach for solution of development problems related to different modes of transport, allocation of freight flows over the network and the rational modal split.

2.1   Main Sources of Research

The development of various models of transport and economic balance has been carried out for a long time worldwide (USA, Europe) during the past 25 years. For example, the Bureau of Transportation Statistics USA (BTS) provided the Commodity Flow Survey (CFS) on a regular basis since 1993 [13]. CFS is based on sample surveys of enterprises and contains information on interstate transportation in the U.S. by type of commodities. The main purpose of CFS is to give the government and business owners an overview of the commodity flows in the United States. On the CFS basis, the U.S. freight turnover is calculated, forecasted and monitored on regular basis under Freight Analysis Framework (FAF).

Similar activity implemented in Europe is provided by the European Commission, for example, in framework of the ETIS - BASE project (European Transport Policy Information System) [14]. The ETIS objectives are the development of metrology of consolidation and verification of national transport statistics data of the EU member-states and analytical support for decision-making process in transport planning in the EU.

Another appropriate study was conducted in the framework of the SUST-RUS Project with the participation of experts from the Russian economic school [26]. The study aims to identification of transport and economic links between the Russian federal districts. It establishes a convenient notation system which was implemented in the TEB framework for describing the basic equations of the interregional transport and economic balance of the Russian Federation. The development of balance methods for modeling transport demand across the country is provided also in the studies of Dutch researchers [11, 12], where an efficient mathematical apparatus for transport and economic balance was developed. These scientific works have had a significant impact on the setting and pursuing objectives of the TEB study.

3   The Structure of the Transport and Economic Balance of the Russian Federation

The TEB describes the actual and forecast origin-destination freight flows between various regions of the Russian Federation by rail, road, inland waterway and maritime transport by types of commodities.

The TEB structure is set by a multidimensional OD-matrix of interregional freight flows, where the rows and columns correspond to the regions of origin and destination, and at the intersection of the rows and columns there are the volumes of freight flows by modes of transport and types of commodities (Fig. 1). Another dimension of the matrix is time that shows the historical volumes and the origin-destination information of cargo traffic from 2007 to 2017. A similar TEB matrix is being built for the forecast period 2019–2030 (Figs. 2, 3, 4, 5, 6 and 7).

The TEB matrices should satisfy the balance equations connecting the transport operations between regions and with the rest of the world across the border of the Russian Federation. The balance equations substantively reflect the balance of exports, imports, production, consumption, trade, import/export of goods between all regions, as well as the transport inside the regions.

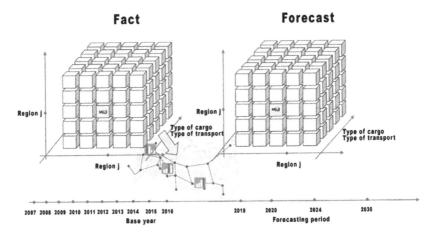

Fig. 1. Multidimensional matrixes of volumes and correspondence of freight traffic between regions by type of cargo and by modes of transport - a actual data and forecast for the period up to 2030.

The basic balance equations of TEB include the following relations:

$$X0_{i,r} = TR_{i,r} + EX_{i,r} , \qquad (1)$$

$$EX_{i,r} = \sum_{rr} \sum_{k} EX_{i,k,r,rr} , \qquad (2)$$

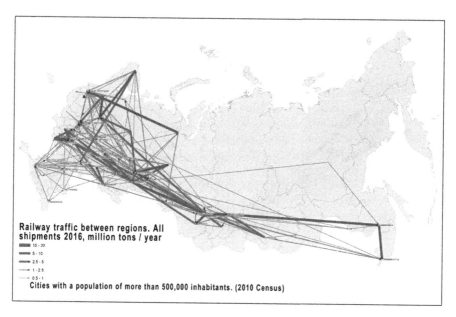

Fig. 2. Freight traffic between regions by rail. All shipments, 2016.

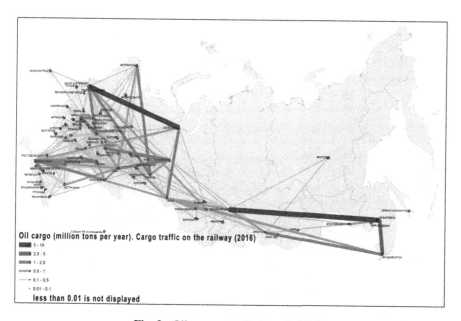

Fig. 3. Oil cargoes traffic by rail, 2016.

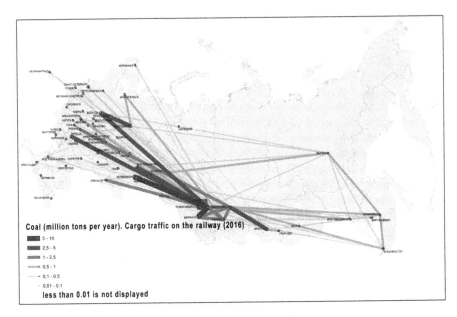

Fig. 4. Coal traffic by rail, 2016.

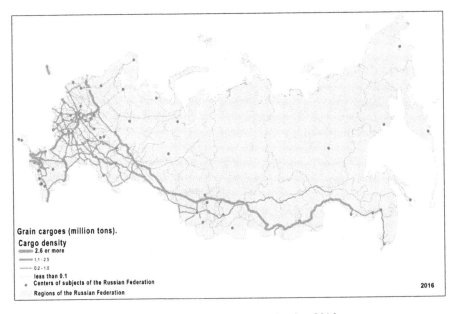

Fig. 5. Grain cargoes and their density, 2016.

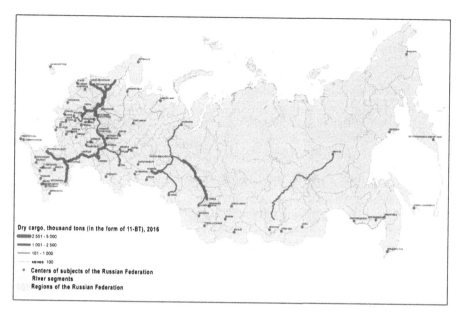

Fig. 6. Dry cargoes by inland water transport, 2016.

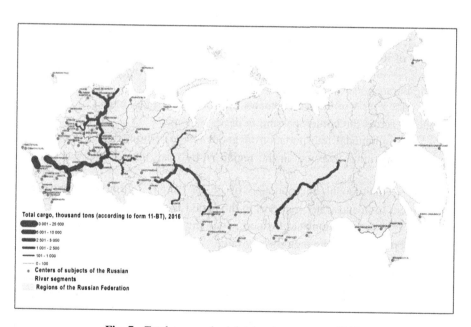

Fig. 7. Total cargoes by inland water transport, 2016.

$$IM_{i,r}^* = \sum_{rr} \sum_k IM_{i,k,r,rr} \,, \tag{3}$$

$$TR_{i,r} = \sum_{rr} \sum_k TR_{i,k,r,rr} \,, \tag{4}$$

$$TEB_{i,r,rr} = \sum_k TR_{i,k,r,rr} + \sum_k EX_{i,k,r,rr} + EX_{i,r,rr}^{MAR} + EX_{i,r,rr}^{IWW}$$
$$+ IM_{i,r,rr}^{MAR} + M_{i,r,rr}^{IWW} + TR_{i,r,rr}^{RAIL} \,, \tag{5}$$

$$EX_{i,r,rr}^{MAR} = EX_{i,r,rr}^{RAIL \to MAR} + EX_{i,r,rr}^{TRUCK \to MAR} + EX_{i,r,rr}^{IWW \to MAR} \,, \tag{6}$$

$$EX_{i,r,rr}^{IWW} = EX_{i,r,rr}^{RAIL \to IWW} + EX_{i,r,rr}^{TRUCK \to IWW} \,, \tag{7}$$

$$IM_{i,r,rr}^{MAR} = IM_{i,r,rr}^{MAR \to RAIL} + IM_{i,r,rr}^{MAR \to TRUCK} + IM_{i,r,rr}^{MAR \to IWW} \,, \tag{8}$$

$$IM_{i,r,rr}^{IWW} = IM_{i,r,rr}^{IWW \to RAIL} + IM_{i,r,rr}^{IWW \to TRUCK} \,. \tag{9}$$

where:

$X0_{i,r}$ – shipment of goods (cargo) i in region r;

$TR_{i,r}$ – domestic transportation of goods (cargo) i from region r;

$EX_{i,r}$ – export of goods (cargo) i from region r;

$EX_{i,k,r,rr}$ – matrix of export transportation of goods (cargo) i from region r through the border of Russia, passing in the region rr, by mode of transport k;

$TR_{i,k,r,rr}$ – the matrix of domestic transport of goods by modes of transport, including intraregional transportation;

$IM_{i,r}^*$ – the matrix of import shipments of goods (cargo) i by modes of transport to the region r across the border, passing in the rr region;

$EX_{i,r,rr}^{MAR}$ –multimodal transportation of goods (cargo) i from region r with transshipment to maritime transport in the region rr by road, inland waterway and rail transport;

$EX_{i,r,rr}^{IWW}$ – multimodal transportation of goods (cargo) i from the region with transshipment to inland water transport in the region by road and rail transport;

$EX_{i,r,rr}^{RAIL \to MAR}$ – transshipment of export goods (cargo) i, delivered from the region r to the seaport located in the region rr by rail;

$EX_{i,r,rr}^{IWW \to MAR}$ – transshipment of export goods (cargo) i, delivered from the region r to the seaport located in the region rr by inland water transport;

$EX_{i,r,rr}^{TRUCK \to MAR}$ – transshipment of export goods (cargo) i, delivered from the region r to the seaport located in the rr region, by road;

$IM_{i,r,rr}^{MAR}$ – multimodal transportation of goods (cargo) i, arrived across the border of Russia to the region by maritime transport, for transshipment to other modes of transport and further transportation to regions of destination rr;

$IM_{i,r,rr}^{IWW}$ – multimodal transportation of goods (cargo) i, arrived via the Russian border in the region by inland water transport for transshipment to other modes of transport and further transportation to the regions of destination rr;

$IM_{i,r,rr}^{MAR \to RAIL}$ – multimodal transportation of goods (cargo) i, arrived across the border of Russia to the region by maritime transport for transshipment to rail transport and further transportation to the regions of destination rr;

$IM_{i,r,rr}^{MAR \to TRUCK}$ – multimodal transportation of goods (cargo) i, arrived across the border of Russia to the region by maritime transport for transshipment into road transport and further transportation to the regions of destination rr;

$IM_{i,r,rr}^{MAR \to IWW}$ – multimodal transportation of goods (cargo) i, arrived across the border of Russia to the region by maritime transport for transshipment to inland waterway and further transportation to the regions of destination rr;

$IM_{i,r,rr}^{IWW \to RAIL}$ – multimodal transportation of goods (cargo) i, arrived via the Russian border in the region by inland water transport for transshipment to rail transport and further transportation to the regions of destination rr;

$IM_{i,r,rr}^{IWW \to TRUCK}$ – multimodal transportation of goods (cargo) i, arrived via the Russian border to the region by inland water transport for transshipment to road transport and further transportation to the regions of destination rr;

$TR_{i,r,rr}^{RAIL}$ – transshipment of goods (cargo) i, within the region r from road to rail and from rail to road.

Equation (1) describes the statement that all produced goods must be transported within the region, or to other regions, or for export. Equations (2), (3) and (4) fix the geographical splitting of exports, imports and domestic goods flows, respectively. Equation (5) is the basic transport balance equation related to the multimodal transport. Equations (6) and (7) determine the procedure for estimating combined export traffic on the maritime and inland water transport, respectively. Equations (8) and (9) determine the procedure for estimating multimodal import traffic involving maritime and inland water transport, respectively.

4 Construction of the Transport and Economic Balance

The source data for TEB construction is the statistical data of Rosstat on the volumes of shipped products of mining and manufacturing industries, trade, construction industry, agriculture, export and import statistics including data from the Federal Customs Service of Russia (FCS of Russia), economic statistics of the fuel and energy complex, as well as transport statistics, including data from Russian Railways, statistics on maritime and inland water transport, road transport.

Industry-specific sources of information are used to construct the TEB matrix of products shipment and origin-destination transportation matrix for the regions of the country. The Rosstat forms are used to compile shipping data, the Russian Railways corporate data warehouse (shipment archive), the maritime transport data of the M-3 and MP-2 forms, the inland water transport - data forms 11-WT and 15-WT. To determine the foreign trade transportation by road, the data of the Federal Customs Service of Russia is used; internal transportation by road is estimated on the basis of the data from the forms 1-export, П-1, 21-CX and the above-mentioned statistics by the modes of transport.

All the initial information is structured and converted to a harmonized cargo nomenclature of the TEB ensuring the comparability and compatibility of all elements of the source data with each other.

The TEB harmonized cargo nomenclature includes the following 44 types of cargo:

- 1 *construction materials*
- 11   sand, gravel and stone
- 12   cement
- 13   construction Materials (bricks, blocks, glass and other except wood materials)
- 14   firelcays and heat resistant materials
- 2 *coal, coke, peat and shale*
- 21   coal
- 22   coke
- 23   peat and shale
- 3 *oil cargo*
- 31   crude oil
- 32   light petroleum products (gasoline, diesel fuel, kerosene, etc.)
- 33   heavy petroleum products (mazut, etc.)
- 34   compressed or liquefied gas
- 4 *ore*
- 41   ferrous metal ore
- 42   non-ferrous metal ore and other ore
- 5 *ferrous material*
- 51   rolled stock of ferrous metals
- 52   steel pipes
- 53   other ferrous metals
- 6 *fertilizers*
- 61   mineral and chemical fertilizers
- 62   raw mineral and chemical fertilizers (ore)
- 63   organic fertilizers
- 7 *timber cargo*
- 71   roundwood (round logs)
- 72   wood process products
- 8   grain and grind products
- 81   grain
- 82   grinding products
- 9 *other cargo*
- 91   chemicals and soda
- 92   non-ferrous metals and products from them
- 93   fluxes
- 94   hardware and metal construction materials
- 95   cellulose
- 96   cardboard, paper, printing products
- 97   agricultural products
- 98   compound feedstuff
- 99   food and drink products (except for mixed fodder)
- 9A   sugar
- 9B   scrap metal, other recyclables, waste
- 9B1   ferrous scrap
- 9B2   non-ferrous scrap
- 9B3   recyclables, waste, garbage
- 9C   textiles, garment production
- 9D   leather, leather goods and shoes
- 9E   rubber products
- 9F   other non-metal products not included in other groups
- 9G   hardware, machinery and equipment
- 9H   vehicles
- 9I   electrical equipment, electronic and optical equipment
- 9J   other goods not included in other groups

Exports and imports of goods (products) for regions of Russia are estimated on the basis of harmonized industrial statistics and foreign economic statistics. The volume of cargo load in the regions is estimated on the basis of production data. Interregional origin-destination transportation matrix for the regions and intraregional volumes of transportation are generated on the basis of transport statistics.

The balance is constructed for all regions of Russia. The calculations are based on the existing practice of statistical accounting in Russia without expensive additional surveys. The sequence of TEB formation is determined by the peculiarities of statistical accounting, the completeness and accuracy of the available source data on production, product shipment, trade and transportation of goods.

It should be mentioned that in Russia there is a well-established statistical accounting of production and interregional trade, as well as transport by modes of transport, but the quality of individual indicators is quite different. At the same time, in each industry and on each mode of transport, statistical recording implies its historically established range of goods (cargo) and its own level of spatial detail of statistical data.

Undoubtedly, the statistics of rail transportation is the best in Russia, it is known for the detailed cargo nomenclature and accounting origin-destination information detailed to the level of stations. These statistics are reliable and easily aggregated at the regional level into TEB harmonized cargo nomenclature. It is important that railway transport provides the vast majority of all cargo turnover in Russia (excluding pipeline transportation).

According to Rosstat, in 2016 the freight turnover of railway transport was 10 times higher than that of road transport, 36 times the domestic water transport and 54 times the cargo turnover performed by Russian enterprises of maritime transport (excluding foreign). The only drawback of the railway statistics is the lack of information on the transshipment of goods from the railway to the road and back. This deficiency is compensated partially by the fact that it is known which enterprises have direct access to the public and nonpublic railways.

The statistics of interport maritime transportation is a little bit less convenient, but still reliable. It is carried out on the basis of consignment notes and therefore is reasonably accurate, easily regionalized, but due to the narrow range of goods, it can be reflected without loss only to the abbreviated TEB harmonized cargo nomenclature. When described in the expanded nomenclature, there are losses in the quality of information, fortunately it has been empirically revealed that they are small. The advantage is the fact that the statistical accounting of cargo handling from the maritime to other modes of transport and back is adjusted.

Reliable is the statistics of production and shipment of large and medium-sized enterprises. The quality of statistics on small enterprises is not so good, but the contribution of small enterprises to the overall cargo shipment of Russia is small, and the methodology for its assessment is stable enough to consider this information conditionally reliable. Regardless of the number of enterprises covered by Rosstat surveys, the statistics of production and shipment of enterprises are easily regionalized and aggregated into the TEB nomenclature without loss.

The statistics of interregional trade in industrial and food products, raw materials and main types of agricultural products is convenient for the purposes of TEB. These statistics are also well regionalized and aggregated into the TEB without loss. Unfortunately, it covers only large and medium-sized enterprises and is not always accurate from a transport point of view. The reason is that the records are kept at the location of the buyer and seller of products, which, under Russian conditions, does not always reflect the actual location of the sender and receiver of the goods. A positive point is that the statistics of trade in the most important for Russia fuel and energy resources and fuel, maintained by Rosstat, is reliably and significantly more closely duplicated by the subordinate organizations of the Ministry of Energy of Russia.

The statistics of inland water transport is much less convenient for the purpose of forming the TEB. The advantage of this statistics is that it represents the OD-matrix of interregional transport by inland water transport. But this statistic has a number of significant drawbacks. First, it relies solely on the declarations of transportation by professional market participants, that is, organizations that declare inland water transport as the main activity. Meanwhile, significant volumes of transportation of timber and petroleum products are carried out by branches of organizations that have a main type of activity that differs from inland water transport. This gives them the opportunity not to be covered by statistical observation. The second drawback is the extremely narrow range of goods, which is recorded. Until 2017, statistics on inter-regional inland water transport was carried out for only 4 types of cargo. Since 2017, it is conducted on 10 types of cargo. This gives some inaccuracies in converting to TEB cargo nomenclature. Nevertheless, the advantage is that there is a statistics of trans-shipment of goods to other modes of transport and back for inland water transport.

The statistics of road transport is the worst in all senses. Until 2017, it did not include division by type of cargo. There is no assessment by Rosstat of the volumes of interregional transportation by road. There is only an estimate of the total volume of transportation by industry in the regions, but it also causes some confidence only in large and medium-sized enterprises. The situation is complicated by the fact that transportation by motor vehicles performed by small and micro enterprises, as well as individual entrepreneurs in the Russian context cannot be neglected, since their share in the road transport market is greater than that of large and medium-sized enterprises.

Thus, the statistical accounting of production, shipment, trade and transportation in Russia determines the specific sequence of TEB calculation.

First of all, when processing initial information, it is necessary to take into account that all sections of statistics may contain errors and inaccuracies. In addition, from year to year, the statistical accounting system in Russia is changing, new accounting rules, codes and indicators are introduced, which require special processing before performing the TEB calculations.

When converting input forms of statistical accounting to a form suitable for machine processing, the TEB operator eliminates obvious errors associated, for example, with the dimension of quantities, units of measurement, incorrect representation of numerical values, etc. Next, an analysis of changes in the regulatory and reference information of statistical accounting is carried out, if the statistical monitoring bodies enacted the changes last year. In order to take these changes into account, a special mechanism is provided to ensure the unification of the original statistical data and bring them to a universal internal form for presenting information on the production and transportation of cargo-intensive products. This mechanism is implemented using the tables of keys for conversion information from the source form to universal harmonized cargo nomenclature used in TEB. Conversion keys provide mapping of the initial information on cargo loading volume and cargo transportation to the internal TEB tables using a harmonized cargo nomenclature. When changing the original forms of statistical accounting, the operator configures the tables of conversion keys, which provide the ability to automatically download and process the initial statistical information for performing the TEB calculations.

Logical control of the initial statistical information is performed while preparing for the calculations. For example, the sums of various quantities in the regions are compared with similar values for Russia as a whole, as well as each other of identical data from different statistical forms are compared also. In case of discrepancy of these data, the operator clarifies the values of the original statistical information with the organization, which is the source of information. The calculation of TEB is performed as follows. First, on the basis of economic statistics, the cargo loading volume of industry, agriculture, trade, and also the recycling industry is calculated. Then, according to transport statistics, using the balance equations of the TEB (1) - (9), an estimate of the interregional transportation by rail, maritime and inland water transport is compiled.

The total volume of interregional transportation by road, including intraregional transportation (for itself), is estimated initially as the difference in the cargo loading volume (production output) and transportation by other modes of transport. Then the estimation of interregional transportation by road transport for each interregional correspondence for each type of cargo is derived from the difference in the known volumes of interregional trade and volumes of interregional transportation by rail, inland water and maritime transport. Other road transportation is considered as intraregional transportation (for itself). Multimodal transportation by rail, inland waterway and road transport is estimated using the statistical proportions of export of products produced by one or another type of transport, as well as balance equations of the TEB.

From the standpoint of the freight turnover of motor vehicles, the OD-matrix of interregional motor transportation obtained in this way can be considered a conservative estimate. This OD-matrix is refined using actual data on the intensity of the movement of vehicles on highways. The refining is performed by solving the optimization problem of minimizing the discrepancy of the estimated intensity of traffic and actual data on the intensity of movement of vehicles. The estimation of interregional origin-destination flows by road transport is specified to an upper value by reassigning a part of transportation previously assigned to intraregional carriages to interregional transportation.

The resultant TEB is represented by spatial input-output tables. It aggregates the actual and forecast origin-destination flows of freight traffic (OD-matrix) between the regions of the Russian Federation by all modes of transport by types of commodities described in terms of harmonized cargo nomenclature. This matrix accurately reflects the structure of interregional transportation by rail, inland water and maritime transport and successfully reflects the structure of interregional transportation by road. At least, the traffic estimation of road transport is consistent with the volume of shipments in Russia, transportation by other modes of transport and data from the traffic metering points on the roads. This means that the TEB is fairly accurate in general.

At the final stage of TEB calculation the results are checked and verified. The discrepancies of the balance are identified taking into account the balance equations of TEB (1) - (9). The obtained estimates of cargo transportation by types of commodities are compared with similar data from previous years. When large discrepancies and deviations are detected the input data is checked against the original data, the information processing errors are detected and the data is refined with provider. After the elimination of errors the transition to recalculation of the refined TEB is done.

The consolidated balance describes the departure and arrival of goods in the regions of Russia. The shipment balance reflects the shipment from some region to other regions of Russia and for export, and the arrival balance describes the arrival of goods in the region from other regions of Russia and by import. A consolidated spatial input-output table of domestic transportation of goods for the region by modes of transport, as well as a table of transportations from the region in export and import by modes of transport is built.

The results are implemented in the Information and Analytical System for Transport Regulation of the Ministry of Transport of the Russian Federation. The constructed transport and economic balance describes the actual and forecast volumes and origin-destination information of 97% of freight traffic between all the regions of the Russian Federation. The discrepancies in the initial data caused by the incompleteness and inaccuracy of the original statistics were corrected when constructing the balance. The criterion for eliminating discrepancies is the convergence of balance equations between regions, as well as for export and import.

The interregional discrepancy averages 3-5%, that is, the balance has an accuracy of 95%. Discrepancies are caused by inaccuracy and incompleteness of official statistical information and differences in accounting technology for various statistical forms, as well as small errors in converting data to unified cargo (product) accounting units used in TEB.

The forecast of cargo load and interregional freight flows of TEB covers the period up to 2030. The forecast model uses economic parameters and scenario conditions of the Ministry of Economic Development of Russia, as well as regional economic development scenarios (Fig. 8).

The software forecast model takes into account changes in technological and transport connectivity of main cargo generating industries, reflecting the technological links of these industries with resource suppliers and consumers of their products. At the same time, the forecast model uses the direct cost matrix of the symmetrical input-output table (inter-sectoral balance) for Russia as a whole.

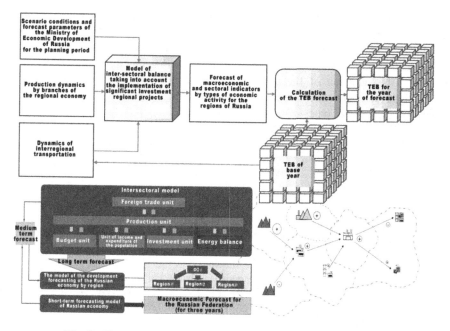

Fig. 8. Forecasting model in the transport and economic balance.

5   The Application of the Transport and Economic Balance

Actual and forecast TEB describing spatial input-output tables of transportation demand between territories of the country as well as export and import by types of commodities and means of transport provides a large amount of important information for transport planning.

TEB forecast together with current transport infrastructure data provides an assessment of imbalances in the use of various types of cargo transport, identification of cargo-intensive transport directions, determination of measures for switching traffic flows to the most profitable for society types of transport and development of the transport infrastructure capacity. For example, in planning of international transport corridors development (ITCs) for these purposes, along with TEB, an electronic passport ITC (EP ITC) can be used [2].

The TEB provides the basis for calculation and justification of the predicted loads on the infrastructure taking into account various options for its reconstruction and development. It will help to optimize distribution of the predicted flows through the network taking into account future characteristics of throughput, speeds and stability (predictability) of cargo delivery time, loading of network elements and bottlenecks. The most effective projects will be ranked and prioritized on this basis. Freight flows optimization criterion include price, time, reliability and safety of transportation, impact on the environment, taking into account capacity constraints. At the same time, the variation of tariffs makes it possible to evaluate various options for the redistribution of flows along the transport network.

Transport planning for certain territories and routes could use the following steps: analysis of the cargo load and traffic flows, search for imbalances, formation of project activities for specific territories and routes, calculation of key performance indicators for each solution, calculation costs and effects, including multiplicative effects in the economy, the selection of the most effective solutions via "cost-benefit analysis". Calculations can take into account various economy scenarios, different transport demand scenarios and types of commodities.

References

1. Evseev, O., Zaboev, A.: Prospects of electronic passportization of transport corridors in the EAEU within the context of transport digitalization. In: Prospects for the Development of the Transport Complex, pp. 9–12. BelNIIT, Minsk (2017). https://transtekhnika.by/upload/%D0%9C%D0%B0%D1%82%D0%B5%D1%80%D0%B8%D0%B0%D0%BB%D1%8B%20%D0%BA%D0%BE%D0%BD%D1%84%D0%B5%D1%80%D0%B5%D0%BD%D1%86%D0%B8%D0%B8%202017.pdf (in Russian)
2. Evseev, O.V., et al.: Transport and economic balance and its role in the coordination of transport planning during the digitalization era. Mod. Inf. Technol. IT-Educ. **14**(3), 717–726 (2018). https://doi.org/10.25559/SITITO.14.201803.717-726. (in Russian)
3. The use of mathematical methods and computers in planning the development and operation of transport. In: Chernomordik, G.I., Kozlov, I.T. (eds.). Transport, Moscow (1967). (in Russian)
4. Kovshov, G.N.: Transport in the system of long-term planning models of the national economy. Econ. Math. Methods **XIII**(5), 1034–1053 (1977). (in Russian)
5. Kovshov, G.N., Mikhailov, A.D.: About the transport factor in the system of optimal long-term planning of the national economy. In: Optimal Planning Challenges, Part II. CEMI USSR Academy of Sciences, Moscow (1973). (in Russian)
6. Livshits, V.N.: The choice of optimal solutions in the technical and economic calculations. Economics, Moscow (1971). (in Russian)
7. Methodical foundations for building a system of models of national economic planning in a sectoral and territorial context. CEMI USSR Academy of Sciences, Moscow (1980). (in Russian)
8. Transport strategy of the Russian Federation for the period up to 2030 of 22.11.2008 no. 1734-r as amended by the Order of the Government of the Russian Federation of 11.06.2014 no. 1032-r. In: Collection of Legislation of the Russian Federation no. 50, art. 5977. https://www.mintrans.ru/documents/3/1009. Accessed 08 Dec 2018
9. Shirov, A.A., Yantovsky, A.A.: Input-output macroeconomic model as the core of complex forecasting calculations. Stud. Russ. Econ. Dev. **25**(3), 225–234 (2014)
10. Brandsma, A., Ivanova, O., Kancs, d'A.: RHOMOLO – a dynamic spatial general equilibrium model. JRC IPTS, Seville, Spain (2011)
11. Ivanova, O.: The role of transport infrastructure in regional economic development. In: TØI Report 671/2003, Oslo (2003) https://www.toi.no/getfile.php?mmfileid=9223
12. Ivanova, O., Vold, A., Jean-Hansen, V.: PINGO: a model for prediction of regional and interregional freight transport. In: Version 1, TØI Rapport 578/2002, Oslo (2002) https://www.toi.no/getfile.php?mmfileid=2346
13. Commodity Flow Survey Overview. U.S. Department of Transportation, Bureau of Transportation Statistics. https://www.bts.gov/cfs. Accessed 08 Dec 2018

14. Core Database Development for the European Transport policy Information System (ETIS). EU Transport Research and Innovation Monitoring and Information System. https://trimis. ec.europa.eu/?q=project/core-database-development-european-transport-policy-information-system-etis. Accessed 08 Dec 2018

15. Dietzenbacher, E., Los, B., Stehrer, R., Timmer, M., de Vries, G.: The construction of world input-output tables in the WIOD project. Econ. Syst. Res. **25**(1), 71–98 (2013). https://doi. org/10.1080/09535314.2012.761180

16. Fachin, S., Venanzoni, G.: IDEM: an integrated demographic and economic model of Italy. In: Proceedings of the 14th International Conference on Input-Output Techniques, CONSIP S.p.A. (2002) https://www.iioa.org/conferences/14th/files/Fachiim.pdf

17. Gaulier, G., Zignago, S.: BACI: international trade database at the product-level. In: The 1994-2007 Version. CEPII Working Paper 2010-23. (2010). http://www.cepii.fr/CEPII/en/ publications/wp/abstract.asp?NoDoc=2726

18. Helpman, E., Melitz, M., Rubinstein, Y.: Estimating trade flows: trading partners and trading volumes. Q. J. Econ. **123**(2), 441–487 (2008). https://doi.org/10.1162/qjec.2008.123.2.441

19. Lenzen, M., Moran, D., Kanemoto, K., Geschke, A.: Building EORA: a global multi-region input-output database at high country and sector resolution. Econ. Syst. Res. **25**(1), 20–49 (2013). https://doi.org/10.1080/09535314.2013.769938

20. Narayanan, G., Badri, A.A., McDougall, R.: Global Trade, Assistance, and Production: The Gtap 8 Data Base. Purdue University, Center for Global Trade Analysis (2012). https://www. gtap.agecon.purdue.edu/databases/v8/v8_doco.asp

21. Measuring material flows and resource productivity. In: The OECD Guide, vol. I. OECD (2008) https://www.oecd.org/environment/indicators-modelling-outlooks/MFA-Guide.pdf. Accessed 08 Dec 2018

22. STAN Database for Structural Analysis. Organisation for Economic Cooperation and Development (OECD). In: ISIC Rev. 3, SNA93. https://stats.oecd.org/index.Aspx? Datasetcode=stan08bis. Accessed 08 Dec 2018

23. Sivakumar, A.: Modelling Transport: A Synthesis of Transport Modelling Methodologies. Imperial College London Working Paper (2007)

24. Sorratini, J.A.: Estimating statewide truck trips using commodity flows and input-output coefficients. J. Transp. Stat. **3**(1), 53–67 (2000) https://www.bts.gov/sites/bts.dot.gov/files/ legacy/publications/journal_of_transportation_and_statistics/volume_03_number_01/jts_ v3_n1.pdf

25. Global Material Flows Database. http://www.Materialflows.net. Accessed 08 Dec 2018

26. Heyndrickx, Ch., Kartseva, M., Tourdyeva, N.: The SUST-RUS database: regional social accounting matrix for Russia. In: SUST-RUS Project Report (2011) http://www.cefir.ru/ index.php?l=eng&id=528. Accessed 08 Dec 2018

27. Tukker, A., et al.: Towards a global multi-regional environmentally extended input-output database. Ecol. Econ. **68**(7), 1928–1937 (2009). https://doi.org/10.1016/j.ecolecon.2008.11. 010

28. United Nations Statistics Division. In: UN Comtrade – United Nations Commodity Trade Statistics Database. New York, NY, USA, United Nations Statistics Division (UNSD) (2012) https://unstats.un.org/unsd/databases.htm. Accessed 08 Dec 2018

29. United Nations Statistics Division. In: United Nations Service Trade Statistics Database. New York, NY, USA, United Nations Statistics Division (UNSD) (2017) https://unstats.un. org/unsd/databases.htm. Accessed 08 Dec 2018

Mobile Technologies in Intelligent Transportation Systems

Igor Malygin[1] , Yaroslav Seliverstov[1,2(✉)] ,
Svyatoslav Seliverstov[1,2] , Mikhail Silnikov[3] ,
Roza Muksimova[4] , Gleb Gergel[4] , Victoria Chigur[5] ,
and Shakib Fahmi[1,6]

[1] Solomenko Institute of Transport Problems of the Russian Academy
of Sciences, 12-th Line V.O. 13, 199178 Saint-Petersburg, Russia
malygin_com@mail.ru, silver8yr@gmail.com,
amuanator@rambler.ru, shakeebf@mail.ru
[2] Peter the Great Saint-Petersburg Polytechnical University, Polytechnicheskaya
Street 29, 195251 Saint-Petersburg, Russia
[3] Saint-Petersburg University of State Fire Service of Emercom of Russia,
Moscow Avenue 149, 196105 Saint-Petersburg, Russia
pr@igps.ru
[4] Saint Petersburg State University of Civil Aviation, Pilotov Street 38,
196210 Saint Petersburg, Russia
K16@spbguga.ru, Glebgergel@yandex.ru
[5] Saint-Petersburg State University, Universitetskaya Emb. 7-9,
199034 Saint-Petersburg, Russia
[6] Saint Petersburg Electrotechnical University "LETI",
Professora Popova Street 5, 197376 Saint-Petersburg, Russia

Abstract. An analysis is made of the use of cellular communication as part of intelligent transportation systems to collect information on traffic flows and population mobility. The model of the monitoring system of urban population social activity is created. The reliability of the model is demonstrated with the City Navigator mobile application. The application is developed in the Xcode 9 environment in Swift3 language, and the data analysis system - in Python 3.X. The application serves as the information source for preferential routing, enables to assess the quality of the urban system facilities and take into account the infrastructure, transport, needs, locations, photo-registration and users GPS tracks. User's GPS tracks are tied to the classifiers of the Unified System of Classification and Codification of Technical and Economic and Social Information (USCCTESI) and the International Classification of Diseases of the Tenth View (ICD-10). The practical guidelines for the further use of mobile applications as part of intelligent transportation systems are indicated.

Keywords: Intelligent transportation systems · Mobile applications · Transport behavior

© Springer Nature Switzerland AG 2020
V. Sukhomlin and E. Zubareva (Eds.): Convergent 2018, CCIS 1140, pp. 384–391, 2020.
https://doi.org/10.1007/978-3-030-37436-5_33

1   Introduction

Approaches to the organization and management of urban transportation systems are undergoing significant changes caused by the growing population of megacities, social processes complication, rapid development of mobile and Internet technologies. Conventional urban and regional transport management requires time critical transition to intelligent and cognitive transportation systems [1] efficient enough to transform the urban environment and population social activity. Such systems should possess comprehensive information on a wide range of activities and enable its "smart" collection, receive-transmit, processing, analysis, storage and use.

Such technological solutions include user applications based on preferential routing methods [2], traffic management methods based on users' targets and transportation system [3], methods for analyzing the classifier structure of the transport flow and individual user characteristics [4, 5], methods for intelligent routing of urban services vehicles [6], methods for prevention of road accidents causes [7], technologies of augmented reality [8], methods for traffic flows modeling [9, 10] based on origin–destination matrix restoration [11] considering transport coverage indices [12] and urban population social activity chains [13, 14], and many others.

Mass development of wireless Internet access points [15] and mobile communication as an everyday active means of electronic communication of city residents enable to consider it as a reliable source of latest statistical information for the city needs.

The information from smart-mobility knowledge bases can later be used to design the preferential routes systems [2], i.e. to lay routes not only the shortest in distance or in time but also take into account a lot of personal criteria. These include: "Non-infectious routes" - routes that are not used by people with infectious diseases; "Routes for acquaintances" - routes on which unmarried people move; "Safe routes" - routes on which no events of criminal nature were recorded; and many others.

Information on the structure of the traffic flow by gender and work (profession, education) characteristics will expand the toolkit of transport and industry modeling and enable to optimize transport flows according to professional criteria. Moreover urban services are able to monitor the quality of public urban services in a timely manner having users' information on the quality of transport infrastructure.

2   Problems

Thus the following is required for the rapid analysis of population social activity:

1. real-time information on the population transport movements in the form of GPS tracks;
2. classification of the population social structure, destinations, and the reasons for the residents transport activity;
3. information about the used transport mode;
4. information on social activities and name of the resident's location in real time;
5. rapid assessment of the quality of transport services and resident's locations.

The information received will enable to reconstruct the matrices of transport correspondence and daily chains of population social activity.

3 Methods

We begin by introducing a formal definition for social activity and building a formal model for the monitoring system of the urban population social activity (hereinafter referred to as the system). By formal social activity of the user we mean a set of socio-economic, consumer, transportation, behavioral, information-network and other user activities that existing mobile information systems are able to register.

The formal model of the system F_M is given by the following set of functional according to (1):

$$F^M = \langle \hat{F}_D; \hat{F}_N\,; \hat{F}_C; \hat{F}_T; \hat{F}_R \rangle_T\,, \tag{1}$$

where $\hat{F}_D : H_C \underset{f_\partial}{\oplus} O_S = H_D$ is the functional of directivization which assigns to each resident from a multitude of city H_C a directive element of the system O_S or a mobile cellular communication device and transfers it into a multitude of users H_D; $\hat{F}_N : H_D \rightarrow N$ is the functional of identification of the elementary multitude H_C which assigns to each object from H_D an identifier or a set of identifiers from multitude N; $\hat{F}_C : H_D \times N \rightarrow CH$ is the characteristic parameterization functional of users H_D which assigns to each user from H_D with a unique number from N sets of characteristics CH inherent to the given user such that $CH = \{ch_\pi^{h_d}, \pi = 1,\ldots,N_\pi\}$ is a multitude of characteristics of users CH, and $ch_\pi^{h_d}$ is given by a tuple $ch_\pi^{h_d} = \langle name, \{value\}\rangle$ where name is the name of the π characteristic, {value} is the value of the π characteristic from multitude of characteristics Π; $\hat{F}_T : H_D \rightarrow \left[\tau_T^{def} \vee (\tau_T; \tau_{T+1})\right]$ is a time operator that assigns to each object from H_D a certain moment or time interval from a multitude of moments or time intervals T on which a relation of strict order is given, i.e. $\tau_1 < \tau_2, \ldots \tau_T < \tau_{T+1}$, $\tau_T^{def} \in T$ is a certain point in time; $\hat{F}_S : H_D \times CH \times N \rightarrow DATE$ is a transaction operator that transfers information about the user H_D with the identifier from N and characteristics CH into data $DATE$.

Thus the objective function of the subjective transport utility Φ^M of users H_D determined by their transport-logistic behavior B_D will tend to the maximum as the information $DATE$ increases from $\hat{F}_S$ according to (2):

$$\Phi^M = B_D \overset{F_S}{\times} DATE \rightarrow \Phi_{\max}^M, \tag{2}$$

The chains of users social activity [17] are given by a multitude of dynamic agent graphs expressed through transport-logistic behavior of users B_D.

Then each user $h_i \in H_D$ can be associated with his transport-logistic behavior (social activity) $B_t^{h_i} \in B_D$ according to (3):

$$B_t^{h_i} \in \Gamma_t^{h_i}\left(\left(\begin{array}{c} \Gamma_t^{GPS}(V;E) \cup \Gamma_t^L(V;E) \cup \Gamma_t^N(V;E) \cup \Gamma_t^T(V;E) \cup \\ \cup \Gamma_t^E(V;E) \cup \Gamma_t^Q(V;E) \cup \Gamma_t^F(V;E) \cup \Gamma_t^C(V;E) \end{array}\right); T\right), \qquad (3)$$

where $\Gamma_t^{h_i}(();T)$ is the graph of the social activity of the user h_i; $\Gamma_t^{GPS}(V;E)$ - the graph of the spatial activity of the user h_i; $\Gamma_t^L(V;E)$ - the graph of the infrastructure activity of the user h_i; $\Gamma_t^N(V;E)$ - the graph of consumer activity of the user h_i, $\Gamma_t^E(V;E)$ - meals schedule of the user h_i, $\Gamma_t^T(V;E)$- the graph of transport activity of the user h_i; $\Gamma_t^Q(V;E)$ - the graph of the quality assessment of urban facilities of the user h_i; $\Gamma_t^F(V;E)$ - the graph of the media-event activity of the user h_i; $\Gamma_t^C(V;E)$ - the graph of the recommendation-news activity of the user h_i.

Thus by allocating compound graphs in the graph of the user social activity it becomes possible to analyze the user social activity through infrastructure, consumer, transport, spatial and other components (3) taking into account the rank evaluation of the quality of each.

4 Software Example and Results

A mobile application to register the users' social activity is developed in *Xcode 9* environment in *Swift 3* language, and the data analysis system in *Python* 3.X. The mobile application was called *City Navigator*. The software-algorithmic development of the application was carried out in several stages.

A conceptual scheme of the application was developed and its main components were defined at the first stage in accordance with the tasks set, namely:

- *Firebase* - a database in. json format;
- *imagesArray []* - image database (photos);
- *commentsArray []* - users comments database;
- *ratingArray []* - evaluation of the event quality by the user;
- *allUsersData []* - all user data;
- *time* - the time of the event registration in the format Date.Month.Year, Hours. Minutes;
- *coordinate* - coordinates of longitude and latitude in GPS-format.

The conceptual scheme of City Navigator mobile application is presented in Fig. 1.

At the second stage, a mobile application interface was created. The mobile application interface consists of 6 "screen-tabs". The layout of 3 out of 6 of the "screen-tabs" is shown in Fig. 2.

Each tab contains response templates and fill-in fields that reflect a specific set of characteristics inherent to a particular activity or user condition. The user independently fills in the necessary information about themselves.

The user also has the opportunity to leave a comment and make a photo-recording of the event which refers to the information reflected in this tab.

At the second stage the application software is developed according to the formal model (1): keys are programmed, logic is specified and event handlers are written.

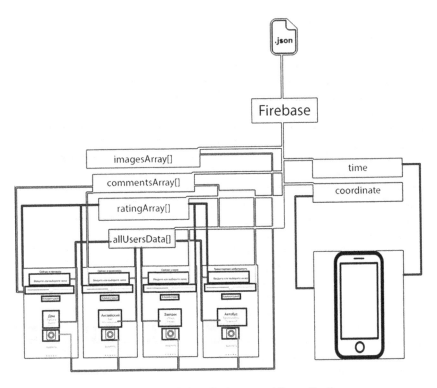

Fig. 1. Layout of *City Navigator* mobile application.

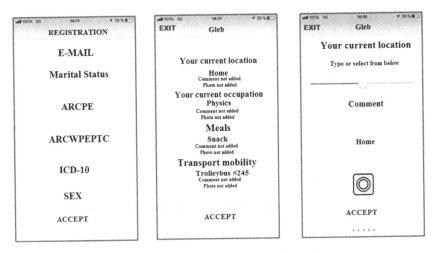

Fig. 2. Interface of City Navigator mobile application.

GPS tracks in the City Navigator application are built in reference to the classifiers All-Russian classifier of workers professions employees posts and tariff categories (ARCWPEPTC), All-Russian Classifier of Information on Population (Sex, Marital status), All-Russian Classifier of Professions by Education (ARCPE) from Unified System of Classification and Codification of Technical and Economic and Social Information and ICD-10[1] (Figure 3).

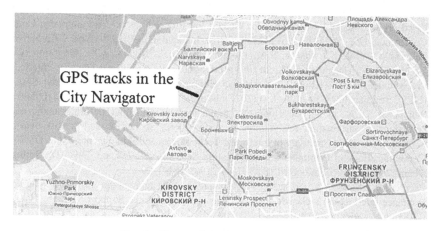

Fig. 3. User social activity (GPS tracks).

Thus City Navigator surpasses the existing pedestrian navigators in terms of informational content. Integration of classifiers from the Unified System of Classification and Codification of Technical and Economic and Social Information and ICD-10 enables using it as a part of the mobile component of the system of state regional operational transport statistics.

5   Conclusion

In the course of this study a model of a mobile monitoring system for the urban population social activity was developed and the possibility of its integration with transport and economic modeling systems was demonstrated. It is proposed to form the social activity of users within the scope of the developed model through infrastructural, transport, consumer, location [16], rating, media-event (photo-registration) and recommendation-news (comments) components of activity. For the first time classifiers from the Unified System of Classification and Codification of Technical and Economic and Social Information and ICD-10 are used as user identifiers. For the first time the use of state classifiers in urban social activity monitoring systems enables to proceed to

---

[1] ICD-10 – 10th revision of the International Statistical Classification of Diseases and Related Health Problems.

the analysis of operational state statistical accounting within the scope of the Unified System of Classification and Codification of Technical and Economic and Social Information at the regional level.

References

1. Diveev, A.I., Sofronova, E.A.: Synthesis of intelligent control of traffic flows in urban roads based on the logical network operator method. In: Proceedings of 2013 European Control Conference, ECC 2013, pp. 3512–3517 (2013). https://doi.org/10.23919/ecc.2013.6669696
2. Seliverstov, Y.A., Seliverstov, S.A., Lukomskaya, O.Y., Nikitin, K.V., Grigoriev, V.A., Vydrina, E.O.: The method of selecting a preferred route based on subjective criteria. In: Proceedings of 2017 IEEE II International Conference on Control in Technical Systems (CTS), St. Petersburg, pp. 126–130 (2017). https://doi.org/10.1109/ctsys.2017.8109506
3. Seliverstov, Y.A., et al.: Development of management principles of urban traffic under conditions of information uncertainty. In: Kravets, A., Shcherbakov, M., Kultsova, M., Groumpos, P. (eds.) Creativity in Intelligent Technologies and Data Science, CIT&DS 2017. Communications in Computer and Information Science, vol. 754, pp. 399–418. Springer, Cham (2017). https://doi.org/10.1007/978-3-319-65551-2_29
4. Paefgen, J., Staake, T., Thiesse, F.: Evaluation and aggregation of pay-as-you-drive insurance rate factors: a classification analysis approach. Decis. Support Syst. 56, 192–201 (2013). https://doi.org/10.1016/j.dss.2013.06.001
5. Seliverstov, Y.A., Seliverstov, S.A., Lukomskaya, O.Y., Fahmi, S.S., Vydrina, E.O., Firstov, A.A.: Application of the trilinear model in the problems of improving the quality of management of inland water transportations. Mar. Intellect. Technol. 1(1), 174–184 (2018). (in Russian)
6. Xin, Q., Fu, R., Yuan, W., Liu, Q., Yu, S.: Predictive intelligent driver model for eco-driving using upcoming traffic signal information. Phys. A Stat. Mech. Appl. 508, 806–823 (2018). https://doi.org/10.1016/j.physa.2018.05.138
7. Seliverstov, Ya.A., Seliverstov, Sv.A., Komashinskiy, V.I., Tarantsev, A.A., Shatalova, N. V., Grigoriev, V.A.: Intelligent systems preventing road traffic accidents in megalopolises in order to evaluate. In: Proceedings of 2017 XX IEEE International Conference on Soft Computing and Measurements (SCM), St. Petersburg, pp. 489–492 (2017). https://doi.org/10.1109/scm.2017.7970626
8. Abdi, L., Abdallah, E.B., Meddeb, A.: In-vehicle augmented reality traffic information system: a new type of communication between driver and vehicle. Procedia Comput. Sci. 73, 242–249 (2015). https://doi.org/10.1016/j.procs.2015.12.024
9. Seliverstov, Y.A., Malygin, I.G., Komashinskiy, V.I., Tarantsev, A.A., Shatalova, N.V., Petrova, V.A.: The St. Petersburg transport system simulation before opening new subway stations. In: Proceedings of 2017 XX IEEE International Conference on Soft Computing and Measurements (SCM), St. Petersburg, pp. 284–287 (2017). https://doi.org/10.1109/scm. 2017.7970562
10. Seliverstov, S.A., Malygin, I.G., Starichenkov, A.L., Muksimova, R.R., Grigoriev, V.A., Asaul, A.N.: Modeling of megalopolis traffic flows with the introduction of a new line of water intercity passenger transport. In: Proceedings of 2017 XX IEEE International Conference on Soft Computing and Measurements (SCM), St. Petersburg, pp. 278–280 (2017). https://doi.org/10.1109/scm.2017.7970560

11. Hazelton, M.L.: Statistical inference for time varying origin–destination matrices. Transp. Res. Part B Methodol. **42**(6), 542–552 (2008). https://doi.org/10.1016/j.trb.2007. 11.003

12. Santos, A.S., Ribeiro, S.K.: The role of transport indicators to the improvement of local governance in Rio de Janeiro City: a contribution for the debate on sustainable future. Case Stud. Transp. Policy **3**(4), 415–420 (2015). https://doi.org/10.1016/j.cstp.2015.08.006

13. Shoval, N.: Monitoring and managing visitors flows in destinations using aggregate GPS data. In: Gretzel, R.L., Fuchs, M. (eds.) Information and Communication Technologies in Tourism 2010, pp. 171–183. Springer, Vienna (2010). https://doi.org/10.1007/978-3-211-99407-8_15

14. Sierpiński, G. (ed.): Intelligent Transport Systems and Travel Behaviour. AISC, vol. 505. Springer, Cham (2017). https://doi.org/10.1007/978-3-319-43991-4

15. Habtie, A.B., Abraham, A., Midekso, D.: Artificial neural network based real-time urban road traffic state estimation framework. In: Abraham, A., Falcon, R., Koeppen, M. (eds.) Computational Intelligence in Wireless Sensor Networks. SCI, vol. 676, pp. 73–97. Springer, Cham (2017). https://doi.org/10.1007/978-3-319-47715-2_4

16. Qin, G., Li, T., Yu, B., Wang, Y., Huang, Z., Sun, J.: Mining factors affecting taxi drivers' incomes using GPS trajectories. Transp. Res. Part C Emerg. Technol. **79**, 103–118 (2017). https://doi.org/10.1016/j.trc.2017.03.013

Digital Railway and How to Move from GSM-R to LTE-R and 5G

Manfred Sneps-Sneppe[1] and Dmitry Namiot[2(✉)]

[1] Ventspils University of Applied Sciences,
Inženieru Str. 101a, Ventspils 3601, Latvia
[2] Lomonosov Moscow State University, Leninskie Gory, 1, GSP-1,
119991 Moscow, Russia
dnamiot@gmail.com

Abstract. The paper is devoted to telecommunication services for digital railways. We discuss a transition from GSM-R to LTE-R and 5G technologies. As a practical use case, we target urban railways development in Moscow, Russia. According to the European Commission, digital railways development should create so-called connected railways by providing reliable connectivity for safe, efficient and attractive railways, enhancing customer experience. It should provide added value for customers, increased capacity by enhanced reliability, efficiency, and performance of railways. In this connection, we discuss the critical elements of 5G deployment and the practical steps to move from the current telecommunication services to 5G. As historical examples, we are considering the largest projects of the transformation of the telecommunications infrastructure. As basic examples for GSM-R transition and switch to digital railways, we discuss Moscow Central Ring and Moscow Central Diameters. The paper highlights several tasks for telecom providers in Russia. In particularly, it is the development of the GSM-R network architecture taking into account existing networks, including interaction with an intelligent network, as well as the need to upgrade existing networks.

Keywords: 5G · Digital railways · GSM-R

1 Introduction

The landscape for railway telecommunications in Europe has changed drastically since the turn of the century. From 35 separate analogue systems in 2000, a single, interoperable railway communications system now exists across much of the European railway network: GSM-R. In 2016, 60 countries on five continents were using GSM-R, with more than 100,000 km of lines covered in Europe [1]. Work is underway now to lay the framework for a new standardized railway telecommunications network to replace GSM-R: the railway sector is ready to replace its existing 2G networks.

The paper presents our attempt to understand the transition from the GSM-R network to the LTE-R and 5G-R - whether it takes place at all? [2]. Communication specialists around the world are facing the same problem: shifting from circuit switching to packet switching.

© Springer Nature Switzerland AG 2020
V. Sukhomlin and E. Zubareva (Eds.): Convergent 2018, CCIS 1140, pp. 392–402, 2020.
https://doi.org/10.1007/978-3-030-37436-5_34

As a prototype, we are considering the evolution of Pentagon telecommunications [3] (in Sect. 2). GSM-R basics and discussion on future of railway radio are discussed in Sects. 3 and 4. Section 5 is devoted to Moscow transport plans.

2 Looking for Parallels: Pentagon Case

2.1 Joint Vision 2010

The Defense Information Systems Network (DISN) has been developing since the early 1990s. This is a global network. Its purpose is to provide services for the transfer of various types of information (speech, data, video, multimedia) for the effective and secure control of troops, communications, reconnaissance, and EW.

When they began to implement the Joint Vision 2010 plan, they analyzed the state of DISN, and many shortcomings had revealed. First of all, this is the low level of integration of many hundreds of networks included in DISN, which significantly limits interaction within a single network and hampers effective unified management of all its resources. In particular, the interaction between stationary and field (mobile) components of the core network was noted due to the difference in: the standards used, the types of communication channels (analog and digital), the services provided, the capacity (for a mobile component, it is significantly lower than for a fixed).

In 1996, "Joint Vision 2010" - a strategic development plan for US military departments for a 15-year period has been approved. Under conditions of technological uncertainty, DISA has made a principled decision to build US military communications networks using the "open architecture" and commercial-off-the-shelf (COTS) products. As a result, the choice fell on the "old" developments of Bell Labs, namely, on the telephone signaling protocol SS7 and on the Advanced Intelligent Network (AIN). Note that by the time the Bell Labs Institute had a long ago liquidated (as well as the Bell System - in 1983).

Signaling System No. 7 is, figuratively speaking, the nervous system of the communication network. SS7 is a set of signaling telephone protocols used to establish telephone connections around the world. The main feature of SS7 is that the transmission of messages for establishing telephone connections use a separate signal channel. SS7 protocols had been developed at Bell Labs since 1975 and in 1981 were defined as ITU standards.

Users of AIN can be both subscribers of the circuit switched network and packet switched. Note that the intelligent network also has a transportable part (shown at the bottom left). For example, in the war in Afghanistan, a telephone stations with SSP/Adjunct functions, Intelligent Peripheral and Database equipment were delivered by air to service Deployed Forces. On the DISN network the connections are established using SS7 signaling, i.e., the SS7 network is full in the core of the network, and devices of any type are used on the periphery. Despite the fact that all new terminal equipment appears on the global military network, it is largely an IP means, SS7 network nevertheless retains its central place.

From this, we make an important conclusion: the presence of the SS7 network does not prevent the transition to IP protocols, but rather the opposite - it facilitates the transition to packet switching, makes it in step-by-step mode.

2.2   Joint Vision 2020: Transition to IP Protocol

Only four years have passed since the "Joint Vision 2010" plan was launched in 1996, as lobbyists of Internet technologies persuaded the Pentagon leadership in updating the weapons program, and a document "Joint Vision 2020" appeared. In 2007, Pentagon published a fundamental program [4], in which we find the key main point: single Global Information Grid (GIG) must be built on the basis of IP protocol as the only means of communication between the transport layer and applications.

The transition from the circuit switched network, where the SS7 protocol prevails, to packet switching and AS-SIP protocol requires the installation of SoftSwitch gateways. The Department of Defense has developed detailed methodological materials on the implementation of AS-SIP (much more sophisticated than SIP one). It is still difficult to predict the time during which the DISN network will finally switch to the AS-SIP protocol.

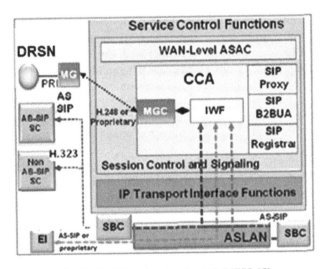

Fig. 1. Multifunctional softswitch MFSS [5].

Let us explain how the multifunctional softswitch MFSS will manage calls (Fig. 1):

- The IWF (ISUP-SIP interworking function) function is used towards the external PSTN or ISDN network.
- The MFSS controller provides "old" PSTN/ISDN signaling, including ISUP, CCS7/SS7, and CAS (Channel Associated Signaling).
- MFSS acts as a media gateway (MG) between TDM channels and IP channels. The media gateway is under control of MGC via H.248 protocol.
- The Signaling Gateway (SG) provides communication between CCS7 and SIP.

In the MFSS environment, there are also EI (End Instrument) in the circuit-switched network and two types of devices in the IP network: AEI (Assured Services End Instrument) operating using AS-SIP protocol, as well as non-standard PIE Instrument. It is worth mentioning two difficulties faced by supporters of the IP transition: DRSN and cybersecurity.

2.3   The Failure of the DISN Cybersecurity Management Project

In June 2012, Lockheed Martin won the largest tender for managing the GIG network (Global Services Management-Operations, GSM-O). The essence of the GSM-O contract is the modernization of the GIG network management system for cybersecurity requirements. The cost of work is a huge amount - 4.6 billion dollars for 7 years. In 2013, the GSM-O team began to study the status of the four GIG network management centers that are responsible for the maintenance and uninterrupted operation of all Pentagon computer networks - 8,100 computer systems in more than 460 locations in the world, which in turn are connected by 46,000 cables. The first deal was to upgrade the GIG management system, namely, to consolidate the operating centers - from four to two.

Cybersecurity targets are the Pentagon's top priority, but the lack of necessary standards hampers the implementation of the entire GSM-O program. In 2015, the world of telecommunications was shocked by the news: Lockheed Martin is not coping with the upgrade of the DISN network management, that is, with the implementation of a multi-billion dollar GSM-O contract, and sells its division "LM Information and Global Solutions" to the competing firm Leidos. The failure of the work was most likely due to the inability to recruit developers capable of combining the "old" circuit switching equipment with the latest packet switching systems as well as taking into account the new requirements of cybersecurity.

2.4   Resume

Let us recall that the shifting from circuit switching to packet switching is one highly expensive and risky deal. Three above named technologies – GSM, SS7 and IN - are part of the gold fund of the inventiveness of human beings but very old. System GSM had invented in the late 1980s by ETSI and until now is the most popular technology. The SS7 protocols had developed at Bell Labs since 1975 and in 1981 defined as ITU standards. The same age – 35+ years passed before Bell Labs developed and in 1982 launched the electronic telephone exchange 5ESS in which the principles of an intelligent network were implemented.

3   GSM-R Basics

3.1   ERTMS System Overview

The definition of European Rail Traffic Management System (ERTMS) was the result of the European efforts to promote interoperability. ERTMS includes three levels [6].

Among them, ERTMS levels 2 and 3 employ GSM-R as the basis that supports communications. In Europe, a 4 MHz bandwidth is reserved for such communications. The main elements of ERTMS are:

- ETCS: it allows for automating train control. It consists of a Radio Block Center and a Lineside Electronic Unit. ETCS can be divided into three levels:
- ETCS level 1: the location of the train is determined by traditional means (i.e., no beacons are used for locating the train), whereas communications between fixed safety infrastructure and trains are performed by means of beacons (transponders placed between the rails of a railway track). GSM-R is only used for voice communications.
- ETCS level 2: the communications between trains and the railway infrastructure are continuous and supported by GSM-R technology. The location of the train is estimated by means of fixed beacons.
- ETCS level 3: the integrity of the train elements is checked at the train, thus no devices are required in the track. Fixed beacons are used to locate the train.
- EURORADIO GSM-R: radio infrastructure.
- EUROBALISE: beacons allowing for locating the trains accurately.
- EUROCAB: on-board management system that includes European Vital Computer, Driver-Machine Interface, and measurement devices such as odometers.

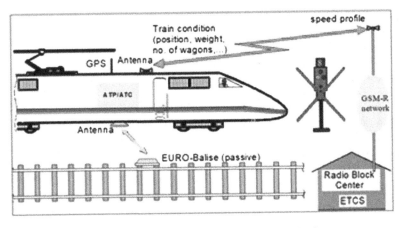

Fig. 2. European Train Control System ETCS [6].

The interface between the fixed parts of ETCS is the RBC (Radio Block Centre) and for GSM-R the MSC (Mobile Switching Centre). This interface is using the protocol ISDN 30B+D that consists of 30 64 kb/s B-connections plus a 16 kb/s D-channel for signaling purposes. Together this makes up a 2 Mb/s connection. Between the MSC and the more outspread part of the GSM-R system, the BSC (Base Station Controller), two 2 Mb/s systems is used for redundancy sake. The same applies for the connection between the BSC and the BTS (Base Transceiver System), but for security reasons the BTS is connected in a loop, always having two possible connections. The transmission media can be optofibre cable, coaxial cables or radio links, the latter often used in rural conditions (Fig. 2).

3.2   Radio Channels and Available Frequencies

Dedicated frequencies are reserved for the use of GSM-R for operational communications by railway companies. For uplink communication, 4 MHz is reserved in the 876–880 MHz band, and for downlink 4 MHz in the 921–925 MHz band. As these frequencies are agreed on a European basis, they allow border crossing and international traffic. The 4 MHz for GSM-R makes 19 frequency channels of 200 kHz each available. One of the frequency channels is used as a guard band.

Each 200 kHz frequency channel has 8 timeslots available to be used as data or voice channels, whereof one is used as the common control channel for the radio system (this concept is called Common Channel Signalling and is used for the internal control of the radio transmission system), and the remaining 7 are used for voice or data communication. One control channel can be used for two frequency channels, making 7 + 8 = 15 timeslots/channels available for communication (Table 1).

Using circuit switching, there are 19 frequencies available. Each frequency contains 7 timeslots for communication, making a total 19 × 7 = 133 channels for communication. If using the concept of one control channel for two frequencies, this makes a total of 142 available. These channels shall be used for both voice and ETCS data communication.

Table 1. GSM-R Services [6].

Service group	Type of service	Cab	Shunting
Voice-call	Point-to-point	MI	M
	Public emergency Broadcast	M	M
	Group	M	M
	Multi-party	MI	M
		MI	M
Data	Text message	MI	M
	General data applications	M	O
Specific features	Functional addressing (FA)	MI	M
	Location dependent addressing (LDA)	MI	O
	Shunting mode	MI	M
	Multiple driver communications within some train	MI	NA
	Railway emergency calls	MI	M

Note: Mandatory for Interoperability (MI), Mandatory for the System (M), Optional (O).

4   Discussion: The Future of Railway Radio

Work is underway now to lay the framework for a new standardized railway telecommunications network to replace GSM-R beginning in 2021 or 2022. But a great deal of uncertainty persists over the technology that this new network will use and whether the railway sector is ready to replace its existing 2G networks [1]. There is a problem. GSM-R is a second-generation telecommunications system, which means it is a long way behind today's 4G technology, let alone 5G, which is expected to emerge around 2020 (Fig. 3). And while providers have committed to maintaining GSM-R up to 2030, beyond this it will become increasingly difficult, and expensive, for infrastructure managers to retain the same quality of service. In response, work is now underway to prepare the industry for the transition to a new radio system and associated technologies. 5G stable products below and above 6 GHz may be available by the time of migration from GSM-R to the next standard radio system.

4.1   The Biggest Challenge

Nevertheless, it is spectrum allocation rather than radio technology, which is described as the biggest challenge facing the deployment of this new technology and the future of railway communications. GSM-R is currently located within the 4 MHz of the R-GSM band.

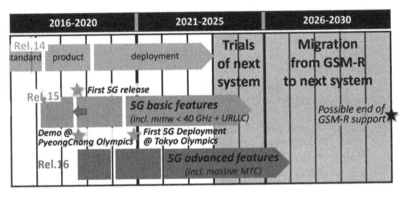

Fig. 3. Roadmap of 5G deployments [7].

However, there is evidence that coexistence of GSM-R and a future system within this band is not possible without a substantial degradation of the level of service. A 2016 study by LS Telecom considered whether LTE/LTE Advanced, as the only practical candidate currently available, could be used effectively in the same band as GSM-R. It found that it is not possible to introduce LTE in the GSM-R band without a number of technical mitigating measures while there is insufficient capacity to allow coexistence without some degradation. The study also concluded that LTE would provide extra data capacity but potentially reduce the capacity of GSM-R. In addition, in areas of high traffic density or border areas, the capacity for both services would be severely reduced.

To counter these problems, railways may be forced to explore the use of a different frequency for the new system, with the frequencies both below and above 1 GHz available as possible alternatives. However, this could drastically increase costs due to the requirements to install new infrastructure compatible with an alternative frequency.

For GSM-R, Kapsch, Huawei, and Nokia have supplied the industry, while Ericsson is currently addressing the market with its LTE solution. Mr, Thomas Chatelet, project officer in the ERTMS Unit at the Agency (the European Agency for Railways), says that for the next generation, it is expected that these vendors will continue to lead the way, but with opportunities for others, including current signalling suppliers, to come up with their own solutions [1].

4.2 Research

Huawei is continuing to push 4G LTE and 4.5G LTE as the preferred solution and is engaged in various research and development activities. Huawei will take a critical step forward with the rollout of 4G LTE on a China Railway main line in 2017. Companies already offer LTE network equipment compatible with GSM-R. The Huawei Technologies strategy consists of three steps: Step 1 - Only GSM-R network, Step 2 - Parallel operation of GSM-R and LTE networks: GSM-R provides reliable (encrypted) communications for the control of trains, LTE transmits unprotected data, Step 3 - A single platform "LTE for railway" is being created.

5 The Great Moscow Agglomeration Case

5.1 Moscow Metro and Wi-Fi and LTE

People can use free Wi-Fi by accessing the Moscow Transport (MT_FREE) network [8]. Several million people use the network daily. All Moscow Metro line trains, Moscow Central Circle (MCC) trains, and Aeroexpress trains now feature the Moscow Transport (MT_FREE) Wi-Fi network. Passengers can stay online during an entire trip.

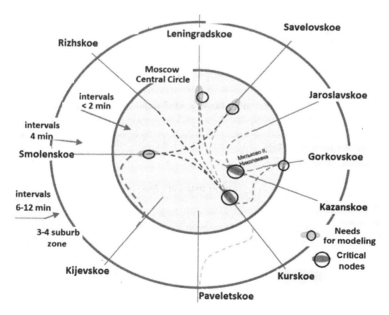

Fig. 4. Nine Moscow railway stations and the projected diametrical connections [9].

People using the network only need to register once, when entering a metro or MCC train, bus, tram or trolleybus. After that, they can use the MT_FREE Wi-Fi network on various transit routes, without text-message identification.

5.2   Moscow Central Circle and GSM-R Network

The Moscow Central Circle line is operated by 61 Siemens ES2G Lastochka trains and controlled by GSM-R. The line opened on 10 September 2016. 130 trains per day will circulate around the circle line, with a frequency of 5–6 min during the rush hours, and 10–15 min at other times. Within MRR project ROTEK Company has supplied more than 700 GSM-R portable stations and 1,200 specifically designed SIM-cards for use in portable and locomotive radio stations, which had installed in high-speed trains "Lastochka" of MRR.

5.3   Moscow Central Diameters

In 2017, Moscow announced plans [9] to create links between the existing radial rail routes into the city (Fig. 4). Modeling the movement of trains taking into account the development of diametrical connections of the railway lines of the Moscow node and GSM-R QoS requirements is extremely important.

Four nodes for throughput modeling, as well as two critical nodes, are shown (Fig. 4) to fulfill QoS Requirements (Table 2). By word, Banedanmark [10] has made a memo about ETCS level 2 solutions for large stations and junction areas. They state that the practical limit is approximately 25 trains per square kilometer, which could be raised to 28, when extensive network planning is done, using sectored and umbrella cells.

At least five such routes are to be developed, with existing lines upgraded and large diameter tunnels bored where required [11]. End-to-end journey times would be about 1 h on both routes, with services running every 6 min, compared with less frequent and less regular services on the current lines [12].

Table 2. Main GSM-R QoS requirements.

Requirements	Value
Connection establishment delay of mobile originated calls	<8.5 s (95%), ≤ 10 s (100%)
Connection establishment error ratio	<10^{-2} (100%)
Connection loss rate	<10^{-2}/h (100%)
Maximum end-to-end transfer delay (of 30 byte data block)	≤ 0.5 s (99%)
Transmission interference period	<0.8 s (95%), <1 s (99%)
Error-free period	>20 s (95%), >7 s (99%)
Network registration delay	≤ 30 s (95%), ≤ 40 s (100%)
Call-setup time	≤ 10 s (100%)
Emergency call-setup time	≤ 2 s (100%)
Duration of transmission failures	<1 s (99%)

6 Further Work

Is it reasonable to talk about 5G? [13] Russia's MTS (Mobile Telephone System) has given a scathing assessment of the emerging 5G mobile standard during an investor presentation in London, decrying the lack of technology progress and the absence of any clear 5G business case: "There is no finalized technology, no network equipment available, no frequency allocation in any of our countries, and it is not in our plans for 2017 or 2018," he said. "There are no terminals – and they don't seem to be coming – and there is no business case behind it."

6.1 Wireless Sensor Network

Infrastructure is usually monitored by using WSNs, which are able to assess the condition of tracks, track beds, bridges and the equipment placed on the tracks. Moreover, WSNs can be used to monitor tunnels or to detect intrusions and abandoned items in stations. It is worth mentioning Structural Health Monitoring (SHM), which is currently an essential field for the railway industry. Traditionally, SHM systems made use of sensors wired to data acquisition systems, but, thanks to the evolution and the lower cost of wireless devices, in recent years researchers have proposed solutions based on WSNs. A relevant requirement is a need for a precise time synchronization with a resolution of microseconds. This requirement is due to the fact that certain measurements, like vibration monitoring, demand accurate timing and synchronized sensing at high sampling rates [14, 15].

6.2 Industrial Internet of Things

IIoT Market is set for tremendous growth in 2015 as more and more businesses are realizing its potential uses and impact it can have on the global economy. Digital railway is one attractive area for IIoT [16].

In conclusion, the nearest tasks of Russian telecommunications:

1. Comprehensive tests of GSM-R technology, especially reliability issues due to interference effects between networks, especially due to Moscow Central Diameters.
2. Development of the GSM-R network architecture taking into account existing networks, including interaction with an intelligent network, as well as the need to upgrade existing networks.
3. Consider the issues of import substitution of GSM-R equipment by own Russian products, taking into account the Russian market volume.

References

1. Smith, K.: Beyond GSM-R: the future of railway radio. Int. Railway J. (2017). http://www.railjournal.com/index.php/telecoms/beyond-gsm-r-the-future-of-railway-radio.html. Accessed 09 Aug 2018

2. Sneps-Sneppe, M., et al.: Digital railway and the transition from the GSM-R network to the LTE-R and 5G-R-whether it takes place? Int. J. Open Inf. Technol. 5(1), 71–80 (2017). http://injoit.ru/index.php/j1/article/view/379. Accessed 09 Aug 2018. (in Russian)

3. Sneps-Sneppe, M.: On telecommunications evolution: pentagon case and some challenges. In: Proceedings of 9th International Congress on Ultra Modern Telecommunications and Control Systems and Workshops, ICUMT 2017, Munich, pp. 251–256 (2017). https://doi.org/10.1109/icumt.2017.8255114

4. Global Information Grid. Architectural Vision for a Net-Centric, Service-Oriented DoD Enterprise. Department of Defense. Version 1.0, June 2007. http://acqnotes.com/Attachments/DoD%20GIG%20Architectural%20Vision,%20June%2007.pdf. Accessed 09 Aug 2018

5. Department of Defense. Unified Capabilities Framework 2013, January 2013. https://dodcio.defense.gov/Portals/0/Documents/DIEA/Approved%20DoD%20UC%20Reference%20Architecture.pdf. Accessed 09 Aug 2018

6. International Union of Railways (UIC) – SM-R Operators Group, European Integrated Radio Enhanced Network (EIRENE). Functional Requirements Specification Version 8.0.0. Technical Report, EIRENE: Paris, France, December 2015

7. Mottier, D.: How 5G technologies could benefit to the railway sector: challenges and opportunities. In: Mitsubishi Electric R&D Centre Europe – France (2016). https://docbox.etsi.org/Workshop/2016/201611_managing_rail_mobile_comms/s03_attractiveness_future_other_techno/benefits_5g_techno_railway_sector_mottier_merce.pdf. Accessed 09 Aug 2018

8. All Moscow metro lines now feature MT_FREE Wi-Fi network, 30 April 2017 https://www.mos.ru/en/news/item/23445073/. Accessed 09 Aug 2018

9. Rozenberg, E.N.: Digital railway - near future. Autom. Commun. Inf. 10, 4–7 (2016). [in Russian]

10. Degnegaard, S.: ERTM level 2 for large stations and junction areas. Memorandum, Banedanmark (2008)

11. Namiot, D., Kutuzmanov, Z., Fedorov, E., Pokusaev, O.: On the assessment of socio-economic effects of the city railway. Int. J. Open Inf. Technol. 6(1), 92–103 (2018). http://injoit.ru/index.php/j1/article/view/527. (in Russian)

12. Putin approves Moscow REP. Metro Report International, 17 November 2017. http://www.metro-report.com/news/single-view/view/putin-approves-moscow-rer.html. Accessed 09 Aug 2018

13. Morris, I.: Russia's MTS: There Is No 5G Business Case. Light Reading, 21 March 2017. http://www.lightreading.com/mobile/5g/russias-mts-there-is-no-5g-business-case/d/d-id/731347. Accessed: 09 Aug 2018

14. Giannoulis, S., Koulamas, C., Emmanouilidis, C., Pistofidis, P., Karampatzakis, D.: Wireless sensor network technologies for condition monitoring of industrial assets. In: Emmanouilidis, C., Taisch, M., Kiritsis, D. (eds.) APMS 2012. IAICT, vol. 398, pp. 33–40. Springer, Heidelberg (2013). https://doi.org/10.1007/978-3-642-40361-3_5

15. Lai, C.C., Au, H.Y., Liu, M.S.Y., Ho, S.L., Tam, H.Y.: Development of level sensors based on fiber Bragg grating for railway track differential settlement measurement. IEEE Sens. J. 16(16), 6346–6350 (2016). https://doi.org/10.1109/JSEN.2016.2574622

16. Fraga-Lamas, P., Fernández-Caramés, T.M., Castedo, L.: Towards the Internet of smart trains: a review on industrial IoT-connected railways. Sensors 17(6), 1457 (2017). https://doi.org/10.3390/s17061457

Applied Optimization Problems

Basic Concepts of the Elective Course on the Hard Computing Problems

Boris Melnikov⬤, Elena Melnikova⬤, and Svetlana Pivneva$^{(\boxtimes)}$⬤

Russian State Social University, Wilhelm Pieck str., 4, Moscow 129226, Russia
bf-melnikov@yandex.ru, ya.e.melnikova@yandex.ru, tlt-swetlana@yandex.ru
http://www.mathnet.ru/php/person.phtml?personid=27967

Abstract. We consider the material of the elective course for the young students, and briefly describe both so-called hard problems and some methods necessary to develop programs for their implementation on the computer. For this, we are considering several real problems of discrete optimization. For each of them we consider both "greedy" algorithms and more complex approaches. The latter are, first of all, are considered in the description of concepts, understandable to "advanced" young students and necessary for the subsequent program implementation of the branches and bounds method and some associated heuristic algorithms. According to the authors, all this "within reasonable limits" is available for "advanced" young students of 14–15 years.

Thus, we present our view on the consideration of difficult problems and possible approaches to their algorithmization – at a level "somewhat higher than the popular science", but "somewhat less than scientific". And for this, the paper formulates the starting concepts which allows one of such "complications" to be carried out within the next half-year.

Keywords: Elective course · Hard computing problems · "Greedy" algorithms · The first step in the science

1 Introduction and Motivation

This paper can be considered as a popular scientific presentation of algorithms necessary for advanced programmers to solve complex search problems. We consider the material of the elective course for the schoolchildren (young students), and briefly describe both so-called hard problems and some methods necessary to develop programs for their implementation on the computer. Just note, that the continuation of this course can be several completely different elective courses – in the following areas:

– the substantially more detailed presentation of any of the problems considered in this article (and also in the elective course described in it);

Partially supported by the research project of Russian State Social University.

V. Sukhomlin and E. Zubareva (Eds.): Convergent 2018, CCIS 1140, pp. 405–415, 2020.
https://doi.org/10.1007/978-3-030-37436-5_35

- the presentation of *mathematical principles* for evaluating the complexity of algorithms – and the application of these principles to solve the problems of discrete optimization considered here;
- the presentation of the *principles of statistical evaluation* of the effectiveness of the created software – and, similarly, the application of these principles to solve the problems of discrete optimization considered here;
- the consideration of software aspects of constructing solvers of discrete optimization problems;
- and so on.

According to the authors, all this "within reasonable limits" is available for "advanced" young students of 14–15 years. And for this, the paper (and, accordingly, the material described in it) formulates the starting concepts which allows one of such "complications" to be carried out within the next half-year.

Thus, we present our view on the consideration of difficult problems and possible approaches to their algorithmization – at a level "somewhat higher than the popular science", but "somewhat less than scientific". Apparently, in Russian, after the closure of the magazine "Computerra" [1] at the end of 2009, there is no full-fledged "paper" popular science magazine; however, this is not a "catastrophe": many such topics are now constantly discussed at forums, at relevant sites, remember at least "Habr" ("Habrahabr", [2]). However, they are difficult to find a popular presentation of the relevant material (creating algorithms for solving complex problems) for schoolchildren – which we expect to do in this paper and, we hope, in subsequent ones.

At the beginning of training of schoolchildren 14–15 years after mastering the basic elements of the programming language, we often consider the approach to constructing simple recursive algorithms (we recall that we are talking about classes with "advanced" young students). Among these algorithms, we consider various algorithms for generating permutations that are close to those described in [3], but not only these algorithms. (We shall not write about other "recursive" programming problems here: we think that this is much simpler than the material presented in this article.) Further, after considering the algorithms for generating permutations, there are necessarily questions about possible *applications* of these algorithms. Here the most "natural" option is the widely known problem of the traveling salesman, [4] etc.; in this case, as the practice of working with schoolchildren shows, the "advanced" students easily write appropriate programs (using already known and already implemented algorithms for generating permutations to solve the traveling salesman problem) for about one lesson (after only 2–3 months of programming classes before this).

Then there is another "natural" question, i.e. the question about the dimension of the problem, which can be solved with the help of similar brute-force algorithms. At the same time, of course, it is surprising for young students, that the increase in the clock frequency of the "average" computer processor by approximately 100 times (to say, from 30 MHz to 3 GHz) over the last 25 years has led to an increase in the dimension of the problem that *can be solved in real time* in such an exhaustive manner, only 2 (in practice, the dimension increased from 13 to 15 only). All this leads to the idea of the need to consider *other approaches* to the solution of this problem, as well as many similar ones, than we actually do in the framework of the described elective course (and within the framework of this paper).

So, we (together with young students!) come to the conclusion that algorithms with exponential time complexity cannot be considered as practically applicable, and algorithms with polynomial time complexity (i.e., $O(n^c)$ for small values c) can. Therefore, it is no exaggeration to say that the most important goal of theoretical informatics (and perhaps *the most intellectual kind of human activity!*) is the development of practical algorithms for solving difficult problems and their good software implementation.[1]

2   Some Simple Examples and Some Terms

In Introduction, there were very few examples: from specific problems we mentioned only the problem of the traveling salesman. However, we can assume that some more examples were us discussed earlier in [5]. Continuing the subject and examples of that paper, we shall continue our consideration of the so-called puzzles and repeat the idea that to them, as well as to intellectual games, cannot be taken lightly: almost any good textbook on artificial intelligence begins with their consideration and description of possible methods for their solution. And, apparently, the most common example is the well-known problem of the Hanoi towers; however, of course, it does not apply to hard problems.[2] Also very interesting are puzzles created on the basis of famous computer games: various solitaires, sapper, tetris, as well as sudoku and nonograms, see [6–8].[3] It is important to note that, despite the simplicity of their wording, all these problems can be viewed from our point of view as the hard ones; and the possible methods for solving them practically coincide with the methods for solving "more serious" problems. In this case, it is sudoku that is primarily considered such a "serious problem", describing NP-completeness, see, for example, [8]. Above we already mentioned intellectual games (it is desirable not to be confused them with puzzles, despite the fact that one of the most famous puzzles is more often called "Sam Loyd's Game of Fifteen"): the choice of the next move in the intellectual game can also be considered as an example of a hard problem.

We now turn to the description of the formulations of the three problems, which we called the more serious. In doing so, we introduce some terms related

---

[1] "Ah, gentlemen, you know why we are here. We've not much time, and quite a problem here" (Andrew Lloyd Webber and Tim Rice).

[2] Although the latter statement can also be disputed, if we consider it not as a problem of *implementing the algorithm of its solution found beforehand by a person* (namely, this problem is usually considered in literature not connected with artificial intelligence), but as a task *of finding* such a solution.

[3] Let us also note, that in the final of the student team championship in programming in the world (according to the ACM version) back in 1992, there was a task about the mentioned nonograms.

to the problems of discrete optimization in general. We note that the order of the problems cited by us, including those already mentioned, roughly corresponds to an increase in the degree of their difficulty. All these problems, similarly to the ones mentioned above, can be solved in real time in the case of small dimensions, but in the transition to large dimensions these real-time problems can not be exactly solved even with the help of simple heuristics.[4] Let us repeat that in our formulations, all the problems we are considering are fully accessible to the "advanced" young students of 14–15 years of age.

2.1   The First Example: State-Minimization of NFA

Let us first formulate *our interpretation* of the problem of state minimization for nondeterministic finite automata (NFA, [10,11]). A rectangular matrix filled with elements 0 or 1 is given. Additionally, such limitations may be required:

- there is no identical strings in it;
- no string consists of only 0's;
- both these limitations are also true for the columns.

A certain pair of subsets of rows and columns is called a *grid*, if:

- all their intersections are 1's;
- this set cannot be filled either with a row or with a column, without violating the previous property.

In this example, a so-called *acceptable solution*[5] is the set of blocks covering all the elements 1 of the given matrix. It is required to choose a feasible solution containing the minimum possible number of blocks, i.e., so-called *optimal solution*.

In Fig. 1 below, we give a simple example to this problem. The table has the following 5 grids:

$$\alpha = \{A, B, C, D\} \times \{U\}; \quad \beta = \{A, C, D\} \times \{Z, U\};$$
$$\gamma = \{B, C, D\} \times \{X, U\}; \quad \delta = \{C, D\} \times \{X, Z, U\};$$
$$\text{and} \quad \omega = \{D\} \times \{X, Y, Z, U\}$$

(we selected the elements of the block in a gray background). To cover all the 1's of the given matrix, it is sufficient to use 3 of these 5 blocks, namely β, γ and ω.

---

[4] The concept of "heuristics" will be briefly discussed below. According to the authors, *the easiest example* of a heuristic algorithm accessible for young students can be QuickSort, [9] etc.

[5] This is a very important concept, but we shall not strictly define it. The meaning *will always be clear from the context*.

	X	Y	Z	U
A	0	0	1	1
B	1	0	0	1
C	1	0	1	1
D	1	1	1	1

Fig. 1. The table corresponding to the given automaton.

2.2   The Second Example: Minimization of DNF

Now, let us give the formulation of the problem of minimizing disjunctive normal forms (DNF). An n-dimensional cube is specified, and each vertex is marked with 0 or 1 elements. An admissible solution is the set of k-dimensional planes of this cube (where the values of k are, generally speaking, different for each plane, not exceeding n), containing only 1's and *covering* all elements 1 of the given n-dimensional cube. It is required to choose a feasible solution containing the minimum number of planes. In this case, as in the previous problem, we will additionally require that none of the planes considered be contained in any plane of greater dimension.

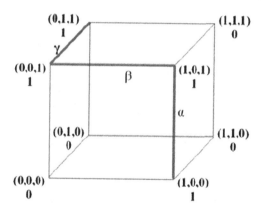

Fig. 2. The example of the problem of DNF-minimization.

A simple example is shown on Fig. 2. Here $n = 3$ (that is, we are considering the "ordinary" cube), and there are 3 planes, each of which has a size of 1 (that is, a segment):

$$\alpha = [(1,0,0),(1,0,1)], \quad \beta = [(0,0,1),(1,0,1)], \quad \text{and} \quad \gamma = [(0,0,1),(0,1,1)].$$

For the coverage, it is sufficient to choose 2 of these 3 planes: α and γ.

2.3   The Third Example: Traveling Salesman Problem

Third, let us consider the traveling salesman problem (TSP). It defines a matrix in which the cost of travel from the i-th city to the j-th one is recorded in the cell located at the intersection of the i-th string and the j-th column. It is required to make a route (tour) of the traveling salesman, passing through all cities, starting and ending in the same city; each of the tours and is an acceptable solution. It is required to choose a feasible solution with the lowest possible cost.

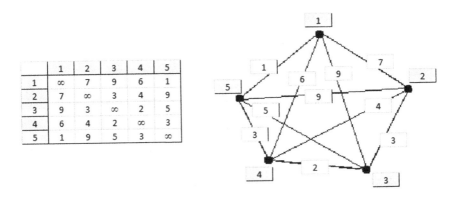

	1	2	3	4	5
1	∞	7	9	6	1
2	7	∞	3	4	9
3	9	3	∞	2	5
4	6	4	2	∞	3
5	1	9	5	3	∞

Fig. 3. The example of traveling salesman problem.

A simple example is shown in Fig. 3, it shows two ways of specifying the same particular case of TSP. For small dimensions, the input data is often represented as a graph. If the cost of travel "there" and "back" for all pairs of cities coincide, then such a graph is conveniently considered not to be oriented; we will consider only such examples. In this case, the matrices are symmetric with respect to the main diagonal, therefore in our example the elements lying below the main diagonal can not be specified.

3   The State Space

The whole set of admissible solutions in other words is called the state space. Practically for each problem, there is the possibility of an effective auxiliary algorithm designed to obtain some new feasible solution based on the already available one; so the entire state space can be considered a graph. Usually, such graph is undirected. Figure 4 shows possible graphs describing the state spaces *for the examples that we already considered*: the figure on the left is for the problem of DNF-minimizing, and the figure on the right is for the problem of NFA-minimizing. We believe that in both examples, a new solution can be obtained on the basis of the previous one by deleting or adding exactly one element (the plane or the grid), but we note that other relevant auxiliary algorithms are often used. In both figures, the optimal solutions are highlighted.

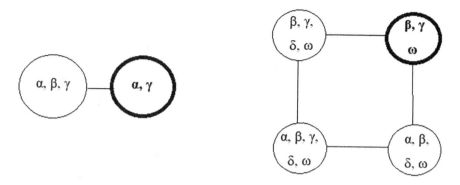

Fig. 4. The examples of the state space.

In the given examples, the state spaces are small. However, in real conditions, their size often exponentially (and more) depends on the size of the input data. Therefore, the search for an acceptable admissible solution in such a graph is the most important point in the algorithmization of hard problems. This search corresponds to the construction (explicit or implicit) of a subgraph that is a so-called root tree. And the natural procedure for constructing (sorting out the vertices) of this tree is called backtracking, simple examples of which can be found in most books on artificial intelligence, [12,13] etc.

The word "heuristic" has already been mentioned above. There are many different definitions of this concept – and sometimes they even contradict each other, and in some (worse) books, they are unsuccessful. For the word "heuristics", there is often ("almost correct") interpretation of "decision-making under uncertainty". Heuristic algorithms usually do not guarantee an optimal solution; but with an acceptable high probability, they give a solution that is close to optimal. At the same time, their variants are often needed, the so-called *anytime-algorithms*, i.e., real-time algorithms that have the best (at the moment) solution at each particular moment of the work; the user in real time can view these pseudo-optimal solutions. The sequence of such solutions in the limit *usually* gives the optimal solution.

4 Greedy Algorithms and Their Drawbacks

The simplest example of heuristic (but not anytime) algorithms is, apparently, greedy algorithms. A little simplifying the situation, we can say that they consistently build a solution in several steps, at each step, including the "part of the permissible solution", which at the moment seems to be the most profitable. For example, in problems of minimizing finite automata and disjunctive normal forms, this is a grid (a plane) adding to the current solution the maximum number of new cells in which 1 is written. And in TSP, it is an element of the matrix (from those that can be added to the construction round), which has a minimum cost.

It seems at first glance, that greedy heuristics are very good. However, for each of the problems we are considering, it is easy to come up with examples when this is not so. We have already considered just such examples, for problems of minimizing disjunctive normal forms and nondeterministic finite automata. Moreover, it can be shown that a greedy algorithm can give solutions whose values are arbitrarily greater than optimal ones.

	X	Y	Z	U	V	W
A	1	1	1	1	0	0
B	1	1	1	0	1	0
C	1	1	1	0	0	1
D	1	0	0	1	1	1
E	0	1	0	1	1	1
F	0	0	1	1	1	1

Fig. 5. The table corresponding to the given automaton.

Let us consider two simple examples. Suppose that for the NFA-minimization problem, the table is given as follows (Fig. 5). At the same time, the greedy heuristics will choose one of two maximum grids, for example, the grid corresponding to the rows A, B and C and the columns X, Y and Z. However, both maximal blocks are not included in the optimal answer: one of such possible optimal answers is 6 "grids-strings", in which for each letter from A to F, we simply "include all possible 1's".

Figure 6 for the problem of minimizing DNF is sometimes called "hedgehog". The plane corresponding to the maximum possible k is not included in the optimal answer: in our case, $n = 4$, $k = 2$, and such a plane is the only square marked with bold lines. The optimal answer is four "fat" segments, not belonging to this square ("the needles").

Of course, both these examples are *specially chosen* so that the so-called "greedy" algorithms work badly here. However, even in the examples we have examined, there are shortcomings of greedy algorithms on small dimensions of the optimization problems we are considering. In real conditions, all the examples are much more complicated than those given here, but from the "small" examples we have chosen very interesting ones. And it is obvious that in the case of large dimensions, these shortcomings should further "spoil life", that is, give non-optimal solutions with much greater probabilities, or give solutions that are farther from optimal ones, etc. The way out of this situation is the use of more complicated heuristics.

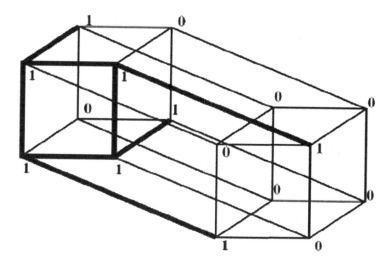

Fig. 6. The example of the problem of DNF-minimization.

5   More Complicated Heuristics

Thus, in real situations, all the examples are much more complicated than those given above. But from the "small" examples we have chosen very interesting; on their basis, many other examples can be considered in real elective courses. It is also important to note that we have considered all the problems – in the described statement – we almost never can not guarantee an optimal solutions it is a result of the so-called *combinatorial explosion* (simplifying the situation, it means a huge increase in the amount of computation with a small increase in dimension of the problem). Therefore "we have to settle for" the creation of anytime-algorithms; as we already said, they are gradually approaching pseudo-optimal algorithms of real-time, giving each user the desired point in time the decision which is best for the moment; of course, the sequence of such pseudo-optimal solutions should converge to the optimal, but the time of such convergence in reality can be extremely large.

In view of the volume limitation for this paper, we shall very briefly consider only *the approach to creating a very complex heuristic* ("metaheuristics", the so-called method of branches and bounds, BBM). The first variants of the description of this algorithm appeared more than 50 years ago. It is based on the backtracking already mentioned before, i.e., it can be considered as a special technology for a complete search in the space of all admissible solutions. As we have already noted, the main problem is that the power of the entire set of admissible solutions for inputs of the large dimension is usually very large and leads to a combinatorial explosion. What should we do in cases where the simplest algorithm "stops before time" and, similarly to the examples we have discussed, gives a solution that is very far from the optimal one? One possible solution to this problem is the following: it is necessary to divide the problem

under consideration into two subproblems. For example, for the traveling salesman problem, we select a certain matrix cell (the so-called separating element);
in one subtask we believe that a trip between the two cities corresponding to
this cell *necessarily takes place*, and in the other one, that it *does not necessarily
occur*. Simplifying the situation, we can say that the iterative process of this
division of some considered problem into two sub-problems is also a method of
branches and bounds.

The most difficult in specific problems is the choice of the variant for the
division of the problem described above. This requires expert opinions ("a priori
estimates"), for example, about when the decision will end in one and the other
case: when will this happen before? And in view of the impossibility of "applying
live experts", for each problem special auxiliary experts-subprograms are being
written that answer this question.

6   Conclusion

In the continuation paper, we propose to give a much more detailed description of BBM, and consider other examples: i.e., the examples of the problems of
discrete optimization considered here, as well as some others. Also, in the following publications, we want to briefly consider a number of additional heuristics
to BBM, which improve (by different parameters) its work. Let us note once
again that the software implementation of such heuristics is quite accessible to
"advanced" young students.

Here are some of the questions that we want to consider further. There are
several subroutines for selecting a separating element – how to choose the only
one from their answers? For this choice, we apply the so-called "game" heuristics
and risk functions. And simultaneously with the last ones for averaging we apply
algorithms from one more area of artificial intelligence, i.e., so called genetic
self-learning algorithms. Where, as in them, there should be "the desire of the
program for self-improvement"? But this is a big separate topic, which we also
want to present later.

(As the latest scientific publications of authors on this subject, we mention
[14–16].)

References

1. Computerra. https://en.wikipedia.org/wiki/Computerra. Accessed 14 June 2018
2. Habr. https://habr.com. Accessed 14 June 2018. (in Russian)
3. Lipski, W.: Kombinatoryka dla programistów. Wydawnictwa Naukowo-Techniczne, Warszawa (2004). (in Polish)
4. Goodman, S., Stephen, S.: Introduction to the Design and Analysis of Algorithms. McGraw-Hill Computer Science Series, New York (1977)
5. Melnikov, B., Melnikova, E.: Some competition programming problems as the beginning of artificial intelligence. Inf. Educ. **6**(2), 385–396 (2007)
6. Nonogram. https://en.wikipedia.org/wiki/Nonogram. Accessed 14 June 2018

7. Sudoku. http://www.sudoku.com. Accessed 14 June 2018
8. 15 puzzle. https://en.wikipedia.org/wiki/15_puzzle. Accessed 14 June 2018
9. Wirth, N.: Algorithms + Data Structures = Programs. Prentice Hall, Upper Saddle River (1979)
10. Polák, L.: Minimization of NFA using the universal automaton. Int. J. Found. Comput. Sci. **16**(999), 335–341 (2005)
11. Melnikov, B.: Multiheuristic approach to discrete optimization problems. Cybern. Syst. Anal. **42**(3), 335–341 (2006)
12. Russel, S., Norvig, P.: Artificial Intelligence: A Modern Approach. Prentice Hall, Upper Saddle River (2010)
13. Luger, G.: Artificial Intelligence: Structures and Strategies for Complex Problem Solving. Addison Wesley, Boston (2008)
14. Makarkin, S., Melnikov, B., Trenina, M.: An approach to solving a pseudo-geometric version of the traveling salesman problem. Izvestia of higher educational institutions. Volga Region. Phys. Math. Sci. **2**(34), 135–147 (2015). https://elibrary.ru/item.asp?id=24254294. (in Russian)
15. Melnikov, B.: The complete finite automaton. Int. J. Open Inf. Technol. **5**(10), 9–17 (2017)
16. Melnikov, B., Melnikova, E., Pivneva, S., Churikova, N., Dudnikov, V., Prus, M.: Multi-heuristic and game approaches in search problems of the graph theory. In: Information Technology and Nanotechnology Proceedings, ITNT-2018, pp. 2884–2894 (2018)

Author Index

Printed in the United States
By Bookmasters